ELIOT AFTER *THE WASTE LAND*

ALSO BY ROBERT CRAWFORD

NONFICTION

The Savage and the City in the Work
of T. S. Eliot

Devolving English Literature

Identifying Poets: Self and Territory
in Twentieth-Century Poetry

The Modern Poet

Scotland's Books: The Penguin
History of Scottish Literature

The Bard: Robert Burns, A Biography

Bannockburns

On Glasgow and Edinburgh

Robert Burns and Cultural Authority
(editor)

The Scottish Invention of English
Literature (editor)

Contemporary Poetry and
Contemporary Science (editor)

Young Eliot: From St. Louis to
'The Waste Land'

POETRY

A Scottish Assembly

Sharawaggi (with W. N. Herbert)

Talkies

Masculinity

Spirit Machines

The Tip of My Tongue

Selected Poems

Apollos of the North

Full Volume

Simonides

Testament

ANTHOLOGIES

Other Tongues: Young Scottish Poets
in English, Scots and Gaelic
(editor)

The Penguin Book of Poetry from
Britain and Ireland since 1945
(editor with Simon Armitage)

The Penguin Book of
Scottish Verse
(editor with Mick Imlah)

Scottish Religious Poetry
(editor with Meg Bateman and
James McGonigal)

The Book of St Andrews (editor)

Eliot After
The Waste Land

ROBERT CRAWFORD

FARRAR, STRAUS AND GIROUX

NEW YORK

Farrar, Straus and Giroux
120 Broadway, New York 10271

Printed in the United States of America
Originally published in 2022 by Jonathan Cape, Great Britain
Published in the United States by Farrar, Straus and Giroux
First American edition, 2022

Owing to limitations of space, all acknowledgements for permission
to reprint previously published and unpublished material can be found
on page 489 of the Acknowledgements.

Library of Congress Cataloging-in-Publication Data
Names: Crawford, Robert, 1959– author.
Title: Eliot after The waste land / Robert Crawford.
Description: First American edition. | New York : Farrar, Straus and Giroux, 2022. |
   "Originally published in 2022 by Jonathan Cape, Great Britain." | Includes
   bibliographical references and index.
Identifiers: LCCN 2022020636 | ISBN 9780374279462 (hardcover)
Subjects: LCSH: Eliot, T. S. (Thomas Stearns), 1888–1965. | Poets, American—
   20th century—Biography. | LCGFT: Biographies.
Classification: LCC PS3509.L43 Z6538 2022 | DDC 821/.912 [B]—
   dc23/eng/20220525
LC record available at https://lccn.loc.gov/2022020636

Our books may be purchased in bulk for promotional, educational,
or business use. Please contact your local bookseller or the Macmillan Corporate
and Premium Sales Department at 1-800-221-7945, extension 5442, or by email at
MacmillanSpecialMarkets@macmillan.com.

www.fsgbooks.com
www.twitter.com/fsgbooks • www.facebook.com/fsgbooks

1   3   5   7   9   10   8   6   4   2

for Alice
with love

Contents

List of Plates

1. T. S. Eliot outside the Faber & Gwyer offices at 24 Russell Square, Bloomsbury. This photograph was taken by his brother Henry.
    MS Am2560 (Box 7: 186), Houghton Library, Harvard University; reproduced courtesy of the Houghton Library and with the permission of the T. S. Eliot Estate

2. T. S. Eliot at his desk at Faber & Gwyer, 1926. This photograph was taken by his brother Henry, and seems to show a marionette hanging from the telephone.
    MS Am2560 (Box 7: 187), Houghton Library, Harvard University; reproduced courtesy of the Houghton Library and with the permission of the T. S. Eliot Estate

3. A studio photograph of Vivien Eliot, inscribed by her to her sister-in-law in 1930.
    The T. S. Eliot Estate; reproduced with the permission of the T. S. Eliot Estate

4. T. S. Eliot, Virginia Woolf and Vivien Eliot, photographed by Leonard Woolf at Rodmell, Sussex, in September 1932.
    MS Thr 560 (Box 1: 87), Houghton Library, Harvard University; reproduced courtesy of the Houghton Library and with the permission of the University of Sussex and the Society of Authors as the Literary Representative of the Estate of Leonard Woolf

5. T. S. Eliot and Vivien Eliot, photographed by Leonard Woolf at Rodmell, Sussex, in September 1932.
    MS Thr 560 (Box 1: 90), Houghton Library, Harvard University; reproduced courtesy of the Houghton Library and with the permission of the University of Sussex and the Society of Authors as the Literary Representative of the Estate of Leonard Woolf

6. Emily Hale performing in a play put on by The Montebanks at Milwaukee-Downer College in 1924.
    From the Archives Department, University of Wisconsin-Milwaukee Libraries (Milwaukee-Downer College Records: Series 7, Box 24, Volume 41); reproduced with permission

7. Emily Hale at Milwaukee-Downer College, circa 1926–1930.
   ARC2015-140, Lawrence University Archives, Appleton, Wisconsin; reproduced with the permission of Lawrence University Archives

8. Emily Hale at Abbot Academy in 1956.
   Commissioned by Phillips Academy, Andover, CC BY-SA 4.0, via Wikimedia Commons, and courtesy of Phillips Academy

9. One of a series of photographs taken on 4 July 1939 at Much Hadham Hall, Hertfordshire, on the occasion of a farewell party for the Morley family, who were leaving for the United States. Left to right in the back row are Richard de la Mare, Catherine de la Mare, Christina Morley, Frank Morley and Geoffrey Faber; in the middle row are the children Catherine de la Mare and Donald Morley; in front is T. S. Eliot.
   Faber & Faber Archives; reproduced with the permission of Faber & Faber

10. Emily Hale with flowers in 1935, probably taken by T. S. Eliot, who called this photograph a 'masterpiece' when he sent it to Emily's friend Jeanette McPherrin.
    The T. S. Eliot Estate; reproduced with the permission of the T. S. Eliot Estate

11. T. S. Eliot and Emily Hale at Woods Hole, Massachusetts, in 1936.
    Ruth George Collection of T. S. Eliot, Ella Strong Denison Library, Scripps College; reproduced with the permission of Scripps College

12. The sloping rear garden of Stamford House, Chipping Campden. The yew tree (no longer present today) is visible at the top of this picture, which is taken roughly from the back door of the house, probably in the 1930s and possibly by Eleanor Malby, who was friendly with Emily Hale's aunt Edith Carroll Perkins.
    Reginald A. Malby / Royal Horticultural Society Lindley Collections; reproduced with the permission of the Royal Horticultural Society

13. The rear garden of Stamford House, Chipping Campden, looking towards the back door of the house, probably photographed in the 1930s and possibly by Eleanor Malby.
    Reginald A. Malby / Royal Horticultural Society Lindley Collections; reproduced with the permission of the Royal Horticultural Society

14. A group in the living room at Shamley Wood, Shamley Green, Surrey, around 1941. Left to right: Constance Moncrieff, Mappie Mirrlees, Hettie James (with tray), Ellen James, Hope Mirrlees, T. S. Eliot.
    The T. S. Eliot Estate; reproduced with the permission of the T. S. Eliot Estate

ELIOT AFTER *THE WASTE LAND*

Introduction

O N a wintry day in the late 1950s, around the time of his second marriage, T. S. Eliot came downstairs from his publishing-house office in London's Russell Square and noticed a restless baby in a pram. The little daughter of Frank and Patricia Herrmann had been left in the office foyer, close to the receptionist, and had kicked off her blankets. When the Herrmanns returned, seeing no pram, they began to panic. 'Where has the pram gone?', Patricia Herrmann shouted, but the receptionist calmed her, explaining that the poet had seen little Camilla looking unsettled, and had tucked her up, then taken the pram outside to push it round Russell Square. Twenty-first-century readers may be disturbed by this momentary abduction as a gesture of appropriation and control, or touched by it as a small example of observant kindness. Whether, as the Herrmanns did later, they speculate that 'the experience' may have represented 'a vicarious substitute for unfulfilled parenthood', and whether or not readers choose to relate it to his poetry, is a matter for each individual.[1] Chronicled much later by Frank Herrmann, and in our own century detailed by Christopher Ricks and Jim McCue in their annotated text of *The Poems of T. S. Eliot*, this was a revealing action performed by the elderly poet, publisher, and internationally lauded man of letters. But it may be more appropriate to regard it as something done by the man whom his family simply called Tom.

Both in America, where he had been born in 1888, and in England, where he lived from his twenty-sixth year, many people found it hard to get to know this poet on familiar terms. Even if they did so, some were unsure what to call him. 'Will he become "Tom"?' Virginia Woolf had wondered in 1921, after she had known him for well over two years.[2] By the time *The Waste Land* appeared in 1922, Thomas Stearns Eliot, the young, London-based, St Louis-born, Harvard-schooled poet who had seemed so formal and reserved, was certainly 'Tom' to her, and in the following year she typeset his remarkable poem for its earliest British publication as a book. Like *Young Eliot* (2015), this second part of a two-volume biography of Eliot offers readers access not just to the poet, public figure, banker, publisher and man of letters, but also and crucially to 'Tom' or, as close American friends and relatives called him, 'Taam'.[3] *Eliot After 'The Waste Land'* is the first full-scale biography to draw on his most important surviving correspondence, the letters to Emily Hale made public in 2020, and on the great scholarly editions of his poetry and his prose (completed respectively in 2015 and 2019) as well as on the vast, ongoing print and electronic edition of the poet's general correspondence, whose ninth volume appeared in 2021. At the same time, I am also the last biographer to interview anyone who knew 'Tom' when *The Waste Land* was first published; and, over several decades, I have gained from conversations with his surviving godchildren and others who remember him in England and America from the 1930s, 40s, 50s, and 60s. No one who met Valerie Eliot, the poet's widow (who died in 2012), will forget how she spoke of him as 'Tom'. In biography, as in poetry and in life, naming is important. The poet of Prufrock and Macavity knew that well. Like its predecessor, this book presents a close-grained, intimate portrait of a man who can still seem to some, as he seemed to Siegfried Sassoon in 1922, intellectually aloof and a specimen of 'cold-storaged humanity'.[4] That is why, throughout, I call him 'Tom'.

Being on first-name terms need not encourage readers to share all of the subject's attitudes, passions, or prejudices. In a book which takes him from his time as an exhausted bank employee during the emotional turmoil of his early thirties, then through his years as a middle-aged firewatcher in bombed wartime London to the personal surprises of his eminent old age, I try to present Tom Eliot's life and work without undue moralising, letting readers reach their own conclusions. Inevitably, in selecting details, I am making a particular individual portrait that tries to delineate how his powerfully resonant, superbly calibrated poetry is linked to the trials of his emotional, intellectual and spiritual life; other biographers will choose differently. My aim is not to neaten his life, or reduce it to one expository template, but to let it emerge in its sometimes complex, contradictory messiness. There is a temptation, to which the poet, his widow, and some biographers have been prone, to describe that life as if it followed a teleological pattern and possessed one stable meaning. This book seeks to reveal the life as it was lived, not as it may have been shaped in retrospect. While conscious that a number of readers may want a biographical 'explanation' – whether psychological, religious, sexual or sociopolitical – I have tried to stay true to my belief that a human life is too rich and subtle to be explained away through one neat interpretative matrix.

Rightly, the subject of *Eliot After 'The Waste Land'* matters most to the world as a poet. The following chapters concentrate particularly on the part of his life during which he wrote poetry, though they address also his work as playwright, publisher, editor, and Christian public intellectual. Not least, I try to show ways in which, however refractedly, the poetry sprang from the poet's sometimes tormented life, from his 1915 marriage to Vivien (sometimes spelled Vivienne) Haigh-Wood, and from his surroundings. I will suggest, too, how this non-combatant produced the greatest English-language poetry of the Second World War. Telling this story requires intense selectivity, or the material would become overwhelming. In its annotated form, *The Poems of T. S. Eliot* runs to nearly 2,000 pages. His *Complete Prose* comprises about 7,000 pages. Including *The Rock*, his six full-length plays await a fully annotated edition. The ongoing publication of his letters in print and online already extends well beyond 10,000 pages, and is perhaps less than half complete. The daunting voluminousness of these writings and activities explains in part why the present book maintains a close focus on the man who generated them, rather than attempting a panoramic survey of the society, figures, and cultures around him. Biographers need to sieve and filter all the published writings, drawing too on further published and unpublished sources, as well as on oral and broadcast interviews. The biographer has to be an editor, a chooser of resonant details, as well as a narrator, companionable guide, critic, historian, and assembler of images. *Eliot After 'The Waste Land'* tries to suggest why this poet and his poetry compel our attention, but the book is not a work of literary criticism or history, so I have avoided puddling the text with critical or historical essays; instead, I have tried to select material that does justice to the full range of this remarkable and difficult man's achievements, and to present him not as a literary monument but as a human being.

The French philosopher Henri Bergson, some of whose classes Tom Eliot attended at the Sorbonne in 1910–11, liked to stress that our experience of time is significantly subjective, and that some moments appear to have a duration and intensity surpassing their measurement on the clock. Before Bergson, the Romantic poets, with their focus on what Wordsworth calls 'spots of time', sensed this too, though intuition of the phenomenon may be as old as poetry itself.[5] Certainly, such perceptions are part of *Four Quartets*. Most people treasure particularly revealing or revelatory instants and incidents, recalling them throughout their lives, and in selecting some moments rather than others, biographers, like poets, have to hone their material. Though, perhaps like many readers, I was first attracted to the poet of 'The Love Song of J. Alfred Prufrock' through reading his great, nervously tensile early poems, it is not just in *The Waste Land* but also in his subsequent poetry that some of his finest accomplishments lie. With its tidal acoustic and intense sense of longing, 'Marina', that great father–daughter poem authored by a childless man, is surely one of the most beautiful of all anglophone poems, while *Four Quartets*, written during times of profound personal pressure, articulates remarkably and simultaneously a sense of struggle and almost limitless endurance. This is the biography of an often astonishing poet, whose life's course conditioned his poems.

I

'I Cannot Go On'

JUST weeks before *The Waste Land* was first published in New York as a book-length poem, a rumour spread that its American author had attempted suicide. In mid-November 1922 the story reached Manhattan where Edmund Wilson was managing editor of *Vanity Fair*. Wilson's friend the American poet John Peale Bishop had been drinking in Paris with Ezra Pound, who recounted how 'Tears Eliot (as some Paris wit has recently christened him)' had at one time 'decided to kill himself', though he had 'funked at the final moment'. Bishop makes it sound as if this incident took place some years earlier; his account claimed wrongly that *The Waste Land*'s author was 'tubercular'.[1] Evidence to corroborate the suicide claim is lacking, but Bishop, who had just been reading *The Waste Land* in the *Criterion* (the supposedly suicidal poet's new, London-published cultural magazine), ran together his interpretation of this poem in which 'everybody is in a hell of a fix' with what he understood Pound to be telling him about its author's precarious psychological state.[2]

If *The Waste Land* struck some early readers as a cry of personal despair, it also spoke to their era. Not least for Americans who had come to Europe, it articulated a shared sense of Great War 'waste'. Pound wrote of 'wastage as never before', while earlier in 1922 Bishop and Wilson (two young Princeton graduates who had served in France with the US army, then survived the global Spanish Flu pandemic) had published their 'book about death', *The Undertaker's Garland*, lamenting how 'the whole world seemed poisoned with decay' so that even 'the winds of spring' had come to be 'tainted now with the foulness of those seven million dead'. Presenting 'April' as 'the cruellest month' and portraying living-dead commuters in modern commercial London, *The Waste Land* spoke for this generation who had perceived that 'All Europe' had recently 'reached a point at last where it could think of nothing but death', while 'in America' too, as Bishop and Wilson put it, 'life had become a sort of death'.[3] *The Waste Land* fused the trauma of a shattered Western world with an appalling personal crisis. '*Le style, c'est l'homme*' quoted Henry Eliot to his younger brother Tom, adding that 'the personality of the artist' was not 'irrelevant, as you claim'.[4] If Tom had already told his mother that 'he had put so much of his own life into' *The Waste Land*, and his English close friend Mary Hutchinson had interpreted it as 'Tom's autobiography – a melancholy one', then soon his old Harvard confidant Conrad Aiken would see the 'brilliant' poem's 'Anatomy of Melancholy' as far-reaching, arguing that its poet's 'sense of the literary past' was 'overmastering'.[5] This far-reaching sense, too, corresponded with deeply personal 'feelings' of 'dispossession by the dead' which Tom had experienced at Marlow in England (where he had rented a house with Vivien and Bertrand Russell for several years from 1917) and at Périgueux in France where he had holidayed with Ezra Pound around the time of writing his 1919 essay 'Tradition and the Individual Talent' which insists that a poet's 'meaning' is defined by 'his relationship to the dead'. Pound recalled Tom's telling him in 1919, 'I am afraid of the life after death.'[6] A keen sense of death, the presence of the dead, and of being at once possessed and dispossessed by past voices, haunts not just *The Waste Land* and 'Tradition and the Individual Talent'; it also haunted Tom, and would continue to do so.

Shortly after appearing in Scofield Thayer's New York avant-garde magazine the *Dial*, *The Waste Land* was first published as a book in December 1922 by Boni & Liveright in Manhattan. Only a year had passed since its author's treatment for a nervous breakdown, and many of the factors surrounding that episode persisted: marital anxieties, overwork as he tried to combine writing and editing with his demanding full-time job in banking, worry that he had messed up his life. Sitting in his upstairs flat at 9 Clarence Gate Gardens in London's Marylebone district, typing a letter to Henry in Chicago, Tom Eliot felt that though both he and his English wife were only thirty-four they were, as he put it on 8 December, 'completely worn out'.[7] Ever eager to help, Henry had congratulated him on the award of a $2,000 prize from the *Dial* – a consequence of *The Waste Land* – but Tom realised Henry did 'not really like the poem'. It 'wearies me a little', Henry confessed: 'too excessively allusive'; 'a scrap book'.[8] Vivien, whose doctors struggled to understand her combination of worsening physical and psychological troubles, recognised the poem's power, but was, like her husband, highly conscious of her own frailty; for months she had lacked the energy even to sit up to take her evening meal. Thinking back, Tom realised she had been 'very ill during nearly the whole of 1922'.[9]

For some of that summer they had lived apart, Vivien in the countryside and Tom in London. Now, back at Clarence Gate Gardens and sometimes heavily medicated, Vivien slept in her own bedroom. After seven years of marriage, she remained resolutely and loyally convinced of her husband's genius, but Tom had realised as early as 1916 that he was still in love with Emily Hale, the young woman he had left behind in Boston when he set out for Europe in 1914. By the time *The Waste Land* was published, it was several years since Vivien's adultery with Tom's predatory former professor, Bertrand Russell, but sexual torment and disgust pervade the poem. At times the Eliots could show mutual affection, but their marriage carried its own freight of 'waste'. As Tom recollected, 'I did try, again and again, to love as I had promised; but failed utterly; and no one could thrive on what I had left to give.' Though he kept the matter a closely guarded secret, in 1922 he too had committed adultery: 'having failed to do right, I tried to do wrong [. . .] I tried to have a love affair with a young society woman who was living apart from her husband, and who was, I am afraid, rather notorious, and in spite of wealth and position was even looked at askance by some.' In part, his action revenged Vivien's affair with Russell: after his own adultery, Tom felt 'I escaped finally from the influence of Bertie Russell.' The affair Tom 'tried' to have was short-lived, 'over almost before it was begun', but it left, as he put it eight years later, 'a taste of ashes which I can never forget'.[10]

His partner in adultery appears to have been twenty-six-year-old Mrs Nancy Fairbairn. She had lived apart from her husband for three years, and had many affairs. Her father, Sir Bache Cunard, was the wealthy English grandson of the founder of the Cunard shipping line. Nancy's American mother Lady Maud (later 'Emerald') Cunard numbered among her lovers orchestral conductor Sir Thomas Beecham, and was one of London's most effervescent society hostesses. In 1916 at 20 Cavendish Square, Lady Cunard's sumptuous, marble-fireplaced Marylebone town house where imposing stairwell paintings depicted fantastic classical ruins, Tom had attended the 'first performance' of Yeats's *At the Hawk's Well*, a ritual drama which, like *The Waste Land*, features a craving for life-giving water.[11] Glinting with gold and emerald green, Lady Cunard's rooms theatrically mixed classical architecture with fashionable Ballets Russes decor, Louis Quinze furniture, lapis lazuli, and antiques featuring 'naked nymphs and naiads'.[12] A lover of Renaissance and Restoration drama (she was said to know *The Duchess of Malfi* by heart, and Shakespeare's work in its 'entirety'), Lady Cunard moved at the heart of high society; assembling political, wealthy, and artistic elites, her parties at Cavendish Square, and then, a little later, at 5 Carlton House Terrace, attracted the Prince of Wales and fashionable aristocrats.[13] They were aromatic with scandal.

Amplified by and fused with literary allusions, Lady Cunard's theatrical and palatial town-house milieu is close to that of the decadently over-whelming classical-yet-modern scenario that opens part two of *The Waste Land*. At her parties Tom remembered wearing fashionable green face pow-der from Paris 'which under artificial light gave a corpse like effect which had a great success'.[14] A decade or so later he looked back on the London beau monde of 'the Asquiths, Cunards, Diana Manners, and such people' as 'intelligent' and 'cultivated even', but also 'corruptly vulgar'.[15] He had not met Lady Cunard's daughter until 1919, around the time when he tried to resume correspondence with Emily Hale, making clear his 'keen interest' in all Emily did; but he mentions Nancy Cunard in an earlier letter and she too appears to have been in his mind while he worked on *The Waste Land*.[16] An extended section, removed from the typescript at the suggestion of Pound, had portrayed in Popeian couplets 'The white-armed Fresca', a modern, sexually promiscuous socialite with a taste for the eighteenth-century fic-tion of Samuel Richardson, for fashionable modern writer Jean Giraudoux, and for 'the Scandinavians' and 'Russians'. This Paris-loving Fresca writes poetry with a 'gloomy tone'. Its awkward fusion of late Victorian and mod-ernist elements is mocked, and she is summed up as 'a sort of can-can salonnière'; in another poem Tom linked 'Fresca' to 'Geo[rge] Moore'.[17] Nancy Fairbairn, like Tom, loved Paris and had spent time in Munich when she was young; well read, well versed in painting and music, and highly intelligent, she had a taste for Scandinavian and Russian as well as French and English writing. Later she would become known as a political activist during the Spanish Civil War, and for her commitment to the artistic achievements of the African diaspora – particularly in her huge 1934 anthol-ogy, *Negro*; but in the early 1920s she was best known as a glamorous, poetry-writing socialite. Recalled by Tom's friend Richard Aldington for her 'unlimited promiscuity', and by Leonard Woolf in terms of 'enchant-ment', Nancy was unusually close to the novelist George Moore, who was one of her mother's lovers, and, according to one rumour, Nancy's natural father.[18] Moore was among the reviewers of her sometimes downcast, self-subsidised poetry collection, *Outlaws*, published under the name Nancy Cunard in early 1921. 'My loves have been voracious' announces the speaker of one of its poems, while another celebrates being an 'outlaw from the rules of life'.[19] Tom's misogynistic depiction of 'Fresca' in the cancelled sec-tion of *The Waste Land* (which Nancy would never have seen) expresses Swiftian disgust at 'the good old hearty female stench' linked to the 'puss puss cat' who is 'Fresca'; but it shows an obsessive fascination.[20]

The fascination was mutual. In the early summer of 1919 when she had been reading George Moore's work and enjoying the company of another of her admirers, 'Hutchy' (St John Hutchinson, husband of Tom's close friend Mary Hutchinson), Nancy had encountered Tom. By that July, over lunch with Nancy, 'Hutchy' had talked about 'an amazing new poem by Eliot' – 'Gerontion', which was then in draft; Nancy had got hold of a copy which she dated 'July 1919'. It mentioned, but did not elaborate upon, 'Fresca'.[21] Mary Hutchinson in 1919 wrote of the sexual outlaw Nancy (who loved avant-garde clothes and jewellery) as 'wonderful, made of alabaster and gold and scarlet, with a face like Donatello's Saint George; a lady who would fit into the early court of Louis XIV or Boccaccio's world'.[22] Smart, and with a taste for 'the good things of life – caviar, plovers' eggs, champagne' – Nancy had looked for Tom in the audience when she sat in her mother's box at the ballet; he was one of the 'intellectual people' whom 'Hutchy' had urged Nancy to see 'frequently'; by 1921, Pound had counselled her with regard to obtaining criticism of her poetry, 'nobody in England knows anything, except Eliot, and he is too weary and too polite to distribute it'.[23] She read Tom's poetry obsessively, and maintained it 'changed my life'.[24] Her book-length poem *Parallax*, published in 1925, though old-fashioned in diction, is suffused with awareness of *The Waste Land*.

Even if details of her relationship with Tom are scanty, it is clear they met on several occasions when Nancy, who liked to cut a dash in Paris, Monte Carlo, and on the Côte d'Azur, was in England. Summering there in 1922, she was again in touch with 'Hutchy' and others of Tom's circle, while Tom in London sometimes took full advantage of Vivien's absence in the countryside. Signed 'with love', his letter to Mary Hutchinson of 23 June 1922, excusing his failure to appear when Mary had '*expected* me to dinner' (and explaining that, with Vivien away, he had been 'to dinner and a dance last night' prior to finishing a bottle of vermouth), hints at wild, 'rather fun' behaviour, and may date from around the time he slept with Nancy.[25]

During her final illness in 1965, Nancy sent Tom's friend John Hayward a mixture of lyrical effusion and recollection, recalling how in a 'red and gold' Parisian Poiret dress 'with cascading white tulle on the hips', she had danced with the Prince of Wales at one of her mother's balls, then encountered dinner-jacketed Tom in the supper room: 'you came in, alone too, for the first time to my eyes'. She remembered her passionate reaction to him: 'Seized was I by your looks, your way, your eyes, at that ball.' She wrote of dining with him, and of their nocturnal 'tryst' at the Eiffel Tower restaurant in London's Percy Street, where, above the Vorticist Room decorated by Wyndham Lewis, Nancy had kept a private apartment. There, when they should have been dining with the Hutchinsons elsewhere, Nancy and Tom had sat on the floor, and had grown, in her words, 'as close as close could be'. Drinking double gins, they had spoken of 'passion and repression' while a gas fire blazed. While this prose 'poem' written just before Nancy Cunard died does not explicitly say that she slept with Tom, and is hazy about chronology, it clearly unsettled Hayward, who feared it might 'hint at "revelations!"' [26]

Though Tom in 1927 confessed he had known 'minor pleasures of drunkenness and adultery', it was not until 2020 that the release of his letters to Emily Hale made public details of his attempted 'love affair' with a 'notorious' young society woman when 'a very brief incident of one evening' in 1922 constituted his 'adultery'. [27] His description of his lover as 'a goodhearted woman' who had been 'corrupted by a bad mother', and who 'found another lover almost at once' is further evidence that she was Nancy Cunard – who soon left for the continent and had a 'brief affair' with Wyndham Lewis in Venice. [28] Long afterwards, Vivien's brother recalled Nancy as one of the women who might have 'lured' Tom away from his marriage; Mary Hutchinson, whose memoir of Tom hints at how she too saw him as a potential lover, was also 'for a brief moment', Tom recalled, 'infatuated (unsuccessfully) with me'. [29] How much Vivien knew of his infidelity is uncertain, but her vituperative question to Tom in a surviving fragmentary letter of 1926 – 'Why can't I even have the freedom & respect which is accorded to Nancy the *real* tart?' – suggests she had some sense of his betrayal. [30]

By the end of 1922, Tom, left with an unforgettable 'taste of ashes' after his experience of adultery, wished the matter suppressed as completely as the 'Fresca' passage that had been excised from *The Waste Land*. In the version of the poem published in 1922 he had, however, embedded references to other people, places, and scenes, including ('almost word for word') Marie von Moritz with whom he had conversed and taken 'walks' in Munich in 1911 – and, more tellingly, Emily Hale. [31] Having acted alongside Tom in amateur theatricals before he left America, 'Miss Emily Hale' had gone on to coach drama students at Boston's Simmons College. [32] There in 1916 she had directed Shakespeare's *The Tempest*, and, among her many performances, in 1917 she had played 'The Marchioness' in a drama of the French Revolution in which her stage husband, 'The Marquis', was well-known Brookline amateur thespian W. Graydon Stetson. [33] Stetson had been on local stages during Tom's time at Harvard, and by 1922, like Tom, he had become a banker. *The Waste Land* incorporates several references to *The Tempest*, as well as featuring 'one I knew' called 'Stetson' (whom Tom later described as a 'superior bank clerk'). [34] It will never be evident exactly how far the poem draws on Tom's longing for Emily, her world, and what she represented for him, but clearly, as the years passed, he wanted her to perceive that she was integral to it. Years later, he urged her to 're-read the hyacinth lines' in part one of the poem, 'and the lines toward the very end beginning "friend, blood shaking my heart" (where *we* means privately of course *I*)', making clear that they were not only autobiographical but also that they related to his love for her: 'I shall always write primarily for you.'[35] Bracketing the 'hyacinth lines' in which a lover is rendered speechless by intense feeling, his quotation in *The Waste Land* of passages from Wagner's *Tristan und Isolde* connects with his painfully vivid memory of being taken to that powerfully erotic opera in Boston years before by Emily and her parents; he would refer to Emily later as 'my dear Isolde'.[36] For Tom, in 1922 when it seemed he might never see Emily again, the poem crackled with a private intensity that other readers could sense, but not fully fathom.

Late that year, the work's publication provoked varied reactions: 'Some of the old timers and old academic critics hate it,' Tom's wealthy patron and meticulous US legal advisor John Quinn wrote from New York in December, 'The live ones delight in it.'[37] Conscious of the unease his jagged, avant-garde poem provoked among his siblings in America, who knew nothing of his still vivid feelings for Emily Hale or his adultery with Nancy Cunard, Tom sent as a Christmas present to his elder sister Charlotte a more conventionally melancholy book of verse: A. E. Housman's death-haunted 1896 volume *A Shropshire Lad* exuded nostalgia for a lost realm of 'blue remembered hills'.[38] He inscribed Charlotte's copy with love, signing it with his wife's first name preceding his own, as if to signal easy, considerate normality.[39] At home, though, ease was in very short supply. Recently delivered to the Eliots' flat was the December issue of *La Nouvelle Revue française* in whose pages Tom paid admiring tribute to novelist May Sinclair's psychoanalytically informed *Life and Death of Harriet Frean*. That tale portrayed a frustrated woman's mental growth and decay. He praised, too, his friend Sydney Schiff's new novel *Elinor Colhouse* for making readers forget they were reading a fiction: '*il semble que l'on repasse simplement en esprit la morne chronique d'existences humaines*' (it seems that one simply relives in spirit the dreary chronicle of human lives).[40] Tom's sense of life as waste and dreary was unabated. In late 1922 and early 1923 he wrote two essays about recently dead women whose demise emblematised his pervasive sense of loss. One was the working-class Marie Lloyd, 'the greatest music-hall artist of her time in England'; the other was the 'great actress' Sarah Bernhardt whose death in France marked 'the termination of an epoch'.[41]

He had been reading, too, the psychologist W. H. R. Rivers, chronicler of the supposedly uncivilised peoples of Melanesia; they were 'dying out' because '"Civilization" forced upon them has deprived them of all interest in life.' Just as in *The Waste Land* Tom had set ancient and 'primitive' rites alongside banal and sophisticated modern urban life, so in writing about Marie Lloyd, he concluded by juxtaposing a deathly vision of the increasingly technological society around him with his interpretation of Rivers's work:

> When every theatre has been replaced by 100 cinemas, when every musical instrument has been replaced by 100 gramophones, when every horse has been replaced by 100 cheap motor-cars, when electrical ingenuity has made it possible for every child to hear its bedtime stories from a loudspeaker, when applied science has done everything possible with the materials on this earth to make life as interesting as possible, it will not be surprising if the population of the entire civilized world rapidly follows the fate of the Melanesians.[42]

This is modernity as a death wish; for Tom in his bleakest moods that waste land was where he was living.

Yet, steeling himself, he persisted. In the 1920s and 1930s only the well-off in Britain could afford the sort of healthcare that his own and Vivien's illnesses seemed to demand. He earned enough to cover medical bills, rent, food, clothing and servants' wages, even if his income continued to be supplemented by gifts from Henry and his mother in America, as well as income from stocks inherited from his wealthy late father. Tom did not live now in the style he had known in his St Louis childhood, but the author of *The Waste Land* had earned considerably more than $2,000 (over $30,000 in today's terms) for a single poem; dressed for the occasion, he could mingle in high society. Some admirers of his work continued to try to raise money sufficient to release him from his day job, but Tom valued a secure income. Despite craving more time to write, he resisted attempts to lure him away from his banker's salary.

Each weekday and on Saturday mornings, in his dark, three-piece suit, he commuted for about half an hour to work in the Information Department of Lloyds Bank at 75 Lombard Street in London's financial district, the City. Right opposite stood the steeple clock of St Mary Woolnoth Church, whose 'dead sound on the final stroke of nine' was, he commented in *The Waste Land*'s notes, 'A phenomenon which I have often noticed.'[43] At Lloyds, he was Head Office employee 'number 239'.[44] He worked – officially for 'forty-four hours a week' – in a small financial intelligence unit, investigating and monitoring settlement of Great War enemy debts in the wake of the Treaty of Versailles.[45] Intellectually demanding, this task required reading 'ten or fifteen papers a day' to keep up with shifts in

'foreign budgets, movements of crops, agricultural banks, oil developments' and other areas. Winning him the respect of colleagues, his bank
work, like his editorial labours on the *Criterion*, involved writing, printing,
and publishing. Circulated through internal bank publications, his regular
reports on foreign financial developments informed Lloyds's legal and
commercial operations. Often he came in early and worked late. Other
responsibilities included supervising support staff – three men and four
young women – plus attending to the bank's 'printing press (which is
always breaking down)'.[46]

In both professional and domestic life a sense of breakdown was never
far away. Bank work offered refuge from intimate troubles, but was also a
burden. For several years he produced measured, dry reports about currency shifts on foreign exchanges, and tracked industrial fluctuations.
Published in *Lloyds Bank Monthly: A Survey of International Trade Conditions*,
in the decade that would culminate in the stock market crash of 1929, these
reports about 'weakness', 'depressed' markets, lack of 'any appreciable alle-
viation', and searches for 'stability' among 'disasters' and 'collapse' used
language that had a bearing, too, on his personal life where again he feared
'complete paralysis' or even 'collapse'.[47] He strove to locate some sense of
order in his existence outside the bank.

Vivien's broken health meant she had no regular paid employment. She
stayed at home in the flat, often chatting with Ellen Kellond, the maid who
had been with them now for four years. Ellen had met several visiting
members of Tom's American family, and Vivien regarded her as a friend.
Nine years older than her employers, Ellen came from a very different
milieu: born in a Camden workhouse, she was the illegitimate daughter of
a servant mother and a labourer-cum-housepainter. Growing up poor in
Kensington and Chelsea, she had worked for years as cook and domestic
servant; in 1912, aged thirty-three, she had married George Kellond, a car-
man three years her senior; but, just over two years later, her husband had
died.[48] Childless like Vivien, Ellen was a lively raconteur: Tom described
The Waste Land's abortion narrative about demobbed 'Albert' and his wife
'Lil' as 'pure Ellen Kellond' – Ellen had 'recounted it'.[49] Along with Vivien
and Pound, she was, albeit unwittingly, among the most important collaborators in the making of his poem.[50]

Frequently by the time Tom returned from work, Vivien was tired, and
saw her husband 'pretty well worn out'; nonetheless, he sat typing late into
the night, corresponding about the editing, proofing, and accounts of the
quarterly *Criterion*. Its financial backer was Lady Rothermere, whose parties Tom sometimes attended. He thought her 'much more like an American
than any English woman I have ever met'. She had 'a great liking for

Americans and America'; he felt 'One of my greatest pulls with her is being an American myself.'[51] Lilian Rothermere, however, considered Tom's new magazine dull. She paid printers' bills and contributors' fees, but, partly to support the journal and partly so Lloyds Bank did not think he was moonlighting, Tom accepted no payment for editorial labours. Soon he felt 'a damned fool ever to agree to run the review without a salary; or, in fact, to run it at all'.[52]

He never seemed to have enough time. While many of London's better-off professional writers enjoyed long literary lunches, he was obliged to stick to bank lunch breaks, which began at noon and were 'strictly limited to an hour'.[53] If he met friends or associates during the week, they had to come to eateries near his City workplace; otherwise, there was no time. Saturday afternoons and Sundays were for catching up, but he was dogged by 'months of insufficient sleep'.[54]

Still, he had an intimidating gift for focusing single-mindedly. 'Selection and concentration' were what he admired most in Marie Lloyd; such abilities had made her not just a great popular entertainer but a superior artist.[55] Having relished ragtime and vaudeville since childhood, he continued to savour music-hall stars. In what little free time he had, he attended performances by English artistes including Little Tich, Nellie Wallace, George Robey, and Marie Lloyd. In her 'last song' as Tom called it – the choral item with which she liked to finish a show – Lloyd had collapsed on stage while singing about herself as a ruin.[56] The audience, however, thinking she was simply acting, had 'shrieked with laughter'.[57] Simultaneously tragic and comic, her death was to Tom an 'important event'.[58]

Ever alert to literal and metaphorical resonance, he admired Lloyd's 'tone of voice'; representing phonetically her cockney singing, he gave the title of her 'last song' as 'One of the Ruins that Cromwell Knocked Abaht a Bit'. He saw the working-class audience's participation in choruses of Lloyd's songs as part of that 'collaboration of the audience with the artist which is necessary in all art and most obviously in dramatic art'.[59] As the chorus of her last number was belted out, singer and audience sang together of themselves as ruins: 'I'm one of the ruins that Cromwell knocked about a bit.'[60] In *The Waste Land*, which, like 'The Hollow Men', often relies on choral effects, the last seven lines that begin with the popular nursery-rhyme song of breakdown 'London Bridge is falling down', and precede the final Sanskrit hush, present an unforgettable acoustic of smash-up. Though it's not at all evident who is voicing its words, one of the poem's most memorable lines is 'These fragments I have shored against my ruins'.[61] Here, as in Marie Lloyd's song, the 'ruins' might be those of physical stonework, but they are also the ruins of a person – 'my ruins' – and suggest that the 'I' here is a ruined self.

The waste, the ruin, seems spiritual, not just physical. With its allusions to the Bible, to ancient fertility ceremonies, to the Buddha's Fire Sermon, Sanskrit sacred texts and legends of the Holy Grail, the poem articulates a desperate search for some frame of belief that may order chaos. For all his biting ironic self-consciousness, and indeed because of it, Tom still quested for a system to which he could give spiritual assent. In different guises and voices, *The Waste Land* articulates a ruined self, because no such system seems strong enough to stave off that terrible sense of ruin.

In its allusive method, its ritual repetitions and consecutive patterns, his poem presents a poetics of reincarnation. Much later he remarked that around the time of its composition he had considered becoming a Buddhist. After studying Japanese Buddhism at Harvard, he had attended a Buddhist society during his Oxford postgraduate year, so this interest was hardly new. He calls the 'Shantih shantih shantih' which concludes *The Waste Land* 'a formal ending to an Upanishad'.[62] Upanishads are ancient Hindu texts, many of which are revered by Buddhists. For a Buddhist the 'shantih' is the peace that lies in a state beyond all the *samsara* cycles of pain and passion; yet in *The Waste Land* such peace is present less as an achieved condition, more as a maddeningly unattainable possibility. Glossing its meaning in one of the notes he added to bulk out the poem when it became a book, Tom, revealingly, translated 'shantih' into a Christian equivalent. Using a phrase from chapter four of St Paul's letter to the Philippians in the King James Bible, he wrote that ' "The Peace which passeth understanding" is our equivalent to this word.'[63]

If the poet's final note to his poem points in the direction of Christianity, no reader of *The Waste Land* is likely to conclude that such a direction has been reached easily. To most people the poem's Sanskrit words sound dauntingly remote. That may be part of the point. When the note suggests what 'our equivalent' to 'shantih' may be, its use of the word 'our' implies some measure of identification with Christian tradition. Perceptively, Henry discerned in his brother's poem an approach to 'Biblical seriousness', adding, with a note of piety and concern, 'Heaven direct your steps.'[64] Their mother, to whom Tom had written in 1922 saying he 'had put so much of his own life into' *The Waste Land*, knew he was planning a new poem. Attuned to Tennyson as well as to Tom, she hoped he might 'supplement *The Waste Land* by its natural sequence "The Coming of the Grail" '.[65]

The Waste Land speaks of ruin, broken-ness, pain and wastage, but, substantially thanks to Pound's editorial guidance, it possesses form and order, repeatedly and tellingly aligning past and present. Overworked and exhausted, order was what Tom sought. It was what his bank work demanded, as he attempted to identify patterns in Europe's financial turbulence; an essay he worked on for a considerable time before publishing it in 1923 argued that the sort of 'mythical method' exemplified by Joyce's *Ulysses* ('the most important expression which the present age has found') offered 'ways of controlling, of ordering, of giving a shape and a significance to the immense panorama of futility and anarchy which is contemporary history'; *The Waste Land* attempted this too.[66] For Tom, faced with potential ruin of all sorts ('He is like a person about to break down', wrote Virginia Woolf in February), this search for order was paramount.[67]

Sometimes it had embarrassing results. On 2 January 1923, eager to humour Lady Rothermere and alert to potential new employers, he met Lord Rothermere to discuss a possible 'position in journalism'.[68] Rothermere, owner of the *Daily Mail*, was a plutocratic, philandering English press baron with markedly right-wing views; he lived apart from his wife, who had conducted an affair with his younger brother. Rothermere agreed to meet Tom, but kept him at a certain distance, telling him 'the political situation was so dangerous' that he should remain in the bank, and get in touch again after a few months.[69] Tom tried to maintain the pressure, telling Lady Rothermere in February, 'I have become more and more convinced that I must leave the bank ultimately.' Could Lord Rothermere 'give me a literary post (even a small one) on one of his journals?'[70] Just days after meeting Rothermere, Tom sent a letter to the *Daily Mail*, expressing 'cordial approval' of that paper's 'attitude on nearly every public question of present importance', and particularly commending 'the remarkable series of articles which you have been publishing on Fascismo'.[71] Reflecting anxieties about Bolshevism in the wake of the 1917 Russian Revolution (which, banker Tom thought in 1923, had seen 'trade and commerce annihilated'), these articles extolled the 'wonderful epic' of Italy's 'Black Shirt' Fascist Revolution led by Mussolini.[72] Lady Rothermere sought a meeting with Mussolini in 1923.[73] Tom's sycophantic 'thank you' to the *Daily Mail* seems part of what he described to his brother as 'solidifying myself with the Rothermeres'.[74] It also signals that, although just a few years earlier he had described himself as inclined to support the Labour Party in Britain, he now found Labour's rise an 'alarming' generator of 'anxiety and confusion' which might herald 'panic and depression'.[75]

Writing to Ford Madox Ford, he sympathised with Ford's Francophile literary stance, and explained his sympathy was 'united (politically) within hereditary and ineradicable toryism'.[76] Tom's familial American Republicanism, his privileged education at Harvard by such advocates of classical order as Irving Babbitt, his long-standing intellectual interest in the French right-wing thought of Charles Maurras, his growing friendship with the old Tory man of letters Charles Whibley (now almost a father figure to him), as well as his need to find some ordering principles in the midst of European chaos and threatened personal breakdown – all these inclined him to the attractions of order as championed by politicians of the right.

Vivien, whose own politics tended in similar directions, disliked Whibley, but did not dissent from her husband's politics. Calling him 'Dearest darling Wing' and then 'Wang' ('wing-wang' is slang for penis), she thanked him in mid-January 1923 for his 'very sweet satisfying letters'.[77] With her aspiring writer friend Irene Pearl Fassett, twenty-year-old daughter of an American-born gramophone company manager, Vivien was staying at Eastbourne on the south coast as part of 'an experiment' – living apart as she tried to regain health in the sea air. She felt some improvement, but was still immensely tired and 'hideous green and blotched'; anxiously, she insisted Tom keep in close touch by letter and telegram.[78] One disturbing piece of news was that Katherine Mansfield had died in France after a long illness. Relations between Mansfield, her husband John Middleton Murry, and the Eliots had been strained and sometimes difficult, but Tom (despite regarding Mansfield's literary reputation as 'inflated') had managed to stay close to Murry while disagreeing with his apparently vague and sentimental ideas.[79] Telling Murry he felt Mansfield's loss 'very very deeply', Tom knew what it meant to be married to a woman tormented by illness.[80] In Eastbourne, leafing through the Boni & Liveright *Waste Land*, Vivien knew better than anyone except her husband how much of their own sense of waste the poem contained. She told Tom the book's technical production was *'very nice'*; all she had to say about the second issue of the *Criterion* (which contained Tom's 'Marie Lloyd' essay) was that it was *'not bad'*.[81]

Struggling to work at home, and 'within measurable distance of the end of my tether', Tom began renting a small office-flat in St Martin's Lane, near Trafalgar Square.[82] This bolthole, 38 Burleigh Mansions, was designed to be a temporary arrangement, known only to Vivien and close friends, where Tom could do *Criterion* work uninterrupted while the Eliots planned to look for a different flat. It had been hard to keep work and home life apart: renting office space was yet another attempt to establish order, though Tom's determination to keep his refuge secret caused some amusement and annoyance. Visitors were told to ask for 'Captain Eliot'.[83]

Sure that the *Criterion* should be international in literary coverage, he also wanted it to signal commitment to principles of order. These, despite his assertion that 'the review can only maintain its literary usefulness by keeping outside of political [discussion]', were at times politically tinged.[84] To one potential contributor he explained privately in 1923 that, while 'independent of party politics', the magazine was 'a Conservative review' which was 'leagued with an ideal rather than with the actual Tory party'. 'I should like', he added, 'to give to Toryism the intellectual basis with the illusion of which Socialism has so long deceived the young and eager. And I believe that the intellectual hold of socialism on the young is weakening, and that there is the chance of establishing an austere classicism.'[85] At his most messianic he saw the magazine's 'main programme' as 'literary, social and political reform', and he even 'toyed' more than once 'with the notion of the formation of a non-parliamentary political party'.[86] Though in print he eschewed much explicit engagement with contemporary politics, he commissioned pieces such as Whibley's two-part study of early eighteenth-century English Tory Viscount Bolingbroke; this material sat awkwardly alongside a contemporary French discussion of 'the vampire of love' and some previously unpublished letters by Dostoyevsky, but the *Criterion* sought to appeal to the conservatively inclined in politics and to readers with a taste for the literary avant-garde, bringing the two together in its pages just as its editor now did in his life.[87]

On weekdays, Tom read foreign (especially European) newspapers, precising news for *Lloyds Bank Monthly* and assembling 'a daily sheet' of selections for *Lloyds Bank Extracts from the Foreign Press*; sometimes he was criticised for perceived Americanisms: 'a superior drew to his attention' to the phrase ' "under the circumstances" '.[88] At home in the evenings, he kept the *Criterion* alert to literary developments abroad, particularly in Europe and the United States; from 1923 onwards, it incorporated summaries of interesting work from overseas periodicals such as the *Dial* or *La Nouvelle Revue française*. Though other people wrote these epitomes, Tom oversaw the work, setting up exchanges with periodicals in France, Spain, Germany, America, and elsewhere. His literary activities and bank work demanded verbal judgement, internationally minded alertness, and commercial sense. Repeatedly he asked his printer to count numbers of words in articles, so he could calculate just how much each contributor should be paid. As an editor in Lombard Street, in St Martin's Lane, and at Clarence Gate Gardens he totted up accounts, able to demonstrate to Lady Rothermere's auditors and to his Lloyds colleagues that he was an astute manager whose sense of order was valuable – even if, on occasion, at the bank 'he had long hours of overwork because his [balance] sheets did not come out right'.[89]

Criterion correspondence reinforced his relations with eminent writers – from Yeats to Paul Valéry, from E. M. Forster and Virginia Woolf to Hugo von Hofmannsthal and Ford Madox Ford – all of whom had work appearing in the *Criterion* during 1923. Yet few of the authors he published offered him their most exciting writing. He steered his magazine determinedly, but nothing had the same impact as his own poem in its very first issue. Vivien's glancing verdict – *'not bad'* – was harsh, but, though often she helped him with the journal, her implication that the *Criterion* was not her husband's greatest achievement is shrewd. Soon, Pound called most of its contributors a 'bunch of dead mushrooms'.[90] Tom regretted the way the magazine threatened to exhaust his creative energies, doing him 'more harm than good'.[91] Producing it proved, however, that this internationally connected young American was a skilled, tenacious editor as well as a poet; his distinction, even if not generally known, was already remarkable. Yet, asked by a fellow London editor in January 1923 if he had any verse to submit, Tom replied truthfully, 'I have not produced the slightest scrap for a year.'[92]

But he knew what he wanted to write. Several years earlier he had told Virginia Woolf he aimed to explore further his disturbing creation, Sweeney. In early 1922 he had discussed Aristophanes with Pound, who had linked that ancient Greek dramatist to 'native negro phoque melodies of Dixee' in the context of raising 'the ball-encumbered phallus of man'.[93] Coming to terms with his own adultery as well as with Vivien's, Tom continued to ponder 'moulding a contemporary narrative upon an ancient myth' in the context of *Ulysses*, Pound's ongoing *Cantos*, and *The Waste Land*, but was determined that 'whatever I do next will be, at least, very different'.[94] He had not, however, left behind the contemplation of order and myth in the context of angst-ridden sexuality.

He had been reading with fascination work by Alfred Kreymborg, a New Yorker who wrote poems in free verse as well as plays for puppets. Kreymborg had visited him at Clarence Gate Gardens the year before, impressed by how the banker poet drank 'Scotch and soda' and 'smiled his sphinx-like smile and nodded in a friendly fashion'. Tom's apparently 'casual question about writing for puppets', had prompted Kreymborg to enthuse about marionette plays. The visitor was struck by Tom's 'English manner, which he wore like a native', and detected connections between his life and poetry:

> The man was as clearly the expression of the artist as the artist was of the man. The suave intelligence was given over to the pursuit of refinements of experience from which unnecessary details dropped away with an ironical though almost imperceptible smile. The man was beautiful to look at as well as to listen to.[95]

Genuinely interested in Kreymborg's puppet work, around early April 1923 Tom was pondering striking differences between realistic acting styles and the technique of an actor able to make 'himself into a figure, a marionette' with a 'mask-like beauty'. Some of his earlier poetry had drawn on the dramatic-monologue genre. Now he gravitated towards three-dimensional theatre, imagining a future stage with actors (like the principal performer he had watched in Yeats's *At the Hawk's Well*) trained in balletic 'movement and gesture'. His ideal was the Ballets Russes dancer Leonid Massine – 'completely unhuman, impersonal, abstract'. In Massine, as in that very different stage artiste, Marie Lloyd, he saw the potential of ritual:

> The realism of the ordinary stage is something to which we can no longer respond, because to us it is no longer realistic. We know now that the gesture of daily existence is inadequate for the stage; instead of pretending that the stage gesture is a copy of reality, let us adopt a literal untruth, a thorough-going convention, a ritual. For the stage – not only in its remote origins, but always – is a ritual, and the failure of the contemporary stage to satisfy the craving for ritual is one of the reasons why it is not a living art.

What was needed too was a new sense of rhythm, allied with at least some aspects of popular culture. With that in mind, Tom turned from the music hall of Marie Lloyd to the cinema of Charlie Chaplin: 'The egregious merit of Chaplin is that he has escaped in his own way from the realism of the cinema and invented a rhythm.'[96] Having bought F. M. Cornford's *The Origins of Attic Comedy*, he read about the roots of Aristophanic drama in fertility rites; his interest in unusual dramatic possibilities afforded by Kreymborg's stylised puppet theatre was real.

His sphinx-like smile, like his wearying sense of having to 'live in a mask all one's life', helped him conceal intimate worries.[97] 'I am worn out, I cannot go on', he told his virulently antisemitic supporter John Quinn, adding splenetically with regard to *The Waste Land*'s publisher Liveright, 'I am sick of doing business with Jew publishers who will not carry out their part of the contract unless they are forced to.' Drawing on his parents' antisemitism and falling in line with Quinn's complaints about 'swarms of horrible-looking Jews', he wished he 'could find a decent Christian publisher in New York'.[98] Displays of despair, anger, and prejudice at this time were symptomatic of his being, as Virginia Woolf put it on 13 March, 'on the verge of collapse'.[99] He seemed to her 'broken down' when she and others plotted to install him as literary editor of the *Nation*; thanking her 'on the telephone' (a means of communication he disliked), he 'couldn't speak for tears'.[100] Yet, not long afterwards, unsympathetic to the paper's Liberal politics, and cleaving to financial security at the bank, he wrote to John Maynard Keynes, the *Nation*'s chairman, making clear this new job would not suit him. Tom was exasperating, Woolf complained: he 'let drop by drop of his agonised perplexities fall ever so finely through pure cambric'. Dealing with him was 'dreary work'. She wished 'poor dear Tom had more spunk in him'.[101] He did show a flash of anger that March when Ben Hecht, a Chicago journalist with a Jewish surname, wrote of *The Waste Land* as 'a hoax on the American public'; its poet was a man who 'hates Americans'. Tom the admirer of boxing denounced Hecht as a 'liar', mentioned 'legal action', and implied he would like to take 'physical action'.[102]

He maintained, though, a determined practicality. In early 1923 the Eliots searched for a country cottage offering a prospect of relaxation for Vivien – and perhaps for Tom, advised 'most emphatically' by a 'specialist in Harley Street' to take several weeks' holiday as soon as 'possible'.[103] They rented an end-terrace two-storey house at 2 Milestone Cottages on the main road at Old Fishbourne, a small West Sussex coastal village two miles from Chichester. Close to Bosham, where they had summered previously, and where Tom had signed the Parish Church visitors' book as early as 14 June 1919, Fishbourne railway station was less than two hours from London Victoria.[104] Vivien hoped to recuperate, but also mentioned to Mary Hutchinson the possibility of 'the poet's wife dying in a humble cot'.[105] As well as 'electric treatment', she was now undergoing 'Plombières'.[106] Developed in France and widely practised at fashionable 1920s English spas, this involved a rubber catheter 'inserted about 9 inches into the intestinal tract' and douches of pressurised warm water in a process of colonic irrigation.[107] Diagnosed with 'Catarrh of the intestines, with occasional enteritis', Vivien seems to have been afflicted with repeated intestinal inflammation.[108] Her ordeals exhausted her, and stressed Tom.

Minor concerns compounded major ones: an official letter from Methuen warned him 'demand for your book *The Sacred Wood* is not very good'; copies would be remaindered.[109] More importantly, he worried, too, about his seventy-year-old widowed mother in Cambridge, Massachusetts. Sometimes using the language of a lover, he reproached her for keeping him 'in unnecessary suspense and deluded hope'. He had mentioned 'in nearly every letter' his 'counting on seeing' her in 1923: 'how I long to see you'.[110] If only she would come to London that summer, then 'I should live here at Clarence [Gate Gardens] with you', while Vivien might spend time elsewhere.[111] Ever anxious about her younger son, Lottie Eliot was distressed by his letters: 'I am sorry for him, more sorry than I can tell'; but she resented his 'reproaching me as bitterly as he is doing', even if he was 'sore tried' by circumstances.[112] Such exchanges strained the patience of Tom's sisters and brother, with whom their mother communed: 'He makes the very best of his marriage', but it had been 'a great misfortune, and becomes more and more so. I can not bear to look forward for him.'[113] Lottie worried she might die without seeing him again: perhaps he might visit her 'if I feel the end approaching'.[114] Each fuelled the other's anxieties. Perceiving his 'nerves' were 'unstrung', she found this hard to reconcile with his appearance in photographs: 'you look so smiling, I cannot realize how troubled you are'.[115] It had become second nature to him to conceal his emotional and mental turmoil from people he met. To his mother he revealed inner ruin:

> I am simply distracted and destroyed – everything seems to be crumbling away about me and under me, and I am faced with most vital decisions deciding my whole future. But those I must tell you about separately and face as best I can: they come at a time when I want you very much. You will never know how constantly I think of you, and how at every moment of anxiety or despair, as well as in success or happiness, I have longed for your presence.[116]

She cabled immediately, and wrote to Vivien, urging her to let Tom come to America. Lottie would pay for his return trip. Admittedly this would involve Vivien in 'some self-denial' if her husband sailed away, but surely it would be 'better than' Tom having 'a nervous collapse'.[117] Vivien, undergoing her Plombières treatment, was experiencing 'utter prostration and general numbness' while wrestling with depression.[118] In the wake of Tom's declining the *Nation* job, Quinn and American banker Otto H. Kahn guaranteed him $600 if he left the bank because of illness. He struggled to reach a decision. 'If Vivian [*sic*] was enough of a support to him, Tom would not need me', his mother opined to Henry.[119] Vivien, who had always found Tom's mother hard to deal with, grew increasingly worn out.

She was looked after by Cambridge-trained physician Hubert Higgins of Culworth House, St John's Wood, where she and Tom had lodged briefly in 1916. Interested in 'neurasthenia', Higgins was a disciple of the 'Great Masticator', American physician Horace Fletcher, whom he had assisted with *The A.B.-Z. of Our Own Nutrition* (1903).[120] Higgins's *Humaniculture* (1906) denounced 'hurried eating', linking healthy digestion to ordered civil government; bad eating could lead to lunacy.[121] Like Tom, Higgins prized order. In 1922 in *The Times*, he had defended 'the authority of the physician' in the face of 'anarchy'.[122] Tom thought Higgins spoke 'quite coldly' but 'clearly and cogently': if Vivien did not '*consider herself*', she would '*certainly die*'. Like all her earlier doctors, Higgins counselled that Vivien '*ought to be alone*', avoiding undue excitation. Her illness's 'root and core' was '*malnutrition . . . of which colitis is only a symptom*'. Tom hoped his and Vivien's health might benefit from time at Fishbourne, but their situation was desperate: 'When we do get to the country we shall simply have to bury ourselves completely in order to save our lives.'[123]

Before they could move house in the spring of 1923, Vivien went completely numb. Gasping for breath, she had severe palpitations. Tom phoned four different doctors. Almost immediately, she 'had a terrific colitis explosion', voiding accumulated matter. Higgins and another physician arrived, concluding 'that this saved her life. Otherwise, she would have died of acute toxaemia, or of the strain on the heart of the effort to resist it.' Since the danger seemed over, the doctors advised she be moved to the country at once. The Eliots 'came down in a car' to Fishbourne, but their cottage on the main road was noisy; Vivien suffered a second, night-long crisis, then a further attack. For three days she was fed 'little drops of milk and teaspoonfuls of brandy to keep her alive'. Tom sent for her elderly mother from London; arrangements were made to hire a nurse. Experiencing 'a series of intestinal crises', Vivien 'wasted . . . to an absolute skeleton'.[124]

As medics struggled to determine the problem, diagnosing not just 'colitis' but 'septic influenza', possible 'pneumonia', and ongoing 'malnutrition', Tom's own health deteriorated.[125] Struggling to maintain the *Criterion*, how could he provide for Vivien ('She will never be strong enough to shift for herself'), especially if he left the bank? Medical bills for twice-daily local doctors and Higgins's twice-weekly visits were 'almost ruinous'; he told Murry he felt at 'an ebb-tide, in *every* respect'.[126] Fortunately, the bank granted him more leave. Investigating a possible lecturing 'connection with Oxford' where Ottoline Morrell had friends, Tom left Vivien and stayed overnight at Balliol College in early May, talking about literary criticism to undergraduates.[127] A little later, he tried to resume work in London, but felt stymied: 'If we could only go *abroad* for a long time and hide and forget everything!!'[128]

In distress, he turned to reading poetry. In mid-May on the train between London and Chichester he devoured the *Poésies de A. O. Barnabooth* by Valery Larbaud, one of the *Criterion*'s European contributors. One particularly striking poem expressed 'a feeling which I have felt myself very strongly'.[129] The persona in 'Le don de soi-même' ('The Gift of Myself') speaks of something '*d'infiniment aride*' (infinitely arid) at his heart: an inner being with a life of its own nonetheless lives the speaker's life and listens impassively to his conscience, appearing

Un être fait de néant, si c'est possible,
Insensible à mes souffrances physiques,
Qui ne pleure pas quand je pleure,
Qui ne rit pas quand je ris,
Qui ne rougit pas quand je commets une action honteuse,
Et qui ne gémit pas quand mon coeur est blessé;

23

Qui se tient immobile et ne donne pas de conseils,
Mais semble dire éternellement:
'Je suis là, indifférent à tout.'

(A being, if it is possible, made of nothingness,
Indifferent to my physical sufferings,
Who does not cry when I cry,
Who does not laugh when I laugh,
Who does not blush when I commit a shameful act,
And who does not groan when my heart is injured;
Who stands stock-still and offers no advice,
But seems to say eternally:
'Here I am, indifferent to it all.')[130]

Vivien admired 'extraordinary detachment' and 'cool indifference' in literary style.[131] Many artists feel in themselves such a phenomenon as Larbaud describes. For Tom this feeling was coupled with acute self-consciousness, and a conviction he had to keep part of himself steeled to go on working, earning, and conducting everyday affairs – otherwise, all would be lost. Though he struggled on while Vivien was cared for, not everyone found his coping mechanisms attractive. When he dined with the Woolfs on 17 May, Virginia, knowing 'Mrs Eliot has almost died at times in the past month', found him 'infinitely considerate', yet also 'perfectly detached'; she likened him to a monk in a 'chilly' cell.[132] Aware matters were dire, Tom had left Vivien in the country, supervised by her mother and a young male carer. On 20 May, writing to Pound who hoped to boost Tom's income, he thanked his old friend, confessing that 'On contemplating suicide a short time ago she [Vivien] was going to leave you a letter.' Then he inked in a one-word sentence: 'Hell.'[133]

Urgently needing help, he arranged with Lady Rothermere to hire Richard Aldington, a writer experienced in literary journalism, as managing editor of the *Criterion* at '£50 a year'.[134] Tom's editorial work continued unremunerated, but Lilian Rothermere increased the magazine's financial guarantee from £600 to £750, offering Tom remuneration of £300 per annum for three years if he left the bank. Conscious he earned much more at Lloyds, and was in line for a pension if he stayed, he secured two further weeks' bank leave, and managed to produce for Leonard Woolf at the *Nation and Athenaeum* a review-essay on Donne's love poems. Tom thought it 'a failure, incoherent, badly written'.[135] He was reluctant to separate Donne's erotic from his religious verse, especially in a modern era when 'we accept the belief that any state of mind is extremely complex, and chiefly composed of odds and ends in constant flux manipulated by desire and fear'. Though he did not say so, *The Waste Land*, that poem of odds and ends in constant flux, could appear a love-poem manqué; but it could also sound religious. Writing about Donne, Tom emphasised again, citing *Ulysses*, the importance of 'myth' as an ordering principle.[136] The need for 'order' was stressed too when he set out the 'function' of the *Criterion* – order as opposed to the 'chaos' of that vaguer term ' "life" '.[137]

With Lady Rothermere's approval, he proposed a series of volumes by *Criterion* contributors, to be published by the journal's printer, Richard Cobden-Sanderson, whose father had produced celebrated collectors' editions. For the first, a translation of Paul Valéry's poem *Le Serpent*, Tom would write an introduction. Pondering myth, he drew on anthropological reading he had done as a student, and solicited *Criterion* essays from J. G. Frazer, Jane Harrison, F. M. Cornford, G. Elliot Smith, and other anthropologically influenced scholars. Some, but by no means all, obliged.

By mid-June Vivien was improving. She informed Virginia Woolf she had been driving in the Fishbourne area, looking for a better cottage. Returning to London, however, she complained to Murry of 'real despair, which isolates and freezes one'.[138] The Eliots met briefly with James Joyce, who was in town with his wife Nora, but Tom, arranging for the Joyces to have tea with him and Ottoline Morrell at sumptuous Frascati's in Oxford Street, thought Vivien 'not strong enough to see many people yet'.[139] Lady Ottoline recommended Vivien consult Dr Karl Bernold Martin, head physician of the Sanatorium Hoven, Freiburg, who was visiting London, ministering to high-society patients. Martin had published work on anaemia; his sanatorium, whose clients included Lady Rothermere, specialised in nervous, digestive and metabolic disorders, offering dietary treatments and boasting of *'langjahrige Erfahrung in Psychotherapie'* (many years of experience in psychotherapy).[140] The Eliots had two 'long interviews' with him. After making 'bacteriological analyses', the reputedly 'great doctor' found 'an extraordinary excess of streptococcus fecalis, and other mischievous cocci', and encouraged Vivien to travel to Freiburg. Fearing 'ruinous expenses', Tom doubted this would be possible.[141] Instead, with Martin's encouragement, Vivien passed into the care of another physician, 'the Swede', Dr Cyriax, but suffered a 'bad relapse'.[142] Her treatment involved her 'having her meat minced in a mincing machine' to make it easier to digest.[143] The machine had to be inspected daily to make absolutely sure it was clean.

She took to bed again at Fishbourne. Tom visited at weekends. He asked Mary Hutchinson (whose nearby country home, Eleanor House at West Wittering, Vivien admired) if she could help them find another cottage, and arranged to picnic with Mary at Fishbourne. Later in the summer, Mary proposed 'to give Vivien a course of reading'; Tom was keen the *Criterion* publish 'caustic sketches of the sort of people who are typical of our time': he had asked Sydney Schiff to author some, and Vivien was turning to writing too.[144] Seeking outlets for her own creativity, she was 'painting furniture very beautifully', Tom told Mary, to whom he felt confidingly – even flirtatiously – close.[145] Sensing Mary's infatuation with him, he was exhausted with Vivien, but knew where his responsibilities lay. He took out a life insurance policy naming Vivien as his beneficiary; his brother paid the first premium, but Tom was unsettled when, as he confessed to Henry, the doctor who examined him in connection with the policy told him that his congenital 'hernia was worse (on the *other* side) and I should wear a truss and perhaps have an operation'. Further consultations were called for. Things were 'very bad'.[146]

His conversation with Kreymborg stayed in his mind, and he read both a manuscript on puppetry and Kreymborg's new *Puppet Plays* volume, with scripts including 'Manikin and Minikin' in which male and female marionettes engage in emotionally edgy, repetitive dialogue whose verse is inflected with jazz-age rhythms:

> SHE. It's been hours, days, weeks –
> by the sound of that everlasting clock –
> and the coming of day and the going of day –
> since I saw you last!
> HE. What's the use of the sun
> with its butterfly wings of light –
> what's the use of a sun made to see by –
> if I can't see you!
> SHE. Manikin!
> HE. Minikin?
> SHE. Say that again!
> HE. Why should I say it again – don't you know?
> SHE. I know, but sometimes I doubt –
> HE. Why do you, what do you doubt?
> SHE. Please say it again![147]

Tom read these plays several times, convinced Kreymborg had 'really got hold of something new and fruitful in rythym [*sic*]'. Asking how to make a puppet, he wanted 'to build a small theatre – a box small enough to stand on a table 3 × 3 ft – and preordain every move and gesture and grouping'. This wish matched his conviction drama must become ritualistic and balletic. He told Kreymborg he proposed a play of his own: 'I am trying to get at a dominant rythym and subordinated rythyms for the thing – I expect it will be called jazz drama.'[148] Drawing on the anthropologically influenced classical scholarship of Cornford, this would become *Sweeney Agonistes*. By early September he informed Pound he had 'mapt out' an 'Aristophanic comedy', but 'must devote study to phallic songs, also agons [conflict scenes]'. In his life, he worried about his hernia; in his poetry, he turned again to structuring an account of modern existence on an ancient fertility ritual, this time manifesting itself in a theatrical form vertiginously balanced between feverish action and strict control. As in his university days, so now any anxiety about his own masculinity could fuel his work in complexly indirect ways; to Pound, in a gesture of male bonding that reverted to another of his student customs, he sent scandalously racist rhymes about 'King Bolo' that flaunted absurdly overassertive male sexual swagger:

> The ladies of King Bolo's court
> They gossiped with each other
> They said 'King Bolo's big black queen
> Will soon become a mother[']
> They said 'an embryonic prince
> Is hidden in her tumbo;
> His prick is long his balls are strong
> And his name is Boloumbo.'[149]

The gulf between the world of Bolo and the world of Tom's hernia problems and Vivien's intestinal agonies was vast, awful and ridiculous. Scandalous humour was one coping strategy, immersion in work another.

Yet in the midst of these troubles, something else had shaken him profoundly that summer, hinting at how different life could have been. He had taken care to find out what had happened to Emily Hale, and she had been unable to forget him. Now she was visiting London and Tom 'saw' her.[150] This encounter brought back and intensified vivid details which haunted him lifelong: how they had met initially as teenagers (she was three years younger) around 1905; how in 'an uneasy fever and dream' he had danced an English square-dance with her in Massachusetts in his early twenties, calling her for the first time by her first name; her party dress blue 'with a scarlet sash', her brown hair, her voice when she spoke and when, lyrically, she sang; how he 'fell in love' with her, as they improvised a charade together at his cousin's house and he stepped on her feet; how they had grown close, rehearsing other amateur dramatic performances; how he had

27

felt 'shaken to pieces' sitting with her at *Tristan und Isolde*; how, leaving America in 1914, he had said to her on their 'last evening' together, ' "I can't ask anything, because I have nothing to offer" ', which had been his way of signalling that his only ambition was to be able to ask her to marry him – and to which, he feared, she had made no response.[151] However much, in the summer of 1923, he maintained his sphinx-like mask of composure; however intensely he felt the pain and duty of marriage to Vivien, whom he had never loved as he loved Emily – and, indeed, whom he thought he might never have loved at all – Emily's coming to London was a shock. He concealed its impact almost completely. Only in the most obliquely coded way he revealed to her what she still meant to him.

This sweetheart whom he had left behind nine years earlier had been 'brought up', Tom recalled later, 'in the same sort of society and tradition' as himself.[152] After he left for Europe, she had lived on in Massachusetts, where her 'saintly' father Edward (who had been, like Tom, Class Poet of his year at Harvard, and, again like Tom, loved small-boat sailing) was Unitarian minister at the First Church of Chestnut Hill in Newton. Unitarian Emily had revered her hard-working, devout, and well-loved father. After writing youthful poems of 'loneliness' and 'weary thoughts that will not cease', and after living for two years in Italy as a young man, he had worked for a time as assistant professor of homiletics at Harvard Divinity School, and spent a decade editing *The Psychological Elements of Religious Faith* (1902) and *Theism and the Christian Faith* (1909) by the Harvard Unitarian theologian Charles Carroll Everett, whose high-toned work hymned a fusion of truth and beauty.[153] Names including 'Eliot' and 'Greenleaf' (Tom's grandfather's middle name) were familiar in Edward Hale's Chestnut Hill congregation.[154] While Tom had been an undergraduate, the Reverend Hale had worked closely with architect J. Lowell Little, whose brother Clarence was one of Tom's closest student friends, to design a new building for First Church, Chestnut Hill, and Emily had grown up in her parents' large, traditional clapboard house on the corner of Middlesex and Circuit roads in leafy, prosperous Brookline. Apparently as a young woman she was painted by the fashionable Boston artist Margaret Foster Richardson, whose sympathies inclined towards the 'New Woman' movement, and who depicted Emily as calm and composed, holding a posy. Years later, Tom, who saw this painting by 'Miss Richardson' at some stage and felt he would 'love to have' it (even if the 'nose' was 'wrong'), would associate Emily with a calm female figure at the start of his poem *Ash-Wednesday*, and with a flower garden in 'Burnt Norton'.[155]

Yet Emily's family had been troubled. When she was five, her only sibling, a one-year-old brother, had died, leaving her mother, Emily Jose (Milliken)

Hale, who gave 'devoted service to the First Church', grief-stricken.[156] After attending Berkeley Street School in Cambridge, Massachusetts, where Tom's cousin Eleanor Hinkley had been a fellow pupil, Emily had studied at the elite Miss Porter's School in Farmington, Connecticut, where she acted together with her 'closest friend' Mary Walker Parker in 'the drama group', and wrote some poetry.[157] A keen singer and public reciter, instead of going to university she had developed her talent for amateur acting, which Tom and others so admired, but which her parents, opposed to their daughter pursuing a professional stage career, regarded with caution. If Tom recalled with intense emotion accompanying Emily and her parents to *Tristan und Isolde* in America, then for Emily the years between her parting from Tom in 1914 and their meeting again in 1923 had been painful. A year after Tom had married Vivien, Emily's father had become seriously ill. He died during the early days of the Spanish Flu pandemic in 1918. In addition, Emily's mother's mental health had grown so broken that she had been institutionalised in the McLean Hospital at Belmont, Massachusetts. One of America's oldest and most respected asylums, the huge, modern McLean complex (which had its own farm, extensive grounds, and whose inmates could worship at its Eliot Memorial Chapel) accommodated its often highly cultured residents in some style. Emily's mother, who would spend the rest of her life there, was able to read and write and was regarded as capable of light work, but Emily, who went on visiting her there for decades, found the situation of the 'Patient' recorded as 'Hale Emily J' intensely upsetting.[158]

Nevertheless, with her welfare overseen by her Unitarian uncle the Reverend John Carroll Perkins and his wife Edith, Emily, who had a passion for elocution, had gone on acting with the Brookline Amateurs, as well as working at a Boston women's college, Simmons, where she had proved her mettle during the Spanish Flu pandemic, serving as 'Assistant Matron of the Dormitories' in difficult times, coaching the student Dramatic Club, teaching elocution and sometimes acting.[159] 'In a heavy moustache and wig', she had been 'unbelievably convincing as the brutal sergeant' in Lewis Beach's Civil War drama *The Clod* in 1918, and her name appeared regularly in Boston press reports of plays.[160] She had taken summer courses in 1920 at Boston's Leland Powers School (which taught elocution as well as acting), and in 1921 at the Cornish School of Music, Drama and Dancing in Seattle, where her uncle and aunt then lived. By 1921 she had become 'the guiding spirit' of the Simmons College Dramatic Club, and was regarded by students as an authority on 'speech' as well as stagecraft.[161] That year, when her Simmons colleague Lucia Russell Briggs (daughter of one of Tom's former Harvard lecturers, Professor LeBaron Russell Briggs) had been appointed president of Milwaukee-Downer

College in Wisconsin, Emily too had accepted a position at that Midwest women's college, where she presided over its Johnston Hall dormitory and taught drama. By 1923 Milwaukee-Downer's 'Dramatic Club' had been renamed 'The Montebanks', and was flourishing.[162]

When Emily met Tom in London that summer she was about to teach four courses during her next session in Wisconsin: 'The Training of Voice and Body', 'Dramatic Reading', 'Voice Training', and 'Stage Technique'. In her own acting she savoured aristocratic roles, and her 1920s students recalled her ability to communicate 'spirit and inspiration'. They relished how she brought to the classroom 'a ladylike air and perfect walk'. 'A marvelous teacher' with 'real flair', she seemed to them 'a director of unusual sensitivity' who could reveal in her acting both 'dry wit' and 'deep and intense feeling'. Though this rather patrician Bostonian Unitarian young woman could appear staid and prim to some of Tom's English friends, Emily's Wisconsin drama protégées saw her as 'exciting' and 'colorful' – 'very lively' and '*always* acting!' These 1920s students' recollections catch vital aspects of the Emily whom Tom recalled and missed profoundly. Like him, too, she had a strong sense of how to play a part. 'Life was an act for Emily.'[163]

During that summer of 1923 Tom and Emily saw each other on several occasions, and in London's Eccleston Square they conversed one evening 'for the last time' before she left the country. Emotionally, he had been feeling 'quite lost'; but now, 'everything had to be reorganized'. Seeking clarification about the nature of their relationship, and aware his marriage was troubled, Emily questioned him. At a crucial moment he 'did not answer'.[164] Not to reply was painful, but his sense of duty, of honour (his own, Emily's, Vivien's, and that of their families), and his habit of masking his feelings all militated against his pouring out his heart to her. As a young man, Tom had described himself as 'suppressed' and had written an early erotic poem, 'Suppressed Complex'; Emily had once enjoyed a 'considerable triumph' in helping stage a Freud-inflected American comedy of marital unhappiness and extramarital longing, *Suppressed Desires*.[165] But this couple's shared and sophisticated awareness of role-playing and concealed sexual feelings were of little help to them. Like many of their encounters, their meeting at Eccleston Square was remembered by each of them as a highly charged, pained occasion. Later, he told her, it was from that point that 'my active spiritual life dates', but at the time he could say nothing that was either appropriate or adequate.[166] They parted.

Since his marriage Tom had made clear to a few mutual friends in America his continuing interest in all Emily did, but to her the nature of that interest was hardly straightforward. After her 1923 London visit, on which she accompanied her 'aunt and uncle' (the Anglophile Perkinses), Emily, conscious Tom's marriage was 'a very unhappy affair', returned to America, to a life very different from that of the banker poet who was pondering his plays with puppets.[167] Her taste in poetry may be sensed from the way that, despite moving house often, she kept for many years a 1920s anthology inscribed to her by 'her devoted Uncle John' Perkins. Edited by the British Poet Laureate Robert Bridges, and emphasising 'spiritual life', it presented English-language poetry since Shakespeare's time 'for the use of schools'; its youngest poet was Rupert Brooke, and it contained only three American poems, with no modernist poetry whatsoever.[168] In early September, however, Tom inscribed in ink for her a copy of his challenging 1920 poetry collection *Ara Vus Prec*, which takes its title from the cry of a soul in torment in Dante's *Purgatorio*:

For Emily Hale
with the author's
humble compliments.
T. S. Eliot
5.ix.23.

and underneath he quoted the words of a poet who speaks of his own poem, then bids farewell, in Dante's *Inferno*:

SIETI RACCOMMENDATO
    IL MIO TESORO
NELLO QUAL VIVO ANCOR
    E NON PIU CHIEGGIO.
POI SI RIVOLSE.[169]

Uncharacteristically, Tom inked these words in block capitals, making them unmistakably clear to read. Emily had inherited her father's love of Italy, but even if she identified the source of this quotation and pondered its meaning, she came to find the communications of her remarkable, allusive, and apparently self-involved admirer less than wholeheartedly clear. The words can be translated as 'Let me entrust to you my Treasure wherein I still survive; I ask no more of you. Then he turned and left.'

Three days after inscribing this book, Tom telegrammed Mary Hutchinson, inviting her to a picnic.[170] He doubled down on editorial, bankerly, and other labours. On 14 September he consulted Ottoline Morrell about Vivien's ongoing problems. It was as if nothing had changed. But that same day he slipped into a letter to Cobden-Sanderson the request that a year's subscription to the *Criterion*, beginning with volume 2, number 1, be sent to

Miss Hale,
Johnston Hall,
Milwaukee-Downer College,
Milwaukee, Wis. USA.[171]

It was one way of maintaining a connection.

The Waste Land had still not appeared in Britain in book form, but he had agreed with the Woolfs they should publish it from their Hogarth Press at Richmond, Surrey, whose list featured other experimental texts including Hope Mirrlees's book-length post-war urban collage poem *Paris*, to which Tom made no surviving reference. Virginia Woolf, whose formally innovative novel *Jacob's Room* had appeared the preceding year, had been typesetting Tom's long poem by hand, not always meticulously. Distracted by so many other compelling concerns, he had proofread it – but not well enough. As a result, when the small book with its blue, marbled boards appeared on 12 September, though he thought its layout 'far better than the American edition', he was embarrassed not to have noticed that on page 7 a crowd 'flowed under London Bridge' when it should have 'flowed over'.[172] Later he spotted other errors, and hurried to correct copies in a bookshop.

The showiest early reaction to *The Waste Land* occurred when an eager student poet, Harold Acton, read it through a megaphone to oarsmen passing below his Oxford college rooms (a scene later fictionalised by Evelyn Waugh in *Brideshead Revisited*), but British reviews were far from universally enthusiastic. In the *Times Literary Supplement* Edgell Rickword anonymously styled it 'a magic-lantern show'; its poet, 'too reserved to expose in public the impressions stamped on his own soul by the journey through the Waste Land . . . employs the slides made by others'. In the *Nation*, Mary Hutchinson's lover Clive Bell (whose review made Tom feel 'as if I was covered with lice') wrote of 'wisps and straws'; J. C. Squire diagnosed 'erudite depression'; alert to the poem's interest in 'phallic symbols', F. L. Lucas detected in it a 'spasm', linking it to the work of 'Victorian "Spasmodics"'; Humbert Wolfe experienced 'thrills' and 'desolate music'.[173] In its first six months, the Hogarth Press edition sold 330 copies, which Leonard Woolf regarded as having 'done extraordinarily well'.[174] Tom earned just over £7 in royalties. Identifying himself, however flippantly, with Christ, he complained in 1923 with regard to *The Waste Land*'s reception that 'one crucifies oneself and entertains drawing rooms and lounges'.[175] All reviewers sensed the poem's communication of intense desolation, but several found it chaotic.

Unsurprisingly, 'the orderly and the chaotic' were Tom's focus in 'The Function of Criticism', written in September for October's *Criterion*. As often, he did public 'battle' with Murry's ideas: ' "Catholicism," he [Murry] says, "stands for the principle of unquestioned spiritual authority outside the individual; that is also the principle of Classicism in literature." ' For Murry, champion of Romanticism, such allegiances were anathema. Tom, having long sided with classicism, disagreed, maintaining that 'men cannot get on without giving allegiance to something outside themselves'. Increasingly, he saw art, criticism, politics and religion in terms of 'a problem of order'. To stave off chaos the modern artist must commit to an ordered set of beliefs:

If, then, a man's interest is political, he must, I presume, profess an allegiance to principles, or to a form of government, or to a monarch; and if he is interested in religion, and has one, to a Church; and if he happens to be interested in literature, he must acknowledge, it seems to me, just that sort of allegiance [to classicism] which I endeavoured to put forth in the preceding section.

Tom was not just reaffirming his commitment to literary classicism. He was demonstrating, too, his increasingly apparent adherence to a politics of order associated with the right, and hinting at his developing interest in the ordering principles of 'a Church'. Where Murry argued that 'The English writer, the English divine, the English statesman, inherit no rules from their forbears', but must depend on 'the inner voice', the American Tom, even as he negotiated with Englishness, denounced this 'inner voice' which meant merely ' "doing as one likes" ' – a phrase from Matthew Arnold's *Culture and Anarchy*.[176] Tom sought to oppose chaos with a view of culture, politics and religion as bound together. If there was an Arnoldian tinge to this (Arnold too had written on 'The Function of Criticism'), then Tom went further and deeper than the Victorian sage whose religious faith had receded. As both *The Waste Land* and this new essay suggested, Tom, afflicted by personal and societal despair, sought the ordering structure of religious belief that offered his individual talent communion with a greater spiritual tradition.

Intensifying commitment to religion went hand in hand with a sharpening of his political allegiances. With undisguised hostility, Richard Aldington recalled dining at the Oxford and Cambridge Club on 23 September 1923 with Tom and the political 'crank' Whibley, 'the very embodiment of the English Tory don'. After 'a good deal of excellent wine', Whibley and a 'witty and scathing' Tom set about denouncing 'Whigs and Whiggism', and criticising the Liberal Lord Morley, who had died that day. Eventually, Whibley felt that Tom, as an American, had gone too far, and retorted, 'There was one good thing about Morley – he always hated Americans.' After an awkward pause, the conversation turned to the recent war, and Tom 'told us gravely that in the next war he intended to join the British army. He worked himself up almost to blood-heat in a fine frenzy of patriotism.'[177] Yet even as Tom protested loyalty to the Crown, Aldington detected signs of his persistent American foreignness.

For years, tensions about religious, personal, national, and political identity had found their way into his poetry, even as they complicated his life. As early as October 1921, Tom, exasperated at the American Consulate and at US 'Income Tax' demands, had mentioned to Aldington a wish to 'get my [British] naturalisation papers in order', a process to which he had returned in 1922, and which he continued to discuss with the right-wing thinker Whibley.[178] About ten days after dining with Whibley and Aldington, and around the time he published 'The Function of Criticism' (which, like Tom and Whibley's dinner conversation, denounces 'Whiggery'), Tom wrote to Charles Maurras in early October 1923, *'Je suis certain que les opinions du groupe du* Criterion *sont celles qui se rapprochent le plus à l'Action Française'* (I am certain that the *Criterion* group represents the body of opinion nearest to the Action Française).[179] He was far from alone in his rightwards trajectory. Now resident in Italy, Pound became a much more extreme devotee of Mussolini, while Wyndham Lewis – with whom Tom had recently holidayed in France and whose work he was eager to publish in the *Criterion* – would develop (like Lord Rothermere) an admiration for Hitler. In 1923 even the poet Hugh MacDiarmid, later a communist, published a 'Plea for a Scottish Fascism'. Closer to home, Vivien too came to feel the attractions of the fascist cause, though she could grow impatient with her husband's accompanying inclination to investigate the principles of religion.

With patrician bite (he would soon maintain that 'Christianity, as I see it, is anti-democratic'), and with the denunciatory vigour of an Old Testament prophet – or perhaps one of his own witch-hanging Puritan ancestors – he ventured in his *Criterion* piece on 'The Function of Criticism' a rhetorical flourish: 'The possessors of the inner voice ride ten in a compartment to a football match at Swansea, listening to the inner voice, which breathes the eternal message of vanity, fear, and lust.'[180] Seeking, with a measure of disgust, to control such urges in himself and others, the tormented husband of Vivien, adulterous lover of Nancy Cunard, and distant admirer of Emily Hale craved the discipline of spiritual as well as political order. If, among other things, *The Waste Land* expresses despair, scepticism, and unsatisfied religious hunger, then 'The Function of

Criticism' approaches religious and other kinds of commitment through tough intellectual argument: 'The question is, the first question, *not* what comes natural or what comes *easy* to us, but what is right?'[181] The essay, like the poem, is a bout of spiritual and intellectual wrestling. Around the time he finished it he said he would like 'very much' to publish a *Criterion* article on John Henry Newman, the most famous nineteenth-century English convert to the Catholic Church; he might write that 'myself'.[182]

Criticism and creativity were fused: 'the larger part of the labour of an author in composing a work is critical labour: the labour of sifting, combining, constructing, expunging, correcting, testing: this frightful toil is as much critical as creative'.[183] Articulating in poetry and prose his craving for order, he constructed a channel that melded literary, religious, and political instincts, thinking, and beliefs. 'The Function of Criticism' has credo-like aspects, yet stops short of absolute commitment: that phrasing, 'if he is interested in religion, and has one [an allegiance], to a Church', leaves open the possibility of having no religion, no Church. Yet elsewhere in the October 1923 *Criterion* Tom argued not just that '*all* European civilisations are equally dependent on Greece and Rome' but that 'Rome' should be regarded as meaning 'the Church' as well as Latin literature and language; 'we have no prejudice against non-European civilisations', he wrote, but just as India and China had to be true to their own cultural forms, so Europe had to be loyal to its, and England (to him a European country) had to be true to the heritage of Rome: 'If everything derived from Rome were withdrawn – everything we have from Norman-French society, from the Church, from Humanism, from every channel direct and indirect, what would be left?'[184]

To argue that one should commit to 'the Church' simply because it was part of a shared, European cultural tradition (that 'mind of Europe' with which Tom as an American in England had come to identify as a mainstay against American or Russian 'barbarism') is not an irrefutable argument.[185] Still, when combined with the interrogation of belief in *The Waste Land*, the hunger for order and ritual expressed elsewhere, and even with such influences as his mother's deep love of Christian forms, his emphasis on 'the Church' here is yet another indication of how, along with his deepening Anglophile and anti-Liberal political convictions, and despite having been 'brought up in a strong atmosphere of the most liberal Liberal theology' and 'never having been a member' of the Catholic Church, he was manoeuvring himself effortfully towards a profession of faith.[186]

'Literature cannot be understood without going to the sources: sources which are often remote, difficult, and unintelligible unless one transcends the prejudices of ordinary literary taste', he wrote in an anthropologically accented review published in October 1923. Aided by Cornford and others, he was tracing the roots of art and civilisation back to 'rhythm', a sense of which must be renewed from age to age. 'Drama', he declared, 'was originally ritual; and ritual, consisting of a set of repeated movements, is essentially a dance.' The origins of rites such as 'beating a drum' lie in 'desire' and 'need'; they may seem 'unintelligible', but, however remotely, underpin the arts of today.[187] '*All* art emulates the condition of ritual', he wrote in an admiring review of Marianne Moore's work published late that year.[188] Within eighteen months, discussing 'ritual' and 'faith', he would contend that the Catholic 'High Mass' was 'one of the highest developments of dancing'.[189] Trying to bring order to the chaos of his personal life, and to articulate a sustaining philosophy of art, he inclined increasingly towards a Church that offered, in the face of his own intensely sceptical education and temperament, an abiding spiritual order.

Meanwhile, encouraged by Wyndham Lewis, who also highlighted primitive urges and patterns underlying modern society, he went 'on with the Sweeney play', at least in terms of planning, and solicited *Criterion* work from writers (mainly men) whose ideas seemed sympathetic. Mentioning 'Charles Whibley', he contacted Stephen Gaselee, fellow of Magdalene College, Cambridge, classical scholar, and right-leaning High Anglican fascinated by ritual and liturgy; Tom also encouraged Aldington to examine Italian Fascism and 'find out whether it has any general philosophy and if so whether its general ideas can in any way be attached to our own' at the *Criterion*.[190] Though the proposal came to nothing, during this time when he described himself as 'an old-fashioned Tory', he had in mind to edit a volume of essays setting out 'the *Criterion* position': as well as including his own 'Function of Criticism', the book might include his mentor Whibley on Charles Maurras, in addition to Aldington on 'Fashismo'.[191] Fascism, it seemed, was going to burgeon.

2

Hell-Broth

WITH Vivien now staying mainly in the cottage, during that autumn of 1923 Tom spent most weekdays alone in London, visiting Fishbourne at weekends. In town Ellen Kellond helped 'look after' him; in the country Vivien had both charwoman and carer.[1] True to his wish for order, and keen to impress his mother who wrote weekly from America, he drew up a list of ten pieces he had undertaken to write, none of them poems; he even attempted a rapprochement with his wife's former lover, Bertrand Russell, who had expressed admiration for *The Waste Land*. Yet his mother discerned persisting problems. Going against her late husband's wishes, she had altered her will to provide for Vivien in the event of Tom's death. He told her Vivien's weight was 'only a little over 80 pounds'; their hopes were pinned on Dr Martin, who had diagnosed 'chronic anaemia and defective circulation'.[2] As regards Tom, Lottie Eliot confided to Henry, 'Vivian is fond of him too, how could she help being, but she eats his life out.'[3] 'Give my love and sympathy to Vivien', she wrote to Tom in England.[4] Though aware his prospects at Lloyds were 'almost "brilliant"', and conscious of the security, salary, and pension 'inducements that enslave one', he was determined to try and leave the bank in January, and then to host his mother in London.[5]

Enjoying Paul Valéry's London lecture on Victor Hugo and Baudelaire, he had inscribed to Valéry a copy of *The Waste Land* on 1 November, but was also fascinated by Gilbert Seldes' championing of jazz in a recent *Dial*. Seeing jazz as an American art form 'grown out of ragtime' such as Tom had known since his St Louis childhood, Seldes invoked both the 'drumming' of 'savages' and the music of George Gershwin and Cole Porter as well as 'the *Sacre du Printemps* of Strawinsky'; he ended up juxtaposing jazz with 'Mr Joyce's sense of form' and the work of 'Mr Eliot' and 'Picasso'.[6] Tom relished this alignment; when Seldes asked about his 'Jazz Oratorio', he replied that this 'play, if it is ever written', would be intended 'for production with an orchestra consisting exclusively of drums'.[7] Yet by the end of 1923 the play remained unrealised, its would-be author '*very* run down'.[8] His situation was not helped by Aldington's resignation from the *Criterion*; Aldington felt treated like a lackey. Wearily, awkwardly, Tom wrote to Lady Rothermere, excusing delays in the magazine's production. For Christmas 1923 he inscribed a copy of the English edition of *The Waste Land* 'with the enduring gratitude of the author' to 'Dr Roger Vittoz', the specialist in nervous diseases who had treated him in Lausanne in 1921, but he remained tense and uneasy.[9] When, without Vivien, he hosted a small mid-December party in the rented flat at Burleigh Mansions, the Woolfs could see he had been drinking. Leonard heard him vomiting in another room, and Virginia observed him return, 'ghastly pale, with his eyes shut, apparently in a stupor'.[10] Next day, embarrassed, he apologised.

Spurred by book-lists supplied by Mary Hutchinson and Tom, each of whom had written short fiction, Vivien determined she too would become a writer. Around the start of 1924 she authored several fictional 'sketches' of contemporary life, presenting them, as she put it, from 'the standpoint of a very interested, and a very *intimate*, outsider . . . who does not actually appear in the sketches'.[11] Returned to London, but finding it impossible to write at Clarence Gate Gardens, she tried working in Tom's rented rooms in St Martin's Lane. Her friend Pearl Fassett produced similar tales at the time, though Pearl used a first-person female narrator. Vivien hoped her own sketches would form a group, perhaps a book. Tom read both women's stories with interest, and gave some encouragement, though, accustomed to sharp editing, he could be a harsh advisor.

In mid-February he went over a sketch of Pearl's, red-pencilling 'parts which I think would be better to omit'; he warned her against making statements on subjects about 'which you have not thought sufficiently'. The thirty-five-year-old philosophically trained Tom admonished Vivien's twenty-one-year-old friend: 'In general your writing suffers very much from the fact that you have never thought enough, and that you have never formed any theories of your own.' Counselling her ('My dear Pearl'), he advised her to theorise, cut, and rewrite. He did not hold back. If she took his advice, however, he would print her story in the *Criterion*. He treated Vivien similarly, and accepted for publication both Pearl's Parisian sketch 'Mrs Pilkington' and Vivien's French-inflected 'Thé Dansant'. Making their *Criterion* debut alongside D. H. Lawrence, the two friends chose similar pseudonyms: Vivien's 'Feiron Morris', matched Pearl's 'Felix Morrison'.[12]

The protagonist of Vivien's story has a close friend called not 'Felix' but 'Felice'. Set at a contemporary tea dance, 'Thé Dansant', like Vivien's other sketches, presents a young woman called Sibylla (sometimes spelt by Vivien 'Sybilla'). The name was more common than it is today; it had featured, for instance, in 'The Ignorance of Sybilla' by turn-of-the-century writer of stories for girls, Mrs George de Horne Vaizey. To readers of *The Waste Land* in book form, however, it was most familiar from that poem's classical epigraph which begins 'Nam Sibyllam', and then has 'Sibylla' (the quotation has the name in Greek letters) exclaim in Greek, 'I want to die.'[13] For the suffering Vivien, who so recently had contemplated suicide, this name may have carried private significance. Her story involves dancing (which she and Tom loved) and the experience of a 'pick up' on a dance floor which might complicate the relationship between Felice, Sibylla, and Sibylla's partner Mike. Brittle relationships characterise many of Vivien's stories. They convey the milieu in which the Eliots circulated, and reflect aspects of Tom and herself. No stranger to 'pain so intense that she lost control', Sibylla readily registers emotional disturbance.[14]

Just as Tom may have drawn on his relationship with Vivien for the exchange in *The Waste Land* beginning 'My nerves are bad tonight' that Vivien thought 'WONDERFUL', so she seems to have drawn on her husband and his friends for her stories.[15] Often writing in faint pencil, she redrafted work and sometimes typed it up, though several stories and fragments were abandoned. In one sketch a couple – Ellison and Antony – share an upstairs apartment in 'Mansions', a large residential block resembling Clarence Gate Gardens – or perhaps the Eliots' old home at Crawford Mansions. Antony returns from work to the flat, aware 'There were many things he dreaded – that Ellison might have a headache, that she might be irritable & hate him, that her old friend whom he disliked might be there (& he would find them quarrelling).' He enters 'almost stealthily', seeing 'Ellison, alone, lying on the sofa'. The unease continues as he approaches her.

> Antony stooped & kissed Ellison rather gingerly. Ellison's smile was strained. They both seemed to wait (uncomfortably). Antony's mind, on these occasions was a blank. Ellison's emotions every evening at 6 o'clock were too uneasy to be borne, & too intricate for her to dwell upon. Rebelling she said harshly & wearily 'has anything happened?' Her tone said –'of course nothing has & nothing ever will.' No, said Antony. He smiled apologetically [. . .][16]

If this 'nothing ever will' is reminiscent of *The Waste Land*'s ' "What shall we ever do?" ' passage, other tonal links connect the Eliots' lives and these writings.[17] Several of Vivien's most developed female protagonists seem both exasperated and exhausted. In one pencil draft Columbina is asked by a man if she is going to the theatre that evening.

'I dont know' she said 'I really haven't thought about it. No, I dont suppose I shall go – why should I?' She felt a vague resentment. Somewhere in her mind there was a fatigue, a fatigue which hurt like physical pain if it were touched. Having to make definite plans touched it. Having to even answer a definite question touched it.[18]

Though only a few were published in the *Criterion*, manuscripts and typescripts of these and several other stories survive. Often, shrewdly and demandingly, Tom edited Vivien's work; sometimes he suggested possible subject matter. Both Eliots were keen that their writings succeeded. When she could, she assisted him with the *Criterion*; in early 1924 they were preparing to publish fiction by Lewis which satirised Bloomsbury and would outrage several friends, but which Tom and Vivien relished. If their own writing activity brought them closer, it also drew on personal anxieties and persistent illness. Tom gave Osbert Sitwell the impression that marriage brought both the Eliots 'despair and hopelessness'; it vexed Tom that Vivien had not revealed until long after their wedding just how extensive had been her history of ill health.[19] In mid-February, just after he had been ailing, Vivien 'got out of bed and *fell down*'; a week later, he wrote, she 'has been sleeping most of the time ever since'. He was at his wits' end; his 'judgment and will', he told Henry, were 'paralysed'.[20] Virginia Woolf, who wrote of Tom on 30 March as having about him something 'hole & cornerish, biting in the back, suspicious', later joked to Mary Hutchinson about his 'marmoreal heart', but, however much he hid his feelings, he was deeply unsettled.[21] Worried he was behaving 'like a frightened rat', he begged Henry to come and advise him what to do.[22]

Continuing to take 'a mild sedative at night prescribed by Dr Martin', Vivien tried other drugs too, including 'Mutaflor', a remedy for bowel disorders obtained by post from a Freiburg chemist.[23] She also attempted to go daily as a private patient for an hour's treatment from Dr Annjuta Kellgren-Cyriax, appointed in 1924 'physician-in-charge of the physiotherapy department' at Bloomsbury's Elizabeth Garrett Anderson Hospital.[24] This Swedish-born physician gave Vivien 'manipulation and hand vibration, getting her digestive organs into place and stimulating them to do their work'. At the same time, Dr Kellgren-Cyriax's husband Edgar worked on Tom several days a week, treating 'the nerves of my head and neck and spine, and stomach'.[25] The Cyriaxes' 1924 *Collected Papers on Mechano-Therapeutics* advocated a system of intense physical manipulation of the body, not least the abdomen. Both Eliots pinned their hopes on them.

Tom thought Vivien's 'colitis' improved, though she was 'beginning to show signs of anaemia again'.[26] While he was still pondering Cornford's anthropological interpretation of ancient Greek comedy, a bout of influenza prevented him attending a Cambridge performance of Aristophanes' *Birds* with costumes designed by Duncan Grant. No sooner had Tom improved than Vivien caught 'a very bad attack of influenza' through which she was 'dragged' to recovery by 'the Doctors Cyriax' who recommended she recuperate in the country.[27] The Eliots' illnesses were a shared wound, and a constant source of friction.

To help keep going, Tom had hired a new *Criterion* assistant. John Reibel Culpin, 'Jack', was the younger brother of Karl Culpin, Tom's good friend at Merton College, Oxford, who had died in the war. Tom had kept in touch with the Culpins, and in the 1920s called Jack's German mother 'Aunt Johanna'.[28] Seven years younger than Tom, Jack 'looked very *young*' according to Vivien, who admired his sweet expression.[29] That spring and summer he became one of her carers, spending time at Fishbourne in May. In London, he helped Tom prepare the magazine for the press, sorting proofs, word-counts, and payments. Though Tom's time remained scarce, at Fleet Street's Cock tavern he set up fortnightly lunches with *Criterion* contributors including poet-critic Herbert Read and 'any sympathizing critics or poets from abroad' (such as his old Harvard friend Conrad Aiken) who happened to be in town.[30] Through such social contacts and his burgeoning correspondence, he encountered a wide range of people from up-and-coming Oxbridge undergraduates, dons and translators to E. M. Forster, the Sitwells, and (at lunch in March with Whibley) Conservative politician Stanley Baldwin. Baldwin was about to become prime minister. Tom 'liked' him 'very much indeed'.[31]

Time with Vivien was more difficult. 'Our weekends always are' a 'strain' she wrote; illness meant she saw far fewer people than her increasingly well-known husband.[32] At times they tried, but too hard, to live more indulgently: in the mid-1920s young poet Basil Bunting spotted Tom 'at a party wearing an enormous cape lined with red and eyebrows painted green'. '"Thought the party needed hotting up",' Tom remarked.[33] Half-echoing some *Waste Land* tropes, Vivien's 'Letters of the Moment' sketch in the February 1924 *Criterion* has an anxiously exhausted-sounding speaker:

Now one begins to beat against the bars of the cage: the typewriter and the telephone, and the sight of one's face in the glass. One's soul

stirs stiffly out of the dead endurance of the winter – but toward
what spring?

Le temps s'en va, le temps s'en va, madame:
Las! le temps, non, mais nous nous en allons,
Et tôt serons estendus sous la lame.

What happy meetings, what luminous conversations in twilit
rooms filled with the scent of hyacinths, await me now? The uncompromising voice of truth inside me answers, None at all. For I am not
the same person who once played – as it seems to one – a leading part
in those spring fantasies.

But, you say, what about the wonderful parties of your intellectual
friends which you used to describe to me so gaily?

I have not been to any.

And why not? You say.

Well, the enjoyment of parties belongs to the Spring that one
has lost.[34]

Vivien did try to get out into society. In late March she saw *King Lear*
performed by the Phoenix Society, one of whose supporters was Lady
Cunard; Tom and his publisher Virginia Woolf were there too, and both,
according to Woolf, 'jeered' the production. However, in the *Criterion*
Tom, who had been pondering how Elizabethan theatre could promote a
'revolutionary' new non-realistic drama, stated that the performance of
this work of 'immense power' was 'almost flawless', then went on to complain about 'that incapacity for surrender or allegiance to something
outside of oneself, which is a frequent symptom of the soul of man under
democracy'. When she taxed him 'lightly' with contradicting his earlier
reactions, Woolf was annoyed at his 'suspicious, elaborate, uneasy' manner.
Vivien recorded simply that going to the play 'has nearly done me in'.[35]
Woolf's frustration with Tom was exacerbated by his having published
Lewis's 'masterpiece' satire on Bloomsbury, apparently without having time to
'read and expurgate' it.[36] Tom tried to smooth things over with a degree of
flirtatious self-mockery, caricaturing himself as someone likely to make Woolf
'expire of boredom', and jokily indicating she knew he had developed a taste
for 'Divine Service on Sunday Morning'.[37] Vivien seemed not to share this religious commitment. Tom knew he could be trying, but, close to the end of his
tether, he made demands on people he trusted. That spring he asked his hard-
worked, Chicago-based brother to go to New York to persuade globe-trotting
Lady Rothermere, who was due there, to pay Tom a guaranteed *Criterion* salary sufficient to let him leave the bank. Henry's New York interview was
'inconclusive'.[38] Soon he offered Tom further financial support himself.

Tom stayed with the bank, but his troubles continued. As a result of an infected abscess under a fingernail, his whole hand grew 'very painful', and on 10 July, in the first of two operations, he had a piece of bone removed from the finger.[39] Supplementing her Cyriax treatment, Vivien continued to receive ministrations from Dr Martin, who was then in England. Knowing Martin's interest in psychoanalysis, both Eliots underwent analyses. Tom had 'half a dozen sittings', recalling wryly thirteen years later that 'as soon as' Martin 'began inquiring about dreams I began having the most complicated and cryptic dreams, such as I had never had before, and these stopped as soon as I left off'. His experience with Martin, who 'did not tell me anything about myself of which I was not already conscious', made him sceptical about the value of psychoanalysis, which he worried could do serious damage.[40] Modern investigations suggest that Freiburg's Sanatorium Hoven, Martin's employer, may have been something of a racket. Certainly, within a decade it developed close links to the Nazi party and Dr Martin worked for years alongside the sadistic Waldemar Hoven (son of the sanatorium's founders) who went on to achieve notoriety working for the Waffen SS Hygiene Institute and serving as 'Lagerarzt des KZ Buchenwald' – camp doctor at Buchenwald concentration camp.[41]

Having his own dreams analysed in mid-1924 may have spurred Tom's production of 'Doris's Dream Songs', published shortly afterwards, as well as other brief, dreamlike poems soon reworked into 'The Hollow Men' which features nightmarish 'dreams', 'death's dream Kingdom', and 'eyes I dare not meet in dreams'.[42] Yet if Tom's psychoanalysis incited a creative response, and, later, could be dismissed in ironic recollection, for Vivien the experience was potentially more threatening. Usually, when she saw Dr Martin, Tom accompanied her, but one day in July he was unable to be there in time for the start of her session and matters went disastrously wrong. As he explained later to his father-in-law,

> She went alone, and he was in some hysterical state, and in a diabolical rage for reasons of his own. He began to psychoanalyse her and poke into her childhood and youth, and told her finally that she was living on Will, that she had a terrific will which kept her alive, and that if this will ever collapsed she would be nothing but a feeble minded little snivelling invalid, asking only for a little pity and led about by an attendant. He even pointed to the corner of the room and said she would be sitting there and painted in words a filthy picture of a semi-idiot. She sat still and looked at him and said nothing at all, and this must have infuriated him more, for when they came out of the room I noticed at once that his forehead was heavily beaded

with sweat. V. seemed quite calm and appeared to take no notice whatever of his words. In fact, she did not tell me what he had said until a long time afterwards.[43]

If Vivien's 'story' is to be trusted, then she seems to have been too traumatised to reveal at once what had happened; she knew, too, that Tom, undergoing surgery on his hand, was distracted.[44] He registered Martin's anger, and Vivien's silence, but did not immediately understand their meaning. Preoccupied, he was trying to arrange for the *Criterion* to occupy the former offices of the *Egoist* magazine, and was preparing, too, for his eighty-one-year-old mother's long-anticipated visit. Vivien's mother-in-law was due to reach England on 14 July. She would stay for several weeks.

Conscious not only of her age but also of her kidney condition, Lottie Eliot had chosen to travel with Tom's sister Charlotte, who lived with her husband and children in Millis, Massachusetts, about twenty miles from Boston. Having been ill the previous year, Charlotte 'dreaded' the journey, but Lottie, eager to see her beloved son, believed mother and daughter might look after one another, savouring a voyage, a change of scene, and a family reunion.[45] Unfortunately, Lottie was taken unwell during the transatlantic crossing and the visit proved a considerable strain for all concerned, including, not least, Vivien. Initially she and Tom moved out into 'temporary slums' to let their visitors take over their flat; soon Tom had to accompany his 'completely exhausted' wife to an apartment at Eastbourne on the south coast where he had arranged for her to stay.[46] He then returned to Clarence Gate Gardens, sleeping in the lounge while Charlotte and Lottie used the separate bedrooms he and Vivien usually occupied. The older Mrs Eliot rejoiced to be so close to her son, and her health improved; Vivien's health worsened.

Torn again between loyalty to his wife and to his mother, Tom felt increasingly strained, but maintained his *Criterion* correspondence and contacts as well as focusing more intently on scoping out his embryonic play. Struggling to reconcile competing demands on his time, he moved his mother and sister to a hotel on Eastbourne seafront, and took time off to be with Vivien nearby. He escorted his family on day trips around the surrounding countryside, including to picturesque Pevensey where William the Conqueror had landed in 1066. If the terrain was historic, it was also newly notorious. During the second half of July newspapers carried accounts of the trial of Patrick Herbert Mahon, a married man who had lured his typist lover Emily Beilby Kaye to the Crumbles bungalow between Eastbourne and Pevensey where he killed and dismembered her. The jury heard how pieces of the dead woman's flesh had been found boiled in a saucepan at the bungalow, while other body parts had been discovered in a hat box, a trunk, and a biscuit tin.

This was hardly the sort of story that Lottie Eliot would have found salubrious, but it had impressed Tom when in early May *The Times* was reporting on the 'Eastbourne Crime' (also known as the 'Bungalow Crime'), and when he joked to Virginia Woolf that, as a result of Lewis's satire on Bloomsbury, the editor of the *Criterion* might be found 'dismembered, like a hero of Grecian tragedy (rather than a bungalow bride)'. The idea of cooked body parts and the murdered would-be bride were probably still in his mind late in August when, using an image from *Macbeth*, he described his own life as being 'boiled in a hell-broth'; such imagery fitted, too, with his ideas for a ritualistic play that, disturbingly, would involve a woman's murder.[47] Seven years earlier, after realising that, despite his marriage to Vivien, he was still in love with Emily Hale, Tom had published his only short story, 'Eeldrop and Appleplex', which mentions an 'unhappily married' man who has ruined his life, and a man who 'murders his mistress', then, in a state of living death, reflects on the medieval world's awareness of 'the eternity of punishment'.[48] Now, in Tom's new drama hell-broth and cannibal stew combined, fusing modern and ancient, personal and ritual, in a work of art that became a refracted public version of his private torments.

Certainly he had been struggling. Planning for his mother's visit, he had negotiated holiday leave from the bank, as well as his considerable sick leave. In 'moments of great distress of mind' he had had to ask assistant general manager for administration, W. G. Johns, for additional time off. Having risen from private to colonel during four years fighting in the Great War in France, Johns was used to seeing men suffering from stress. He cared about 'the human element'.[49] Tom appreciated his 'generous patience'.[50]

In Eastbourne, though, his health faltered again: 'an attack, or a recrudescence, of influenza' he termed it.[51] A doctor, with whom Lottie discussed her son's health, was clear Tom should 'remain in bed and rest for some time', giving up work for 'as long as possible'.[52] Recording this in her journal, Lottie decided it was best for her to leave Tom with Vivien whose 'lady' Dr Cyriax Lottie also met, and considered a person 'of culture and charm'.[53] In warm August weather Lottie and Charlotte headed for London's art galleries. On 4 August Tom too returned; soon he was back at the bank, catching up with *Criterion* correspondence, liaising with Vivien at Eastbourne – who took to her bed for a further 'ten days' – and conferring earnestly with his mother who decided he was 'a little better, though not very strong'.[54]

Striving to be attentive to his mother and sister, he introduced them to Osbert Sitwell, who thought Lottie 'strait-laced', though 'kindly'. Tom was very aware of their foreignness in England. He feared Virginia Woolf might not welcome 'a charabanc of American visitors', even if Woolf's works had their admirers (who included Emily Hale) on that 'dark Continent'; to F. S. Flint, an English *Criterion* contributor who thought Tom 'so little of an American', he remarked slyly, 'I dislike Americans, as a rule.'[55] However assimilated as an immigrant in England, he acknowledged his immediate family roots lay elsewhere. Ottoline Morrell thought Tom's 'studious courtesy' towards his mother, which included 'carrying her bag, etc. struck Eng[lish] people as ridiculous'.[56]

With Lottie he debated earnestly whether or not to leave the bank. They discussed her financial trust, from which he derived income, as well as his own prospects. Summarising matters to Henry, he considered what would happen (not least to Vivien) were he to predecease his mother, or were she to die before him. If both he and Vivien died, his money would revert 'to the family' in America.[57] He thought a lot about death and wills, as did his ageing parent. With bankerly clarity he set alternative financial scenarios. Efficient and clear-headed one moment, he was upset the next. What did his mother and sister really want? At Eastbourne Charlotte had been complaining of 'indigestion'; was this simply 'a pretext'? Was Lottie 'not well'? Often labyrinthine in his own emotional and intellectual dealings, he found it hard to accept that he might share such traits with his family. He knew them intimately, yet had grown unaccustomed to their presence. To Henry he complained, petulantly, 'I am used to people who deal openly and directly.'[58] Yet he loved them, and wished they would stay longer. When they left for America on 23 August he accompanied them by train all the way to Liverpool, then conducted them aboard their transatlantic vessel. He would never see them again.

Oddly, but in a characteristically Eliot family way, his elderly mother's concerns touched not just on her own and her children's money and health but also on religious poetry. She had sought Tom's help in publishing her dramatic poem about the ascetic fifteenth-century Florentine Catholic poet-preacher Girolamo Savonarola, most famous for his Bonfire of the Vanities. Planning his own very different, yet also intense verse drama, Tom wanted to help. A problem was that his mother's work, for all it shared some of his own preoccupations with vision and spiritual commitment, was written in an antique idiom unlikely to find modern readers. The acerbic critic in him evaluated *Savonarola*; but, a dutiful son, he assured Lottie he would give his support. He would supply an introduction, and do what he could to secure a publisher (soon he tried Knopf); she was astute enough to realise a prefatory 'essay on the poetic drama' by the author of *The Waste Land* would help, and left him with a copy of her manuscript when she sailed.[59]

How could he catch up? He had not even finished last year's tax return. For October publication he owed the Woolfs *Homage to John Dryden*, a small book comprising several *Times Literary Supplement* essays, fragments of a larger project on seventeenth- and eighteenth-century poetry. Lady Rothermere required mollifying. The bank was considering sending him to Basle on business, and Tom, soon after parting with his family visitors, noted with 'intimate and private grief' that the subject of his doctoral dissertation, F. H. Bradley, had just died.[60] More urgently, he had to work out his future with Vivien: the Fishbourne cottage had become intolerably noisy after a motor garage had set up opposite; and Vivien now found Jack Culpin, as she put it in some impromptu verses, '*secretive* & bitter & rude'.[61] Tom, who had just managed a rapprochement with his erstwhile *Criterion* assistant Aldington, now found that relations with his new assistant Culpin were strained almost to breaking point, and his situation with Vivien worse than ever.

Not for the first time, while under extreme mental and physical stress Tom found that poetry burst from him. In late September, in 'a hell of a sweat' he worked on 'Doris's Dream Songs', perhaps considering them momentarily as interludes for his planned play: its 'agon' would feature the characters of Doris and Sweeney, and would end with singing about 'a sweat and a hell of a fright'.[62] On 5 October he sent these new songs to Harold Monro for his magazine, *Chapbook*; on 6 October Tom asked for them back to revise amidst a slew of *Criterion* correspondence; he had been reading Gertrude Stein's work, which he found 'extremely interesting', not least because of its 'peculiar hypnotic effect' which he connected with his own ongoing attempts 'working in a method of repetition and variation'.[63] 'Doris's Dream Songs' repeated words including 'Eyes', 'tears', 'death', 'dream' and 'kingdom' in a hypnotic way, articulating another emotional waste land. Though the poem's 'tears' and 'death' are hardly specific, Tom had spent months facing up to what might happen if he, his wife, or his mother were to die. His 1923 meeting with Emily Hale had brought renewed intensity, but she was gone; his relationship with Vivien lay in tatters. He wrote of the pain of 'Eyes I shall not see again' that seemed filled with derision. The voice of these 'Songs' seems trapped 'in death's dream kingdom'. Images of death mix with 'supplication' to 'stone images' – drawn, perhaps, from his anthropological reading or from those unsettling dreams prompted by his psychoanalysis. The songs are shot through with torment and loss, including erotic loss:

Waking alone
At the hour when we are

Trembling with tenderness
Lips that would kiss
Form prayers to broken stone.[64]

However indirectly, this spoke to and from his own sense of emotional damage and 'paralysed force'. Another poem written around the same time, and printed separately, articulated a terrifying sense of an inner nothingness worse than that of the 'being made of nothingness' ('*Un être fait de néant*') of Larbaud which had so impressed him. He had been struck, too, by a recollection of Stravinsky's ballet of puppets and failed love, *Petrushka*, and later wrote that his bleak new poem, which presented effigy-like figures, owed 'a great deal' to that work.[65] Tom's articulation was simple, desperate, and chant-like: 'We are the hollow men'.[66]

While working on these poems he consulted the well-connected novelist and dramatist Arnold Bennett about his play. On 10 September he had gone to the Reform Club in Pall Mall to ask Bennett for a response to Virginia Woolf's recent *Criterion* essay on 'Character in Fiction' which took Bennett as its starting point; more urgently, Tom sought advice about a 'drama of modern life' with 'furnished flat sort of people'. The meeting started awkwardly: Bennett inquired whether the notes to 'Wastelands' were 'a skit'. Soon, though, Tom, whom Bennett thought 'Pale, quiet, well assured' and likeable, explained his proposed drama: it would be in rhythmic prose, though Bennett was struck by Tom's saying ' "perhaps with certain things in it accentuated by drum-beats" '. The older playwright expressed an interest in seeing 'the scenario and some sample pages of dialogue'.[67]

By 8 October, just after sending 'Doris's Dream Songs' to Monro, Tom had come up with his scenario and 'five or six typed pages of dialogue'.[68] A surviving typescript shows he was uncertain what to call the work. One possibility was 'The Marriage of Life and Death: A Dream', but he settled on *The Superior Landlord*, giving the work an epigraph from Shakespeare's *Julius Caesar* about 'a hideous dream'.[69] A dozen years later, he told an interviewer his drama was 'written in two nights . . . from ten o'clock at night until five the next morning . . . with the aid of youthful enthusiasm and a bottle of gin'.[70] If composed at speed, it had been long in gestation, its structure carefully plotted according to Cornford's argument that Aristophanic comedies derived a distinctive form from primitive 'ritual performances' involving 'conflict and death' as well as 'resurrection and marriage'.[71] Tom's scenario fused this structure with modern-day London apartment life and American-accented jazz-age culture of singing, banjos, drumming, and the gramophone. At a supper party Sweeney, after badinage with Doris and a balletic interlude, debates with, then murders, Mrs Porter; later she is resurrected and marries Sweeney before loud knocking is heard and a tenant revealed waking up in bed. All the foregoing action 'has been his DREAM'.[72]

In the play's surviving 'agon' (not published until 1926, after 'reconstructing'), Sweeney threatens to become the 'cannibal' who – like the bungalow-bride murderer who had boiled his lover's body parts in a saucepan – will 'convert' the 'missionary' Doris into 'a nice little, white little, soft little, tender little, / Juicy little, right little, missionary stew'. Sweeney's vision of life on a 'cannibal isle' as monotonous to the point of death recalls also Tom's fascination with the looming fate of the Melanesians as reported by the anthropologist and psychologist Rivers, and leads Sweeney to the bleak conclusion that 'Life is death'. Doris is told by him, 'That's all the facts when you come to brass tacks: / Birth, and copulation, and death.'[73]

Though the play fizzes with crazy, jazzy, jagged wit, it also portrays sexuality as a bleak conflict – a marriage of life and death. Sweeney maintains 'Any man has to, needs to, wants to / Once in a lifetime, do a girl in'.[74] Picking up on contemporary stories from 'the papers' like the bungalow-bride murder, the play draws, too, on accounts of the notorious Dr Crippen who had dissolved his female victims in acid in a bath: Sweeney claims to have known 'a man once did a girl in' by keeping her 'With a gallon of lysol in a bath'.[75] Tom had not met Crippen but, as he had written to Dorothy Pound in October 1923, he had known a doctor who could 'do somebody in' and who 'nearly put V. in her grave'.[76] Unable, despite his best efforts, to save Vivien from her continuing torments, Tom came to feel in some moods that he was responsible for her sufferings, even that he was in a sense her killer. Both he and Vivien found Murry's obsessive writing about the death of Katherine Mansfield repulsive, but it was to Murry some months later that Tom would confess that his own behaviour in steeling himself to persist had brought about a kind of death and had '*killed* V.'[77]

The work he produced in the later part of 1924 let him make memorably disturbing artistic patterns out of the chaos of his life. Two of 'Doris's Dream Songs' were relegated to lie among his 'minor poems', but a third found its way into – and gave the title to – what became his most widely quoted as well as his most desolate poem, 'The Hollow Men' – that work which, more devastatingly than any of his others, articulates near-total despair.

Yet alongside this expression of inner turbulence came a reinforcing of his public achievement. Supported by Herbert Read, he sought to shape the *Criterion*'s principal contributors into a 'phalanx' of 'persons who have an impersonal loyalty to some faith not antagonistic to my own'. 'At the present time', Tom explained to Read, 'we need more dogma.' He did not expect every *Criterion* contributor 'to subscribe to all the articles of my own faith, or to read Arnold, Newman, Bradley, or Maurras with my eyes', but for himself he required 'as precise and clear a creed as possible'. He declared himself untroubled by an 'apparent inconsistency' between his prose championing of order and his verse articulations of chaos; and he was wary of being seen as 'leader' of his 'phalanx'. His instinct was often, he told Read, to stay silent, aware that 'I sometimes give people an impression of arrogance and intolerant self-conceit.' Yet he did recognise that as a ' "leader" ' or ' "organiser" ' he might provide 'a particular function' that allowed 'others to do their best work'.[78]

In this model of leadership, Tom echoed some of the conduct of the right-wing philosopher-poet Maurras, who had begun by editing a monthly magazine which served as a rallying point for his Action Française followers. Aware of Maurras since his student days (Tom had bought Maurras's *L'Avenir de l'intelligence*, in 1911), when referring in 1924 to his own running of 'the *Criterion* for two suicidal years', he quoted Dante's lines about a steward whose great and noble work was ill-rewarded: '*e cio gli fece / Romeo, persona umile e peregrine*' (and this was made / By Romeo, a lowly and foreign person).[79] These words, one of Tom's favourite Dante passages, were cited towards the climax of *L'Avenir de l'intelligence*, which Tom, conscious of its important 'influence', recommended to *Criterion* readers in 1926; Maurras applied the words to the guiding force of 'Intelligence' itself, whose role was threatened in the modern world but whose function was bonded to that of an intellectual elite.[80] Writing in French in 1923, Tom had said of the *Criterion* that '*si la revue peut satisfaire une petite élite internationale, je serai recompensé du travail*' (if the review can satisfy a small international elite, I shall be compensated for the work involved).[81]

He did not always feel sufficiently compensated. Yet he stayed resolutely faithful to the mission of his elite periodical whose subscribers numbered only 'about 200', even if a few hundred more copies were sold in shops.[82] Honing his 'creed', he led the *Criterion*. Like the late poet-philosopher T. E. Hulme whose works Read edited in 1924 and who had championed classicism and the doctrine of original sin – and like the French writer on myth and violence Georges Sorel, about whose work he also enthused – Tom was attracted by the anti-democratic right. In France ardent right-wing thought was often nostalgic for the Middle Ages and for France's status as a great Catholic monarchic power. However, Tom was not quite Maurras. Maurras had developed his right-wing political force as an antisemitic, anti-German French nationalist; in the early 1920s, despite his admiration for Catholicism (to which he later converted), he was a staunch agnostic. As a foreign immigrant, a 'metic', in London, Tom, however, believed, as he put it in 1925, that 'the metic, like the Jew, can only thoroughly naturalize himself in cities'.[83] He thought, too, that the 'critique of the school of Maurras' had a 'weakness' in that it 'cannot support, correct, or develop any of the actual creative writing in France'.[84] Still, his long-standing interest in Maurras, who had been presented in *La Nouvelle Revue française* (in 1913, when Tom subscribed) as '*l'incarnation vivante de trois traditions "classique, catholique, monarchique"* ', certainly dovetailed with the *Criterion*'s editorial line.[85] Tom may not have been Maurras, but he adapted Maurras's credo.

Now to help with his magazine he hired Pearl Fassett, who had also been doing 'odd jobs' for Vivien who herself continued to assist her husband with the *Criterion*.[86] In the backbiting world of literary London, where one minute the Eliots might mock Murry and the next treat him as a close friend, it was hard to remain cordial towards all *Criterion* contributors. After Sydney Schiff (who had been supporting Wyndham Lewis financially) fell out with Lewis, Tom refused to reproach his artist friend. Schiff got angry. 'Disagreeable words passed between us.'[87] Publication of his own *Homage to John Dryden* in November cheered Tom somewhat; he joked to Virginia Woolf, 'The book gives me great pleasure – if I do not read it.'[88] His preface, referring to 'perpetual oblivion' and 'the infirmities of age', made its author sound geriatric. Privately, he admitted to a 'rather rheumatic pomposity' in 'my prose'.[89] Still, Vivien's health was sufficiently improved that she and Tom went to Paris on 14 November for what might have been a reviving weekend – had not Tom needed 'to see Lady Rothermere', cram in a meeting with at least one *Criterion* contributor, then return to London on the Sunday evening.[90] As soon as he got back he was floored for four days by further 'influenza', then 'up for three days, and then in bed again!'[91]

Overwork was habitual. Just a week before Paris he had been in Cambridge, giving an invited paper to the Cam Literary Society about Renaissance playwright George Chapman, a verse dramatist of 'dream' and 'shade' who seemed to the author of 'Doris's Dream Songs' to illustrate, like Donne, 'an internal incoherence, as of an era of transition and decay'. To Tom, Chapman's characters appeared to consciously act their roles 'in *this* world', while accepting that 'the real centre of their action is in another Kingdom'. He linked this to Dostoyevsky's awareness both of 'two planes of reality' and of people involved in 'conversation with spectres'. Veering aside, he told his listeners that Dante 'and some of the Spanish mystics' had 'arrived at a theory of love and sex' that '*worked*', though it was hard for modern people to comprehend in an era when 'psychology' led 'either to glands or to theology'. Though he spoke neither of Dr Martin nor Vivien's problematic glands nor his own engagement with theology, he told the Cambridge undergraduates that 'You should not conceive of me in this context as the apologist of Christianity', but argued, nonetheless, that

Chapman and Donne and Dostoevski, and also James Joyce, accept Christian problems; they are operating with Christian categories; and that they are all inferior to Dante because they do not draw Christian conclusions. This is I think the great distress of the modern world, that it is neither Christian nor definitely something else.

Emphasising human and divine as 'inseparable and eternally in conflict', Tom added that 'this recognition of duality is the Doctrine of Original Sin'.[92]

Though his student listeners may not have realised it, in Tom's mind such assertions were closely bound up with the 'longer sequence' of poems that became 'The Hollow Men'.[93] There mention of the 'dream kingdom' leads to words from the Lord's Prayer, '*For Thine is the Kingdom*', only for the prayer to break down. These Hollow Men seem trapped in a condition 'neither Christian nor definitely something else'. Their 'quiet and meaningless' voices are surely part of a 'conversation with spectres'.[94] The 'Multifoliate rose' of Dante's *Paradiso* (whose petals comprise the tiers of the redeemed) is presented as 'The hope only / Of empty men.'[95]

Years afterwards, Tom said this 'rose' also alluded 'to the rose mentioned in the Litany of the Blessed Virgin', a text to which he would return.[96] Invoking Hulme and 'Original Sin' when he spoke to the Cam Literary Society in the Tea Shop, Cambridge, on 8 November 1924 he said simply, 'it is difficult for us to understand the Mystery of the Adoration of the Blessed Virgin'.[97] If 'The Hollow Men' articulates craving for religious certainty, its 'empty men' appear cut off from that. As he wrote unflinchingly in his introduction to Valéry's *Le Serpent*, 'One is prepared for art when one has ceased to be interested in one's own emotions and experiences except as material.'[98] Determinedly, even chillingly, he sculpted his suffering into verse.

Yet right at this low point a chance encounter changed his life. The bibliophile Whibley (whom Vivien detested as 'the devil') had been a guest at Oxford's exclusive All Souls College. Chatting with its recently appointed estates bursar, Whibley mentioned Tom's name.[99] The estates bursar, a year younger than Tom, looked after the college's substantial land and property holdings. He had been privately educated at Rugby School before taking a top-flight classics degree at Oxford. Author of two books of poetry, after an apprenticeship in publishing at Oxford University Press and distinguished war service in France he had been elected to an All Souls prize fellowship. This granted him dining rights and college rooms, but, since All Souls has no undergraduates, he was not required to teach. Instead, like some of the other fellows, he pursued a career in the wider world, visiting the college and helping with its governance. By 1923, after business experience as a brewery director and qualifying as a lawyer, he had begun negotiating with an All Souls colleague about expanding the Scientific Press. His colleague's wife had inherited this publishing house based at 28–29 Southampton Street in London.

The estates bursar's name was Geoffrey Faber; his colleague was Maurice Gwyer. In class, cash and education both were 'chaps' from the upper echelons of English society. Faber, who had hoped to become a Conservative MP, mentioned to Whibley the possibility of recruiting someone able to move the Scientific Press into areas beyond its current profitable line – medical texts and related publications including the *Nursing Mirror*. Tipped off by Whibley, on 25 November 1924 Tom, signing himself 'Your obedient servant', typed Faber a short, formal note saying he would be happy to call on him.[100] On the evening of 1 December, recovering from bronchitis, he went by invitation to Faber's elegant town house, 21 Ladbroke Grove, Notting Hill, hoping to gain employment that would let him leave the bank. Faber, however, had a less secure arrangement in mind: more of 'an informal adviser and, in fact, a "talent scout"' with 'some reputation among the young', who might help attract promising writers to the embryonic firm of 'Faber & Gwyer'. Yet, gradually, as the formal, Harvard-educated *Criterion* editor and banker-poet talked at length with the cultivated, introspective Oxford-educated bursar-poet about the *Criterion* and publishing possibilities, Tom recalled, 'we took to each other' with the result that 'our two designs became identical'.[101]

Next morning, beginning his letter with 'My [dear] Eliot', the legally trained Faber sent Tom a 'short memorandum' of their conversation.[102] Though he warned there were obstacles to overcome (Faber needed to discuss matters with colleagues), he hoped something positive might result. Tom was excited. That very same day he mentioned to Lewis 'a new publishing firm which is promising, but it won't even be formed for six months or so'.[103] Yet he had to go on wrangling over *Criterion* arrangements with Lady Rothermere, wary of her 'violent temper' as he and Cobden-Sanderson planned how to placate her.[104] Faber, a more experienced businessman, guided Tom how best to present his case to the 'Directors' of the new publishing house, and counselled him about getting testimonials.

Bruce Richmond, editor of the *Times Literary Supplement*, could supply one, Arnold Bennett another.

What we do not want them to say is: 'Mr Eliot is a profound and scholarly critic.' What we want them to say is: 'Mr Eliot is a brilliant editor, as well as a brilliant writer and critic.' What will impress my directors favourably in the scheme, if anything will, is the sense that in you we have found a man who combines literary gifts with business instincts, who has a wide circle of literary friends, and who is quite as much at home on the lower levels as on the lonely peaks.[105]

Though negotiations lasted several months, this opportunity would let Tom leave the bank for congenial work with a substantial salary and likely long-term security.

While he was being piloted into publishing, he continued to guide Vivien's literary aspirations. Several of her prose sketches appeared in the *Criterion*. At the start of 1925 the couple went to Eastbourne, apparently for the sake of Vivien's health, but Tom's health was still precarious and his temper frayed. Both Eliots had been finding Jack Culpin hard to deal with, as had Pearl Fassett. If Vivien's versified account of Jack's 'rudeness' is to be believed, then around Christmas or very early in 1925 he and Tom had a physical 'row':

Tom blacks Jacks eye
But does no good,
Then turns Jack out
In sullen mood
Incited thereunto by Pearl
Who is, at least, a 'vengeance girl'[106]

Whereas such physical venting of pent-up emotion impressed Vivien, it did Tom little good. He was ill in mid-January. Vivien blamed the 'dark airless basement' in which he had been working at Lloyds for the last six months.[107] Tom's doctor agreed, but there were other anxieties too, making him feel a hollow man – 'a shell with no machinery in it'.[108] Enthusiastically, Faber was already suggesting Tom edit a new quarterly magazine for the emergent publishing house, but Tom still had the *Criterion* to cope with, and as yet had signed no contract with Faber. By mid-February he was still off work ('influenza and breakdown'); Vivien, as so often matching him worry for worry, was '*very* ill', her temperature soaring after even 'a few minutes' conversation'.[109] It was, he told Murry, 'the *blackest moment in my life*'.[110] Yet suddenly Murry came to his rescue, putting his name forward for the Clark Lectures at Trinity College, Cambridge. These would earn Tom £200, making it all the more feasible for him to abandon the bank.

But not yet. For months, still popular with 'the boys and girls' at the bank (as his colleagues styled themselves to him that April), he had to slog in Lloyds basement by day, edit and write by night, and assist Vivien.[111] The stories she was writing, including 'Medicine à la Mode' (which went through several drafts), drew closely on her experience of her Cyriax treatment. 'Sibylla' stands with 'thin keen face & startled eyes', her hair unkempt, in a doctor's surgery, 'her thin hands clasping & rubbing her emaciated body in the places where the treatment has been most severe'. Sibylla encounters the opulently dressed 'Lady Rotherbrooke', whose life is redolent of luxurious Paris and chauffeur-driven outings in a Rolls-Royce; Sibylla longs to find 'at last, the treatment, the cure, the one perfect certain treatment'.[112] Suggesting small verbal sharpenings, and even letting her use material left out of *The Waste Land*, Tom, though he insisted some names be changed, did all he could to help Vivien shape these stories which drew so closely on their shared experience. In March, however, her illness worsened: 'terrific rheumatism all over her body'. Her doctor was puzzled. 'In the greatest pain' and 'almost delirious' for three days, she seemed to Tom as if about to 'simply expire from exhaustion'. 'Life', he confessed to Virginia Woolf, 'is simply from minute to minute of horror.' He found the 'anxiety', which dragged on for weeks, 'terrible'.[113]

As her physician was aware, Vivien's condition seems to have been made worse by a sexual assault. For many months she had been subject to the attentions of her mentally unstable American friend Lucy Thayer, Scofield Thayer's cousin, whom she had known for almost twenty years. Lucy had been a witness at the Eliots' wedding. According to an account apparently derived from Vivien, in 1923, two years after Lucy had let the Eliots stay in her London flat, she had horrified Vivien by announcing she intended to kill Vivien's father. Undergoing prolonged psychoanalysis, Lucy seemed to have developed a sexual obsession with Vivien. By 1925 a letter from Tom to Lady Rothermere complained that for two years Lucy had been 'persecuting my wife . . . with her very obscene attentions'. Then, in early 1925, according to this account written in June, Lucy

> lay in wait for my wife at her doctor's, when she was very ill, and told her in so many words that she had killed her father at last. I have another witness for this. She then made violent love to my wife,

kneeling at her feet. She is perverted. My wife was *prostrated* by this shock, especially as she was then in a state of great anxiety about her own father. She has been very ill ever since, and nearly lost her reason for a time.[114]

Vivien's most recent biographer, Ann Pasternak Slater, argues that this letter to Lady Rothermere, ostensibly written by Tom, was authored in fact by Vivien, and that it is Vivien 'who sounds' insane.[115] Certainly Vivien's version of the Lucy Thayer incident corroborated the account sent to Lady Rothermere: Vivien informed Pound that Lucy 'nelt [*sic*] down beside me and asked me if I loved her, & made love. I could not get at anyone to help me & so nearly went mad. Helpless. Not dressed. Alone.'[116] Convinced Lucy was '*mad*', Tom 'forbade the woman the house and forcibly removed her'.[117] Whatever had happened, Vivien was clearly shattered. Night after night Tom saw his wife exhausted and in pain.

So, what was really wrong with Vivien? Though she admits that the 'suggestion is inevitably hypothetical' and retrospective, Pasternak Slater maintains that 'she fulfils all the diagnostic criteria once specified for chronic Munchausen's Syndrome – a condition only described, and named, after her death'. Pasternak Slater explains that 'This is a psychiatric disorder whose sufferers feign disease in order to draw attention, sympathy, lenience, or reassurance to themselves.'[118] However, as Pasternak Slater and others make clear, Vivien had suffered in early life from at least one serious physical ailment – tuberculosis – and was prone to recurrent anxiety. So was Tom. Pasternak Slater, who establishes the young Vivien as 'highly strung, rather spoiled' and 'bossy and manipulative', goes on to call her 'a hysteric, a neurotic', and shows how over the years she grew increasingly addicted to several drugs, including the sedative chloral hydrate and, later, a variety of other sedatives, anaesthetics, and painkillers.[119] But psychological and physical diagnoses conducted almost a century afterwards by biographers who lack medical qualifications and access to full records of the patient are at best speculative, and can risk sounding reductively judgemental. For Vivien and Tom, part of the problem was that, while the acute pain and suffering were evident, it was so hard to work out with real certainty just where their cause or causes lay. Over time different doctors would suggest various physical and psychological causes and remedies. The Eliots, like many of their twenty-first-century readers, had to struggle with the apparent irresolvability of Vivien's tormenting and worsening condition, and those struggles only intensified the worry.

Meanwhile, to the outside world Tom pretended as far as he could that all was well. He held long business conversations with Geoffrey Faber about launching a new quarterly. Faber wanted it to contain more creative work, and less criticism than the *Criterion*, to avoid 'a dulling of interest'.[120] He counselled his new Francophile American friend to avoid any 'rigid, dogmatic' attitude as a publisher: 'That is not the natural English way.'[121] Tom's unEnglishness was a sensitive point, but Whibley had already written to Faber, assuring him Tom was 'strongly anti-American, as you would suppose', and was 'now being naturalized' as a British subject.[122] Without denying his family or his background, Tom was doing all he could to conform to his adopted country. Working with Faber would further that assimilation.

What Faber wanted from his new venture was 'the active, continuous combination of the young men under the unifying principle not of a new dogma, but of a personality, and if our scheme comes to anything it is you who will supply that'.[123] A publisher, Faber told Tom, 'is not either a preacher or a philosopher; he is a tradesman'.[124] Knowing little of his poetry, Faber perceived that while Tom might have proved he possessed editorial abilities, he needed to be coached and coaxed away from rigid 'dogma' to succeed as a publisher beyond a niche intellectual market. Confiding to Tom that he had religious convictions and belonged 'to that dwindling band which reads this world in the light of another', Faber was very shrewd.[125] Tom responded that Faber's sense of 'the "other world" in poetry' came very close to hints he had given in his recent Cambridge talk on Chapman, and to what he intended to say about seventeenth-century metaphysical poetry in his forthcoming Clark Lectures.[126]

Faber's emphasis on 'personality' rather than 'dogma' may have grated with Tom; but, already struggling to convince Herbert Read that he was not an editorial 'autocrat' while trying to make peace with the quarrelsome Lewis, he told Faber he was 'in agreement' about publishing.[127] Both men were increasingly aligned. 'The Editor', Tom confirmed, 'has to combine and reconcile principle, sensibility, and business sense. That is why an editor's life is such a bloody sweat.'[128] Hoping Tom's contacts as magazine editor would attract authors to the new publishing house, Faber would match Lady Rothermere's £750 guarantee against loss for the magazine, and looked likely to offer a substantial salary. As it turned out, Tom would receive £325 a year for editing 'a Quarterly Review', plus remuneration of £150 per annum as a 'Director of the Company'.[129]

To the fledgling publishing house Faber's new hire committed exclusively not just his editorial talents but also his poems. 'A blow to us' at the Hogarth Press, thought Virginia Woolf, sensing, like others, a certain self-advancing ruthlessness in Tom.[130] He now aimed to collect his poetry from *Prufrock* onwards in a single volume. Along with Geoffrey Faber's soon forgotten prose fantasy *Elnovia*, this would be among the first books scheduled by Faber & Gwyer. To Faber, Tom maintained his high-functioning professional demeanour; yet to Murry he confessed his agony:

> In the last ten years – gradually, but deliberately – I have made myself into a *machine*. I have done it deliberately – in order to endure, in order not to feel – *but it has killed* V. In leaving the bank I hope to become less a machine – but yet I am frightened – because I don't know what it will do to me – and to V. – should I come alive again. I have deliberately killed my senses – I have deliberately died – in order to go on with the outward form of living – This I did in 1915. What will happen if I live again?[131]

1915 was the year of his marriage. Part of what lies behind this letter seems to have been his continuing but concealed feelings for Emily Hale. He asked Murry whether it was possible to 'exorcise this desire for what I cannot have, for someone I cannot see'. Such feelings only intensified his sense of guilt towards Vivien. If he had 'killed' her by living as if dead, then equally he might kill her by coming to life again, 'wanting something' he could not get from her. His letter never uses the word 'love', but evidently the 'desire' he feels is not for Vivien, though he feels bound to her by duty, anxiety and guilt. He suggests a couple's lives can be 'absolutely hostile'. Yet he was shaken by Vivien's intense hurt. 'She really *went away – for three days she felt that she had left her body. Is this wrong?'* He wondered, 'Does she want to die?' He felt like her murderer. 'Must I kill her or kill myself? I have *tried* to kill myself – but only to make the machine which kills her.'[132] This was his personal agon, his marital agony of life and death.

'You must cease to sacrifice your inviolable self', advised Murry, whose Lawrentian view that 'A woman's direction is given only by her man: that is the law' was more absolute than any of Tom's strictures.[133] Tormented, Tom could not abandon Vivien. She was terrified of loneliness, and grew fearful every time he left the house. He felt she had experienced 'years of loneliness since marriage'; yet, conscious of the damaged, damaging nature of their relationship, he wondered if it might benefit her 'to live quite alone – if she could'.[134] In anguish, he turned for advice not just to Murry who had seen his own wife die but also to Violet Schiff (who endured chronic ill health), to the Woolfs (who lived with mental and physical breakdown), and even to Bertrand Russell who had stepped in to assist before, with ruinous results. When Vivien wrote a very lightly fictionalised story involving 'B. R.', Tom scored out those initials and styled this character 'the mathematician'; Vivien's fictional treatment suggested she now regarded her 'dessicated & pedantic' former lover with scorn. After 'B. R. enters' in one story Sibylla reflects, 'There had been a time when she had seen much of this aristocratic heretic, but he had changed his milieu & for the past few years she had seen him hardly at all. Missing him, she yet wasted no time on regrets.' There was not any 'question of revenge'.[135]

In desperation, calling him 'a great psychologist', Tom approached Russell. Unsure if Vivien would become 'criminal or saint', Russell had written in 1915 about her mixture of affection and cruelty towards Tom. Now Tom sought not revenge, but guidance about how Vivien might recover. He told Russell, 'everything has turned out as you predicted ten years ago'.[136] Though they had sought so many physicians' advice, Tom now blamed himself for their 'criminal maltreatment'.[137] The Cyriax regime had left Vivien's 'stomach . . . *out of place*' and 'exhausted every nerve in her body to breaking point'.[138] 'Making the most shocking faces and hypnotising herself', she feared being diagnosed as 'an idiot'. 'Paralysed', Tom 'had very grave fears that her reason would go altogether'.[139] Dr Martin, 'tampering' with her psychology, had directed her mind 'inward and backward', inviting 'introspection' which 'paralyses action'.[140] If the Hollow Men's horrors of 'Paralysed force' were Tom's, they were also Vivien's.[141]

'The Paralysed Woman', a story she wrote around this time, is rooted in her sufferings and the state of their marriage. Tom thought it 'wonderful', conscious it drew terrifyingly on her time at Eastbourne the previous summer when she had 'continued to starve, and most unfortunately there lived opposite her window a paralysed woman, who somehow joined up in her mind the horrible ideas that the German doctor [Martin] had planted there'.[142] In Vivien's story Sibylla, staying with Felice in a 'seaside flat' and growing 'thinner' while reading seventeenth-century Jeremy Taylor's *Holy Dying*, obsessively watches a pretty, rich, paralysed woman, neatly dressed, like a 'doll', and wonders 'how can she *bother*? – If I was paralysed . . .' The narrative, with its human 'mechanical figures', epitomises 'Horror' and 'pain'. Mike, a leading character, travels backwards and forwards to London, finding Sibylla 'weak; highly strung, over sensitive, too easily stimulated and excited.' André, bowler-hatted like banker Tom, comes at weekends 'carrying as usual two large suit cases – one filled with books and periodicals and the other with medicine bottles', as if replenishing 'a desert island'. They go to 'tea and dance' at the 'Queen's Hotel' – clearly Eastbourne's Queen's Hotel. Sibylla speaks of longing to be 'an exhibition dancer', an aspiration Vivien had held. André grows 'liverish and ill-tempered'; there is talk of medical 'Bacteria', 'oil' and 'cachets'. Amidst Sunday 'chaos', Sibylla lies in bed watching the paralysed woman, argues over dirty laundry, then suddenly loses her temper, falling back 'exhausted on her bed'.

> 'I can't bear it. I can't go on.' She relaxed her body and appeared dead; but her mind went on as fast as ever.
> 'I must, somehow I must be independent.'

Staring at the paralysed woman, 'inert' Sibylla waits for André to come 'and get them away'.[143]

Sibylla's 'I can't go on', like Tom's 'I cannot go on' a couple of years earlier, is a cry of despair. 'I know that I have killed *her*', Tom wrote again to Murry in mid-April 1925, 'And this terrible sense of the most subtle form of *guilt* is itself paralysing and deadening.'[144] Meanwhile, just as she had done for him, by deploying his controlling intelligence he did his best to shape and spur her creativity, maintaining 'she is a *very* clever and original writer, with a mathematical and abstract mind which ought to be trained – and I intend that it shall'.[145] He suggested to Virginia Woolf how good it would be if Virginia 'advised or instructed her about *writing*'.[146] Virginia, while sympathetic, found Vivien exhausting, and showed no enthusiasm for her literary efforts. Only the *Criterion* published her stories, which had been rejected elsewhere, leaving her 'bitterly disappointed'.[147]

Tom might praise his wife's writing and intelligence, but, like the character in her story who thinks the female protagonist 'too easily stimulated and excited', Tom found Vivien 'naturally immoderate'. When she put off writing and tried to rest, ideas went on 'fermenting in her brain' and, he fretted, 'with this neuralgia, she thinks and thinks the whole time'.[148] He convinced himself she had experienced 'purely a nervous, *not* mental breakdown', but confessed to Russell he found her 'perpetually baffling and deceptive'.[149] In her story 'Desert Island', Vivien described a sense of 'arrested development in adolescence caused by shock'.[150] Tom wrote, 'She seems to me like a child of six with an immensely clever and precocious mind.'[151] He asked for guidance about psychiatric help – for himself as much as for her, and hoped they could simply 'disappear this summer', pinning their hopes on 'a long rest'.[152] Vivien's feelings seem encapsulated in a poem she published in April 1925. 'Necesse est Perstare?' ('Is it Necessary to Endure?') glances at Bloomsbury 'inanities', then presents a pained relationship:

> I looked at you and you looked at me.
> I longed to speak to you,
> But I didn't. I longed
> To come and stand beside you at the window and

Look out at the fleering
Cold English sunshine and say,
Is it necessary –
Is it necessary –
Tell me, is it *necessary* that we go through this?[153]

Less obliquely than Tom's, Vivien's writings drew on their marriage. Reducing Dostoyevsky-reading Mike to tears, Sibylla says menacingly 'that you are indifferent as to whether you are dead or alive'. Playing with a knife, she adds, 'You would not be indifferent, for instance, if I were just to wipe this knife round your throat.'[154] In what came to be called *Sweeney Agonistes*, a work that, like Vivien's fiction, juxtaposes London and an exotic island, Sweeney complains to Doris, 'I gotta use words when I talk to you', then tries to explain the situation of a murderer who has done 'a girl in':

He didn't know if he was alive
and the girl was dead
He didn't know if the girl was alive
and he was dead
He didn't know if they both were alive
or both were dead[155]

Though Tom's schematic conventionalising of character in *Sweeney Agonistes*, and his alignment of jazz-age apartment life and music-hall turns with ancient fertility rituals has the effect of making his work both disconcerting and impersonal ('my own aim is to suppress my own biography' he told Kreymborg), he, like Vivien but with more profound artistry, writes out of a personal hell.[156]

Both of them were haunted by thoughts of Lucy Thayer's assault on Vivien. Tom probably oversaw the severe typed letter Vivien sent her on 25 May after receiving Lucy's semi-legible communication. 'I do not think yours is a mind I should ever understand, nor a mind which I particularly wish to understand', declared Vivien. 'In so far as there is any relation to break off it is an impossible one on every count.'[157] Still, she and Tom worried that Lucy (now in Paris) might spread malicious gossip about them. Outlining to Lady Rothermere what had happened, Tom (in a letter probably overseen – or maybe even ghostwritten – by Vivien) worried that his wife's former friend, not content with attacking Vivien, was also 'anxious to injure me'.[158]

As this row developed, aware Geoffrey Faber was vital to his future plans, Tom agreed to dine at All Souls on 23 May; Faber hoped that Tom, although an American, might be elected to the college, and Tom around this time renewed his efforts to take British nationality. But fulfilling business and social engagements became ever more difficult. When he missed the Faber & Gwyer directors' meeting on 28 May, Tom had to inform Faber how serious Vivien's condition was. He had found her a new, American physician, Dr West, who had advised Dorothy Pound. Examining Vivien, West diagnosed starvation and extreme liver problems. Vivien, sure she had suffered a 'nervous breakdown', had experienced 'trances': '*Enjoyed trances*. Went off for 2 or 3 weeks at a time. (Had *very queer* experiences in sum other Place.)'[159] Seeing Dr West three times a week, she disliked him intensely, but admitted he improved her health. He wanted her to go for a French health cure in the spa town of Vichy; still 'very unwell', she favoured Paris instead. Tom, who would soon consult both Virginia Woolf's specialist Dr Henry Head and the psychoanalyst Dr James Glover, could not decide what was best. 'Spouse all of a dither', Vivien complained to Pound.[160]

Unsure about Vivien, he confidently agreed to edit a 'quarterly literary periodical' for the Scientific Press, soon to become Faber & Gwyer. This magazine would be called the *New Criterion*. After lengthy tussling, and the possibility that Tom might run two separate titles simultaneously, Lady Rothermere (whom Geoffrey Faber found 'exasperating') agreed with Faber & Gwyer to supply one more year's support for the *Criterion*, then withdraw.[161] There might be a hiatus in publication, but Tom would graduate to his *New Criterion*, backed by Faber & Gwyer. This was reassuring, but Tom felt obliged to write to Vivien's father about her 'nervous breakdown and idiot-mania symptoms'. Recommended by the Schiffs, Dr John Davis Barris, a 'surgeon-consultant' specialising in gynaecology and highly critical of the Cyriax treatment, had advised that many of her problems had been caused by starvation; for the next few years she would need constant nursing. Tom confided to Vivien's father that Barris 'considers her extraordinarily undeveloped, in fact all doctors do, every one has commented on her extreme youth and almost childishness'. Both Barris and Dr Glover thought three or four months abroad (probably in Rome where Vivien's brother Maurice was living) were 'advisable'; even 'almost necessary'. Tom agreed Maurice's companionship would be good for her, but, working himself into deepening distress, he wrote to her father (who had helped financially during Tom's nervous breakdown) both about her health and about cash: 'I really am nearly ruined.' Confessing he had 'bled my mother white for money', then listing his and Vivien's woes, he stated that 'The future fills me with horror. I do not know what I shall do.'[162] It is hard to know how high the Eliots' medical costs were, but surviving details of

Dr Higgins's bills show that in December 1925 alone, Vivien's care 'expenses' must have cost over £138 – nearly a third of the annual salary that Tom anticipated for his work as publisher and editor at Faber & Gwyer.[163] Ever loyal, Henry, who had just become engaged, cabled him $1,500.

Though in August 1925 he visited the concerned Fabers at their Welsh holiday home, he had to excuse himself from the July directors' meeting. But he drew up a long, impressive list for a proposed book series on 'Foreign Men of Letters', suggesting he write the volume on Maurras.[164] 'Poor Tom', thought Vivien, 'He is not well. He seems to me again to have involved himself in too much work. It is so hopeless – one can't *live*, like this.'[165] She complained that 'Tom's terrific life takes all my energy, and I can only lie still and wait for it to end.'[166] They hoped to move house, but she caught shingles.[167] Virginia Woolf recommended earplugs, which helped her sleep; soon she was being given 'injections' for anaemia, and Tom too was receiving jabs – for iron deficiency.[168] They consulted doctor after doctor.

'The Paralysed Woman' story had been submitted (awkwardly and optimistically) to Lucy Thayer's sister Ellen at the *Dial*, but was rejected by Marianne Moore there, precipitating outrage in the Eliot household. 'Ill, harassed', Tom had 'to be gassed' so five teeth could be extracted.[169] Next came an operation on his jaw which had become infected; but he sang his wife's praises to Violet Schiff, explaining how she had had to give up careers in dancing, painting, and music, all because of her health. 'She is quite aware, as I am aware, that she is not primarily and primitively a *writer* – this has only come to her (lately) as a *partial* compensation for what she wanted.' Her pursuing a literary career represented 'an immense victory of will'.[170] Yet when, fifteen years later, Tom recalled his hope around 1925 'that if she could develop expression in writing it would help her to recover a grasp on life', it was painfully clear no victory had been won.[171]

Having outlined Vivien's situation to Violet Schiff, Tom went on to suggest that there were also weaknesses in himself that might have driven him to find refuge in writing poetry.

> You may say that even if you and Vivienne know these things, that I have no right to discuss them – because I have had a straight road, with no obstacles and no substitutions. It may be so, certainly it looks so, and I have *no grounds for regret*. I am not sure however that I have not been *forced* into poetry by my weakness in other directions – that there is not something else that I want – but at all events, I took this

direction very young, and learned very early to find my life and my realisation in this curious way, and to be obtuse and indifferent to my reality in other ways. So it has been much easier for me. The admission of this fact may help you to admit that I understand in part the tragedy of others. But your letter seemed to require my explaining to you for Vivienne – as she never explains herself – the degree of resignation and the force of will and character which her present activities represent.[172]

Recovering from his jaw operation, he feared for the precariousness of his achievements. Aldington, disappointed in his own hope to edit a series of books similar to Tom's proposed 'Foreign Men of Letters', was annoyed at him again, convinced Tom used other people as 'his stepping-stones to higher things' and exhibited 'condescension'.[173] When, instead of letting the Hogarth Press reprint *The Waste Land*, Tom (without formally cancelling his Hogarth contract) took the poem to Faber & Gwyer for his forthcoming *Poems, 1909–1925*, the Woolfs were sore at him: 'Tom's character is sadly aspersed,' Virginia confided to Mary Hutchinson, though she knew his woes:

> I shall stick to the rags and tatters that remain (of Tom's character) with the tenacity of a leech, but get little help from Leonard. But suppose a little boy was beaten every day, and had his fingers shut in doors, and dead rats tied to his tail coat – that is Tom's predicament I maintain – he might fail in that manly and straightforward conduct which we all admire.[174]

Granted some reluctant absolution by the Woolfs and successful in patching things up with Aldington later in the year, Tom was keen to stay on good terms with as many literary colleagues as he could. Increasing his commitments, his pool of correspondents widened and deepened. Now it included his Connecticut-born cousin Marguerite Chapin – who had become Marguerite Caetani, on her marriage to Roffredo Caetani, the Prince of Bassiano in Lazio, about forty miles from Rome; Tom had published the first part of what became 'The Hollow Men' in *Commerce*, a review whose editors included Larbaud and Valéry and which was sponsored by Marguerite Caetani. Along with another of his correspondents, wealthy Paris-based American writer Natalie Barney, Marguerite had offered financial support if he left the bank.

Tom took on too much. He agreed to 'collaborate' with Robert Graves on a book about modern poetry, but had to pull out; he mulled over – but never wrote – his proposed volume on Maurras: more pondering of 'order', 'disintegration' and Catholic 'religious belief'; as well as planning his Cambridge Clark Lectures, he let his name go forward for the All Souls fellowship.[175] He could not keep everyone happy. When in October twenty-year-old Cambridge undergraduate John Hayward invited him to address the Heretics literary society, Tom pleaded 'illness', mentioning 'an enormous amount of writing and organising work ahead of me'.[176] To Pound, however, he devoted more time, following up the publication of a swathe of *Cantos* in the *Criterion* with assembling a suggested table of contents for Pound's *Selected Poems* – a volume to match his own. Eventually, Pound's poems would be published by Faber & Gwyer. Always conscious of his '*debt*' to Pound as 'tutor and critic', Tom sent his friend a version of 'The Hollow Men', as yet unpublished in full.[177]

By 2 November 1925 when, after several months' leave from the bank, Tom submitted his official resignation, Vivien had 'been sent to a nursing home in the country by Sir William Willcox', a senior physician at St Mary's Hospital. Tom himself was embarking 'on a voyage by the insistence of my doctor and the kindness of friends'.[178] Willcox, who had testified at the Crippen trial and the 'brides in the bath' case, specialised in curing narcotic addictions. In effect, under medical advice, the Eliots were being separated in the hope such a split might improve their health. Both could be short-tempered, and they seem to have quarrelled around this time. She told him in early December 'we must both do our *own* thinking. Alone.' She apologised 'for having upset you'.[179] Apparently referring to Tom's life with Vivien, Dr Higgins told Tom he had been suffering from a mental 'imprisonment': 'you were forced, by your higher instincts of protection and chivalry, into a region of restricted contacts with reality'. Tom must try to see things 'from the aspect rather of comedy than tragedy', and 'rest as much as possible and grin and bear it'; Higgins thought his American patient needed a warm climate, lots of rest, as well as tips on 'learning to relax' and 'thought control'.[180]

This sounded not uninviting. Tom was to sail for France on 6 November. He would stay for over a month at La Bluette, Lady Rothermere's holiday home near the well-appointed Savoy Hotel, La Turbie, at the foot of a Côte d'Azur hillside. Lady Rothermere was one of the 'friends' seeking to aid his recovery. Before setting off, he wrote to Faber, explaining his situation with Vivien and how he was at his wits' end. Supportively, Faber assured him, 'you have done your best and the responsibility is now on other people's shoulders'; he hoped the Eliots might heal while apart.[181] Apparently, as requested, Faber burned Tom's letter.

Vivien was bound first of all for a Southampton 'nursing home' under the supervision of Dr Thomas Ayscough Hawkesworth whose interests included 'chronic ill health' linked to 'emotional states'.[182] Then she transferred to The Stanboroughs, a converted mansion on a 200-acre wooded estate near Watford offering treatment for 'Digestive Disorders, Rheumatism, Arthritis, Heart Trouble, Diabetes, Neurasthenia'.[183] At Southampton, Hawkesworth found her 'acutely restless and hysterical'; 'her will to take drugs' was 'being systematically opposed'.[184] Visited by the Schiffs in December, she spoke openly about 'her habit of taking chloral during many years' as 'the cause of all her troubles'.[185] Chloral hydrate treated anxiety and insomnia; repeated use led to addiction. At Southampton where she appreciated 'good clever nurses', Vivien seems to have been asked not just about drug use but also about her relationship with Tom. She wrote to him in early November, requesting he confirm to Hawkesworth 'the truth, that we have had sexual relations' and that 'our married life . . . *had* been good' – these tenses are revealing. She had scars on her back, probably caused by earlier medical treatment, and asked Tom to explain them to her new physician. In an incomplete letter, 'I am sorry', she wrote, 'I tortured you and drove you mad. I had no notion until yesterday afternoon that I had done it. I have been simply raving mad.'[186]

At The Stanboroughs, an institution run by Seventh-Day Adventists and whose 'kindly, competent' matron was 'an old friend' of Dr Higgins, Vivien felt 'worry and fear and torment,' begging the Schiffs to visit her.[187] They found her agitated, then 'perfectly reasonable' as their visit progressed.[188] On 18 December she sent Tom a letter he was 'very pleased' to receive. He wrote to her – 'My dear Wee' – saying he would wire when he returned from France around Christmas Eve and signing off lovingly.[189] At Nice that month he was photographed with slicked-back hair, sporting a small moustache, 'trying to look French'.[190] Before returning from La Turbie he visited Pound at Rapallo: the first time the two had met for four years. Vivien had urged Pound on 14 December to '*make*' Tom 'rescue' her, maintaining she was 'well', then telling Pound that Tom, in thrall to Dr Higgins and Lady Rothermere, '*is*' unbalanced'.[191] Around the same time she wrote to Ellen Kellond, pleading with her to '*beg*' Tom 'to come *quickly* and fetch me away and have me with him for Xmas.' Her position was '*awful*'. 'Dr Higgins is very angry, and I fear Mr Eliot will be angry. *O don't let him.*' Her letter ended, 'If Mr Eliot does not arrive till night, what shall I do? I shall go mad Ellen.'[192]

Vivien veered between protesting that Tom 'no longer wants me and no longer cares for me', and feeling tremendous gratitude towards him. To Ellen, to Higgins and probably to others she said she meant 'to take my life'.[193] She was desperate to be out of The Stanboroughs by Christmas. On 22 December she wrote to Higgins,

When I think of all that my husband has done for me, and of all the life I smashed up (as I do think of it, all night and much of the day) I do not know why I dont go out and hang myself.

There is so much opportunity for sorrow and brooding here and the atmosphere fosters it. I feel *absolutely* *done*.[194]

Yet her letters are vertiginously inconsistent. Next day she told Ottoline Morrell, 'I feel so much better', and looked forward to 'leaving here in a few weeks, and going to Brighton, to finish the cure'.[195]

Across the English Channel, Tom had received copies of his newly published *Poems 1909–1925*. 'The book gives me no pleasure', he wrote to Leonard Woolf; its contents were merely 'an ejection, a means of getting all that out of the way'.[196] The volume's concluding poem, 'The Hollow Men', ended with his most famous lines, born from his and Vivien's shared suffering. Fusing distortedly apocalyptic nursery rhyme with the last sound heard from a disgraced, executed man in Kipling's poem 'Danny Deever', these final lines sing a chorus touched with madness:

This is the way the world ends
This is the way the world ends
This is the way the world ends
Not with a bang but a whimper.[197]

3

Crisis

INCANTATORY and searing, 'The Hollow Men' marked both an emotional nadir and the start of a new phase. It would round off his forthcoming *Poems*, whose publication by Faber & Gwyer would signal a career change from banking to books. His new poem's desperate bleakness was answered by his latent religious commitment. Intensified by recent meetings with Emily, the poem's frustrated longings would spur his willed, disconcerting transformation of her into a symbol invested with spiritual yearning. While he considered himself bound to his disastrous marriage, separation from Vivien brought temporary relief, encouraging his search for fresh purpose. In France his accommodation had 'damp patches on the walls'. 'The Côte d'Azur is DAMNED COLD', he complained that December.[1] Yet his enlivening visit to Rapallo, and the chance to ponder his forthcoming Clark Lectures initiated a period of intense composition.

Between late 1925 and late 1927 he wrote more than ever. Though much correspondence has not survived, even in published form his letters run to 900 pages; lectures, book reviews and essays occupy 600 more. This period brought *Poems, 1909–1925* plus extended translation work and the fragmentary verse play *Sweeney Agonistes*, as well as the poems 'Journey of the Magi' and 'Salutation'. Those poems announce decisively his imaginative commitment to Christianity, a move beyond what Murry termed *The Waste Land*'s 'self-torturing and utter nihilism'.[2] Eventually 'Salutation' became part of the book-length *Ash-Wednesday*, named after the day when in many Christian churches the approach to Easter's crucifixion season begins with fasting, contemplation of sins, and appropriate penances.

At La Turbie Tom drafted several of his Clark Lectures on the varieties of metaphysical poetry. Somewhat eccentrically, he contextualised these 'varieties' as part of an assumed 'Disintegration of the Intellect'.[3] He contended that in Dante's poetry, in that of Donne and seventeenth-century English metaphysicals, and in later nineteenth-century French verse by Baudelaire's successors – including Laforgue, Rimbaud, and Tristan Corbière – there was intense 'fusing sense with thought' in 'distinctly "metaphysical" manifestations'.[4] Concentrating on the English metaphysicals, but incorporating Dante and French Symbolists, Tom reeled in other texts that haunted him, arguing that 'Sappho's great ode, for instance, is a real advance, a development, in human consciousness'.[5] Sappho's 'Ode to Anactoria' presents a lover rendered speechless and blind by the excitement of love. Not so long before, Tom had been unable to speak when Emily questioned him about their relationship. Readers might relate *The Waste Land*'s earlier, erotically excited words, 'I could not / Speak, and my eyes failed', to Sappho's sentiments; but for a lecture audience expecting to hear about seventeenth-century poetry, Tom's references would be disconcerting.[6]

Having suffered at least one breakdown, and fearing Vivien had 'nearly lost her reason for a time', his preoccupation with 'disintegration of the intellect' is unsurprising.[7] What he projects as large-scale analysis of the history of poetry can seem, at times, a wrestling with his own and Vivien's demons. 'Dissolution so frequently begins within', he argued, calling Donne 'in a sense a psychologist'.[8] Ranging across the erotic, religious and political, lectures drafted at La Turbie considered the torment of excessive 'self-consciousness' when trapped inside one's own 'cranial lodging'.[9] Tom's discussion of love soon moves from 'Donne's lighter' moods to the 'impossibility and frustration' of Racine's jealous, suicidal Phaedra; making this odd transition, he likens Donne's metaphysical 'bringing to light' of 'curious aspects and connections' to an infusing 'as it were, the dose of bismuth which makes the position of the intestine apparent on the X-ray screen'.[10] This image derives, surely, from Vivien's 'intestine' having been diagnosed recently as 'so nearly dead'.[11]

Pressured by private anxieties, Tom's lectures reveal a nexus of ideas including original sin, sex, psychology, and illness. At the end of the second lecture's typescript he finds in late nineteenth-century English prose 'more than a trace of intellectual psychologism, and just the faintest, undefinable perfume of femininity'; this femininity has troubling associations with 'low fever' and 'a slight temperature'.[12] Linking the feminine to the fevered anticipates a view of erotic love as insufficient in comparison with love of God: 'whether you seek the Absolute in marriage, adultery or debauchery, it is all one – you are seeking in the wrong place'.[13]

By 11 December 1925 Tom was describing his lectures' centuries-long trajectory that tracked 'the disintegration' of Dante's 'unity' of imagination, belief and world view 'partly as the history of corruption'.[14] Attentive to 'disillusion and disgust', Tom is alert to a love poet whose 'experience' has 'made and spoilt his life'.[15] As 'a modern poet', Donne is 'even a very great poet, of chaos'; Laforgue, however, 'had an innate craving for order' and so 'The only world in which he could have satisfied himself, therefore, was a world such as Dante's.'[16] Donne and Laforgue, with whom Tom had identified, and from whom he had learned, lack the fusion of poetry, theology, and social order exemplified in the Dante who can sublimate erotic love most perfectly into love of the divine. It was early 1926 before Tom finished these lectures; he wrote 'only three' at La Turbie and was still composing later ones after he delivered the first in Cambridge on 26 January.[17] His final lecture would conclude by quoting the last stanza of Chaucer's *Troilus and Criseyde*, a long poem of intense, unhappy passion which ends by transcending earthly love and embracing the love of God.

At La Turbie he worked intensively and rapidly, wanting as many of his lectures as possible ready before he returned to face challenges in England. He pored over theological texts. Reading a discussion of intellect and the conduct of life by Maurras's admirer Jacques Maritain, a Catholic convert, Tom thought 'Maurrasism, an excellent thing within its limits', but was less interested in 'political activity' linked to it than in its admiration for Catholicism and St Thomas Aquinas's medieval 'thomist' philosophy: he longed for 'a thorough historical defence of thomism or of the Church – to show that *any* philosophy except that of the church leads to heresies which ordinary common sense condemns'. Long fascinated by ritual and Christianity, yet so temperamentally loath to commit to decisive action, Tom craved 'some tentative scheme which shall simply go far enough to make action possible, and give to action a kind of moral and liturgical dignity'.[18] He believed the intellectual 'disintegration' he located in literary and intellectual history might lead to a new 'form of generation' – but not yet.[19]

Back in England, Vivien, still at The Stanboroughs, had been assigned a nurse 'who sleeps in my room', an apparent indication her suicide threats were regarded seriously.[20] Tom arranged for her to receive a copy of his new *Poems* with his ink inscription, dated Christmas Day, 'For my dearest Vivien This book, which no one else will quite understand.'[21] Yet she telegrammed him on 30 December expressing a fear of Dr Higgins, who suggested she might move, temporarily at least, to convalesce at Brighton. Earlier, Higgins had helped fix things so that, after La Turbie, Tom could 'live at' Lady Rothermere's London residence, rather than returning to his marital home.[22] Through telegrams Vivien communicated evident distress: 'TERRIFIED ISOLATION MELANCHOLIA'.[23] The same day, Geoffrey Faber wrote to Lady Rothermere, assuring her Tom's French vacation would let him return as 'a different man after the change. But I fear he has a difficult time ahead of him.'[24]

He distracted himself by reading *The Great Gatsby*, one of the first novels to draw on *The Waste Land*. Inscribing it 'For T. S. Elliot [*sic*] Greatest of Living Poets', his self-styled 'enthusiastic worshipper', Scott Fitzgerald had sent a copy which arrived just as Tom left for France. Now he read it 'three times', and wrote to Fitzgerald on 31 December to say it had 'interested and excited' him 'more than any new novel I have seen, either English and American, for a number of years'. It seemed 'the first step that American fiction has taken since Henry James', and he wanted Faber & Gwyer to publish it in England.[25] Though Tom was too late to secure the rights, Fitzgerald's contemporary tale of privilege, marital hurt, and obsessive love resonated with aspects of his own situation, and impressed him deeply. Like his own recent writings, it articulated and was shaped by intimate disaster. Though Tom grew interested, too, in the fiction of another of his American readers, Ernest Hemingway, no comment of his survives on Hemingway's 1924 story 'Mr and Mrs Elliot'. Recently republished by Boni & Liveright in Hemingway's 1925 *In Our Time*, it depicted the tormented marriage of a sexually inexperienced Harvard-educated poet in Europe who seems unable to satisfy his wife.

In early January Vivien accused Higgins of trying 'to put as great a distance as possible between me & my husband'; she was convinced her physician believed she was '*persecuting*' Tom. '*I understand*', she told Higgins, 'your desire to protect my husband.' Clearly, she did not trust Higgins, but was considering whether she might '*make* a life without my husband' in some way.[26] To Tom she wrote accusingly and anxiously: 'I am trembling all over. I am doomed.' Detecting persecutors circling – 'You *know* Higgins wants to make out I am *common*, & *beneath you*' – Vivien felt trapped and abused: 'The net is being drawn bit by bit, so stealthily, so *cunningly* round me. You, with your head in the air, in your splendid isolation are leaving yr wife to be most vilely & cunningly ruined.'[27]

Return to London precipitated Tom into a Phlebas-like 'whirlpool' of publishing business, with several Clark Lectures still unwritten, but he sought 'counsel & general information' from Leonard Woolf, another man whose wife was afflicted by mental health problems.[28] By 12 January Vivien was back at Clarence Gate Gardens with Ellen Kellond and 'a nurse to help her'. Tom saw her 'every day'.[29] Not until 22 January, however, does his correspondence suggest he was co-habiting with her, and four days later he needed to be in Cambridge for his first lecture. Still, the Eliots planned to move in March to a London property they were already renting at 57 Chester Terrace (today Chester Row). As Vivien showed initial improvement, they promised to holiday together overseas that spring. 'I am really well!' she wrote to Mary Hutchinson with a hint of surprise; 'Tom & I have not disappeared. I mean we did disappear but we are coming to light again.'[30]

To Tom, however, there seemed little chance of relief. When his old friend Conrad Aiken was undergoing a series of operations involving an anal fistula, Aiken (to whom Tom had sent recently his *Poems 1909–1925*) received in January a page torn from the 28 November 1925 issue of the *Nursing Mirror and Midwives' Journal*, a publication recently taken over by Faber & Gwyer. The page featured an article on 'Vaginal Discharges', and Aiken recalled that 'certain words and phrases' such as '*Blood – mucous – shreds of mucous*' and '*purulent offensive discharge*' had been underlined in ink.[31] Aiken was convinced that this page (which he recalled vividly decades later) had been sent by Tom; long afterwards, puzzled and embarrassed, Tom professed he had no memory of the incident. Ann Pasternak Slater argues that the page could 'easily' have been 'posted' to Aiken by the erratic Vivien, whose brother Maurice recalled her anxieties about menstruation.[32] Maurice Haigh-Wood remembered how on occasion, worried about soiling, 'Vivie stole sheets' from 'hotels, had them washed and sent them back. Sometimes she went along to the Post Office and posted the clean sheets back to the hotels. Tom went *mad*.'[33] Whatever the truth behind the incident that upset Aiken, it signals continuing disturbance within the Eliot household.

For Tom work was in part an escape. Yet, with mounting doctors' bills, it was also a lifeline. Over one long mid-January weekend he wrote '(i.e. dictated) 50 business letters'.[34] He attended too, with nervous, meticulous attention, to the publication of *Savonarola*. 'Designing a wrapper' himself, he liaised with Cobden-Sanderson over printing, finished his rather awkward introduction, and made sure costs were kept below the £100 'limit' his mother had guaranteed to finance her book.[35] Though Lottie's drama about a noble heretic manifested some 'opposition to ecclesiasticism', Tom, writing about it, drew ever closer to the Church. His mother deployed nineteenth-century idioms, but he knew 'verse drama' of the future needed 'new verse forms'. If, as he argued, 'Dramatic form may occur at various points along a line the termini of which are liturgy and realism', then *Sweeney Agonistes* was structured like a ritual, a rite. 'The play, like a religious service, should be a stimulant to make life more tolerable and augment our ability to live' – such high-mindedness his mother might relish. Yet his own play, like his domestic problems, indicated the sheer difficulty of making life 'tolerable'.[36] As he prepared *Savonarola* for publication, his mother's drama showed how close, but also how far apart, they were; again, when he encouraged and edited Vivien's stories, there was both a closeness and a gap.

Tom was prepared to organise publication of his mother's book, bankrolled by Eliot money, but there is no evidence he or Vivien considered asking Cobden-Sanderson to publish a collection of Vivien's prose sketches. As a publisher, Tom reflected the following year, 'there is no sale whatever in this country for volumes of short stories'.[37] In any event, after Marianne Moore's rejection of 'The Paralysed Woman', Vivien's writings lay in her notebooks, except perhaps for a now lost pamphlet of her poems.

From late January until late March 1926 Tom visited Cambridge weekly, lecturing on Tuesday afternoons. Usually he stayed over at least one night since F. L. Lucas – a don at King's College, next door to Trinity where the lectures were held – had arranged informal get-togethers on Wednesdays at which a small, select group of undergraduates, including William Empson and John Hayward, might meet the Clark Lecturer. The lectures' venue, the high-ceilinged, cavernous, wood-panelled Renaissance college dining hall, was daunting. Tom stated he spoke not as an academic but as 'a crafts-man who has attempted for eighteen years to make English verses'; but the nervous thirty-seven-year-old lecturer tried to sound as venerable and learned as possible: within his opening ten minutes he name-checked thirty poets of the past.[38] Later he quoted Dante in Italian, Racine in French, and 'read or chanted' passages of medieval Latin. At his first lecture the hall was full; by his third, numbers were 'dwindling'; very few folk attended the last.[39] 'The impact seemed negligible', recalled graduate student T. R. Henn; Tom was 'not a lecturer of any technique'. Joan Bennett found him 'difficult to hear and rather difficult to follow'.[40]

Though years later Tom dismissed his Clark Lectures as 'immature and pretentious', in 1926 I. A. Richards, who along with others in the newly founded Cambridge English Faculty had encouraged Tom to apply for a fellowship, was considerably more enthusiastic.[41] Richards breakfasted with him, discussing Donne and Dante; but in London Virginia Woolf heard reports Tom was 'not creating a good impression'.[42] The Reverend Hugh Fraser Stewart, fellow of Trinity, expert on Boethius and Blaise Pascal, and sometime collaborator with Tom's old Harvard teacher Ken Rand, invited him to stay at his home; Stewart and his wife Jessie befriended him. By the last lecture, on 9 March, Tom spotted in his modest audience both Henry and Henry's bride Theresa. Honeymooning in Europe, they had come to lend support. Theresa sketched the bespectacled lecturer standing, eyes down, gripping his large lectern tightly, solemnly reading from a typescript in which he insisted on 'the role of the artist in the development and maintenance of the mind'.[43]

As his lectures proceeded, Tom continued seeking medical advice about Vivien. Accompanied by a nurse, she seems to have gone 'to Cambridge' more than once when Tom was at Trinity.[44] When Henry and Theresa arrived in early March, she felt unable to discuss her condition with them, but encouraged them to contact her physician; he explained, 'she took drugs, and had started at 16 under some doctor's orders'.[45] Both she and Tom had been consulting Dr Reginald Miller of 110 Harley Street. Fearing that, though she was again 'paying visits to her friends', there was little 'improvement', Tom had written Miller a 'sad' letter in February.[46] Eight years Tom's senior, Miller had a 'shy and sensitive disposition'. Sympathetic and astute, yet suspicious of much 'psychiatric teaching' and the 'Freudian school', this 'sincere Catholic' had, like Tom, 'much of the Puritan in his nature and was almost ascetic in his habits'.[47] He advised Tom that Vivien's 'fears' were likely to diminish; he had urged her 'to get on with the settling of the new house, to get in there with you, and have the proposed holiday abroad with you'. Yet even as Miller encouraged the couple to reunite, he cautioned Tom, 'there is an attempt on both of your parts to make the two circles of your lives too coincident'. Vivien's 'sphere' was 'far too closely superimposed' on Tom's. 'Perpetually in her mind' was the conviction 'that she must dominate you, or you will dominate her'.[48]

Soon noticing something of this, Henry was pleased when Tom refused to be dominated. He reported to Lottie, 'I am glad to discern a firmer attitude on Tom's part, in that he insisted in playing the phonograph when Vivien objected slightly, and that he maintained that she was in excellent health, in contradiction of her faint protests.'[49] Vivien told Mary Hutchinson, 'Tom's brother & his new wife are a bother.'[50] The American visitors dined with Ottoline Morrell in London, then visited her at Garsington on 20 March. Lady Ottoline complained Vivien (then suffering from 'influenza') was 'hysterical' about her health, making Tom cancel engagements at the last minute. 'She said that Tom never admitted Vivien's faults but that people understood his problems.'[51] Around this time Vivien told Ottoline she would sue Tom for inveigling her into a mental home; next, she said she had relished the home where she had met 'Haden Guest' (presumably the philandering Labour MP, war hero and writer Leslie Haden-Guest) who 'appreciated' her as Tom had never done. Ottoline observed Tom watching Vivien with a look of fright, and understood why he had 'taken to drink'.[52]

In mid-March the Eliots, planning to sublet their Marylebone flat for its lease's remaining two years, moved to a terraced property in elegant Belgravia. Vivien immediately pronounced 57 Chester Terrace 'a terrible house'. It stood, Tom told Henry, 'somewhere back of Buckingham Palace', but Vivien felt plunged 'into the outer suburbs'.[53] She was annoyed when her concerned elderly parents, after holidaying in warmer climes, 'bore down on me & settled down in a hotel with nothing on earth to do but interfere with me & shout advice in my ears & sit over me & make my life a hell'.[54] Still accompanied by her live-in nurse, she was also distressed because forty-eight-year-old Ellen Kellond ('my greatest − best − almost only friend for 9 years') was leaving to get married again.[55] William Leonard Janes, the 'mad ex-policeman aged 70' whom Tom hired 'to help' around the new house also irked Vivien.[56] It hardly consoled her that Henry and Theresa, heady with visits to Oxford, Warwick, and other historic sites, thought the Chester Terrace house (still being painted) absolutely admirable:

> It is on a charming little street, full of little houses in a row, all much alike, with iron fences in front of each and pretty doors. There is a little living room on the first floor and a bedroom back of it. Below (in the basement) is a neat and light kitchen. You go out of the kitchen into a back yard which is below the level of the street. The back yard is paved with old flagstones with a garden bed running around three sides, and a brick wall also. All the houses in the row have such back yards.[57]

These yards seemed ideal for the two Yorkshire terriers Vivien and Tom now owned: Lulu shared her name with the scandalous dancer made famous by German dramatist Frank Wedekind; Henry, more prosaically, shared his name with Tom's brother. Enthusiastically, Henry Eliot photographed the occupants in their Belgravia property, and Tom at his new Faber & Gwyer office at 24 Russell Square, Bloomsbury. Inside the office Tom sat at a desk piled with typescripts; leaning against his telephone was a tiny puppet, perhaps connected with his planned puppet plays − Tom mentioned to Henry the ongoing *Sweeney Agonistes*. Outdoors in Russell Square he posed beside the Faber & Gwyer nameplate, leaning on his cane, his double-breasted, three-piece chequered suit tightly buttoned, a bowler hat on his head. He smiled for Henry's camera, but his face was slightly drawn. In another photograph his complexion looks perhaps eczematous. It was, again, a time of strain.

Now, maintaining she had 'always hankered after the Law', and imagining she might 'yet turn into a barrister', Vivien immersed herself in 'Law, statistics, Constitutional history', only to find 'nothing interesting'. Tom attempted encouragement, thinking it good for her (as she put it) to have 'some very *hard* food for my mind', but she soon gave up. Instead, sick of 'miserable doctors' and '*great* difficulty with servants', and driven 'to desperation' by the presence of her parents, she retreated temporarily to

Clarence Gate Gardens. There, she told Ottoline Morrell, she was 'laid up with shingles . . . & am all stuck up with bandages & ointments & loathsomeness'. Her letter is peppered with words such as 'fearful', 'catastrophe', and '*horrible*'; if only Tom (who was 'learning at a motor school') could afford a car, they might flee to Garsington.[58]

Mid-morning on Saturday 3 April they dressed up and travelled to Paddington Register Office to witness Ellen's marriage to William Fisher Sollory, unemployed former foreman of an 'iron foundry'.[59] Kindly but awkwardly the Eliots took the newly-weds to lunch at Frascati's, a venue famous for jazz, dining, and dancing, whose orchestra played on radio programmes for the recently established British Broadcasting Corporation. Lunch proved stressful; 'V. was quite knocked out.' The following Saturday Tom was committed to 'giving away' at her wedding the 'ex-nurse who has been living with us to help V. with massage etc'.[60]

He sought solace in work but also in regular dinners with male associates from the *New Criterion* as it was now called. These cronies included Herbert Read, Aldington, music critic J. B. Trend, minor poet Humbert Wolfe, and literary critic Bonamy Dobrée. All of them, along with Yeats and E. M. Forster, contributed to the April issue. After one such dinner, in a private room with a piano at the Commercio restaurant, Tom complained to Dobrée about 'a frightful attack of rheumatism the next day. I'm afraid I sang too much.'[61] If dining and alcohol offered release, deeper preoccupations gripped him. Privately and publicly he discussed theology with Aldington, Murry, and others. Aldington respected and admired the Roman Church, but did not 'much like Christ' – Tom agreed 'about Christ'; Murry suggested that to 'order' Tom's professed classicism and perceived romantic angst might require 'joining the Catholic Church'; to Father Francis Yealy, who had criticised a point in his Clark Lectures, Tom regretted 'the intellectual break up of Europe and the rise of Protestantism . . . One might approve of the maintenance of the Church of England in our time and yet deplore its origin.'[62] Slowly he advanced his official application to become what the Tory Anglican Geoffrey Faber called not a British but 'an English subject'.[63] Sympathy with Maurras and the Action Française encouraged Tom to favour Catholic forms of religion with a distinctly national cultural inflection; he was also increasingly preoccupied with what he termed in 1926 'the permanent condition of the soul'.[64] Ritual seemed less a surface phenomenon than something which could channel that permanent condition; increasingly the rites that mattered to him most were those of Anglo-Catholicism.

Having proposed him for election at All Souls, Faber told the fellows that Tom was 'at present, writing a monograph on *Dante*'.[65] Stressing the candidate's work as critic, Faber's letter of proposal enclosed Tom's lengthy, ill-judged account of his ongoing work on Elizabethan drama, literature and religion; these labours, the would-be fellow stated, needed 'not less than fourteen years' to complete.[66] Testimonials arrived from Whibley and Bruce Richmond, but nobody mentioned Tom wrote poetry. When the dons discovered he did, and got hold of his *Poems*, several denounced it as 'obscene and blasphemous': attracting fourteen out of thirty-five votes, he failed to make the grade.[67]

Instead, taking a risk, he set out with Vivien, Henry and Theresa for the continental holiday doctors had advised. Problems started even before they left. Panicking, on 15 and on 16 April Henry, who had gone ahead with Theresa to Paris, received cables signed 'TOM': Henry must return to London where there was 'REAL DANGER'.[68] Vivien complained of 'great trouble' and 'great fear'.[69] A few years later, she gave a friend (who wrote it down) an account of a row with Tom around this time:

> T's brother and wife were here and leaving for Paris. They wanted Eliots to go too, but V. didn't want to. Tom did. They quarrelled and fussed all Sun. p.m., V. saying, 'If we were normal people, you'd go and I'd stay.' Suddenly he left, went to bedroom, slammed door, and was gone. She waited. He didn't come back for tea. Nor dinner. She went to her mother's and told her. Father ill. 'Don't tell your father or it will kill him.'[70]

Yet, a week later they were all in Paris 'on a secret errand to the Pope' as Tom put it in his short, jaunty postcard to Virginia Woolf.[71] At 10.20 p.m. on Friday 23 April all four Eliots boarded the overnight 'Rome Express'.[72] In the Italian capital they rendezvoused with Vivien's brother Maurice, an employee of the Banca Italo-Brittanica.

At first all seemed well. They stayed at the Pensione Prey 'near the Hotel Boston', an institution in the Via Lombardia 'patronized by Americans', close to the Villa Borghese gardens.[73] Henry told his mother, 'Tom & Vivien's room overlooks a beautiful villa.'[74] They strolled in the gardens with Maurice, dining outdoors at a terrace restaurant above the Villa with the Vatican dome of St Peter's Basilica on the skyline beyond. As Easter approached, like most tourists they visited great sites in the Holy City. Theresa recalled that, when they entered the ordered magnificence of St Peter's, regarded by many as the central church of Christendom, 'Vivien, who wasn't really impressed, said something like "It's very fine."' Then they looked round and 'suddenly saw that Tom was on his knees praying'.[75] Uncertain what to make of this, they were unsettled. Was Henry's ex-Unitarian brother, this admirer of

Dante's 'fusion' of the Ovidian 'Art of Love with the Worship of the Virgin', about to become a Roman Catholic?[76]

Theresa and Henry went off to tour Italy. Tom and Vivien remained in Rome. Tom cabled Pound, who arrived from Rapallo, urging them to follow his example and abandon England for inexpensive, delightful Italy: Tom could visit London four times a year to edit his quarterly *New Criterion*. Vivien was 'keen' on that.[77] Tom already dealt with work by correspondence; besides, London was now in the grip of the General Strike. In Rome, though, Vivien grew extremely anxious. Tom recalled their time there as 'intensely unhappy'.[78] 'Soaked in bromidia' (a sedative), Vivien was convinced 'the police were pursuing her from country to country'.[79] 'What shall I do, where go. What *can* I do', Vivien wrote to Murry in whom she increasingly confided.[80] At short notice, taking a considerable gamble, she and Tom headed for Freiburg to consult once more the dubious Dr Martin. '*Do not mention*' to Vivien's mother and father '*that we are going to Germany*', Tom urged Henry.[81] Though evidence is scant, Vivien's sense of persecution seems to have intensified. Henry, convinced his brother could do more to control her, sent Tom a letter that referred to Dr Miller's advice; Tom showed Vivien this correspondence. She responded, 'The mastered wife is the happy wife. Dr Miller knows all this as you say.' Vivien contended she had encouraged Tom to dominate her, but had not succeeded:

> I wd like to add, & Tom will witness it – not that the signature of such a 'poor whipped dog' signifies anything – that within the last 3 months I have implored Tom to throw his boots at me, to shout at me, & to demand every possible & impossible thing of me.[82]

The tone of this is close to an epigraph Tom added to the typescript of his Clark Lectures: 'I want someone to treat me rough. / Give me a cabman'.[83] Apparently, like Gershwin's later 'Treat Me Rough', this referred to a 'Popular Song' circulating in America after 1916 and derived from Berton Bradley's poem 'The Atavistic Maid':

> Listen, sweetheart, to my plea
> Cut this highly cultured game.
> All this fine gentility
> Grows to be exceeding tame.
> What I want is low-brow love,
> Heavy, knock down, cave-man stuff!
> I'm no cooing turtle-dove.
> Treat me rough, kid! Treat me rough![84]

Prefacing his Clark Lectures, Tom arrestingly juxtaposed the female-voiced 'treat me rough' quotation with a very different, male-voiced passage from Dante's *Vita Nuova*; in the latter, Dante addresses some ladies – though, misquoting, Tom presented the passage as if addressed to one particular lady:

Madonna, lo fine del mio amore fu già il salute di questa donna, forse de cui voi intendete; ed in quello dimorava la beatitudine, ch'e il fine di tutti li miei desiri.[85]
    [Lady, the end and aim of my love was but the salutation of that lady of whom I conceive that you are speaking; wherein alone I found that beatitude which is the goal of desire.]

Tom contrasted a woman who (like the Vivien who had urged him 'to throw his boots at me') craved someone to 'treat me rough', with a man who, in 'salute' or 'salutation', addresses with sublimated holy adoration his pure 'Lady' – a term of address Tom would use later to Emily. In May 1926 Vivien told Henry she felt she had 'shattered' her husband.

I don't *think* any woman really enjoys mastering her husband. It humiliates her extremely, it's a great strain on the character & the health.
    Anyhow, unless Tom had had that something so intensely delicate & rare in him he wd never have been so shattered. And anyhow I am at the end of my tether, & I knew it before we went away with you, & I shall just hang up somewhere & keep out of his way now.[86]

A decade later, Tom maintained to Geoffrey Faber that 'Between any two people (and the more intimate their relations the more important this becomes) there is always an unresolvable element of hostility which may be only further incubated by the dominance of one over the other.'[87] In 1926, whatever the rights and wrongs between Tom and Vivien, and whether or not it had been a mistake to consult Dr Martin again, it was Vivien who emerged more 'shattered' than Tom. Writing from the Hotel Restaurant Foyot in Paris on 3 June, apparently after Vivien, in a suicide attempt, had tried to swallow poison, he gave Henry his side of the story:

My dear brother
    So much has happened that I have had no time to write. We *intended* to join you in Milan.
    The German doctor took a very serious view. But I think things had already gone too far for his methods to avail. Her ideas of per-

secution grew rapidly. When we got back to Basel she was in such a state that I encouraged her to believe that the best thing was to go straight to England. We got as far as Paris, to this hotel where the Pounds are living. P. took her in hand & I left for England in the hope that she might pick up without me. In 3 days the Pounds were at the end of their resources & wired for me. The hallucinations (voices etc.) had got worse etc. She had been sleeping on the floor of their room, in terror. I intended to take her back to London but she was too ill. Thanks very much to Pound's great help I got her out to a home near Paris – I believe the best in France – & she is being cared for under the direction of Claude, the Professor of Psychiatry at the Sorbonne.[88]

Henri Charles Jules Claude, a psychoanalyst familiar with Freud's work, specialised in mental illness at the Sainte-Anne Hospital, Paris's lunatic asylum. That summer he was preparing a paper on dementia praecox and schizophrenia; later he would study hallucinations. Tom was told Vivien needed 'continuous guarding, night and day, & a special room for suicidal cases'; it was 'possible that she will recover', but less than certain.[89] The 'home' in which she was now on suicide watch was not an asylum but the exclusive Sanatorium de la Malmaison in Rueil, about eight miles west of central Paris. Established in 1910 by Louis Bour and André Antheaume (an expert in mental illness), its well-appointed buildings occupied parklands with a lake. Specialising in nervous diseases and eating disorders, it was, too, a rest home for the troubled: Valéry, Maurice Ravel and Léon Bakst had spent time there; Zelda Fitzgerald was a later patient. Alongside Bour and Antheaume its senior medical team included Charles-Louis Trepsat. Influenced by Freud, he had published on anxiety, hallucination, and persecution mania. Several Malmaison doctors examined Vivien. Given the seriousness of her case and that she had been admitted thanks to Professor Claude – arguably France's leading psychoanalyst – it is likely she and Tom, 'impressed with the intelligence of the French doctors, and their humanity', had access to the finest physicians.[90]

Returned to London, Tom went on working as editor and publisher almost as if nothing was wrong. Living 'in a mask all one's life' became second nature.[91] However, having missed several meetings of the Phoenix Society (which revived historic plays), he resigned his post as one of its directors. His most striking public gesture was marching alongside Dobrée and others in protest against the 'Disposal of Churches' bill which was going through Parliament that summer; in theory this bill would permit demolition of City churches including St Magnus the Martyr whose

'Inexplicable splendour', at an earlier period when 'demolition' had been mooted, featured in *The Waste Land*.[92] Tom was recalled as having 'frequented' St Magnus the Martyr in the early 1920s.[93] Its Anglo-Catholic rector, Henry Joy Fynes-Clinton, who was among those opposing the 1926 bill, claimed the 'weekly congregation' of his church 'was between 2,000 and 3,000'.[94] To Tom's and Fynes-Clinton's relief, the bill was defeated, but its discussion concentrated the minds of many interested in the future of Anglo-Catholicism. Now Tom, having knelt in St Peter's, and recalling what stepping inside a City church might mean to a 'passing penitent who has saved a few minutes from his lunch hour', cared about that future intensely. It was 'bad enough' that 'St Magnus Martyr' had 'been concealed' by new building which relegated it to 'museum piece' status; 'demolition' must be averted. Saving a church was not only a matter of 'Christopher Wren' architecture; it involved the sacred '*beauty of holiness*'.[95] Physical destruction meant spiritual destruction.

Tom tried to stave off other, unignorable perils. If asked, he told friends, 'V. has not been at all well and is staying abroad for a rest cure'; he feared she was – or might be thought – mentally ill: 'it is so well known that the word "Malmaison" is almost synonymous with insanity'.[96] To Henry, who helped him pay the £10 weekly medical bills, he confessed on 13 June that he had received news she 'has been devoured by self-accusations' and continued to be 'watched day and night'. What most upset him was that she still heard voices constantly. 'The doctors do not allow me to be very optimistic.'[97] Her frail, elderly parents had travelled to France; neither they nor Tom were allowed to see her.

Back in Paris to consult her physicians, he distracted and exhausted himself by seeing relatives and friends. These included Maritain with whom he discussed theology, and Jean Cocteau, whose *Orphée* updated the ancient tale of the poet Orpheus attempting to rescue his wife from Hades: hoping to save his own spouse from torment, Tom attended, but did not much enjoy, this play. He also met Pound, whose protégé the atonal composer George Antheil premiered his avant-garde *Ballet Mécanique*; a top-hatted Tom (who liked it) escorted Lady Rothermere amid a restive audience that included James Joyce, Sergei Diaghilev and Constantin Brancusi. More sedately, he dined with Marguerite Caetani and her husband in their 'beautiful villa and garden' at Versailles.[98] Earlier that year Marguerite had persuaded cousin Tom to translate *Anabase*, a long prose poem by French diplomat Saint-John Perse whose extensive knowledge of China conditioned his writing. Tom had made relatively little progress. Circumstances were hardly conducive. Still, *Anabase* came to fascinate him, though its

Asian-inspired landscapes affected him less immediately than the polemic
of Henri Massis, whose recent *Criterion* essay 'Defence of the West' warned
against Russian-led 'Asiaticism'. Massis had invited Tom to an Action Française dinner honouring Maurras. Tom explained to his mother that

> The more one sees of the disorganisation and bad government of the
> republic since the war, its corruption and lack of continuous policy
> and the utter selfishness of so many politicians, the growing power of
> socialists under Russian influence, the more one sympathises with the
> movement which aims to replace the republic by the kingship. And
> since the Russian revolution socialism has come to mean more and
> more definitely not only anti-clericalism but anti-religion. The 'for-
> eign agitator', sometimes Russian and often Jew, is no longer confined
> to America; he is conspicuous in England and still more so in France.[99]

In political opinions his patrician manner, laced with familial antisemitism, came to the fore; he knew how to look the part of a top-hatted man
about town, but he realised his situation with Vivien was dire. By late June
he reported, 'She is very affectionate and gentle, and her regrets and self-
accusations are terribly pathetic.' He was facing the possibility that she
might have to 'remain' at the Malmaison or in a similar institution 'indefinitely'. If this happened, he estimated, it would cost 'something like £500
a year' – a great part of his income – but 'I can live quite inexpensively by
myself'. Yet if she were 'at large', could he cope?

> She does not want to leave, so far; the worry will begin when she
> does. Her beliefs in persecution are unshaken, and she still hears
> voices. But she has not made any attempt on her life for over a
> fortnight.[100]

He began alternating week-about between Paris and London, still managing to review books, edit, dictate letters – but only by periodically
sealing off awareness of Vivien's predicament. Murry, who had lived
through Katherine Mansfield's death in a sanatorium, had been writing to
Vivien, sending her some Mansfield work to translate, urging her to 'Keep
calm & quiet', and discussing '*The annihilation of personality.*' Distraught,
Vivien brooded on her own annihilation.

> I can't help myself & I can't ask God to help me. I don't ask Tom to
> help me now. I am quite alone & I have nothing at all inside. It is
> absolutely dark.

Sure he might understand, she made Murry her confidant, but was unable to follow his advice:

I can't keep calm & quiet John. It's no use. Why does Tom love me? You know I love Tom in a way that destroys us both. And it is *all* my life. Nothing remains.[101]

In London, Tom had to deal with Murry writing to him, encouraged by Vivien, offering to discuss her situation. He sought further advice from Leonard Woolf. Struggling, he undertook to consult Murry, who was receiving a succession of letters from Vivien about having 'been in hell' with 'hallucinations' while 'completely out of my mind'; she wished she had stayed in Rome alone; in Paris she had taken 'poison'.[102] In her desperation she saw Murry as her possible saviour, a 'John the Baptist', even a 'Christ'. Returning to the theme of whether she or her husband dominated each other, she now contended not that Tom was a 'poor whipped dog' but that he oppressed her, caging her, depriving her of freedom and air. She could not fathom all 'his interests, work, thoughts, desires' that she '*simply*' could not '*understand*', so that

sometimes, when I am tired or overwrought, it gives me the sensation that he is mad. Sometimes that he is mad or else that he is most *frightfully* & subtly *wicked* and *dangerous*. That he is a terrible *menace*. That I must either somehow cut free & run, run, run to somewhere where there is a clear sky & open fields & *air*. Or else that I shall be stifled, that I must sink down, down into a heavy vapour, & so gradually be stifled to death.

You know he is fond of me. Very very fond. I don't think he ever was fond of me until he got me, somehow, under. Don't mistake me. I am not being cruel, I am not bitter & venomous, now. I love him, & I want to see him happy & successful in the way he sees, because there is no other way for him my dear John. But O my dear, I want air.

But if I have air, will he love me, or will it spoil everything for him? To lose me, would, I believe make him bitter. I don't mean really lose me. But I don't know. You see I simply don't understand him, it's no good. I got to the point when I felt the only thing I could do was to get out of his life in that way. A sort of sacrifice.[103]

As well as pouring out her heart to Murry, Vivien wrote about her troubles to her ex-lover Russell in letters now lost. Her extant correspondence gives no indication she was aware that Tom still thought about Emily.

When Vivien and he were together, however, she was convinced he felt *'exactly as lonely'* as she did herself. She maintained people kept suggesting to her 'why *don't* you go away & do what you like?' She knew she and Tom were hurting each other; but knew too that, even as they struggled to dominate each other and she felt caged, neither of them could bring themselves to leave the other:

> John, I never *dared*. First, it meant losing Tom. (*Losing my hold* on Tom). Now, it means hurting Tom, & *losing myself, doesn't it?*
> What is my duty?
> What shall I do?
> Tell me, please.[104]

4

Birth or Death?

Vivien's mother and father had been married for decades. Tom's parents' marriage had lasted over fifty years. Eliots did not divorce. Trying to hide his worst woes from his mother, Tom let Henry tell his sister Charlotte what was going on, and strove to appear in control. Accepting his play would remain unfinished, he readied what there was of it for publication. 'Fragment of a Prologue' would emerge in October's *Criterion*, 'Fragment of an Agon' the following January. The 'Agon' included Sweeney's statement, 'That's all the facts when you come to brass tacks: / Birth, and copulation, and death.'[1] How close these bleak words came to Tom's own situation was clear on 29 July 1926 when, surveying his upbringing, he reflected to Henry, 'Unitarianism is a bad preparation for brass tacks like birth, copulation, death, hell, heaven and insanity.' For Unitarians these simply fell 'within the classification of Bad Form'. Suffering, Tom needed something deeper; his life was 'like a bad Russian novel'.[2]

At the Malmaison, where he had just visited Vivien, her doctors had judged her well enough to be accompanied by a nurse into Paris. One cloudy Thursday in July 1926, after both Eliots agreed the nurse might depart, they took tea. A thunderstorm broke. Vivien made clear her conviction that Henry and Theresa disapproved of her: they might 'annul our marriage' or 'kidnap' Tom and take him to America. He sought signs of her 'calmness and stability', accepting she needed 'a long period of physical building up and nutrition'. Relieved, he convinced himself 'The doctors agree that of insanity, that is of *mental* disease proper, there is no trace.' Apparently, he told Henry, 'The trouble' was 'wholly emotional' – her 'delusions' were 'projections of a state of emotional anguish' – but 'she may have a similar attack in a few years time'.[3] Living with such strain was daunting. Tom decided he too should undergo a 'rest cure', occupying a room in a separate

Malmaison building. This would be close to Vivien, whose 'doctors' would 'be able to observe the effect on her'.[4] Seeing Tom 'very *very* tired indeed', Vivien had 'urged him to come', sure that their '*both* being here will be a good thing – for us both'. Later, if all went well, he would accompany her (with financial support from her parents) to the splendid art-deco Grand Hotel in Divonne-les-Bains where her doctors had arranged she could stay under medical supervision. Vivien explained to Murry that she wanted 'my liberty – I mean my *equality*, with Tom'.[5] He might remain in Divonne-les-Bains all winter, though, once she had settled, he aimed to return to London. 'But if she wishes she shall come back too.'[6]

Each of them was uneasy about how much 'liberty' they would have from one another, but hoped for the best. Writing to Henry, Tom sounded more convinced about the long-term prospects of the 'group of men' he had assembled as *Criterion* editor: this fellowship might 'hold together, and persist in the same direction, after I am gone'. Albeit imperceptibly, 'such a group of young men might have considerable influence on even the political future of England'. His words suggest his cadre was the *Criterion*'s own Action Française; but what did he mean by 'after I am gone'? He sounded exhausted. 'One realises that one never arrives at anything, but must just go on fighting every day as long as the strength lasts.'[7] Ostensibly, he was discussing political influence, but his phrasing also fitted the struggle to make his marriage something bearable for both partners. Aldous Huxley, lunching with him in London shortly before Tom joined Vivien at the Malmaison, found him as urbane and sophisticated as ever, but 'terribly grey-green'. Tom 'drank no less than five gins with his meal'.[8]

Through the carapace of his disciplined, hard-working, increasingly hard-drinking self, he perceived the seriousness of his wife's condition. He strove to find top-flight medical help, to spend time with Vivien when she wanted him, and to give her space when that might help. Having experienced breakdown himself, he was better placed than many to understand something of her pain. Yet, for all they sympathised with each other, their marriage contained a cavernous sense of mutual isolation. Consciousness of this had undergirded the section of *The Waste Land* first called 'In the Cage', then later 'A Game of Chess', whose lines Vivien thought 'wonderful'; originally she had scribbled a simple 'Yes' beside the line where an edgy couple resolve to 'play a game of chess' in a relationship so filled with isolation that 'The ivory men make company between us'; later, before the poem became public, 'This line was omitted at Vivien Eliot's request.'[9] When Vivien, maintaining in 1926 that 'for 11 years' she had been in 'One cage after another', writes about feeling 'utter isolation' in 'his presence', and sensing that 'he feels *exactly as lonely* with me', she articulates a sense of loneliness within marriage very close to that of *The Waste Land*.[10] She mentions neither Russell nor Nancy Cunard – nor Emily.

All along, Vivien had supported Tom's talent. She had stuck with him in his exhaustion, ill temper, and breakdown; he had supported her too, emotionally, intellectually and financially, encouraging her search for a vocation and helping her through illness after illness. Though he missed Emily, he repressed his intense 'desire for what I cannot have, for someone I cannot see'.[11] The Eliots were bonded by shared experience. Yet Tom's outburst to Russell in 1925, 'I need the help of someone who understands her – I find her still perpetually baffling and deceptive', parallels Vivien's plea to Murry, 'I do not understand Tom [. . .] I simply don't understand him.'[12] Increasingly these spouses shared a mutual misery they exacerbated in each other. After 1925 the indications are that when apart they communicated regularly, but their later letters and telegrams to one another are almost all destroyed. In December, when Vivien was in 'worry and fear and torment' at The Stanboroughs, Tom had written with evident affection, confirming he would wire her as soon as he reached England from France, and sending 'My love till then'.[13] Now in 1926 she still expressed 'love' for Tom.[14] Yet it is hard not to conclude that, despite their efforts, their marriage was facing its death throes.

So much of society's power lay in the hands of men – whether in medicine, education, politics, publishing, or finance. An ill woman unable to earn her living and with few formal qualifications was vulnerably dependent on her husband (if she had one), on male relatives, male doctors, and an overwhelmingly male establishment. Tom's young niece 'Dodo' – Theodora Eliot Smith – who visited the Eliots at the Malmaison (and naively thought Vivien 'steadily getting better') noted her aunt's half-flippant wish to 'adopt me': perhaps another indication of loneliness.[15] Vivien's female confidantes, including the wealthier, more socially secure Mary Hutchinson and Ottoline Morrell, tended to be women she had met through Tom. That she and Ottoline had shared Russell as a lover hardly helped, while Mary (married and with a lover of her own) did not always hide her infatuation with the poet. Vivien maintained that her oldest friend Lucy Thayer had sexually assaulted her; even if they had made up over time, Lucy suffered acute psychiatric problems. After Ellen Kellond left, Vivien was never as close to any of her servants. Sometimes in doctors' letters to Tom there are hints of a collusive man-to-man tone when his wife is discussed. When the isolated Vivien told Murry in 1926 that 'people have always said to me, but why *don't* you go away & do what you like?', she added, 'John, I never *dared*.'[16]

Tom showed his wounds far less openly. To many who met him, he looked impeccably dressed and strikingly successful: a brilliant avant-garde poet and an essayist with a stunningly Olympian intellectual reach; his background in banking and now in publishing readily won him friends in the English establishment, and by 1926 some of his stray remarks ('Shakespeare may have been, and very probably was, in practice a Conservative in politics') hint at his ease among Tories as well as among artistic radicals.[17] Though his United States passport had been renewed the previous year, he had converted his American patrician inheritance into a close approximation of upper-middle-class Englishness, and while in France that August, with support from Whibley, he tried to advance his application for British nationality, only to be told he must wait until he returned to Britain. Yet, despite his essays' injunctions against doing so, anyone able to examine his intimate biography alongside his remarkably artful and pliant poetry might perceive the two as interlinked. Increasingly, afflicted by his sense of the 'waste' and 'hollow', he turned towards the suffering Christian God.

This was easy neither for him nor Vivien, with whom he tried to talk about faith: 'I have not found religion of any use to her, either mine or anybody else's', he told Murry in August.[18] Tom's religious commitment grew stronger, but also increased his distance from his wife. Several prose pieces he worked on in 1926 reveal interest in sublimating the sexual instinct, and rechannelling it through religion. He aimed to write a 'Hymn to the Virgin', but told Marguerite Caetani in August he had not 'got on with' it.[19] Though its composition cannot be dated precisely, what he produced was 'Salutation', first announced for publication in autumn 1927; its title draws on the 'salute' or 'salutation' mentioned in his Clark Lectures' epigraph from *La Vita Nuova* about the 'beatitude which is the goal of desire'.[20] His 'Hymn to the Virgin' would praise a pure 'Lady of silences', located 'Where all loves end'.[21] A few years later, calling her 'my Lady', he would tell Emily he had 'no need' to explain such poetry 'to *you*', adding (in phrasing which recalls his words to Vivien when he inscribed her copy of his 1925 *Poems*), 'No one else will ever understand it.'[22]

In mid-1926, preparing 'Fragment of a Prologue' for publication, he gave it two epigraphs: one is from the ancient Greek dramatist Aeschylus whose tormented Orestes must 'move on' to flee female furies 'hunting' him 'down'; the other is from Spanish mystic St John of the Cross: 'the soul cannot be possessed of the divine union, until it has divested itself of the love of created beings'.[23] Tom's religious commitment did not involve wholly divesting himself of Vivien. His 'spiritual steps' seemed to him 'tentative' as well as 'obscure and doubtful', and he felt responsible for her; but when he moved closer to her at the Malmaison, she felt 'in a horrible state of mind'; when they went together to Divonne-les-Bains, Tom found it 'dreadful'.[24]

Gordon George (later known as Robert Sencourt), a New Zealand-born Anglican writer in his mid-thirties who later converted to Roman Catholicism and had interests in Donne, Dante and mysticism, was also resident at Divonne-les-Bains, recuperating from insomnia and 'nerves'. Conversing with the Eliots, he observed 'that the strain from which my new friends were suffering was that they no longer lived together in deepest unity'.[25] Reflecting on his own religious development that summer, Tom told Murry, 'the end like the beginning is solitude. And the difficulty in the end is to keep one's solitude in humility and not in pride.'[26]

At Divonne-les-Bains, Sencourt recalled, 'The doctors on the whole deprecated drugs and avoided psychoanalysis.' Instead, the Eliots, Sencourt, and others underwent 'a variant of the *douche écossaise*, in which strong gushes of hot, alternating with icy cold, water were played on the naked body'. This did Vivien, whose recent woes included pleurisy, little good. Sencourt recalled her walking 'almost as though in a trance', her hair 'dank' and 'her white face blotched' as 'her dark dress hung loosely over her frail form'.[27] By 19 September, Tom told Murry (who was trying to secure a cottage in England to which Vivien might return) she was 'now so unwell that we dare not look *one inch* ahead'.[28] Observing Tom around this time, Humbert Wolfe wondered 'how a body so thin and white goes on living', but was struck by Tom's animation when conversation turned to the *Criterion*.[29]

From France Tom liaised with Faber and others in London, ordering books including Bishop Charles Gore's *Can we then Believe?* and discussing publishing possibilities, but Henry urged him to distance himself from Vivien. Henry maintained she fed off Tom's concern for her, and that her 'emotional anguish' was 'self-induced' – a way of seeking his attention.[30] 'You', he told Tom 'are the worst person in the world for Vivien to be with.' Tom's 'natural elasticity' restored his 'poise' when relieved of Vivien's presence. 'Do not be too much together,' Henry urged, 'mix with people, and relax and regain strength – you as well as she.'[31]

Tom had had 'a great shock'.[32] During his preoccupation with his own affairs his sister Charlotte in Massachusetts had died at fifty-one. He had given her some details of Vivien's plight, but before Charlotte could reply she underwent an urgent 'very serious and dangerous operation' for peritonitis.[33] Though Charlotte had seemed tired during her last English visit, it was Tom's elderly mother whose health had seemed at risk. Now Charlotte, 'my favourite sister', was gone.[34] Suddenly, too, Charlotte's daughter Dodo had to 'return to Boston'.[35]

Vivien's situation, his mother's illness, Vivien's parents' frailty, and now Charlotte's death all intensified Tom's awareness of mortality and craving for religious consolation. Writing about the seventeenth-century Anglo-Catholic Bishop Lancelot Andrewes for a *Times Literary Supplement* leading article, he summarised the Church of England's history, presenting Andrewes as 'one of the community of the born spiritual' – a rather elect-sounding group which surely included Tom's mother, sister, and himself. Since at least 'Gerontion', which draws in part on Andrewes' 1622 Christmas sermon, Tom had used that Reformation writer's work. Now, echoing his own poetic ideal, he called Andrewes someone whose 'Intellect and sensibility were in harmony', adding that 'those who would prove this harmony would do well to examine' Andrewes' published private prayers, the *Preces Privatae*.[36]

In 1927, just before mentioning 'Vivien' and 'her sanatorium', he told his mother about 'a tiny book which has been of great value to me: Lancelot Andrewes' *Private Devotions*', explaining he liked 'to turn to them during the night whenever I cannot sleep'.[37] 'It was the Anglican forms of Lancelot Andrewes to which', Sencourt recalled, Tom 'had first been attracted'.[38] Certainly in 1926–7 and afterwards, Andrewes' work impressed him. He sent Lottie a copy of *Preces Privatae* small enough to fit under a pillow. Frequently invoking biblical or liturgical prose, and drawing (in English translation) on Latin, Greek, and Hebrew originals, it recast these as verse prayers. Andrewes' work let Tom repeat prayers that were universal in scope yet touched on his own – and his wife's – private anxieties.

> Remember, Lord, infants, children, growing youth,
> the young, the middle-aged, the old, the decayed,
> the hungry, thirsty, naked, sick,
> captives, friendless strangers,
> the possessed with devils and tempted to suicide,
> the distressed in soul or body,
> the fainthearted, the despairing,
> all in prison or chains, all under sentence of death,
> orphans, widows, foreigners, travellers, voyagers,
> women with child, women who give suck,
> all in bitter servitude, or mines, or galleys,
> or in loneliness.[39]

Sending his mother these prayers, Tom retained a larger edition. Commending its introduction, which presented the *Preces* not just as biblical and liturgical but also 'in a measure an autobiography', he quoted the editor's emphasis on these prayers as 'hymns' set out in 'steps' and 'stages'.[40] Pondering his own 'Hymn to the Virgin', Tom too would draw on biblical and liturgical cadences; eventually dedicated to Vivien, his new work would be in part refractedly autobiographical. One critic who was close to Tom came to see his 'poems, since "The Hollow Men"' as 'a series of Preces Privatae'.[41]

When Tom returned to London in early October 1926, Vivien remained in France, sojourning at Cannes before joining him at Chester Terrace in November. As well as working on an overdue essay on Seneca and Elizabethan drama, he liaised with *Criterion* contributors, sidestepped a Cambridge debate ('What on earth is "modernist verse"?' he asked), and mollified an indignant Lady Rothermere after the *Criterion*'s advertisement manager – who soon got 'the sack' – allowed an ad for Luvisca shirts to feature inappropriately in that highbrow journal.[42] The magazine's 'every-other-Tuesday dinners' continued, but Tom's relations with Vivien remained edgy.[43] In early December, mulling over her old affair with Russell, she asked Tom to return to him a 'packet' containing 'jewellery' Russell had once given her; Vivien cautioned Russell not to 'speak of it' to Tom, since 'it wd be very painful to him'.[44] Pound thought Tom ' "under a curse" ', and told him so.[45] Christmas arrived, 'wrapped in the usual fogs and glooms'.[46] Hosting Lucy Thayer complicated matters: surprisingly, only eighteen months after 'permanently' splitting from her, Vivien now found Lucy 'sensible, good-tempered'.[47] The festive season brought awkward reconciliations, not to mention presents including a cheque from Henry, but it was emotionally complicated.

Each Christmas, Tom's separation from his American family was unignorable. Shocked by Charlotte's death, he had at least managed to see his determined, ailing mother's *Savonarola* through the press, thanks to help from Cobden-Sanderson, who understood such gestures of filial piety. Cobden-Sanderson was also publishing his own late father's *Journals*, so they might appear while his strong-willed mother, a veteran 'suffragist', was still alive. Reading in 4 November's *Times* 'a notice of the death of Cobden-Sanderson's mother', Tom sent condolences 'immediately'.[48] Earlier, Cobden-Sanderson had been liaising with his close friend William Force Stead, an English-based American Anglo-Catholic priest; that summer Cobden-Sanderson had published Stead's *The Shadow of Mount Carmel*, which detailed 'a pilgrimage' that had led Stead 'to Rome at Easter'.[49] Cobden-Sanderson had been thinking intently about faith, and in December, a few weeks after his mother's cremation, he was baptised by Stead in the Church of St Mary and St Nicholas, Littlemore, Oxford, where Stead was then Acting Curate. Next day, as Stead had arranged, in the chapel of the Bishop's Palace at nearby Cuddesdon, Cobden-Sanderson was privately confirmed into the Church of England by the Bishop of Oxford.

Cobden-Sanderson had first introduced Tom to Stead at a 1923 lunch. The two Americans had much in common. Four years older than Tom, Stead had moved from 'utter and practical atheism' to become 'a Tory and a High Churchman'; according to his friend Sencourt, he had a taste for 'the writings of seventeenth-century Anglicanism, and especially those of Lancelot Andrewes' towards which he 'steadily drew Tom'.[50] Educated at the University of Virginia, Stead had arrived in England around 1910 as a United States vice consul. After marrying and starting a family, he had attended Oxford University, pursuing interests in the philosophy of religion. He wrote poetry, befriended poets and, like Tom, could play the mandolin; since the early 1920s he had visited Ottoline Morrell at Garsington. Stead was surprised one day when, confessing a longing for mystic visions, she showed him in her library copies of Plotinus, Christian Platonists, St Francis, St John of the Cross, and other mystics whose works he too had been reading. Like Tom's, Stead's marriage was insecure. By 1926 he had confessed to a friend he was 'in love' with a woman who was not his wife.[51]

In 1923 Stead's conventional taste in poetry had made him wary of Tom; but after Tom's conversations about religion with Sencourt at Divonne-les-Bains, Sencourt passed back reports of 'seeing a good deal' of Tom, and in October 1926, following Cobden-Sanderson's publication of *The Shadow of Mount Carmel*, Sencourt sent Tom a copy with an invitation to visit. Tom responded, saying he would 'very much like to see' Stead.[52] Sometime after mid-November Tom read Stead's book, which he later called 'a classic of prose style in its kind'.[53] The gossipy Sencourt gave Stead the impression Tom had 'conquered' his 'sceptical mood' and was 'going to come out clearly on the side of theism'. Stead seems to have suggested to Ottoline Morrell that Tom had 'repudiated' his earlier poetry and the 'mood' of *The Waste Land*. Assured by Sencourt that Tom now held 'a well reasoned belief in something very much like the theology of the Church of England', Stead anticipated 'a great fluttering of the dove-cotes'.[54]

Over Christmas 1926 the temperature in the south of England sank 'below the normal'.[55] Perusing Stead's book, Tom kept in mind words about 'the wise men come from the East' in Andrewes' Christmas sermon. Recast, they would form the beginning of his own Christmas poem published the next year:

It was no summer progress. A cold coming they had of it at this time of the year, just the worst time of the year to take a journey, and specially a long journey in. The ways deep, the weather sharp, the days short, the sun farthest off, *in solstitio brumali*, 'the very dead of winter'.[56]

Two days after speaking to Cobden-Sanderson, on receipt of Stead's letter about fluttering dovecotes, Tom replied saying he 'might as well repudiate infancy and childhood' as repudiate his earlier poetry; he had no interest at that time in 'fluttering dovecotes or any form of publicity'. Nevertheless, he found the rest of Stead's letter 'extremely sympathetic'. Stead's 'more important impressions', Tom assured him, 'were correct'.[57] About a month later, doggedly maintaining that 'I *hate* spectacular "conversions"', and that the matter concerned 'not even those nearest me', Tom asked Stead for 'advice, information & your practical assistance in getting Confirmation with the Anglican Church'.[58]

In retrospect, Stead, who came to relish lunching with Tom and Cobden-Sanderson, claimed 'no credit' for Tom's conversion.[59] Yet he was exceptionally well placed to understand its course: 'a change from scepticism to belief, from a state of mind in which he could hardly affirm anything to a state of mind in which he can say the Athanasian Creed with conviction'.[60] In *Sweeney Agonistes*, and other recent writings, Tom returned to his interest in anthropological texts. In January 1927 he corresponded with *Criterion* contributor Frederic Manning, who had argued that the anthropologist J. G. Frazer might 'be held to have established' human 'ideas of God, of immortality, of sin, and of atonement' as being 'natural and necessary assumptions'. 'I think that I agree with you about Frazer', wrote Tom.[61] Reconsidering another writer who had long meant much to him, he contended to Read that Henry James 'directed to the intensification of social values feeling which is properly religious'.[62]

In the same month Tom further advanced his slow-moving process of becoming a British subject by signing a formal declaration of his wishes, and grew eager to write about Baudelaire, another abiding preoccupation: like the eyes of 'The Hollow Men', Baudelaire's 'horrified eyes' perceived a 'chasm between the real and the ideal', whereas Walt Whitman 'had the ordinary desires of the flesh'.[63] When Tom's piece on Baudelaire appeared, it argued that the French poet, in attempting 'to explain, to justify, to make something of' his passions, was 'almost on a level with the author of the *Vita Nuova*'. Baudelaire, whose 'tendency to "ritual"' sprang, Tom argued, from 'a soul that was *naturaliter* Christian', was 'a Christian, born out of his due time, and a classicist, born out of his due time'. The French poet had 'had to discover Christianity for himself' and constantly sought 'sublimation of passion'.[64] Though Tom maintained 'the best aspect of Unitarianism' was 'a kind of emotional reserve and intellectual energy' to which he often conformed, ultimately his ability to commit himself to Christianity emanated from deep feeling, hard thinking, and a matching desire to sublimate his own sexual longings into a convert's dedication to a life of faith.[65] His

Anglo-Catholicism marked a decisive rejection of Unitarianism, the faith in which he and Emily Hale had grown up. Yet, tellingly, Boston's Unitarian King's Chapel which Tom had visited 'twice or thrice' in his youth was the Unitarian church most closely linked to Anglicanism, while he also recalled attending Boston's 'Arlington Street' Unitarian church.[66] Its splendid Tiffany windows included a Madonna of the Flowers, and its minister, Paul Revere Frothingham, had admired, like Tom, Arthur Symons's *The Symbolist Movement in Literature*.

Pieces Tom was now publishing in the *Criterion* – whether Ramon Fernandez in 'The Experience of Newman' discussing that famous convert's *Grammar of Assent*, or Maritain comparing poetry with divine grace in 'Poetry and Religion' – clearly reflect his intellectual interests. He sympathised with 'people who believe in the spiritual askesis and the discipline and development of the soul'.[67] This trajectory is evident, too, in the Clark Lectures; discouraging him from publishing them, the critic Mario Praz, whose writings on metaphysical poetry had stimulated Tom, argued those lectures mattered principally for their 'history of your own mind'.[68] Yet, for all his intellectual commitment, his conversion was emotional and spiritual. Provoked by Tom (who called him a Unitarian), Murry thought him 'an impossibilist', but a feeling that assent was now possible carried him beyond reason alone, letting him commit to a church.[69]

He did so aware 'there is always *doubt*; and in doubt we are living parasitically (which is better than not living at all) on the minds of the men of genius of the past who have believed something'. For him now, though, 'doubt and uncertainty' were 'merely a variety of belief'.[70] While recognising Christianity as supranational, he was conscious of a recent 'growth of the spirit of nationalism'. Interested in that, as well as in 'The European Idea', he liked to view those Reformation theologians Richard Hooker and Andrewes as 'fathers of a national church' as well as 'Europeans'.[71] Commitment to the 'High', Anglo-Catholic wing of Anglicanism accompanied his growing wish to commit formally to England. Headed by the monarch, the Church of England was, after all, the official state church of his adopted nation. In March Whibley signed a further declaration of support for Tom's application to become a British subject, though the modern scholar Elizabeth Micaković whose researches unearthed the application papers at the National Archives in Kew, points out that the arduous process (which involved Tom in being interviewed by the police in September) was not concluded until 3 November at what he described to Whibley as 'a very inferior ceremony'. Tom had imagined being summoned 'before the Throne'.[72] Ironically perhaps, his adherence to the linkage of church, king and country was shaped partly by his Francophile sympathy with the Action Française. He argued English 'Toryism is essentially Anglican', whereas 'Roman Catholicism, which in our time draws its greatest support from America, is more in harmony with Republicanism'.[73] Nonetheless, to Henri Massis, whom he associated with 'intense nationalism' and who had invited him to the Action Française dinner in Paris two years earlier, he wrote in March 1927 that *'Je crois que votre point de vu est plus près au mien que vous ne pensez. Il n'ya a pas grande différence entre votre Catholicisme et notre Anglo-Catholicisme, parceque je devine en votre Catholicisme une certaine partie inévitable de Gallicanisme . . . Je crois qu'une politique pareille doit s'allier avec une théologie pareille'* (I believe that your point of view is nearer to mine than you think. There is not a great deal of difference between your Catholicism and our Anglo-Catholicism, because, in your Catholicism, I sense an inevitable element of Gallicanism . . . I believe that similar political views must be allied to similar theological attitudes).[74] Guided by Action Française tendencies, the spirituality he articulated in the months prior to his conversion could sound elitist: 'The majority of people live below the level of belief or doubt. It takes application, and a kind of genius, to believe anything, and to believe *anything* (I do *not* mean merely to believe in some "religion") will probably become more and more difficult as time goes on.'[75] There may be a note of spiritual pride here, but he was aware, too, of humility as something to strive for – often with difficulty.

As he listened to Anglican liturgy he treasured *'incantation'*, a phenomenon he had always appreciated in poetry – and not just ostensibly religious poetry; he heard it insistently in Poe and Mallarmé in whose work it seemed to him partly to replace 'philosophy', insisting on 'the primitive power of the Word ("Fatum")'. Quoting a line of Mallarmé that would haunt him – *'Donner un sens plus pur aux mots de la tribu'* (Bestow a purer sense on the language of the tribe) – Tom discerned 'The effort to restore the power of the Word'.[76] His capitalisation of 'Word' links the term not just to the pre-Christian classical 'Fatum' (a term used several times in Virgil's *Aeneid* and which can mean prophetic or divine utterance, destiny, doom, or death) but also to the Christian 'Logos', the Word of God incarnated in Christ. As Tom's Christianity deepened, he saw the aim of poetry as attempting to let words approach the Word.

Unlike Matthew Arnold, or, he asserted, I. A. Richards, he did not think poetry 'capable of saving us'. That, he maintained, was 'like saying that the wall-paper will save us when the walls have crumbled'.[77] Elsewhere, writing again about George Chapman, that poet to whose work he felt unusually close, he argued Chapman was 'like other poets, a man of emotional rather than "intellectual" power'.[78] Wrestling with 'the relation between *truth* and *belief*, between rational and emotional assent', Tom, invoking Newman's *Grammar of Assent* in his mention of a 'Grammar of Belief', felt he must confront 'the immense problem of the relation of Belief to Ritual'.[79] Doing so, he was ready to assent to the process of conversion, and ritual forms of baptism and confirmation.

With Vivien, who scarcely shared his religious enthusiasm, he went to the grand Warrior House Hotel in St Leonards-on-Sea near Hastings 'for a few weeks' in late February.[80] This let her visit her gravely ill seventy-two-year-old father. Juggling commitments, Tom commuted to London two or three days a week and reviewed several detective stories (a genre he loved) as well as reading E. G. Selwyn's collection of *Essays Catholic and Critical*, which Stead had recommended, and T. A. Lacey's 'extremely convenient' guide, *The Anglo-Catholic Faith*.[81] Her seaside stay close to her father did Vivien little good. Her 'condition', Tom told Henry in mid-March, was 'anything but satisfactory, her delusions are very serious indeed'. Henry tried to convince Tom she needed 'severe handling'. Tom countered that her 'delusions' were in no sense a pretence and were 'quite beyond the point of "severe handling". They are quite genuine.'[82] She was suffering, also, symptoms of 'bronchitis'.[83] She and Tom returned to London. Trying not to make things worse, he kept from her how extremely unwell her father was, and hid from his mother 'how ill V. is'.[84]

Vivien's father died on Friday 25 March from 'cancer of the mediastinum' – 'a kind of tumour on the lung'.[85] His burial took place the following Tuesday. Vivien lay ill in London. 'The doctor said that if she got up and went down to Hastings she would very likely get pneumonia, so there was no question about it.'[86] Tom had agreed to be one of his father-in-law's executors. The two men had got on well; Charles Haigh-Wood had 'made the primary declaration' supporting Tom's application to become a British subject.[87] Now Tom needed to oversee legal work concerning Haigh-Wood's estate because after the funeral Vivien's brother had returned to Rome, while the third executor, Tom's mother-in-law, remained frail. Coinciding with the illness of his secretary Pearl Fassett, and an announcement that in an attempt to increase sales the quarterly *New Criterion* would become the *Monthly Criterion*, this was a daunting challenge. Haigh-Wood's estate included ancestral property in what was now the Irish Free State, as well as English investments. Legal complications would drag on for many months, requiring delicate liaising with lawyers, tax authorities, the other executors, and Vivien. With characteristic determination, scrupulousness, and slog, Tom embarked on this complex task.

His mother too had death on her mind. She was arranging to dispose of private papers, books, and other items her children might appreciate. Tom knew she had kept most of his correspondence ever since his high-school days. Sorting through Vivien's father's papers, he was absolutely sure he wanted his own private life kept utterly confidential.

> About my letters. For heaven's sake don't send them to me. If there is one thing more depressing than reading other people's old letters it is reading one's own. What I suggest, even beg, is that you keep all or any that you want to keep, but leave instructions that they be destroyed after your death. I do not want my biography, if it is ever written – and I hope it won't – to have anything private in it. I don't like reading other people's private correspondence in print, and I do not want other people to read mine.[88]

Though much later he modified this view somewhat, it reflected his sense of 'impersonality'. Perfectly happy to plan to publish studies containing biography, and to read biographies (a few days later, he was looking forward to 'a Biography of [Archbishop William] Laud'), he wanted no spotlight on his own life.[89] 'I do not say that poetry is not "autobiographical"', he wrote that year, 'but this autobiography is written by a foreign man in a foreign tongue, which can never be translated.'[90]

While trying to help Vivien and her family, he also gave his employer emotional as well as editorial support. Worried by the turbulence around the General Strike, Geoffrey Faber feared for his company's 'commercial success'. Faber had been full of confidence when the firm started. As older board members retired and new directors were hired, he was transforming the business from a specialist into a general publisher. Yet by 1927 when, in the wake of the commercial failure of his own *Elnovia* and an unsuccessful attempt to write plays, he was undergoing a lengthy course of psychotherapy, he feared this might be too much for him. 'May God help me to win through', he prayed in January. Several of his forebears having held ecclesiastical positions, Faber, like Tom, was fascinated by Newman; he would go on to write a history of the Anglo-Catholic Oxford movement. By April, when his wife Enid was in the late stages of pregnancy, Faber showed strain. 'Upon instinct', Tom wrote him a heartening letter. Most of their daily interactions involved book pricing, cover designs, practical matters, but Tom saw Faber struggling to balance 'absorption in the business' with home life, and sought to reassure him. Faber treasured Tom's wise friendship. Tom consoled him that 'after ten days or so' when the birth of the Fabers' second child was expected, Geoffrey would 'feel lighter in heart'.[91] When the baby arrived on 25 April, his parents called him Thomas: 'your namesake'.[92]

Though the birth brought joy, Faber now had two children to support. 'Business' presented 'insuperable obstacles'; his 'anxieties' became 'acute'. Drawing on his own experience, Tom, struggling with the *Monthly Criterion* and sure they were living through 'political and economic anarchy', tried to steady his senior colleague: 'I find myself, when I am tired, that I become more absorbed in administrative work.'[93] Now he also sought to take Faber out of himself. In early May Tom invited him to dinner at the Commercio, then to a boxing match at the Albert Hall where East Ender Teddy Baldock took a beating from New Yorker Archie Bell but fought on to clinch the world bantamweight title. Faber found this an 'amazing sight'.[94] Having taken boxing lessons in his Boston youth, Tom liked to surprise and cheer up his English friend; and he took a certain glee in likening writers who practised 'theological debate' to 'highly paid pugilists'.[95] Tom was a staunchly reliable colleague; in print, whether defending 'the impersonality and innocence of Machiavelli' or championing Renaissance dramatist Thomas Middleton's scandalous Moll Cutpurse as an example of 'free and noble womanhood', he liked to be unpredictable.[96]

Young poets sought him out, finding him astute but daunting. Peter Quennell, a Francophile Balliol graduate, noticed 'He still wore the short black coat and pin-striped trousers of an old-fashioned City gentleman, had a long sallow face, sympathetic brown eyes and a slightly twisted smile. His manner of speaking was quiet and precise, and his whole appearance "*un peu clergyman et correct*", as Gustave Kahn said of Jules Laforgue, when he first encountered him.'[97] Yet to his inner circle at *Criterion* dinners Tom showed another side, singing comic songs and circulating schoolboyishly risqué material. As he prepared for baptism and confirmation he discussed with Stead the difference between Unitarianism and Trinitarianism – and mailed Dobrée ridiculous letters outlining Bolovian theology: having 'two Gods, named respectively Wux and Wux', the Bolovians made do with just one idol. 'In the Forenoon, they worshipped it as Wux, from the front; in the Afternoon, they worshipped it from Behind as Wux. (Hence the Black Bottom.) Those who worshipped in front were called Modernists; those who worshipped from behind were called Fundamentalists.'[98]

Anglicanism offered an ordering of his spiritual life. Meanwhile, regularising the financial affairs of his late father-in-law, he also tried to order his own. To Bertrand Russell, whose *Why I Am Not a Christian* Tom denounced that summer as 'a pathetic document' but whom he continued to address cordially as 'Dear Bertie', he wrote 'at Vivien's request', returning £3,500 in shares.[99] Russell had presented these to him years earlier to stave off financial emergency – and perhaps in an attempt to salve a guilty conscience while infatuated with Vivien. Tom's awareness of 'the problem of sex' stayed strong; making reference to Russell's heirs, he made it clear 'I have, and shall have, none.'[100] Sublimating his own sexuality, he went on publishing in the *Criterion* controversial work by D. H. Lawrence – a 'demoniac with a gospel'. Still, Lawrence's sensual story 'Sun' proved too much for the Tom who regarded the evolutionary origins of sex as 'some hideous coition of protoplasm'.[101]

The sharpness of his scorn can be sensed in his agreeing with Aldington in May 1927 'that England is sterile, but quality as well as fecundity is valuable, and one cannot encourage the feeble-minded to breed'.[102] None of this stopped mild flirtation with Virginia Woolf in whose work he detected both flaws and 'astonishing beauty' and whom he introduced to American jazz and ragtime records.[103] 'I should be very glad to show you what little I know about the Grizzly Bear, or the Chicken Strut. I should not dare to bring you any more records without being sure that you have not got them already, but have you got The Memphis Shake?' He signed himself, 'Ever yours affectionately'. She enjoyed taking tea with him 'very much', and responded to his tone: 'We might dance.'[104]

He had been enlivened by an unexpected letter from Emily. Still employed by Milwaukee-Downer College, where that year she would be granted the title 'assistant professor', and still active in the Unitarian church, she was now enjoying several months' sabbatical in Italy, with a side-trip to Switzerland.[105] Most of her time was spent in Florence – the city of Dante and Beatrice – and later that year in a published piece she enthused about the delights of 'the old quarter of the city today, as Dante knew it'.[106] Stead, who met Tom the day Emily's letter arrived, recalled much later,

> Eliot and I were walking round Russell Square on our way to lunch.
> It was May and the sun was bright and the leaves were coming out
> and the tulips in flower. I made the rather inane remark that it would
> be nice to be in love on a day like this. 'Perhaps it is the weather,' said
> Eliot, 'but I had a letter from a girl in Boston this morning whom I
> have not seen or heard from for years and years – it brought some-
> thing back to me that I have not known for a long time.'

Stead carefully added, 'Those are the words of a celibate: a man given to loose living does not have those delicate feelings.' Stead also remarked that '*Not a trace* of his sex life (whatever it may be)' appeared on the surface; while Tom possessed 'a warm and romantic heart', Stead associated him with 'strict chastity'. Prefacing his account of the letter from the Bostonian 'girl', Stead recalled talking with him about Dante and *La Vita Nuova* 'in which Dante's love for Beatrice passed over into a love of God'.

'I have had that experience,' Eliot said eagerly and rather shyly, and then lapsed into silence. Other men might have gone on to say more of the experience, but Eliot keeps his secrets to himself. He made this remark apparently before he realised its implications and then felt that he had said too much.[107]

Before he received Emily's letter, Tom had already been planning his 'Hymn to the Virgin' and pondering *La Vita Nuova*. Associating Emily with love, he was very glad she had contacted him, but maintained his focus on divine rather than human love. He wrote to her 'in 1927', but was not deflected from what he saw as his husbandly duty.[108] If there was contact between him and Emily around this time, it was epistolary and restrained.

For Vivien's sake he accompanied her to her familiar haunts at Eastbourne, staying at 55 Meads Street for much of June and July. They were together at weekends, but Tom spent most weekdays working in London. It was hard to fix a date for his baptism and confirmation. Vivien would not accompany him. Eventually, he went alone to Oxford, where Stead, resident eleven miles away in the seventeenth-century manor house at rural Finstock, had been appointed chaplain at Worcester College. On 29 June, a cool summer Wednesday, Tom approached Finstock's part-Victorian, part-Edwardian Cotswold limestone village church on the edge of Wychwood Forest.

To be godfathers, Stead had brought his own close friend, Worcester College don Vere Somerset, and a theology don from Queen's College, Canon B. H. Streeter, a former agnostic who had become an Anglican and of whom Tom already held 'a very high opinion'.[109] Having baptised Cobden-Sanderson the previous year, Stead was aware private adult baptisms were sensitive occasions. 'It seemed odd', he recalled, 'to have such a large though infant Christian at the baptismal font, so, to avoid embarrassment, we locked the front door of the little parish church and posted the verger on guard in the vestry.'[110] The Church of England had a special, quite lengthy ceremony for adult baptism. At one point during it, the person being baptised was asked by the priest, in words from the Book of Common Prayer, 'Dost thou renounce the devil and all his works, the vain pomp and glory of the world, with all covetous desires of the same, and the carnal desires of the flesh, so that thou wilt not follow, nor be led by them?' To which the formal answer required from Tom was 'I renounce them all.'[111]

While in Finstock, he stayed overnight with Stead, Somerset, and Streeter, and at twilight they traversed Wychwood Forest, Tom 'pacing under the mighty oaks and pushing his way through hazel thickets attired in a smart suit, a bowler hat, and', Stead recalled, 'grey spats'. Next morning Tom went to the Bishop's Palace at Cuddesdon, and was 'confirmed privately' as a member of the Church of England by Thomas Banks Strong, Bishop of Oxford.[112] Geoffrey Faber, one of the few people who knew what had happened, was pleased when Tom agreed to be godparent to baby Tom Faber.

With all this in mind, Tom, as he explained to Conrad Aiken that September, wrote a new poem 'in three quarters of an hour after church time and before lunch one Sunday morning, with the assistance of half a bottle of Booth's gin'.[113] This was 'Journey of the Magi', whose opening and several later lines draw closely on Andrewes' Christmas sermon about 'the very dead of winter'. In gestation, perhaps, before Tom's father-in-law's death and Tom Faber's birth, the recently baptised Tom's poem sets birth and death beside one another, seeing them in a Christian context as inextricably intertwined.

The poem's speaker, one of the 'Magi' or wise men said to have visited the infant Christ, comes from the old, pre-Christian 'dispensation' terminated by the Saviour's birth. Where Sweeney in 'Fragment of an Agon' had maintained bleakly that 'Death is life and life is death', now in this new poem a wise man on the cusp of the Christian era struggles to decide whether he and his fellow journeyers have been led 'all that way for / Birth or Death' since now the two seem disconcertingly similar.[114] For the speaker, the only way to resolve things may be through 'another death' – his own.[115] The poem's nativity scene is part of a painful process, and only partially reveals what Christianity may offer. Published in a series of 'Ariel Poems' which Faber & Gwyer produced as Christmas cards, it also drew on Tom's experience translating *Anabase*, a work filled with images of journeying, desert landscape, and arresting details. Scrutinising Saint-John Perse's French tilted Tom decisively towards an imaginative engagement with landscape which had been present only fleetingly in his earlier poems. While partly constructed from echoes of older writers, and voiced by an ancient magus, 'Journey of the Magi' was also a poem articulating Tom's individual religious commitment. Where once he might have sought to connect death and rebirth in Buddhist terms, now his focus was intensely Christian. One of the first people to receive his new poem was his infant godson.

In late July 1927, alongside Vivien in Eastbourne, he avoided work. They drove around Sussex, visiting Winchelsea, Portsmouth, Dover, and Canterbury. Reconciled with Vivien, Lucy Thayer brought a tent to be erected at the end of the month in the back garden at Chester Terrace so she, Vivien and Tom could have tea or supper outdoors among the hollyhocks, lupins, and vines which Janes, their handyman, 'tended so carefully'.[116] But it seems Tom went alone to be godfather to Thomas Erle Faber at his christening in Hampstead Parish Church on 27 July. Years later, Tom recorded that his own conversion afforded 'a fresh reason for domestic persecution'.[117] Having motored round Sussex, joined a church, and brooded on sex, Tom sent Dobrée news of 'a complete new theory of Bolovian Theology' along with 'an inventory of the God wux' which included

4 Legs
4 Feet (Duck)
4 Arms
4 testicles
2 Penisses
1 speedometer
1 clock
1 dash lamp
4 wheel brakes
extra wheel and toolchest[118]

Around the same time, though the letters do not survive, he appears to have given his mother an account of his conversion, as well as writing to his sisters. He understood that his mother – whom he kept up to date with his published pieces, including a recent essay on Wilkie Collins – had 'about six months or a year' to live.[119]

Though her son's theology was hardly hers, nonetheless Lottie, who had written at least one poem about the Magi coming to Christ and who had longed for an explicitly Christian sequel to *The Waste Land*, lived long enough to notice Tom outlining 'theological work' to sit alongside a book on Dante, a volume of literary essays and his revised Clark Lectures.[120] She implied she would never see him again; 'very sad', he replied he hoped he might visit her in America next year and that 'in the second place I have a much more positive conviction than you have that I shall see you in another life'.[121] In some ways, conversion brought him even closer to her; he described how the sitting room at Chester Terrace was decorated with photographs of 'you and father and grandpa and grandma' along with other ancestors; but he still concealed the seriousness of his difficulties with Vivien, even if his words of attempted consolation may be ghosted by his own marital problems:

Many people believe that they love each other, and understand each other, who are in reality utterly isolated from each other. But I believe that you and I understand each other and are like each other perhaps more than we know, and that we shall surely meet. And whenever I have done anything that the world has thought good, or that the world is likely to think good for a generation or two after I am dead, I have always felt that it was something that you and I did together, or even something that you had dreamt of and projected before I was born. I often feel that I am merely a continuation of you and Father, and that I am merely doing your work for you. Anyway, you are the finest and greatest woman that I have ever known.[122]

While she lived, he wanted her to believe in him. He sent a typescript of his Clark Lectures, and, desperate to justify himself to his 'dearest dear mother', told her, 'I have still – though I know that I am getting old – ambitions of things to be done: I think that I can still do more, that if I am spared to strength and activity I can make a deeper mark on English and European civilisation; but if this is a delusion I am resigned to it.'[123]

To Henry, whose wife was also ill, he explained why he could not cross the Atlantic. The problem was Vivien's condition: 'In the present delusion stage, you and Theresa are "great enemies", but not so much so as her brother Maurice and her aunts.' Tom added, 'Judge how I am torn', but felt he could not leave his wife: 'it has got to the point where staying here is not a mere matter of sentiment or conscience, but a matter of duty and almost daily anxiety and necessity. When things get *better,* or when they get much *worse,* I can come; meanwhile I must try to put the best face on it I can.'[124]

So he went on, reporting on typescripts, putting together issues of the *Monthly Criterion*, seeing books through the press, and meeting authors. Revealingly, at a time when both Vivien and Emily were in his thoughts, he told Faber that he had 'always felt a particular sympathy and (probably) illusory understanding' of Jonathan Swift in connexion with Stella and Vanessa, the two women with whom Swift had long-lasting relationships; 'I do think Swift's sexual life ought to be studied carefully & sympatheti-cally, because he is a spiritual type, *not* a mere abnormal.'[125]

Though arguably his most emotionally intense connection around this time was with his far-off mother, he remained committed to helping Vivien. Yet on 16 August, formally but thoughtfully, he inscribed 'for Emily Hale from T. S. Eliot' a copy of 'Journey of the Magi'. He sent her also (writing on it more familiarly 'E.H. from T.S.E. 1927') his new *Shake-speare and the Stoicism of Seneca* in which, among other things, he remarks on 'having my biography invariably ignored in what I *did* write from per-sonal experience' and argues that 'What every poet starts from is his own emotions', pointing out Dante's 'nostalgia, his bitter regrets for past happiness – or for what seems happiness when it is past – and his brave attempts to fabricate something permanent and holy out of his personal animal feelings – as in the *Vita Nuova'*.[126] Prepared that summer, the Faber list for autumn 1927 announced that 'Salutation' would appear 'in the near future' in the *Criterion*.[127]

Later revised and incorporated into *Ash-Wednesday*, 'Salutation' presents a speaker who has been torn apart. Its first published version mentions a 'Rose / With worm eaten petals', reminiscent of 'The Sick Rose' attacked by a 'worm' in William Blake's poem of love gone wrong – Tom read books on Blake while pondering the 'erotic-devotional' in mid-1927.[128] 'Salutation' goes on to speak of the 'torment / Of love unsatisfied' and 'The greater torment / Of love satisfied' as it pursues its 'endless / Journey' and offers 'Grace to the Mother'.[129] Tom gave an early draft to Stead, and on 2 September informed his mother he had 'just written another small poem', which he would send.[130]

Eventually becoming the first part of *Ash-Wednesday*, and originally called 'All Aboard for Natchez Cairo and St Louis' (a line from an American song Tom loved), this other new poem was later retitled 'Perch'io non spero'.[131] That Italian title came from a medieval poem by Guido Cavalcanti on which he drew for his opening line, 'Because I do not hope to turn again'. In his 1912 Cavalcanti edition (for a proposed new version of which Tom wrote a Faber reader's report dated '6 Sept. 1927') Pound had singled out 'that matchless and poignant ballad, "*Perch'io non spero di tornar gia mai*"', twining Cavalcanti's erotic work with Dante's poetry of Christian worship.[132] That is what Tom would do in *Ash-Wednesday*, but where Pound and Cavalcanti invoke a 'Lady' who is an erotic beloved to whom the speaker has no hope of returning, Tom's 'Lady' seems a divine emblem.[133] Even if in his mind she was in part Emily, turning to this celestial 'Lady' avoided the difficulties of sexuality. Tom turned, and did not hope to turn again.

Probably his mother was spared seeing American literary pirate Samuel Roth – who had reprinted work by Tom and by James Joyce without permission – denounce her son as 'a prig and a blackguard'.[134] 'Brer Possum,' Pound urged, 'you keep away from that polecat', but Tom engaged in literary pugilism with Roth in the *New York Evening Post*.[135] Tom could act as peacemaker: he tried to calm Robert Graves, who reacted splenetically to a piece by Faber poet John Gould Fletcher in the *Criterion*; Tom mollified Aldington, who was insulted by a novelisation of his domestic affairs by fellow *Criterion* contributor John Cournos; Tom strove yet again to placate Lady Rothermere, who continued to offer quasi-editorial advice. But sometimes Tom just vented his annoyance. *Criterion* dinners afforded some

relief: drinking port at one that August brought on 'a fearful Headache';
light relief came, too, from bantering with Dobrée, to whom Tom sent
Bolovian verses rhyming 'THE VIRGIN MARY' with 'Seamen brown
and hairy'.[136]

'So long as Vivien is as she is,' Tom wrote to Henry, 'I do not see how I
can leave. You will say: kinder to her, and far better for me, to put her away
in a Home at once. But that is difficult in England, except when the patient
is willing.'[137] Though he had clung to the idea that Vivien was not mentally ill, now he was prepared to hint that she was, even if at this point she
did not regard herself as requiring hospitalisation. Tom told Henry that,
some years earlier, English doctors had been bankrupted by a male 'violent
lunatic' who had sued them after they institutionalised him. 'As it is, no
doctor will commit anyone to an asylum unless they have either manifestly
tried to commit suicide or committed a criminal assault upon someone
else.' This meant there was

no likelihood of getting Vivien into a Home at present. We must
therefore wait until she either annoys people in the public street
(which I am always expecting) or tries to take her own life, before I
can do anything about it. Meanwhile I feel that I must not leave her,
even for a night, as this sort of thing might happen at any time.

As he sat typing these grim words, Tom warned that 'at any moment I
may be obliged to cut this letter short'.[138]
Feeling intensely his own and Vivien's torment, he continued to hide it
as best he could. Now, ironically, the friend who seemed to understand his
wife best was Lucy Thayer. Her own mental fragility gave her insight. The
Eliots went with Lucy 'in her car' to Dunstable, Bedfordshire, for tea on 28
August; otherwise Vivien stayed close to home.[139] By September her
brother was in London. Tom consulted him in detail about settling the
estate, but found him little help with Vivien.
A seasoned magazine editor, Tom was less experienced as a publisher of
books. As Faber tried to steer his firm into general literary publishing, it
continued producing volumes such as essays by the chief medical officer
and a physiological study called *Nerves*. Such titles appeared alongside traditional and avant-garde fiction – from American C. Kay Scott's *Siren* (whose
heroine is 'a woman who can express herself only through sex') to Allen
Upward's English murder mystery *The Domino Club*.[140] With the list of the
'new firm' evolving, its logo metamorphosed from the medical healing-
rod emblem of Asclepius to an image of a monk reading a book.[141] This
change did not mean Faber was becoming a religious rather than a secular

publisher, but did reflect some of his and Tom's interests. Though he developed a hunger for book-trade statistics, Geoffrey Faber became a publisher ready to assert that 'The real book – to borrow a metaphor from religion – is the soul incarnate in all this print and paper.'[142] By 1927 the increasingly heterogeneous Faber list took in not just H. W. Yoxall's *Modern Love* (a novel of ' "incompatibility of temperament" between husband and wife') but also George Ryland's edition of *The Psalms of David*, plus a study of *Northumbrian Crosses*, a volume on poet-mystic Francis Thompson, and *Parsons' Wives* by Myfanwy Price.[143]

Sadly, with the exception of Tom's own work, the poetry list was unspectacular. Early in 1927 the *Times Literary Supplement* had devoted its lead review substantially to his achievements as a 'metaphysical poet' – an 'obscure' one – and had been rather dismissive of his fellow 'metaphysical' Herbert Read, whose *Collected Poems* featured on Faber's list. So did American John Gould Fletcher's long-lined biblically attuned *Branches of Adam* – 'A poem in four books and an epilogue', which, Tom admitted later, failed 'conspicuously'. There were also anthologies: *The Poetry of Toil* covered 'the dignity, the pain, the joys, and the infinite diversity of labour', while *By What Sweet Name* offered poems 'associated with a particular feminine name'.[144] Seeking to balance marketable with rather more adventurous poetry, Tom hoped the two might sometimes coincide. But his bailiwick extended beyond poets. Writing reports on fiction and non-fiction alike, he brought to Faber European intellectuals including Henri Massis. Conscious, however, that poetry was Tom's speciality, Faber worried his colleague's taste was too exclusive. Faber admired Tom's verse, but struggled with it: 'Are you conscious of your own obsessive obscurity?' Perhaps Tom could make 'greater effort' to 'meet the reader half-way'. Faber feared 'the rigidity' of Tom's 'way of life' might 'divorce' him 'further & further from the common man.' Awkwardly, he wrote Tom a long letter saying so, recommending 'the good things of life' which, for Geoffrey, included 'a comfortable house, a car, good food, some sport, domestic interests, pleasant companionship, practical curiosities'; these might, 'in time', extend to 'metaphysics'. [145]

Tom was stung by this. For him, he replied with convert's fervour, 'the good things of life' were 'primarily, heroism and saintliness'. Motivated by his 'awareness of God', he sought to inspire others towards these. Before citing St John of the Cross and the *Sweeney Agonistes* epigraph about the love of 'created beings', he used language pertinent to *Ash-Wednesday* as well as to his own erotic and religious life:

if one makes the relation of man to man (or still more to woman) the highest good, I maintain that it turns out a delusion and a cheat. But if two people (say a man and a woman in the greatest intimacy) love God still more than they love each other, then they enjoy greater love of each other than if they did not love God at all. I have found my own love for a woman enhanced, intensified and purified by meditation on the Virgin.[146]

Surely his relationship with Vivien was in his mind when he wrote this remarkable letter, but also his feelings − or the ghost of them − for Emily. It was not long since he had written of the 'loveliness' of the 'Lady' who 'honours the Virgin in meditation' in the 'Salutation' that later (retitled in Vivien's handwriting) found its way into Emily's collection.[147] Responding to Faber's letter, Tom mentioned experiencing 'minor pleasures of drunkenness and adultery'.[148] It is clear from Stead and others that on occasion, though 'comparatively Sober', he was drinking quite heavily.[149] His response to Faber stands out for its allusion to his adultery with Nancy Cunard, and perhaps to his thoughts of Emily which he hoped he had 'purified by meditation'. He knew, too, the words of St Matthew's Gospel: 'whosoever looketh on a woman to lust after her hath committed adultery with her already in his heart'.[150]

Trying to convince Faber he was neither 'a Puritan ascetic' nor professed 'a fantastical puritanical catholicism', Tom cited his love of French cuisine.[151] Shortly afterwards, he spent a week in Paris, but hardly gave himself over to uninhibited hedonism; instead, he accompanied Vivien again to the Malmaison. Her condition had become so serious that he had induced her 'to return to her excellent sanatorium'. 'My poor wife', he called her in a letter to Dobrée. Rhyming 'Passover' and 'Tea-kettle-arse-over', this letter's casually racist, antisemitic, calculatingly obscene Bolovian versifying about 'Tail' and 'Penis' served both to disguise and to vent deep-seated anxieties about sex and theology.[152]

Mischievously, when he heard that Mary Hutchinson's lover Clive Bell would be in Paris, Tom tried to put Bell in touch with jazz-age artistes the Dolly Sisters, one of whose acts involved dancing with collie dogs at the Casino de Paris. 'Introduce yourself as a friend of M. Eliot de la Malmaison', suggested Tom.[153] Hinting she was not 'quite normal', he mentioned to Russell his relief when Vivien 'returned to her sanatorium'.[154] The Woolfs had him to dinner, and Ellen (now Ellen Sollory) wrote to say she was sorry about 'Mrs Eliots Illness'.[155] From other people he completely concealed the issue. Alone at Chester Terrace, he did his best to look after Peter and George, his and Vivien's new small dogs. Cooking little, he often ate at a nearby restaurant.

In October 1927 at Sencourt's instigation, he accepted an invitation to Yorkshire to visit Viscount Halifax, a leading Anglo-Catholic layman whose principal residence was Hickleton Hall, near Doncaster. President of the English Church Union, Lord Halifax was closely involved in controversial discussions about union between the Church of England and the Church of Rome. Then in his late eighties, Halifax had devoted his life to Anglo-Catholic causes. He and Tom debated the Action Française which the Pope had condemned and Tom now regarded as 'dangerous' but not 'immoral'.[156] Tom got on well with this elderly aristocrat, whose theological passions were counterpointed by mischievous humour and whose London house at 88 Eaton Square was a short walk from Chester Terrace. Both men stayed in touch, and in 1928 Tom declared concerning his own faith, 'I owe a great deal in my present position to conversation with Lord Halifax.'[157] The viscount had long held the position of churchwarden at the very 'High' Anglican parish Church of St Mary the Virgin in Graham Street, just round the corner from Tom's house; since the other nearby Anglican church was 'Low', and since the vicar of St Mary the Virgin visited 57 Chester Terrace later in the year, it is evident Tom worshipped at St Mary's – the 'local church' in whose 'repair' (it was then being extended) he had begun to 'interest' himself in 1927.[158] The previous year Lord Halifax had laid the 'foundation-stone' for the 'enlargement of the Church of St Mary the Virgin', and work to beautify its interior was ongoing.[159]

Tom continued discussing theological 'opinions' with established friends including Cobden-Sanderson, and with newer chums such as the likeable, erratic botanist Geoffrey Tandy, but Vivien's situation in France was constantly on his mind.[160] On 24 October he lunched with her mother in London; that same day he thanked Marguerite Caetani for sending Vivien flowers. Because during her previous Malmaison stay Vivien had sent letters which some recipients (including Osbert and Edith Sitwell) found 'long and incoherent', the Malmaison doctors now passed her correspondence to Tom 'to look at first'.[161] She wrote to her husband 'twice a week', and he received 'reports from the sanatorium'. Though this correspondence seems lost, Tom concluded Vivien showed 'some improvement', but 'the condition is still bad'.[162]

He felt 'in a rather tense state', but Faber hosted him at All Souls one weekend, which he relished.[163] Next, don and *Criterion* contributor Kenneth Pickthorn invited him to Corpus Christi College, Cambridge. Tom busied himself with work, attending lunches and dinner parties. In his 'white waistcoat' he seemed to Virginia Woolf 'much the man of the world'.[164] Confessing to Henry – 'don't tell mother' – that he was waiting to receive his 'British Passport', he hoped his brother would not be too shocked.[165] Becoming British was regarded by his friends as becoming English, and matched his joining the Church of England, even if an

Irish-American visitor that month, Mary Colum, thought he looked 'a little alien in London' and 'aware of his own alienness'.[166]

He still wondered if he might visit his mother in America before Christmas. He was supervising a dissertation for literary critic E. M. W. Tillyard at Cambridge: knowing what would please Lottie, he told her 'I should like, and even hope, eventually to get a job or an honorary Fellowship in Cambridge; I like Cambridge much better than Oxford.'[167] As ever, he felt torn between duty to her and to Vivien. By 10 November he told Whibley, who had just married a woman forty-three years his junior (which Tom thought 'may be a very good thing for both of them'), that the passport had arrived, 'so that I can visit my wife or my mother at any time'.[168] Whibley was 'delighted' Tom was 'an Englishman at last'.[169] Unrealistically, this new-minted Englishman thought he might fit in business and family visits to Switzerland, Paris, Dublin, and Boston over the coming weeks.

With 'dread' he went to Paris in mid-November. He saw friends, but mainly visited his wife 'each day'. He told his mother Vivien looked much 'stronger'; however, she was not ready to return to London.[170] He journeyed on to Switzerland for difficult discussions with Lady Rothermere about the future of the *Criterion*: she told him it and his own work were 'dry' – products of 'lack of emotion in your life'.[171] They quarrelled. Her Ladyship decided to withdraw her capital from the magazine.

London held trouble too. While Tom was travelling, his handyman Janes 'tripped over the cat on the stairs' at Chester Terrace and lay unconscious for some time.[172] When Tom returned, he visited Janes regularly, paying his doctor's bill. Wanting female company, Tom cheered himself up by going to the theatre with Mary Hutchinson in December, and inviting Virginia Woolf to tea at Russell Square. He promised to 'buy a Cake'. Virginia responded, 'A penny bun is what I like most of anything in the world.'[173] Throughout the month, the illnesses of his mother and his wife preyed on him. 'I should be very glad to be joyful,' he wrote in a piece published just after Christmas, 'but I should not care for any joy to be obtained at the price of surrendering my life's experience.'[174] Reassured by Henry that Lottie was stronger and would even accept his change of nationality, he decided to travel now to Paris, not Boston. To Frank Morley, a *Criterion* colleague, he joked about trying to avoid 'litigation' from Lady Rothermere, whose husband, Sidney Harmsworth, was among England's richest men.[175] To Cobden-Sanderson he was forthright: 'To Hell with the Harmsworths.'[176] The *Criterion* would go on without them.

On 21 December he went to France with Vivien's mother to spend a week close to his wife. Lucy Thayer was 'staying in Paris too', though Maurice Haigh-Wood had decided he was too 'busy' to spend Christmas with his sister.[177] As well as seeing Vivien, Tom attended several church services. Punctiliously, he informed William Force Stead afterwards that he 'did not make any Christmas communion'. However, '(strictly private) I communicate three times a week anyway, so I hope that does not matter'.[178] Zealous in his Christianity, he showed as much in an anonymous tribute to the philosopher F. H. Bradley, published that month. Tom linked Bradley (subject of his doctoral thesis) to the great convert Newman, arguing in terms that indicate something of his own journey towards belief, that 'scepticism and disillusion are a useful equipment for religious understanding'. Bradley represented the 'catholic, civilized, and universal'. In Arnoldian tones infused with new-found zeal, Tom contended that

> there is no such thing as a Lost Cause because there is no such thing as a Gained Cause. We fight for lost causes because we know that our defeat and dismay may be the preface to our successors' victory, though that victory itself will be temporary; we fight rather to keep something alive than in the expectation that anything will triumph.[179]

Tom deployed Bradley to champion 'the individual in communion with God'.[180] His determination as a philosophically trained Christian was almost matched by growing commitment as a publisher. He intended to add to his list work by his old friend Pound: Faber & Gwyer, he told Aldington that December, was 'too bloody respectable'. Tom aspired 'to make them less' so.[181] If recruiting Pound might help, Tom had also been genuinely 'interested' in an Oxford undergraduate who had been in touch earlier in the year – even though he had turned down the young man's poems.[182] The student's name was Wystan Hugh Auden.

5

Churchman

Soon Auden would become the most striking young English poet on Tom's list. He would be joined by contemporaries including Stephen Spender, consolidating Tom's reputation as a poetry talent-spotter. In late December 1927, as Tom visited Vivien at the Malmaison, however, none of this was clear. On his first Christmas as an Anglican, he went to the grand, ornate Catholic church of Saint-Sulpice in the Latin Quarter, close to where he had been in student lodgings seventeen years earlier. A worshipper but not a communicant, he heard Latin Mass under the high ceiling of Saint-Sulpice, whose Lady Chapel featured on its dome's interior an impressive mural showing the assumption into heaven of the Virgin Mary, depicted in pigments of intense blue. Next morning, after breakfast, he worshipped on the other side of the Seine at St Michael's, the Anglican 'British Embassy Church'.[1]

Returning to England, for the first time since his conversion he experienced the Epiphany feast day, 6 January, on which many Christians celebrate the visit of the Magi to the infant Christ. Unfortunately, the author of 'Journey of the Magi' was still getting over a bout of seasickness. Ten days later he sailed back to France for five nights before crossing again to London. Vivien remained at the Malmaison. On 24 January Tom and Stead – two unhappy husbands – went to St Martin-in-the-Fields in Trafalgar Square to attend the high-society wedding of Ottoline Morrell's daughter Julian, who was marrying war hero Victor Goodman.[2] Julian, with whom Tom had played croquet at Garsington, smiled in her 'dress of white chiffon with a pearl girdle'. It was a blustery day. When photographs were taken the twenty-two-year-old bride's white 'tulle veil' blew in the wind.[3] Tom knew the family well enough to realise Julian's parents had made her end her relationship with her 'true love', a brilliant young historian, Igor Vinogradoff.[4] Of the wedding, Tom recalled 'a bottle of not very good champagne'.[5]

Not marriage but faith was his mainstay, though several friends found that difficult. In January Virginia Woolf wrote to her sister, Vanessa Bell,

> I have had a most shameful and distressing interview with poor dear Tom Eliot, who may be called dead to us all from this day forward. He has become an Anglo-Catholic, believes in God and immortality, and goes to church. I was really shocked. A corpse would seem to me more credible than he is. I mean, there's something obscene in a living person sitting by the fire and believing in God.[6]

Woolf and Tom remained friends, but, conscious of 'innuendoes about Vivien's sanity', she had little time for what she saw as his 'pomp', religious or otherwise.[7] Yet, if his demeanour and beliefs could appear pompous, he craved support. Accustoming himself to a regime of thrice-weekly communion, early that year he 'very much' relished a 'small book', *The Life of Prayer in the World* by Father Francis Underhill, cousin of mysticism scholar Evelyn Underhill.[8] This Anglican priest's volume explained how 'each of us is two persons': one with an 'outward life', one with a 'hidden life'. 'In our outward life we can and do disguise much from others', but 'our spiritual life is what we really are'. For Underhill 'spiritual life' was 'founded on strict rule, on unwearying inner self-discipline, on heroic unseen battles'.[9]

To Tom, who wrote on 'The Life of Prayer' later in 1928, this rang true.[10] 'We must let nothing prevent the keeping of our rule of Confession and Communion, of Meditation, Intercession, Examination of Conscience, Retreat', urged Underhill. Denouncing 'the fatal modern habit of reading only easy and shallow books', and championing not just 'theological works' but also 'the best literature, history, poetry, and novels', he sounded like a high-minded publisher well suited to 24 Russell Square. '*Pray always*', he counselled, advising regular 'meditation' in which by 'resolute effort . . . the soul detaches itself from worldly things', sometimes by taking 'some passage of Holy Scripture' and 'picturing to ourselves the scene'. Tom had done that in 'Journey of the Magi', and would do so again in his next 'Ariel Poem', 'A Song for Simeon'. For Underhill 'serious reading' was 'a necessity, and chiefly reading of the Bible'. He encouraged slow, quiet scrutiny of a passage from spiritual writing, until 'we try to make it our own and apply it to our own life, breaking into prayer as God helps us.' This focus on incorporating into prayers fragments of scripture and spiritual texts appealed to Tom, and was already underway in his poetry, but Underhill's disciplinarian strictness also matched Tom's temperament: 'The first necessity of the spiritual life is discipline – self-control – the watchful guardianship of every thought, word, and act.' Underhill emphasised 'punctuality' was especially 'valuable' in 'the spiritual life'. 'Getting up at a FIXED TIME' mattered, as did regular religious observation both in private and in public worship: 'Happy are those who are near their church.'[11]

Tom's church was only about 200 yards away. Built of plain red brick in the 1870s, the Church of St Mary the Virgin in Graham Street was a beacon of Anglo-Catholicism. One of its priests, flamboyant Maurice Child, had helped found the Society of St Peter and St Paul (SSPP), an Anglo-Catholic movement fascinated both by Roman Catholicism and by Thomas Cranmer's sixteenth-century liturgy, on which the Church of England's Book of Common Prayer is based. The most prominent priest at St Mary the Virgin, Father Humphrey Whitby, had 'perfected the SSPP method of saying Mass using the words of the Anglican Prayer Book but in such a way that an observer would think that he was at a Roman service'.[12] One of Whitby's 'sidesmen' or assistant churchwardens, Kenneth Ingram, ran 'the Society of SS. Peter & Paul' press, and became friendly with Tom.[13]

St Mary the Virgin was an appropriate church where Tom could worship. Father Whitby had commissioned an elaborate altar, candlesticks, and other ecclesiastical adornments from Martin Travers, the enthusiastic Anglo-Catholic artist responsible for restoration work at St Magnus the Martyr. From 1926 onwards, Whitby extended and reconfigured his church, with a new Bourne Street entrance and an arcade of arches framing a large gilded statue of Our Lady of Peace. Designed by Travers in 1920, this statue seems based on a thirteenth-century Golden Virgin in Amiens Cathedral. At St Mary the Virgin Tom was impressed to hear 'the Litany of our Lady' sung 'with the greatest gusto', and to see 'the humbler people' taking 'great pleasure in the Adoration office' – the adoration of the Virgin.[14]

With 'diffidence and desperate reserve' masking 'a sparkling sense of fun', Whitby led a congregation used to high-level discourse that ranged from 'George Herbert and Nicholas Ferrar', the theology of Baron Friedrich von Hügel, and modern scholarship on Donne to 'the Vedanta and the Greeks, and St Thomas Aquinas'.[15] Though more than familiar with all those names, Tom was initially undecided what to make of his parish priest, but stated in early 1928, 'I like Whitby more as I know him a little better.'[16] When Tom wanted someone to explain English prayer-book arguments to 'the French', Whitby suggested Kenneth Ingram; with Whitby, as with fellow churchman George Bell, Tom (sniffy about John Masefield's May 1928 Canterbury 'mystery play' *The Coming of Christ*) also discussed religious drama. 'Well read' and 'artistic', Whitby had a strong sense of theatre. Along with his faith, this had 'inspired him to institute the "Pageant of the

Holy Nativity"'' that had been performed 'by a group of anonymous players from St Mary's Graham-street, at the Chelsea Palace Theatre' in
December 1927.[17] Supported by Lord Halifax and his congregation, Whitby
wanted the Church of St Mary the Virgin to become a remarkable shrine.

Given this church's name, the day termed in the Book of Common
Prayer 'The Purification of Saint Mary the Virgin' was special in its calendar. Each 2 February (sometimes called 'Candlemas'), up and down the
land the officiating priest at Church of England services read from St Luke's
Gospel a passage about 'a man in Jerusalem, whose name was Simeon' and
who had been promised by God 'that he should not see death, before he
had seen the Lord's Christ' in the temple. Traditionally imaged as aged, the
devout Simeon blesses Joseph and Mary. Telling Mary something of what
lies in store for Christ, Simeon signals in a parenthesis that this will be hard
for her: '(yea, a sword shall pierce through thine own soul also)'.[18] Tom was
familiar with the 'Nunc Dimittis', often called in English the 'Song of
Simeon', which forms part of the Anglican liturgy for compline – the formal prayer at the end of the day; this 'Song of Simeon' begins, 'Lord, now
lettest thou thy servant depart in peace: according to thy word. / For mine
eyes have seen: thy salvation.'[19]

Tom wove together these texts in 'A Song for Simeon'. Opening with
the word 'Lord' and spoken by 'one who has eighty years and no to-
morrow', this wintry poem 'written at Chester Terrace' was completed
sometime before the end of May 1928.[20] In several ways, it fitted the Church
of St Mary the Virgin where the devout churchwarden, Halifax, was then
in his late eighties and the priest Whitby was so devoted to the Virgin Mary
whose Seven Sorrows (first of which is the prophecy of Simeon) are
depicted in his church. In its parenthesised lines '(And a sword shall pierce
thy heart, / Thine also)', Tom's poem comes very close to the reading prescribed for 'The Purification of Saint Mary the Virgin', but it also involves
that mixing of life and death which characterises 'Journey of the Magi'.
Tom's Simeon 'Song' hardly makes Christianity sound easy. Its voice is that
of an exhausted man, but one who has found hope.

Poems he wrote around this time are suffused with words and images
encountered in church, or read in the Bible or the Book of Common
Prayer. *Ash-Wednesday* draws on those texts, fusing them with other echoes and memories. I. A. Richards recalled the poet on visits to Cambridge
during this period carrying 'a large new, and to us awe-inspiring, Prayer
Book', and Tom was keenly interested in arguments about Prayer Book
reform.[21] The epistle which the Book of Common Prayer specifies for
reading on Ash Wednesday, the first day of Lent, begins, 'TURN ye even
to me, saith the Lord, with all your heart', and encourages the hearer to

'rend your heart, and not your garments'.[22] *Ash-Wednesday* starts with talk of a decisive 'turn', but if the final title of that work inclines readers towards Christ, then the earlier title of what became its first part – 'Perch'io non spero' – comes from that first line of Cavalcanti's sad *ballata* (ballad) of erotic love.[23]

Articulating its turn towards faith, *Ash-Wednesday*, most of which seems to have been written in 1928, wrestles with itself, struggling to find what Tom, writing of Dante's Beatrice that March, calls a 'means of transition' between 'human and divine love'.[24] The poem's struggle connects with his marital situation, and feelings about Emily. Seven years later he told Spender *Ash-Wednesday* was 'an exposition of my view of the relationship of *eros* and *agape* based on my own experience'.[25] In 1928, however, he was not so forthright.

Now, though Tom maintained she liked her psychiatrist Henri Claude 'very much', Vivien was begging to come home.[26] Tom had reservations – 'she is not fit' – and Vivien still suspected his family and friends of plotting against her.[27] Marguerite Caetani, to whom he would send 'Perch'io non spero', was a trusted confidante. Tom kept from Vivien his fears the *Criterion* might collapse; she had enough troubles, and regarded him as one of them. Not long before heading for France in mid-February he listened in a London street to Scots Guards bagpipers playing the 'Lament for Flodden' at the funeral of Great War Field Marshal Earl Haig. 'There is nothing more dismal and melancholy than the pipers playing that tune. It tears your nerves to pieces.'[28]

Signing herself 'Your outcasted friend', Vivien had written 'Lovingly' from the Malmaison to Ottoline Morrell. She asked not just about Julian's wedding but also about Russell: 'Was Bertie there? Do you see Bertie much now?' As for her marriage, she complained, 'I am very miserable, & it is all quite *useless*. You must have gathered from Tom what a *horrible* mess all this is. But as you can see, he simply hates the sight of me. And I *don't know what to do*.'[29] Sex and religion were again awkwardly compounded as Tom argued solemnly with Dobrée that refraining from true commitment to 'a system' of disciplined religious commitment was 'a kind of *coitus retractatus*'.[30] Religious observance was now a deep need. 'One has to take risks.'[31]

On 21 February 1928, Shrove Tuesday, he had made his first confession. Just days before, he had returned from France with Vivien to London where, she recalled seven years later, they were greeted off the boat train by her mother and brother. Tom had hired a female nurse, E. A. Gordon, who met Vivien briefly that evening then came next day to stay with her at Chester Terrace. Vivien remembered feeling scared, sensing Tom's reluctance to bring her home from France: 'I was out *of my* mind, & so behaved *badly* to Tom & got very excited.' Years later, she recollected it had seemed to her then 'everything he said was a *sneer* or an *insult*'.[32] Whether or not this was persecution mania on her part, the situation was evidently disturbing, adding to Tom's sense of anxious responsibility as he prepared himself for his first confession.

Shrove Tuesday, the day before Ash Wednesday, has associations with feasting before Lent, the season of renunciation, begins. But Tom knew enough ecclesiology to realise that the 'shriving' which gives Shrove Tuesday its name means confessing one's sins and receiving absolution. 'It is a costly experience to make a First Confession', wrote Underhill in a book he worked on in 1928; private confession to God might be 'difficult and purging', but 'for most people the telling out of one's troubles to God in the presence of any other human being is more humiliating, by far, and also more fully liberating'. So 'wonderfully liberating' was confession, Underhill maintained, that 'many eminent doctors now regard it as at least a perfectly normal form of spiritual treatment'.[33]

Underhill was the priest Tom chose as his spiritual counsellor. Two days after Shrove Tuesday, Tom went to stay overnight with Dorothea and I. A. Richards in Cambridge, looking 'gaunt & grim – as if he had burnt himself out', then got 'absurdly drunk – not talkative – just fuddled', listening to gramophone records until about 4 a.m.[34] Nevertheless, Tom's recollection of confession accords with what Underhill described. Writing to Stead in March about his first confession, he felt 'as if I had crossed a very wide and deep river: whether I get much further or not, I feel very certain that I shall not cross back, and *that* in itself gives one a very extraordinary sense of surrender and gain'.[35]

That sense of decisive crossing surely informs the determination not 'to turn again' in *Ash-Wednesday*, the poem whose eventual title sets it in the church calendar immediately after the day Tom chose for his first confession. Though what he confessed to Underhill was utterly confidential, as usual in writing poetry he drew on his emotions and anxieties, as well as on the faith and forms of the church. Since 1988 several scholars have asserted that Tom took 'a vow of chastity' or 'vow of celibacy' during 'March 1928', but no clear evidence for this has been supplied.[36] Certainly, the poet who worshipped at St Mary the Virgin and who had told Faber a few months earlier, 'I have found my own love for a woman enhanced, intensified and purified by meditation on the Virgin', was very much the poet of *Ash-Wednesday*.[37] Explicitly at times, that poem seems to articulate a prayer – one close to a confession of sins, determined to

> pray to God to have mercy upon us
> And I pray that I may forget

These matters that with myself I too much discuss
Too much explain
Because I do not hope to turn again
Let these words answer
For what is done, not to be done again
May the judgement not be too heavy upon us[38]

The voice of the 'I' not only prays but, conscious of sin, asks others to pray too: 'Pray for us sinners now and at the hour of our death'.[39] This 'I' is not directly autobiographical, and the sins are unspecified, though clearly later in the poem the speaker tries to move beyond the 'Distraction' of sexuality and sensuality.[40] Underhill warned against 'Distraction in prayer', and in the Anglican Prayer Book tradition prayers are spoken sometimes by one individual, and sometimes collectively.[41] This was what Tom was used to.

In Whitby's Mary-dedicated sanctuary and elsewhere Tom was familiar, too, with the 'Hail Mary', requesting the Virgin to 'pray for us sinners now and at the hour of our death'.[42] Readers of *Ash-Wednesday* participate in a ritual, a prayer, in which, voicing the poem, they inhabit its 'I' in a manner both moving and disconcerting. Whether or not its readers are wholly in sympathy with the 'Lady' dressed 'In a white gown' (like Dante's lady of *La Vita Nuova* '*vistita di colore bianchissimo*') who 'honours the Virgin in meditation', *Ash-Wednesday* envelops its audience in a dream-state through language drawn from several eras to sound at once timeless and habitable.[43]

Though he professed hostility toward the surrealism then becoming fashionable in England and elsewhere, Tom later admitted he had put images from 'a dream I had' into *Ash-Wednesday* alongside textual echoes and hints of personal memories.[44] Not so long after watching the veiled bride Julian Morrell, he wrote of 'The silent sister veiled in white and blue'.[45] But, as it neared completion, *Ash-Wednesday* with its 'Sister, mother / And spirit of the river, spirit of the sea' would incorporate fragmentary family memories too: if it was decades since Tom's childhood at Gloucester, Massachusetts, where there had been a 'wide window towards the granite shore', then it was still painfully recently that his favourite sister had died, and much of the poem was written while he knew his mother, the Eliot family's other religious poet, was dying.[46] He wrote to her about feeling so 'closely in sympathy' just two weeks before his first confession and while parts of *Ash-Wednesday* and 'A Song for Simeon' were being written or in gestation.[47]

Not for the first time, he felt 'approaching old age', as he joked on the day of his first confession.[48] If some of *Ash-Wednesday* is pressured by what he was undergoing, then others of its long-digested images confirm that

Tom's 'mind' – as he wrote of John Webster's in early 1928 – 'was of the reservoir type'. The Jacobean Webster 'needed to accumulate for a long time before he could transmute into original poetry'.[49] Tom remained pre-occupied with memory and desire: 'debts of poets to their own earlier work are apt to be overlooked'.[50] He stayed uncertain about his work's value, confessing to John Gould Fletcher, 'I often have very grave doubts about my own merit as a poet, but I console myself with the reminder that I often have doubts about everybody else, and that after all it doesn't matter and that none of us will ever know.'[51] Demandingly but also lyrically, *Ash-Wednesday* enacts attempts at spiritual progression. It has proved able to speak to men and women who have undergone their own intense inner struggles; a fine account by A. D. Moody describes reading it with people who have experienced drug addiction.[52]

Underhill's statement that 'each of us is two persons' was particularly true for Tom at this time. Laying bare his most 'hidden life' in confession, he coped, too, with his 'outer life' at Russell Square, where he began working more closely with fellow publisher Frank Morley, eleven years his junior. Born to English Quaker parents in America, Morley had written a PhD on mathematics at New College, Oxford. Afterwards, he had worked for Richmond at the *Times Literary Supplement* before becoming London manager for the New York-based Century publishing company, whose offices were twenty minutes' walk from Russell Square. Like Tom, Morley loved small-boat sailing. Experienced in journal editing, he had helped found – and still co-edited – New York's *Saturday Review of Literature*, the periodical that on 10 December 1927 had first published Tom's 'Salutation'.

Sociable and astute, Morley was a familiar face at *Criterion* dinners. Since at least 1926 he had been important to the magazine's day-to-day financial management. A year later Tom had joked to Dobrée about making portly 'Morley President of the newly founded Bolovian Club' which would require 'Top Hat and Morning Coat at Dinners (Trowsers facultative)'.[53] Yet if Morley was someone to whom he grew close, much of Tom's publishing work, though congenial, was drily formal. He dictated correspondence in businesslike tones: 'Thank you for your letter of the 11th instant.'[54] He attended meetings. He read manuscripts, appraised volumes from Julien Benda's new *La Trahison des clercs* ('a book of the day') to Wilkie Collins's Victorian classic *The Moonstone* ('best of modern English detective novels'), wrote numerous blurbs, and met authors and would-be authors.[55] He regularly perused *The Times* and *Church Times*, defending Maurras in the latter. There were always further obligations. During late February 1928 he 'ruined' his 'peace of mind for two or three days', preparing a lecture to deliver on 1 March at Harold Monro's Poetry Bookshop in Bloomsbury's Great Russell Street.[56]

Having taken British nationality, Tom was required to detail his life to the American vice consul, who had to 'cancel' his 'former citizenship record'.[57] He wrote grandly and approvingly in a *Criterion* commentary piece that Britain as 'the only member of the European community that has established a genuine empire' which, like 'the Roman Empire', was 'world-wide', was crucial as 'the connection between Europe and the rest of the world'.[58] Yet how simple, stark, and revealing was his description of his marriage: 'My wife was British born. We have no children.'[59]

Schooled to repression, he kept Vivien's illness and his inner struggles private. Few saw behind the mask. 'T. S. Eliot, pale, cold and speaking slowly with his soft persuasive voice like a white kid glove', recalled Humbert Wolfe, who accompanied him in an unsuccessful attempt to interest Arnold Bennett in the *Criterion*'s long-drawn financial plight.[60] 'If nothing turns up I propose to stop March', Tom told Read bleakly on 14 January 1928.[61] Yet, slowly, his determined efforts to keep the journal afloat began to succeed. On condition that the now monthly magazine would revert to a quarterly, and might prune its 'excessive amount of philosophy', he secured financing ('£250 per annum for three years') from wealthy Scottish writer and retired businessman F. S. Oliver, biographer of Alexander Hamilton.[62] Other, smaller pledges came too. Once again, the magazine he proudly defended as 'far more international than any literary review in England' looked viable.[63]

Ottoline Morrell visited Vivien at Chester Terrace. Vivien, having 'spoken against' Tom 'so much', thought the encounter went awkwardly. Having a nurse in the house to mind her while he was out cannot have been easy. 'I am very unhappy,' she told Ottoline, '& as you agreed with me – *quite* defenceless. So there it is. If you hear of me being murdered, don't be surprised.'[64] She craved further visits, but Ottoline found her difficult. By mid-March, while builders redecorated three rooms at Chester Terrace, Vivien took to bed: 'influenza'.[65] Though invited, she did not accompany Tom to lunch with Underhill ten days later.

'If Easter is a season of hope, it is also a season when one wants to be given hope', Tom wrote to Stead, adding he was managing 'only to "keep my soul alive" by prayer and regular devotions'. Clearly stressed, he worried his spiritual life might falter. 'I do not know whether my circumstances excuse my going no farther or not.' The two celibate priests to whom he was closest mattered to him increasingly as he continued *Ash-Wednesday*. 'I like Fr Underhill very much; but I feel that Whitby, when I can see him, is more in my line. I feel that I need the most severe, as Underhill would say, the most Latin, kind of discipline, Ignatian or other. It is a question of compensation. I fear that nothing could be too ascetic, too violent, for my own needs.'[66] Years earlier, he had resigned himself 'to celibate old age'; now celibacy could become a discipline.[67] Nothing suggests he and Vivien any longer had a sex life. Long afterwards, he spoke of how 'she had only one emotion: fear, and was terrified of having children'. According to this later account, 'On medical advice they ceased relations.'[68] As for Emily, shortly before Holy Week he had inked 'for Emily Hale from T. S. Eliot' on a copy of his new *Dialogue on Dramatic Poetry*.[69] *Ash-Wednesday* transmuted but did not extinguish his longing. He sublimated, disciplined, and sculpted it. Where Whitby beautified his Belgravia church of the Virgin, Tom made in *Ash-Wednesday* a tribute to his 'Lady' who was part Holy Virgin, part Emily. To him this made an obsessive kind of sense. Despite her occasional visits to England, Emily lived an ocean away, which made her all the safer to correspond with. But Emily, a flesh-and-blood woman in her late thirties, striving to make a living from insecure academic employment and bemused by her strange, distant admirer, was scarcely ready to be confined within a poetic religious reliquary.

'The human soul, in intense emotion, strives to express itself in verse', Tom wrote in his *Dialogue*. 'The Mass is a small drama' as is 'the ritual of the Church during the cycle of the year'. 'The more fluid, the more chaotic the religious and ethical beliefs, the more the drama must tend in the direction of liturgy.'[70] Emily, with her passion for drama, might ponder such words. Linking religious ritual to drama and the 'askesis' of ballet might appeal also to Father Whitby whose style of worship at St Mary the Virgin followed SSPP precepts. The SSPP's *English Holy-Week Book*, which Tom admired, argued that 'The traditional services of Holy Week, as they have been used in the Western Church for well nigh a thousand years, form a single dramatic scheme, as coherent and artistically perfect as an Aeschylean trilogy or a Wagnerian cycle.'[71]

If Whitby's sense of 'beautiful rites' appealed to Tom, then Underhill's understanding of ritual matched his own, encouraging awareness of 'the influence of Greek poetry and drama on the Christian offering of the Eucharist'. Having 'read through *The Golden Bough*', Underhill could relate 'baptism' to 'a rain charm'. He believed the church had 'taken over many primitive ideas, which are embedded deep in man's experience'. 'My faith and prayer are rooted far back in the history of the race.' 'Primitive rites' foreshadowed Christian communion.[72] An attentive reader of anthropology and Newman as well as an enthusiast for poetry, Underhill, perceiving poetry and prayer as connected, was well placed to understand how Tom (who maintained in his March 1928 preface to a second edition of *The Sacred*

Wood that poetry 'has something to do with morals, and with religion') had progressed from *The Waste Land* to *Ash-Wednesday*.[73]

Yet in the long run it was less Underhill's literary tastes than his emphasis on 'constant discipline', 'prayer', and the need to 'saturate our minds with the Word of God' which made him so important to Tom.[74] In Ignatius's '*Spiritual Exercises* he teaches that the very highest perfection of the Christian life is open to lay people no less than to priests', wrote Underhill.[75] Stressing that 'confession must issue in amendment of life', he highlighted the need for 'penitence'.[76] Tom's Anglo-Catholic convert's fervour grew problematic not only for the Woolfs' circle but also for other literary friends including Pound and Aldington. It would be hard, too, for his Unitarian family – and his wife, and, not least, Emily.

Bolovian spoof-theology, boozy *Criterion* dinners, and even the mock-ecclesiastical title Tom gave 'Father Tandy', his bibulous botanist pal from the Natural History Museum, all acted as safety valves.[77] Yet, however subjected to discipline, his personal difficulties persisted, and literary business was hardly straightforward. At Faber & Gwyer, where he soon suggested 'to the members of my Board a series of small books of English Theology', he needed all his diplomatic skill to mediate between Faber and Alsina Gwyer, whose husband Maurice was being sidelined.[78] Worse, Tom's loyal secretary, Pearl Fassett, ill with tuberculosis, intended to resign. Tom and fellow board member Charles Stewart arranged for her job to be held open. She took extended leave, but grew worse.

His mother's health was deteriorating too. Noticing on 23 April that it was St George's Day, the festival of England's patron saint, he felt a heightened awareness of his background: the 'granite, lichens, clapboards etc.' of coastal New England; the 'nigger drawl' he recalled bringing from Missouri as a child; American memories of birdlife, 'bay and goldenrod' – all flood his preface to a 1928 Faber & Gwyer book, *This American World*, just as his sensing 'golden-rod' and 'lost sea smell' heightens *Ash-Wednesday*.[79] Committed to England and England's national church, he remained a son of the United States. He had considered writing a memoir about his American background, *The River and the Sea*, but, as with other plans for longer prose volumes, no book emerged.

'Come & lunch' was his frequent suggestion.[80] In a golden age of publishers' lunches, midday eating and drinking were crucial. He lunched or had tea with literary men – from Cambridge-trained philosopher C. K. Ogden to Orcadian poet-critic Edwin Muir. Sometimes the venue was the Royal Societies Club, St James's Street, where, among the 'old and deaf', he became a temporary member that April.[81] More demanding were social events conflating business with domestic life. In May Vivien was 'extremely nervous' on first meeting the Cobden-Sandersons, along with Alsina Gwyer and Dorothy Pound.[82] Using the phrase 'my wife & I', Tom tried hard to reintegrate her into society.[83] He told Mary Hutchinson Vivien 'has been pining to see you'; he assured Marguerite Caetani 'Vivien has been running her house well and we have seen a good many people', but he worried lest over dinner 'V.' might 'make some statement' that disconcerted people.[84] Virginia Woolf was one such disconcerted guest, and wrote to her sister about the experience:

> Tom is in a great taking with Vivien as mad as a hare, but not confined, and they give parties, where she suddenly accuses him of being in love with Ottoline (and me, but this Ott: threw in as a sop), and Vivien suddenly says when the talk dies down 'You're the bloodiest snob I ever knew' so I have refused to dine there.[85]

Fretting about his wife and her effect on others, Tom often declined evening engagements, but did make several overnight visits alone to Oxford and Cambridge where he spoke, sometimes revealingly, to student societies.

At University College, Oxford, on 16 May Stephen Spender remembered an inebriated undergraduate arguing there could be no 'absolute aesthetic criterion unless there was God'. Bowing his head 'in that almost praying attitude which I came to know well', Spender recalled, Tom 'murmured something to the effect of "That is what I have come to believe." '[86] His faith gave him a sense of absolute and ultimate values, which, as a younger man, he had examined so sceptically; but it did not make life easy. Visiting Cambridge a few days earlier, he 'drank all' his host's whisky on Saturday night, then attended 'Communion the next morning'.[87] In July, in line with Underhill's insistence on 'the importance' of a religious 'Retreat', he participated in one.[88] 'It is, for some,' he reflected that year, 'easier to believe in God than to love Him.'[89]

Over the summer, while coping with decorators, the Eliots hosted at Chester Terrace 'successions of American visitors, my nieces, and various other friends and relatives'.[90] There were also tea parties with the Hutchinsons, but then, in late July, Pearl Fassett died. Though Vivien had a servant to help her and Tom assured people she was 'very well', she grew 'very tired'.[91] They took no holiday. He too found it 'a long tiring summer', and sometimes sought 'asylum' at the Royal Societies Club.[92] Discussion of fascism was in the air. Though Tom continued defending the Action Française, he was more sceptical about rising fascist movements in Italy, England, and elsewhere. These, like communism, he saw as surrogate religions. He devoted space to debates over fascism in his magazine, would write about 'The Literature of Fascism', and went on to correspond with Mary Hutchinson's brother, Jim Barnes, a Catholic convert who covered 'Fascism' for the *Criterion* and enthusiastically supported Mussolini; but Tom would become neither fascist nor communist.[93] Still, his politics could sound scornful: 'Even the *Criterion* public is largely made up of well-meaning intellectual weaklings!'[94] Support for democracy came with a patrician caveat: 'A real democracy is always a restricted democracy, and can only flourish with some limitation by hereditary rights and responsibilities.'[95]

Despite his attraction to Irving Babbitt's ideas on democracy and leadership, theology compelled him more than politics. He urged Richards (with whom he considered co-authoring a book on poetry and belief) to meet American thinker Paul Elmer More, whose *Christ the Word* Tom 'especially' admired. More was in England, visiting Cambridge. 'Of course he has gone over almost entirely to theology, but is still, I think, the most interesting critic in America after Babbitt himself.'[96] Babbitt too was in England. He and Tom — his former Harvard 'disciple' — dined together.[97] Babbitt reproached Tom for being excessively 'secretive' about his beliefs.[98] Tom wrote 'The Humanism of Irving Babbitt' that summer, but, however much he owed them, he had gravitated away from Babbitt and Maurras. While he worked on *Ash-Wednesday* stray remarks in his prose indicate appreciation of a 'good Collect of the English Church' and 'Ave Maris Stella and . . . many another Latin hymn.'[99] He read books on Dante and Beatrice, sure that 'with Dante there is always a foundation of personal human feeling', albeit transmuted through poetic craftsmanship.[100] Dante was his abiding example.

Yet business and temperament bound him to contemporary literature. Joining with 'Mr Forster and Mrs Woolf' and others to contest the suppression of Radclyffe Hall's lesbian novel *The Well of Loneliness*, he resented, too, 'censorship in Boston' and America: 'Censorship has made impossible a critical estimate of Joyce's *Ulysses* for at least a generation.'[101] As critic and publisher he opposed treating literature as if it was pornography. Stung by Babbitt's charge of being 'secretive', he declared his allegiances. Introducing Faber & Gwyer's edition of his friend's *Selected Poems*, he championed Pound's wildly heterodox work. However, collecting several of his own essays on seventeenth-century literature, Baudelaire, Bradley and Babbitt, and dedicating *For Lancelot Andrewes* to 'My Mother', he pronounced his 'general point of view' as 'classicist in literature, royalist in politics, and anglo-catholic in religion'. Doing so, he explained, would 'refute any accusation of playing 'possum'.[102] His phrasing here winks towards the American-inflected nickname, Old Possum, he used in correspondence with Pound. His statement's inflection winks, too, toward Maurras. Even as Tom made himself sound thoroughly English, he did so guided by the Americans and French.

For his fortieth birthday on 26 September 1928 Vivien wanted a *'large gathering'*.[103] He persuaded her a private dinner with her family would suffice. While he assembled *Ash-Wednesday*'s sections, Shakespeare's isolated Coriolanus was in his mind, alongside his own unhappy erotic experiences. Vivien, left *'frightfully* lonely' by Pearl Fassett's death, mourned for her friend. She thought Tom did too, but 'he is *so* reserved & peculiar that he never says anything about it, & one cannot get him to speak. That makes one much more lonely.'[104]

Mary Hutchinson, to whom she confided, suggested to Vivien 'meetings to read Tom's poems & criticize them'. Vivien welcomed this, but went on feeling 'so very very lonely over here in *Chester Terrace'*. She missed their old flat; 57 Chester Terrace was 'too small', 'horribly lonely', 'cut-off'.[105] That September she spent about a shilling a day on cigarettes, trying to cheer herself up with the *Daily Mail* and popular women's magazines *Home Chat* and *Home Notes*.[106] Tom's nervousness about her increased: 'I should not like V. to think that you wished to see me and not her', he told Ottoline Morrell. Vivien was becoming 'feverish', he confided to Mary Hutchinson.[107] Dutifully, the Eliots totted up joint household expenditure. Awkwardly, they tried too hard to socialise. In October Virginia Woolf, who had not severed her contact with the couple in Chester Terrace, confided to her sister that she felt awkward about going

> to the Eliots to discuss Tom's new poems; but not only that – to drink cocktails and play jazz into the bargain, Tom thinking one can't do anything simple. He thinks this makes the occasion modern, chic. He will, no doubt, be sick in the back room; we shall all feel ashamed of our species. He has written some new poems, religious, I'm afraid, and is in doubt about his soul as a writer.[108]

Others, though, were more sympathetically attuned. That autumn, having suggested a new Faber & Gwyer series, 'The Poets on the Poets', he found himself encouraged by Geoffrey Faber to write for it a short study of Dante. Already contracted to produce a full-length volume on Dante for Routledge's 'Republic of Letters' series, he had some delicate negotiating to do. The outcome was that authoring *Dante* for Faber dovetailed neatly with completing *Ash-Wednesday*. Tom never did write the book for Routledge.

He kept up his American connections, encouraging young Southern poet Allen Tate (who thought him 'a Sphinx'), and Harvard student

Lincoln Kirstein whose *Hound and Horn* was modelled on the *Criterion*.[109] He enjoyed meeting Robert Frost and Fletcher, but told Leonard Woolf (who had published it) that Robinson Jeffers's *Roan Stallion, Tamar, and Other Poems* was 'the best verse out of America for a long time'.[110] Soon he would assist Louis Zukofsky, whose poetry struck him as 'honourably Jewish', as well as young Boston-born Ed Dahlberg – who was slightly surprised, after being warned by the poet F. S. Flint, 'Tom does not like Jews.'[111] Long afterwards, when he was asked about this aspect of Tom, Leonard Woolf, his closest Jewish friend and a man alert to the antisemitism that pervaded much English society (including that of Bloomsbury), replied that Tom 'was slightly anti-Semitic in the sort of vague way which is not uncommon', adding that Tom 'would have denied it quite genuinely'.[112] Woolf 'did not know why' Tom was antisemitic, 'and he had never shown any sign of it in his presence'.[113]

To young writers especially, he could seem intimidating, but also shrewdly and dutifully attentive. A little later, Spender recalled being taken to lunch by him at a London club. Spender was then in his early twenties, Tom just over forty. 'His appearance was grave, slightly bowed, aquiline, ceremonious, and there was something withdrawn and yet benevolent about his glance.' Tom's scrutiny of the menu produced a hush, and his pondering the soup seemed a wry yet 'priestly' act. At one of their first meals together, Spender disturbed him a little by choosing smoked eel. 'I don't think I dare eat smoked eel,' Tom opined, and Spender was struck by how close 'the poet's own idiomatic voice' was to that of the Prufrock whom he was 'unconsciously paraphrasing'. Tom's conversation did not 'give the impression of exceptional energy', but had, nevertheless, 'a kind of drive all its own' as it proceeded 'along its rigid lines', making it hard to interrupt or change the subject. Tom asked Spender what he wanted to do. Spender replied, 'Be a poet.' Tom's response was, 'I can understand your wanting to write poems, but I don't quite know what you mean by "being a poet"', and he went on to state gravely that 'poetry was a task which required the fullest attention of a man during his whole lifetime'.[114] Spender was unsettled, unsure he could commit himself so entirely.

Tom's dedication and sense of vocation were intense, partnering his religious commitment, which also involved duties and obligations. For Father Whitby he wrote the introduction to *The Merry Masque of Our Lady in London Town*, the drama which 'the Players from St Mary's, Graham Street' were to perform 'at Chelsea Palace Theatre' in December.[115] The play opens with a 'Tree' one of whose branches 'hangs over Pimlico' in London. Beneath it is 'Mary Virgin' in her 'blue cloak'. Incorporating what Tom called 'immediately recognised' religious language ('Hail Mary, lady full of grace') and biblical passages (Tom highlighted 'O my people, what have I done unto thee'), the masque was written by Charles A. Claye and published by the Society of St Peter and St Paul.[116]

With its '(Bless me father)' and biblical graftings, *Ash-Wednesday* too celebrates its 'Lady'.[117] Claye's verse is of nothing like such a high order. Nonetheless, writing an introductory pamphlet to be given away at performances and bound in with the *Graham Street Quarterly* not only exemplified Tom's devotion to his church; it also dovetailed with his thinking about religious drama. Certainly, during the masque's theatrical run, Tom explained to Herbert Grierson in Presbyterian Edinburgh, 'there is plenty of unpleasant Sainte-Sulpicerie in Anglo-Catholicism' and 'a disposition to feel that whatever is Roman is right'. He confessed, too, that 'the Immaculate Conception' was something 'which I cannot swallow'.[118] But he was committed to Claye's masque.

Claye, he maintained, was doing something 'new'. He was not merely imitating 'an antique form of literature' but 'wishes to revive something of the mediaeval popular attitude towards the divine story'. Tom paraded his own close familiarity with Bible, liturgy, and ritual: 'the *Magnificat* . . . the offices of Holy Week . . . *Tenebrae* – the Mattins of Maundy Thursday, Good Friday, and Holy Saturday . . . The Reproaches . . . the hymn of *Pangue lingua gloriosi* and the other allusions to the Mass of the Pre-Sanctified'.[119] Such a full, committed awareness would shape his writing, helping propel him towards religious drama of his own.

His talent, he joked, was now 'autumnal'.[120] In the wake of the All Souls debacle, why 'waste time' standing as Oxford University's Professor of Poetry? 'I am too disreputable a figure anyhow.'[121] Vivien did not object that he had 'taken up dancing again, & is quite enjoying it (gramophone)'.[122] At home their handyman Janes helped with 'heavy work'.[123] Other servants came and went, Vivien finding them hard to get on with. Social events remained tense. She worried she was ugly; had no new dress; her hands were too rough. 'Dining out is apt to tire her,' Tom told Richards.[124] She put things more forcefully. 'I had a horrible affair at a hair-dresser's last Monday week,' she wrote to Mary Hutchinson, '& I *very nearly died*. All last week I felt terribly ill, & I had to have 2 interviews with doctors. I have been afraid to go out, as I keep on having queer "turns" and feeling faint.'[125]

As Vivien's illnesses depressed them both, Tom found Andrewes' private prayers 'almost indispensable'.[126] Contacting Underhill, he said he 'would very much like to see' him.[127] On the same day as excusing himself from 'serving on the Parish Council' of St Mary the Virgin, he explained to Whitby, 'for reasons which are partly known to you, it is difficult for me to make engagements'.[128] By early January 1929 he was asking Leonard Woolf about a 'matter' concerning psychoanalyst Adrian Stephen, Virginia's brother.[129] Tom's delicate phrasing suggests he was seeking further help for Vivien.

A general election loomed. In an 'intolerable winter', he denounced it as an 'undesirable luxury'. Politicians, judged by their rhetoric, were found wanting. Liberal Lloyd George was 'busy'; Labour's Ramsay MacDonald produced 'dreary sermons'. 'And if we proceed from bad to worse, we arrive at length at the prose style of Mr Winston Churchill.'[130] Though Tom still found 'the sixteenth and seventeenth centuries . . . the most exciting period of English literature', his own prose in the Clark Lectures – 'the weary Donne book' – seemed to him increasingly disappointing, even if he assured his mother those lectures would sell decently when published.[131] Meanwhile, in Bloomsbury, Geoffrey Faber was establishing a new company to take over from Faber & Gwyer. Gwyer, who disagreed with Faber's plans for the company, would stand down, but Faber would remain as chairman, with Tom, Frank Morley, Richard de la Mare, and Charles Stewart as directors. Tom and Morley would run most of the editorial work. Though there was only one Faber, the relaunched firm's name would be 'Faber & Faber' – at least as solid-sounding as Faber & Gwyer.[132]

Tom's proposed directorial salary was '£600' per annum.[133] Soon that metamorphosed into '£400', with an assumption that hours might be highly flexible.[134] The cash was welcome, but the work challenging. With his meticulous diplomatic gifts, he became involved in long-drawn efforts to publish the translated memoirs of Polish politician General Jósef Pilsudski. Unenthused, he turned to Sherlock Holmes for relief, but as international politics on the eve of the Great Depression grew more volatile, the Pilsudski tome deepened his knowledge of Polish and European affairs.

As ever, he was keen to impress his mother: 'My Poems have sold about 3,000 copies, which is very good for poetry.'[135] He signalled dissatisfaction with the 'tiny' rooms of the London house, and explained he was looking for somewhere new.[136] Vivien was surely behind this. 'Never quite sure of being able to keep any engagement', Tom planned to consult psychiatrist Bernard Hart, author of *The Psychology of Insanity*.[137] Vivien's doctor had sent over her clinical notes from France. Visiting her, Ottoline Morrell felt 'trembling', and, 'fearing a scene', took her leave.[138] Perhaps the Eliots should separate?[139]

From Paul Elmer More and other admirers Tom was receiving invitations to lecture in the States. Accepting would allow him to see his mother, but, as things stood, he declined, with some annoyance. 'By the time I am ready to lecture in America, I shall be despised as an old fogey – that time is not far off.'[140] Still, he read 'with great enjoyment' a book prized by several Anglo-Catholic friends. Baron von Hügel's *Letters to his Niece* impressed him by its contention that 'there seem to be certain persons for whom religion is wholly unnecessary'. Not mentioning Vivien, he wrote to More about 'the void that I find in the middle of all human happiness and all human relations, and which there is only one thing to fill. I am one whom this sense of void tends to drive towards asceticism or sensuality, and only Christianity helps reconcile me to life, which is otherwise disgusting.' To him it was 'bewildering' that other people found life easier.[141] Dental extractions worsened his mood. Vivien was exhausted with 'nursing' him.[142]

In late February 1929 he submitted to the recently established British Broadcasting Corporation synopses for a series of six radio talks on seventeenth-century poetry – his Clark Lectures reworked. The BBC wanted 'Tudor Prose' instead. Sometimes he was impatient with requirements to simplify his thinking for non-specialist listeners, but his unrelenting focus on clear analysis, his command of the material, and his attentive ear meant he was good at radio work. It paid well. The talks would appear in the BBC's magazine, the *Listener*, and Tom thought that an agent, David Higham at Curtis Brown, might sell them in America. Soon, intrigued by this modern medium, he bought his first 'wireless'.[143]

By April, however, citing 'mental health' and 'nervous exhaustion', he informed Murry 'we are not seeing anybody at present; we are neither of us well, and Vivien is very worn out'.[144] Fobbing off Massachusetts relations who were visiting London, he struggled to find a suitable new dwelling. His bad temper showed in his journalistic writings. Though hardly enthusiastic about socialists' 'sunset glory', he asserted that the Conservative Party had 'what no other political party at present enjoys, a complete mental vacuum'.[145] Pondering communism and fascism, he declared, 'Man can *believe* almost anything: his capacity for credulity is unlimited.'[146] Still, he could be incisively shrewd: 'I cannot see very much fundamental difference between Nationalism and Internationalism . . . The wise man will pay due respect to both, the fanatic to one.'[147] When Spender asked him that year how he saw the future of Western civilisation, Tom's reply was 'internecine conflict'. He glossed this as 'People killing one another in the streets.'[148]

Virginia Woolf, for whom Tom remained 'a man of genius', found his domestic situation painfully absurd. In May, after a half-hour phone call, she reflected,

I stand for half an hour listening while he says that Vivien cant walk. Her legs have gone. But whats the matter? No one knows. And so she lies in bed – cant put a shoe on. And they have difficulties, humiliations, with servants. And after endless quibbling about visiting – which he cant do these 8 weeks, owing to moving house & 15 first cousins come to England, suddenly he appears overcome, moved, tragic, unhappy, broken down, because I offer to come to tea on Thursday. Oh but we dont dare ask our friends, he said. We have been deserted. Nobody has been to see us for weeks. Would you really come – all this way? To see us? Yes I said. But what a vision of misery, imagined, but real too. Vivien with her foot on a stool, in bed all day; Tom hurrying back lest she abuse him . . . [149]

Frustrated after trying 'Miller's Foot Arches', Vivien (visited, Woolf reported, by 'ten doctors') now appeared 'practically crippled' by 'steep stairs'.[150] She could not go to view the new flat Tom had found at 98 Clarence Gate Gardens – back in their old street, which Vivien missed – but she clamoured to quit Chester Terrace. Tom's attitudes towards women could be intolerant: 'Of course this is a feminist age and one must put up with that', he told Thomas McGreevy, one of several critics now writing books on him.[151] Still, he did his best to consider Vivien's health. He was struggling to meet deadlines for his BBC talks. Not pre-recorded, they went out live. He had to deliver his Dante book for 30 June, five days after he and Vivien were due to move house. Realising that the BBC required him to broadcast one talk on the day of the move, he begged them to change the time 'if humanly possible'.[152] They could not.

Making 'superhuman efforts', he finished *Dante* in late May.[153] It is his most impressive piece of extended prose. Dante is 'a master – I may even say, *the* master – for a poet writing to-day in any language'.[154] Dante was also associated with several of the people he cared about most: Tom's copy of the *Purgatorio* bore his name 'written in Mother's hand'; prefacing *Dante*, he acknowledged her supporter the Harvard Dante scholar Charles Grandgent, as well as the writing and 'table-talk' of '*il miglior fabbro*', Pound.[155] Inscribing *Ara Vus Prec* to Emily, inscribing *The Waste Land* to Faber, and thanking Mary Hutchinson for a gift of books, he drew repeatedly on the same '*tesoro*' passage from Dante.[156] In words Tom published in 1929, 'The experience of a poem is the experience both of a moment and of a lifetime.' His 'familiarity' with Dante had lasted 'twenty years'. Sections he had underscored at Harvard in his Temple Classics edition were passages quoted, later, in his poetry, and now, again, in *Dante*.[157] Though his student editions languished in America, he had bought fresh copies, and pored over them.

Long before committing himself to Christianity, he had marked in his copy of the *Paradiso* the words *'la sua volontate è nostra pace'* (His will is our peace).[158] Now he put his trust in surrender to that divine will. Yet he wrote about Dante not simply out of belief, but as a poet bringing profound trust and insight, so that his comments are singularly perceptive. He contends, for instance, 'that genuine poetry can communicate before it is understood'.[159] Elsewhere, he merges arguments about poetic language with assertions about cultural politics. In English poetry

> words have associations, and the groups of words *in* association have associations, which is a kind of local self-consciousness, because they are the growth of a *particular* civilization; and the same thing is true of other modern languages. The Italian of Dante, though essentially the Italian of today, is not in this way a modern language. The culture of Dante was not of one European country but of Europe.

Surrounded by clamour about 'nationalism', Tom cleaved to Dante as representing what he had called in 'Tradition and the Individual Talent' 'the mind of Europe'. Through the *Criterion* and elsewhere he sought to nurture that mind in the wake of 'the Treaty of Versailles'.[160] 'To enjoy any French or German poetry, I think one needs to have some sympathy with the French or German mind; Dante, nonetheless an Italian and a patriot, is first a European.'[161]

His writing here may hint at unresolved tensions, not least involving English nationalism, but Tom's interest in Dante was also psychological. Dante possessed a 'visual' imagination 'in the sense that he lived in an age in which men still saw visions. It was a psychological habit, the trick of which we have forgotten', but which, 'as good as any of our own', came from a 'disciplined kind of dreaming'.[162] *Ash-Wednesday* attempts to create a modern equivalent of this visionary Dantescan mode, but, like *Ash-Wednesday*, Tom's reading of Dante was pressured by private experience. His *Dante*, he explained to Richards in May, also drew on 'a few notions discussed with you: the idea of the *Vita Nuova* as a manual of sex psychology'.[163] Though this put matters bluntly, Tom's consideration of Dante, again like *Ash-Wednesday*, engages with transmuting 'the recrudescence of an ancient passion', an *'antica fiamma'* (old flame), into 'a new emotion' bound up with 'renunciation'.[164] Discussing the *Vita Nuova* in language that both recalls his thoughts on Baudelaire and anticipates his 1930 poem 'Marina', he stated 'the fact that the love of man and woman (or for that matter man and man) is only explained and made reasonable by the higher love, or else is simply the coupling of animals'. He highlighted Dante's transition from 'Beatrice' to 'the Cult of the Virgin'; the *Vita Nuova* was 'a very sound psychological treatise on something related to what is now called "sublimation" '.[165]

'One outgrows and outlives the majority of human passions', Tom wrote, discussing the *Divine Comedy*.[166] Seeking to move beyond the 'Distraction' of erotic passion ('brown hair over the mouth blown'), *Ash-Wednesday*, as Dante had done, strives towards the 'holy': 'His will is our peace.'[167] Tom's poem can be seen as purgatorial, and in *Dante* – which he described to Pound as 'a small autobiographical fragment' – he quoted lines from the *Purgatorio* on which he had drawn in his poetry more frequently than any others:

> '*Ara vos prec, per aquella valor*
> *que vos guida al som de l'escalina,*
> *sovegna vos a temps de ma dolor.*'
> POI S'ASCOSE NEL FOCO CHE GLI AFFINA

['And so I pray you, by that Virtue which leads you to the topmost of the stair – be mindful in due time of my pain.' Then he dived back into that fire which refines them.][168]

These four lines had yielded him a 1920 book title, a provisional section title plus an embedded quotation in *Ash-Wednesday*, and a line for *The Waste Land*. A further provisional section title for *Ash-Wednesday* came from the line that precedes this Dante passage. Its words are spoken by the poet Arnaut Daniel who is doing penance in Purgatory for lust, and whom Dante had termed '*il miglior fabbro*'. Tom's obsession with these lines may be linked to a long-lasting association of sexual desire with sin. More immediately they connect with his sense of his own 'sensuality' and need for 'severe . . . discipline' at a time when he was conscious not just of his old flame Emily but also of his tormented wife.[169]

Dante was a significant achievement. Further books he planned – *The Outline of Royalism*, *The School of Donne* (based on his Clark Lectures), *The Principles of Modern Heresy* (Tom thought 'humanism' a 'heresy') – were displaced by other pressures.[170] A few days before his 25 June radio broadcast, the Eliots managed to move house. Vivien, 'up to her eyes' in 'getting things straight' at 98 Clarence Gate Gardens, was 'nearly at the end of her strength'. Tom feared the move was 'much more frightful than was anticipated'. The new flat seemed 'a huge barrack and we don't know how we shall ever run it'.[171] In nearby Baker Street tall modern apartments were being built, 'so the clanging of steel goes on all day'.[172] With 'committee meetings every Wednesday and Thursday afternoon', Tom had his Russell

Square office as a refuge.[173] Vivien did not. While he corrected his *Dante* proofs she was 'taken ill' in July; 'pleurisy', Tom told his mother. Vivien's doctor suggested they 'take a two weeks holiday as soon as she can get out'.[174] Writing to Lottie, Tom was, as usual, eager to impress. He informed her in strict confidence that her old acquaintance Professor John Livingstone Lowes, who had moved from Washington University in St Louis to Harvard, was working to ensure 'that I should be nominated at some time for the Charles Eliot Norton Professorship', a prestigious Harvard visiting appointment. Conscious of his mother's frailty, forty-year-old Tom reminded her he was still her boy:

> I have been wearing, what I always keep for very warm weather, the two pairs of white pyjamas you made me. Do you remember them? I do not wear them a great deal, because I want to keep them to wear for a long long time; and even when they are too worn out to wear I shall still keep them![175]

Not for the first time, he was 'going to have lessons in driving a motor car', and hoped Vivien might too. 'She needs to get out of doors more.'[176] Their vacation, predictably, did not materialise. Tom declined a weekend invitation from Read, not wanting to leave Vivien alone in the flat during 'our maid's holiday'.[177] Algar Thorold, editor of the *Dublin Review*, found him 'extraordinarily intelligent' over lunch on 14 August, but 'looking ill'.[178] He had been working hard on an essay, 'Religion without Humanism', where he explained he had found 'discipline and training of emotion' was 'only attainable through dogmatic religion'. Having dedicated *Dante* to Maurras, he addressed, too, his own specific denominational affiliation. He dismissed American Catholicism as often 'vulgar' as well as 'narrow and bigoted'. Protestantism was equally so, or else 'liberal, sloppy, hypocritical and humanitarian'.

> The great majority of English speaking people, or at least the vast majority of persons of British descent; half of France, half of Germany, the whole of Scandinavia, are outside of the Roman communion: that is to say, the Roman Church has lost some organic parts of the body of modern civilisation. It is a recognition of this fact which makes some persons of British extraction hesitate to embrace the Roman communion; and which makes them feel that those of their race who have embraced it have done so only by the surrender of some essential part of their inheritance and by cutting themselves off from their family.[179]

Tom had risked severance from his own family when he married Vivien. Now he wanted them – and especially his mother – to understand his chosen course. 'Suffer me not to be separated' are almost *Ash-Wednesday*'s last words. In one sense they are a prayer to God, but are addressed directly to 'Sister, mother / And spirit of the river, spirit of the sea'.[180] That phrasing suggests Tom's aborted memoir of childhood 'which I was going to call "The River and the Sea"'.[181] *Ash-Wednesday* attempts to combine loyalty to family, including the dead and dying, with loyalty to God, at the same time as transmuting his feelings for Emily. Its sense of difficult torque is its strength. For Vivien, immured in her own struggles, the tangled mesh of Tom's loyalties cannot have been easy. But in his contorted way he tried to make things work: 'For Vivienne with love from her devoted husband' he wrote on her advance copy of *Dante* on 28 August.[182] But duty more than love kept him with her, and the strain was growing too much.

Work, more than alcohol, was his outlet. He read intensely for a 'Five Reviews' short-story competition run by the *Criterion* in collaboration with four other European journals. At last, after many months, a signed agreement arrived from Saint-John Perse, meaning Tom's version of *Anabase* could progress towards publication. Already in 'Journey of the Magi' and elsewhere it had 'affected' his own poetry, and Perse, a lover of '*les mystères essentiels de l'incantation*', knew he had found in Tom a great translator.[183] Busy at Russell Square, Tom lunched with Auden. He issued invitations to another young friend, Donne editor and *Criterion* contributor John Hayward from Cambridge, as well as to visiting Harvard academic Theodore Spencer, who knew Tom's family and would edit a book on Donne. Business activities filled his diary, but at home Vivien pronounced their new flat 'most terrible', '*enormous*', 'hideous'. Desperate to move from Chester Terrace, she had 'left it to Tom to choose it. Very stupid & unfair of me.' Now, after less than three months, she pressured him to 'move again'.[184]

Before they could do so, on 10 September 1929 a cable arrived from America: Lottie had died. 'I fear for Tom', Vivien told Mary Hutchinson, but he had to keep going, even although, a friend recorded later, 'After his mother's death he wanted to stop writing. Why should he go on? What for?'[185] The day after hearing of Lottie's death, he lunched with his elderly friend Whibley, in whom he had confided about his feelings for Emily. She had been in Europe again that summer, as she had been during the previous two summers; but if Tom had any contact with her, it was slight. Having given up her job in Wisconsin, she was returning to Boston where later that year she would 'coach the play' at Simmons College and prepare to deliver several public lectures.[186] For Tom, Lottie's demise clarified things starkly. Later he would tell Emily that 'From the day I married until certainly after my mother's death, nothing held me but the sense of guilt.' He came to believe, or so he told Emily bitterly, that he had spent 'barren unproductive years' with Vivien, 'trying to love someone whom I loathed body and soul'.[187] But in the immediate aftermath of his mother's death he and Vivien did what they could for each other. Recriminations came later.

Tom was due to see Joyce, who had been holidaying with his family in Torquay, and whose *Anna Livia Plurabelle* – part of what would become *Finnegans Wake* – Faber & Faber hoped to publish in 1930.[188] More BBC work was coming Tom's way, but, confronting the loss of his mother, he felt 'suddenly and irrevocably middle-aged'.[189] 'Not very eager to appear in public during the rest of this year', he needed to muster his energies for yet another house move – along the road to 177 Clarence Gate Gardens – on 1 October.[190]

While all this was going on he had to sign 400 copies of a limited edition of his new Ariel Poem, 'Animula'. 'O my God! I forgot there would be 400 of 'em.'[191] But he signed dutifully. The poem, whose Latin title means 'little soul', was written before his mother's death, around the same time as *Dante*. In *Dante* he ponders connections between poetry and biography, and quotes lines about '*l'anima semplicetta*' (the simple soul), linking them to Aristotle's *De Anima*. Alluding to Dante's *Purgatorio* in its first line, ' "Issues from the hand of God, the simple soul" ', 'Animula', which Tom called 'rather depressing', goes on to present the soul as a small child in a rich, happy, privileged, bookish environment, rather like that of his own childhood, yet one suffused too with 'the pain of living'. Disconcertingly, the reader glides from childhood imagery to awareness of haunted age, 'Denying the importunity of the blood, / Shadow of its own shadows, spectre in its own gloom'. Immediately afterwards comes death, though also possible salvation, and encouragements to 'Pray'.[192] Informed by autobiography, but also ghosted by echoes and memories of other people, real and imaginary, 'Animula' signals evasions, transience, and vulnerability, as well as spiritual need. It dwells on childhood, and features death, but omits almost everything between. A copy 'for Emily Hale from T. S. Eliot' crossed the Atlantic.[193]

'I believe we are now settled for some time at 177, Clarence Gate Gardens', Tom informed Sacheverell Sitwell.[194] Vivien relished displaying flowers against its 'black & gold curtains'.[195] After meeting Aldous Huxley, Tom told Marguerite Caetani, 'We like his wife very much.'[196] Not all his contact with authors was enjoyable. He complained that in publishing 'There is a perpetual struggle between one's ideals and the necessity of hitting the market; most of the books one publishes are intellectually and morally worthless; you are interested in poetry and you have to sit up planning the "lay-out" of a book on cricket, or the memoirs of some eminent nincompoop; and insensibly it becomes harder to read any book for profit or enjoyment, or to judge any book except commercially.'[197]

As for his own poetry, now he had all six parts of his new sequence, provisionally titled *Ash Wednesday Music*, and he went on pondering childhood: 'as I get older, I find myself turning more on St Louis', he told Henry, longing to see him again. He was happy Henry would inherit all the copies of his books he had sent to his mother. Tom hoped Lottie's poems might be published, but wanted to make sure all his own letters to her 'should be destroyed; I do not want to read them again, and I do not want anyone outside of the family ever to have access to them'. Telling Henry about life in the 'rather close correct Oxford atmosphere of Faber & Faber', Tom explained he had to supplement his earnings with literary work of all sorts. 'I begin, I confess, to feel a little tired at my age, of such irregular sources of income. I have begun life three times: at 22, at 28, and again at 40; I hope I shall not have to do so again, because I am growing tired.'[198]

On the advice of her doctor, to cheer Vivien up, he bought a Morris Minor, 'a minimal car' which she drove alarmingly. Tom's map-reading and advice infuriated her. 'You'll have to drive like hell', he urged, approaching a long incline.[199] Typing private letters, he boasted to his old Harvard room-mate Howard Morris about becoming 'more & more dissolute and shady', sending Morris verses about 'Chris Columbo', 'the Chaplain', and buggery 'on the alter [sic]' to prove it.[200] His translation of *Anabase* advanced to proof stage, but 'a variable though slight influenza' dogged him through November.[201] Not for the first time, he considered translating one or two of Hugo von Hofmannsthal's German 'Jacobean verse plays back into Jacobean', but as little came of this as had come of hopes he might some day complete a full-length *Sweeney Agonistes*.[202] Though he disliked the translation, he produced an introduction for Christopher Isherwood's Englishing of Baudelaire's *Intimate Journals*. Strikingly, Tom argued that 'Baudelaire's Satanism' was 'an attempt to get into Christianity by the back door' through his awareness of 'Sin in the permanent Christian sense'. Baudelaire's 'suffering' implied 'the possibility of a positive state of beatitude'. His linking of Baudelaire to Laforgue and to Hulme on 'Original Sin' implies that his own journey towards faith via scepticism, despair, and suffering may have led to Christianity by a 'back door' route.[203] Recognising that Baudelaire's 'insistence upon the evil of love' and 'the sexual act as evil' might have 'psychopathological causes', he saw 'no need to pry' into these. Instead, 'the correction to the *Journaux Intimes*, so far as they deal with the relations of man and woman, is the *Vita Nuova*'.[204] This, from the poet of *Ash-Wednesday*, is revealing.

Gifts arrived: from Mary Hutchinson a cherry-wood bowl for Tom and a necklace for Vivien. But the discontented Eliots were already resolved to shift from 'this dismal flat'.[205] Tom smoked himself hoarse on a Christmas cigar. At least his driving was progressing somewhat. He explained to Mary's husband Jack he could drive as far as the Hutchinsons' house, provided Jack would 'turn the car round so that I can drive back'.[206] After a Christmas Day excursion, Vivien thought Tom 'perfect master' of the car. Another 'nice short drive' ensued.[207] Excusing himself from an invitation to Dobrée's 'HOGMANY HILARITIES', he planned a get-together of *Criterion* cronies (all-male as usual) for later in January, typing the programme for an 'OPEN WIRELESS VAUDEVILLE' whose cast would include

T. S. Eliot
The Bellowing Baritone
With Bolovian Ballads
'The Blue Baboon'[208]

More seriously, he told Livingstone Lowes in Massachusetts that he had turned down the invitation to lecture at Harvard, partly because he did not want to 'visit Cambridge so soon after my mother's death'.[209] He felt able neither to leave Vivien in London, nor to ask her to accompany him. Religion was his sole mainstay, but he confessed to Murry that 'the more confidently I accept the dogmas of the Church – the more puzzling and mysterious they become'.[210]

6

Love and Separation

THOUGH Anglo-Catholic rather than Roman Catholic, Tom developed lasting friendships with several Roman Catholic priests in England and America. Sometimes mocked for it, he admired monasticism. His Jesuit contemporary, Father Martin D'Arcy, a *Criterion* contributor teaching at Oxford's Campion Hall, shared his admiration for Aquinas, that philosopher whom Dante revered. Tom had acquired through subscription sixteen volumes of the 'Desclée edition' of Aquinas.[1] Seeking to follow Dante in drawing on 'the "truest"' philosophical and theological thought, he wanted a Christian 'humanism' sufficient 'to reconcile the mystic and the ecclesiastic in one church'.[2] Sure where he stood, he established foundations for his future work.

Intelligence always attracted him, and he attracted intelligent people, not least on his regular visits to the narrow confines of Oxford and Cambridge. At those almost exclusively male, increasingly secular universities many of his younger supporters, including Richards, Spender, and William Empson, were atheists or agnostics, disconcerted by the *Waste Land* poet's conversion. Others, however, sympathised with his January 1930 statement 'that you must either take the whole of revealed religion or none of it'.[3] Tom was stringent yet generous towards Missouri-educated Father F. J. Yealy, whose Cambridge thesis on Ralph Waldo Emerson he had examined in 1928. In 1930 for an expanding Criterion Miscellany pamphlet series he commissioned the older, Mayfair-based Jesuit Charles Martindale to write on censorship and Catholic readers. Like Lord Halifax and other Anglo-Catholics, Tom sought deeper dialogue between Anglicanism and Roman Catholicism. He liked to style himself Catholic, rather than Protestant.

'Heresy', he proclaimed, 'is always with us', but as poet and publisher he resisted simplistic policing of his imagination.[4] He was quite clear that the communist Auden, whose 'verse play *Paid on Both Sides'* he called 'brilliant' in January 1930, was 'about the best poet that I have discovered in several years'.[5] Other discoveries, including Joseph Gordon Macleod (whose *The Ecliptic* came from Faber in 1930), were less sure-fire. Still, Tom hoped his own work, alongside that of Pound and other Francophiles, had changed the literary climate. He asserted it was 'now taken for granted that the current of French poetry which sprang from Baudelaire is one which has, in these twenty-one years, affected all English poetry that matters'.[6]

Yet poetry made his firm little money. Tom was keen they try to 'capture' a 'market' for crime fiction. Sharing his Sherlock Holmes enthusiasm with fellow directors, he wondered, 'Is not the proper game in this line to get a man who can turn out one good book a year, and back him for a long period?'[7] His question was astute, but misguided in terms of gender. In the golden era of English detective stories, instead of publishing Dorothy L. Sayers or Agatha Christie, Faber made do with the likes of Stacey Bishop (pen-name of Pound's musical protégé George Antheil) and Richard Hull. In detective theology they were more successfully innovative: assessing A. H. Ross's typescript about Christ's resurrection, *Who Moved the Stone?*, Tom found it 'as absorbing as a detective story'; it sold outstandingly.[8] Publicising it, he contacted influential clerics including D'Arcy, as well as Bishop George Bell, *Church Times* editor and president of Britain's Religious Drama Society. Strategically, but sometimes a little awkwardly, he dovetailed faith and business interests. Dating his letter 'Charles King & Martyr' (i.e., 30 January) 1930, he wrote from his office to the Reverend Charles Harris, chairman of the book committee of the English Church Union, based nearby in Russell Square.[9] Next, Tom joined Harris's Committee, agreeing to help edit a new *Encyclopaedia of the Christian Religion*. Soon Tom gave the Church Union's Russell Square address as that of Faber & Faber.[10]

Happy to have been introduced to Harris by Stead, he appreciated, too, Stead's 'solicitude' in 'more personal matters'. He informed Stead in early February he was seeing 'Francis Underhill pretty regularly', finding him 'helpful to me personally'.[11] In a BBC talk on 7 March, Tom recommended 'the *Exercises* of Ignatius, and something of St John of the Cross, such as *The Dark Night of the Soul*, or *The Ascent of Mount Carmel'*.[12] He joked to All Souls don A. L. Rowse that 'an editor's existence is very ascetic'; for Ash Wednesday he contemplated eating 'dried haddock'.[13] His Christian asceticism, much modified by alcohol and cigarettes, underpinned his difficult life. His old mentor Whibley ('my dearest friend') died in France that March.[14] Aware Tom was experiencing strain and 'financial worries', Faber (whom Tom sometimes considered dully respectable, but on whose shrewd loyalty and leadership he came to rely) raised his salary.[15] Having 'moved twice in the last year, and recently having gone as far with three houses as giving references' before withdrawing, the Eliots prepared for yet more relocation.[16] Virginia Woolf informed Clive Bell, 'Tom by the way writes today that he is just moving to a house, from a flat, – the 5th move in 6 months; which means I suppose that the worm in Vivien turns and turns, and not a nice worm at that.'[17]

In the aftermath of their mother's death, Henry had sent an autobiographical fragment she had written, along with his father's 1863 graduation address, 'Philosophy: The Science of Truth'. Tom reflected on 'the characters of two very wonderful people' whose happy marriage shamed his own.[18] Aware he and Vivien would have no children, he pondered paternity, amongst 'an inferno of private difficulties and embarrassments'.[19] Their April Fool's Day move to 43 Chester Terrace returned them to the area Vivien had scorned – though now she maintained their previous house there had been 'nice'.[20]

'Very sick', she was annoyed: they were moving 'not with much *hope*'.[21] A sofa, tables, bedroom furniture, and 'All my pictures', had to go into storage, at least until their new house was renovated.[22] Quite apart from the removal, she was upset that in Italy her thirty-three-year-old brother had married twenty-five-year-old dancer, Emily ('Amhé') Cleveland Hoagland. 'A fearful shock', it had happened 'suddenly'. Now Maurice 'arrived back with a sick wife. An American. Very young.'[23] Vivien's own marriage to an American had been hasty; her brother's vexed her. Sympathetic to the new bride's appendicitis, but struggling to combine moving house with his weekly radio broadcasts, Tom wrote tetchily to the *Nation and Athenaeum* about D. H. Lawrence, who had died recently, and expressed 'vexation' that *Ash-Wednesday*, which might have been published on Ash Wednesday, would not appear until 29 April.[24]

Unsettled, he had had to decline an invitation to deliver the Turnbull Lectures at Johns Hopkins University, but his mind kept turning to America, and not just to his family and Emily Hale, who, having left Milwaukee-Downer College by now, and, having returned to Massachusetts, was trying to live as a freelance speaker, lecturing in Boston (where her uncle John Perkins had become minister at the Unitarian King's Chapel) on such topics as 'The American Theatre, From Both Sides of the Footlights'.[25] His old Harvard philosophy teacher James Woods received a fond letter from him in April, and Tom's cousin, naval historian Samuel Eliot Morison, helped ensure Tom was elected to the Colonial Society of Massachusetts whose published proceedings detailed local history, traditions, and New England sailing expeditions. It was fifteen years since Tom had seen Massachusetts. He and Vivien holidayed 'at the seaside' in Eastbourne in late April.[26] Before they left, he sent out advance copies of *Ash-Wednesday*, including one to John Hayward, now a 'great friend'.[27] When Hayward thanked him, and outlined his own psychological struggles, Tom replied he too had known

> very well that sort of discouragement and almost panic. I don't think I have so much of it now; but then it has taken me nearly forty-two years to acquire a faint perception of the meaning of Humility – the first of the virtues – and to see that I am not a person of any great importance. It is exactly as if one had been living on drugs and stimu-lants all one's life and had suddenly been taken off them. I know just enough – and no more – of the 'peace of God' to know that it is an extraordinarily painful blessing.[28]

Returned from holiday, by early May 1930 he had drafted – even if he feared it might be 'only half baked' – one of his most beautiful poems.[29] Full of images of sailing, 'Marina' draws on his youthful voyages up the New England coast. 'The scenery in which it is dressed up is Casco Bay, Maine.'[30] It is suffused, too, with meditations on loss and parenthood. Though he and Vivien expected no children, this poem is intensely parental.

Its 'theme is paternity', Tom told his English-domiciled American friend, artist Edward McKnight Kauffer, who illustrated this new 'Ariel Poem'.[31] Years later, having experienced being a godparent, Tom confessed to Hayward (who was also childless) that in the past he had felt 'acutely the desire for progeny'.[32] In an era when such male wishes were seldom articu-lated in literature, 'Marina', whatever else it does, articulates a longing for a child. Suggestive of boats and the sea, its title is also the name of a father's lost, miraculously rediscovered daughter in Shakespeare's *Pericles*. Reread-ing that play, Tom had come across interpretations of it in a typescript whose young scholarly author, G. Wilson Knight, was fascinated by pat-terns of imagery. Later in 1930 Tom wrote an introduction for Knight's *The Wheel of Fire*, and inscribed a copy of 'Marina' to him 'with, I hope, some appropriateness'.[33] Along with its title, the poem's epigraph, Tom explained to Knight, suggests 'a crisscross between Hercules waking up to find that he had slain his children, and Pericles waking up to find his child alive' – so one man finds himself utterly childless, while another, Pericles, discovers he has a living child.[34]

Like much of Tom's poetry, 'Marina' works through suggestion and allusion. In no way directly autobiographical, it nevertheless draws on personal experience, nourished by deep feeling, astute intelligence, and a remarkable poetic ear. Its opening is suspended between stunned disloca-tion and longing for relationship:

> What seas what shores what grey rocks and what islands
> What water lapping the bow
> And scent of pine and the woodthrush singing through the fog
> What images return
> O my daughter.[35]

Alternating in length, these lines let their surprisingly unpunctuated elements float. Line-breaks guide and are guided by syntax, while them-selves acting as punctuation. This opening is crucial to the poem's acoustic. 'Marina' is so striking a sound system because of the way its lines ebb and flow. The whole poem is filled with tidal movement, most obviously in its second verse paragraph when four different long lines up to fifteen syllables in length alternate with the repeated monosyllabic line, 'Death'. Aspects of 'Marina' may be ghosted by Kipling's short story of hidden children, 'They', and by Walt Whitman's whispering sea in 'Out of the Cradle End-lessly Rocking' with its 'Death, death, death, death, death.'

Yet 'Marina' has a soundscape all of its own. Its internal rhymes are incantatory and astonishing. Rhymes are placed not only within a line – 'By this grace dissolved in place' – but also across the division of the verse para-graphs, so that, traversing the gulf between sections, the rhyme is picked up again, mid-line: 'What is this face, less clear and clearer.' Here and else-where, end-rhyme, so often confined within one verse or verse paragraph of a poem (other than, say, in a villanelle), is continued across the verse paragraphs, bridging the separation. This acoustic of separation, apparent disjunction, that is overcome by an act of joining – of rhyme – parallels the way the separation, the loss, of forgetting is balanced against the recall of memory. Sounds and images in 'Marina' seem far off, only to emerge close up. Remote, they re-emerge as internal – 'more distant than stars and nearer than the eye'.[36] Islanded yet joined, scattered but netted, they are lost but found. For many readers, it is in his finest poetry rather than in social or critical writings (which are most compelling when closest to the music and making of poetry) that this poet best sets out his deeply held ideas of order. The word-music, the sound system, most fundamentally carries the meaning. 'Marina' became Tom's favourite among his poems.

It may be right to relate this poem of longing to his transmuted sense of Emily, who was crossing the Atlantic with her aunt and uncle to England that summer, and who received a signed copy. Yet the poem's paternal use of the word 'daughter' points in a direction different to that of *Ash-Wednesday*'s 'Lady'. Biographically, 'Marina' is all the more moving for coming from a childless male poet able to articulate so feelingly longing for a child. For some, it is predominantly a religious poem of 'hope'.[37] Like Tom's other 'Ariel Poems' it works through paradox, confusing birth and death to imagine a rebirth, however painful. But it is also the finest father–daughter poem in the English language.

The day after sending manuscripts of 'Marina' to Sir Michael Sadler, master of University College, Oxford, who craved an Eliot manuscript for the Bodleian Library's archives, he wrote with habitual courtesy, honesty and wry humour to an Indiana high-school student. The boy had sent questions. 'I am sorry for you', Tom replied, 'for being a senior in high school, which is a painful moment in life.' By 1930, Tom was used to enduring painful moments. The boy, James Nixon, had asked if he ever intended to 'make a lecture tour of the United States'. Tom answered, 'I should very much like to give some lectures in America.'[38] But the poet who had recently deleted from 'Marina' a specific Maine place name (that of densely wooded Roque Island with its beautiful beach), did not yet feel able, except in memory and imagination, to revisit his and Emily's native land.[39]

Instead, at last, Faber & Faber were publishing on 22 May his *Anabase* translation. This long poem in cadenced prose brims with awareness of displacement, migration, and landscape, but is devoid of place names. Considering *Anabase* 'one of the most remarkable poems of this generation', Tom had been 'paid to translate it'.[40] Doing so nourished several 'Ariel Poems' but his own awareness of landscape was subtly different. To Kauffer he confessed, 'no scenery except the Mississippi, the prairie and the North East Coast has ever made much impression on me'.[41] As his childhood memories sent to a St Louis newspaper that year testify, his internalised America held deep 'intensity'.[42] Yet day-to-day America could be annoying. Contractual wrangles over republishing *The Waste Land* in New York prompted possible 'legal' action. Involving Henry and Faber colleagues in negotiations, he determined to retain copyright of 'my longest and most profitable poem'.[43]

Poetry and publishing needed toughness. Aldington was not best pleased when Tom requested clarification about how many copies of Aldington's poetry titles for which Faber acted as agent on behalf of the former Egoist Press should be 'destroyed'. Like volumes by Marianne Moore and by Pound (thirty-five copies sold in six years), they lay in limbo. Concerned lest Aldington's 'feelings' towards him had changed, Tom expressed 'affection and gratitude' for past help, but was undeflectable.[44] Aldington's powerful war novel *Death of a Hero* (1929) had mocked Tom as the 'very great man' and Tory snob 'Mr Waldo Tubbe' from 'the Middle Western districts of the United States' who championed 'Royalism in Art, Authority in Politics, and Classicism in Religion'.[45] Tom made no reference to that when writing about destroying Aldington's books.

Commercial and writerly experience helped him advise emerging writers. 'Poetry should be discouraged', he told a young priest. 'Those who can bear that burden will assume it in spite of everybody and everything and in spite of what they themselves, in lucid moments, recognise as best for them.'[46] His advice could be daunting, but shrewd. 'Of course being at Oxford is paralysing to you', he told Spender. 'Residence in a University, enforced for three or four years, is unpleasant to anyone who is eager for artistic expression; but my belief is that it is best to put up with it. It may take you a year or two to recover; but the experience, and even the holding-back is useful in the long run.'[47] His personal experience haunted him, but he hid its intimate aspects. Touched to receive from Henry family mementoes left by their mother, including a 'little old Bible', perhaps 'the one we read from on Sunday mornings' in St Louis, he made sure his own letters home became 'ashes', recalling them as full of 'folly and selfishness'. 'If I could destroy every letter I have ever written in my life I would do so before I die. I should like to leave as little biography as possible.'[48]

He informed Henry that for the umpteenth time they were relocating, now to '68, Clarence Gate Gardens'.[49] After just two months, this involved abandoning their Chester Terrace house which Tom now thought 'perfectly unsaleable'.[50] Maurice Haigh-Wood sympathised – 'filthy luck'.[51] Tom continued helping Vivien's mother with her late husband's estate, in addition to discussing cars with Maurice. Vivien was still, Tom told Virginia Woolf in late June, 'not . . . at all well'.[52] She drove around London, though, visiting her ailing mother. About a month later, citing his wife's 'poor health', Tom turned down an offer of hospitality from George Bell.[53]

He confided to Paul Elmer More that religion had brought him 'not happiness, but the sense of something above happiness and therefore more terrifying than ordinary pain and misery'; perhaps explicating this, in the context of 'important decisions', he explained that for certain individuals these 'have consequences for all the rest of our mortal life. Some people find themselves consequently in circumstances such that the whole of their mortal life *must* be a torment to them.'[54] More was not his confessor, but this has the ring of confession; Tom's most tormenting decision had been to marry Vivien. Gloomily, he contemplated 'death' and 'the end of the world'. 'I live, so far as I live at all, in that sense of imminent peril.'[55] He was hardly cheered by reviews of *Ash-Wednesday* which he felt misunderstood it, or treated it simply as ' "devotional" verse'.[56]

At work, where Tom was arranging with Joyce to publish *Haveth Childers Everywhere* (a further instalment of what became *Finnegans Wake*), a new director joined Faber in August. George Blake, a novelist, was a friend of Morley's. After journalistic work in Glasgow and London, he ran Edinburgh's Porpoise Press with fellow Scot George Malcolm Thomson whom Tom later encouraged 'to come out as a [Scottish] nationalist'.[57] Morley appreciated the 'very interesting Scottish nationalistic movement' which was 'producing some brilliant writers'.[58] For the next two years Blake would take charge of Faber's fiction list, before returning to Edinburgh where Faber & Faber took over the Porpoise Press. Tom liked him, and admired Thomson's 1930 pamphlet *Will the Scottish Church Survive?* Though he had not visited Scotland, he praised 'these young men' who were 'really ambitious to do something for their country, ardent nationalists – I share the views of my friends of *Action Française* about local self-government – and if they can get together other writers as good as Thomson himself I think they may do something interesting.'[59] Certainly Tom enjoyed adopting the accent of upper-class London clubmen ('a lunch depends on the happy combination of host, guests, cooking, wine, brandy and cigars') and drinking with his *Criterion* chaps at Poetry Bookshop evenings, or joining the 'Temple Bar Club' organised by Kenneth Ingram from St Mary the Virgin to debate 'religious and philosophical questions'.[60] However, his interests ranged beyond metropolitan and Oxbridge elites.

Neither he nor Vivien holidayed that summer, but they did see friends, including female companions from Tom's youth. His cousin Eleanor and her mother did not visit as they had done in 1929, but Eleanor's friend Penelope Barker Noyes met Tom and Vivien several times. Penny had been at the Berkeley Street School in Cambridge, Massachusetts, with Eleanor and Emily. Later, while at Radcliffe College, she had moved in amateur-dramatics circles when Tom fell in love with Emily. Tom knew Penny carried back 'reports' of his married life. More consequentially and riskily, he and Vivien met Emily herself once 'this summer' (probably in early September) when she came 'to tea'.[61] Tom made clear to her he was happy Vivien had liked her 'so much – to the point of infatuation!' Clearly the visit had been awkward ('a great shame to me at the time'), but he was glad it had taken place. 'Far better, in the circumstances, than seeing you alone.'[62]

Emily's dear friend Mary Parker had married her sweetheart Leon Foss (a Harvard graduate and war veteran) and was now a young mother. Emily, still single, was conscious her own situation was very different, but, reciting, lecturing, performing, and coaching actors, she valued a certain spirited, sometimes lonely, independence. Tom thought that Emily's love of acting had helped liberate her from some of Boston society's restrictive atmosphere, and, as the twenty-first-century commentator Paul Keegan has pointed out, he came to regard Emily at times as someone with a rather theatrical 'plurality of personae – "the Emily of Fire & Violence" – like a closely kept hand of cards'.[63] In 1930, as well as holidaying in the Cotswolds, she was attending a Shaw drama festival in Great Malvern during late August, and visiting London where she gave some lectures. When they met, she and Tom spoke, among other things, about modern poetry. Afterwards, he mailed at least three transatlantic 'parcels of books' to her at 41 Brimmer Street, Boston, where she then lodged with the wealthy elderly Unitarian Mary Lee Ware whose cosmopolitan elegance, high standards, and dedication to young people she regarded as exemplary.[64]

Later in the 1930s, Emily wrote her only free-standing publication, an extended obituary for Miss Ware whose love of 'music, painting and poetry' and whose passion for reading poetry aloud 'with an underlying reverence for thought and word audible in her voice' the elocution enthusiast Emily shared. Like Emily's father and Emily herself, Miss Ware loved Italy, and Emily's account suggests that the two women may have travelled together there, as well as having a mutual love of New England landscapes from New Hampshire (where Emily was familiar with Miss Ware's farmestate at West Rindge) to Boston's Charles River. Best remembered today for her family's role in gifting to Harvard University its famous collection of glass flowers, Mary Lee Ware, who had 'worshipped since a child' at 'the historic King's Chapel in Boston', loved botany, the religious art of Fra Angelico, and European travel. Writing of Miss Ware in a rather mannered, old-school Bostonian style, Emily saluted and shared this mentor figure's love of 'high resolve and sensitive consciousness', her deploring of 'lowering of standards in a great Democracy', and her fondness for transatlantic friendships on 'both sides of the water'.[65] In some ways, for all her independence, Emily, while she might deploy phraseology from the Anglican Prayer Book, remained a committed Unitarian, and represented, like Miss Ware (at whose Boston home Tom, in 1931, recalled dining 'once or twice, years and years ago'), the high-toned, familial Boston Unitarianism against which he had reacted, and which he, the son of Henry Ware Eliot, could never forget.[66] But Emily meant much more to him than that, and, however decorously he concealed his emotion, he was overjoyed to see her again.

For her part, however interesting she found Tom, Emily had reservations. Surviving notes for one of her lectures (apparently from around 1929) present this poet as 'Gifted, so much to say he falls down under it – *ironic incisive complex bitter.*'[67] But now he made it clear he wanted her to understand him better, and sought to be useful to her as she developed her lectures. Mailing her books, he made sure to include René Taupin's *L'Influence du symbolisme français sur la poésie américaine, de 1910 à 1920*, which contained discussion of his own verse. Having taken trouble to get her this volume, in which (he explained to her in a letter dated 17 September) F. S. Flint had made 'marginal notes for your benefit', Tom also arranged to send poetry by Roy Campbell whose 'flamboyant vigour' he singled out. Signed 'yours in haste' and initialled 'T.S.E.', his letter shows him going further than 'haste' might imply. Trusting her discretion, he was edging towards making her again, as she had once been, his trusted confidante: 'I am afraid that I find the Sitwells hopelessly dull, although they are very nice people.'[68] He wrote to her several times in October. Soon, encouraged by her replies, he corresponded incessantly.

He mailed her, too, T. E. Hulme's *Speculations*, singling out Hulme's 'very beautiful' poem 'Conversion'. Its 'hyacinths' accompany a sense of overwhelming 'beauty', thwarted sexuality and awkward, lost 'loveliness'. Tom made clear to Emily, as she prepared her script for lecturing, 'I hope that I may, in some way or another, see the text of your lecture and of anything you write.'[69] Close trust, deep familiarity, but also an implied carefulness: all these he sought to encourage, telling her, 'I have no really intimate friends, though a vast acquaintance.' But he went much further. As early as the start of October, using his business rather than his home address, he posted her what was clearly 'a love letter'. 'Praying' it would give 'no offence', he described his love as 'as pure and unsullying as any love can be'.[70] Nine days later, anxiously awaiting her response, he sent *London: A Poem and The Vanity of Human Wishes by Samuel Johnson with an Introductory Essay*, inscribed simply 'for Emily Hale from T. S. Eliot 15.x.30'.[71]

On Friday 31 October Tom went to confession. Next day, All Saints' Day, he went to communion, then stopped by his office, looking for mail. There, as he had hoped, he found a 'lovely and saintly' letter from Emily. It seemed to him 'a Gift of Divine Grace'. Greatly relieved, he explained to Emily afterwards that he had been told by Underhill at confession that 'it was not wrong for me to love you and to cherish your thought and image in my heart, but that it was a gift of God to help me in troubles and for spiritual development'. After a month of waiting in 'torment', suddenly reading her letter made him 'happier than I have ever been'. He saw stretching ahead of him 'the only kind of happiness now possible for the rest of my life'. Even though it was 'the deepest happiness which is identical with my deepest loss and sorrow', it brought him, he informed her in his passionate reply, 'a kind of supernatural ecstasy'.[72]

Calling her 'Love' and 'Lady', hymning her 'blessed face', his letter set the tone for innumerable further letters, its 'intense and strong devotion' mixing erotic frisson (he longs to 'stroke' 'radiantly beautiful' Emily's 'forehead'; he protests, 'I love you'; he would be 'extremely jealous' of any other man who 'cared for you as I have') with a rhetoric of heightened friendship approaching worship. He protested she was central to his inner life: 'I want you to know how utterly, from now, I shall depend upon you as a friend, and as long as you are in this world I shall want to stay here too.'[73]

Across the Atlantic, in Boston, juggling engagements as a freelance lecturer, and coping with the constant worry of her institutionalised mother alongside her own ever-precarious employment prospects and acting engagements, Emily was not entirely sure what to make of these outpourings from her unhappily married admirer who now assured her 'my love for you has been the one great thing all through my life'. He perceived she had suffered. He felt guilty: when they had first met, 'immature for my age', Tom had been 'timid, discouraged, and intensely egotistical'. Now he asked her forgiveness. Without naming the woman, he confessed his affair with Nancy Cunard, then made clear the terrible 'price' he had 'paid' for his marriage. Assuring Emily, 'I like to believe that I am capable of knowing you and appreciating you as no one else can', he praised her 'spirituality' as 'something very rare and precious indeed', then proceeded to explain, disconcertingly,

Since my mother died I have felt very much alone, and you will take some of her place for me too. I loved her very much, and felt much sympathy with her, and like to think that you and she are somewhat alike.[74]

Did he want a mother, a muse, a lover, another wife, or a Blessed Virgin? Apparently, all of them. Emily's being an ocean away, coupled with his transformation of her into an 'exceptional object' of devotion, helped license his lonely, needy outpourings.[75] For her, this worshipper's letters created dilemmas. Excited, she responded positively, but worried lest Tom, seeing her as other than she really was, might over-rate her. He wanted to know what she was wearing. When was her birthday? He dreamed of acting on stage alongside her. He craved to learn everything that had happened to her in the last fifteen years. Emily treasured his letters, carefully preserving them, but did not feel able to match his ardour, or even fully to understand him.

Hiding this passionate correspondence from his wife, he repeated over and over in his head treasured passages from Emily's letters. Soon he was hoarding them with other confidential papers in a 'locked tin box' at Russell Square. Geoffrey Faber, whom he made his literary executor, was to take charge of this in the event of Tom's death. Some contents must 'be burnt at once', others 'given to the Bodleian library'.[76] Tom urged Emily to reread his poetry and realise how versions of 'my love for you' featured there, refined into 'something finer and finer. And I shall always write primarily for you.'[77]

Not privy to some of its hidden aspects, Vivien found her celibate husband's intense religious devotion hard to accept. When gossipy Sencourt, whom she disliked, came to stay for a spell that autumn, not long after Emily's visit, he found Vivien 'positively hostile' towards Tom's 'church filiations, deriding them as "monastic"'.[78] Sencourt's Oxford thesis had analysed metaphysical poetry and seventeenth-century religious thought; his interests spanned India to the monarchy, Anglo-Catholicism, and English traditions. Tom sometimes found his 'chatterbox', camp manner and love of cultivating important people trying, but appreciated his help with Vivien.[79] 'So many people hate him', she reflected.[80] Still, Sencourt showed patience, persuading her to join him in doing embroidery. Visiting the Eliots, Conrad Aiken considered Sencourt a 'fairy', and noted that Tom excused Vivien ('in bed') from lunching with them.[81] Another visitor realised she often lay in bed until 2 p.m., even after inviting a lunch guest for 1.30, and perceived that Sencourt could annoy her: 'But aren't you mistress of your own house?' he asked her one day in conversation at a dinner party. 'She flashed back with anger, "I'm not mistress here. I'm Mr Eliot's legal wife."'[82] Vivien was sensitive about the word 'mistress', and accused Ottoline Morrell on occasion of being Tom's mistress. If she suspected that his erotic attentions were directed elsewhere, there is no evidence that she knew of his burgeoning correspondence with Emily; but she intuited something was wrong.

When Tom asked Ingram and Stead to lunch at the English-Speaking Union in October, he was eager to consult Stead 'privately for a few minutes some time too, for there is so much between us that is strictly private'.[83] Stead's own marriage had failed. His wife had entered a convent. Vivien showed no sign of doing that. In November Ottoline Morrell thought the Eliots' residence stank of ether, to which Vivien risked becoming addicted. 'Half-crazed', Vivien addressed Tom as if he were a dog; he looked 'grim'.[84] That same month, Virginia Woolf maintained 'raving mad' Vivien made Tom's life 'a torture'. Woolf thought Tom, when with Vivien, was 'all suspicion, hesitation & reserve'.[85] Woolf wrote to her sister on 8 November, 'worn out with half an hour' of the Eliots' company,

She is insane. She suspects every word one says. 'Do you keep bees?' I asked, handing her the honey. 'Hornets' she replied. 'Where?' I asked.

'Under the bed.' Thats the style, and one has to go on talking, and Tom tries, I suppose, to cover it up with longwinded and facetious stories. And she smells; and she throws cheap powder over the bread; and she opens his letters, suspects me of being his mistress, so far as we could gather; and finally said that I had made a signal which meant that they were to go.[86]

To Mary Hutchinson, whose 'pain' Tom sensed, and whom he asked to 'ring up V. Preferably while I am *out!*' he explained he wrote 'private letters' at his office rather than at home.[87] Several visitors to the Eliot household noted that life there was almost intolerable, and wondered how Tom could stand it. Emily, real and imagined, was his consolation: 'it is terrifying, for the first time at the age of forty-two, suddenly to find that one trusts one person absolutely'.[88] She wrote to him with 'candour'.[89] They shared their sufferings. She became 'My Emily'. He felt a 'new life'.[90]

Yet just as all this was going on, Father Underhill published an article stating that 'the Anglican Church is closely bound, by her documents and traditions, to the entire indissolubility of Christian marriage'.[91] Underhill was adamant. Tom, whose opinions on this point coincided with Underhill's, was adamant too. Sleeping badly, and writing to Emily about the 'interpenetration' of their souls, he confessed he was 'trying to fight the craving for alcohol'.[92] Even if he pondered a separation, he would not – could not – consider divorce.

His religion, however, quickened his growing preoccupation with literature's moral force. Sin – particularly sexual sin – was considered at the Church of England's 1930 Lambeth Conference, in which Tom, who would author *Thoughts after Lambeth*, took considerable interest. When his friend Ingram opposed the idea 'that the sex-act is a sin whenever it is potentially dissociated from the purpose of procreation', Tom found Ingram's view 'very unsatisfactory'.[93] People struggling with 'sexual matters' should 'consult properly ordained spiritual advisers'; in Tom's case, this meant Underhill.[94] Tom saw Baudelaire, regarding sex as evil, as more morally astute than the English Victorians Matthew Arnold and Walter Pater. His preoccupation with Baudelaire's sense of man as 'essentially bad' chimed with his interest in Swiftian disgust, and in satire as exemplified by Johnson's *The Vanity of Human Wishes*.[95] Original sin explained life's bleakness, its vanity.

The Vanity of Human Wishes, Tom wrote, was as superb as Juvenal and 'among the greatest verse Satires of the English or any other language'.[96] The 'satirist' was 'a stern moralist'. In *The Vanity of Human Wishes* Johnson's brief verse biography of a military leader, Sweden's Charles XII, was exemplary 'as poetry'.[97] Excited but disillusioned in private life, and in contemporary politics ('I am terrified of the modern contempt of "democracy" . . . I am as scared of Order as of Disorder'), Tom, who had renewed his subscription to *L'Action Française* newspaper in October, now envisaged his own unlikely fusion of satire and military verse-biography.[98] His never-to-be-completed 'Coriolan' was encouraged by a long-standing interest in Shakespeare's lonely, mother-fixated general, Coriolanus; also by Beethoven's *Coriolan* overture and by a 'convincing' *Coriolanus* essay by Wilson Knight.[99] As Tom wrote to Knight in late October, 'the real motive of the play is the astonishing study of the mother–son relation: "he did it to please his mother . . ." I think of writing a poem on this and on Beethoven's version *Coriolan*.'[100]

Work on this, and correspondence with Emily, offered partial refuge from Vivien, whose 'self-esteem' he recognised (in a cutting insight that might be turned back upon himself) was 'always in need of support and sustenance'.[101] His days gained structure from disciplined religious observance and from his work as publisher. Sometimes those two coalesced: he mentioned Joyce (whose eyesight was worsening) in his 'prayers'; and, though the scheme did not come off, he explored the possibility of setting up through Faber & Faber a society of subscribers who might purchase gramophone recordings of authors (precursors of today's audiobooks), beginning with a recording of Joyce.[102] Tom kept a quasi-paternal eye on younger *Criterion* contributors such as Hayward, and on Faber poets: Spender was 'a mere nurseling, and I think it is very bad for children to be pushed ahead too fast'.[103] He encouraged Scottish nationalist writers, including Hugh MacDiarmid, commenting with wry superiority: 'I am wholly in sympathy with this movement, if only to relieve the kingdom of England from the dominion of Northern adventurers.'[104] He supported the English Church Union's publishing arm, but came to feel George Williamson's *The Donne Tradition* (1930) had made publication of his own Clark Lectures 'superfluous'. Anyway, he now decided Donne exhibited 'a manifest fissure between thought and sensibility'.[105]

At home, though Vivien, whom Tom considered 'not a very economical housekeeper', did what she could to help, expenditure increased.[106] Her ex-banker husband attempted to guide her in bookkeeping, but sometimes he was late in paying bills. On 24 October she headed a new page in their joint household account book '*A FRESH START*', but still spent roughly £2 that day.[107] Routine living cost them £5 or £6 a week, including payments for whisky and beer, and constant outgoings on cigarettes. Both Eliots had bad teeth, making them look older: to thirty-year-old critic Austin Warren, Tom 'no longer was the handsome, elegant young man familiar from his earlier photographs: he now was spectacled and his teeth had become carious'.[108] Counterpointing medical bills, their laundry bills were high – occasionally over £1 a week. Several times Tom took over the domestic accounting, but usually he and Vivien shared the job, however tense relations between them.

Soon he would describe himself to Emily as a man 'who has to ration his own whisky'.[109] He drank, but managed to cope with work. On 21 November he joked to the Cobden-Sandersons about cocktails, sherry, and gin; to Richards he recalled having shared rooms at Dunster Hall, Harvard, 'with an eccentric French count, who eventually died of alcoholic psychosis'.[110] Paying a 'very delightful and happy weekend' visit to Bell at Chichester in mid-December, he went alone.[111] Again, after a Christmas and New Year when both Eliots were ill, he went by himself to spend what Underhill called a 'time of quiet' at the Society of the Sacred Mission at Kelham, Nottinghamshire.[112] By then, encouraged by Stead and others, he seems to have been seriously considering separation from Vivien. To Stead he wrote in December,

> I want to talk to you – as for your suggestion – my dear – it has been put *strongly* by my wife's R. C. doctor – by Underhill – and by others less qualified. But I shd like to talk to *you* because *you* know how difficult it is. I will say that I have now a certain happiness which makes celibacy easy for the first time. I think you will know what I am speaking of.[113]

Before going to Kelham in January 1931, Tom wrote to his 'dearest Lady', Emily, about her 'saintly soul' and 'complete spiritual possession and union', but was unsettled by her suggestion there might be something 'abnormal' about their situation. While he now felt 'completely freed from the sexual strain of celibacy under the conditions under which I live', he soon began to worry lest his renewed feelings for Emily might 'harm' her.[114] He felt compelled to speak again to Underhill, telling Sencourt soon afterwards, 'On really vital matters I should never trust my own conscience unless I had at least put it to the test of spiritual counsel.'[115] A review by New York-based Peter Monro Jack pleased him with its perception that *Ash-Wednesday* was 'indirectly a poem for the Virgin Mary' and had a focus 'on the theme of penitence'.[116] 'Penance' was on his mind, but his temper snapped when Virginia Woolf, after refusing to sit for a portrait by Cecil Beaton, complained she had become one of Beaton's 'victims' when the photographer published an image of her without her consent: 'Mr Beaton is a very insignificant, though malodorous, insect', ranted Tom to the

Nation & Athenaeum, whose editor worried his angry complaint was libellous.[117] Feeling a 'need to confess everything to you', Tom had recently confessed to Emily not only his 'pride and vanity', but also 'occasional fits of hysterical temper which not even frayed nerves can extenuate'.[118]

Preparing for Kelham, he contemplated ecclesiastical rites. Though now he attended the Church of St Cyprian, just along Clarence Gate Gardens, Tom (whose birthday, he remarked more than once, coincided with the Feast of St Cyprian) explained to Bishop Bell that his taste had been shaped at St Mary the Virgin:

> the form of Lenten Offices to which I am accustomed (and to which I am strongly attached) is in *The English Holy Week Book* published by the Society of SS. Peter & Paul (2/6). That contains Tenebrae, the Mass of the Pre-Sanctified and the Blessing of the Font, Blessing of the New Fire, and preparation of the Pascal Candle on Holy Saturday, as we had them at St Mary the Virgin's. Of course the regular Mass of Ashes is equally 'essential'. For the Mass of the Pre-Sanctified, I like both the transference of the Host from the Lady Chapel to the High Altar, and the Procession to kiss the Crucifix, after the unveiling.[119]

The ideal church Tom described in 1931 is one such as Father Whitby had developed: 'a church which shows the loving attempts of generation after generation, each according to its own notions of beauty, to leave visible testimony of its devotion'.[120] Later that year, after meeting his confessor's cousin, Evelyn Underhill, he proposed to write about churchman-poet George Herbert, author of 'The Temple'. Tom came to believe, as he put it in early 1931, reflecting on 'that oddest of institutions, the Church of England', that

> The World is trying the experiment of attempting to form a civilized but non-Christian mentality. The experiment will fail; but we must be very patient in awaiting its collapse; meanwhile redeeming the time: so that the Faith may be preserved alive through the dark ages before us; to renew and rebuild civilization, and save the World from suicide.[121]

Oppressed by such thoughts in England, his imagination turned to America where Richards had gone with his wife to teach at Harvard. 'I should like Emily to meet them if possible', he wrote to Eleanor Hinkley, who decided Richards was 'effeminate' but who was well placed to know how much Emily mattered to Tom.[122] Continually conscious of 'private anxieties', childless as he was, he found an outlet in writing to his godson.[123] On 20 January 1931, the same day as he corresponded elatedly with Emily, dwelling lovingly on her 'ears' and 'neck' and protesting how 'very proud' he was 'of simply *belonging* to you', he sent Tom Faber a jaunty illustrated account of 'JELLYLORUM', a cat so small it could sit on Tom Eliot's (admittedly large) ear.[124] A few months later, 'Silly Uncle Tom' sent four-year-old Tom a birthday poem about 'Pollicle Dogs and Jellicle Cats': from such beginnings a book for children would develop.[125] Its cats guard their own secrets, and sometimes fight.

Pondering anew relationships between son, mother, and wife, he chatted with Wilson Knight about Coriolanus. That heroic battler, Knight contended, did not so much '*neglect* his wife' as give 'always . . . more attention to his mother'.[126] Tom read 'very touching and painful' old letters of his own mother's, which Henry had copied and sent.[127] Later that year, he assessed Murry's *Son of Woman: The Story of D. H. Lawrence* as 'brilliant', a 'definitive work of critical biography, or biographical criticism . . . so well done that it gives me the creeps'. Throughout *Son of Woman*, Tom responded to 'the emotional dislocation of a "mother-complex"'. In trying to convince himself that 'he was right to be as he was', self-deluding Lawrence, guilty of 'spiritual pride', had twisted his art. What would have saved him was 'orthodoxy'. Instead, Tom argued, Lawrence had believed two people could be 'spiritually united' in a 'greater intimacy than is possible between human beings'. For Tom 'the simple truth is that of any two human beings each has privacies which the other cannot penetrate, and boundaries which the other must not transgress'. Only in 'the love of God' could 'the love of two human beings' be 'made perfect'. This reflected his private thinking about Emily. Though the love of God was difficult and there was 'no good in making Christianity easy and pleasant', however awkwardly, with the Atlantic between them, he and his strong-willed mother had shared their love.[128] Now transatlantic love involved Emily. For Vivien, sharing a marriage, but hardly love, with Tom, his preoccupations and religious 'asceticism' only emphasised their mutual apartness.

Where Tom's sense of 'privacies' was strong, and his most intense emotions found release in poems and secret love letters to his 'saint', Vivien struggled to separate what was in her mind from behaviour around her.[129] Subject to hallucinations, she unsettled interlocutors who saw her twisting their words to fit her own anxieties. Effortfully, Tom sought to fortify and police the border between private and public. In Vivien that border risked breaking down. She had been relishing freedoms afforded by her car, but now, with bronchitis succeeding gastric flu, she spent almost three weeks in bed, and wrote unnervingly to Mary Hutchinson from 'this strange flat',

> We have a man staying here. I only see him for a few minutes late at night when all the servants & nurses have departed. He sometimes stays with us. Tom can bear him. Perhaps you could find out why.[130]

Perhaps this man was Sencourt, whose piece on St John of the Cross Tom would soon publish in the *Criterion* and who remained in early 1931 a regular visitor, but it is odd that Vivien does not name him. Was this 'man' real or unreal? 'If I were a bishop', Tom quipped to George Bell, 'I should go very quickly into a nursing-home for Nervous Disorders'; but it was Vivien, with 'all' her 'nurses' in the flat, who came closer to needing such care.[131]

At Russell Square he now had an office to himself. Small, and high up at the back of the building, it had cream walls and contained a desk, bookcases, two hard chairs, an armchair, and an electric stove for heating. Its third-floor window, third from the right, overlooked the lilac trees and 'pleasant green of Woburn Square' towards Christ Church (now demolished), which, Tom informed Emily, was 'the rather ugly church where Christina Rossetti used to worship'.[132] Office-bound, he found solitude to write to his 'Dove', signing himself 'Your Tom', and hungering for replies; he was intensely disappointed when there were delays in her answering his long and frequent letters, but, as always at Russell Square, he could revert to his 'clam-like' self and do office work.[133] Apparently endlessly, he dictated business letters to a secretary – and notes of thanks, including one to the president of the International Mark Twain Society, which had made him an Honorary Member. 'Especially as a Missourian', he felt pleased.[134] His correspondence reveals a man weighing words meticulously; but his missives to Emily have an intimacy and passion lacking in most of his other letters, and as their correspondence developed he went on to send her many enclosures – photographs, and letters from such luminaries as Joyce, Woolf, Pound, or Murry. He was regarded as a canny metropolitan publisher ('lunch with me at my club at 63 St James's Street'); as a committed churchman 'concerned with the problem of making a cathedral a living centre of the life of the people'; and as the busy thinker who hoped 'to be able to attend' a two-day meeting in February 1931 at Student Movement House, 32 Russell Square, where ecumenical Presbyterian J. H. Oldham was planning a new, Christian-accented discussion group.[135] Many perceived only Tom's professionalism. He managed his public image carefully.

Yet he knew, as he put it in a memorial address for Whibley delivered that February at Westminster School, that 'anyone who would write must let himself go, in one way or the other, for there are only four ways of thinking: to talk to others, or to one another, or to talk to oneself, or to talk to God.'[136] Just occasionally, especially to close friends whose own stresses were apparent, he revealed his vulnerability and how he coped. Hayward, whose muscular dystrophy was worsening, wrote about having 'very, very slowly come to know you better' over the previous five or six years. Mentioning Tom's 'austerity' of 'attitude' and 'interpretation of asceticism', Hayward expressed sadness at failing to apply to his own 'experience of suffering' the 'solution' that Tom had 'found through Faith'. Tom explained he did not 'want to "convert" anyone: it's an impertinence, to begin with; and one man's route is of no use to another; and in the end all conversion is self-conversion'. Yet he also described his own coming to terms with pain:

As for suffering, it is very queer indeed. Of course, I admit that I know little, perhaps less than most, of physical suffering, and I am sure that you know much of both. But I have had considerable mental agony at one time or another, and once or twice have felt on the verge of insanity or imbecility (I mean two quite different experiences). And I never found that I could make any conscious deliberate *use* of suffering – for one always feels that one must turn it to account in some way, and can't. If I had died even five years ago, everything that I had suffered up to then would, so far as I can see, have been just waste and muddle. Then a pattern suddenly emerges from it, without one's seeming to have done anything about it oneself. And I don't suppose it is ever the same pattern for any two people.[137]

A little later, Tom discussed seventeenth-century dramatist Thomas Heywood, whose domestic tragedy *A Woman Killed with Kindness* features a wife who commits adultery with her husband Frankford's close friend and then, frozen out by her husband, seeks to starve herself to death. Tom highlighted 'that fine speech of Frankford which surely no man or woman past their youth can read without a twinge of personal feeling:

O God! O God! that it were possible
To undo things done; to call back yesterday . . .'[138]

Others perceived patterns in Tom's work that made him feel his sufferings had not been fruitless. After Thomas McGreevy's 1931 *Thomas Stearns*

Eliot was published, Tom found its reading of *The Waste Land* 'extremely acute': 'I supposed that I was merely working off a grouch against life while passing the time in a Swiss sanatorium; but apparently I meant something by it.'[139] Might Emily too come to appreciate the way that, however blighted, his life had a meaningful pattern? Tom urged her to write to him candidly and openly, with minute details of her life. In Boston, talking to clubs, societies, and student audiences about such topics as contemporary drama, and continuing to perform on stage, she was coming to realise in this, the year of her fortieth birthday, that in the longer term she would need to return to full-time employment. She began to share with Tom her own anxieties, worrying she might have harboured homoerotic feelings for a student. Tom reassured her 'nothing' was 'more natural' than for people of 'refinement' to experience this. 'I once, when I was a schoolmaster at Highgate, had something of that feeling towards one of my boys, but it was not reciprocated.'

> The only danger in such a relationship seems to me to be this: In the more intimate relation of a man and a woman there is a kind of equality which comes from a reciprocity of power. Each one has both the sense of dominating and the sense of being dominated – at least in a right adaptation of two congenial persons, – and is both dominant and submissive. But in the other relationship, with the same sex and considerable difference of age, the power is all on one side – or mostly.[140]

He went on to reveal how he had felt an 'awful' kind of 'mystical crisis' in Paris in 1910–11, experiencing intense 'fascination' and 'aversion' towards Matthew Prichard, the original of 'Mr Silvero' in 'Gerontion'. Prichard, with whom Tom had gone travelling, had influenced his views on philosophy and art (examination of correspondence reveals Prichard and Tom read several of the same novels by Charles-Louis Philippe around that time), but Tom had worried that the aesthete Prichard was seeking somehow, terrifyingly, to possess him. 'The man had an abnormal love of power over younger men which sprang from some sexual distortion.'[141]

He explained to Emily that his solution, even if no 'real sexual inversion' were involved, was to separate himself from the person in question. He had acted similarly when, around 1919, the flamboyantly homosexual Lytton Strachey, who liked flirting with him, had gone

> down on his knees and kissed me – I was completely taken aback, and in such a shock my first impulse was to laugh, for there was something farcical about it; and then I felt terribly ashamed for him – and

sometimes it is more painful to feel ashamed for another person than for oneself. I am afraid he was really hurt; he is a sensitive person, and after all he can't help being like that, and I do like him otherwise, and like all his family very much. We have never met again except in company.[142]

In an era when, even if Bloomsbury saw things differently, the British state regarded active male homosexuality as a serious crime, Tom's views were relatively enlightened. With the exception of certain clergymen pledged to celibacy, he may have found overt lesbians easier to associate with than flamboyantly gay men. But his principal concern in sharing such details with Emily was to spare her undue guilt. He, like she, had a reservoir of guilt and suffering.

He worried not just about personal hurt, but also about turmoil in wider society. Writing disapprovingly about 'the reproduction of the least desirable', for all that he was aware of 'Anti-Semitism' as one of the 'problems, related to Eugenics', he could sound like a eugenicist.[143] Casual antisemitism features in his letters to Emily, and she seems to have shared it. Yet, unlike his friends Pound and Jim Barnes, Tom did not commit to Fascism. Wyndham Lewis had published *Hitler* in March, and at Russell Square there was discussion of the German general and military theorist Erich Ludendorff's *Weltkrieg droht auf deutschem Boden*. Predicting imminent 'world war', this book urged Germans to 'take the sword and regain their liberty'.[144] Faber & Faber published *The Coming War* in June 1931. Contemplating 'English politics' ('depressing as German at present, though not so uproarious'), Tom read German philosophy by Martin Heidegger whose *Sein und Zeit* (*Being and Time*) had appeared four years earlier. It brought to mind the 'great' Edmund Husserl whose *Ideas* were then appearing in English.[145] 'As things are drifting at present, it seems to me only a question of time before there is a popular movement towards *some* form of Hitlerism in England, and I want to think about it before it happens.'[146]

Tom wrote those words six days after former Labour MP Sir Oswald Mosley formed his New Party on 1 March 1931; Mosley's financial backer, car-maker Sir William Morris, was disliked by Tom. On 3 March *The Times* reported Mosley's aspiration for a 'National-Socialist programme' and 'Government of the Right'.[147] Just over a year later Mosley founded his black-shirted British Union of Fascists; but Tom, about to publish in April's *Criterion* Thomas Mann's Berlin speech, 'An Appeal to Reason', sensed how political developments might go, even if he detected 'at least some germs of intelligence' in 'The Mosley programme'.[148] 'Coriolan' and Tom's later work engaged with politics more directly than before.

Increasingly he favoured kinds of 'regionalism', whether in Scotland, England or America. Admiring the 1930 Southern 'Agrarian' manifesto *I'll Take My Stand*, which championed 'the culture of the soil' against 'unrestrained industrialism', he wondered 'how far it is possible for mankind to accept industrialization without spiritual harm'. He regretted that

> The American intellectual of to-day has almost no chance of continuous development upon his own soil and in the environment which his ancestors, however humble, helped to form. He must be an expatriate: either to languish in a provincial university, or abroad, or, the most complete expatriate of all, in New York. And he is merely a more manifest example of what *tends* to happen in all countries.[149]

Though London might be Tom's equivalent of New York, he enthused, nevertheless, about 'local and spiritually living districts or *enclaves*'. This led him to side with impulses towards the local, including some tinged with racism and social snobbery. He linked 'Maurras, Ireland, Scotland, Southern States of America', connecting *I'll Take My Stand* to what 'impels Mr George Malcolm Thomson and his Scottish friends to affirm that Scotland ought to be something more than a Suburb of Greater London, or a confined industrial district populated by lower class Irish immigrants'.[150] He came to believe that MacDiarmid, though 'erratic', had 'a touch of genius'.[151] He admired work by Fife socialist miner Joe Corrie so much that, several years afterwards and rather manipulatively, he edited Corrie's poems.

Yet London was Tom's centre of gravity. Its interlocking literary, social, and ecclesiastical circles made sense to him as an intellectual elitist, in a way that other aspects of English life did not. ' "County people" ', he explained to Henry later, were 'the stupidest, most intolerant and most intolerable part' of English society. 'Intellectual activity, and interest in art and letters, is found in isolated individuals all over the country, but otherwise is confined to a limited society, drawn from various natural classes, and most of the individuals composing which, I probably know.'[152] Possessing his own snobberies, he felt at ease, he explained to Emily, with Virginia Woolf's family who were 'more like our Cambridge (Mass.) society than anyone I know here', and 'snobs in their own way'.[153] Still, always alert to talent in the capital, he encouraged a young schoolteacher, Michael Roberts, who had submitted an essay on Hulme to the *Criterion* and a typescript, *Critique of Poetry*, to Faber & Faber. Expanding his network helped attract authors. Tom joined the editorial committee of the *English Review*.

At home, towards the end of March 1931, he listened to late Beethoven. He remembered his eldest sister, Ada, playing Beethoven in 1890s St Louis.

Familiar with 'the better known symphonies, sonatas and overtures', he had heard some of these while going out with Emily at Harvard.[154] Now

> I have the A minor quartet on the gramophone, and find it quite inexhaustible to study. There is a sort of heavenly or at least more than human gaity [*sic*] about some of his later things which one imagines might come to oneself as the fruit of reconciliation and relief after immense suffering; I should like to get something of that into verse once before I die.[155]

Beethoven's A minor quartet, Opus 132, was composed after recovery from serious illness. Its beautifully tender third movement is the 'Heiliger Dankgesang eines Genesenen an die Gottheit, in der lydischen Tonart' ('Song of thanksgiving to the Deity on recovery from an illness, in the Lydian mode'). For forty-two-year-old Tom thoughts of illness were omnipresent. Lawrence, whose biography he had just been reading, died at forty-four; Vivien had contemplated suicide several times; his sister Charlotte had died in her early fifties. 'My life is a kind of struggle to prepare for death, or to try to die and be reborn while still in this life', he wrote to Emily that April. He felt sometimes as if holding on 'desperately with both hands sweating like one undergoing a major operation without an anaesthetic'.[156] He steadied himself with music – and by contemplating again the life of the 'great poet' John Dryden, who had lived until almost the biblical age of three score years and ten, experiencing 'apparently little domestic happiness', as Tom said in an April radio broadcast. 'By close application of a first rate mind', Dryden had 'made himself a great dramatist', despite being 'not *naturally* a dramatist' like Shakespeare or Congreve.[157] Tom outlined a trajectory he too might follow. He admired Dryden, also, as 'the first great English poet to set down carefully his theories about the practice of his own art' – something else Tom had accomplished.[158]

'Some people maintain that a good religious play cannot be written nowadays; I believe, as I believe of religious painting and sculpture, that if the opportunity is given, the work will be done.' That spring he wrote these words in 'If I Were a Dean' for Bell's *Chichester Diocesan Gazette*. Having prefaced Claye's 1928 religious pageant, and aware Bell had commissioned a pageant from Masefield for the 1928 Canterbury Festival, in a sense Tom was touting for business. Convinced English cathedrals should also 'encourage and stimulate first the local spirit of that part of England', he was also articulating in a Christian accent his strengthening commitment to regionalism.[159]

Drafting an essay about Pascal and 'conversion', Tom saw him as linked to Hulme, who had presented some of his own work 'as a prolegomena [*sic*] to the reading of Pascal'.[160] Tom's Pascal was no 'mystic', but 'what can only be called mystical experience happens to many men who do not become mystics'. Drawing on personal knowledge, Tom wrote, 'it is a commonplace that some forms of illness are extremely favourable, not only to religious illumination, but to artistic and literary composition. A piece of writing meditated, apparently without progress, for months or years, may suddenly take shape and word; and in this state long passages may be produced which require little or no retouch.' Pascal's *Pensées* impressed him as 'spiritual autobiography'.[161]

Drawing on Newman's *Grammar of Assent*, he reflected that 'the man who is trying consciously and conscientiously to explain to himself the sequence which culminated in faith' finds the nature of the world (including particularly 'the moral world within') most explicable in terms of Christianity: 'thus, by what Newman calls "powerful and concurrent" reasons, he finds himself inexorably committed to the doctrine of the Incarnation'.[162] In Pascal, whose 'scepticism' led eventually to 'faith', Tom detected how 'despair' might act as 'a necessary prelude to, and element in, the joy of faith'. He could 'think of no Christian writer, not Newman even, more to be commended than Pascal to those who doubt, but who have the mind to conceive, and the sensibility to feel, the disorder, the futility, the meaninglessness, the mystery of life and suffering, and who can only find peace through satisfaction of the whole being'.[163] In part, Tom's writing about this Pascal who avoided the risk of 'spiritual pride' by maintaining a 'fast . . . hold' on 'humility' reveals aspects of his own journey towards belief.[164] Loving Emily for being 'a proud and reserved person', he confessed to her his own 'pride'. She censured his 'stubbornness of will'.[165] However, it is mistaken to see his poetry straightforwardly and exclusively as 'spiritual autobiography'; rather, through crafted intensification, it fuses aspects of his experience with the matter and tones of other texts.

To many people Tom seemed to resemble his Pascal – 'a man of the world among ascetics, and an ascetic among men of the world'.[166] However, retaining his intellectual agility, he was not quite ready to become a venerable ancient. That spring his young protégé Auden, school-teaching in Helensburgh on the Firth of Clyde, sent him a typescript of *The Orators*. Written in Scotland, this *English Study* reflected on Englishness, discourse, and politics. Tom admired its brilliance, but found 'lumps of undigested St Jean [*sic*] Perse' in it.[167] Some passages appeared incomprehensible. Yet Tom knew that 'the poet who fears to take the risk that what he writes may turn out not to be poetry at all, is a man who has surely failed, who ought to have adopted some less adventurous vocation'.[168] Besides, he admired Auden. Bafflingly, *The Orators* included parodies, lists and diagrams. Auden mailed his publisher an 'explanation'.[169]

Later, Tom maintained 'Triumphal March', the first part of 'Coriolan', was 'not concerned with contemporary politics'.[170] In 1931, however, it was for him 'a political satire'.[171] As if spurred by Auden's *Orators*, it incorporated verbatim an inventory of military paraphernalia (surrendered in 'self-emasculation') from Ludendorff's *The Coming War* plus a sentence from Husserl about the 'Ego'.[172] Where Ludendorff had listed weapons surrendered by Germany after the Versailles Peace Treaty, Tom presented them as paraded by victors. This embedded material was fused with contemporary elements from Britain and France, some discordantly absurd. Martial might jostles with 'golf club Captains' and 'the *societé gymnastique de Poissy*'.[173] Tom, who had golfed as a child, noted that summer the election of J. Beaumont Pease, Lloyds Bank chairman, 'to the captaincy of the Royal & Ancient Golf Club of St Andrew's [*sic*]'; and his Missourian eye was caught by La Saint-Louis de Poissy, a sports club situated on the boulevard de la Paix in Paris's Poissy district.[174]

After conversing with Tom, critic Hugh Ross Williamson saw 'Coriolan' as summing up 'the post-Peace world'.[175] To contemporary details were added glances towards *Anabase*, Maurras, the biblical Isaiah (who 'succeeded in being both' poet and prophet), Lottie Eliot's *Savonarola*, and *Coriolanus*.[176] 'Triumphal March' and its companion piece 'Difficulties of a Statesman', completed by late August 1931, evoke surface splendours of militarism, and hidden insecurities that resist suppression. Eventually, in a world that values 'salary' and 'annual increments' more than any 'church', Tom's Coriolanus-like statesman among 'family portraits' is reduced to crying (with desperate, part-ironic echoes of Isaiah) both to and for his 'mother' as he faces the stark injunction 'RESIGN RESIGN RESIGN'.[177] The poem features not only a Coriolanus-like statesman, but also some fragmentary biography of one Arthur Edward Cyril Parker, who, like Coriolanus, connects the surviving parts. Tom planned at least two further sections. The third, he told Murry in October, seemed 'writable'; the fourth ('largely derivative from S. John of the Cross') already looked unlikely.[178] Only sections one and two survive.

Gradually, he unburdened himself to Emily about Vivien: since early in their marriage she had come to seem to him 'more and more just a child'. He could 'really like her' in her 'good child flashes'; occasionally she talked 'in quite a mature and very intelligent way', but showed 'a deeprooted fear: fear of growing up.' Another 'older man, an Englishman and a man of the world', he mused, might have accepted her 'prettiness and dependence' with 'no deep emotion'.[179] Vivien was his burden, whereas Emily was someone 'of exceptional sensibility, emotional power, and intelligence, confined in too narrow an environment for their powers'.[180] He sympathised with Emily's 'exhausting' visits to her mother at the McLean Hospital, making clear he too found 'constantly' that being with such a 'patient' brought 'complete exhaustion of spirit'.[181] By early May, unable to think of Vivien as 'an adult', and conscious both of her loneliness and her 'self-deception', he was discussing with Emily his possible marital separation. 'I cannot assure myself that a separation would be better for her as well as for me; which leaves me to look for substantial certain reasons only on my own side – and that makes it more difficult.'[182]

Ironically, Emily too was lonely and vulnerable to breakdown. And so, for all his great abilities, was Tom, one of whose sisters, Margaret, was (he explained to Emily) 'a nervous invalid'.[183] Something may have attracted him to vulnerable women – and they to him – with mutually damaging results. In late May, eager to speak with Mary Hutchinson's fascist brother Jim, Vivien was convinced 'God' had sent her a malign 'birthday present' on her forty-third birthday by causing their dog to injure itself through falling off the coal-house roof. Meanwhile, she perceived Tom was very 'upset', apparently by something to do with the Hutchinsons. He 'was quite beside himself' at the start of June.[184] His tetchiness and prejudices were close to the surface: 'I dislike religious fiction by hysterical women', he sniped in an internal Faber book report.[185]

Adding to domestic difficulties, harsh economic conditions brought work-related problems. That summer he felt obliged to ask Henry (who was out of work in New York) for further help over copyright issues. Tom told John Gould Fletcher, whose poetry he had had to reject and who was heading for America, 'I should like to be going myself at this time.'[186] He had to decline, too, a collection by his old friend Aiken, while among other poetry submissions was a title he would appropriate for his own use, 'The Rock'.[187] An 'extremely interesting' memoir Faber republished that year was *An Adventure* by C. A. E. Moberly and E. F. Jourdain, in which modern-day visitors strolling around Versailles find themselves transported back in time to its gardens as they were in an earlier era; the late Philip Jourdain, philosopher brother of one of the book's authors, had been 'a friend' to Tom, who sent Emily this 'absorbing' volume.[188] Impressions of walking through a garden haunted by past possibilities while meditating philosophically on time would come to matter in Tom's later poem 'Burnt Norton', and in 1931 he wondered what life would have been like had he made different choices, becoming, say, a Cambridge don. James Joyce and his wife were in London, and Tom enjoyed humming Wagner with Joyce over lunch in a fish restaurant, but his gloom persisted. 'Though I am a tired little journalist,' he wrote to More in July, 'I still fancy that I might have made a brilliant corporation-lawyer, and of course I wish I had been.' Dejectedly, and without mentioning Emily or Vivien, he used an expression signalling illusory promise: 'whatever one does, I imagine that we all like to think of ourselves as connoisseurs of Dead Sea Fruit'.[189]

Emily's fate was adoration: Tom wished in June he could have 'taken your hand and knelt at your feet'.[190] Feeling at times 'glorified and transfigured through you', he fed off her letters, fearing he was 'rather a vampire!'[191] In her very different situation, Vivien's edginess shows in her letters to Mary Hutchinson about small matters: 'I was so sorry not to be able to go to the telephone when you rang up this morning. Do forgive me. I am dreadfully sorry.' After a further 200 words about phoning and appointments, her letter ends 'I MUST see you, SOON.'[192] Mary kept Vivien's correspondence, brought her small presents, and was sympathetic as Vivien entertained Tom's visiting nieces; but Vivien, sure she was being persecuted, wearied people, not just Tom. On 14 July the Eliots 'quite successfully' hosted a dinner for the Morleys, the Joyces, and the Hutchinsons, but such let-ups were short-lived.[193] 'There is no particular acute problem at the moment', Tom explained to Mary with regard to his wife later that year, 'only the permanent one'. He hoped Vivien might 'be persuaded to believe that people she likes want to see *her*'. He realised, too, it would be good for them both to be more independent – 'the more people she can see without me the more people I might be able to see without her!' – but this seemed unachievable.[194] Sometimes, not long after Tom had arrived in his office, Vivien would telephone, demanding he return home; he would 'apologise' to his secretary, and go.[195]

Empathetically, Tom did all he could to help Lilian Donaghy, an Irishwoman whose poet husband's 'persecution mania' made the man believe 'every one', including his spouse, was 'in league against him'. John Lyle Donaghy could seem 'apparently normal', Mrs Donaghy explained, 'but we never know when he will take exception to something one of us may say or do'.[196] Donaghy sent Tom verse from a private asylum, Northumberland House, Green Lanes, Finsbury Park. Tom corresponded with him and his wife, with whom he was unusually open:

You will, I hope, excuse me for writing about the matter as if I knew you, but it is only because I happen to have more knowledge of this type of nervous illness than most people. Such cases are very difficult to handle, because they rarely want to stay in a sanatorium voluntarily, and no one wants to go as far as certification. In your case, I think that it is merely a question of how difficult it becomes, especially in view of the children. All the symptoms you describe are known to me. I am quite certain that people in such a state ought not, as much for their own sakes as for that of others, be with their family and friends. The manifestations of mania are always more pronounced with the persons they know best than with others. Furthermore, those near can do no good but only harm; and it is a heartrending business to wear oneself to shreds for anyone when one knows all the time that he or she only becomes the worst for it.[197]

If this letter reveals his thinking about Vivien, and his growing inclination towards separation, Emily encouraged that idea. Learning from her in August that American critic Willard Thorp and his wife Margaret (former neighbours of the Hinkleys) would visit London for the winter, Tom helped them relocate. Confident and well connected, the highly educated feminist Margaret Thorp (née Farrand) was an author, academic, and a long-standing close friend of Emily's; for many years they exchanged confiding letters, on the understanding that each would burn the other's correspondence. At Clarence Gate Gardens, Willard Thorp, a Princeton professor, thought Tom and Vivien like 'a patient father with a fractious child'.[198] Explaining to Emily late in August that Vivien's 'actions' when the Eliots married 'can be explained by vanity, fear, immaturity, weak physique, weak nerves, drugs and disappointment', Tom added, 'I should have separated from her a year after our marriage.'[199] However, while asserting that he might once have been prepared to endure 'the horrors of the English divorce court', he made it clear to Emily that 'now, of course, I belong to a church which does not recognize divorce in any circumstances or for any reason'. He had wanted to spare his mother the full truth about his marriage, but that, after Lottie's death, he

> several times raised the question of separation with V. – sometimes in fits of hysteria, but also when quite calm; but have never made the slightest impression. It produces a quarrel, but in twentyfour hours she has quite put it out of mind; in short, it seems as if the only way to arrive at a separation would be for me to make a bolt.[200]

To Emily Tom continued, 'I yet feel almost unclean to go on living in the same flat, feeling towards her as I do. It is not even as if I had ever cared for her; to have felt any sort of passion, even had its duration been very brief, would impose a continuing bond; but as it is I don't feel that I have ever been married at all.'[201] But he *was* married. Unitarian Emily, conscious of her own needs and responsibilities, and undergoing her own 'acute spiritual crisis', was aware that some Anglicans did divorce.[202] Trying to decide whether to accept a two-year post as assistant professor of oral English at Scripps College in California, she was less than delighted with Tom's reasoning about either divorce or her future. Despite an instinctive aversion to California, he was annoyed when, feeling inadequate, she declined the Scripps post. Soon, however, ardent but attempting jocularity, he sent her 'a good kiss instead of the smack of another kind which I felt like giving you'.[203] He wanted to feel they always had, and always would, understand each other fully. But his inflexible attitude towards divorce brought lasting strain between them, and it was around this time that Emily wrote – and sent to him – a sonnet, 'An Etching'. It presents a troubling image of a couple, the woman veiled and the man preoccupied 'As if in prayer', with hands 'caught / In a steel like grip of self-control'. If this was Emily's oblique comment on Tom and his relationship with her, he did not see the poem in that light, and criticised its 'too conscientious' focus on the etching and Emily's 'subduing' of herself. 'You should really be talking about yourself and your own feelings.'[204] Perhaps he did not realise that she was.

Though it was 'unlikely that I shall get to America this year', and his situation threatened 'mental impotence', he soon informed Emily he was 'interested' in coming to Harvard as Norton Professor in 1932.[205] He would come alone. This, she speculated, might 'force any issue' between them.[206] Meanwhile, privately begging Emily for a lock of her hair, in public Tom made the most of camaraderie in Faber's offices and at meetings of *Criterion* friends, sometimes in Monro's Poetry Bookshop. Time with cronies could lift his spirits, but gossip about the Eliots was circulating. One rumour, which demanded contradiction, was that Tom was becoming a Roman Catholic. Another tale – about his primly meticulous speech – was apocryphal, but so congenial that Tom wished it were true:

> The story goes that he was at dinner, with a gushing young woman beside him. She turned to him and said, 'Don't you find D. H. Lawrence's latest book [whatever it was] is *too* amusing?' Mr Eliot is reported to have thought this over in silence, and then to have replied, 'And just what do you mean by "*too*"?'[207]

Further rumours were believable. Ottoline Morrell (whose 'insight into my domestic life' Tom thought considerable) recounted how, talking about sport, Tom expressed 'a strong desire when seeing a man down in boxing to trample on him, tear him . . .' Ottoline informed an American visitor that 'Eliot is not very vital', detailing how Vivien, 'sexually dissatisfied', had 'carried on a kind of love affair here with B. Russell'. A 'drug addict' though 'witty at times', Vivien showed 'extraordinary vacillations of mood' and had been 'once confined'. Her house was 'heavy with ether odors'. Furthermore, 'When she was in confinement someone tried to talk to him about separation, for he was much happier.' However, 'he regards it [marriage] as a serious sacrament and is angelic to her – masochistic, seemingly – won't separate'. Ottoline's American guest recorded, 'Lady O. said Eliot is 1/8 devil; rest a saint and very pleasant', though he had some 'Extremely sadistic impulses' and a 'Bad temper'. Usually, Tom was ' "angelic" ' to Vivien 'in her various moods', but once when Lady Ottoline had asked him 'how to keep young', his answer had been 'by drink', which had prompted 'Mrs Eliot' to 'come out with, "How can you say that? you've upset me . . ." '[208]

Worse was an attack from someone else intimate with the Eliots. First published in a Florentine limited edition advertised in the July *Times Literary Supplement* as 'A FEROCIOUS SATIRE ON AMERICAN LITERARY ADVENTURERS, ENGLISH INTELLECTUAL SNOBBERY AND CONTEMPORARY RELIGIOUS FADS', Richard Aldington's *Stepping Heavenward: A Record* was destined for London publication later in 1931 in Chatto & Windus's respected Dolphin Books series.[209] That series already included McGreevy's *Thomas Stearns Eliot* and *Richard Aldington*. Described as 'a delicious parody' of 'the solemn pompous biography', Aldington's volume chronicled the ruthless rise of 'the late Jeremy Pratt Sybba, afterwards Father Cibber, O. S. B.', an American intellectual of New England descent born in 1880s 'Colonsville', 'an important railway junction' situated 'between the Ohio and the Mississippi'. Reared by a proud, suffocating mother (' "Never forget, Jeremy," she would say to him, "never forget you are a Pratt" '), then educated in America and Europe, Cibber authors ' "A Plea for Royalism in Western Europe" ', a clever paraphrase of Maurras.[210] This ambitious intellectual faces 'financial worries' and family disapproval as well as 'the acute personal problem of Miss Adèle Paleologue' whom he marries (after she rejects 'an American footballer'), only to discover she is becoming insane.[211] Enduring 'slow silent misery', Cibber is regarded as a saint; Adèle, though among the first 'to proclaim Cibber's peculiar genius and to push him on in the world', cannot 'dwell happily on the austere mountain heights of' his 'spiritual elevation', and is driven by her husband's 'presence' into 'wild neurasthenia'. 'It must be rather a shock to think you are marrying a nice young American and then to discover that you have bedded with an angel unawares.'[212]

In *Stepping Heavenward* gossip about Adèle fascinates literary London:

'Oh, it's that awful wife of his.' 'How I loathe that woman!' Bowler-hatted Cibber receives lucrative offers to lecture 'across the Atlantic'. He is honoured by 'Julien Benda' and the Pope. Yet in a marital home festooned with religious emblems, his wife's condition worsens:

> So, many a time poor Adèle gazed into the mirror, clutching her hair distractedly, and whispering: 'I'm going mad, I'm going mad, I'm going mad.' Cibber invariably stood up when she came into the room, and their quarrels were conducted on coldly intellectual lines.[213]

Aldington's book ends with Adèle running off with another man, begging Cibber 'to divorce her'. Yet, Cibber's being ' "received" ' into the church makes 'divorce impossible'. Eventually, after joining the Pope to launch a 'war' on 'paganism in Europe', Cibber dies.[214] He is beatified.

Though Bruce Richmond's *Times Literary Supplement* claimed in its November 1931 review that *Stepping Heavenward* gave readers 'no clue' about 'the real person' castigated, Geoffrey Faber recognised it immediately as 'a bitter and indeed a malevolent attack on Eliot' and 'what is worse – on his relations with his wife'. Outraged at this '*incredible* thing', Faber protested to a Chatto director that the book was 'unpardonable'.[215] Chatto refused to back down, reprinting *Stepping Heavenward* the following year. Tom was deeply hurt. Over thirty years later, recalling Aldington's 'scurrilous and offensive lampoon', he complained that 'one could do nothing about [it] because to take him to court or take any other such step would have been merely to give more publicity to a painful situation'.[216] The day after *Stepping Heavenward* appeared, he wired Harvard, accepting the lucrative Norton visiting professorship. He contacted Emily, his family, old American friends, and Harvard contacts including Theodore Spencer about how best to arrange things. Preparing to act in a play called *Berkeley Square*, Emily reminded him they 'both' knew 'how to play parts'.[217] He explained to his Aunt Rose in St Louis that Vivien would not be 'strong enough to be able to come with me'.[218]

After the Aldington bombshell, Faber, who received a long business letter from Tom on 9 December expressing dissatisfaction with the firm's 'advertising', with its publishing 'too many books', and with its 'overdone' committee system, 'dined with the Eliots' the following day – a gesture of support.[219] Tom had been reading an essay on 'Nicholas Ferrar and George Herbert' which he would publish in the following year's *Criterion*, following Faber's agreement to continue the magazine's financial backing.[220] Tom was tense. 'Horrified' at how the dinner party went, Vivien had 'a fearful time, with T. All of a sudden.'[221] He was under pressure to make a radio broadcast a few days later, exactly when she proposed to hold a party. She postponed her party until New Year's Eve, sure he would enjoy hosting Ottoline, Sencourt, and other friends. Vivien had taken a fancy to a 'delightful' new visitor, poet Ralph Hodgson, and to Samuel Koteliansky. This Russian translator thought Christianity mere 'escapism' – which grated on Tom. Hoping soon to serve twice-weekly at Mass, he retorted that 'Christian faith, far from softening the edges of life, made each of them more cutting.'[222]

This was the Cibber-like figure Aldington had lampooned. Though he could write charmingly to his godson about 'Another Cat' called 'MIRZA MURAD ALI BEG', Tom admitted to Virginia Woolf he was 'irritable'.[223] It hardly helped when 'newspapers and press bureaux' started 'ringing up' about his Harvard appointment. After it was mentioned 'on the wireless', several papers misreported it. Tom assured the *Times* he was 'not returning permanently to America'.[224] 'Worn out by Christmas', Vivien had what she called 'a sort of breakdown'.[225] She changed the date of the forthcoming party again, to 12 January, and, thanking the increasingly deaf Ottoline for some presents, sent a disturbed letter,

> They are very beautiful, & also they have some strange connections in my mind, which I could not possibly put in writing to you but which I am sure have some meaning which certainly if I tried to explain to anyone, they would either not hear me, or else say what ridiculous & childish nonsense & please do not say anything more about it as I refuse to listen to you. But it is difficult to communicate with you privately – as you do not hear me when I speak in a low voice & writing is always a risk. And if there is anything I do hate & fear it is communicating by *signs*. I think it is *low & brutal & degrading*, & rather than that, I think it would be better to go & 'live' alone on the top of a high mountain.[226]

Perhaps Vivien was trying to get at Tom. Her phrasing may indicate she had read Aldington's account of Cibber's dwelling on 'austere mountain heights'. Ottoline remembered the Eliots' January party as 'a ghastly evening' with Vivien 'talking wildly in the street outside'.[227]

As 1931 became 1932, Tom wrote to Emily ('My dear Bird') about having 'flashes of perception of a kind of "pattern" in life, in my life, which are like mystical moments; flashes which do not give peace "as the world gives" but which, while they last, reconcile one to all the mystery of fault and suffering in the past'. He felt, too, 'a kind of flash of anticipation of my future'.[228] Such insights would come to fuel his verse, but now, as he contemplated visiting America, he thought not just of Emily but also of his dead parents. With Joyce, whose father's death caused that novelist intense 'remorse', Tom shared memories of his own father: 'he died still believing, I am sure, that I had made a complete mess of my life – which from his point of view, and possibly quite rightly, I had done. I cannot forget him sitting in the railway station before my last departure, looking completely broken.'[229] At times, for all Tom's remarkable achievements, breakage seemed his terrible bequest to those closest to him. Vivien was broken. Emily, still delivering public lectures on such topics as 'Competitive Stages – Broadway and Hollywood', and now staying with her friend Penelope Noyes, had had 'a little breakdown'.[230] News from England can hardly have helped. Solicitous about her reputation as well as his, Tom made clear that when he came to America he proposed to ration strictly their face-to-face meetings. 'What I feel is, frankly, that as I can't have what I want, which is of course to have you with me day and night always, then all that I want is to pursue and develop the mutual sympathy and understanding and companionship through letters.'[231] Life for Emily was hard.

Though relocating involved putting a whole continent between herself and her mother in Belmont, Massachusetts, she decided to go to Scripps after all. Tom, to whom Scripps seemed 'a nunnery', planned to visit her there, but began turning his thoughts towards Harvard.[232] He could handle professors with finesse, assuring the warden of All Souls where he had been rejected for a fellowship that a review of the warden's Latin poems was sure to appear in the *Criterion*. Just as easily, he could advise the churchman Oldham about theologians and academics who might participate in a discussion group. Tom excelled at this sort of intellectual management. Trained in intellectual fisticuffs and business etiquette, he maintained good editorial relationships with poets as different as Auden (precocious) and Pound, who told Tom the 'American academy' was 'old bloody clogged sewage'.[233] Strategically, the ambitious, soon-to-be Norton Professor proposed 'to bring out a volume of collected essays in the autumn'.[234] To his admirers, he epitomised success, though he told Basil Bunting he was 'even accustomed to personal attacks'.[235] Still, dealing with his domestic situation was demanding, so he was delighted his wife had taken not only to the much-travelled Englishman Ralph Hodgson, but also to Hodgson's cultured, piano-playing American partner Aurelia Bolliger, and their '*nice puppy*' (Vivien's emphasis), Pickwick.[236] Portly and witty, Hodgson, like Tom, found 'England & Englishness' fascinating.[237] Hodgson's poetry had dried up, but Tom tried to coax new work from him. Like Vivien, Tom responded to this couple's vivacity. Admitting them to their domestic milieu, both Eliots were unusually open.

For Aurelia Tom signed a copy of 'Marina' – 'the poem that he likes best of all he has written'. Inscribing *Ash-Wednesday* for Ralph, he spoke in detail about childhood, recalling how at prep school he was 'too fastidious' to bathe in other boys' bathwater; how memories of 'the moment of boyhood when he first discovered the curve of a girl's cheek' were 'too painful'. Hodgson thought Tom 'carries his boyhood with him, and has carried it longer than most men. It explains the man.' Meeting these Anglo-American visitors, reviewing his life, and anticipating return to Harvard, Tom shared other recollections. Talking of his graduate-student days, he took down a volume of F. H. Bradley and read aloud 'passages of his prose, to show his rare clarity'. He enthused about favourite foods: New England fish balls ('ambrosia'), oysters, cheeses, and 'asparagras': 'there's no day of the year when I couldn't eat asparagras'. Becoming more relaxed and American, he complained about aspects of English cuisine: 'I loathe their damned boiled puddings.'[238]

'She is good for me', Vivien told Aurelia Bolliger about the 'paid companion' who helped look after her. 'I can always get along well with people who come from a parsonage.' Yet, Tom's wife maintained, 'Christianity gives T.S.E. no comfort.' Aurelia, a former missionary, became one of Vivien's companions, and minutely recorded the Eliots' home life:

> *Mr Eliot* – tall, quite broad-shouldered, well-filled out, inclined to round cheeks. Sallow color. He was well set up and well developed, quite different from my hazy conception of a spare, monkish type. He had the back and mouth but not a good nose for boxing, but never indulged it much because of chronic hernia (we learned later). His hand clasp was warm and cordial, not at all the bored, formal shake of a man who endures receptions and invitations. He looked younger than his years (43).

Tom's lack of exhibitionism impressed Aurelia: 'He is [an] inconspicuously dressed, well-bred man indistinguishable from the ordinary run of men except for his very intelligent, responsive face.' Vivien was 'an exceptionally slight frail little lady' with 'a thin, drawn face, with quasi-pockmarked effect – round shouldered, tho some costumes hid it'. Her eyes had disconcerting 'Oscillating pupils'. 'Ralph noticed the odor of ether about her.'[239]

These visitors' 'First call on [the] Eliots' was intriguing but unsettling:

> We two appeared for dinner, with Pickwick at 7 o'clock. I was taken into a small bedroom to leave my wraps, then Mrs Eliot came to greet

me. I asked 'how are you?' 'Not at all well. I've been in bed all day. I just got up.' 'Oh, Mrs Eliot, I'm so sorry.'

'I knew you'd be.' (a reply which startled me)

'Truly, it would have been all right to cancel tonight's dinner. To think that you got out of bed, just because we were coming!'

'It's an old trouble, a kind of nervous breakdown.'[240]

Yet after the visitors' dog misbehaved, Vivien, accustomed to the ways of her own Yorkshire terrier, 'laughed heartily as the waterfall continued, and got a cloth'; later, she 'cleaned it up herself' with paper and a shovel. Trying to reassure his visitors, Tom 'just remarked calmly, "We're used to it. Sometimes I get down on the floor myself and scrub away the marks." '[241]

Vivien complained that her own family, the Haigh-Woods, made her 'furious': 'They think I'm a raving lunatic and treat me like one.' Several times, Aurelia saw her 'furious' at Tom; he made people 'furious', Vivien claimed. Aurelia noted 'his embarrassment' when subjected to Vivien's 'tone of sharp criticism'. When conversation turned to the nineteenth-century Primogene Duvard and her mocking poem 'The Boys', Vivien 'spoke up emphatically, "I agree. I loathe men – all men, just loathe them." ' An embarrassed silence ensued, until a male guest's laughter 'covered it up somehow'. Vivien interrogated Aurelia with 'vehement energy'. 'She showed too much emotion for the subject, and her mind leapt so quickly from one thing to another.' Aurelia thought that with male friends Tom 'was free bright and witty, quicker in speech and he laughed deep spontaneous laughter'; with Vivien he was attentive, but very careful. Once, speculating about time travel, Ralph Hodgson asked Tom 'whether he'd like to go into the future or the past', Tom answered 'Into the past. It's finished.' To which Vivien responded, 'It's never finished. It always follows us.'[242] Aurelia took this to refer to Vivien's sense of her own 'haunted life'; it became, too, a recurring theme in Tom's imaginative work.[243]

Despite hearing from Ottoline that 'both of the Eliots were cruel', Aurelia enjoyed their company. Sometimes she spent nights at their flat, effectively becoming another of Vivien's carers. Tom filled a hot-water bottle for her. She heard him 'stirring' – apparently working – late into the night. Helping Vivien undress for bed one evening, she noticed marks on her back 'like measles' and wondered if they might have been caused by 'injections'. Vivien's eating was disordered. Though Aurelia found lunch at the Eliots' flat 'delicious', Vivien

ate little herself, usually passing up meat very lightly if not altogether. Her habit was to have breakfast very late, after her nurse had given her the massage treatment (every other day). But what a light meal – a shredded wheat biscuit and tea – and then she'd have no genuine appetite for lunch. Some days she grew really hungry by tea time and asked for sandwiches, or an egg, as well as cakes. Then she'd mince about her supper plate! It's no wonder that she needed a bowl of soup at 11 (though that also served to hide the taste of her 'drug,' as she called it to me), or that she kept a plate of sandwiches or left-over pudding handy to eat during the night if she was restless. She couldn't quite understand it that I didn't eat late at night, and some-times she brought me too a dish of jelly, or a glass of milk.[244]

The Eliots' home life struck Aurelia as messy: pyjamas rolled up in the living room where there were faded, 'oft-laundered' pillows. She helped tidy Tom's books. Walking from room to room, she saw several paintings by Vivien's late father, but most Haigh-Wood family portraits remained in Vivien's mother's house. Tom's pictures, however, were prominent. As well as images of ancestors, going right back to a reproduction of a Hol-bein portrait (probably of Sir Thomas Elyot), there was a large drawing by Lewis, another by Kauffer, and one by Tom's father, the 'Vision of Julius Caesar'.[245]

At night Aurelia found the living room 'comfortable', its 'wall space taken up by book cases. T.S.E. explained, "I can work better with a lot of books around me." The windows were covered with black brocaded-stuff; the wall lights were shaded; the fire burned brightly.' She observed 'no table prayers, no family worship', but 'on the table' lay 'always books of devotion and meditation'. 'Over the mantelpiece hangs a carved crucifix; and below it, suspended on a black ribbon over the handles of a brass tea-pot, is a small dark crucifix. On his dresser is also a small velvet case, wherein lies another one. The case always seems to lie open.' More than once, getting up late at night to fetch something, she encountered Tom alone, with a rosary on the table, and felt embarrassment at interrupting his devotions. To Emily, who was feeling lonely, Tom wrote about suffering nightmares, and about his daily religious exercises (which he linked to the suppression of desire), but Aurelia sensed a lack of 'missionary zeal' in the part of him that was 'the social man'; he had no apparent 'desire to convert' others, stating 'I hope I never get so old that I think someone else ought to agree with me.' Arranging his books, which included many theological volumes, she noticed a newly published one. It dealt with pre-Christian and Christian solitaries from John the Baptist to 'Charles de Foucauld, the nineteenth-century hermit of the Sahara'.[246] Its title was *The Quest of Solitude*.

Vivien remarked that, when he considered notions of the English gentleman, Tom was convinced neither he nor his brother were gentlemen. Yet to Aurelia he did seem gentlemanly. Despite seeing the Eliots quarrel – or perhaps *because* of that – she thought Tom

> Vivienne's constant protector, and in her presence his conversation was dictated by what he wished her to hear or know. I always felt uncertain of the opinions he expressed then, that they might not represent the man himself.
>
> He was ever anxious about her. From the office he would telephone home at least once to ascertain that all was well. If she had gone alone to her mother's or her aunt's, he telephoned to make sure of her arrival. She always used her little car. She loathed walking, buses and Tubes. It took her two years to learn to drive, and the purchase of the car had been a doctor's suggestion. She was cautious and slow in coordination, but had had no accidents. Nevertheless, I grew quite afraid of being with her. I think he was too, for he was quite nervous after her two long trips and needed whisky to pull himself together. The little car jerked and bounced when she drove, and the gears screeched maddeningly.[247]

Solicitous towards Vivien, yet preparing for Harvard, Tom sounded out museum director Eric Maclagan – a former Norton Professor who attended the Church of St Mary the Virgin – about Harvard's expectations. As for 'correcting papers, setting examinations etc', Tom wrote to Richards, 'drudgery of that sort . . . I don't want to do'.[248] He sought to return to Harvard on his own terms, which included earning 'as much money as I can in America' without 'over-work'.[249] Pleased to have London literary agent David Higham trying to sell some of his radio broadcasts to New York publishers, Tom intended to take Spencer's advice about renting a suite of rooms in the appropriately named Eliot House, a new and swanky college. There Tom, a white son of nineteenth-century Missouri and a patrician used to Oxford's porters or 'scouts', joked he might have 'for my service a nice negro scout whose name ought to be George'. Spencer replied that might be 'difficult'.[250]

Some attitudes Tom retained from his upbringing, albeit with a certain ironic inflection. Yet he could also be critical of social assumptions, not least in his adopted country. Despite inclining towards conservatism, he told Tory propagandist Douglas Jerrold that 'people who wish to promulgate Conservative ideas today must be up against a very serious obstacle indeed, that is to say the Conservative party and its followers'. What was 'of first importance' to Tom was 'to have doctrines and to understand them'.[251] He valued institutions, provided they appeared thought-through and credible. The most important was the church. To Aurelia Bolliger it appeared that by 1932 his

> church habits weren't painfully regular. He got to at least one service on Sunday if it wasn't one of his week-ends in bed. Oftenest it seemed to be the early communion service. Then he would come home, have breakfast, and go back to bed till noon. He had the ability to sleep too even after that interruption.
>
> Vivienne and I often planned to go together to either [the Roman Catholic] Brompton Oratory or Westminster Cathedral together, but it never came off. She wasn't well enough. Those she called 'my church': 'it wasn't the same church he attended' she explained, 'but almost the same thing.' The only time she went during the months that I saw most of her, was to Easter communion.
>
> Mr Eliot also attended communion (or morning prayers, or something) once or twice a week on week-days, sometimes at 8.30, sometimes at 10. This was particularly on special days.[252]

As well as praying and attending services, he went each Friday to confession at Liddon House, an Anglican centre headed by Underhill in fashionable Mayfair. 'Confession regularly', he told Emily that summer, was of 'capital importance'.[253] Though she does not seem to have done so, Vivien told Tom she too might confess to Underhill.[254] Tom wanted, also, 'to come down to St Mary's again for the Holy Saturday offices' in his former parish church.[255] Some other institutions, however, seemed to him dubious: 'there are institutions in England like the Royal Society of Literature which I believe would not, in the ordinary sense of the phrase, bear exposure to the light of day'.[256]

At times in conversation, he could appear sympathetic towards that emergent institution, Mosley's New Party. In March 1932 he lunched with Jim Barnes, who had been talking to Mosley about developing a 'movement' beyond the New Party itself, and with Harold Nicolson, who was then a fascist sympathiser.[257] Tom, who had just accepted MacDiarmid's 'Second Hymn to Lenin' for the *Criterion*, appeared to accept Barnes's invitation to contribute to a proposed essay collection that would be 'New Party or fascist in tendency' – or at least he seemed ready to write in response to Barnes's pro-fascist introduction that would show where Mosley had 'made mistakes'.[258] Yet the book proposal came to nothing, and Tom, who registered Mosley's 'cleverness and slickness' but thought he lacked depth, wrote no such essay.[259] Nicolson ('a hearty booby', Tom thought) remembered him at lunch on 2 March looking 'very yellow and glum'. With his 'perfect manners' he was 'like a sacerdotal lawyer – dyspeptic, ascetic, eclectic. Inhibitions.'[260] However fond Tom was of Mary Hutchinson, he was guarded in responding to her brother Jim's fascist zeal, and his polished manners helped conceal his domestic distress. 'Ascetic' was how he appeared to many: that same day he had written to Charles Harris of the English Church Union, approving their support for F. P. Harton's *The Elements of the Spiritual Life: A Study in Ascetical Theology*. Still, he relished playing possum.

Vivien worried about his American plans. To provide reassurance, perhaps with her encouragement, he drew up a formal letter detailing his engagements. Beginning, 'My dear Vivienne', and ending 'Affectionately yours, your husband', this document made clear that he would leave in September, returning next May, and would continue as a Faber director and as the *Criterion*'s editor.[261] It looked likely Vivien would remain in England with nursing care. She aimed, she told Mary Hutchinson, to 'keep things going for him *here*'.[262] Meanwhile, Tom's secret obsession with his 'saint', to whom often he wrote twice each week, encouraged him to discuss with Emily the fate of their correspondence. Her eager replies were almost as frequent as his, but, unsurprisingly, their views did not always coincide. He hoped his 'papers' might go to the Bodleian Library, 'to remain unopened for sixty years after my death'. He explained to her that he wanted their relationship to be known, eventually.

> There will be so much in existence to give a very false impression of me, and so few clues to the truth. Can I make clear to you my feeling, I wonder. I admit that it is egotistic and perhaps selfish; but is it not natural, when one has had to live in a mask all one's life, to be able to hope that some day people can know the truth, if they want it. I have again and again seen the impression I have made, and have longed to be able to cry 'no you are all wrong about me, it isn't like that at all; the truth is perfectly simple and intelligible, and here it is in a few words.'[263]

However painful the outcome, he was prepared to leave to Emily the decision about the fate of their correspondence. Yet these sometimes Prufrockian words suggest his focus was more on himself than on her. Surely Emily, however modest, could not wish her name to be omitted forever from his history? 'It does canker,' he wrote, 'to feel that so long as there is any interest in me at all, if there is, my life and work will be misunderstood to the end of time.'[264]

Beginning to plan American engagements, including his visit to Scripps, he went on working hard in London. He joined 'the committee of the Old Vic and Sadler's Wells Society', and two letters written in that connection (but not included in the published Eliot *Letters*) show that he and Vivien, despite all the tensions between them, could still co-operate.[265] On 27 April, after they visited the Morrells' London home, each of them wrote to Philip Morrell, about how the Society's membership might be expanded. Spelling his forename wrongly, Vivien sent suggestions, and gratitude: 'What a glorious tea party it was today at your house. I did love it[.] Thanking you both a million times.'[266] The following day Tom's rather different note to Morrell about adding Society members was typically businesslike (he suggested 'circulating the Members' of the Shakespeare Association, of which he was a council member), and just one tiny part of his still substantial workload.[267]

Attempting to stay on top of his correspondence, as publisher he inquired about a 'Jewish Rabbi' who might write 'a history of the Jews'.[268] Each Monday and Thursday he attended Faber committee meetings. One of these featured a forty-five-minute discussion about Auden's use of the words 'fuck' and 'bugger' in his soon-to-be-published *Orators*.[269] Rather than risking prosecution over the expression '*A fucked hen*', Tom suggested Auden might substitute '*A June Bride*' – 'sore but satisfied' was Tom's explanation.[270] More solemnly, he sent Underhill's cousin, Evelyn, his *Spectator* essay 'George Herbert' which praised Herbert for going much further than Donne 'on the road of humility', and stated,

All poetry is difficult, almost impossible to write: and one of the great permanent causes of error in writing poetry is the difficulty of distinguishing between what one really feels and what one would like to feel, and between the moments of genuine feeling and the moments of falsity.[271]

With customary clarity, he wrote, too, about reading Charles-Louis Philippe's *Bubu of Montparnasse*, and feeling 'I have sinned exceedingly in thought, word and deed' – words that sound like a phrase from the confessional.[272] Alert to unemployment, communism, and political dilemmas, he argued in a March BBC talk on 'Christianity and Communism' that 'all our problems turn out ultimately to be a religious problem'.[273] Murry, whose newly published *The Necessity of Communism* presented communism as 'a religion' to which Murry had '*converted*', might have agreed.[274] But Tom chose the New Testament over Marx. Referring once more to Newman's *Grammar of Assent* – and, tellingly, to Stendhal's classic analysis of erotic adoration – he set out the nature of his own conversion:

Towards any profound conviction one is borne gradually, perhaps insensibly over a long period of time, by what Newman called 'powerful concurrent reasons'. Some of these reasons may appear to the outside world irrelevant; some are purely personal; and each individual, perhaps, has some reasons which could concern, some influences which could have influenced, no one but himself. At some moment or other, a kind of crystallisation occurs, in which appears an element of *faith* not strictly definable from any reason or combination of reasons. I am not speaking, mind you, of conversion to Christian faith only, but of conversion in general; there are some interesting remarks on the subject of conversion in a book by the great French novelist Stendhal entitled *On the Subject of Love*. In my own case, I believe that one of the reasons was that the Christian scheme seemed to me the only one which would work. I hasten to add that this is not a reason for believing; it is a tenable hypothesis to maintain that there is *no* scheme which will work. That was simply the removal of any reason for believing in anything else, the erasure of a prejudice, the arrival at the scepticism which is the preface to conversion. And when I say 'work', I am quite aware that I had my own notion of what the 'working' of a scheme comprehends. Among other things, the Christian scheme seemed the only possible scheme which found a place for values which I must maintain or perish (and belief comes first and practice second), the belief, for instance, in holy living and holy dying, in sanctity, chastity, humility, austerity. And it is in favour of the Christian scheme, from the Christian point of view, that it never has, and never will, work perfectly.[275]

Not long after this expression of belief, one sharpened perhaps by the demands of radio, by feelings for Emily, and by awareness of how much his 'Christian-slimy' (Aldington's term) turn had alienated friends, Tom was intensely saddened to hear Harold Monro had died.[276] He feared Emily would think him morbid. 'We are sad & need your company', he wrote to Hodgson, who accompanied him and Flint to Monro's funeral.[277] At Golders Green Crematorium Edith Sitwell 'saw Tom Eliot, for one moment only, and he looked broken'.[278] Heading home, Tom slept all the rest of that day.

Though she would 'not have gone' without Aurelia Bolliger, Vivien went to Marylebone Church on Good Friday 1932, before listening to Tom broadcast on the BBC on Easter Sunday about 'Building Up the Christian World'.[279] Denouncing 'the movement away from Christianity, which is for me the fundamental evil', he sounded at his most preacherly: 'we have got to a disorderly condition in which life seems to have lost all meaning and value'.[280] Vivien's dating letters to Aurelia 'Good Friday' and 'Easter Sunday' suggests she was now considerably less hostile to Tom's faith; she, her mother, and other family friends were proud to hear Tom's broadcast.[281] 'We must bear the responsibility for our ancestors, for we are of them and they are in us', he had stated a short time before, sounding not unlike a New England divine, and perhaps rather like Aldington's caricature.[282] Only months earlier he had confided privately that New England's famous son, Ralph Waldo Emerson, 'was such a damn prig. All his essays are sermons.'[283] Emily thought Tom's constant advice to her could sound like 'sermons', and told him so, but sermons ran in his blood.[284] His Easter Sunday broadcast ended with 'the words of Pascal, to be recalled even, and perhaps especially, on the day of the Resurrection: "The Christ will be in agony even to the end of the world." For sin and evil-doing we cannot abolish; but we can surely labour towards a social justice in this world which will prepare more souls to share not only here but in the Resurrection.'[285]

Vivien's ill health remained an almost constant anxiety. In early April Aurelia, after visiting the Eliots the day before, received an 'urgent' telegram from Tom. Aurelia explained she could not come until the afternoon. When she arrived, she and Vivien had an odd conversation about their shared affection for canaries.

> I entered the dark room. V. explained the telegram. After we had left Friday night, she had got desperately ill, with repeated vomitings. She thought it might have come from accumulated poison in her system from the medicines or drugs she took. Something like that happened periodically: but the worst fear was that she remembered a doctor saying another attack of continued vomiting might kill her. And she wasn't ready to die.[286]

Vivien had been 'haunted' overnight by anxieties about some canaries.[287] Aurelia tried to reassure her. Next day Vivien said she felt 'a little better, but of course have not been able to go out yet', and urged Aurelia to telephone.[288] Before long, recovered, she relished seeing *Wings Over Europe*, a play about a highly strung scientist and European war ('I *must* go again').[289] Her nurse-companion was now a Mrs Dixon Davies, a capable woman active in the Catholic Study Circle for Animal Welfare chaired by the rector of the Church of the Holy Rosary, Marylebone. This carer grew 'very fond of V.' Sencourt had 'established the connection'. Tom thought Mrs Dixon Davies 'extremely kind and persistent', but feared 'she may have the hope of accomplishing more than she can'.[290] He knew Vivien needed care, but, worn out, he could not cope much longer.

Mrs Dixon Davies was being lined up to help Vivien while he was abroad. Tom felt persistent 'Worry' about his wife's situation, and about the state of the world. 'Worry', Ellen Kellond's husband William Sollory told him, 'takes the vitality out of one'.[291] In this Depression era, Sollory, a boilerman, was having to sell off furniture to make ends meet. Tom helped him out with parcels of old clothes, and sought legal advice in connection with Sollory's pay, then helped him settle his debts. Sollory treasured Tom's kindness. 'You have been a *God send* to me.'[292]

He wished he could do more for Joyce. The Faber board examined the possibility of publishing *Ulysses* for the first time in Britain, but reluctantly shelved the idea: 'prosecution and serious penalties' seemed likely.[293] Rejecting submissions and communicating unwelcome news was part of Tom's job; he did it with his customary finesse. In April he had to decline a typescript by Maurice Reckitt, editor of *Christendom*, where some of Tom's own writings appeared. Tactfully, and with feeling, he wrote the *Times* obituary on Monro, who had once (though Tom did not mention this) turned down 'Prufrock' but whose 'ideal of poetry and of fraternity among poets' was exemplary.[294] Not long afterwards, Tom visited novelist and *Criterion* contributor Frederic Manning, who lay dying of bronchitis in a St John's Wood nursing home, 'coughing violently and smoking cigarettes'.[295] Emily too was depressed. The poet of *The Waste Land* tried to console her, explaining that spring and autumn were the most upsetting seasons. He found light relief in the all-male capers of 'a *Criterion* meeting' 'in the Board Room' at Russell Square on 3 May. The spoof cast list included 'F. V. Morley', whose home was Pikes Farm, Lingfield, Surrey, as 'An honest downright farmer' – and 'T. S. Eliot' (who 'very much' disliked 'being addressed as Professor') as 'A student'.[296]

Though he did not offer to publish it in Britain, Tom pronounced himself impressed by *The Rumble Murders*, a 'very good' 'detective story' that Henry (writing as 'Mason Deal') had published with Houghton Mifflin in New York.[297] Tom omitted mentioning his brother's sometimes clunky prose, praising, instead, his 'skill in plot'. Like Henry, he loved crime stories – Arsène Lupin, Sherlock Holmes, and more recent sleuths; but Tom was sure he could 'never' author one. 'My only possible resource for adding to my income would be to write children's verses or stories, having had a little success in writing letters to children (and illustrating them of course).'[298] Influenced not least by Edward Lear, he continued practising on the Faber children.

He told Henry that though 'it will be expensive keeping V. in England during my absence', he was looking forward to separating himself from her: 'even the most active life will be restful if I am alone'. He had already arranged lectures at Harvard, Bryn Mawr, Princeton and Johns Hopkins 'probably before Christmas'; then visits to St Louis and probably 'as far as the west coast', not to mention New York. 'This is the only opportunity of a lifetime to explore America a little at moderate cost.' Henry, with whom Tom shared many personal details, but who was not privy to his letters to Emily, was sure 'Your visit here will do you immense good nervously and physically.'[299]

Suddenly Ralph Hodgson's brother died. Vivien commiserated on 12 May, telling Hodgson he had seemed to her a 'tower of strength & reality' in a world 'of ghosts & shadows & unrealities'. Over the forthcoming Whitsun holidays Tom, exhausted, would spend '3 days in bed'.[300] His wife had come to regard Aurelia as 'one of the family', good company while 'Mr Eliot . . . read and grumble[d].' Vivien wanted them all to go 'to the country in the car to see my Aunt Lillia at Hindhead'.[301] Before long, they had a 'beautiful day in the country' – '*perfect* – & I shall never be able to say enough about it'. Aurelia must stay with them in their flat while 'Mr Hodgson' was away.[302]

Concerned to do her best for Vivien, Aurelia, though, had other commitments. So did Tom. Emily had suggested that in America he might go on holiday with her 'as many couples do in all morality these days'. Fearing 'scandal', he was not so sure.[303] A May *Times Literary Supplement* featured his piece on Jacobean dramatist John Ford, recalling dramas of sexual relationships gone wrong, a 'fine passage given to a crazed woman', and Ford's lines,

> Remember,
> When we last gathered roses in the garden,
> I found my wits; but truly you lost yours.[304]

Easily incensed, Vivien complained to Aurelia on 19 May, 'Mr Eliot is playing on the Wireless & driving me *MAD* '.[305] Just two days earlier Aurelia had observed the Eliots:

> V. drying hair, knees and elbows on floor. Asks T.S. about her engagements on Th[ursday] Night, the one he took by telephone. He in corner of bedroom in dressing gown (invisible from where I stood) couldn't remember. Grabbing hair: 'By Cripie, how I *do* hate a fool,' with tremendous emotion. He silent. 'Sat. is my birthday. What will you do to celebrate? Tom, you must do something.' 'You girls settle

everything. No, you girls do it.' I awkwardly get behind door to avoid his face and embarrassment.[306]

As it turned out, Tom had got presents for his wife. However, though he encouraged her to see friends and noted in his diary when a 'Big Tea Party' was due, he was wary of making arrangements she might find fault with.[307] She had accused her aunt of 'insulting' her, and warned Aurelia not to do so. Tetchy, Tom sought refuge in literary high-mindedness. He had been reading Q. D. Leavis's *Fiction and the Reading Public*, which led him to think about 'our *élite*, such as it is'. While believing that 'Anyone who is committed to religious dogma must also be committed to a theory of art which insists upon the permanent as well as the changing', he felt that 'the labour of the few at the top, their labour in developing human sensibility, their labour in inventing new forms of expression and new critical views of life and society, is largely in vain'.[308] Sounding off to Spender about 'Original Sin', he was more scornfully forthright: 'the vast majority' of the world's 'population will always be a compound of knave and blockhead, chiefly moved by vanity and fear, and kept quiet by laziness'.[309] Auden and Spender, whose work fascinated him, also nonplussed him. 'Modern youthful poets', he thought, 'are so devilish clever, much cleverer than we ever were.' Aurelia Bolliger heard him say he couldn't 'follow them'.[310] Nonetheless, helped by Morley, he assembled his *Selected Essays* for publication by Faber & Faber on 15 September, just before he was due to leave for America. Simultaneously, it would appear also from Harcourt, Brace in New York along with the first American edition of his *Poems, 1909–25*. He knew how to manage his career.

Vivien was having an 'Inventory taken of the *whole* flat', and Tom wanted his books listed before he moved out.[311] The separateness of the couple's lives surfaces in passing remarks. Vivien told Mary Hutchinson, 'Tom had to go to Church' – reinforcing Sencourt's observation, 'She did not join in his worship.'[312] Recalling stays with the Eliots, Sencourt recorded, 'it was apparent that the sharing, trust and companionship essential to any marriage were sadly lacking'. In Vivien he saw 'mental illness'. Sometimes 'her mood would verge on the very abyss of despair'. She quoted with 'zest' Thomas Hardy's lines about '*One who, past doubtings all, / Waits in unhope.*' For Sencourt 'Tom's decision to go to America without her certainly pushed her further over the confines of sanity', even if Tom had been 'the most devoted of husbands' throughout their seventeen-year marriage.[313]

Visiting Vivien on 8 June, Aurelia Bolliger noted an angry exchange when Tom telephoned.

Over tel. to T.S.E. (She had called me to come to her during the call.) 'Tell me what to do . . . You've given me 3 choices. Tell me, you cautious, over-cautious coward!' She screamed over tel. banged table with her fists in her tantrum, and cut him off. Then meekly: 'I'm sorry, Tom. I'm over-wrought. Now tell me what to do.'

Immediately after tea: I'd wish he'd go off and die somewhere. I'm tired. I'm thru. Mrs Monro knows. She said he was a sadist. He wants to make me squirm on a pin . . . squirm and squirm. Have you read Prufrock? There it is. He was squirming on a pin then. Let him go off to Am[erica] alone, and squirm again.

I think mother's right. He ought to go to see a doctor, a mental specialist, I mean. Don't you think so? What does R[alph] H[odgson] think about him? ('He has great affection for Mr Eliot. And for you too.') He can't. Nobody can.

Then she stared at me with a mad intensity. I looked away and ate sandwiches, lest another tantrum break out.[314]

Women familiar with Vivien tended to side with Tom. Hope Mirrlees, who stayed friends with both the Eliots, recalled decades later, with regard to Vivien,

she gave the impression of absolute terror. Of a person who'd seen a hideous ghost, a goblin ghost, and was always seeing a goblin in front of her. Her face was all drawn and white; and wild, frightened, angry eyes, and an over-intensity over nothing, you see: over some little thing you'd say. Suppose you were to say to her, 'Will you have some more cake?' And she'd say in a wild voice, 'What's that? What's that? What do you mean? What did you say that for?' She was terrifying. At the end of an hour, when she used to come and see me, I was absolutely exhausted. Sucked dry. And I felt to myself: poor Tom. This is enough.[315]

Tom felt that too, confessing to Marguerite Caetani he was still unsure 'what to do with Vivien while I am in America'. He made financial arrangements to ensure she was comfortable, though his lawyers would oversee his British bank account. It might, he told his cousin,

be cheaper to leave her in the Malmaison, even now; but I do not think it advisable that she should be so far away from her family and friends while I am away; nor do I think that it would be good for her to stop as long as eight months in any sanatorium. I hope to persuade her to accept some paid companion, but she is rather refractory. Meanwhile I am feeling increasingly tired and look to the sea voyage for a little rest (I suppose there is no prospect of your visiting America this winter?) Vivienne has continued in as normal condition as she is ever likely to attain, and has been able, though with dwindling resources, to keep her small car in which she gets about.[316]

Elizabeth Bowen saw a good deal of the Eliots around this time. Tom impressed her as 'very funny and charming and domestic', but confided that 'without alcohol he would never have got into the mood for his poems'.[317] She noticed 'poor little Vivien's wild eyes!' Bowen thought there was 'something about the atmosphere of the flat that I find exceedingly sinister and depressing', and decided it was 'the atmosphere of two unhappy and highly nervous people shut up together in grinding proximity'.[318] Visiting from America, Penelope Noyes 'said that one afternoon with V. used her all up, and what must it be to live with'.[319] Eager to leave, but grateful to anyone who was patient with his wife, Tom thanked Ottoline Morrell for 'kindness to Vivienne throughout this past year especially', and Vivien told Ottoline, 'You *know* that it is entirely due to you that I have been able to keep up.'[320] He confessed to long-suffering Emily that he hoped to experience in America some periods of '*complete* solitude'.[321] He felt his present life was 'a prison cell', but trusted that soon he might go alone for spells in 'monasteries'.[322] He wanted to go to Mass 'nearly every morning' at 'the Cowley Fathers' house' near Eliot House.[323] He took Vivien to the seaside for a short holiday, hoping it might do her good.

Writing flirtatiously to Mary Hutchinson as her self-styled 'lover', Vivien, '*worn out*', felt she too needed 'a change'. Though she worried it was '2 years & 2 months' since she had last 'left', she could not 'endure my present servants any longer'. She complained, 'I can't stay here, I really hate it', even as she dreamed of spending the winter making 'rooms' (perhaps in Bloomsbury's Tavistock Square or Gordon Square) just 'perfect for *Tom's return*'.[324] As his departure approached, he made sure to see various friends – Stead, Auden, Read, Dobrée, Sencourt (who had lent him a fur coat for the Massachusetts winter) – before leaving. He advised Joyce, whose daughter Lucia had had a nervous breakdown, about the Malmaison's care for 'that sort of trouble', though Tom worried 'French diagnoses seem to me very often an ingenious way of avoiding diagnosis.'[325] As ever, he felt dogged by potential decline. Aurelia Bolliger wrote,

He feels that he has already done his best work on the Criterion, and that it would be injurious – probably to both – if he continued too long. He is ready for a change. The winter at Harvard would give him a temporary rest, at least . . . The Criterion has only once as I recall run above 800 copies, average is 600. Only 1st and 2nd issues are now completely sold out. R[alph] H[odgson] thought subscription list would be 7,000–8,000. T.S.E. was silent a minute. 'If it were that, I wouldn't be living in this flat.'[326]

Very soon 'this flat' would be left behind. Through Sally Cobden-Sanderson, who worked for a travel agency, he had booked a passage on the *Ausonia* from Southampton to Montreal on 17 September 1932, planning to travel by train from there to Boston, avoiding reporters, unwanted contacts, and fuss. He longed to see his American relatives, and had already invited Eleanor Hinkley, whose play about Jane Austen he had tried unsuccessfully to place in London, 'to come with me to the Yale football match'.[327]

The start of August brought painful goodbyes. Hodgson and Bolliger were off to Japan. 'Viv will miss you terribly', Vivien's mother told Aurelia, wishing that the younger woman had been able to stay as 'a sister' to Vivien 'until Tom comes back from the USA'.[328] Tom would miss Ralph Hodgson too – not just his enthusiasm for dogs, but also his belief in poetry as a channel for visionary experience. After Tom had admired Hodgson's Malacca walking stick, Hodgson had given Tom an identical one; each time the two men met they exchanged walking sticks, and when Hodgson eventually departed he took Tom's with him, leaving his with Tom. To the end of his life, this became Tom's 'principal walking-stick'.[329] On 16 August he posted Hodgson two illustrated Edward-Learish poems. The first began 'How Delightful to Know Mr Hodgson! / (Everyone Wants to Know *Him*)'.[330] The second, under a sketched self-portrait (thin, upright, wearing a clerical-looking hat), opens

How Unpleasant to Know Mr Eliot!
With his Coat of Clerical Cut,
And his Face so Grim
And his Mouth so Prim
And his Conversation so Nicely
Restricted to What Precisely
And If & Perhaps and But.[331]

An astute self-depiction, this balances mischief and imaginative release with an awareness of how other folk perceived his meticulously chosen words. It incorporates an element of self-loathing. Aurelia Bolliger heard him say, 'Poetry has never brought me any happiness.'[332]

People who met him saw aspects of what he saw in himself. The child Jeremy Hutchinson detected something 'prim' in his speech; English poet Richard Church noted his 'nervous intensity', thinking his accent lacked any 'trace of its American origin'. It sounded 'old-fashioned, in the Edwardian mode of such English precisionists as Max Beerbohm and Osbert Sitwell', though Church heard in Tom's voice, too, 'a cutting edge . . . a hint of merciless satire' which he found attractive.[333] Vivien could be wounded by that cutting edge; not infrequently Tom turned it on himself.

As summer advanced, there were further engagements. On 2 September, when they visited the Woolfs at Rodmell in East Sussex, Virginia Woolf wrote in her diary how 'Tom, poor man, all battened down as usual, prim, grey' was 'making his kind jokes' with his wife.[334] Vivien seemed disturbed: 'On a wild wet day she dresses in white satin, and exudes ether from a dirty pocket handkerchief. Also she has whims and fancies all the time – some amorous, some pornographic.'[335] Virginia was surprised to find herself suddenly in Vivien's 'amorous embrace', and remembered how Vivien grew 'increasingly distraught as the afternoon wore on, changing her mind every second, and flying from one extreme to the other'.[336] One of the photographs taken by Leonard Woolf that afternoon shows Vivien pointing at Tom with apparent anger. The tension in it can still be felt today.

Trying to put a brave face on things the Eliots drove to Surrey for the christening of Tom's new godchild, Frank Morley's daughter Susanna. There were also many goodbyes, some face-to-face, others by letter. He wanted to meet his old bank colleague, H. C. Crofton, for 'a cold lobster and a bottle of hock' at the United University Club.[337] He contacted Bishop Bell about 'church building'. In October Bell was organising a Chichester conference on religious drama, bringing together poets, churchmen, and theatre people. Tom asked him to pass on material to Bell's Advisor on Religious Drama, Martin Browne, whom he had met at Chichester in 1930.[338] In due course, he and Browne would collaborate. Tom informed the managing director of the Clarence Gate Mansions Company that he would be absent in America, but 'Mrs Eliot expects to be in residence in my flat'; other plans for Vivien had fallen through.[339] He arranged that his bank manager would go on paying the Clarence Gate Gardens rent of £55 per quarter. There was another flurry of farewells, to Spender, the Woolfs (Virginia thought Vivien seemed 'wild as Ophelia'), Wilson Knight, the Morrells, Dobrée, the poet George Barker, Stead.[340] Most Tom saw personally, but he was running out of time, so some like Stead received letters only. He and Vivien spent time with the Faber family.

Giving some people four days' notice, and others just a few hours, Vivien urged the Morrells, Hayward (who thought her 'mad, quite mad'), and additional guests including Richard de la Mare and his wife to attend an 'AT HOME' on 15 September at 8.30 p.m. She asked that 'Morning Dress' be worn, assuring Ottoline Morrell she wanted to make 'Tom's Good-bye party' an event for people who wished 'his *absolute safety & ultimate good* in every possible way – above all spiritually'.[341] Tom, having dictated numerous letters at work, with numerous more to follow next day, did his best to look cheerful. A day or so later, as Alida Monro recalled, Vivien attempted to sabotage Tom's departure by locking in the bathroom a suitcase containing 'all his papers & lecture notes'.[342] Setting out at the very start of his long journey, Tom realised what she had done only when he was already sitting beside her in a taxi bound for Waterloo Station. Fortunately, Alida Monro was with them, and able to speed off to Clarence Gate Gardens to retrieve the suitcase. Tom and Vivien caught the train at Waterloo. Maurice Haigh-Wood remembered how on Saturday 17 September he, his wife, and Vivien waved the poet off at Southampton Docks. The Eliots 'walked a little while on the liner's deck'.[343] Then Vivien returned to the quayside, before, one by one, the ship's ropes were cast off. He was gone.

7

America

'A FRAID of Falling over Board' at night on the transatlantic crossing, 'a young lady' accosted Tom, asking for help walking round the deck. He assisted, but she complained his 'Support' was insufficient.[1] The image of a woman lost overboard mid-Atlantic would feature years later as a guilt-ridden husband craves atonement in his play *The Family Reunion*. Sailing towards his own family reunion in September 1932, he also anticipated seeing Emily – though not until January in California. Their reunion, he suggested to her, would 'be like the meeting of two people who have only just, full grown, come into existence', though he reminded her that 'the date' of their earliest 'meeting was, I think, 1905' when they had been 'children' and 'both too shy and reserved to have real conversation'.[2] Emily, the former schoolmate of Tom's cousin Eleanor, would have been about fourteen then, and Tom around seventeen. That first meeting does not seem to have struck her as very important, though in retrospect it may have seemed to him like Dante's first encounter with Beatrice. Now, however, she was excited, and had mentioned her relationship with Tom to Margaret Thorp.

On reaching Montreal, Tom headed for the old Bonaventure Station, then boarded his Boston train. The day-long route wound through Vermont and New Hampshire mountains in 'brilliant' autumn colours. 'More beautiful than I remembered', and so different from the long-domesticated terrain of southern England, this landscape's 'inhuman natural beauty' astonished him. New England's 'bird life' now seemed 'the most wonderful in creation'.[3] Cambridge, Massachusetts, too, was foreign yet familiar. Eliot House had not existed in his student days; opened in 1931, this 'very handsome' red-brick college with its ornate, white-domed clock tower was 'infinitely luxurious', but, with his eye accustomed to Oxbridge colleges, its 'vulgarity' appeared 'an effect of burlesque'.[4] ' "Home" to me', he told

Emily, 'has come to mean London in general, and my office and my club in particular.'[5]

Shy, poetry-writing Ted Spencer, Eliot House's thirty-year-old resident tutor in English, was 'extremely kind', promising, in Prohibition-era America, 'all the gin I may need'.[6] Spencer and Tom would teach a modern-literature course in semester two. While Spencer had an eye for the ladies, his colleague in English, F. O. Matthiessen, Eliot House's head tutor, was discreetly homosexual. Tom remembered his 'repressed excessive intensity'; his cat, George, a favourite with students, lived 'on terms of cold tolerance with the mice that disport themselves about the dining hall'.[7] Tom would get on well with these human and feline colleagues. He went swimming with Spencer and was photographed strolling with him along a beach in vest and trunks. Other company, however, proved less congenial. He was welcomed back by Harvard's President Lowell, a political scientist whose sister was poet Amy Lowell. President Lowell was intolerant of Jews, African Americans, and homosexuals, and Tom had always scorned him: 'an affable, mediocre, uninteresting Boston businessman, almost pathetically too small for the role he has to fill'.[8]

Determinedly undaunted by the alma mater he had left behind eighteen years earlier, Tom had his own demanding roles to fill. 'The only way I can manage my life here is on terms of the most formal social correctness', he told Emily.[9] With his family he relaxed – somewhat. His sister Ada had a party planned for the day of his arrival, his birthday. Gradually, over ensuing weeks, Tom revealed to her his 'domestic affairs', making clear he would travel to see Emily.[10] Encountering many other relatives, including his sisters Marion and Margaret, his cousin Eleanor, two uncles, and old student friends like Bill Castle and Leon Little, he was more circumspect. He felt awkward with Emily's aunt and uncle, the Perkinses, unsure how much they knew about his relationship with their niece. Nervously, in early October, he telephoned her. Hearing her voice rendered him 'nearly speechless, and partly imbecile, and afraid of being too emotional'. Delighted to hear her 'laugh a little', he sensed, though, she was 'forlorn' in 'exile'. In California, where her students found her a stylish, charismatic teacher, she was learning to ride; he wished he could give her a dog. If only he could touch her hand or take her to a symphony concert where they might 'have a good cry'.[11] Mostly, they continued exchanging letters.

He had written no lectures and prepared no teaching. Yet immediately he must play the eminent professor in an academic hothouse where several of his former teachers – philosopher James Woods, the venerable Irving Babbitt, and the shallower rhetorician Charles Copeland – remained presences on campus. Sitting in Eliot House library on 4 October, rereading

Coleridge's *Biographia Literaria* to fuel his lectures and making the air 'thicker with the aroma of English tobacco', he told a *Harvard Crimson* interviewer, 'Harvard looks very different at first sight, but it is gradually taking on its traditional appearance for me.'[12] Less guardedly, he confessed to Faber his initial 'sense of alienation' was 'painful'. Isolated by an 'invisible barrier', he worried 'there may be no one with whom I can wholly communicate, except the sister with whom I am staying'.[13]

His family helped him acclimatise. Ada and her husband 'Shef' Sheffield, a Wellesley College English professor, lived in Cambridge, and soon Henry (who found him 'grateful for personal affection after so much distant veneration') came to stay for several days.[14] Tom joked with his former room-mate Howard Morris about modern Harvard students: 'They don't seem to be the natty dressers that they were in our generation, and their mild and studious looks differ strangely from the hard & bestial faces of most of our old friends.'[15] When the topic seemed unavoidable, he stated, 'I have by the way, left my wife in London.' His explanation was partly financial, and partly that 'her doctor did not advise her coming, in view of the climate and the conditions of life'.[16] He and Vivien corresponded. Lucy Thayer spent time with her, but left; another companion, hired in part for her 'understanding of psychological abnormality' and whom Tom had hoped might 'become a permanency', also left, unable to 'endure this situation any longer'.[17] Virginia Woolf, aware of Vivien's 'running amok', had already expressed the private hope that Tom's 'separation' would be 'complete and final'; but Tom was still not ready to commit to a total break.[18] As the weeks passed, Vivien's letters gave him a sense of someone 'hopelessly infantile', even when she was 'in a well-behaving mood'.[19] He arranged for his secretary to visit her, and urged other friends to do likewise.

Soon he had moved from the Sheffields' home into a well-appointed suite of raised ground-floor rooms at B-11, Eliot House. Outside, on the quadrangle's lawns, stood substantial trees; to the rear the view was towards the Charles River. Tom's suite included two bedrooms (Henry used the spare one when visiting) and a 'marble shower bath'; however, still judging by English standards, he found the dining-hall food odd: 'tomato cocktails, fried pineapple, and strange salads'. Tea was in scarce supply. Unsatisfying 'near-beer' and a complete lack of Wensleydale cheese (his favourite) were alleviated, he confessed to Morley, by Scotch and gin – some supplied by the 'Master of this House', historian Roger 'Frisky' Merriman, a Harvard alumnus of 'aloof geniality' who, like Tom, had sojourned at Oxford and the Sorbonne.[20] In lofty academic company, even if his anglicised habits grated on some, Tom knew how to fit in. All-male, and characterised, as the *Crimson* put it, 'by a certain feeling of complacency', Eliot House had 'oligarchic' aspects, a strong intellectual life, and a comical abundance of Eliot heraldic crests which Tom found positively embarrassing.[21] He had his own Eliot House notepaper – minus the crest. Adding an exclamation mark after 'Eliot House', he sent young Tom Faber a letter filled with comical drawings, the last of which shows him typing at his desk, puffing on a cigarette.[22] He looks like a smoking concert pianist.

People's expectations were daunting. That November More would write him up in the *Saturday Review of Literature* as 'perhaps the most distinguished man of letters today in the English-speaking world'.[23] To others he was a pseudo-English charlatan. Journalists requested interviews; authors pressed books on him; audiences clamoured to make up their minds. 'I know I shall hate giving lectures and readings', he confided days before reading at Wellesley on 17 October; but, having lined up an ambitious schedule, he kept adding further engagements.[24] He sought to consolidate his American reputation, and his bank balance: Vivien's care requirements would be costly; if they lived apart, expenses would be even greater.

It became his habit to be 'At Home to students' each term-time Wednesday at 5 p.m.[25] By late October he was on the fourth rewrite of 'The Relationship of Criticism and Poetry', his first public lecture, announced for 8 p.m. on 4 November. He strove 'to make it pellucid'. He combed his slicked-back hair and felt 'very nervous about lecturing', but, introduced by Professor Livingston Lowes, he survived unscathed: 'large hall and big crowd, moderate applause; nobody tried to kiss me but Lowes seemed satisfied'.[26] Numbering several hundred, with people 'sitting on the floor in the aisles and on the steps' in the New Lecture Hall (today the Lowell Lecture Hall), his audience was agog, but many struggled: 'difficult to hear him beyond the first few rows'.[27] One-to-one or in small groups, students often found him less strained, warmer, more encouraging. Invitations proliferated: at a St Botolph Club dinner Robert Frost seemed 'a good soul', but 'to me not very interesting'; then came cocktail parties, more dinners, a 'Negro Spiritual Minstrel Show', Chamber Music Club concerts.[28] Circulating politely, he hid his troubles, which included a visit to his old ally Scofield Thayer, now suffering 'incurable' persecution mania. 'He had some symptoms quite familiar to me', Tom informed Emily; this disturbing 'disease' was 'patently an exaggeration of extreme egotism'. Tom missed England. 'I have never had a happy moment there; but my attachment is quite profound.'[29]

For the rest of his first semester's Friday-evening Norton Lectures on 'Poetry and Criticism in the Time of Elizabeth', on 'The Classical Tradition: Dryden and Johnson', and on 'The Theories of Coleridge and Wordsworth', his strategy was to mix protestations of modesty with intimidating flourishes of erudition.[30] In his second lecture, on 25 November, he presented himself as 'the grasshopper at the end of Lafontaine's fable – a species of insect associated by the early Greeks with lively music and poetry, rather than with learning and regiment'.[31] Yet in his mind the grasshopper was linked also to melancholy lines in the Old Testament book of Ecclesiastes which he quoted in a Boston lecture just days later: 'they shall be afraid of that which is high, and fears shall be in the way, and the almond tree shall flourish, and the grasshopper shall be a burden, and desire shall fail: because man goeth to his long home'.[32] This 'grasshopper' passage, well known to scripture readers of Tom's generation, haunted him.[33] He had cited it in his 'Notes' to *The Waste Land*, drawn on it in *Ash-Wednesday* where 'bones sang chirping / With the burden of the grasshopper', and would return to it again when he considered 'Fear in the Way' as a possible title for what became *Murder in the Cathedral*.[34] His likening himself in 1932 to the grasshopper, used by Lafontaine to portray an improvident singer dancing towards extinction, and connected in Ecclesiastes with failing desire and death, hints at a melancholy underlying his Harvard lectures.

He used those to advocate his aesthetic standpoint, carefully alluding (sometimes with a wink) to his own poetry as well as books by other Faber authors; but a persistent solemn sadness is evident. On 9 December, speaking of the *Biographia Literaria*, he discussed Coleridge's 'lament for lost youth', quoting a substantial passage of 'passionate self-revelation' from 'Dejection: An Ode' when Coleridge's 'afflictions bow' him 'down to earth' and where, eventually, the poet seems hollowed out:

And haply by abstruse research to steal
  From my own nature all the natural man –
  This was my sole resource, my only plan:
Till that which suits a part infects the whole,
  And now is almost grown the habit of my soul.

These lines, which Tom marked in his personal copy of Coleridge's poems, constituted, he told his audience, 'one of the saddest of confessions that I have ever read', and came from 'a haunted man . . . a ruined man. Sometimes, however, to be a "ruined man" is itself a vocation.'[35] Eventually, in his concluding lecture the following semester, Tom would leave the New Lecture Hall stage with what was for him a theatrically rhetorical gesture when, after quoting James Thomson's 'lips only sing when they cannot kiss' (words he had drawn on in 'The Hollow Men'), he proclaimed, as if heading for the Underworld, 'The sad ghost of Coleridge beckons to me from the shadows.'[36] Yet in December 1932, he told Emily that he thought, though there were 'always spectres at my back', in 'so far as "happiness" can be wholly dissociated from hope (hope in this world) that I am "happier" than I have ever been in my life'.[37]

In part, during this period at Harvard when he wrote little poetry, his stance was that of a poet fearful lest too much academia and 'abstruse research' threaten the poetic impulse in him. But his identification with 'ruined' Coleridge's 'saddest of confessions' ran deep. Regularly in early mornings Tom walked from Eliot House a short distance along Memorial Drive beside the river to worship with his own confessor, Father Spence Burton, in St Francis House (as it was then known), the monastery of the Society of St John the Evangelist. Linked to the Oxford-based 'Cowley Fathers', this monastery belonged to the first Anglican male religious community established since the Reformation. One student noticed Tom 'was a daily communicant at the monastery chapel', attending 'seven o'clock mass'; he also sought advice from the superior, Father Burton.[38] Tom's connection with this monastery would be a lasting one; he would return several times in later life. In addition, he told Emily, he planned to go 'once a month' to Boston's King's Chapel, and more frequently to the Anglican St John's Bowdoin Street.[39]

Regular participation in these services fits with his 1933 self-description as 'a rather fanatical Catholic', and his assertion that 'It is imperative that the next generation shall see to the restoration of the monastic life in society.'[40] Several times he stated, 'The ascetic ideal is essential to Christianity.'[41] His spiritual preoccupations during this period can be sensed not just from his possessing *The Quest for Solitude* by Peter Anson (later the historian of the Society of St John the Evangelist) but also from his use of F. P. Harton's *The Elements of the Spiritual Life: A Study in Ascetical Theology*. Tom had read Harton's 1932 volume, which stressed the value of the spiritual director, before it was published. He obtained the book before leaving England, and quoted from it in revising his American lectures. His marginal annotations highlight passages about the need to 'make constant forced acts of Faith' to 'build up the soul', and sections about 'mortification' – the religious practice of subduing passions through austere living – including the requirement that 'mortification must not be confined to the imagination, but also to the intellect'. He marked, too, material on purgative and illuminative spiritual experience, and Harton's quotation from R. C. Moberley's *Atonement and Personality*:

> Consciously or unconsciously, love is imitative. What I am really in love with I must in part be endeavouring to grow like, if the love is really on fire, even more than I consciously endeavour. What I am

really in love with characterises *me*. It is that which, I, so far, am
becoming.[42]

His American confessor and spiritual director, Father Burton, had published *The Atonement* in 1931, and had particular interests in this area of
theology, the reconciling of God and sinners through expiation of sin.
Seven years Tom's senior, this celibate Harvard graduate came from a well-
off Midwestern family, had studied in Oxford, and spent time in California.
Used to counselling Harvard men and well-heeled Bostonians as well as
prisoners on death row, Burton had experienced suffering when his brother
died young. His sermons manifest intense spirituality and love of incantatory language shaped by liturgical and biblical rhythms:

But I am not alone, for the Father is with me; I am not alone in the
darkness of life's tragedies, in the darkness of life's problems, for the
Father is with me; I am not alone in any dereliction, though I have no
one to turn to, no one to speak to. I may be alone in some hall bedroom
with myself and with my God. There is a God, and He is my God, and
the powers of darkness are routed by that final profession of faith.[43]

Surrounded by Harvard society, yet alone in dealing with feelings of
guilt about Vivien, Tom prepared to visit Emily in California just after
Christmas, and to see for the first time his parents' graves in St Louis. Burton's advice bolstered his religious commitment, his convert's ardour, and
his hunger for austerity, mortification, and atonement.

'A daily communicant', Tom received the sacrament at early-morning
Masses in the small Holy Spirit Chapel of Burton's monastery where, to
the left of the altar, stood a statue of the Virgin Mary. One of Tom's students, Wallace Fowlie, who helped ' "serve" the seven o'clock mass' each
Tuesday, recalled how 'he and I were often the only ones with the priest in
the chapel'. An incident stuck in Fowlie's memory:

Only the three of us were present. At the time of the communion
Eliot had risen and come up to the altar to receive. The priest and I
had turned back to the altar, and I could hear Eliot rise and return to
his place. At that moment there was such a heavy thud, as if Eliot had
fallen, that the priest and I turned round. Eliot was flat on his face in
the aisle, with his arms stretched out. It was obvious at a glance he
had not fallen.

Under his breath, and as if speaking to himself, the priest said,
'What shall we do?'

I suggested, 'Let's finish here first.' So, we turned back to the altar.

The one aisle in the chapel where Eliot lay was so narrow that the priest and I could not have walked there in order to reach the sacristy. The priest finally said to me, 'I think you should help him up. Something may be wrong.' I went on ahead and put my arm under his shoulder. He came with me easily. Almost no physical effort on my part was required to help him back to his seat. As I preceded the priest into the small room at the end of the aisle, I realized that Eliot had just undergone a mystical experience.[44]

Rather than trying to define this experience, it seems best to link it to Tom's falling to his knees in St Peter's in 1926; it was a prostration before God. Whether encouraged by stress or other factors, it signals the intensity of his religious commitment.

If this was less immediately apparent to some lecture-hall audiences, his erudition was inescapable. The 'grasshopper' poet could sound too professorial as he flitted from asserting that 'Everyone has read Campion's "Observations in the Art of English Poesie" and Daniel's "Defence of Rhyme"' to invoking in the space of a few minutes Pound, Milton, Spenser, Pope, Dryden, Shakespeare, *Chevy Chase*, Chaucer, *The Changeling*, *The Witch of Edmonton*, and Racine's tragedy of love versus duty, *Bérénice*. How many in his audience had read all these texts? Straining to catch Tom's drift, an anonymous *Harvard Crimson* reporter struggled to keep up:

> 'Many poetic and dramatic geniuses flourished during this period,' Professor Eliot continued, 'but I regret that some of the plays are not better than they are. The desire for comic relief on the part of the audience is a craving of human nature, due to an inability to concentrate. An audience which can maintain its attention on pure tragedy is more highly civilized than any other audience. Racine's "Berenice", in this respect represents a peak of human civilization.'[45]

Bérénice is unusual among tragedies because it ends not with death but with the painful separation of lovers and a renunciation of love. In a few weeks, still corresponding with Vivien but inclining towards a separation from her, Tom would travel to meet Emily.

If on the lecture platform he could voice regret that 'comic relief' was a 'craving of human nature', nevertheless he craved it for himself. A few days after uttering these words, he left an envelope for Spencer. Inside it Spencer found 'Two selections suitable for a Christmas (or Yuletide)

Reading.' Both were in verse, and each began "Twas Christmas'. The first concluded:

> The Chaplain was so very scared
> His breeches he manured,
> And Columbo slid along the deck
> And raped the smoke-room steward.[46]

The other 'reading' was almost as filthy. By now, Spencer, like some of the other Eliot House tutors with whom Tom exchanged 'obscene limericks' over dinner, knew him well enough to understand that this venting of obscenity was a safety valve that did not negate his conduct elsewhere.[47] In late December Tom and Spencer went to a Christmas Eve midnight Mass with Gregorian chant at St John's Church, Beacon Hill. 'It was snowing outside. The ladies wore fur coats. The liturgy was performed slowly and reverently, and the mass was beautifully sung by the Cowley Fathers.'[48] Annoyed by a clever-clever student who quoted to him the Cavalcanti line that underpins the start of *Ash-Wednesday*, Tom spent Christmas Day with family in Cambridge, before typing many letters on 26 December – some in response to notes and cables from and about Vivien. Then he took trains via New York and St Louis ('stay 4 hours'), and on through Kansas and New Mexico for his much-anticipated Californian rendezvous.[49] Calling Emily 'My dear Dove', and using a favourite nickname, 'My dear Bird, Birdie', he had written, honestly but awkwardly, to say, 'You cannot possibly realise how terrified I am of confronting you – but I do wish you would try – so as not to be exasperated by my sheepishness.'[50]

By the time he stepped off his Santa Fe railroad car at 6.20 a.m. on Thursday 29 December at the recently built Claremont railroad depot, whose oddly Spanish baroque concrete frontage and cruciform doors made it look part train station, part church, Tom was tired and unshaven. Emily was there, but not alone. Her colleague Professor Paul Havens, whom Tom had met in England, had brought his car to drive the VIP guest to lodge at the home of wealthy local educationalist Mary Eyre at 1132 North College Street, close to the recently opened Scripps College. At this privately funded women's liberal-arts establishment Emily as 'Assistant Professor of Oral English' was acting (she played the imposing Lady Bracknell in a production of Oscar Wilde's *The Importance of Being Earnest*), teaching drama, and supervising Eleanor Joy Toll Hall, a Spanish Colonial-style student residence.[51] Claremont, a small town whose population then numbered under 3,000, lies among the foothills of the San Gabriel Mountains about thirty miles east of Los Angeles. The Scripps campus grounds were still being developed by landscape architect Edward Huntsman-Trout. This admirer of Italian Renaissance gardens had recently laid out a special, geometrically patterned garden of flowers and shrubs outside Toll Hall. Tom associated Emily with flowers and gardens, and her college, with its recently chosen motto from Dante ('*Incipit Vita Nova*'), could have been the setting for a new life to begin.[52] Here, Tom told his 'Beautiful Lady', he felt 'suspended between heaven and earth', and came 'as near to happiness as one can come in 10 days – and nearer than ever in my life'.[53]

His visit proved to him 'I am happier in your company than in that of anyone else'.[54] They relished intimate conversations, each sensing anew how difficult the other's life had been. He noticed the Henry James works in her bookcase; she observed his bad teeth. He assured her she was his 'one Fixed Point in this world'.[55] Soon, he learned 'what a kiss is', and 'what companionship is'; but their time alone together was limited, and Tom the visiting celebrity, who intrigued staff and students alike, was hardly, as he admitted to Emily, 'the *homme moyen sensuel*'. For her part, she made it apparent she did 'not feel exactly' towards him as he did towards her.[56] Their closeness increased, but each sensed the other's wish to do nothing compromising, either in the eyes of the college, or of Tom's wife, or of wider communities, or even in the eyes of one another.

Within Scripps, which had produced its first graduates only the year before, there were tensions over gender: college president Dr Ernest Jacqua had appointed more male professors than some governors of this women's college thought appropriate. Its whole set-up – from afternoon tea gatherings and imitation baronial hall to the 'Gutenberg Window' in the chapel-like Ella Strong Denison Library dedicated not to the glory of God but to 'the greater wisdom of women' – was brand new; Claremont itself was only a year older than Tom. Everything disconcerted him. The winter weather was 'very hot', but, on a drive, he 'got stuck in a snow drift. The trees are full of oranges.'[57] California, he told English correspondents, had 'no *country*, only *scenery*'; it was 'a horrible place' – 'a nightmare'.[58]

Yet displaced Bostonian Emily was his dream, even if she still found him strange. Teaching his poetry shortly before, she had called him 'a man of undoubted faults and highest virtues'. She looked forward to his visit, which was, a friend reflected, 'primarily a private one'.[59] At one point she had hoped to go travelling with Tom as far as Yosemite, but that did not happen. Tom had gone to some trouble to compose a special lecture which, after chatting with students and faculty (who recalled his prodigious tea-drinking), he delivered in Scripps's Balch Hall on 5 January. Conscious of the elocutionist Emily's musicality, he chose as his keynote Walter Pater's statement that 'All art consciously aspires towards the condition of music.'

He stressed the importance of poetry that pleases the ear and has a strong emotional effect; his lead came from Aldous Huxley, who over a decade earlier had called Edward Lear a 'genuine poet': 'Change the key ever so little and the "Dong with a Luminous Nose" would be one of the great romantic poems of the nineteenth century.'[60] Tom saw the 'romantic' Lear as a 'more adult' poet than Lewis Carroll. A poet of 'pure poetry', Lear was comparable not just with his contemporaries Tennyson and Swinburne but also with supposedly 'unintelligible' moderns including Mallarmé, Auden and, by implication, Tom. Though the full text of his lecture no longer exists, evidently two of the poems he discussed were 'The Courtship of the Yonghy-Bonghy-Bo' – a nonsensical account of a romantic relationship that founders because one partner has a 'mate' in distant 'England' – and 'The Owl and the Pussy-cat', that poem about a pair who 'went to sea / In a beautiful pea-green boat' ('O let us be married! Too long we have tarried!'), but whose mix of fun and pathos depends on readers realising that in the real world no bird would ever marry a cat.[61]

Tom and Emily went to sea 'in a motor boat' on 10 January, towards the end of his Californian visit.[62] Scripps student Marie McSpadden drove them to her mother's cottage on Balboa Island, so they could spend uninterrupted time together. Tom had just lectured at UCLA and the University of Southern California, with Berkeley to come the following day. After leaving Emily at Scripps, he had felt in Los Angeles 'a slight emotional collapse', but McSpadden, who remembered how Emily's 'dear friend' Tom 'loved his boat ride on the Pacific that day', sailed the couple to the sandy beach at Corona del Mar so they could enjoy being alone beside the ocean.[63] 'Self knowledge is the most important factor in knowing what we really feel', he had told his UCLA audience a few days earlier.[64] Some weeks later, naming no names, he was reported as saying in a public lecture,

> An ideal correspondence, according to Mr Eliot, will be with a person of the opposite sex, not one with whom the writer is in love, for love letters are monotonous. The recipient of the letter should be a mature friend, sufficiently understanding so that a good deal need not be said, but not to the point where letters will be obscure to others. There should be sufficient sentiment to release the writer's mind to speak freely, without fear of betrayal, for the greatest pleasure derived from letter-writing is being indiscreet. The two correspondents should have interests in common and should be able to be brutally frank.[65]

'If you don't see my private joke in talking about how a poet should write letters, no one will', he told Emily.[66] Recently he had been reading

Keats's love letters to Fanny Brawne, and comparing them awkwardly with his own. Having spent years making sure his love for Emily was either converted into friendship or rechannelled and disciplined through the love of God, Tom went on writing to her – at least sixty-four times in 1933 alone. Following his Scripps visit, she sent him a 'dear *unexpected* letter'. Signing himself 'Emily's Tom', he replied, 'I would go around the world for such a letter', and he urged her to write to him without reserve, as if he were a doctor or priest.[67] But he wrote to her a month later, on Valentine's Day, about 'sublimation' and the need for an almost sacerdotally disciplined religious routine; after time had passed she came to feel he had given her 'a false impression' in California.[68] Long afterwards, one of her drama students recalled how, in a clever reworking of a traditional Boston saying, Emily had remarked, half-jokingly, to her select undergraduates, 'Emily Hale speaks only to Eliot, and Eliot speaks only to God.'[69]

Clearly he had been thinking again about whether he could divorce, but 'even if there was some law by which the Church could grant a nullification', Vivien seemed most unlikely to agree to divorce, and might resist even separation.[70] At Scripps, Tom was happy to kiss Emily and savour her presence, but just what might that mean? He soon wrote to her about his preoccupation with '"doubleness" of appearances', and of living 'on two planes at once'.[71] To Tom, in the context of spiritual insight and religious belief, this was attractive and positive. It recalls both what he had admired in the dramas of George Chapman, and what his English spiritual director, Underhill, believed about 'each of us' as 'two persons': one with an 'outward life', one with a 'hidden life'.[72] But could such doubleness shade towards duplicity? It would be hard to blame Emily if she wanted more straightforwardness. Her Unitarianism and his Anglo-Catholicism were a cause of conflict – but sometimes Tom seemed to relish that.

Emotionally, he relied on his correspondence with her and the relationship that went with it. Lorraine Havens, the shrewd wife of Emily's Scripps colleague, Paul, observed the couple together: Emily 'spoke of him often, always as "Tom", and was obviously much in touch with him'. Tom, for all he appeared 'somewhat reserved and formal, but very courteous', was 'obviously devoted to Emily'.[73] The Scripps students had sensed this too, speculating there was something between them. Yet the pair's behaviour was always decorous. From Scripps the Havenses, Emily and Tom went together to a nearby High Episcopal church. It unsettled Tom that Emily as a Unitarian was relaxed about participating in Anglican communion; he could not approve of her attitude. When he inscribed a copy of the recently published *Sweeney Agonistes* for her, he wrote formally, 'For Emily Hale / from the author / T. S. Eliot / Claremont / California / January 1933'.[74]

Emily did not think *Sweeney Agonistes* would work on stage, but in her Toll Hall room (where, sometimes clad in a black silk dressing gown decorated with golden Chinese dragons, she entertained favourite students) she kept a leather folder containing two signed photographs of Tom; he, in turn, begged her for photographs, and treasured those she gave him. After leaving Claremont in January 1933 he felt 'pain' come 'in violent twinges'. For most of the journey back across America, which included his first visit to his parents' graves in St Louis, he told her he felt 'utterly numb'.[75]

Carefully and formally, Emily (later recalled by Marie McSpadden as 'a lonely person') presented Tom's visit as a quiet rest between demanding lecture engagements.[76] Now his schedule became unrelenting. In January in St Louis he addressed 900 people at Washington University on 'The Study of Shakespeare Criticism'. After staying with family in his native city, he proceeded to engagements in Minnesota, Buffalo, and in Baltimore where he stayed with an old Harvard acquaintance, George Boas, and enjoyed his sole meeting with Scott Fitzgerald. Fitzgerald and his wife Zelda were living on the estate of the Turnbull family, sponsors of Tom's Baltimore lectures. For Tom, Fitzgerald filled 'a medicine bottle marked "one teaspoonful every three hours" with whisky – it tasted like varnish.'[77] The two men enjoyed each other's company. Yet Tom thought Fitzgerald, whose marriage to the mentally troubled Zelda was tempestuous and whose alcoholism was becoming chronic, 'a very sick man', while Fitzgerald thought Tom 'Very broken and sad + shrunk inside.'[78]

In Baltimore Tom delivered his Turnbull Lectures at Johns Hopkins University, using a truncated, hastily revised version of the unpublished Clark Lectures. He had added some new material – for instance, a passage about Mallarmé's 'Tonnerre et rubis aux moyeux' ('Thunder and rubies up to the wheel hub') which, he contended, showed that 'Poetry is *incantation*, as well as imagery.'[79] His lectures served to condition the reception of his own poetry. Addressing a large audience in Hopkins's Latrobe Hall, he held forth positively messianically:

The world always has, and always will, tend to substitute appearance for reality. The artist, being always alone, being heterodox when everyone else is orthodox, and orthodox when everyone else is heterodox, is the perpetual upsetter of conventional values, the restorer of the real. [. . .] the important poets will be those who have taught the people speech; and the people had in every generation to be taught to speak: the function of the poet at every moment is to make the inarticulate folk articulate: and as the inarticulate folk is almost always mumbling the speech, become jargon, of its ancestors or of its newspaper editors, the new language is never learnt without a certain resistance, even resentment. '*Donner un sens plus pur aux mots de la tribu*', Mallarmé said of Poe; and this purification of language is not so much a progress, as it is a perpetual return to the real.[80]

Back at Harvard, his orations sounded less messianic, but his religious commitment was certainly proclaimed. 'Good poetry', he told a *Crimson* reporter in advance of his fifth Norton Lecture (on Shelley and Keats) 'should be written by good Catholics and good atheists; not by a man with a religion of his own.'[81] His audience was left in little doubt of Tom's stance when in early March he spoke of Arnold's constant tone of 'regret, of loss of faith, instability, nostalgia', then quoted lines about 'isolation without end' and 'Prolonged [. . .] loneliness.' The lecturer's retort to Arnold was, 'if you don't like it, you can get on with it', and Tom concluded that 'A man's theory of the place of poetry is not independent of his view of life in general.'[82] Developing his Norton Lectures by considering 'The Modern Mind' on 17 March, he hoped he had indicated 'changes in the self-consciousness of poets thinking about poetry'. He attempted to question Richards's contention that '*The Waste Land* "effects a complete severance between poetry and *all* beliefs".' Moving towards a 'Conclusion' in late March, he agreed that 'there is an analogy between mystical experience and some of the ways in which poetry is written', though he was wary of equating the two in a straightforward way: 'ill-health, debility or anaemia' could also give rise to 'an efflux of poetry' after a 'long incubation' and a 'sudden lifting of the burden of anxiety and fear which presses upon our daily life'.[83]

Here and elsewhere he linked such sensations to texts on which he had drawn in his own verse, showing how poetry comes from 'reading' and 'organisation' as well as from any mystical 'inspiration'.[84] His procedure involved fusing all of these. 'The "meaning" of a poem, in the ordinary sense', he argued, was present just to divert the reader's mind 'while the poem does its work upon him: much as the imaginary burglar is always provided with a bit of nice meat for the house-dog'. Hinting at his interests in 'the "long poem"' and 'the theatre', he told his Harvard audience with regard to ' "difficult" ' modern poetry that the problem was 'half-educated and ill-educated', not 'uneducated' readers: 'I myself should like an audience which could neither read nor write.' He wanted to produce work that 'cut across all the present stratifications of public taste', though, after trying to hint how *Sweeney Agonistes* attempted that, he confessed that 'poetry is not a career, but a mug's game'.[85] In private, he indicated that one pleasure in being with his family was being 'with people who were fond of me before the malady of poetry declared itself'.[86]

As always, his lectures asked a lot of audiences. On reading the printed versions, many people have been struck by his perceptive emphasis on 'the musical qualities of verse' – whether in Edward Lear or Arnold. Drawing on anthropology as well as poetry, he memorably summed this up:

> What I call the 'auditory imagination' is the feeling for syllable and rhythm, penetrating far below the conscious levels of thought and feeling, invigorating every word; sinking to the most primitive and forgotten, returning to the origin and bringing something back, seeking the beginning and the end. It works through meanings, certainly, or not without meanings in the ordinary sense, and fuses the old and obliterated and the trite, the current, and the new and surprising, the most ancient and the most civilised mentality.[87]

If here Tom was the oracularly insightful poet, in smaller gatherings he strove to sound less grand, 'banging the piano and singing a huge number of limericks' – some of which 'he had written himself', rhyming 'young girl of Siberia' with 'tempting posterior'.[88] When one of his male students brought an actual 'pretty girl' to one of his Eliot House teas, she so distracted the Harvard chaps that Tom requested future gatherings should be men-only.[89] In an Eliot House where 'only male guests' were invited to an 'unexpurgated' performance of the Elizabethan comedy *The Shoemaker's Holiday* directed by professors Spencer and Matthiessen, such 1930s attitudes were not unusual.[90] Tom relished his 'undeserved reputation for limericks', and liked that when dining at an undergraduate club to which he had once belonged he was 'presented to the company with the words, "Tom Eliot is a member we are all proud of, but I want to say that he is really just a good old Fart like the rest of us."'[91] By turns ascetic, messianic, bawdy, brilliant, and shy, he fascinated his students.

> We were proud to have Eliot there and hear him speak to us each week. We became almost childishly curious about him, about his life, and we developed the outrageous habit of following him in the street to see where he walked, where he ate, what he ate. If he went into the Coop, what did he buy?[92]

The fifteen undergraduates in the class he taught with Spencer in Sever Hall – English 26 'English Literature from 1890 to the Present Day' – were a select bunch. Parading his prejudices, Tom had informed Emily, 'I want as few graduate students as possible, a number of men specializing in other subjects than English, preferably scientific, a few oarsmen or football players, and a quota of not more than 20% Jews.'[93] Those admitted to this group heard him denounce Lawrence as a 'Heretic Messiah', and were certainly stretched.[94] Telling them he did 'not intend to supply any information that can be got out of books', but would operate in a 'Seminar spirit – free discussion', he ranged across topics from Flaubert to the medieval Scots flyting of William Dunbar, taking in also modern fiction, drama, and poetry.[95] His ascetic absolutism prevailed: Hardy revealed a 'Cesspool of unsatisfied desires'.[96] Tom discoursed intensely about evil, which could not 'even be perceived but by a very few'. Praising Conrad and James for their ability to suggest evil, he highlighted 'The perception of life as on several planes at once, noticeable in Chapman and Dostoevski.' His notes show he contended that 'Intersection of planes of reality has been problem of fiction ever since *Bleak House* and *Armadale*. Becomes final with Joyce', who was, he declared in March, 'the greatest writer of the age'.[97] Later, he discussed *Ulysses* in terms of '*The Synchronisation.* (cf. Pound and myself). Several periods of time and several planes of reality at once.'[98] And he praised the late, ritualistic plays of Yeats, whom he had encountered recently at an academic gathering. Students familiar with the ritualistic *Sweeney Agonistes*, whose tormented protagonist seems to perceive a horrible reality that other characters miss, may have seen connections with Tom's own work. Yet surely no student would have caught his allusion to '*An Adventure*', with its figures from the past in a haunted garden.[99] People from his own past preoccupied his mind.

Sensing he was spinning further and further from her orbit, Vivien had been alarmed by his going to California. In turn, her behaviour troubled people in England. She sent Tom cables. In distress, she wired Mary Hutchinson, Morley, and others. She drafted 'a new Will': '*I have left everything to Tom.*'[100] He wrote to her. She delayed replying. Was that 'a good sign'?[101] He sought third-party reports of her health. Considering returning 'to the Sanatorium de la Malmaison for a time', she avoided washing, and felt 'in a most terrible state of health'.[102] Women who knew her advised Tom to stay away. Alida Monro counselled him in February never to put his 'feet over the threshold' of his London flat again. Heeding her opinion, he now favoured 'a sharp sudden break'. 'This is a step which I have contemplated for many years.' Such a move could frighten Vivien, but little or no 'affection' remained. Almost twenty years afterwards, Tom recalled that he had thought the failure of the marriage was 'my fault for a period', and that going to America had been his way of getting away: 'The difficulty is that you either suffer too much or too little with the sufferer.' In late February 1933, though, for all he loved being with his siblings, he felt 'real dislike of America as a habitat'. Still, being there convinced him 'I can be comparatively happy *solely* by being away from V.'[103]

Without explicitly mentioning Russell's adultery with Vivien, or his own adultery or his relationship with Emily, he reflected to Ottoline Morrell in March that 'Bertie' had 'done Evil'. He made it sharply clear his mind was made up.

> I entirely agree with you that she would flourish better without me. I also think that the present time, after my absence, is the best time for a break. For my part, I should prefer never to see her again; for hers, I do not believe that it can be good for any woman to live with a man to whom she is morally, in the larger sense, unpleasant, as well as physically indifferent. But I am quite aware of putting my own interests first. I will ask you not to give any indication of what I have said, not only to her, but to anyone else. I want to arrange matters in such a way as least to injure her vanity.[104]

Tom's harshness here was matched by the tone of lectures he delivered during the rest of his American sojourn. Conscious he would rile them, and telling Unitarian Emily (to whom at times in letters he imaged himself as a jungle beast or a stubbornly defiant, puritanically minded pugilist), 'you know I am by way of being a fanatical narrow bigot', he informed Boston Unitarians in King's Chapel that 'the sense of sin' was 'absolutely essential to Christianity' – as was belief in the supernatural. Anticipating 'a period in which Christians in Western Europe and America will be persecuted', he contended that 'We can have no ideal, for all human beings, lower than that of saintliness.' 'Celibacy' represented 'the highest life', and if some people thought that 'inhuman', so be it.[105] His patronising remarks about a 'Young Females' Seminary', like his longing for a 'monastery', and various comments to Emily about religion, all seem bound up with his persistent sense of sexual relationships as power struggles.[106] To Emily, using language reminiscent of his struggles with Vivien, he wrote in late February,

> What I desire with you is as much Conflict as Unity. I know both the desire to dominate, to influence, to make someone else into my own image; and the desire to be ruled, to be dominated, to be influenced, to make myself into someone else's image. The desire to be a master, and to be a slave. The desire to be an idol, and a worshipper. But these conflicting desires are only harmonized by a third (everyone goes by trinities) the Desire for Conflict. The more I love you, the more I want to quarrel with you. Over small things, mostly. But over big things too. The fact that I am a Trinitarian, and that you are a

Unitarian, matters very much to me. It means a Fight. Of course I mean to win. Very likely I shant.[107]

His sense of conflict with – and love for – Emily ran alongside his marital anxieties. 'Emily should not work but merely exist', he wrote to her, worried she was overworking.[108] Within ten days, accusing her of being 'Silly', he told her, 'If I cannot be of any use to you, I had rather do without you.'[109] Her replies do not survive, but tensions are evident. Between March and May, he advanced arrangements for a clear separation from his wife. Though much 'intimate correspondence involving Vivien' was destroyed, he enlisted help from Geoffrey and Enid Faber, from Morley, and from solicitors as well as from others including Ottoline Morrell, before Vivien received any formal notification.[110] As he steeled himself for repercussions, his public steeliness grew more pronounced. As always, though, he found ways to release tension by adopting jocular voices towards trusted friends.

At the lectern – and sometimes privately – his tone communicated absolutism. With the Norton Lectures ending, between mid-February and early May he filled his calendar relentlessly with engagements: at Yale, Brown, Princeton, Smith, Mount Holyoke, Amherst, Haverford, Bowdoin, New York, Bryn Mawr, Wellesley, Milton Academy, and Vassar (where *Sweeney Agonistes*, with some new, Audenesque lines by Tom, was performed for the first time, and he was interviewed by student poet Elizabeth Bishop). Furious travelling required coming up with lectures at speed, and reflected his ambition. In March he listed to Emily several English 'trifles' he would like to collect, including a senior Cambridge University professorship, and a royal award, the Order of Merit.[111] In America, too, he was signally ambitious. One welcome 'trifle' would be the award of a Columbia University honorary degree in June.

Eager to address American audiences, and to be paid for doing so, he recycled material: his most frequently delivered lecture was that on Edward Lear. He drove himself hard, meeting innumerable people, but could not escape his sense of isolation: 'one's solitude in life becomes more and more evident to oneself'.[112] He pressed ahead with public engagements, and with 'some form of *private* but definitive marital separation'.[113] Harassed, he asked Father Burton at the monastery for 'an appointment for confession' during Holy Week.[114] Apparently shortly after this he wrote to Emily on 'Holy Saturday' (15 April), making it clear he could not divorce. Denying any 'vanity or vainglory', he explained that he had become 'a kind of symbol' to a number of people, including writers, 'strangers', and committed Anglicans like his English friend the Reverend Geoffrey Curtis.

Not only strangers, I feel that I am a symbol for instance to John Hayward or to Geoffrey Curtis; even to Stephen Spender perhaps – who is all that I should dislike, being a half-Jew, an invert and a communist, but in whom I feel a curious physical attraction in spite of all that. It means a restriction on behaviour in some ways; things that other people could do I can't: I can say wholly without overestimating my importance that if I had a divorce it would be the greatest misfortune to the Anglican Church since Newman went over to Rome – and Gladstone called that a 'catastrophe'. It also means a peculiar loneliness – a loneliness which I recognize sadly in Joyce and Lawrence, and interestingly enough, I don't see in Pound, though I do not say that it is not there because I fail to see it – yes, there is something of it in 'Mauberley', so far his greatest poem. And the only consolation, and at the same time a correction towards humility, is contained in the words, 'can ye drink of the cup that I drink of?'[115]

Tom aligned his own loneliness with that of fellow male writers, and with Christ. Self-involved, he paid considerably more attention here to his own predicament and standing than to those of Emily, to whom he was trying to explain why he could not divorce. She wanted him to divorce. She wanted a less abnormal relationship with him, whereas he sought now to 'sing a new song' and 'arrange' his 'life as it is to be to the end', desiring 'self-directed austerity instead of torment'.[116] He argued with her that this course was right, that 'in one way I understand you better than you can understand yourself'; that he was 'leaving Emily free', not 'trying to impose a future upon her so that she may conform to my ideal'. His discussing her in the third person in this letter sounds strangely detached, even as he calls her 'dearest'.[117] She did not give up.

By early May 1933 he was finalising arrangements to come and stay at the Morleys' Surrey farm, and so avoid Vivien. He could sound pally corresponding with Morley, or with 'Rabbit' (Pound), who wrote to him as 'Possum' at 'Possum House', Massachusetts, but he was under strain.[118] After a long train journey, he reached Charlottesville, Virginia, 'a beautiful place' set in 'sad country' where he was to deliver the Page-Barbour Lectures at the university.[119] His host, Professor Scott Buchanan, introduced him to faculty and their spouses; Tom downed mint juleps, and excursed to Thomas Jefferson's Monticello plantation, noting 'immobile negroes' and 'poor white' folk, 'people waiting for nothing to happen'.[120] Encouraged by Buchanan to reflect on tradition and the American South, when Tom emerged to lecture on 'The Meaning of Tradition' in Madison Hall on 10 May, he spoke not as a Missourian but 'as a New Englander' conscious of the Civil War – 'a disaster from which the country has never recovered'. He expressed sympathy for that neo-agrarian movement whose 1930 manifesto *I'll Take My Stand: The South and the Agrarian Tradition* had championed a 'culture of the soil'.[121] His first lecture admired 'blood kinship of "the same people living in the same place"', and praised the desirability of 'stability' in a traditional society.

> The population should be homogeneous; where two or more cultures exist in the same place they are likely either to be fiercely self-conscious or both to become adulterate. What is still more important is unity of religious background; and reasons of race and religion combine to make any large number of free-thinking Jews undesirable.[122]

While the lectures went on to discuss 'heresy' and 'orthodoxy' as applied to literature ('I have my own log to roll'), these were the sentences which, more than any others, became controversial.[123] 'Race' was a bitter topic. Virginia's 1924 Racial Integrity Act had brought de facto segregation. The Klu Klux Klan was active in Charlottesville, and Tom (who, like many at that time, happily used the word 'niggers' in private correspondence) was speaking at a university which did not admit African American students.[124] His invocation of 'race' and 'blood kinship' might have appealed to many in his immediate audience, but it used language likely to be incendiary. More specifically, his describing 'any large number of free-thinking Jews' as 'undesirable' played directly into that strain of antisemitism he had inherited from his parents, and which is visible at times in his published and unpublished writings. More widely, in 1933 it connected not just with widespread prejudices but with the anti-Jewish rhetoric of Hitler and his followers. Less than a month earlier at Kirkland House, just yards from Eliot House, in a meeting of the Liberal Club of Harvard, speakers (reported in the *Crimson*) had argued over 'anti-Semitism' in Germany, a sensitive topic in a Harvard not short of antisemitic members.[125] While in Virginia, Tom spoke with a woman who 'doesnt like Hitler'; he was aware of Hitler's Germany.[126] The lecturer, who would soon describe society as 'worm-eaten with Liberalism', was more sensitive than most people to nuances of language.[127] But he spoke these words about 'race' and 'free-thinking Jews' nevertheless.

Later, in 1940, he would argue his view did 'not imply any prejudice on the ground of race'; later still, challenged by Isaiah Berlin in 1952, he said that 'the sentence of which you complain (with justice) would never have appeared at all at that time, if I had been aware of what was going to happen, indeed had already begun, in Germany'. In 1952 he could 'not understand why the word "race" occurs in the sentence, because my emphasis was on the adjective "free-thinking"'.[128] Probably this was the emphasis he had intended, but he could not get himself off the hook. When George Boas, with whom he had lodged in Baltimore, read the Page-Barbour Lectures in print, his reaction to the passage about 'free-thinking Jews' was that, if the lecturer felt that way, then 'I could relieve him of one of them.'[129]

In his other two Charlottesville lectures he developed his topic of 'heresy' by examining ways in which contemporary writing diverged from 'orthodox' religious positions. So, for instance, Pound's presentation of hell was weakened by being 'a Hell for the *other people*', while Hardy and Lawrence showed 'the intrusion of the *diabolic* into modern literature'. Lawrence, obsessed with class and sex, was 'a very sick man indeed', a writer whom 'daemonic powers' made to produce a vision that is 'spiritual, but spiritually sick'.[130] Tom had been reflecting to Emily about his 1911 memories of the 'Evil influence' of Matthew Prichard who had wanted to 'dominate' and 'possess' the 'soul', and whose activities had given Tom a 'vision of hell'.[131] Private preoccupations seethed under his lectures, which touched on demonic possession. Publishing them the following year as *After Strange Gods: A Primer of Modern Heresy*, he stated he had experimented by ascending 'the platform of these lectures only in the role of moralist', rather than literary critic. The lectures were 'composed for vocal communication to a particular audience' and the sponsoring 'Foundation' had required their publication.[132] He came to regret this, and never republished *After Strange Gods*. Its absolutism, disgust, and prejudice reveal rebarbative aspects of his psyche.

His strain was evident. Sensible of 'the terrible temptation to *despair*', he felt 'miserable'.[133] He had grown addicted to intellectual and spiritual 'Fighting' as a 'drug'.[134] He sensed, he told More, 'the vulture on the liver'.[135] He wanted a holiday. He argued with Emily, and she with him, about their 'peculiar' relationship.[136] Vivien cabled on 7 May: 'Will come to America like a shot remainder of your visit cable yes or no', to which he wired his reply from Charlottesville: 'Your proposal quite impossible very busy and shall be travelling about until middle June'.[137] He wanted to break with her, but not with Emily, however austere he resolved to become. He sent Emily jewellery, including a ring, making it absolutely clear he hoped their relationship would last. He wondered if the ring might fit her fourth finger, but thought she might 'prefer one for the middle finger' – not the appropriate finger for an engagement or wedding ring.[138]

His 'travelling about' included receiving his Columbia honorary doctorate on 6 June. In New York he also recorded poems for a gramophone record, bequeathing his voice to posterity, but more attractive was some time off. On 27 May he had gone with friends to visit Matthiessen at Kittery, Maine; then, as if back in boyhood, had sat birdwatching 'in a canoe' on the Ipswich River in Massachusetts.[139] Now, in June he had the chance to spend several days reminiscing with Henry, Theresa, Ada, Shef, and Marion in Randolph, New Hampshire, at Mountain View House. From one angle, Tom felt his ten months in America had allowed him 'to be myself, to be perfectly natural with people as I never have been able to be before'; but from another perspective, he told Emily, 'the only interval which did me any good was the week in California'.[140] Relaxing in New Hampshire, Henry read Tom's lectures, copying out passages for his own pleasure.

Tom's time in America and his life in England seemed to him like different, largely separate existences. Boston was so familiar, but struck him as inbred, and, as far as he was concerned, 'Unitarianism had to go sooner or later.'[141] He wrote to Emily, making clear he was consulting Alfred James, the Haigh-Woods' solicitor, about breaking to Vivien his desire for a separation. 'I wish, for myself, that a divorce were possible. Or rather, that an annulment were possible.' But 'in canon (Church) law there is no divorce', and annulment looked very unlikely. Anyhow, Vivien would not allow it. Still, he promised Emily he would talk things over again with Underhill in England. He felt towards her 'like a contaminated person, who ought to keep out of your way altogether'. Should they stop corresponding? Tom wondered. But neither he nor she had forgotten their shared kiss in California, and he dreamed of some other 'possible reality' in which they might be happy.[142] For all his asserting 'you can't beat Beethoven', on his New Hampshire holiday he enjoyed the popular 'A Little Love, A Little Kiss' on the 'phono':

> Night will pass and day will follow after,
> Other griefs and joys will come with day;
> Yet through all the weeping and the laughter,
> You will ever hear the words I say –
> Just a little love, a little kiss,
> Just an hour that holds a world of bliss.[143]

But it could not last.

'See what a mess you have made of things', he imagined saying to the teenage ghost of himself on 17 June as he delivered the commencement address at Milton Academy with several of his former schoolteachers in the audience.[144] The English master's wife, Emily Perry, looked on critically. Tom, just back from New Hampshire, had arrived 'dishevelled', having had to be 'awakened out of a sound sleep' by a teacher 'who had driven into Boston to pick him up'. As Tom delivered his oration, Mrs Perry could see his bare legs where his ungartered stockings hung down. 'You would think anyone who was going to give a lecture would not be sleeping late in the morning', she complained half a century later.[145] Tom urged the Milton boys to prepare for the testing time 'when you have to stand quite alone'. In life 'some choices', he explained, 'are irrevocable' so that 'there is no going back'. It was also 'very difficult even to distinguish between success and failure'. He ended his address by telling the schoolboys the story of the British Antarctic explorer Captain Oates, who 'said one evening "I am just going outside and I shall be gone some time"', before Oates walked towards certain death. It was an image of heroic isolation. 'It does not really matter whether we succeed or fail in life. That is as it happens, but what does matter is that we should find out the right thing to do and then do it, whether it leads to success or celebrity or obscurity or even to infamy.'[146] A few days afterwards Tom sailed back alone across the Atlantic, determined not to go home.

8

Irrevocable

IN late June 1933, having disembarked in Greenock, Scotland, Tom travelled to Glasgow. From there he headed south by train for eight hours: time enough to anticipate what faced him. As arranged, Morley met him at London's Euston Station, and drove him to the Oxford and Cambridge Club in Pall Mall. After the two men had a drink together, Morley went ahead to Pikes Farm with Tom's luggage. Tom stayed overnight at the club, dining with his solicitor, Ernest Edward Bird, who advised him on 'matrimonial affairs'.[1] Bird's firm, Bird and Bird, would liaise with Vivien's solicitor, with Geoffrey Faber, Maurice Haigh-Wood, and Vivien's mother. Enid Faber, who had got used to having tea with Tom's wife 'regularly once a week', would try to 'help V.'[2] Enid knew Vivien's 'electric wire'-like volatility, but recognised, too, her 'knowledge of European culture', and did her best.[3] Tom had hoped his decision could be communicated to Vivien either by her lawyer or by Maurice or Mrs Haigh-Wood. None was willing to oblige. Tom must write to Vivien, intimating his intention. His letter had been approved by Bird, who conferred with Faber before passing it to Vivien around the time of Tom's return.

This letter does not survive, but it may be the 'document' that Jack, Mary Hutchinson's lawyer husband, mentioned to Virginia Woolf, and which Woolf, for all she thought Tom should make a complete break, described as 'very cold & brutal'.[4] Tom had long feared telling Vivien would result in 'Hell popping'.[5] Now he sought 'concealment' at Pikes Farm.[6] Before leaving America he had confided to Faber, 'I have a feeling that V. will assume that I have been beguiled and seduced by evil counsellors here, and that if she could see me at once she could bring me to my senses; and I especially wish to avoid a private and unexpected interview.'[7]

It was made clear to him, however, that there must be an 'official interview' between himself and Vivien with lawyers present. 'I dread it', Tom told Henry.[8] Over dinner Bird counselled him how to behave. Next morning, he went to Pikes Farm and steeled himself. He hid his address even from some of the Faber & Faber staff, who were briefed on how to deal with Vivien. She, meanwhile, told Ottoline Morrell that, fearing Tom was '*in danger*', she had been 'nearly insane with anxiety for 2 weeks'.[9] Where was her husband? She rang Geoffrey Faber to ask if Tom was 'dead' or 'insane' or 'had been kidnapped'.[10] By then, as Tom made clear to Henry on 8 July, she had been 'officially notified of my decision'.[11] Virginia Woolf on 10 July was convinced that Vivien, who shut Tom's letters up 'in the cupboard with the sealed string', was 'clearly concealing something'.[12] What Vivien hid from others, and tried to hide from herself, was that Tom would not be coming back.

In mid-July he consulted Underhill, and met Vivien 'at the solicitors' so the situation could be made absolutely clear: he had left her ' "irrevocably" '.[13] Having drawn up his legal letter to his wife, Tom sent Emily in late July a 'LAST WILL AND TESTAMENT' in Edward Lear-like verse, bequeathing her 'the last Lock of his Hair' and a brooch 'like a small Teddy Bear'. Changing tone, he described his 'sole interview' with Vivien 'at the lawyers". His impression was that, for all her protestations about his having been 'entrapped and practically kidnapped by enemies', nonetheless, 'she really knows quite well the true situation; and it has been put before her as clearly as words can make it'.[14] As Virginia Woolf related it, a distraught Vivien told the Hutchinsons how in the lawyer's office Tom 'sat near me & I held his hand, but he never looked at me'.[15]

As soon as the meeting ended, Tom fled to Pikes Farm. Vivien, wrote Woolf, 'seems to have gone crazy'. She lived 'in a flat decorated with pictures of him, & altars, & flowers. Sometimes she prevails on a stranger – like E[lizabeth] Bowen to believe her story, at others lapses into sense.'[16] A week or so later, Woolf asked if her nephew had heard how 'Mrs Eliot is on the war path, said to have a carving knife with which first to skin Tom; then Ottoline, finally me?'[17] To Mary Hutchinson, who had sent him a 'kind note' after contact with Vivien, Tom expressed regret that the Hutchinsons had 'had such a bad time – I did not anticipate this, and I do not know how else I could have managed'. He feared 'it may take some time to make V. realise that my decision is irrevocable'.[18]

Though he would venture occasionally into his office and elsewhere, he aimed to be 'socially invisible for as long as is practicable'.[19] At Pikes Farm he dined with the Morleys, but lodged next door with Mr and Mrs Jack Eames and family. Tom nicknamed his two rooms 'Uncle Tom's Cabin', and sought solace in the countryside. Eames, foreman of the local brickworks, found him an odd guest: 'so engrossed in what he was doing that you could almost touch him and he wouldn't realise that you were there'.[20] Tom's window overlooked 'a rose garden' where he watched thrushes; he played Patience, read theology and crime fiction, picked blackcurrants, and wrote jokey letters to America, confessing he was 'terrified of Cows'. He enjoyed the physical work of pumping a compressed-air machine which controlled the petrol-gas that was the Morleys' energy supply, and he looked forward to learning 'bricklaying'. Growing 'quite good' at Monopoly, he devised elaborate crosswords, and contributed to the Morleys' family newspaper.[21] To the Morley children, who liked him, he was avuncular, yet Morley felt in some way he 'never *saw*' them, or '*saw* country things'.[22] For young Tom Faber he wrote a poem about an 'Awefull Battle' between 'the Pekes and the Pollicles' – 'proud and implacable passionate foes'.[23] He had his own painful battles and preoccupations. 'Oh my dear, I do long for you here', he wrote to Emily, his 'Raspberrymouth'.[24] More meditatively, he shared with her perceptions that would find their way, eventually, into poetry:

> One simply could not live if one's emotions and sensibility were wholly awake all the time; there may even be a certain periodicity in it. Do you feel conscious of fluctuations and changes of rhythm, like that? Occasionally, very rarely, the periods of heightened life pass for a moment into a mood of peace and reconciliation, a momentary perception of a pattern in life, which one just accepts. This never lasts more than a few moments, with me. At present I have rather an awareness of the possibilities of spiritualising my ordinary life a little more, and of how far I have to go.[25]

Later, in a different vein, he would suggest to his sister-in-law that Vivien might have been 'a victim of demonic possession'.[26] Original sin seemed rife, even omnipresent. Revising his Norton Lectures for publication, he added a footnote announcing a companion volume (*After Strange Gods*) that would illustrate 'the influence of the devil on contemporary literature'.[27] In late 1933 he sent the *Virginia Quarterly Review* one of his Page-Barbour Lectures, entitling it 'Personality and Demonic Possession'. To some who saw him he appeared in torment, however much he dismissed 'my unfortunate private affairs'; at least one man who knew them both regarded Vivien as Tom's 'cross'.[28] Expressing apprehension to Emily at the 'terrible' prospect of 'life after death', Tom felt 'extinction would be a relief'. His affairs were 'not progressing, at present, and are afflicting me with that almost physical nausea'.[29]

He could be tolerant of other people's extramarital relationships or divorces. The previous year Aurelia Bolliger, while living with the still married Ralph Hodgson, had been surprised by Tom's acceptance of her situation. Tom had written from America to Morley about the married Herbert Read's affair with Margaret Ludwig, saying Read's 'Divorce wouldnt make any difference in this goddam pagan country.'[30] Over a year later, while arrangements over his own separation were still being discussed, Tom would write revealingly to a *Criterion* contributor with marital problems,

> I hope a divorce will follow quickly. In such cases it seems to me, where there are no religious prohibitions to prevent, the only satisfactory conclusion. One strong reason is that I believe that any union in which having children is wholly out of the question – I mean has to be prevented deliberately from the start – is a great strain; and has less hope of being permanent.[31]

In his own case, however, the 'religious prohibitions' on divorce still seemed absolutely compelling. He would separate from Vivien, but they could never divorce. He could not ask Emily to marry him. 'Having no claim upon you', he told her on his forty-fifth birthday, 'I am the more easily inclined to believe that you have lost, or will lose, interest in me.'[32]

Morley was his protector. However, corresponding with Pound, Morley could not resist nicknaming Tom 'The Deacon' or 'The Rt. And Rev. Prelate'.[33] To Ottoline Morrell, when she was feeling ignored by him, he seemed 'the Frozen Rev. T. S. Eliot'.[34] In this era when MacDiarmid wrote his 'Second Hymn to Lenin' and Pound succumbed to Mussolini-worship, absolutism was to the fore. Yet Pound may have touched a nerve when, reviewing *After Strange Gods* in early 1934, he aligned its author with an 'organized Christianity' where 'The sacerdos [priest] has been superseded by the (often subsidized) ecclesiastical bureaucrat.'[35] Increasingly immersed in church committees and conferences, Tom had signalled he had the measure of his old friend when, some months earlier as part of their voluminous, capering correspondence, he had sent Pound a letter beginning, 'Dear Child of Satan'.[36]

His American stay had produced just a few short poems, but they indicated a new direction. For the first time this notably urban poet had named works after specific rural places. His earlier engagement with American landscape in 'Marina' and *Ash-Wednesday* had avoided place names; now, in 'New Hampshire' and 'Virginia', as he would in important later poems, he named a place and built the poem in subtle ways out of his complex, refracted relationship with it. 'New Hampshire' mischievously echoes the title of Frost's 1924 volume, but draws, too, on Tom's initial sense of estranged re-engagement with what America meant to him – one of those meanings being his twenty-year-long relationship with Emily. 'Twenty years and the spring is over; / To-day grieves, to-morrow grieves', says the poem's speaker, reviewing past, present, and future. Yet any note of lamentation is curbed by the quickening excitement of the poem's bird life, and by the acoustic bower that the soundscape weaves and in which the speaker ('Cover me over') is immersed.[37] This immersion in nature, which Tom sensed both in America and at his Pikes Farm hideout, is in part an escape, a further seeking of refuge. The phrase 'Cover me over' comes from the start of Carl Sandburg's 'Bringers', which had first appeared in *Poetry* in 1917:

Cover me over
In dusk and dust and dreams.
Cover me over
And leave me alone.[38]

To the landscapes of his new, short poems (which he had sent Emily before leaving the States) Tom brought both an observing eye, and his precisely musical, profoundly acquisitive ear for language, proving what he had asserted at Harvard:

I should say that the mind of any poet would be magnetised in its own way, to select automatically, in his reading (from picture papers and cheap novels, indeed, as well as serious books, and least likely from works of an abstract nature, though even these are aliment for some poetic minds) the material – an image, a phrase, a word – which may be of use to him later. And this selection probably runs through the whole of his sensitive life.[39]

In that lecture, Tom had gone on to give the example of a 'sea anemone' seen by a boy; but the passage applies equally well to his incorporation of a phrase from Sandburg – hardly one of his favourite poets, though a singer appropriate to this poem of immersion in an American locale. If, covertly, 'New Hampshire' also signalled Tom's sense of a past that was 'over', then its companion poem 'Virginia' hinted at personal 'Iron thoughts' he had not been able to escape when he went to that Southern state.[40]

By early September 1933, for a Welsh trip, Tom had purchased a 'rather immodest' bathing costume, with a rubber cap for his hair.[41] He was holidaying with the Fabers in their substantial country house, Ty Glyn Aeron, at Ciliae Aeron in Cardiganshire (present-day Ceredigion), a few miles inland from Wales's west coast and about fifteen miles south of Aberystwyth. This vacation kept him in rural seclusion, while also affording the Morleys (one of whose children had special needs) a break from looking after Uncle Tom. From 'wholly foreign' Wales he went for a short retreat at Kelham, Nottinghamshire, at the Society of the Sacred Mission, strengthening his commitment to participation in a dedicated religious community.[42] Though Vivien was maintaining to Bird that 'my only wish is that my husband returns to me under any conditions' and that 'he has been and always will be my only interest and reason for existence', Tom, with regard to 'what is to become of her', was aware of needing 'to force myself to consider that that is not my business any more'.[43]

Through their legal representatives, attempts were underway to draw up a formal deed of separation with full financial provision for Vivien's care. At times she seemed businesslike, instructing her solicitor to argue that Tom 'assume complete control over my income and personal property', and that the couple share 'a joint Banking account'; but at other times people questioned her sanity.[44] Mary Hutchinson thought 'she only likes to see people who will accept that unreal world of hers'.[45] On 9 September Virginia Woolf, aware that 'dear old Tom', just back from Wales, looked 'to years younger: hard, spry, a glorified boy scout in shorts & yellow shirt', was struck, nevertheless, by how, maintaining 'some asperity' towards Vivien, he would not 'admit the excuse of insanity for her – thinks she puts it on'.[46] Woolf described Tom as now 'tight & shiny as a wood louse', but she detected both 'well water in him, cold & pure' and an exclusive hardness. 'Yes I like talking to Tom. But his wing sweeps curved & scimitar like round to the centre himself. He's settling in with some severity to be a great man.' Later in the same diary entry Woolf added, with a rhetorical flourish, 'when you are thrown like an assegai into the hide of the world – this may be a definition of genius – there you stick; & Tom sticks. To shut out, to concentrate – that is perhaps – perhaps – one of the necessary conditions.'[47] Woolf was sensitive about her (not entirely inaccurate) intuition that Tom, even though they had published each other's work, substantially shut out her own writing. But, as sensitively as he could manage, he was also shutting out his wife.

Addressing her as 'My dear Vivienne' and signing himself 'Affectionately your husband', he wrote in mid-October, urging her to accept 'a definite financial arrangement' of '£5 a week' plus other allowances.[48] Soon he estimated her annual income would be around £600. As the solicitors battled on, and after Tom had spoken to her doctor (who advised him, despite Vivien's pleas, not to meet her), he admitted that, though 'the amount and rate of mental deterioration' were hard to assess, it was 'possible that eventually – perhaps not for years – she will have to be looked after in a home'.[49] In the short term he had hoped she might 'go for a time' into nursing care.[50] Vivien, however, would not be persuaded. She had taken to her bed 'in a state of siege' at 68 Clarence Gate Gardens, and complained to Ottoline Morrell that she 'was expected to *agree* with & *acquiesce* in a *wicked plot*. And *still am* – ! *Bombarded. Threatened.*'[51] By early 1934 she was continuing to refuse to sign any deed of separation.

Tom's elaborate domestic arrangements meant mail sent to Russell Square was forwarded to him within twenty-four hours. As winter arrived, he hoped to lodge in London at an address to be withheld from Vivien. As a distraction, Morley proposed Tom accompany him and George Blake along with the visiting New York publisher Donald Brace to Inverness, setting off 'on November 10'.[52] They would visit Faber-published novelist Neil Gunn, who, along with MacDiarmid and others, helped establish the Scottish National Party. Morley planned this substantial excursion in advance, aiming to compress it into a November long weekend. It brought Tom closer to Brace, whose firm, Harcourt, Brace, as well as publishing J. M. Keynes, Virginia Woolf, and E. M. Forster, had published Tom's *Poems* and *Selected Essays* in America the year before, and would go on to publish the US editions of much of his later work. In Scotland the company was good and the drive through snow-capped Highland mountains 'very beautiful and exciting', but Tom felt low. Glasgow seemed 'dismal', Rannoch Moor bitterly 'cold and grim'; Glencoe, site of the famous massacre, and the clans' war-graves at Culloden confirmed his impression of Scotland as 'a ruined, ravished country'.[53] Still, the whisky got 'better the further north you go', reaching 'superb' in Inverness.[54] Conversation at the Gunns' house covered the work of MacDiarmid (whose *Stony Limits*, with its verse meditations on cosmological time, would soon be published), and lasted into the small hours. As Gunn, a whisky connoisseur, wrote to MacDiarmid, 'We were talking about you the other night when a car load of tough guys, including T. S. Eliot, descended upon us. I didn't get to bed until 5 a.m.'[55] Almost immediately after this marathon, Tom and Morley headed for Paris where they spoke with Joyce (whose *Ulysses* they still hoped to publish in Britain) and Tom met French *Criterion* contributors. Soon, he was back in London, writing to Spender on notepaper of the Oxford and Cambridge Club.

To different people he presented different selves. His imaginative life remained largely hidden, but increasingly, revising his Harvard lectures under the title *The Use of Poetry and the Use of Criticism*, he sought to harness it to public usefulness, valuable practicality. Soon Emily received his poem, 'The Practical Cat'.[56] Given his religious beliefs and interests in drama, this intensifying commitment to the usefulness of poetry involved the possibilities of verse on stage. In America he had deepened his connection with Emily, that actress and teacher of drama, and with his cousin Eleanor, an aspiring playwright, while his closest Eliot House friends – Matthiessen and Spencer – had co-directed the Elizabethan prose-and-verse play about upper- and lower-class London life, *The Shoemaker's Holiday*; he had watched, too, *Sweeney Agonistes* at Vassar – the first time he had seen his own work staged. Just before going to the States, Tom had paid attention to Bishop Bell's programmes both to support 'church building in Sussex' and to develop religious drama.[57] Bell had shown 'keen interest' in the pageant backed by Father Whitby at the Church of St Mary the Virgin some years earlier, and such enthusiasms had led in 1930 to his appointment of Elliott Martin Browne in Chichester as England's first diocesan director of religious drama.[58] Now Tom entered into discussions with Browne, whom he had first met with the churchman J. H. Oldham at a 1930 dinner hosted by Bell.

Browne, an Old Etonian, had studied history and theology at Oxford, before working in English and American theatres. A participant in Bell's 1932 religious drama conference (which absence in America had prevented Tom from attending), he had produced several religious dramas, most recently *The Acts of St Richard*. Performed outdoors before 2,000 people during June 1933 at the Bishop's Palace, Chichester, with 'the cathedral spire' behind and Bell in the audience, this eight-scene verse 'play' was a pageant by E. Werge-Oram depicting both the life of medieval St Richard of Chichester and modern-day events.[59] Involving trained as well as amateur actors, Browne's production used a 'processional method' that made audiences participants in a rite.[60] It culminated with cast and audience processing together into the cathedral to pray and sing. Encouraged by this success, and with Bell's approval, Browne had suggested to Tom that summer the 'very interesting' idea of collaborating on a new 'historical pageant' play to raise money for building churches in the diocese of London.[61]

'I have just been invited to write a play!' Tom exclaimed to Emily in an 11 August letter: 'some sort of religious show'.[62] Tom readily accepted, and in the autumn met 'Browne and his wife'.[63] Browne was eager to move beyond earlier suggestions of a conventional pageant and create a more ambitious 'Spectacle of London Church Building'. He supplied Tom with ideas for scenes, some ancient, others modern, that would feature a team of cockney bricklayers, and for which Tom wrote prose dialogue. As the 'Spectacle' (to Tom 'a *revue*') developed, scenes were sometimes reshaped by other participants – from the Reverend Rosslyn Webb-Odell, organising director of the Forty-five Churches Fund, to Morley, Dobrée, and the spirited Reverend Vincent Howson.[64] Playing a leading role, Howson criticised Tom's use of cockney English. If this collaborative venture diluted some of the poet's writing, it served to induct him into practical stagecraft. He drew on what he had learned from reading, drama criticism, his spell on the committee of the Old Vic and Sadler's Wells Society, and his abandoned fragmentary Sweeney drama, but moved beyond all these. This new project, he explained to Emily, offered opportunities 'for practice and experiment'. If 'results' were encouraging, 'I shall try my hand at something of my own.'[65] Drawing not least on traditions associated with London's oldest parish church, the Priory Church of St Bartholomew the Great, where the Virgin Mary was said to have appeared, he developed a 'revue' that, like *Sweeney Agonistes*, built on music-hall turns as well as religious rites and deployed the device of the chorus.

As the son of a leading American brick manufacturer, Tom, living in the brickworks foreman's house beside Pikes Farm while first pondering this new collaborative venture, was qualified in unusual ways to shape a drama of church-building bricklayers. It would also contain dialogue between 'contractors and foremen', plus Latin chanting, music-hall-style songs, and liturgically cadenced choruses.[66] These last were the only elements which, after the revue's publication by Faber in 1934, Tom chose to keep in print alongside his own poems. In performance, however, the strange mixture of verse and prose, lowbrow and highbrow, vernacular and liturgical impressed audiences. By November 1933, with an Old Testament flourish, he was planning to have his chorus (speaking as '*the voice of the Church of God*') intone, 'Remembering the words of Nehemiah the Prophet: "The trowel in hand, and the gun rather loose in the holster." '[67] Elsewhere, spoofing a once ubiquitous advertisement for an Edinburgh pen company – 'They come as a boon and a blessing to men / The Pickwick, the Owl and the Waverley pen' – *The Rock* (as his revue came to be called) presented satirically a '*military formation*' of Blackshirts who proclaim, '*We come as a boon and a blessing to all / Though we'd rather appear in the Albert Hall.*'[68] Browne, wanting audiences to 'look into the past and into the future', was 'dead set on the Crusades' being part of the drama, so Tom mugged up on them. He wondered in late November, however, whether a different 'episode' might represent 'that general period' instead: 'I have thought of Thomas a'Becket, of course, but even that takes us further from London than I like.'[69] Later, he would dismiss *The Rock*'s non-choral dialogue as 'hack-work' containing 'a few gags which I thought amusing'; but, at the time, it constituted a significant apprenticeship: 1933 was 'the year in which I broke into Show Business'.[70]

Though his favourite actress, Emily, thought him somewhat 'improved', Tom told her he worried he 'must have struck you in the past as a very crabbed and distorted person!'[71] They enjoyed sending one another detailed accounts of their lives, and exchanging photographs. He wanted to 'understand' her 'better and better', and feared that over the last year she might have seen in his behaviour 'a divided allegiance of weakness or cowardice, indicative of imperfect devotion'. 'Bitter' that he could 'go so far and no farther', he was 'appalled' by the 'violence' of his feelings. Her letters could affect him 'like a physical stab of exquisite pain, a sort of ecstasy of death'.[72] Yet as the issue of divorce continued to trouble them both, he stated in November, 'I should like you to know once and for all, that there is nothing in this world that I would not give up without hesitation if I had even the slightest hope that you would accept me as your husband.' He would need no urging in this direction, he protested, but had preferred 'not to try to make' Emily 'realise my full feelings – I could not go on living if I realised them continuously myself'. Nevertheless, no sooner had he raised expectations about future marriage, than he proceeded to dash them – as, evidently, he had done in California.

Here is what I tried to say on New Year's Eve – though even up to then I swear I took for granted that you knew it already. The position of the Church is completely uncompromising about the indissolubility of marriage. Frankly, I doubt whether the future of my own single soul would be enough to weigh with me, though theoretically it ought to. I think that my responsibility to society counts more with me. I am – I can say it without the slightest vanity – the most conspicuous layman in the Church to-day, and my defection would be all the more significant because I was not born into it. I should of course be excommunicate, I should no longer take any part in Church affairs, and if I ever raised my voice to speak for the faith or attack paganism I should meet only with ridicule and contempt.

So, explaining he could not divorce, and that Vivien would never agree to divorce, he worried lest Emily might think he had been 'deceiving' her by 'establishing a relation of "friendship" under false pretences'. He said he had not meant to do so, but feared she might 'condemn' him. 'No woman in the world', he made clear, could have given him what she had given. 'You have never disappointed my conception of you, and I am happy in the knowledge that my conception of you is not an "idealisation".' If she judged him unfavourably, 'for God's sake let me disappear from your life'.[73] She did not wish to stop corresponding; her hopes for eventual marriage persisted. Later, when a former student made an unfortunate marriage, Emily advised her forthrightly, 'you *must* free yourself from a crippling alliance while there is yet time to save yourself'; and she cited the example of 'A very dear friend of mine' who was 'involved' with 'a weak and selfish and seriously unstable partner' and who suffered 'disastrous effects'.[74] But if Tom's relationship with Vivien was deadlocked, so in a different way was his liaison with Emily.

Meanwhile, he kept hunting for London lodgings. Various people offered advice. Pound even tried to lure him to Fascist Italy; po-faced, Tom responded his 'only objection' was 'the Climate'.[75] Nowhere seemed ideal. 'My present intention is to look at a room in Kensington (a district which I dislike)', he told Virginia Woolf glumly in late October.[76] John Hayward had moved to a flat at 22 Bina Gardens, South Kensington, that March, and waspishly informed Tom about the area's 'frayed respectability' and 'outmoded conventions'.[77] Tom called on Hayward there in November. Becoming a Bina Gardens regular, he enjoyed Hayward's cognac, chess, and conversation. By December Tom was 'on the Job again from 10 to 6 daily except most Saturdays', with temporary accommodation 'in a polite boarding house in South Kensington' while seeking 'two furnished rooms' to rent.[78] He felt 'much alone'.[79] *The Use of Poetry* had appeared – on 4 November he inscribed Morley's advance copy with thanks 'for counsel, penance, and absolution' – and *After Strange Gods* was imminent.[80] He came to regard both books as 'potboilers', written to avert 'bankruptcy'.[81] Vivien still importuned him to return home, 'ignoring the reality', despite Geoffrey Faber assuring her, 'Tom is irrevocably determined upon a separation.'[82] Morley recalled him at this time as 'a disturbed, tormented fellow'.[83] He begged Emily for letters. As 1933 turned to 1934, he felt he was 'living in a suspended vacuum'.[84]

Though he tried to cheer himself up by skewering Winston Churchill's oratorical prose style ('we seem to observe the author pause for the invariable burst of hand-clapping') and by typing a poem for Pound ending with the words 'a r s e spells arse', matters were not going well.[85] 'In my worst states of depression my past life seems only a nightmare of things ill-done and undone', he wrote to Emily, apparently prefiguring a passage about 'things ill done and done to others' harm' in his later poetry.[86] However painful it would be, should they 'break off anything like regular correspondence, at least for a few years?'[87] But their letters bound them together in suffering, and, not without elements of moral blackmail, their intense correspondence continued. Tom 'kissed' Emily's 'signature'.[88] Hiding his turmoil from other folk, he confessed to her, 'people still tell me how well I look'.[89] At work, after tortuous legal investigations, Fabers again declined to publish *Ulysses*, so the modern novel which Tom admired above all others was lost to the rival firm of Bodley Head. Joyce came to call Faber & Faber 'Feebler and Fumbler'.[90] Tom's landing a book by young poet Louis MacNeice hardly offset the disappointment. After work, he returned to his 'boarding house' at 33 Courtfield Road, still hoping for a more permanent abode.[91]

Near Bina Gardens, the tall, red-brick Courtfield Road establishment had been recommended by Sencourt. It was presided over by a tetchy seventy-year-old ecclesiastic, William Edward Scott-Hall, and his younger friend, cat-loving Freda Bevan. She liked 'only public school men' as lodgers.[92] Her boarding house was handy for Gloucester Road Underground station and for a High Anglican church, St Stephen's, where Tom began attending Mass. The area attracted High Anglicans. Next door to 33 Courtfield Road lived Anglo-Catholic actress-dramatist Muriel Forwood. Her drama *The Great Day* had been performed by the Greater London Players in 1932 along with a play by Irene Gordon, *The Rock* – whose title may have encouraged Tom's. Miss Forwood occasionally obliged her poet neighbour by driving him to engagements. Her enthusiasm for theatre was shared by the St Stephen's vicar, Father Eric Cheetham. A Francophile who was enthusiastic about lanterns, dressmaking, and 'odd people', Cheetham knew Freda Bevan and 'came to dinner' one evening, falling into conversation with Tom whom he recognised as 'a new member of his congregation'.[93]

A small suite of two rooms in Cheetham's presbytery at 9 Grenville Place, just along the road from St Stephen's, had fallen vacant, and in January he offered it to Tom. Though concerned about noise from 'the District Railway' behind, Tom became Cheetham's 'Paying Guest'. Three guineas per week secured the accommodation, use of a bathroom, and '7 breakfasts and 7 dinners a week served in my room'.[94] Tom had just been to Kelham again and was in discussion with a monk there, Father Gabriel Hebert, about Hebert's proposed book on 'the Liturgical Revival'.[95] The near-monastic conditions of his new lodgings suited Tom's tastes. He told Aurelia Bolliger not long afterwards that he expected to live 'alone' for 'the rest of my natural life', and went out of his way to write (for publication on a National Portrait Gallery postcard) a tiny biography of Coleridge, that 'Metaphysician and poet' who had 'contracted an unhappy marriage' and penned 'his great *Ode to Dejection*'.[96] Visiting 9 Grenville Place with Alida Monro the following year, Virginia Woolf, while appreciating Tom's tea and 'rolls in frills on paper', found his 'small angular' room 'not a lovely' one. It had 'dark green blotting paper wall paper'; bookcases with missing shelves contained 'rather meagre' books; there was a gas fire, and a bathroom shared with the curates: 'The hot water runs very slowly.' Tom sat on a 'hard chair'. Conversation was difficult. As the women left, he showed them his small bedroom 'with the railway under it'. He seemed to Woolf 'priestly', ill at ease with the presbytery's 'maid in cap & apron'. It 'all', she wrote in her diary, 'somehow depressed me'.[97]

Ottoline Morrell feared Tom was now 'a queer lonely isolated figure' in '*complete* removal from the ordinary world' – 'an *Ostrich* who hides his head to prevent himself seeing Life'. She blamed his American 'Calvinist forefathers'. They had made him, for all his 'kind side' perceptibly 'cruel', and 'a very sick man'.[98] Yet as publisher and editor he had to deal with day-to-day work in a way that Lady Ottoline did not. His massive brain-power, stamina and nimbleness – one minute considering 'The Theology of Economics', the next magisterially surveying eighteenth- and nineteenth-century Shakespearian criticism – remained dauntingly effective.[99] Still, Morrell was hardly wide of the mark. 'To surrender individual judgment to a Church is a hard thing', Tom stated in an early 1934 *Criterion* 'Commentary'; but he was sure 'What ultimately matters is the salvation of the individual soul.' Later that year he described himself to Faber as 'by temperament but not in doctrine, an old-style hellfire calvinist'.[100]

In early February 1934, lunching with Father Mayhew, his former vicar at St Cyprian's, he found Mayhew 'keenly interested' that St Cyprian's parishioners would be participating in *The Rock*.[101] As Tom's play advanced, his associates came increasingly from London's Anglo-Catholic community. Visiting Ely Cathedral with him, Richards was struck by how Tom 'bows to the High Altar every time he goes by'.[102] The poet whom Pound called 'the Rt/Rev/bro/in Xt/T.S. the Possum of Eliot' was fusing his voice more and more with that of his church.[103] On 9 February he read his work from the pulpit of St Martin-in-the-Fields, Trafalgar Square. 'What an *Ecclesiastical* mind he has. – Rule – Order – paramount – none of the good old English Compromise', wrote Lady Ottoline the following day, attributing all this to Tom's being 'so American'.[104] Later that month, she recorded an incident at dinner when Spender, discussing the recently published *After Strange Gods*, asked Tom with regard to 'the Jews' whether 'he realised that these things could be taken by the Nazi – to cite him as sympathising with them'.[105] Occurring around the first anniversary of what a German Jewish writer whose work Tom admired, Joachim Brander, called 'Hitler's boycott against the Jews', this was an awkward moment; but Tom had already stated he was 'indeed doubtful whether the principles of the Church and those of fascism are not wholly opposed'.[106] 'Practically, a daily communicant' at St Stephen's, and sometimes an inflexible guest ('fish is only compulsory on Wednesdays and Fridays'), he saw his religion as a bastion against fascism.[107] Distrusting Pound's support for Mussolini, he stated, 'Mr Pound is not interested in the survival of the Christian Faith.'[108] 'Don't go involve yourself with that Mosley', he counselled Pound.[109] None of which stopped him describing the Marx Brothers to Emily as 'low class Jews', or asking her (while expressing annoyance at 'these beastly fascists') 'why is there something diabolic about so many Jews?' He thought, he told her, that 'the German intelligence is an hebraicised intelligence and in turning out the Jews the Germans are merely cutting out their own brains'.[110] His vehemence was undiminished.

A milder soul, Father Cheetham wished to make use of his eminent new parishioner. In March, Cheetham invited him to become a St Stephen's churchwarden. Tom, who had confided to Emily (with regard to Vivien) that he was suffering from 'nightmare dreams' and felt a 'hunted feeling in the streets, and at my office', sent Cheetham 'a list of all the reasons why he was unsuitable', though it concluded, as Cheetham recalled, 'of course, if you need me, and are in any sort of fix, then here I am, use me'. Cheetham did, finding him 'invaluable'. As the priest summed up years later, 'His previous experience in the City means that he has a very good head for business, etc. Like most authors he is a very shrewd judge of character, and frequently amazes me by summing up people he has only met once or twice in the most surprisingly accurate way. You wouldn't find a more amazing contrast than the two of us.'[111] After High Mass on Easter Monday, slightly irregularly, the nervously autocratic Cheetham had Tom declared vicar's warden. Jokily listing his ancestors in a letter to Virginia Woolf, and awarding each an appropriate number of 'points' for gravitas ('10' for 'Founder of a University or College'), Tom – who would soon have his grandfather's 'T. Stearns' doorplate affixed to his Russell Square office door – added a postscript: 'I have just been made a Churchwarden. That ought to count 3 points.'[112]

After another short holiday with the Fabers in Wales, he was pleased to find that, despite some hesitation over its hostile treatment of Mosley's Blackshirts, *The Rock* had been cleared by the Lord Chamberlain for performance, and approved by the Bishop of London. Rehearsals grew busy. Reading about insurgent 'young roughs in Germany' and convinced 'the authority claimed by a fascist state would conflict with ecclesiastical authority', Tom wondered how the public would respond to *The Rock*'s 'political allusions'.[113] He had been tinkering up until the last minute, adding, among other things, lines to be spoken by eleven-year-old Patricia Shaw Page who played Dick Whittington's 'little cat' in one scene: 'And what's a pantomime without a Cat?'[114] In the event, reviewers of the pageant's short run at Sadler's Wells Theatre from 28 May until 9 June seemed less interested in cats or political overtones than in the phenomenon of this modern poet working for a church campaign. They were intrigued, too, by his impressive choruses, 'well spoken by masked persons dressed like stone figures from a niche'.[115] Rushing *The Rock* into print, Faber & Faber quoted the *Daily Telegraph*: 'A great theme greatly handled and there is nothing more impressive to be seen in a London theatre.'[116] At the premiere the *Times* critic thought 'The theatre, that long-lost child of the English Church, made a notable reunion with its parent at Sadler's Wells.' The poet of *The Rock* had 'created a new thing in the theatre and made smoother the path towards a contemporary poetic drama'.[117]

Not everyone agreed. Angrily, Tom wrote to the *Spectator*, asking if its reviewer would 'have wished me to tax my poetic resources by making my Chorus declaim about Birth-Control?'[118] Some commentators linked the choruses to the work of Sean O'Casey, others more perceptively to verse drama by Auden, whose *Dance of Death* Tom had seen through the press; in February he had thought its staging by Rupert Doone 'rather a mess'.[119] Critics questioned *The Rock*'s use of cockney, its attempts at 'The shading of one sort of reality into another', and its awkward 'action scenes'. Despite this, there was agreement that 'with his use of the chorus he has regained a lost territory for the drama', and hopes were expressed he might write further plays.[120]

Several of the reviewers knew Tom personally; most had absorbed his other writings. Publishing three books with Fabers in 1934 – *After Strange Gods*, *The Rock*, and *Elizabethan Essays* – kept his name in the press, ensuring his presence registered far beyond the *Criterion*'s readership. His ally Bruce Richmond saw that the *Times Literary Supplement* paid the 'harsh' *After Strange Gods* relatively little attention (though its reviewer did quote the 'free-thinking Jews' passage), but discussed *The Rock* and covered it, too, in a follow-up essay, 'New Poetic Drama'. Though that essay's praise was qualified, it presented Tom as leading a 'movement' towards a 'new poetic drama'. Covering Yeats, Auden, and O'Casey, along with work by Mona Swann on 'choral speech' and arguments by Gordon Bottomley about poetry regaining 'its right of entry to the theatre', this survey positioned Tom just where he wanted to be.[121]

Virginia Woolf went on sensing 'the heavy stone of his self esteem'.[122] Later in 1934, after they dined together, she recorded how he sat 'very solid – large shoulders – in his chair, & talks easily but with authority. Is a great man, in a way, now: self confident, didactic. But to me, still, a dear old ass.'[123] Eminent within the literary world, he knew how to operate its levers of power. Yet his judgement was not infallible. Few today would choose to read Wyndham Lewis's *One-Way Song*, which Tom selected for Faber's 1933 poetry list, rather than the poems of the Eliot-detesting

William Carlos Williams which, Tom confessed in 1934, 'mean very little to me'.[124] Not only *Ulysses* but also the poetry of Dylan Thomas (which Tom encouraged as likely to 'survive the test of time') slipped through his editorial hands.[125] If he was too slow to catch Thomas for Faber's poetry list, he did, however, sign up poet George Barker to whom he would devote enormous patience, generosity, and guidance; and he took under his wing the young poet-critic Michael Roberts and Roberts's future wife Janet Adam Smith, assistant editor of the *Listener*. He had an unsettlingly insightful way of presenting the 'dark embryo' that develops into a poem, and he discussed sympathetically with authors on his list the challenges, droughts, and demands that accompanied the writing of poetry – including (as he put it in words published in 1933) his concern that the poet 'may have wasted his time and messed up his life for nothing'.[126] Often uncompromising, even as he strove to be fair, through his writings, taste and networks he shaped the poetry of his era. Few, however, saw the full, culverted complications of his personality. To Woolf, who had his measure, he revealed more than most; to Emily, an ocean away, he showed himself in a manner at once free and self-preoccupied. He knew her vulnerabilities, but also exploited them, eager to maintain a relationship where he could be less the great man, featured in London's New Burlington Galleries 1934 *Exhibition of Sculptured Celebrities*, than simply Emily's Tom.

Now Emily, who had lingering health concerns, was leaving Scripps, where tensions with the college president had worsened. She planned a long sojourn with her Boston aunt and uncle, the Perkinses, including a much-anticipated visit to England. Knowing she would be travelling with the elderly Dr Perkins (whom Tom styled 'a specimen of the almost extinct Right Wing American Unitarian minister') and his wife Edith, Tom offered assistance, though it was Mrs Perkins who secured the rental of Stamford House and adjoining Stanley Cottage in the small Cotswold market town of Chipping Campden for three months that summer.[127] 'We have cabled Emily Hale to that effect', wrote Dr Perkins in June, adding that they hoped to see Tom 'there one day'.[128] This suited Tom, who was concerned about 'propriety', though he did hope to introduce Emily to the Woolfs, Lady Ottoline, and others in London.[129]

It was a hot summer. He went to Pikes Farm for two weeks in June, typing a chatty letter to Henry about their American and English ancestors: 'Our people, you remember, went to Coker, near Yeovil, in Somerset.'[130] Longing 'to lie in a deck chair, on the lawn, in as few clothes as possible – shorts and no stockings', he complained that soon he had to speak at a school prize-giving in Rochester, where Underhill was now cathedral dean. Fondly remembering New Hampshire, Tom told Henry he wished 'we could repeat the week at Randolph every year!'[131] His mind was on the past, too, as he continued the legal wrangling to recover from Vivien various possessions including 'a framed worsted cat made by myself as a child' – an emblem of the lastingness of that feline impulse still manifested in those cat poems he wrote for his godson, for the Tandy family, for reading to Emily and her new friend and protégée Jeanette McPherrin, and for his own amusement.[132] 'Pollicle Dogs and Jellicle Cats' were in his mind, even as he typed a jokily grumbling letter to Dobrée that July: 'I don't think my poetry is any good; not *The Rock*, anyway, it isnt; nothing but a brilliant future behind me.'[133]

Not long after the Perkinses reached Chipping Campden in mid-July, they invited Tom to spend a weekend with them and their niece. Chipping Campden was 'only a name' to him, though he knew 'its reputation'.[134] Historic, touristically picturesque, it was regarded as 'a monument to local English architects of the past', exemplifying 'perfect harmony between landscape, building material, and style of architecture'.[135] Emily would remember its 'beauty and peacefulness'. She loved its 'long curving street flanked by the weathered houses of the warm grey-yellow Cotswold stone'.[136] In some moods, Tom came to like the place, though in a flash of bitterness he thought it suited the Perkinses all too well – 'an olde worlde atmosphere stinking of death'.[137] It had links to the Arts and Crafts movement, and in the 1930s conservationists were active, preserving and beautifying buildings and landscape. At Kiftsgate Court, beside a manor house, formal gardens were being developed, and next door, at Hidcote Manor (today a National Trust property) about two miles north of the market town, American-born Major Lawrence Johnston had created extensive, lovely gardens maintained by twelve gardeners. About Hidcote, Tom later told Edith Perkins, 'of all the gardens I have visited (mostly with you) that was the one I loved the best'.[138] Chipping Campden had many horticultural connections: Thomas Archibald Bennet-Clark, professor of botany at King's College London, had a house there with his wife Elizabeth, whose garden was one of several Mrs Perkins photographed. Botanist and writer on gardens Ernest Henry Wilson, assistant director of Harvard's Arnold Arboretum from 1919–27, had been born in Chipping Campden, and American visitors – then as now – admired its floral displays. Among the specific attractions of Stamford House were its 'beautiful and intelligently planted garden' laid out on the slope behind, and its views to the Church of St James surmounted by a noble 120-foot tower.[139]

Enthusiastically citing Juvenal, Amy Lowell, Wordsworth, and other poets, Emily's Aunt Edith had once published an article on 'Beauty in Gardens'.[140] She had given, too, photographically illustrated lectures in

America on 'English gardens in the Cotswolds', and was passionate about horticulture – a passion to which Tom was not immune. It may have been conversation with her in London that summer which, combined with his time at Pikes Farm, resulted in his floral assertion in a 26 July *Times Literary Supplement* essay that Jacobean dramatist John Marston had a distinctive 'tone, like the scent of a flower, which by its peculiarity sharpens our appreciation of the other dramatists as well as bringing appreciation of itself, as experiences of gardenia or zinnia refine our experience of rose or sweet-pea'.[141] Over a year later, in a poem addressed to Edith Perkins at Stamford House, he would rhapsodise about her garden, mentioning again both 'zinnia' and 'rose' as well as the 'Clematis Jackmanii' that grew there.[142] Tom's July 1934 weekend visit to Chipping Campden reunited him with Emily and immersed them in a beautiful garden. In August he was back in the Cotswolds with other American visitors – his sister Marion and his niece Dodo – staying at Lechlade's seventeenth-century New Inn and excursing to villages including Fairford where he particularly admired the church with its medieval stained-glass windows. Possibly he met Emily on this excursion, but it is unlikely they had much time alone together. After his relatives' departure on 30 August he returned to Gloucestershire for a weekend. Because Hayward later dated the visit to '1934', it has been thought that this was the time when Tom and Emily walked out of Chipping Campden and visited another garden, at nearby Burnt Norton.[143] However, his letters to Emily (released from embargo in 2020) imply that the Burnt Norton visit was in 1935.

What is certain is that meeting her again in the summer of 1934, and 'taking' Cotswold 'walks' with her, made his feelings 'stronger and more intense than ever before'.[144] Once more, they discussed divorce and marriage. 'I would literally give my eyesight to be able to marry you', he protested. 'But, my love, my love, what do you think I CAN do?' He would talk again to his spiritual advisor. He felt he was 'a blood-sucker', causing her 'pain'.[145] She felt 'terribly unhappy' to make his 'misery more acute'.[146] They found it both wonderful and heart-rending to spend time together. Lavishing praise on her 'very perfect nose', he wondered if, perhaps, he could stand it if she married 'someone else'. He told her he admired her 'dominating personality', and that he had been surprised to hear some people thought he had a 'dominating personality' himself.[147] She held back, worried there was 'inequality' in their 'abnormal' relationship, and that she lacked sufficiently strong feelings, though she invited him to write 'as much of a love letter' as he felt inclined to do. He wanted to worship her 'for what you are'. It was hard for each to fully understand the other. 'I am not an intellectual, but an emotional', he maintained. 'If I ever *am* free I shall ask you to marry me.'[148] She reproached him for his 'microscopic analysis' of his feelings, hers, and their situation. 'I know I am a very twisted creature', he responded, confessing also to 'a violent temper'.[149] He wished he could 'live more easily on two very different planes at once'.[150]

In London he went on with the never-ending expensive legal mess, striving to convince 'deranged' Vivien (whom he told Emily he had long 'loathed body and soul') that he would never be back, and to retrieve his possessions – not least books.[151] He proposed taking out 'a writ' against her.[152] Sometimes consuming dangerous 'doses' of sleeping draughts and painkillers, she would soon attempt to convince her banker she had 'no proof that my husband ever returned from America'.[153] She sent Tom a postcard on his birthday, having earlier tried to place a small ad in *The Times* (which did not publish it): 'Will Thomas Stearns Eliot Director of Faber & Faber 24 Russell Square return immediately to his home & his wife at 68 Clarence Gate Gardens which he left on September 17 1932 if he is free to do so.'[154] But in London Tom's focus was on Emily. He wanted her to come and 'visit my church', and meet several of his friends.[155] For her birthday in October he bought her a ring – a 'star sapphire' mounted in white gold.[156] Meanwhile, Vivien went on trying to catch him at Fabers' offices. The secretaries always politely told her he was not there.

He used his office for writing to Emily, but principally for official tasks. Expert in publishing and promoting poets, he produced a blurb for MacNeice's forthcoming *Poems*: 'The most original Irish poet of his gener-ation'.[157] Yet for himself he stated more bleakly to another correspondent, 'It is equally undesirable to think oneself a poet and to think that one is not a poet. That is something that we never find out.'[158] He went on dictating letter after business letter; producing occasional mischievous rhymes for friends; preparing to lecture in Leeds; authorising the writ to recover his property – 'Framed worsted cat' and all.[159] Vivien, who let him know she left her door open for him every evening, was terrified when, more than once that year, bailiffs entered her flat to recover goods. Tom found she had deposited some of his belongings in banks. While all this went on, he con-tinued not only corresponding with Emily but taking her to places he liked, including Bosham and Chichester. Sometimes, as when he week-ended with Bishop Bell in Chichester in late October, Emily and the Perkinses were present too. She stayed for about a month in a Kensington hotel. Tom accompanied her to dinner, to plays (including to the Group Theatre's *Sweeney Agonistes*), and to London sites. He felt 'happy', despite 'cravings for what I can't have'.[160] Emily was, Tom assured Ottoline Mor-rell, 'quite an exceptional person, though it may not be immediately obvious'.[161] He told Emily how much he admired her 'ability to hold your own in any company and appear the most distinguished and patrician woman in it'.[162] He informed her how Hayward admired her as 'charming, entertaining, and a remarkable mimic'.[163] Yet, whatever they said to him, neither Lady Ottoline nor Hayward took to 'that awful American Woman' whom Tom called his 'friend'. Hayward, vaguely thinking of her as Tom's 'cousin', summed her up later to Morrell as a 'grim, prim, school-ma'amish female who takes a dreadful proprietary interest in poor Tom'.[164] Having known Emily so long and seeing in her what others could not, Tom wanted his English friends to like her. This was part of his effort to fit 'various pieces of my life together, in order to make sure that they belong to one real world'.[165] Also, he was keen to help Emily circulate free of the constricting presence of her uncle and aunt – 'a drain upon her vitality'.[166] But he failed in his attempts. She left for Italy in early December, planning to spend several months in Europe. 'London is very very lonely', he complained.[167]

Nonetheless, he hoped he would have a 'worthy' play for her next year, and may have begun scoping what became, considerably later, *The Family Reunion*.[168] More immediately, renewed contact with Bell had reinforced something proposed earlier that summer: that Tom, building on the success of *The Rock*, write a play for the Canterbury Festival. This excited him. As he argued soon afterwards,

> The possibility of a religious drama depends upon a kind of reciprocity. The dramatists must be able to provide a drama which will be really useful to the Church; and the Church must be ready to make itself useful to those who want to write drama.[169]

Now he was under contract to deliver a new religious drama whose subject would be Thomas à Becket. He strove to clear time to work on the project, but engagements piled up: in late November he was in Hull, Hampton, Newark, and Canterbury. His London commitments ranged from liaising with Rupert Doone, reviver of *Sweeney Agonistes*, to lunching with Yeats, whom he liked better and better. With Yeats he discussed ways each of them might have plays produced, as well as publication of a new translation of the *Upanishads* on which, eventually, Yeats would collaborate with Shri Purohit Swami, some of whose translation Tom had been reading. On a lighter note, furthering his imaginative engagement with the feline world, he had a work, provisionally entitled ' "Pollicle Dogs and Jellicle Cats" (unfinished at this time)'. There were, he told Polly Tandy in November, chiefly '4 kinds of Cat the Old Gumbie Cat the Practical Cat the Porpentine Cat and the Big Bravo Cat'. Mrs Tandy, whose cats had names such as Nimrod and Dorabella (which Tom changed to 'Dolabella') liked this sort of thing.[170] Yet, wherever his imagination might be, at Faber book committee meetings he focused on his job. He was seeing through the press Father Hebert's ambitious account of liturgy and society, as well as the Reverend T. S. Gregory's wide-ranging survey of 'Christian philosophy of history' from the Middle Ages to the era of 'modern illusion'.[171]

Doone's Group Theatre revival of *Sweeney Agonistes* had been seen by many literary figures, including Bertolt Brecht, Yeats, Hope Mirrlees, Virginia Woolf, and Tom himself. Watching the actors, Woolf thought of Tom and wife-murderer Dr Crippen, and decided Tom had it in him to write a whole play. *Sweeney Agonistes* helped demonstrate his contention that 'what distinguishes poetic drama from prosaic drama is a kind of doubleness in the action, as if it took place on two planes at once'.[172] This matched his sense of his own existence. Later Vivien would attend a performance too, finding it both terrifying and impressive. The playwright and his work overawed some men and women, but not all. According to Sencourt, the formidable Muriel Forwood, who drove Tom to a poetry reading that December, heard him say, 'I hate reading my poetry aloud like this', before he added, 'It's like undressing in public.' 'You needn't worry,' she told him, 'You never take off too much.'[173]

He was keen that his cousin, Marguerite Caetani, meet Emily, 'one of my nearest friends', during Emily's European tour.[174] Determined to live the 'celibate life' he had 'envisaged' for himself, and to champion 'love beyond desire', he was equally eager to keep her as his special companion: two aims which caused them both strain.[175] In her absence, he was short-tempered, dismissing people who annoyed him as 'rats and pigs', though, more sympathetically, he sent condolences to Emily after the death of her music-critic uncle, Philip Hale.[176] He tried to knuckle down to his Canterbury play, scheduled 'for the middle of June'.[177] Having secured Elsie Fogerty's agreement to train another chorus, he spent a weekend with Browne at Rottingdean in mid-December, aware 'the writer with dramatic ambitions must be ready to co-operate', and 'acutely sensitive to the fact that his play would be staged only about fifty yards from the spot where Becket died'.[178] Browne took Tom to see *The Revolving Year* by Mona Swann who used the language of the Authorised Version of the Bible to create community drama. They also attended performances of mystery plays and 'Aldington's translation of the Liège Nativity'.[179] Tom sought out historical reading about Becket.

As always, he found his imaginative freedom pressured by other demands. He joshed about this with Virginia Woolf, but she and Leonard also had a much more serious conversation with him when 'suddenly T. spoke with a genuine cry of feeling. About immortality: what it meant to him – I think it was that: anyhow he revealed his passion, as he seldom does. A religious soul: an unhappy man, a lonely very sensitive man, all wrapt up in fibres of self torture, doubt, conceit, desire for warmth & intimacy. And I'm very fond of him – like him in some of my reserves & subterfuges.'[180] Even though Woolf found his religion hard to take, she understood him with a perspicacity few could match.

According to Browne, Tom first conceived of his new play as including, like *The Rock*, substantial amounts of 'prose'.[181] Yet poetic drama was now his calling; he wanted to 'try play writing' not 'more pageants', and his intense religious commitment, more than any historical reading, impelled him sometimes in unexpected directions.[182] 'Today (December 29)', he wrote at the end of 1934,

> is the Feast of St Thomas of Canterbury, better known to most people as Thomas Becket; and I seize the opportunity to mention that fact, because it is hardly likely that anybody else will. I have discovered his Mass in a curious volume called *The English Missal* (curious because it includes Joseph of Calasanz and the Blessing of Eggs, but has nothing to say about Charles, King and Martyr). The Introit is *Gaudeamus*, 'Rejoice we all in the Lord'; but I suspect that St Thomas himself might have preferred to be remembered with the Introit for Boxing Day: *Sederunt principes*, 'Princes, moreover, did sit and did witness falsely against me.'[183]

Tom the churchwarden had recently purchased a 1933 *English Missal for the Laity*, which was used at St Stephen's. Based closely on the Roman Catholic missal – which sets forth the liturgy for Masses throughout the year, detailing passages to be read aloud on saints' days, church feasts, and other occasions – this English-language volume of over a thousand pages was used in Anglo-Catholic churches. It helped give Tom's life structure and meaning, affording solidarity with the church of earlier ages. His own path to belief had involved intense scepticism, and not long after buying his new *Missal* he wrote that 'the church offers today the last asylum for one type of mind which the Middle Ages would hardly have expected to find among the faithful: that of the sceptic.'[184] He still pursued arguments with philosophically trained intellectual determination; but now church-wardenly duties deepened his understanding of ecclesiastical ritual and practice. 'An Anglican of my type', he quipped in 1935, is '*permanently* on the verge of the Roman journey.'[185]

Like Tom's, Cheetham's Anglicanism was very High Church. The rites at St Stephen's accorded with Cheetham's 'great love of the theatre'. Cheetham had in him, Tom recalled, 'just enough, but not too much, of the showman', and was 'a master of pageantry'.[186] Following his church-warden, and helped by Elsie Fogerty, Cheetham, in 1936, would devise a 'pageant'. Featuring a 'choragus', 'Blessed Virgin', and numerous partici-pants, its Royal Albert Hall cast would number several hundred. At St Stephen's, Cheetham's combination of ritual ceremony with theatrical flourish reinforced Tom's sense that the drama of church and stage might meaningfully fuse; 'ritual' was vital because it might shape and even pre-cede 'belief'.[187]

In regular contact with Cheetham, he still kept in touch with his 'friend' Father Mayhew of St Cyprian's, where Vivien was now an occasional wor-shipper; he continued, too, visiting Underhill at Rochester, though the scholar John Haffenden points out that he went, also, 'for confession to Father Philip Bacon' at St Simon's, Kentish Town, where another friend, Father V. A. Demant – a former Unitarian – had worked as assistant priest.[188] Bacon, who was speaking out in early February 1935 about 'How retreats profit the Church', had helped found the Society of Retreat Con-ductors. It advocated the use of Ignatian spiritual exercises, and Tom became a lay member. This accorded well with his liking for retreats at Kelham where his House of the Sacred Mission friends now included the 'charming and saintly' Brother George Every, an aspiring writer. [189] Tom was part of an international network of poets, publishers, and academics, but belonged also to a local – and international – religious community. This shaped his attitudes, bringing him closer to his namesake and dramatic protagonist, Thomas – a man surrounded by priests. Henry would come to see Tom's new play about the medieval Thomas as 'a sort of *apologia pro vita sua*', with Becket as 'a projection of T. S. Eliot'.[190]

Used to moving between religious and secular milieux, and detecting implications of each for the other, in January 1935 Tom was conscious of 'not only the shadow of the Totalitarian State abroad, but smaller creeping shadows at home'.[191] This awareness, too, nourished his play. It was quick-ened by friendship with Bell with whom he shared literary and theological interests (Bell loved Andrewes' *Preces Privatae*) as well as antagonism towards totalitarianism: Bell's colleague A. S. Duncan-Jones, with whom Tom li-aised, had met Hitler in 1933 and became 'an implacable critic of the Nazi state'. Bell argued it was 'monstrous' to 'regard Christianity as unrelated to present-day life'. He befriended anti-Nazi pastor Dietrich Bonhoeffer, and had extensive conversations with Hitler's future foreign minister, Joachim von Ribbentrop, in London discussions during November 1934.[192]

Such experiences shaped Bell's determined opposition to the Nazi regime which, in September 1935, would go on to pass the Nuremberg Laws, depriving Jews of their citizenship.

If Bell was a guiding spirit behind his play, Tom had also been hearing from a very different source. While living in Germany, Spender had written to him in 1932 about the 'disturbing possibility' Hitler 'might be elected'; in 1934, taking Tom to task about *After Strange Gods*, Spender had been aiming to write a 'play for Faber' about 'German justice'.[193] Throughout 1934 *The Times* had reported 'National-Socialist State' attempts to 'dominate' awkwardly 'rebellious pastors'.[194] Now, in early 1935, Tom wished 'to recommend' J.H. Oldham's *Church, Community and State: A World Issue* for which Bell had supplied an introduction.[195] Though Oldham and Bell were involved in attempts to confront Nazi tyranny, *Church, Community and State* presented the dangers of Russian and Italian as well as German totalitarianism: 'The new absolutism of the state is a warning signal of dangers which confront the Church everywhere' when the 'state declares itself to be not just a state but a church'.[196] In England one ecclesiastical faction, led by the Bishop of Gloucester, maintained 'outright support' for the Nazi-backed 'Reich church'. Oldham and Bell sympathised with 'the Confessing Church' that the Nazis opposed. Oldham was, as Tom put it later in 1935, 'very well informed about the situation in Germany'.[197] Tom engaged deeply with his 'friend' Oldham's arguments in an address to an Anglo-Catholic audience on 31 January.[198] More tellingly and dramatically, he staged such arguments in *Murder in the Cathedral*, or, as he called it in late January, 'the "Archbishop Murder Case"'.[199] By that time, Tom was finding it relatively easy, he told Emily, to get his characters 'to TALK, but the trouble is that they don't DO anything.' He hoped 'murder' would 'mean action'.[200]

Doone was trying to persuade him to have the play staged in London, but Tom wanted it premiered at Canterbury. By 1 February he was sending Browne 'the first 396 lines', anticipating the whole play might be about four times as long: Browne could have it 'cut down'. 'So far', however, the drama remained 'stationary', and Tom feared he was 'apt to overlook the importance of the visual effect'.[201] Yeats remained for him 'a lyric poet in the theatre', though Dublin's Abbey Theatre by keeping 'poetry in the theatre' had 'maintained literary standards which had long disappeared from the English stage'. Still, Tom found it hard to generate theatrical dynamism.[202] His move towards performance accorded with his longing for 'the recognition of poetry as something other than exquisite pleasure for a small number of people who have the taste for it – as something having a function of social value. The poet must assume his role of moralist, and thus manifest his relation to society.'[203] Yet his way of presenting drama was to conjure up elements of his own deepest psychological struggles, rather than generating physical activity. Writing the play, he suffered 'anxiety dreams'.[204] Pitting an increasingly isolated priest against demands of the secular state, he drew on his own sense of alone-ness. 'There are moments, perhaps not known to everyone, when a man may be nearly crushed by the terrible awareness of his isolation from every other human being: and I pity him if he finds himself only alone with himself and his meanness and futility, alone without God.' He valued divine 'Grace' for saving and sustaining people in such moments, and cleaved to a necessary 'balance' which the Church maintained in the face of the secular world's 'endless seesaw of political tendency between anarchy and tyranny'.[205] This was what he sought to articulate on stage. His increasingly isolated twelfth-century archbishop faces, as the first draft put it, an 'unending battle' that is essentially psychological and theological while, seeking to get rid of him, 'the king confers with advisers of State'.[206]

In February, finding 'some of the writing very difficult to manage', Tom tried to incorporate glances towards modern rites (including one from the Sherlock Holmes story, 'The Musgrave Ritual') alongside medieval 'Morality play' aspects, and appearances (later cut) by Becket's early biographer Herbert of Bosham.[207] As was often the case, a spell of illness assisted his imagination, offering an excuse to avoid administrative demands at the Faber offices where Auden's new dramatic work lay on his desk. Pressing ahead, he determined not to 'break the thread of my typing until I have killed the Archbishop'.[208] The play touched on issues deeply personal to him in more than one way: 'I *joined* up, & am now a Fascist', Vivien had written in her journal six months earlier.[209] Though she did not buy her so-called fascist 'uniform' – which she wore to a performance of *Sweeney Agonistes* – until June 1935, it is likely that Tom (who decided around this time to revise his will, 'leaving her nothing' beyond the considerable income she enjoyed) knew of her new allegiance, and of her wish that Mosley recruit him too.[210] At least once in 1935 Vivien gave him her address as 'c/o British Union of Fascists'.[211]

Tom was aware his play dealt with 'Spiritual Pride', a weakness he sensed in himself.[212] He knew, he confessed to Emily, that he could sound 'unctuous and preachy' and could manifest 'Olympian hypocrisy'. Perhaps this was an Eliot family problem – a belief that 'God took more notice of us than of ordinary people.'[213] Tom was corresponding with his fourth cousin, Harry Eliot Scott in Massachusetts. After time in Hitler's Munich, Harry had 'converted' to fascist principles. Mosley's 'political philosophy is claptrap', Tom told him, referring to a 'disgraceful' meeting where Mosley supporters had assaulted hecklers. Still feeling loyalty towards Maurras and the Action Française group, Tom was less forthright about antisemitism, telling his cousin, 'As for the question of the Jews in Germany, I can't speak of them with any authority, but certainly anti-Semitism is not, and cannot be, a serious political issue in England, nor does it seem to be a very practical way of inflaming popular passion.'[214] Yet he interrupted work on his play 'to go to the Home Office' to try to help 'a German boy they want to deport'.[215]

Act I of the play was complete by early March 1935, but seemed all 'entrances and no exits'.[216] A crowded stage might help in one regard: 'I meant to emphasise his loneliness', Tom explained to Browne, 'but you can only do that by showing a man in a crowd of people who from different points of view dont understand what he is after.'[217] His Archbishop Thomas's challenges were Tom's too. 'One has got at the same time to unite oneself with humanity, and to isolate oneself completely', he told Spender with regard to writing.[218] Almost everyone he met – poets, priests, relatives, professors, students, lawyers – wanted something from him: his backing, his imprimatur, his agreement, his time. Giving unstintingly, he still appeared warily guarded. 'It was like meeting a bank director rather than a poet', one supplicant complained. Tom listened 'gravely'. He 'always seemed to have a puzzled expression', and sometimes conveyed a quality of scorn – 'his horror of the mob, the yah-hoos as he called them' – even as his interlocutor glimpsed something much more 'sensitive and intense' beyond his defences.[219] To oblige Oldham and Bell, while working on the play he joined yet another committee, their 'Advisory Council' for a 1937 World Conference on Church, Community and State.[220] Yet, necessarily, he steered his own course. An early 1935 photograph by Man Ray shows him staring, indeflectible and intense, right into the camera lens, eyes very slightly hooded, hair impeccably parted. He thought Ray's photographs of him 'better likenesses than any I have ever had taken'.[221] Emily disliked them.

'Let the audience adjust planes of reality for themselves', he told Browne. Returning to a favourite trope, he saw his play as dealing with intersecting kinds of reality: the political was perhaps a surface level; deeper was the spiritual struggle.[222] Yes, the play's subject was medieval, but he wanted it to appeal to modern audiences who, like him, relished detective stories. Might he call it *Fear in the Way*? Geoffrey Faber – who a few months earlier had opined with regard to 'past . . . present' and 'future' that a publisher 'lives on several different time-planes at once' – possessed enough biblical background to recognise an allusion to one of Tom's favourite Ecclesiastes passages, but thought not.[223] Tom swithered. Eventually, prompted by Browne's wife, actress Henzie Raeburn, he opted for *Murder in the Cathedral*, and by early April thought it 'nearly finished'.[224]

Around this time, he added, and then deleted, several short passages. One, about past, present, and future, was to have been spoken by the Second Priest, reacting to the Second Tempter. As the critic Helen Gardner summarised it later, the temptation of Thomas's Second Tempter was 'to retrace one's steps, to try to go back to the moment when a choice was made and make a different choice'.[225] The passage which Tom deleted comprised thirteen lines. Beginning with the words 'Time present and time past', it considered 'What might have been' as well as 'what has been', and deployed the image of a 'passage which we did not take' that led to a 'rose-garden'.[226] Though, as Tom later suggested, the image of this 'passage' might be linked to the first chapter of *Alice's Adventures in Wonderland*, Alice's garden is not specifically a rose garden, and Tom may have drawn, too, on familiar experiences of walking with Emily in any one of several formal gardens – whether at Scripps, or in Gloucestershire, or elsewhere.[227] He would continue to associate her with roses. She came to London in May 1935, residing in his rooms while he moved out. When she departed, he loved the roses she left behind, and, though he had cut the passage from his play, he did not forget about his lines concerning the rose garden. Eventually, by mid-May *Murder* was 'off' his 'hands', though he felt very uncertain about its quality.[228] By late May, tired, he had haemorrhoids and an infected wisdom tooth. But soon he was enjoying an evening with a benign Yeats, discussing 'poets more modern than ourselves', and was advising friends and acquaintants, including Hope Mirrlees's mother Mappie, when to come to see his play in front of the Chapter House at Canterbury, where it opened on 15 June.[229]

Many people were – and still are – vestigially aware of Archbishop Becket's story, thanks to a famous question traditionally attributed to England's King Henry II: 'Who will rid me of this turbulent priest?' Divided into two substantial acts separated by a central 'interlude' taking the form of a sermon about peace and martyrdom preached by Becket, Tom's play was intensely ecclesiastical. It drew on religious texts from the Lord's Prayer to Boethius's *Consolation of Philosophy* and sections of the *English Missal*. Yet as its protagonist steered his way through temptation towards martyrdom, watched over by 'A Chorus of Women of Canterbury' who comprised the only female presence, the poetry of *Murder in the Cathedral* held its audience. That poetry sounded like Tom's earlier verse made more immediately accessible, if less disconcertingly exciting. Instead of 'April is the cruellest month', the chorus chanted how 'Ruinous spring shall beat at our doors' while 'Destiny waits in the hand of God'.[230] 'Extremely happy' with the first performance, Tom felt lasting satisfaction.[231] 'Unless I am mistaken, my choruses are the first thing of the kind that has ever been attempted.'[232] Ambitiously, his play set out to show, as Browne put it much later, 'human action . . . subordinated to the divine, the action in time to the timeless movement of God's will'.[233]

Other than Becket, the principal characters are three priests, who argue with Thomas, and four tempters in the form of armed knights who eventually kill him as a 'traitor' guilty of 'treason'.[234] Facets of the play parallel medieval drama; in the 'Crucifixio Cristi' section of the York mystery plays (which Browne would later produce) four soldiers abuse Christ as a 'traitoure' tainted with 'treasune'.[235] Yet at one point in the writing Tom thought of the tempters as Bertrand Russell, D. H. Lawrence, Aldous Huxley and others. Audiences were left in no doubt of the play's relevance to contemporary European politics and political rhetoric. Descending into politicians' prose, the Knights confront the audience with their case: 'No one regrets the necessity for violence more than we do. Unhappily, there are times when violence is the only way in which social justice can be secured.'[236] The title *Murder in the Cathedral* had a popular, detective-mystery accent too; Agatha Christie's *Murder on the Orient Express* had become an instant hit the previous year.

Not long before *Murder* was performed, Tom was sharing with Emily his 'ecstatic memory' of a recent evening: 'attending to her headache' had been 'the great event of my life'. He rejoiced to have stroked her 'forehead' and been kissed by her.[237] Yet his play emerged from his sombre, St Stephen's churchwardenly side. Its archbishop's sermon mentions Christ's 'first martyr, the blessed Stephen', whom Tom had linked to 'St Thomas' of Canterbury when discussing the *English Missal*; and at least one member of the St Stephen's congregation, Lettice Haffenden, was a member of the play's Canterbury chorus.[238] Reading 'magnificently' as Browne put it, this churchy drama fascinated its Canterbury audience, but it also impressed London theatregoers later in 1935.[239] Premiered in the year when Hitchcock's film of *The Thirty-Nine Steps* opened in cinemas, Tom's two-act drama about a medieval archbishop may have seemed an unlikely success; but in London two years earlier the young John Gielgud had made his name acting in a two-act modern drama of medieval English knights, 'treason' and 'European politics', *Richard of Bordeaux*, by Elizabeth Mackintosh, best known as the detective-story writer 'Josephine Tey'.[240] Tom knew of this play. His own fusion of crime narrative, medieval theme, and modern political overtones found a large and ready audience. On Saturday 22 June three-piece-suited Tom was filmed at Canterbury Cathedral by amateur moviemaker Sydney Bligh, attending a performance of *Murder*. In the footage (the earliest film of him that survives), he looks thin, benign and shy as he blinks, chatting with Martin Browne and the play's prompter, and looks, in another brief shot, directly at the camera with a mixture of confidence and wariness.

At first critics were uncertain. Though Robert Speaight (who would act Becket over a thousand times) played the archbishop with power and understanding, the Woolfs and Spender disliked what they saw. At Canterbury the *Times* reviewer welcomed the poet's move away from 'private symbols' towards 'lucidity' and 'vigour', but was bothered by what seemed 'pantomime' rhymes.[241] For Tom, whose 1935 exploits included letting off small fireworks at one of Hayward's tea parties, and giving guests chocolates containing soap, the slapstick of pantomime was not always objectionable. A more cheering July *New Yorker* piece thought *Murder* a 'triumph of poetic genius' that 'may well mark a turning point in English drama'.[242] By the end of the year, Browne had spoken about the play's 'verse in drama' on BBC radio and, earning Tom an 'inadequate' thirty guineas, an 'excellent' version had been broadcast.[243] Once *Murder* opened at London's smallest theatre, the Mercury in Notting Hill, advertisements were quoting a new *Times* review hailing 'The one great play by a contemporary dramatist now to be seen in England.'[244] Still with Speaight as Becket, *Murder* transferred to the Duchess Theatre, then to the Old Vic. Its London run continued until 1938, by which time audiences in Dublin, New York, and elsewhere had welcomed it. One critic in the popular *Daily Mirror* argued this drama should be 'performed all over the country, and special performances given for school children'. 'POET'S PLAY SUCCEEDS' ran the advertising strapline. As Tom and Faber & Faber (whose sales of the text were rewardingly substantial) knew, that summed it up.[245]

At the height of its run, he earned nearly £40 a week from *Murder*. More impressively, he achieved what no other English-speaking poet has ever managed: having become recognised as arguably the leading poet of his era, he gained almost immediate international success as a popular dramatist. Some, including Tom, might have regarded Yeats as 'the greatest poet of his time', but Yeats's plays lacked a mass audience.[246] When Tom's position as critic and publisher was taken into consideration, his eminence was unassailable. As soon as *Murder* succeeded on stage, he knew he wanted to write further '"religious drama"', and had in mind as a model Corneille's martyrdom tragedy about a love triangle, *Polyeucte*.[247] Yet, as ever, the public and intensely private planes of his life intersected in complex ways, and his relationship with Emily preoccupied him. An abandoned verse fragment probably dating from around the composition of *Murder* uses language implying masturbation as it speaks of 'Pleasure' that has been 'greedily grasped' but is less 'real' than 'Lust' that might be 'Held in the hand, matchless a moment' before it 'Fades fast, perishes in impotence' as 'Light lives / Slip from fingers slip / When freely fingered'. Ending with mention of a 'silken smell', this fragment states baldly, 'All men have their ghosts from the past'. It carried the title 'Bellegarde', the name of the ancestral house of the woman whom the St Louis-connected young American protagonist in Henry James's early novel *The American* longs to marry before, rebuffed, he has to give her up.[248] Tom, who told Spender in April 1935 that he felt 'very much more American' than James, had known this book since youth.[249] Aspects of it parallel his relationship with Emily, who shared his enthusiasm for James. Though Henry Eliot noted that part of 'Bellegarde' was 'nearly identical' to one of several passages about temptation that Tom cut from *Murder*, the only apparent links between 'Bellegarde' and his much longer 1935 poem 'Burnt Norton' are in the idea of degrees of 'reality' (one of Tom's old preoccupations) and that sense of 'ghosts from the past'.[250]

The bleak side of his emotions is evident in another poem tied to the period of his play and 'Burnt Norton', though it was the product of an enjoyable jaunt. In late April 1935 he had been in Scotland again with Morley. Reprising the 1933 visit to Neil Gunn took them through Glencoe, but this time warmer weather encouraged a 'pause' on vast Rannoch Moor.[251] Tom sent Emily's friend and former student Jeanette McPherrin ('a very intelligent and sensitive girl' who resembled a younger Emily, and with whom Tom could be gently flirtatious), a postcard of Glencoe, site of the infamous seventeenth-century massacre when, having accepted the hospitality of the MacDonald clan, visiting Campbells put them to the sword.[252] 'Some weeks later' Tom handed Morley 'Rannoch, by Glencoe'. Presenting its lunar 'moor' as both 'hot' and 'cold', this poem fuses experiences of the recent trip with its wintry 1933 precursor.[253] Its sense of 'confused wrong' and 'Memory' that is 'strong' connects with both *Murder in the Cathedral* (where killing is also a violation of 'hospitality') and with 'Burnt Norton', that poem of memory that recognises a failure fully to connect.[254] For some Scots, including the Eliot-influenced Edwin Muir whose 1934 *Variations on a Time Theme* was reviewed in the *Criterion*, Tom's view of a Scotland damaged by lack of 'concurrence' was problematic.[255] Tom's painfully personal awareness of lost concurrence and 'confused wrong' was not confined to Rannoch and Glencoe. He sent Emily the poem on 23 August.

During summer and autumn 1935, from late July onwards, he made several visits to Chipping Campden. The most important was a week in late July. Quoting to Emily language she would recognise from *The Waste Land* (' "my eyes failed" '), he was in 'ecstasy' to feel her 'head on my shoulder for what was either one second or eternity'. He loved walking with her round local villages, lunching with her 'under the hawthorn tree in a field', then having tea at the Crown Hotel, Blockley, where the 'inn yard, and the iron teatable on a slant and the hollyhocks, are snapshotted on my memory charged with a great significance'. He sat out in the garden of Stamford House until almost midnight with his princess-like 'nightingale' Emily, feeling intense 'glory' after she spoke to him words it was his 'craving desire' to hear.[256] Several times that week he photographed her, but, though he sent Jeanette McPherrin a 'masterpiece' photograph of Emily crouching beside flowers in a garden, emotionally charged mental snapshots were what underpinned his poetry.[257] While he does not mention it in letters until 10 September, it may have been during his July visit that they walked to Burnt Norton, but if mention of 'autumn' in his poem 'Burnt Norton' is taken as evidence, then it seems the visit took place during the weekend of 7–8 September. In a letter written shortly afterwards that refers to that 'weekend', Tom wrote, 'Our being in the rose-garden at Burnt Norton is one of the permanent moments for me.'[258] There was a five-week gap between Tom's July visit and three further visits in September. Emily filled her time with flower-arranging, visiting a Shaw drama festival, seeing friends, and travelling up to London. Tom's times alone with her were short, but intense. In London he was hosting his uncle Christopher, niece Dodo and other relatives, who also met the Perkinses and Emily at Campden, and who drove to ancestral 'Eliot country' in south-west England, 'from Port Eliot to East Coker'.[259]

He told Emily he looked 'forward with hope and joy towards a gradual greater assimilation between us', but did not define exactly what that might mean.[260] The presence of the Perkinses bothered him. He feared Mrs Perkins, dependent on Emily but 'with an unconscious desire to dominate', was trying 'to take the place' of Emily's institutionalised mother.[261] He thought Mrs Perkins 'stupid', her husband 'a pawn in her hands'; for himself, the 'only way to save oneself' from the Perkinses was 'to run away'.[262] Not immune to jealousy, he observed that the Reverend Perkins seemed 'happier in Emily's company than he is with Mrs Perkins'.[263] In September, however, he sent Edith Perkins a note of thanks, saying he 'had come to feel "at home" in Campden in a way in which I had not felt at home for some twenty-one years anywhere'.[264] He also included a long, mannered poem set in 'autumn's season of regret' in which the 'tardy rose' is sparkling 'not with dew, but tears'. Cataloguing flora found in Stamford House's garden and nearby, the poem with its 'Clematis' and other 'happy flowers' gone to 'oblivion' despite the gardener's 'love' shares something with that other poem of roses and clematis, 'Burnt Norton', especially as it asserts that 'Houses remember' and 'gardens have long memories; / Like houses, have familiar ghosts'.[265] Yet this poem written to charm Emily's aunt, the hostess through whose hospitality Tom had enjoyed sequestered access to Emily, glides across the surface, whereas 'Burnt Norton' is not only deeply philosophical but also charged with intense, refracted emotion.

The way Tom later mentioned having 'wandered through the grounds' and 'happened upon' the house at Burnt Norton, about a mile north-west of Chipping Campden, suggests he and Emily did not walk up its main driveway but instead approached – trespassed might be a better word – via a path through the woods. Even today, approaching from this angle, it is easy to get lost, encountering head-high nettles or startling a deer in under-growth off an uncertain track. What Emily and Tom saw was, as he put it later, an old 'third-rate manor house' with 'gardens'. The main property looked 'unoccupied'.[266] Adjoining it was a rose garden and, beside that, two dry pools. The pools looked odd because (though Tom did not know this) they had been constructed out of the wrong kind of concrete and so would not hold water. Their metaphorical resonance was strong, however, and the image of an empty, dry, concrete pool, brown-edged with moss or lichen, stuck in his mind. As he indicated later, he knew nothing of the house's history, but, as he put it, 'I daresay that I found some obscure attraction in the name.'[267]

To someone so sensitive to names and their connotations, this was unsurprising. The name Burnt Norton suggests loss – destruction by fire; in terms of word association, it might call to mind that colloquial expression of the irrevocable, 'burnt bridges'. As for the name 'Norton', recently Tom had been a Norton Professor. As he examined the rose garden with Emily, who loved roses and had lived in California beside an ornamental rose garden, there was a temptation to reflect on what was and on what might have been, much in the way Tom had done in those 'rose-garden' lines deleted from *Murder in the Cathedral* a year or so earlier. Walking with Tom 'at Campden', Emily liked to pick flowers for ' "us" ', some of which she gave him as buttonholes. That autumn, writing to her about 'how one man's life and work has been formed about you', he let her know he had 'stored' these flowers in envelopes, along with a yew sprig she had picked.[268] As her forty-fourth birthday (27 October) approached he focused on much earlier memories of her too, even though their effect was to 'gnaw like acid'. He remembered her in a fur-edged 'apricot dress'; he went over old details of their time together.[269] In October she came to London, accompanying him to the theatre. They dined with the Maritains. He intuited they had never been closer – felt, he told her, ' "possessed" by you'.[270] Until recently, he could enumerate the number of times he had 'kissed' her; now he was losing count.[271] From 18 November he found all Emily's letters to be fully '*love letters*'.[272] He felt they had crossed a rubicon. She was still in London in early December, when he sent her the opening lines of 'Burnt Norton', a poem he hoped to add to his forthcoming *Collected Poems*. When he wrote to her at Liverpool, just before she was due to sail to America, she was his 'Emily in Whom Tom lives'. Other people seemed 'faint and ghost-like'. He signed himself 'Emily-Tom'. He asked her, 'How shall I speak to My Love? Or of Her?'[273] One way was in his intimate letters: 'when I go to bed I shall imagine you kissing me; and when you take off your stocking you must imagine me kissing your dear dear feet and striving to approach your beautiful saintly soul'.[274] Another way of speaking was encoded in 'Burnt Norton'.

Beginning with lines almost identical to those about a 'rose-garden' which he had deleted from *Murder*, the new poem lacked his letters' sometimes awkward erotic adoration, and pointed in a tellingly different direction. A narrative that had haunted him was Lawrence's story 'The Shadow in the Rose Garden'. In *After Strange Gods*, quoting from its denouement and linking it to 'cruelty', he had attacked this tale in which, after years of separation, a woman encounters her 'former lover' in a sunlit rose garden but finds him now a 'lunatic'.[275] In 1933 Tom had noted that Lawrence's story's 'emphasis on physical relationship' was 'true enough to life', and had taught this narrative of loss alongside Mansfield's 'Bliss' (in which a woman discovers her husband is in love with someone else) and Joyce's 'The Dead', where a woman remembers lost love.[276] Tom and Emily were acutely familiar with loss, love, and mental illness. Keenly conscious of Vivien's disturbance, and knowing both Emily's and his own tendency towards 'self-preoccupation', Tom wished Emily would not 'go to see' her 'hopelessly insane' mother, since visiting Mrs Hale in the 'mental hospital' in Belmont, Massachusetts, upset her so much.[277] Emily could seem 'glamorous', an actress playing 'beautiful roles in her associations with other people' on 'the stage of her outward life', as her friend Jeanette McPherrin put it. Yet McPherrin came to see Emily's glamour as 'unconscious compensation for the sufferings and disappointments of her family life', and suggested later that she would not 'have been able to put aside her preoccupation and give herself fully to a life shared with another human being after the death of her father with whom she had shared so much'.[278] Did Emily see something of her poet-priest father in Tom? Conscious of sexual immaturity, did Tom seek a lover or a surrogate mother? Tellingly, though his detestation of J. M. Barrie stopped him from using the nickname, he liked to hear McPherrin in 1935 call Emily 'Wendy', the forename of Peter Pan's gently mothering companion.[279] Throughout that year Tom tried

'Again & Again' to suggest ways Emily might improve her situation.[280] Partnering her 'at Campden', he thought of Claremont where she had been 'much better off' than with the Perkinses.[281] He wished so many things might have been different. Marianne Moore, for a Faber edition of whose poems he had written an introduction, had mentioned to him in late 1934 Barrie's once popular play *Dear Brutus*, which was also a favourite of Emily's. In it, lovers are given a second chance, and a childless man meets the child he never had – his 'might-have-been' as Barrie several times puts it.[282]

All this is part of the context in which, not for the first time, he repurposed older lines to make a new poem. Now, in the context of the Burnt Norton visit, he redeployed the words about 'what might have been' and 'footfalls' that 'echo in the memory' down a 'passage' into a 'rose-garden' which in 1934 he had intended to be spoken by a priest in *Murder in the Cathedral*. Echoing the thinking about 'past' and 'future' in J. W. Dunne's *An Experiment with Time*, which had impressed Tom when Faber reprinted it in 1934, the deleted passage from his play was redeployed to become part of a philosophical poem whose opening section in particular is deeply inflected by his relationship with Emily. For decades readers detected no female presence – the pronoun 'she' is never used; if Emily is present, it is only in the poet's use of 'we' and 'your', rather than simply 'I'. Yet biographical knowledge has altered readings of this poem. Its vision of a garden both denied and granted becomes in part a refracted account of Tom's relationship with Emily. To the 1934 'rose-garden' lines, Tom now added the words, 'My words echo / Thus, in your mind', and then three lines mentioning 'dust on a bowl of rose-leaves'.[283] This dusty image may derive from verses by Shelley, whose poem of idealised love, 'Epipsychidion', was in his mind around this time. Shelley's lyric, 'Music, when soft voices die', contained lines Tom had known from childhood (then had quoted for their 'beauty' in 1920), and which mingle love and loss:

> Rose leaves, when the rose is dead,
> Are heaped for the beloved's bed;
> And so thy thoughts, when thou art gone,
> Love itself shall slumber on.[284]

As the first part of 'Burnt Norton' develops, the 'dry' and 'drained' concrete pool (accurate in terms of the specific Burnt Norton environment) again images loss, but is momentarily transfigured when 'filled with water out of sunlight', and a 'lotos' is seen rising out of 'heart of light'.[285] That last phrase echoes the 'heart of light' from the 'hyacinth girl' moment in *The Waste Land*, while the 'lotos' may have come from mentions of the 'lotus' within the heart and the 'white lotus' of God in the Yeats/Purohit Swami translation of the *Upanishads* that Tom had seen through the press not long before. He had also pored over notes about the 'lotos', 'sunlight', 'past present and future', and varieties of reality much earlier when studying Eastern philosophy at Harvard while he was going out with Emily in 1913–14.[286]

Some might argue that Tom 'disappeared' Emily into 'Burnt Norton', concealing her in the pronoun 'we', and that this disappearance was a kind of exploitation, involving a cruelty as sharp as that sensed in Lawrence's 'The Shadow in the Rose Garden'. Emily, who valued the religious poetry of her friend and Scripps colleague Ruth George as well as that of Tom, seems to have made no explicit objection to being folded into 'Burnt Norton', which Tom saw as a poem specially for her. Yet his brother, writing him a long, unsettling letter in 1935, detected in a different context a determination in Tom to appear unsullied by everyday life: 'Sometimes you remind me of a gentleman in full evening dress and white gloves attempting to put something right with the kitchen plumbing without soiling his attire.'[287] On occasion, this was indeed how Tom attempted to deal with issues in his emotional life. Henry's letter stung him, and, in a short poem written late that year and linked to 'Burnt Norton', he created an 'irritable' speaker brooding on a sensation 'More bitter than the love of youth'.[288]

Pasts and presents, futures and memories intermix in 'Burnt Norton' as they did for Tom and Emily during the period of the poem's germination. He continued working on it in late 1935 and well into 1936, grafting into it a 'kingfisher' he glimpsed near Kelham monastery, and a 'Chinese jar' around the time he published Hugh Gordon Porteus's *Background to Chinese Art*; his asceticism and aestheticism as well as his love for Emily guided the poem.[289] Later he connected it echoically with other texts, too, including 'They' by Rudyard Kipling ('the greatest writer of short stories in the language') and his own 'New Hampshire'.[290] 'Burnt Norton' was his secret tribute to Emily, but it was also about impossibility, about a road not taken, and about 'Cleansing affection from the temporal', transcending the 'twittering world' of ordinary physical life, and moving into a world of 'Love' that is 'Timeless, and undesiring'.[291] 'You know that in a way I did not want you to love me, but now that you do, I can't possibly wish that you should love me less in order that you should suffer less', he wrote to her on 12 December, conscious of 'the agony of being apart'.[292] 'Burnt Norton' celebrated the intensity of their moment, their closeness, and sensed, with a note of disturbance, the possible presence of children; but it was and is a philosophical meditation without love's physical contact, and it possesses a heightened awareness of 'waste sad time'.[293] That, linking with Tom's 1935 reflection that 'a great deal of my life has been wasted', is its final note.

In one draft version the poem ended with just two words, one per line: 'Light / Gone'.[294]

Even though Tom decided against publishing those last two words, and even though, so often separated by an ocean, he and Emily would remain bonded for decades more, each of them unable to relinquish a mutual sense of intimate closeness, he was recording a sadness about something 'gone'. In talk and letters, he protested his love for Emily, and hers for him; but in poetry he turned that into something else, something transmuted by his religious asceticism. Indirectly but intensely recalled, the early feeling of his love for Emily, however much it seemed renewed and transfigured, was in a crucial sense irrevocable, gone.

Vivien, however, remained convinced there was nothing irrevocable about Tom's split from his wife. She had enrolled for piano and singing lessons at the Royal Academy of Music, hoping to reinvent herself, and Enid Faber remembered how, around this time, 'She had her hair, normally a lank brown, peroxided to a brilliant gold, and waved.'[295] Self-deludingly, Vivien dreamed of giving a piano concert with an orchestra, of singing at the New York Opera House, and of reuniting with Tom. Eventually, in November, she ambushed him when he was speaking at a *Sunday Times* Book Exhibition in London's Dorland Hall: when she got face-to-face with him as he approached the platform, he shook her hand and said, she recalled, 'how do you *do*, in quite a loud voice', then continued to the stage.[296] Afterwards, during a book-signing, Vivien let her dog off its lead and it ran to Tom. She remembered standing 'beside him on the platform, with my hands on the table, & I said quietly, will you come back with me? He said I cannot talk to you now. He then signed my three books, & went away with Richard Church.'[297] Vivien still hoped to regain her man. 'As to Tom's *mind, I am* his mind', she told Jack Hutchinson.[298] She believed an almost telepathic bond persisted between herself and her husband. But he was sure his bond was with Emily, with whom he had visited various London friends. Virginia Woolf, after having Tom, Emily, and Spender to tea in November, had described Emily inaccurately as a 'dull impeccable Bostonian' who was 'Eliot's rich American snob lady'.[299] Perceptively, Emily, scrutinising the 'mask-like' face of this novelist whom she admired, had sensed Woolf's 'cool, half mocking detachment'.[300]

For Tom, heady with Emily's physical presence but conscious she was wary of what she called his 'idealisation' of her, these days were intoxicating.[301] Knowing she would be returning to America, he studied and memorised 'every contour' of her face and expression.[302] He held her on his lap and kissed her. He wanted to write plays for her. She told him on the platform at Gloucester Road Tube station that they 'should become more and more alike'.[303] When, eventually, they said their farewells and she left her room, she ran back upstairs to assure him, 'When I'm gone I'm here.'[304] She had given him a ring. He told her it 'means to me all that a wedding ring can mean' and would 'always bind' his finger.[305] They exchanged flurries of letters. She was his 'tall girl', his 'Raspberry Mouth'.[306] He was 'her dearest, her darling, her love', in all his foot-kissing, neck-kissing ardour.[307] When she left, 'Only in writing poetry' could he 'find any relief' and be 'alone' with her.[308] But 'Burnt Norton' told a different story, one that registered the inalienable regret that stayed part of their relationship. When she departed London, he saw her off at her South Kensington hotel. 'I watched you go down the street, turning and waving, and I waved too, but my handkerchief was blue and I fear you did not see it wave.'[309]

9

Pursued

AFTER Emily had so clearly expressed her love, Tom wrote to his sister Ada about the relationship. Ada, whom Frank Morley regarded as 'formidable', had her concerns about Tom, worrying lest his '"Way of contemplation"' might 'divorce him from "human" relationships and drive him into a shadow-world of "dramatism"'.[1] When Emily returned to America, she tried to explain matters face-to-face, asking Ada to 'Please think of me as one of the family.'[2] But what might that mean? Ada remained very discreet. Meanwhile, Tom added ink postscripts – 'I kiss your toes and the soles of your feet' and 'I kiss my ring' – to the love letters he typed to Emily about enfolding her in his arms and touching his lips to her neck.[3] Yet, resolving 'to suffer with you, as you suffer', he presented not sex or marriage but faith as 'the only real consolation'. The immediate context was the suffering Emily endured because of her mother's mental illness, but more generally Tom argued he and Emily should seek Christ-like 'joy, but not in the things of this world'.[4]

Holding out no hope of divorce, he remained a married man, which made her position all the more vulnerable. Wanting to supplement her 'very meagre income', Tom emphasised his deep dependency on her, describing their spiritual connection as 'now and until death and forever'.[5] He felt they should 'learn to live – it is easier to begin now while we are apart – as if things would always be as they are'.[6] Ultimately, Emily desired more. She worried she was 'pushing' him towards divorce. He kept explaining why divorce was impossible, and that it pained him if she experienced resentment 'against the Church' as a result.[7] Yet his letters continually expressed physical longing: 'I resent, and always shall, every occupation and engagement – except writing verse – that takes my mind from you; yet you are always with me when I wake and when I go to bed, and I stretch out my arms to where you ought to be, and at this moment you look over my shoulder and put your cheek against mine and I feel the rhythm of your body.'[8] Their lovemaking was excitedly epistolary.

Despite protesting resentment at obligatory engagements, Tom fulfilled them. As with Vivien, so with Emily he could suppress his emotions sufficiently to get on with work, finding outlets, especially in creative projects, which let him manage and control apparently insoluble problems. In that spirit, he began 1936 full of good intentions. He assured Faber, 'Mr Eliot's Book of Pollicle Dogs & Jellicle Cats (As Recited to Him by the Man in White Spats) should be completed by Easter'; he made sure a selection of his recent prose, *Essays Ancient and Modern*, was ready for publication by Faber & Faber in March and by Harcourt, Brace in New York that summer; and he went on revising 'Burnt Norton' ('can't get the last four lines right') so that it might conclude his new, expanded *Collected Poems* to be published by Fabers at the start of April.[9] The initial print run would be 6,000 copies, with a Harcourt, Brace edition (nearly 5,000) in May. 'Burnt Norton', he told Emily, 'is I think a new kind of love poem, and it is written for you, and it is fearfully obscure'.[10] On occasion Tom called Italy-loving Emily by the Italian version of her name, and he explained to her that, teasingly, he had considered giving 'Burnt Norton' an epigraph from Shelley's 'Epipsychidion', a poem addressed to another 'lady named Emilia'.[11] Chafing against marital unhappiness, the partly autobiographical 'Epipsychidion' (whose Greek title means 'about a little soul') celebrates Shelley's Italian Emilia as an adored, spiritualised, but unavailable soulmate, and the twenty-first-century critic Frances Dickey has argued that Tom's early and lasting fascination for this and other nineteenth-century erotic poems shaped his attitudes and behaviour towards Emily and other women, with 'Epipsychidion' 'clearly a source for "Burnt Norton"'.[12] Certainly, Tom presented 'Burnt Norton' to Emily as a love poem with a secret meaning he and his own 'Emilia' might share. Yet, however much he called it *'our* poem', explaining that its five-part structure was 'similar to "The Waste Land"', that it referred to Heraclitus, St John of the Cross and 'Flaubert's "Tentation de S. Antoine"', and that it was like a late Beethoven quartet, nevertheless there was surely a disjunction between the passionate protestations of his letters, and the difficult philosophical tone of his poem.[13] That disjunction reveals something messily irresolvable.

At Russell Square his small, 'eyrie'-like office was messy too. Reached by steep stairs or a 'creaky lift', its 'clutter of books' was 'piled up on floor and table'. Anne Bradby (later Mrs Anne Ridler) first entered it in 1936. Soon to become his secretary, she surveyed the scene, noticing among the clutter 'a necktie made of marzipan lying on the desk' – apparently a practical joke between Tom and Morley.[14] The desk itself was relatively small. Snapshots, including one of his mother, filled the mantelpiece. He had grown addicted to small ancestral pictures: 'I collect them as some do postage stamps.'[15] Yet, surrounded by mess, Tom was fastidious. With commanding judgement and a daunting ability to marshal names and percentages, this Ordinary Director of Faber & Faber (salary £500 per annum) dictated innumerable letters, often standing while his secretary sat in the room's sole armchair. 'In dictation he was measured but fluent: as with his normal speech, the sentences were perfectly formed – there might be a pause, but no humming and ha'ing.'[16]

He called meetings with authors 'interviews'.[17] Stringently, he dispensed advice about typescripts: 'Make Chapter 1 an INTRODUCTION to what is to come afterwards, not a MANIFESTO. You should be TALK-ING TO PEOPLE, not merely talking to yourself to clear up your own ideas.'[18] Yet, even if the young Dylan Thomas felt patronised by him, Tom could be appropriately supportive. He was kind to hard-pressed, exiled Russian psychologist Nikolai Iovetz-Tereshchenko on whose behalf he wrote many, many letters; and to twelve-year-old Denise Levertoff (later a celebrated poet): 'your notions of poetry will change'.[19] Some correspondence he typed himself, urging Emily to 'be childish with me, because I have a very childish side which I can only expose to you', or joshing with Pound in their shared Brer Rabbit idiom (with accompanying references to 'lil brown bros' and 'coons') that might have baffled the nimblest English secretaries.[20] His old friend was not just hard to handle, but also prodigiously productive: 'my position', Tom explained to an agent when declining to publish Pound on 'economics and boosting Mussolini', 'is that to deal with Ezra's poetry and literary criticism is as much as can be expect[ed] of any one firm, unless we decided to open a special Ezra Department, and I shouldn't care to be the head of such a department myself, at any salary whatever'.[21] Sometimes standing at the typewriter, he preferred typing his own book reports. When he liked a book, he could fight for it: he and Morley co-operated to convince a reluctant Faber in 1936 that Djuna Barnes's lesbian Gothic prose fantasia *Nightwood* was a great work, dealing with what Tom called, revealingly, 'the universal malady of living of which Lesbianism is only one species, as ordinary heterosexuality is another'.[22] He worked hard on Barnes's manuscript. Though initially scared of one another, he and she became fast friends. Poetry, detective stories and theology typescripts remained his specialities, and he took up the idea of books to encourage 'teaching divinity' in schools, not least private schools.[23] Often, too, volumes in French or German came to him as potential candidates for translation. He was a stalwart blurb-writer, and could be called on, if necessary, to pronounce on arcane works: no one else in the building had studied as much ancient Indian philosophy.

'Goddamb it, I have had a hell of a time lately, what with the jobs they give me to do, reading mss and cleaning latrines and so on', he complained to Pound that January, but to fellow chaps at the Oxford and Cambridge Club (whose 1936 members wrote to *The Times* about everything from contemporary politics to the history and functions of the English butler), he appeared a regular member of the metropolitan elite.[24] In this mode, he had written on club notepaper to the *New Statesman* about cheeses and other foods ('American salads are barbaric') as well as joining in a related *Times* correspondence: 'if cheese is to be brought back to its own in England, nothing less is required than the formation of a Society for the Preservation of Ancient Cheeses'.[25] Even if he never acted on that suggestion, continuing to organise *Criterion* contributors' suppers he had 'taken to the vice of Dining Clubs'.[26] Ecclesiastically accented, all-male discussion groups – the All Souls Club, the Chandos Group (whose members discussed Christian sociology) – increasingly attracted him. Making his own routine, he had, according to a society palm-reader who analysed his large hands that year, 'a feeling for ritual and regular custom'.[27] He got into the habit of working at home in the mornings, then sometimes taking an author to lunch – a fine French restaurant, 'the Etoile in Charlotte Street', was a favourite – before coming into Faber & Faber after he had eaten.[28] On Wednesdays, though, he arrived earlier for the weekly directors' lunch (roast lamb and apple pie, prepared by the building's resident caretakers) that preceded the book committee's boardroom meetings. At these, manuscripts were discussed, formal written reports read aloud, and strategy formulated. There were also occasional practical jokes – indoor fireworks a speciality. Tom could seem inscrutably distant, as if preoccupied by the *Times* crossword, but 'his business judgements were as shrewd as anyone's'. His characteristic fastidiousness manifested itself in telling ways. When afternoon tea was served he did not take sugar; Miss Bradby noticed how he 'would carefully remove the teaspoon from his saucer before it became slopped with tea.'[29]

His outer, professional life seemed public property: he was about to sail to Dublin to lecture at University College on contemporary literature, colonialism, Catholicism, and especially on Joyce ('the most universal, the most Irish and the most Catholic writer in English in his generation'); but his inner life was sealed.[30] He praised Yeats: 'a poet should go on developing, making new discoveries and taking new risks throughout his life', but, he told an interviewer, 'a writer should turn to poetry with a fresh eager mind and this is possible only if he treats his poetry as a side-issue and not as a profession'.[31] Side issues mattered. Before going to Dublin in January, he had sent Tom Faber a verse letter containing 'The Naming of Cats'. 'A Cat', this new work explained, 'must have THREE DIFFERENT NAMES'. Detailing these, and used to being waited on, he mentions 'the name that the servants use daily' as the first, everyday name; the second is more 'peculiar' ('Such as Munkustrap, Quaxo, or Capricopat'); but the third, unnamed name is the fascinating one:

> And that is the name that you never will guess;
> The name that no human research can discover –
> But BUT BUT
> BUT the *Cat himself knows*, and will never confess.
> When you notice a Cat in profound meditation,
> The reason, I tell you, is always the same;
> His mind is engaged in intense contemplation
> Of the thought, of the thought, of the thought of his NAME.
> Not his everyday name,
> Not his personal name,
> But just his ineffable
> Effanineffable
> Deep and inscrutable singular Name.[32]

'Tom', the addressee of this verse letter, had three different names (Thomas Erle Faber); so did Thomas Stearns Eliot, who signed himself 'Uncle Tom'.[33] Yet this epistle transcends mere wordplay. Written by someone accustomed to going to confession each week, and who, feeling 'zeal towards the ascetic and the contemplative life', regularly engaged in 'intense contemplation', this feline passage on names and naming reinforces the importance of names not only to day-to-day business life but also to the depths of the religious and poetic imagination – that part where effable and ineffable intersect as the poet mounts what he would later term 'a raid on the inarticulate' or where he contemplates what *Ash-Wednesday* terms 'The Word without a word, the Word within'.[34] The 'deep and inscrutable singular Name' – emblematised as the invisible, unspoken, though perhaps 'effable' signature-name of the cat – remains this poet's goal, glimpsed in his lighter as well as more serious poems.

His new volume of essays contained a recent, brilliantly perceptive piece on Tennyson, quoting a passage about 'the mouse / Behind the mouldering wainscot' from that Victorian poet's great poem of frustrated desire, 'Mariana'. Tom praised Tennyson's hymns to lost love *Maud* and *In Memoriam* as 'series of poems, given form by the greatest lyrical resourcefulness that a poet has ever shown'. These works showed 'blackest melancholia' and 'lack of serenity'. Discussing this author whose poetry might be regarded as 'not religious because of the quality of its faith, but because of the quality of its doubt', Tom might have been surveying some of his own earlier work: 'It happens now and then that a poet by some strange accident expresses the mood of his generation, at the same time that he is expressing a mood of his own which is quite remote from that of his generation.' Tennyson was 'the saddest of all English poets' as well as 'the most instinctive rebel against the society in which he was the most perfect conformist'.[35]

In private, pondering his life, Tom was bleakly open to Henry about 'guilt in having married a woman I detested'.[36] Now, trying to move beyond his 'sordid domestic affairs', he was 'desirous of ridding myself, as rapidly as my means permit, of all the clothing that I had before October 1932'.[37] Preparing his *Collected Poems* encouraged him to review his past and retrospectively shape it: 'my abortive attempt to make myself into a professor of philosophy was due to a religious preoccupation', he maintained, explaining that, except for people who have never before encountered the Christian message, 'a man is not converted: he converts himself'.[38] Rebutting some of Henry's criticisms, this letter sounds assured, but also reveals notes of bitterness that his animal poems and jokey letters to friends helped deflect or conceal. Using words Conan Doyle applies to Sherlock Holmes's arch enemy, Moriarty – the 'Napoleon of Crime' (the same words Tom would deploy at the end of 'Macavity: The Mystery Cat') – he presented himself with schoolboy humour in a letter to Hayward as endlessly elusive, signing off with a joke familiar to readers of Maurice Leblanc's early twentieth-century *Arsène Lupin versus Herlock Sholmes*:

> Very sincerely yours,
> Herlock Sholmes.
> P.S. I sign in this way, as this letter may be intercepted.[39]

Other spoof-Holmes letters to Hayward would be signed simply with a blank. If Tom, like his cats, had an everyday name, and a 'peculiar' name (Old Possum and variants thereof), then he also liked to play with this notion of a completely secret name, and to present himself, like Holmes, as hunted, elusive, under threat: 'No, when the blow falls, it will come in some totally unexpected manner: no one but myself will be prepared for it. Useless to notify Scotland Yard.'[40]

Early February brought 'bronchial influenza': 'hell pangs Chest like nutmeg grater'.[41] Wondering if he was being 'captured' by his 'powerful Calvinist heredity', and convinced 'We need a *really ascetic* (and from an

English point of view, quite *useless*)' religious order, he turned to writing Hayward another unsigned letter: 'The shades are closing in on your old friend, and soon, I fear, there will be nothing left but the closing chapter of the Reichenbach Falls.'[42] On 21 February he mentioned to Doone a 'new play' he had in gestation, and a few days later expressed awkwardness about an invitation to visit Elizabeth Bowen who lived near Regent's Park, close to Vivien: 'I have such a horror of that neighbourhood and a real fear of it in the daytime.'[43] Imaging himself as a hunted victim, and living in terror of encountering his wife, Tom signed himself 'Dolefully', and, after listing many work and social commitments, added the words 'o o otototoi' – an ancient Greek cry of grief found in tragedies including Euripides' *Orestes*.[44] He had used Orestes imagery of himself as a hunted man when writing to Emily the previous year. Where Orestes in Greek myth was pursued by the Furies after committing matricide, in Tom's new play the harried modern-day protagonist, Harry, would be haunted both by a vision of the Furies and by guilt as he wrestles with the idea that he may have killed the 'restless shivering painted shadow', his wife.[45]

In early March Tom felt irritated by the 'chorus' of Auden's new verse play, *The Dog Beneath the Skin*.[46] He knew, too, that MacNeice was translating Aeschylus' *Agamemnon*. His own verse-drama success brought him submissions from many other aspirants: 'it is dangerous to try more than one shift of the planes of reality', he cautioned his acolyte George Every, though Tom could have been addressing himself.[47] Of *Nightwood* he wrote that 'as with Dostoevski and George Chapman, one feels that the action is hardly more than the shadow-play of something taking place on another plane of reality.'[48] That was what he sought to suggest in his new play. For the modern dramatist, 'Shakespeare' was 'the worst possible model – he is too great.' Conscious of his own temptations, he counselled, 'The less action there is, the more important the versification becomes – so that the audience can get a stimulant that way if no other.'[49] With Emily he discussed 'going back to Aeschylus'.[50] He wanted his play-writing to impress her, and even had thoughts of writing a play in which she and he might act.

Though he snatched a few days' holiday before Easter, questions of theology and love still preoccupied him. Emily went with Eleanor Hinkley to see *Murder in the Cathedral* in New York, but Tom worried about Emily's religious views, and her letters' forlorn tone. Her health was worsening. That spring she booked into Senexet House, a Unitarian retreat in pinewoods near Woodstock, Connecticut. Established as 'a place for spiritual refreshment and the deepening of religious life' by Velma Chickering Williams, Boston-reared Unitarian editor of the hymnal *Amore Dei*, this House was in some ways Emily's Unitarian counterpart to Tom's Anglican retreat at Kelham.[51] At one time, before he quashed the idea on grounds of impropriety and theological differences, Emily had hoped that she and Tom might go on a Unitarian retreat together. Now at Senexet she participated in communion services and worship; feeling a sense of access to the infinite, but also a consciousness of closeness to distant loved ones, she experienced episodes of weeping, but felt soothed. Keeping up their constant correspondence, Tom had sent further glossing of 'Burnt Norton', explaining he had been 'trying to convey the sense of certain very rare instants in my life – an instantaneous feeling of being out of time, of being relieved for a moment of the burden of living in time, a sense of love which is not a craving, but something perfectly still and ecstatic'.[52] An ocean away, he worried she thought him 'intolerant and oppressive'.[53] He explained differences between Unitarianism and his much less flexible faith. Reprinting *Ash-Wednesday* within his *Collected Poems*, he had removed its original dedication 'To My Wife'.[54] Elsewhere, however, he had not revised his commitment to the epigraph from St John of the Cross requiring the soul to divest itself 'of the love of created beings'. That epigraph still stood alongside Orestes' line about the Furies 'hunting me down', prefacing *Sweeney Agonistes*.[55]

The St John of the Cross passage was also in his mind in April when he wrote about it to Dobrée. Connecting it to the 'Way of Contemplation', Tom maintained that 'merely to kill one's human affections will get one nowhere, it would be only to become rather more completely a living corpse than most people are. But the doctrine is fundamentally true, I believe.' This illumines his relationship with Emily: 'I don't think that ordinary human affections are capable of leading us to the love of God, but rather that the love of God is capable of informing, intensifying and elevating our human affections, which otherwise may have little to distinguish them from the "natural" affections of animals.'[56] Not long after finishing 'Burnt Norton' he told Faber that poem expressed 'something' of his 'belief' that 'the "illusion" of love is something to pass forward through'.[57] But, wrangling with Emily over the issue of divorce, and knowing she felt ill, he used different terms to her, maintaining that the 'poem is about *you*', though 'also, incidentally, about time.' She was, he assured her, 'my Tall Girl grown up to fit exactly into my shoulder. I hold you now.'[58]

'Do you know any good treatise on Original Sin?' he asked the elderly Paul Elmer More.[59] On the surface, Tom was prepared to grant that already he 'had received more credit than anyone has a right to expect during his lifetime', and that, 'if I have not had a happy life, that is my own doing'.[60] At a deeper level, he thought all human beings stained with original sin. His new play's Harry is an example of the sinner's torment. The drama

Tom had started to envisage would also accord with his May 1936 conviction that 'Between any two people (and the more intimate their relations
the more important this becomes) there is always an unresolvable element
of hostility which may be only further incubated by the dominance of one
over the other.'[61] Was he thinking of Emily or Vivien? Vivien still asserted
she and Tom would be reunited. Presumably referring to their encounter
at the book-signing, but distorting it with wishful thinking, she assured
her brother, 'I met Tom again, and everything was perfectly allright.' Then
she lamented having 'to go about the streets so much', adding 'that I never
had any children in my life, I thank God, and never wished to, since I was
a little girl of about twelve'.[62]

Tom encountered people, including Enid Faber and Hope Mirrlees,
who stayed in contact with Vivien, but his concern remained to avoid
being ambushed. He had an office telephone, but disliked using it. Miss
Bradby learned that 'barring' the way of visitors was 'certainly one of the
chief functions of his secretary', especially when it concerned 'the pathetic
figure of his estranged wife'. Sometimes she saw Vivien

> hover in the waiting-room till he came past the window on his way to
> the entrance. I would be warned of her presence when I came back
> from lunch myself by the firm's telephone controller, 'Miss Swan in
> the box', who was devoted to TSE. I would deal with the matter as
> best I could, having failed on an appeal to Geoffrey Faber, who
> admonished me that it was wrong to try to 'draw a ring-fence round
> Mr Eliot'. Telephone callers were rarely put through to him, and if he
> had to speak, his voice had a curiously strangled sound.[63]

To people who did not know him well he appeared 'immaculate,
impenetrable, inscrutable'.[64] His elusiveness could grow almost patho-
logical, but was bound up, too, with genuine busyness, not all of it Faber
& Faber business. As examiner for a thesis on George Herbert and Nicholas
Ferrar, Tom, though 'unfamiliar' with Ferrar, headed to Cambridge in late
May to meet the candidate, Bernard Blackstone.[65] His fellow examiner, old
acquaintance Hugh Fraser Stewart, and Stewart's wife Jessie were keen that
Tom weekend with them, but he had already promised to stay with J. M.
Keynes. Nonetheless, about a decade after it had first been suggested, he
was 'delighted' that, after the thesis examination, the Stewarts would take
him on a 'long promised visit to Little Gidding'.[66] During the seventeenth
century in that rural Huntingdonshire hamlet Nicholas Ferrar had established a small religious community. Tom had read about it in Mario Praz's
work, and in J. H. Shorthouse's Victorian novel *John Inglesant* which he had

bought in 1927. Shorthouse's account of the 'strange and holy life' of Little Gidding's 'manor house and church' where, along with several men and women, Ferrar lived 'in mortification and devotion', had once been popular, particularly among Anglo-Catholics. It gave an account of poet Richard Crashaw and of Ferrar's other 'dear friend Mr George Herbert, and of his saintly life'.[67] In the *Criterion* Tom had published T. O. Beachcroft's 'Nicholas Ferrar and George Herbert', which explained how without the intense friendship between Ferrar (who had chosen a life of 'self-effacement, whose sole end was religious devotion') and the poet-priest Herbert, the latter's collection *The Temple* 'might never have been published or perhaps even written'.[68]

Little Gidding had been in Tom's mind earlier in 1936 when he read in manuscript George Every's drama, *Stalemate – The King at Little Gidding*. It dealt with a nocturnal visit to the settlement by the hunted King Charles I after the English Civil War Battle of Naseby in 1646, the year when the chapel was partially burnt by Cromwellian soldiers. Now, on 'the only really lovely day' of that summer so far, Tom and the Stewarts saw this 'very much out of the way' place that 'few people' ever went to. 'The countryside', he recounted to Emily, 'was at its best: snowcovered with hawthorn, elder, and scented lilac.'[69] With Blackstone's research and discussions about Ferrar, whom Blackstone championed as a religious genius, at the forefront of his mind, Tom walked past the nearby piggery to the small restored chapel with Ferrar's tomb outside bearing a Latin poem by Crashaw. The facade (of which Tom took 'snapshots', soon sent to Emily) is surmounted by a triangular ornament, below which hangs the old bell.[70] Today above the church door visitors can read a recently renovated inscription from the Book of Genesis: THIS IS NONE OTHER BUT THE HOUSE OF GOD AND THE GATE OF HEAVEN. This inscription may not have been visible in 1936. Nevertheless, Little Gidding was a place Tom would never forget.

Another much-anticipated trip was to the site he regarded as most closely connected to his distant English ancestry and family name. He was used to being quizzed about his surname, especially by Scots. April 1936 brought a lengthy encounter with 'an elderly Scottish gentleman' who had brought a manuscript about Shakespeare for him to see 'Because your name is Eliot' and because the old gentleman's 'mother was an Elliot of Galloway':

> I heard you lecture to the Shakespeare Association, and I said, that man is a true El(l)iot – he is obviously hot tempered, obstinate, and determined to disagree with everybody.[71]

Though Tom politely retorted that his 'people' came 'from the West Country', his Scottish visitor informed him in no uncertain terms that this was because the Norman Michael de Aliot, William the Conqueror's right-hand man, had obtained 'a number of manors in Northamptonshire, and from there the El(l)iots spread into Devonshire and Galloway'. He went on to ask, 'do you mind [remember] the Elliot marching song[?]' Tom replied 'Yes', and, erroneously substituting 'maun' (must) for 'daur' (dare), misquoted,

My name is little Jock Elliot
And wha maun meddle wi' me?[72]

This misquoted 'Elliot Marching Song' fairly soon found its way into 'The Marching Song of the Pollicle Dogs'. Written to the Scottish 'tune of *"The Elliots of Minto"*', this poem would become a less celebrated canine companion to *Old Possum's Book of Practical Cats*.[73]

'Our people, you remember, went to Coker, near Yeovil in Somerset', Tom had reminded Henry a couple of years earlier, nudging his brother towards the genealogical *Sketch of the Eliot Family* by 'Walter Graeme Eliot of New York'.[74] Tom remembered the *Sketch* in their father's library, and had tracked it down in the British Museum. His father was listed among its original subscribers. After complaining, 'It has been disappointing to find how little importance has been attached to the spelling of the family name', and setting out extensive 'Ramifications of the American Eliot Tree', the book began with

COKER

Nestled among the hills and meadows of the heart of Somersetshire, the garden spot of England, is the little hamlet of East Coker, three or four miles SW from Yeovil, on the London & Southwestern Railway. Here, almost under the shadows of a fine old parish church, dating back to the fifteenth century, was the home for a century or more to the Eliot family prior to their departure for America and religious liberty.

Walter Graeme Eliot proceeded to explain that as 'members of the Established Church of England' during the Civil War, the Eliots, 'well educated, highly respected, well-to-do members of the landed gentry of the shire', had been attracted by the promise of emigration. The first family member whose name had been found in extant parish records was one 'Thomas Elliott'.[75]

Aware of this genealogy, after spending the weekend of 13–14 June 1936 with Bruce and Elena Richmond at their Salisbury home, Tom headed west by train to Yeovil where (as he put it in a letter to Polly Tandy, imitating the idiom of diarist Samuel Pepys) 'I lay for one night.'[76] Yeovil, according to his Somerset pocket guide, offered 'many interesting walks', but was 'rapidly increasing'.[77] Through its expanding outskirts Tom walked three miles or so south-west towards East Coker, with its historic church, nearby manor house, and a webbing factory. The village was bypassed by main roads but accessible directly from Yeovil by an older track which once ran beside an open field but nowadays begins among modern bungalows as Lower East Coker Road. This soon narrows to a single-track lane between steep, overgrown banks, making it risky for pedestrians if vehicles approach at speed. Even in the 1930s Yeovil's growth had brought increased motor traffic. Tom recreated in 'East Coker' the atmosphere on a sunny day of a

> deep lane
> Shuttered with branches, dark in the afternoon,
> Where you lean against a bank while a van passes,
> And the deep lane insists on the direction
> Into the village[78]

Highlighting antiquity, darkness and death, as well as summer light, life, and the modernity of the 'van', details in his poem (not completed until 1940), were true to his initial impressions, and 'taken from the village itself'. Just days after his visit he wrote to Elena Richmond that 'East Coker was delightful, with a sort of Germelshausen effect.'[79]

'Germelshausen', a story by the nineteenth-century German author Friedrich Gerstäcker, tells how Arnold, an artist walking alone through the countryside on a sunny day, comes across a beautiful young woman, Gertrud, who has lost her sweetheart. Hearing the peal of a cracked church bell, Arnold accompanies her to her old village, Germelshausen, where her father is mayor. Despite the sunny weather, quaint, grey-stoned Germelshausen is shrouded in mist and weird, yellowish light. Entranced by Gertrud, Arnold makes it clear he would like to stay with her in her father's house. He notices a funeral procession, and hears there will be a village dance that night. Walking through the oddly quiet hamlet, he sees, near its ancient church, medieval gravestones, and is surprised when Gertrud tells him one of these is her mother's. It emerges that as a result of a religious quarrel, the Pope has placed the village under an interdict: Germelshausen with its dancers, inn, and farmers, is trapped in time. Though she loves Arnold, Gertrud tells him he must go, just as the church bell stops ringing at midnight and a storm rises. He leaves, but can never find his way back to the village. The land around it has become overgrown: Germelshausen has disappeared. An old man tells Arnold that this cursed place sank into the ground centuries ago, though local folklore claims it reappears every hundred years. Arnold walks onwards, along a main road, weeping for his Gertrud. The story is one of irrevocable loss.

East Coker had featured in a 1934 *Times* list of the 'Fairest Villages in England'. Tom's guidebook presented its 'church and hall' as attractively 'grouped together on rising ground'. Soon after visiting, Tom called it 'pretty' and 'delightful'.[80] His poem, however, would present its golden stone as 'grey' and light-absorbing in a 'haze', while he linked the place not just to reconnection but also to the Germelhausen story of a love which cannot be regained.[81] By 1936 the poet of the as yet unwritten 'East Coker' had embarked on the drama of lost love that would become *The Family Reunion*. On Tom's East Coker visit, the landlady of the New Inn (today the Helyar Arms) 'asked if I was not a cousin of Colonel Heneage'.[82] The poet enjoyed being mistaken for a relative of the 'local magnate' (whose Tudor mansion, Coker Court, stood nearby), and recounted this incident several times.[83]

Walking uphill past East Coker's row of Civil War-era almshouses and Coker Court, Tom passed through the graveyard of St Michael's Church. He entered the church by its still extant hasped medieval wooden door, the same door his ancestors would have used long before the family left for America. Opposite, he saw a brass plaque 'To the memory of WILLIAM DAMPIER, Buccaneer, explorer, hydrographer'. Dampier, born 'at East Coker in 1651', 'thrice [. . .] circumnavigated the Globe' and explored Australia. Unveiled by Mrs Heneage nearly thirty years before Tom's visit, the plaque culminates with Dampier's words, 'The World is apt to judge of everything by the Success and whosoever has ill Fortune will hardly be allowed a good Name.'[84] Later, in 'East Coker', Tom would maintain that 'Old men ought to be explorers' and would list an array of apparently successful figures, including 'eminent men of letters' like himself, making clear they 'all go into the dark'.[85] If he had come partly in search of his surname, he was disconcerted to find it in the church not on some ancient stone but on a brand-new, 1936 stained-glass window, whose plaque read:

THE ABOVE WINDOW HAS BEEN ERECTED AS A TOKEN OF THE LOVE OF THE TESTATOR WALTER GRAEME ELIOT LATE OF THE CITY OF NEW YORK IN THE UNITED STATES OF AMERICA FOR ST MICHAEL'S CHURCH EAST COKER AND ITS PEOPLE HIS ANCESTORS HAVING BEEN INHABITANTS OF THE PARISH[86]

Tom was taken aback. This window, with its Eliot 'family arms incorrectly inscribed', appeared 'the only ugliness in the place'. It had been 'recently erected by some cousin of mine'. Its designer 'should be infamous'.[87] Rather than being accepted as 'cousin' to the local English squire, Tom had to face up to being 'cousin' to the American commissioner of this window. He told Emily he had felt 'at home' in this ancestral site, but that the inn landlady, while linking him to Colonel Heneage, had also 'identified me with the dreadful glass window'.[88] If he had come as an Anglo-Catholic British subject in search of English kinsfolk, he was confronted instead by his inescapably American filiations linked to an insistent blemish that came with the name of Eliot.

He was aggrieved. In Yeovil he had viewed 'the worst pictures I have ever seen'. Mass there involved 'the most repulsive curate ever I have seen'. Though later he recalled its female figures as 'dancing on the head of an Elephant', just why the East Coker Eliot window, depicting 'Faith Hope & Love with malignant faces', struck him as 'the ugliest that ever I saw' and so unsettled him, is not entirely clear, but his view of its less-than-perfect depiction of 'Love' and her 'villainous sisters' hints at his unhappy state.[89] With its 'vacant interstellar spaces, the vacant into the vacant', 'East Coker' would be a poem of bleakness as well as of faith and determination.[90] Into his summer poem of a Somerset Germelshausen he would incorporate lines about marriage drawing on the sixteenth-century *Governour* authored by another Thomas Elyot, whom Tom saw as 'a grandson of Simon E. of East Coker'.[91] So, 'In daunsinge, signifying matrimonie – / A dignified and commodious sacrament', dancers hold one another as they move in apparent 'concorde', but their 'mirth' is that of 'those long since under earth', and brings sombre awareness of 'Dung and death'.[92] With his own love of dancing (but not folk-dancing) and his fascination with his ancestral name, Tom could be teased: a few weeks after the East Coker visit, a fellow Faber director, in a practical joke, sent him a letter reproaching him for lending his name to a London dance venue, 'Eliot's Club'. Tom responded at absurdly excessive length, suggesting that the firm of Faber & Faber might change its name to 'Eliot, Eliot, Eliot & Eliot Ltd'.[93] But in the much more serious 'East Coker' the 'daunsinge' that for Thomas Elyot was so positive becomes a dance of death, and there is an inescapable, pervasive consciousness of 'empty desolation'.[94] The Eliot name could be a burden.

Shortly before visiting East Coker, in early June 1936 Tom had been to Paris with Frank and Christina Morley. They met Joyce, 'who wanted to stroll, which was,' Tom told Emily, 'a little alarming with anyone so blind, but there was fortunately little traffic; and we sat on a bench in the Square St Clothilde, while he again talked about his daughter'.[95] Later, Tom read at Sylvia Beach's bookshop. He enjoyed dining with André Gide and other intellectuals, discussing, among various topics, the Orient and Indic texts. Morley, unable 'to talk a word' with these 'French people' during the five-hour meal, had less fun.[96] During that summer of 1936 when Jesse Owens won four gold medals at the Berlin Olympics and a hit movie was *Show Boat*, that musical of enduring, tragic love featuring Paul Robeson's memorable singing of 'Ol' Man River', the most famous song about the Mississippi, Tom's mind was turning purposefully to America. Emily had secured a new job, teaching at Smith College, the elite women's liberal arts institution in Northampton, Massachusetts, at which her friend Margaret Thorp had taught some years earlier. Eager to see her but uncertain how much they should be seen together in public, Tom inquired about a transatlantic passage in August.

Yet even in this desire, he could not elude Vivien. Bizarrely, that June she was, as she put it, 'allowing it to be supposed, in various quarters, that I have gone to America, with a friend of my husband's', whereas actually, moving among temporary lodgings in London hotels, she was preparing to sit an examination for the Royal Academy of Music.[97] Sometimes, 'to reduce the strain on my brain', she asked to be communicated with 'c/o Miss Daisy Miller', whom she had 'become'.[98] Was this some strange attempt to 'become' her husband's American 'friend'? It is not clear how much Vivien did or did not know about Tom's relationship with Emily, but it is evident that Vivien's creation of 'Daisy Miller' signals an unsettled state of mind. The name came from Henry James's *Daisy Miller* whose vivacious, flirtatious American heroine, careless of social norms upheld by her American suitor, sickens and dies. If Vivien worried she might die, Tom feared this too; but he also feared what she might go on to do in life. After several days at Kelham and giving a reading 'in a harsh voice' (mainly to 'females') in a 'Student Christian Movement Camp' at a Derbyshire country house where his agonised manner impressed an admirer in her late thirties called Mary Trevelyan, on 28 July Tom got a sudden shock.[99]

Vivien caught him. He blurted this out in a letter to Dorothy Pound:

> I am rather shaky at the moment, because I ran into my late wife in Wigmore Street an hour ago, and had to take to my heels: only people who have been 'wanted' know the sort of life I lead. If I could afford to live anywhere but London I would. Only I mustnt have any address from which I cannot decamp quickly.[100]

Most shockingly revealing here is his use of the phrase 'my late wife'. Vivien, whose very name he avoids mentioning, was not his former wife;

they were still married. One can understand why, after several years of sep-aration, he called her 'my late wife'. Yet the phrase implies a dead woman, not a living one, and recalls his fear, so shockingly expressed to Murry over a decade earlier, of having '*killed* V.'[101]

Already prominent in *Sweeney Agonistes*, the nightmarish scenario of a man who has killed a woman would be at the heart of Tom's new, as yet unwritten, play where Harry fears his having 'pushed' his wife has led to her drowning on a transatlantic voyage. Despite argument over that verb 'pushed', Tom would be determined to retain it, and so leave 'in doubt' the answer to the question, 'did Harry kill his wife or not?' The protagonist, he maintained, 'is really expiating the crime of having wanted to kill his wife'. Only after being visited by 'the Furies' does Harry come to understand his 'Way of Liberation'.[102] Yet if Tom might fear he had somehow killed Vivien, he also saw further contact with her as intolerable. The day after the Wig-more Street encounter, he joked to Hayward about being nicknamed 'White Cargo' – the husband in a crudely sub-Conradian 1920s theatrical melo-drama who is saved, but only just, from his deadly wife.[103] To Emily, whose health remained uncertain, and who, after experiencing 'alternations of feeling', was spending time at Cataumet on Cape Cod and in Cambridge, Massachusetts, Tom sent on 30 July 'love and adoration and devotion', assuring her he would come and give support. 'At present, what you have to do is to become a jelly, and be massaged and looked after.' He prayed 'every night to the Blessed Virgin Mary to help us', but had an odd way of trying to cheer Emily up: 'As for my own sins, I take comfort from the fable of the man who went to confession, and said agitatedly, "Father, I have committed murder." "Yes, my son," said the priest gently, "and how many times?"'[104]

However readers may regard his intimate relationships, no one who peruses Tom's voluminous correspondence and published prose can doubt his stamina or ability to maintain numerous professional and social rela-tionships. During that summer of 1936 which saw the outbreak of the Spanish Civil War (drawing Spender, Auden and others to the anti-Franco cause) he drafted pages of complex arrangements to organise *Criterion* busi-ness during his planned absence in America. Wary of having his name used to support political causes in Spain or elsewhere, he busied himself in everything from liaising with his authors to answering tax queries and entertaining a relative visiting from the States. On a week's holiday with the Fabers in Wales he balanced on the edge of 'a precipice', read Arsène Lupin crime novels, and swam.[105] But he was concerned by Emily's ongoing 'illness'.[106] It had involved 'spiritual struggles' and culminated in 'a sort of a breakdown' from which she continued convalescing.[107] For a time she felt unable to write, though the Perkinses informed him about her condition.

He crossed the Atlantic in late August, but before he could be alone with Emily for any significant time, there was a family reunion in Cambridge, and a reading at Wellesley. Then, sensing a need for familial privacy, Ada had arranged a vacation in Randolph, New Hampshire, for which she, Shef, and Tom set off in early September. Later, Tom and Emily went for a week's seclusion at Olcottage, the well-appointed Cape Cod beachfront home of Emily's old friend, Dorothy Olcott Elsmith, a wealthy Smith College graduate active in the local Episcopalian church. When Tom 'first saw' Emily on this trip, she seemed 'very much changed', exhibiting 'a kind of numbness to the external world'. He worried her tendency to ponder what she perceived as 'her own shortcomings' had intensified.[108] She 'picked up a bit' while in the small community of Woods Hole, where the Elsmiths' large clapboard house looked across to Martha's Vineyard and distant Nantucket.[109] Emily and Tom listened to a 'bell-buoy', 'tolling' in the waves. Tom loved sharing with her 'the long beaches, the sea-gulls, the pine grove'.[110] In beautiful surroundings they relaxed, enjoying buffet breakfasts, and tray suppers 'in front of the open fire' after 'beach walks'.[111] Tom appreciated Dorothy Elsmith's 'tact and hospitality'.[112] Kind to the Elsmiths' children, this poet who could strike some Americans as 'dandiacal in appearance' was photographed in the sunshine, smiling in plus fours, cap, tightly knotted tie, and jacket sporting a breast-pocket handkerchief.[113] Beside him stood Emily in her walking outfit, wearing a small, neat hat. They look every inch the smart 1930s middle-aged holiday couple, though he, looking directly at the camera, is clasping his own hand, not hers, and she stands almost side-on to him, happily looking at his smile.

By 21 September he was back at Ada's Cambridge home, and Henry, now living nearby, was hoping to help organise Tom's forty-eighth birthday party on the 26th. Tom asked if the party might be on '*Ada's* birthday – the 30th'.[114] This let him spend more time with Emily. 'It seems to me that I am more deeply and strongly in love with you than ever', he assured her; but, alert as usual to the appearance of propriety, he made sure their most intimate time together was spent in out-of-the-way places.[115] As always, too, he had other social obligations – some of them solemn. He visited his now 'shockingly emaciated' old friend More, whom Tom found seriously ill, 'lying on a couch in his library' in Princeton.[116] More, an American ' "anglophile" ' from a Calvinist background, had revolted 'against a particular formulation of theism rather than against the spirit of Christianity', before finding his way towards 'sacramentalism'. He was someone to whose 'spiritual biography' Tom, a 'convert' who had made 'a long journey' to 'the English Church', felt very close.[117] Though they did not agree on everything, they shared what Tom termed belief in 'the excellence of English institutions'.[118] It was the last time the two men would meet.

Concerned for her welfare, Tom went also to Northampton, about sixty miles west of Boston, where Emily started as Smith College's assistant professor in the Department of Spoken English. Moving into an attractive clapboard house opposite the red-brick college quadrangle entrance, she seemed to him now 'a good deal better'. She did not yet exhibit 'any lively interest in the work', but he was confident that would 'come'.[119] Smith had about 2,000 students, faculty numbers were growing, and the study and practise of drama expanding. Though junior and still hampered by her lack of a college degree, Emily had prospects. The campus they viewed together was beautiful, well resourced, and much closer to her relatives than Scripps had been. Tom would incorporate into his new play details about working 'Alone, among women, in a women's college', and other aspects of Emily's experience – academic job-hunting, patient endurance, trying to understand an unhappily married man to whom she had been close when young – also found their way into the drama.[120] At the start of October he sailed home reassured about Emily's health, refreshed by contact with those he loved, and reinvigorated by time 'at the mountains and the sea'.[121]

London, by contrast, was noisy, crowded, and complex. That summer's International Surrealist Exhibition had brought quickened interest in what he came to call 'the Surrealist racket'.[122] The philandering new king, Edward VIII, privately sympathetic towards Hitler, was conducting a very public relationship with an American divorcee, Mrs Wallis Simpson, which would lead in December to the announcement that he would abdicate. Tom, who would soon mention with distaste the notion of a 'Fascist King' like a '*Fuehrer*', settled back into customary social pursuits: an 'old buffers evening' at Hayward's flat, or discussing the *Times* crossword with another 'old buffer' at the Oxford and Cambridge Club.[123] When not attending committee meetings, or dictating letters, he was writing references and blurbs for poets or for Elizabeth Bowen's forthcoming *Faber Book of Modern Stories* (which he had helped shape), or else making arrangements to weekend with friends including Hope Mirrlees and her mother (whose pampering household he found 'an ideal one to be ill in'), between duties connected with St Stephen's Church.[124] Being an 'old buffer', enjoying 'snuggling in my club by myself', was an identity he could readily assume. Old-bufferishly, he confided to Henry, 'We are catarrhal: I always use up a handkerchief before breakfast.'[125] He sounded off to Hayward, 'You know my aversion to Modernism in all forms, and especially in Poetry; and you know that Movements like Surrealism are things that I cannot make Head or Tail of.'[126] 'I seem to be degenerating into an Old Buffer', he confessed to Virginia Woolf some months later, with resigned self-mockery, and some relish.[127]

He still lived without a home telephone or radio. In South Kensington when Father Cheetham planned to move to a two-storey flat, Tom considered apartment-sharing with Hayward at 22 Bina Gardens, or setting up 'for myself'. Eventually, in early 1937, he moved to Flat 3 'at the top' of Cheetham's new residence, 11 Emperor's Gate.[128] Tom's two rooms had a cold, northerly exposure. Cheetham agreed he could have new gas heaters, and, in his bedroom, a gas ring, though Tom worried about fire. To reach the flat involved climbing '79 steps. Must get a rope ladder.'[129]

In America Emily's former landlady and mentor, Miss Ware, had died at the start of the year, and in March Emily had published a fulsome, detailed obituary for this woman who (as Emily high-mindedly put it, using language from the Anglican Prayer Book) 'gave herself to all sorts and conditions of men'.[130] In keeping with her use of such Anglican language, at Smith the still Unitarian Emily was attending St John's Episcopal Church on the edge of the campus, and was considering taking communion there. Disturbed by this thought, Tom suggested she consult the 'Vicar or Rector and ascertain his views'.

> He might, or he might not, want to know that you had had what we call a 'valid baptism', which means a baptism with the sign of the Cross in the Name of the Father and of the Son and of the Holy Ghost; and he might or might not ask about Confirmation. The rule in England is similar to that of the Roman Church; but the Episcopal Church in America is independent and I dare say has freer regulations.[131]

Unwavering in his sense of religious correctness, Tom also recommended to Emily theological reading. When she told him she had 'of course' been baptised 'in the Name of the Father and of the Son and of the Holy Ghost', he asked how, then, she could be both 'Unitarian and a Trinitarian' at once.[132] She took his advice, and consulted the rector, Albion Ockenden. Soon she was considering Episcopalian 'confirmation', but did not proceed with it, and Ockenden died the following year.[133] Used to dispensing authoritative counsel, Tom seemed to assume Emily might follow his religious advice, but her Unitarian heritage mattered to her. On 16 October she attended a dinner in Chestnut Hill to mark the twenty-fifth anniversary of the dedication of her father's church there. Tom realised that in discussing theology with this Unitarian minister's daughter he was 'on very difficult and delicate ground'.[134]

Since at least the nineteenth century, London's Kensington district has had marked social divisions: South Kensington is rich, North Kensington deprived. Tom made a BBC appeal on behalf of 'North Kensington Community Centre'.[135] Doing so was just one of many obligations he fulfilled. He wrote a perceptive, commissioned essay on 'Byron as a Scottish poet'; he praised the 'brilliance' as well as the 'horror and doom' of Djuna Barnes's *Nightwood*.[136] But he made room, too, for his own imaginative writing, and continued adding to his growing collection of cat poems, some sent to young Alison Tandy, whose wayward father Tom had helped to get work reading them on the radio. He hoped seriously to set 'to work on another play'.[137] Giving an invited talk after a performance of Charles Williams's verse play *Seed of Adam*, he told the audience,

> Religious drama is not there to give you the effect of the mass-manufactured plaster saint, or the comfortable deadness of the second-rate religious Christmas card. Religious drama ought to supply something in the religious life of the community that cannot be supplied in any other way and when it is fine drama and poetry, it can have a missionary power that is incalculable.[138]

The work of Williams, a friend and fellow publisher as well as fellow author, attracted him increasingly. The two met regularly, spurring each other's imaginations. In *Descent into Hell*, Williams's new novel, for which Tom wrote an enthusiastic blurb in early 1937, a leading character is a contemporary 'great poet' whose verse dramas rely on the use of a chorus. Structured round a quotation from Shelley beginning 'The Magus Zoroaster, my dead child, / Met his own image walking in the garden' (a passage Tom would deploy over a decade later in his modern-day play of martyrdom, *The Cocktail Party*), *Descent into Hell* involves martyrdom, doubles –'meeting an exact likeness of myself in the street' – and self-delusion about obsessive love. It mixes the real, supernatural, and phantasmagorical as many of its main characters, some 'living in at least two time schemes', head towards infernal torments.[139] 'I am interested in hell, and I must think it out' were words Tom gave his protagonist in a draft of his new play.[140] *Descent into Hell* was 'the most impressive' novel by this 'best living writer of the thriller with a supernatural element'.[141] Its themes and details would find their way into both Tom's poetry and his drama.

Europe was slowly descending into hell. In December 1936, Tom described the continent to Emily as 'one great international civil war, both overt and latent'.[142] She experienced 'depression' that Christmas, not for the first time, and international events did nothing to lighten the mood.[143]

A month or so after Tom turned again to his play, April 1937 brought aerial bombing of Guernica's civilians by Spanish and German fascist forces. Still, though, with his fastidious dislike of sloganeering, Tom avoided public denunciation. 'I feel still no more sympathetic to one side than to the other', he confessed to Emily, and when Nancy Cunard sent him a questionnaire that asked writers to take sides, Tom's brief response was that he still felt 'convinced that it is best that at least a few men of letters should remain isolated'.[144] In Britain, that spring would see Conservative Neville Chamberlain elected prime minister. Tom's intellectual Toryism sat readily alongside his Anglo-Catholic orthodoxy, but, like Williams, he had come to see horror and salvation not in terms of politics but of original sin and deep spiritual struggle. In his apparently successful middle age he had grown unsure what 'success' meant; he sensed a 'mysterious pattern of one's life', perceptible only in retrospect and shaped by 'mysterious Divine Grace'. In a way, he told a school prize-giving audience that summer, 'one's whole life is a process of learning to pray'.[145]

'East Coker' was then underway, judging by Tom's dictating in an April 1937 letter the words 'This is a periphrastical way of putting it', which echo one of its lines.[146] In that poem as in his new play he sought to reach 'the kind of point that *poetry* has to get to, the point at which thinking stops and something is just apprehended or contemplated'.[147] His training and temperament made him ponder 'the contrast between the flux and the eternal' that his old teacher Babbitt (whose recent work he read attentively) insisted was 'as vital to Buddhism as to Christianity'.[148] Though he found it strange that Babbitt had turned to Buddhism rather than Christian faith, in his poems of the next few years Tom too would draw on Buddhist and Indic materials as well as on his Christian commitment. Articulated in his verse, the intensity of that commitment impressed priests who knew him. Donald Nicholson, the ardent Anglo-Catholic curate who assisted Father Cheetham at St Stephen's in the later 1930s (and afterwards became vicar of the Church of St Mary the Virgin, Bourne Street) recalled of Tom that 'It was a spiritual experience to administer the Bread and the Wine to so devout a worshipper.'[149]

Immediate distractions took the form of work-related excursions to Rochester, and to 'that goofy country', Scotland, where Tom visited Robert Burns's grave in Dumfries and Burns's Ayrshire birthplace.[150] Writing to Hayward in the snooty tones of eighteenth-century Scotophobe Samuel Johnson about 'the uncouth manners, the barbarous repasts, and the heady liquours of our northern neighbours', Tom nevertheless did his best to republish medieval Scottish poetry as well as that of modern Scots miner Joe Corrie.[151] Southern distractions ranged from a dentist's assault on Old

Possum's recurrently problematic teeth ('year by year, they are extracted. / His agony is more protracted') to sitting through a talk on 'Adult Baptism' at yet another 'Old Buffers dining club'.[152] Yet Tom brought back from Scotland a hint from 'wild and goofy Highlander' Neil Gunn about incantations in the Gaelic *Carmina Gadelica* that offered a model for incantations in his new play, and he managed to complete a draft first act about an 'unhappy family and their birthday party' by mid-April.[153] 'It is', he told Faber that month, 'a gloomy play, I rather think it is going to be much the grimmest thing I have ever written.'[154] 'Very grim', he assured Emily, adding he had 'revived the Furies of Aeschylus', and there would be 'a nice little part' either 'for you or Edith Evans'.[155] For a break, he went to Salzburg in May. The Woolfs had toured Nazi Germany two years before, and Tom's 1937 'fortnight's holiday in Austria' included side trips to Berchtesgaden, near which Germany's Austrian-born dictator was already refurbishing his Berghof, and to Munich, where Tom had summered in 1911 and where Hitler would soon open the House of German Art. Tom noted a 'contrast between Austria and Germany': the former still enjoyed 'an agreeable democracy'.[156]

Like the earlier fragmentary 'Aristophanic Melodrama' *Sweeney Agonistes*, Tom's new play, subtitled in one draft 'A Melodrama', invoked the Aeschylus of the *Choephoroi* and combined ancient ritual with modern life. Surface aspects of his recent experience – a family reunion, a sister's birthday party, visiting a women's college – correspond to details in the drama. At a deeper level, this play, which came to be called *The Family Reunion*, deals with themes of insanity, marital disharmony, a controlling widowed mother, family disapproval of a marriage, lost love, anxiety about an absent, perhaps murdered wife, guilty terrors brought on by a conviction of being pursued, and a sense of original sin and expiation. All these, too, drew on personal knowledge. Initially, his protagonist was nameless. He was simply 'A' who had 'been abroad for some time'; his 'marriage was not approved of by the family'. 'A' reveals 'he thinks he is being followed'. 'Pursuit' of 'A' by 'THE EUMENIDES' is at the play's heart, but most of its characters cannot see the pursuers at all, and his family 'suspect nervous breakdown'. A doctor 'believes him deranged'. 'The horror of being thought insane grows upon him', though it transpires 'A' is not the only character to perceive these Furies who relentlessly pursue him.[157]

This schematic prose outline, with characters identified as 'A', 'B', or 'C', implied problems that would dog the play's development. Were the characters sufficiently realised? How could the Eumenides be portrayed? Was the play a diagrammatic ancient ritual, or a modern-day country-house drama? As far as this last question went, Tom was determined his play must be both: awkwardly, he was following Aeschylus, but also 'perhaps' Chekhov, whose *Uncle Vanya* he had watched that year.[158] As for the other questions, he struggled. In June he attended an outdoor performance of Sophocles' *Oedipus Tyrannus* presented in Greek by an all-male cast in the 'beautiful' amphitheatre at Bradfield College, Berkshire. Hayward thought Tom would have to 'pretend' to understand it: 'he's no classical scholar!'[159] Tom, though, was thinking hard about Greek drama, perceiving in it 'not so much a dramatic as a religious decline' from Aeschylus through Sophocles to Euripides.[160]

Hayward, to whom he showed a draft of part of his play, also confided to Ottoline Morrell that 'that mysterious lady-friend of his' was due to arrive 'from America' in late June.[161] Emily had been ill again. Tom urged her not to 'worry too much about fluctuations of faith'. 'All we can demand of ourselves is to keep the struggle going.'[162] Extricating himself from publishing business that included corresponding with Shri Purohit Swami about Patanjali's *Aphorisms of Yoga* (one of several Indian translations by the Swami that Tom saw into print with Yeats's support), and launching David Jones's 'fascinating' *In Parenthesis*, Tom was planning to meet Emily on 22 June.[163] At her insistence, she would accompany him in early July to Edinburgh University where he would receive an honorary degree. Thereafter, she went to Chipping Campden with the Perkinses while Tom spoke on 'The Church as an Ecumenical Society' at 'Church, Community and State', the vast World Conference of Churches held in Oxford and organised by his friend Oldham. More and more, he wrote and orated on such themes, hoping, for instance, that 'our cathedrals' might 'become centres, each of its own characteristic dramatic activity'.[164] In general, compared with his critical writings on poetry or drama, his ecclesiastical prose seems drab.

His Oxford visit dovetailed neatly with visiting 'American friends in Gloucestershire' – a 'very happy' time, though he felt it necessary to counsel Emily that 'despair' was 'perhaps the deadliest of the sins', and to extol the virtue of patience.[165] Then, in early August, before holidaying with the Fabers in Wales, he made his second visit to East Coker. This time he took photographs to send to Henry, including an image of a narrow, deep road overhung by branches; several times his snapshots may have nourished his poetry around this period. Tom walked 'from East to West Coker in great heat' to call on the vice president of the Somerset Archaeological Society. Lieutenant Colonel the Right Honourable Sir Matthew Nathan, retired civil servant and local antiquarian, lived at the Manor House, West Coker.[166] Nathan, 'a remarkable man' with a vast library, told Tom about 'local feuds during the Wars of the Roses', during which, as Nathan put it later, a 'timber' house, later rebuilt, was 'feloniously and traitorously burnt'.[167] Tom's

'East Coker', with its 'Houses' that 'rise and fall, crumble, are extended', as 'Old stone' gives way to 'new building, old timber to new fires' presents a universalised epitome of local history.[168] He described Nathan to Henry as 'Squire of West Coker, an impressive old Jew'.[169] A fund of local information, Nathan confided to his diary that Tom seemed shy and 'quiet'.[170] The historian's interest was not principally in this poet's ancestors, and when, at long last, Nathan's 600-page *Annals of West Coker* was published posthumously, although East Coker featured in it many times, it mentioned no Eliots. As 'East Coker' developed, it relied on Tom's distilled perceptions of the village and on his own religious sensibility more than on local antiquarianism. Perhaps better attuned to him was the sexton of St Michael's Church, who chatted for a few moments, deciding Tom was 'a nice kind of bloke. Quite religious, you could tell.'[171]

Back in London, he met Lawrence Durrell, whose writing he encouraged. Durrell, in turn, encouraged 'TSE Lio T' to meet Henry Miller, who had been hoping in vain that Tom might publish the erotic writings of Anais Nin.[172] When Miller and Tom met eventually, Durrell recalled, 'they got on famously'.[173] Conscious that people expected him to be strait-laced, Tom liked to surprise them, on occasion; but he also enjoyed playing up to his image, presenting himself Edward Learishly to Alison Tandy as an absurdly clerical 'Possum': 'At home, he is dressed in a mitre / And a cope, or a cape and a cowl.'[174] Close friends, including 'Father Faber', continued to play along, addressing him as 'the Rev. Uncle Possum'.[175] Emily accompanied him sometimes to St Stephen's, and had his measure as much as anyone. When she sailed to America in September, he told her Father Cheetham had 'asked the prayers of the congregation for "Emily Hale, travelling by sea"'.[176] Tom's High Churchiness was associated by some with that upper-middle-class awareness of 'social suitability' in which he had been schooled in America as well as England: 'upper-middle through and through' he described himself to Virginia Woolf in October, and in lines sent to Faber, with a wink towards the creature on the Eliot family crest, he wrote that 'The *Elephant*, of beasts alive, / Is quite the most *Conservative*.'[177] Going that month to lecture in Edinburgh on 'The Development of Shakespeare's Verse' (with concealed nods towards what he was himself 'interested in doing in the theatre') he decided 'Edimbourg is nearer to being my spiritual home than is Glasgow', and enjoyed confessing to Henry that 'One does feel a Swell leaving by sleeping car & walking up and down the station platform in a dinner jacket.'[178]

By this time Emily was critiquing a typescript of his play. On one of several drafts, when 'The Eumenides appear in the window embrasure', Tom scribbled that they should be wearing 'Evening dress'. Hesitating over whether this meant 'Black tie' or 'White tie', he decided on black.[179] The setting was the country home of Amy, Dowager Lady Monchensey, whose surname Tom adapted from a Browning epigraph, having checked there were no Monchenseys 'in *Burke's Peerage*'.[180] The play's milieu was 'fox-hunting' and aristocratic, rather than 'upper-middle'.[181] He had hoped it would be ready for production and publication in spring 1938, but it was not. Tom might have championed 'working regularly for two or three hours a day', preferably 'after breakfast' when the task was 'a long poem, or a play', but this was a demanding ideal for any poet-dramatist-publisher-lecturer to live up to.[182] Now 'Ashley Dukes and Martin Browne', his theatrical 'bosses', insisted he saw Eugene O'Neill's modern version of Greek tragedy, *Mourning Becomes Electra*, which was attracting plaudits during its London run.[183] O'Neill's example was encouraging, but also reason for delay: it was debatable how many fusions of Greek tragedy and modernity audiences might welcome. Now Tom aimed to finish redrafting 'by Easter.'[184] He cheered himself up by expanding his gang of literary felines ('Eternal chats / About Cats' were 'Bliss'), and by sending Virginia Woolf 'delightful reading' – a new Faber book by the 'Duke of Portland' which 'surpasses his previous books in fatuity'. 'Just my line', replied Woolf, and Tom, signing himself 'her devoted & obedient servant', fulsomely inscribed a copy to her as his Christmas present.[185]

He had, he explained to Pound, several rules for playwriting. The most fundamental were

1) You got to keep the audience's attention all the time.
2) if you lose it you got to get it back QUICK.[186]

Convinced that 'If the audience gets its strip tease it will swallow the poetry', he tried to follow these rules, but there were perennial worries about whether his plays contained enough action.[187] The Greek model involved offstage events being recounted by messenger figures, by the chorus, and by principal actors, but audiences used to Shakespeare and modern popular plays had limited appetite for hearing about offstage action. Like Emily, those audiences enjoyed the dramas of Shaw and Noël Coward much more than did Tom. They appreciated Wilde's wit and Chekhov's profoundly nuanced sadness, but Tom could match neither, and, in any case, was committed to a distinctively poetic drama. 'I refuse to write PROSE damb it you know I cant write PROSE' he joked to Pound.[188] He relished planting a short passage of journalism to be read aloud by one of *The Family Reunion*'s characters, embedding it as the sole piece of prose in his verse play.

Under Browne's direction, *Murder in the Cathedral* was to be staged again in America. At the start of 1938 Browne received from Tom a few small textual changes. The way that play, nurtured by ecclesiastical commissioning, had transferred to the commercial stage was remarkable; but now, writing directly for the mainstream theatre while still insisting on ritual aspects of a dramatic mode underpinned by religious conviction, Tom was attempting something more daring. Other people wanted to dramatise his poetry. The BBC broadcast a radio dramatisation of *The Waste Land* in January 1938, but Tom, though he granted permission and pocketed a fee, was not enthusiastic. Curiously, though – or perhaps unavoidably – he would draw on his own earlier poems in his plays.

Living alone, and regarded by many as intimidating, he was growing set in his ways. Emerging media culture meant little to him. Shown a television set for the first time, he thought it 'a truly remarkable toy', but dismissed its '"cabaret show"' content.[189] When the Tandy family (who soon offered a generally favourable 'Report on *MACAVITY: THE MYSTERY CAT*') presented him with new slippers, he realised with embarrassment that his old, torn ones, left behind at their house, were stained with 'Philips's Dental Magnesia froth'. 'I am a slattern.'[190] His *Criterion* was now regarded by some as 'academic and stuffy', but he sought to maintain its conservative, panoptic emphasis on what he treasured as civilised values.[191] He was happy to manufacture for Geoffrey Faber private 'degenerate verse' mentioning 'a Haarlem coon', but Mulk Raj Anand, an Indian student who had overheard him conversing about 'lesser breeds', was understandably resentful.[192] Where once Tom had mocked the Victorian sage, now he quoted 'Arnold' approvingly, and bewailed the 'pseudo-science' of '"the Social Sciences"' represented by Oxford's new, lavishly endowed Nuffield College.

> Higher education is not research, or technical accomplishment however difficult: it is the acquisition of wisdom. This is what it meant in Greece and in China in the past; and to some extent also at Oxford in the past.[193]

As Hitler moved to take control of the German army, then to annex Austria and Czechoslovakia, Tom made sure to publish in the *Criterion* a review of *English Constitutional Affairs in the Fifteenth Century* and a theological article on 'A Pattern for Reality'.[194] Amid 'excess of order' in 'the disorderly state of Europe' he strove to preserve traditional values; but, though conscious of shifting attitudes (he declined to publish the antisemitic French writer Céline, commenting there was 'a less favourable reception in this country for Jew-baiting than ever previously'), he could seem wilfully out of touch.[195] In creative work, however, he understood the need to try new things: *'nothing is worth doing twice'* he counselled George Barker, whose poetry and livelihood he kept supporting staunchly.[196] Still developing as a poet in his seventies, Yeats was inspirational; but Tom struck out in his own distinctive directions. Who would have predicted *The Waste Land*'s author would write a children's book? Or that the medievalist of *Murder in the Cathedral* would gravitate to contemporary country-house drama?

Now 'provisionally called *The Family Reunion*', the new play deployed the device of the chorus in a different way.[197] Rather than forming a separate group commenting on the action, instead this chorus comprised several principal characters uniting to utter *Carmina Gadelica*-style ritual incantations. Audiences might find themselves one moment listening to routine upper-class chatter – 'We might as well go into dinner' – only to be jolted very soon afterwards towards choral chanting:

May the three be separated
May the knot that was tied
Become unknotted
May the crossed bones
In the filled-up well
Be at last straightened
May the weasel and the otter
Be about their proper business[198]

Tom was determined that, to avoid appearing derivative, his lines should not sound at all like Shakespeare's, and audiences should not be continuously aware his characters were 'talking verse'. More remote than Shakespeare, Greek drama offered more possibilities for development. He explained to Dobrée:

I have kept in mind two assumptions:
1. If you can't make the most commonplace remark and still make it sound manifestly VERSE and not prose,
2. If you cant utter the most exalted sentiments, express the most rarified or intense emotions, without the audience thinking at once: 'this is poetry!'
then it isnt dramatic verse.[199]

Working within these assumptions, he did produce stage verse, but it can seem a thinner version of his poetry. Today his poems are quoted frequently; almost nobody quotes his plays. Adequately malleable, their verse lacks memorability. 'The verse', he contended, 'ought to be a medium to look THROUGH, and not a pretty decoration to look AT.'[200] Harder to forget is the onstage jolting between apparent realism and ritual drama. This was his way of showing several 'planes' at once – a surface, and much deeper levels. Some of his characters perceive only the veneer; others, like troubled Harry, see a deeper, often horrific reality. To Emily he worried that *The Family Reunion*'s 'emotions' might be too 'rare' for audiences to comprehend.[201] Browne seemed unhappy, but at least, after considerable redrafting, the play was almost finished. Several times in his life, Tom confessed to George Barker, he had 'felt *almost* convinced that I should never be able to write again'.[202] Now, theatre work offered expansive new possibilities, while, however slow, the progress of 'East Coker' from distilled experience to embryonic draft assured him he was still a poet.

He found it striking that his old sparring partner, John Middleton Murry, was now a Christian preoccupied with religious and national identity. He liked 'very much' Murry's pamphlet, *God or the Nation?* and told Emily, with surprise, that Murry intended 'to study for Anglican orders and become a country parson'.[203] Convinced a 're-birth of the Christian religion' was essential to 'the continuity of civilisation', Murry wanted the church 'to break with Nationalism'.[204] Yet as Murry's work, which Tom followed closely, developed, it emphasised not just the need for 'supranational authority' but also a particular, traditionally English identity. Murry's *Heaven – and Earth* (1938) stressed 'village-community' and English identity; *The Price of Leadership* (1939) asked, 'What does the effort to re-establish the authority of God *mean* for an Englishman?'[205] In the 'few pieces of Chamber Music, somewhat along the same lines' as 'Burnt Norton' that Tom now had in mind, he would strive to present a supranational faith while articulating, too, a deep sense of traditional Englishness drawing on village culture as well as London life.[206] This sense was present also, even at the risk of cliché, in the country-house drama of *The Family Reunion*. Tom might glance to Glencoe, or to Usk in Wales, and could give occasional encouragement to Scottish nationalists, but, like many of his friends, he was markedly more English than British. While unenthusiastic about the founding of a 'National Theatre', and conscious of being nourished by his American filiations, he had a convert's fervour in his conservative Englishness as much as in his Anglo-Catholicism.[207]

Warning her he might need 'three double' gins to prepare for the encounter, he met Djuna Barnes again in London in February 1938. She had been described to him once as like 'Mae West', but told him that she, too, was bound to be 'in a state of the jitters'.[208] They got on well. He introduced her to Hayward, 'a cripple and most intelligent'.[209] These two men were now so close that Tom asked Hayward to become his 'Literary Executor'.[210] While they shared tastes in literature and humour, one important factor bonding him to the wheelchair-bound Hayward was perceived isolation. Tom might feel he belonged to Emily, but a key part of that relationship was that, most of the time, she was thousands of miles away. Scrupulous in his dealings with Maurice Haigh-Wood over Vivien's finances, Tom felt, nevertheless, there was 'no obvious person or persons to leave all my worldly goods to, in the long run'.[211] He trusted Hayward, who was commenting on *The Family Reunion*, as a male, London-based literary judge who understood him. As executor, Hayward might be relied on to prevent reprinting of 'junk' Tom had written for periodicals ('F. & F. might be tempted, and your job would be to say no'), or publication of any letters 'prior to 1933'. Hayward must honour Tom's 'mania for posthumous privacy', and discourage books about him: 'I don't want any biography written.'[212] When, that February, Emily expressed an intent to write about Tom, Tom's response was, 'Well, my dear, why shouldn't you write anything about me that you like! So long as you keep it strictly private – as private as our letters – for unfortunately the interesting things cannot be said until everyone is dead – but I suppose that is true of most people.'[213]

In succeeding years Hayward would become a gatekeeper figure. 'Possum' (aka 'Elephant') could relax at this bibliophile crony's Bina Gardens flat where evenings of gossipy, game-playing, smoky and bibulous conviviality involved Hayward ('Tarantula'), Faber ('Coot'), Morley ('Whale'), and sometimes other invitees including John Betjeman and Ted Kauffer, with, occasionally, society ladies 'Vom innern Mayfairkern' (From Mayfair's inner core). At late-1930s 'Binagarten', Tarantula, Coot, Whale, and Possum/Elephant circulated in-group 'poetical effusions' in patinated literary English, French, German, and Latin that would be collected by Hayward in the privately printed 1939 *Noctes Binanianae*.[214] Twenty-four copies of this volume by 'the Choicest Wits of the Age' went to men, and the twenty-fifth to a woman outside their charmed circle – Tom's loyally discreet, hard-pressed secretary, whom 'Elephant' (a contributor in English, French, and German) had asked to type a 'fair copy'.[215]

By February 1938 Tom was sending Ashley Dukes and Browne (who worried it was 'weak in plot') a 'complete text of *The Family Reunion*', now on its 'third revise'.[216] The protagonist's having 'PUSHED' his wife troubled Frank Morley, but, conscious of Tom's distinction, he helped arrange that the poet sit for a portrait by Wyndham Lewis 'for the [Royal] Academy'.[217] During this period while Tom was 'rather stuck' with 'Skimbleshanks: The Railway Cat' for whom all are 'searching high and low', he added further touches to his drama of haunted, pursued Harry.[218] Lewis thought Tom looked exhausted. Yet the painter also recalled how his subject, 'when he had taken his place at a table, given his face a dry wash with his hands, and having had a little refreshment' would then 'rapidly shed all resemblance to the harassed and exhausted refugee, in flight from some Scourge of God. Apparently a modest reserve of power, prudently set aside, would be drawn on.'[219] Lewis made two paintings: a small-scale oil study, now at Harvard, and a powerful full-size portrait. It showed the dark-suited, solemnly intense yet impassive poet in an armchair, with shadows under what Virginia Woolf called 'his wild hazel eyes', and his hair parted with customary, geometrical sharpness.[220] This portrait, which Tom thought 'very fine', became notorious in April when rejected by the Royal Academy, prompting resignations, scandal, and excited press reports.[221] Eventually, after the Tate Gallery declined to buy it, it was purchased for the large sum of £250 by South Africa's Durban Art Gallery.

If Tom could seem 'harassed' and 'in flight', he could also cry. He did so that February – 'my only experience, I think, of weeping visibly in a theatre' – when watching Chekhov's melancholy 'great play' about ageing, family, and lost hopes, *Three Sisters*. In his own *Family Reunion*, he explained to Enid Faber, 'The tragedy, as with my Master, Tchechov, is as much for the people who go on living, as for those who die.'[222] His Furies, the Eumenides, pursue guilt-ridden Harry, who, like other characters, has seen his hopes and loves frustrated. Yet the dramatist wanted audiences to understand that, ultimately, his Eumenides might lead Harry to salvation: 'there is Hope for Harry – the hope of learning to want something different, rather than of getting anything he wanted'.[223] Though it is not directly autobiographical, Tom's explanation to Browne of Harry's relationships towards Mary and Agatha surely draws on aspects of his own experience with Emily and religion after his marriage to Vivien.

> The effect of his married life upon him was one of such horror as to leave him for the time at least in a state that may be called one of being psychologically partially desexed: or rather, it has given him a horror of women as of unclean creatures. The scene with Mary is meant to bring out, as I am aware it fails to, the conflict inside him between this repulsion for Mary as a woman, and the attraction which the *normal* part of him that is still left, feels towards her personally *for the first time*. This is the first time since his marriage ('there was no ecstasy') that he has been attracted towards any woman. The attraction glimmers for a moment in his mind, half-consciously as a possible 'way of escape'; and the Furies (for the Furies are *divine* instruments,

not simple hell-hounds) come in the nick of time to warn him away from this evasion – though at that moment he misunderstands their function. Now, this attraction towards Mary has stirred him up, but, owing to his mental state, is incapable of developing: therefore he finds a refuge in an ambiguous relation – the attraction, half of a son and half of a lover, to Agatha, who reciprocates in somewhat the same way. And this gives the cue for the second appearance of the Furies, more patently in their role of divine messengers, to let him know clearly that the only way out is the way of purgation and holiness.[224]

Revealing, too, is Tom's intense sense of inwardness with this Harry who is 'expiating the crime of having wanted to kill his wife' and must be saved by a religious 'Way of Liberation'.[225] Tom, who was trying to counsel Emily about 'unsatisfied desires' around this time, sees things here very much from Harry's angle and far less from the points of view of Mary or Agatha.[226] Both Emily (to whom Tom sent drafts) and Browne tried to persuade the dramatist to develop the character of Mary more fully, but he resisted. His argument to Browne that 'the character most like myself' is the eventually perceptive yet generally old-bufferish Honourable Charles Piper, who likes 'a comfortable chair' in his London club and maintains that 'All that a civilised person needs / Is a glass of dry sherry or two before dinner', is not convincing.[227]

Ottoline Morrell, who knew much about the Eliots' hurts, died on 21 April 1938, aged sixty-four. Tom, to whom she 'meant a good deal', was one of the last people outside her close family to visit her during her final illness.[228] Like his visit to the dying More, this was an act bound up with friendship, but also conditioned by faith that 'what happens to a man after death is more important than what happens to him in this life'.[229] He could not attend Ottoline's funeral on 25 April, however, because he was travelling to Lisbon. Tom admitted this trip sounded 'rather silly', but a paid-for holiday had attracted him.[230] In Lisbon, having agreed to help judge the Camoens Prize for writing about Portugal, he was fed nine-course lunches ('a torture when repeated regularly'), and met Portugal's ascetic, right-wing, pro-Franco Catholic dictator, António Salazar.[231] To a degree, he admired Salazar, a 'Christian at the head of a Christian country' who had criticised the Nazis and whose biography he encouraged Faber to publish.[232] With further European conflict looming, the British government – as Tom knew from *Criterion* contributor Sir Stephen Gaselee of the Foreign Office – was keen to preserve Britain's 'Ancient Alliance' with Portugal.[233]

Tom was abroad when, ominously, the recently formed 'Kensington

Air Raid Precautions Committee' practised responses to 'an assumed air raid on the borough', but he was back before, later in May, 'a crowd of several thousand' watched 'all branches of A.R.P. work at Kensington'.[234] Like so many, Tom followed events anxiously. 'Distressed for the fate of the Jews in Vienna', he had expressed to Emily, nevertheless, his hope 'that all the university professors will not come and settle here: there are enough Jews in the English universities as it is'.[235] On returning from Portugal, after he had lectured in Salisbury about George Herbert and distributed prizes to Methodist schoolchildren in Truro and Penzance, he thanked his Portuguese host, Salazar's biographer António Ferro, and praised Portugal's 'enlightened and far-seeing Government'.[236] Then, soon afterwards Tom's '*PRIVATE AND CONFIDENTIAL*' letter to Gaselee explained that Ferro was due in London with his wife and 'ought to be flattered' by the Foreign Office. Calling the couple 'two great black babies', he added, 'They both, incidentally, have more than a lick of the tar brush in them, and are absurdly fat.'[237] The poet of 'King Bolo and his Big Black Queen' was, as he had reminded Pound months earlier, 'a N. Englander born south of M. [Mason] & Dixon's line' (the traditional border between the Southern and the Northern United States), 'and I DEW draw a kind of a colour bar'.[238] Though his grandfather had written the biography of a freed slave, Tom had deep veins of American and English racism to draw on.

Emily and the Perkinses came to summer in Chipping Campden, but mid-July found Tom enmeshed in calamity. Scrupulously, he had suggested he might withdraw from being a trustee of Vivien's late father's estate, but Maurice Haigh-Wood (finding Vivien 'hopeless' to deal with) had wanted him to stay on.[239] Now, suddenly, while Tom was in Chipping Campden, a letter dated Thursday 14 July arrived from Maurice: 'V. was found wandering in the streets at 5 o'clock this morning & was taken in to Marylebone Police Station.' A policeman told Maurice 'she had talked in a very confused & unintelligible manner & appeared to have various illusions, & if it had not been possible to get hold of me or someone to take charge of her, he would have felt obliged to place her under mental observation'. She had been 'wandering about for two nights, afraid to go anywhere', and for the previous few months had been toing and froing between Eastbourne and London, giving no one her address. Dr Miller, her physician, had heard she was 'in a deplorable condition'. Miller felt she '*must* go either to Malmaison or to some home'. Vivien, Maurice reported to Tom, was 'full of the most fantastic suspicions & ideas. She asked me if it was true that you had been beheaded. She says she has been in hiding from various mysterious people, & so on.' Having left her 'much calmer' in a flat she was renting at 21 Burleigh Mansions, the St Martin's Lane block where Tom had had his 1923 bolthole, Maurice proposed to visit her again that day. She told him she 'never' slept there and was 'rarely there at any time'.[240] Vivien, too, felt pursued.

About to go on holiday, Dr Miller advised that if Vivien developed further 'serious' symptoms, a 'mental specialist' should be consulted: either Dr Robert Dick Gillespie or Dr Edward Mapother or Dr Bernard Hart.[241] All were eminent. Tom went to London to meet his lawyer, Maurice, and Miller. After discussing Vivien's situation, and offering to pay the specialist's fee, he then returned to Chipping Campden. Very soon Maurice was contacted by Vivien's banker who, after hesitations over confidentiality, revealed she had been behaving erratically, spending large sums, and was £500 overdrawn. With her mental condition prompting serious concern, Maurice arranged for Dr Hart – author of *The Psychology of Insanity* and former medical superintendent of Northumberland House, the private asylum in London's Finsbury Park district – to examine her on 10 August with a view to possible certification.

Back in Chipping Campden, Tom, who had known of Northumberland House since at least 1931 when he corresponded with Lilian Donaghy whose husband was a patient there, consulted his lawyer by letter. Tom made clear he was willing to increase his £5 weekly payments to Vivien but only if her 'financial affairs were taken completely out of her hands, and put under the control of some responsible administrator, presumably Haigh-Wood himself'. He was concerned that if Vivien checked in voluntarily to an institution such as the Malmaison again, she might, while still disturbed, 'terminate' her stay there 'at will'. To pay large bills for this would be 'to throw money away'. While Tom was content to continue paying her £5 per week (payments which had 'slipped' Maurice's 'memory'), 'supplementing of her income seems inseparable from certification'.[242] On 9 August in Chipping Campden, in response to a letter from Maurice and after consulting lawyers, who thought there was now 'only' one 'real solution of this most unhappy business', Tom (who kept a carbon copy) typed a short, legally worded letter to his brother-in-law. It stated that 'so far as my authority is concerned and so far as my authorisation is necessary, I give you my authority to apply for certification of your sister, Mrs T. S. Eliot, if Dr Bernard Hart thinks advisable, or to take any steps leading thereto which he thinks advisable, which may require my authorisation as well as yours'.[243]

Vivien was examined by Hart on Wednesday 10 August. Having telephoned Maurice, Tom's lawyer informed Tom that the psychiatrist was 'satisfied beyond all doubt that she is certifiable'. However, the case did not seem 'of sufficient immediate urgency to justify the issue of a certificate without a second opinion'.[244] Accordingly, on that Friday, when Vivien, who had returned to Dr Anna Cyriax for further 'massage' treatment, was with Dr Cyriax she was examined by Dr Edward Mapother, medical superintendent of the Maudsley Hospital and professor of psychiatry at King's College London.[245] A quarter of a century earlier Bernard Hart had acknowledged Mapother for 'much valuable assistance' in preparing his *Psychology of Insanity*, and the two physicians had worked together before.[246] Mapother, who had made it clear in 1936 that he customarily opposed 'admitting mental cases to the wards of a general hospital', seconded Hart's judgement that Vivien should be committed.[247] Maurice took these doctors' certificates to a magistrate, then visited Northumberland House. That Friday evening a car with two nurses called at Compayne Gardens, the Haigh-Woods' family home in Highgate. 'After a good deal of discussion', Vivien 'went very quietly' to the vehicle.[248] She was driven to well-appointed Northumberland House Mental Hospital whose high walls enclosed substantial grounds. There, under the care of Dr Frederick Dillon, Hart's successor as medical superintendent, she was to stay.

Dr Dillon was a humane physician. His interests included psychotherapy and 'phobias and obsessions' that could precede suicide.[249] A few days after Vivien was admitted, he expressed approval of 'Dr Bernard Hart's well-known *Psychology of Insanity*'.[250] It is clear that these male psychiatrists Hart, Mapother, and Dillon knew each other, but to suggest they conspired against their female patient would be unfair. Patients at Northumberland House were 'graded according to the severity of their case', and Vivien began as someone admitted to 'the nicest part, the Villas', whose residents were thought to need least observation.[251] When Maurice spoke to the doctor on 13 August, he reported to Tom that Vivien 'had been fairly cheerful, had slept well & eaten well, & had sat out in the garden & read a certain amount'.[252] Maurice soon discovered she had rented several properties in different parts of London, apparently moving between them to elude her supposed pursuers. At Northumberland House he hoped she would find 'some peace'.[253]

Tom remained in Gloucestershire where, albeit with interruptions, he had been spending 'very happy' days with Emily.[254] According to a later account, probably derived from his own recollections, he was told by 'the doctors' that he 'mustn't' visit Vivien.[255] Having separated from her so decisively, he was as determined to avoid encountering her again as he was to ensure he did his duty in contributing to her maintenance. He wrote to Henry and Ada, telling them what had happened. Henry replied they were 'glad to hear that Vivien has been placed in an asylum', and that he was reassured 'it was Maurice that took this step and that you are relieved of the responsibility'. Moreover, Henry was pleased Tom could now 'come and go without fear of annoyance or attack'. He added that he was 'of course glad' for Vivien's sake, too, 'since the next thing she would have been hit by an automobile while wandering around demented'.[256]

This was what Tom needed to hear. Guided by his lawyer, and by Maurice Haigh-Wood, an application was made for an 'Official Solicitor' to oversee Vivien's affairs; neither Tom nor Maurice wished to be responsible for them.[257] When he could, Tom sought refuge in congenial company, not least with Emily. On 18 July, a few days after receiving Maurice's letter about Vivien being at Marylebone Police Station, Tom inscribed a draft typescript of *Old Possum's Book of Practical Cats* 'for Miss Emily Hale, / this not quite final text, / from Old Possum. / 18.vii.38'.[258] The two of them enjoyed quiet time together in the garden of the house at Chipping Campden. 'Dear Love', he called her.[259] Still in Gloucestershire a few days after Vivien was committed, he wrote a short, kindly, witty letter to Hayward for whom he had bought a specially constructed new wheelchair. The Fabers hosted him in Wales from 26 August until 3 September.

On his return, he and Emily did something they had long discussed. They bought a dog. The large, fifteen-month-old Norwegian elkhound – 'very gentle' yet 'formidable'-looking – was, Tom believed, 'just the right kind of dog for her to have'.[260] Sensing he might not see Emily again for some time, 'with the political situation what it is', he 'felt acute relief' when she left for the States.[261] The dog would accompany her, protecting her where he could not; its name was Boerre (which Tom seems to have pronounced to rhyme with 'burr'), a name derived from a word in Old Norse that has the same root as the present-day Norwegian term '*berge*', and means 'rescue' or 'keeping safe'.[262] If the elkhound's name was a kind of private joke, then Emily, the admirer of Virginia Woolf's writing, may have known, too, that the protagonist of Woolf's *Orlando* turns to 'elkhounds' when 'done with men'.[263]

Tom and Emily had argued again about religion. She hoped he might gain 'an education in lines of new breadth, new vision, new understanding'. Prickly on such topics, he made clear that the inflexible 'dogmas of the Church' were 'no invention of mine'.[264] For his fiftieth birthday, 'in spite of doctrinal differences', she gave him a rosary.[265] When she was home in Massachusetts, he wrote to advise her 'in the event of war' to 'stick' to her 'job at Smith'; 'another war might well be a long war'.[266] Worried he would be 'quite useless for active warfare', he sent her his 'perpetual love'.[267]

Janes, the old handyman whom he and Vivien had employed, and whose recent medical bills Tom had paid, wanted to call on Vivien. Tom thought it could do no 'harm'.[268] Enid Faber would see her also, as would Vivien's elderly aunt. Tom came to worry 'frequent visits from her relatives' did no good.[269] At least twice that autumn she attempted 'escape' from Northumberland House.[270] Apparently, she hoped to find sanctuary with a friend, Louie Purdon, at a refuge for escaped psychiatric patients, but she did not get far. Convinced her condition was 'incurable', Tom wondered if she might 'be removed to some institution situated in the country at some distance from London'. This, he put it to his lawyer, 'should not only be pleasanter and healthier, but a further removal out of London might make her more docile and less restless', though he added that Hart and Mapother might be consulted.[271] Messages from her found their way to him. He did not reply. As it turned out, the Master in Lunacy, one of the oddly titled British officials overseeing the insane, was also of the opinion that perhaps rural seclusion might suit Mrs Eliot. Neither the Master nor Tom pressed the issue, however, and Vivien remained at Northumberland House. She would never see her husband again.

IO

War

G LAD Emily and the Perkinses were back in the States, Tom told them he thought if war came it would involve each side trying to starve the other out, rather than 'anything so quick and spectacular as air raids'. He suggested that unless he could 'be of any use here', he might 'go to America'. Having Foreign Office contacts, he contemplated that official 'government service' might send him 'somewhere abroad'.[1] In early September 1938, as Europe waited to see whether Hitler would annex Czechoslovakia's Sudetenland, Tom planned to seek some peace by visiting the monastery of the Community of the Resurrection at Mirfield in Yorkshire, but was conscious 'if war broke out' his first priority would be 'to finish my play'.[2]

The international situation's seriousness was brought home to him by reports and conversations, but also through participating in a group that included German Jewish refugees. Dismissed from the University of Frankfurt am Main in 1933 under Nazi laws against 'non-Aryans', professors Adolf von Löwe and Karl Mannheim along with Tom, Murry, Catholic sociologist Christopher Dawson and several other thinkers had joined 'the Moot'. This discussion group focused on relations between Christianity and social organisation. Its lynchpin, J. H. Oldham, had made clear at its initial April 1938 meeting that he hoped it might lead to the formation of a new religious 'Order'. Members discussed a 'crisis' involving 'increasing divorce between the life of the Church and the life of the community'. Tom advocated not 'a Christian totalitarian state' but the ideal of 'a local community within a nation and having wider relationships'.[3] He was interested increasingly in rural communities. Setting them against 'urbanization of mind', he maintained 'it is necessary that the greater part of the population, of all classes (so long as we have classes) should be settled in the country and dependent upon it'.[4]

Now, at the Moot's second, late-September meeting, he agreed with Löwe's statement that 'current events proved the breakdown' of ideas that the 'nation' was the 'final temporal unit'. For Tom, in the era of National Social-ism, it was 'more essential than ever' society 'should be Christian'.[5] Reacting to Murry's suggested 'Christian Theory of Society', and conscious of A. S. Duncan Jones's recent book *The Struggle for Religious Freedom in Germany*, Tom highlighted the 'Church' as 'a supra-national body'. He worried Murry offered no 'safeguard against the *national* Church becoming a *nationalistic* Church'. 'England', Tom contended, still represented 'the nearest approach to a Chris-tian State'.[6] Oldham then steered discussion towards attempting 'to define a Christian society'. Having heard from Löwe and others about Nazi zeal, the group pondered 'what we should do if war broke out'. Tom's hope, recorded in the minutes, was to find 'occupation in some form of national service with-out that official status which might shut his mouth'. Not adopting the line that creative artists must seek positions of safety, he sought 'to take part in any work for the future that was possible'. Even if war did not break out, 'We should still be in crisis and on the edge of war, for war was an integral part of our social system. Hence the need for intensifying thought and activity in an interval which might be marked merely by deterioration.'[7]

The Moot's concerns helped underpin the Boutwood Lectures he had been invited to give at Corpus Christi College, Cambridge, 'on any subject in political or religious philosophy or in the borderline between these'. His provisional title was 'The Idea of a Christian State'.[8] Participation in the Moot also nourished his poetry over the next few years, while his sense of contemporary 'deterioration' was bound up with his decision to terminate the *Criterion*. He confessed to Faber he had 'run it without conviction for several years'. With 'war' on the horizon, it seemed right to stop.[9]

'Deeply shaken' by the Munich Agreement which saw Prime Minister Neville Chamberlain agreeing with the leaders of France and Italy that Hitler should be allowed to annex the Sudetenland, Tom read with approval Oldham's October letter to *The Times* which argued that 'the spiritual foundations of western civilisation have been undermined'. After resigning as a British government minister, Alfred Duff Cooper, a fellow member of the Literary Club, received a supportive message from Tom.[10] To considerable popular acclaim, Chamberlain had announced 'peace with honour', but Duff Cooper had maintained in the House of Commons that 'one great Power should not be allowed, in disregard of treaty obligations, of the law of nations, and the decrees of morality, to dominate by brutal force the continent of Europe'. He argued that instead of the 'sweet rea-sonableness' offered by Chamberlain, Hitler was 'more open to the language of the mailed fist'.[11] Convinced Duff Cooper was right, Tom praised his 'courage and integrity'.[12] In October Emily heard from Tom how some London Tube stations were being converted 'into bomb shelters', while men worked day and night 'digging up trenches in the parks and public squares'.[13] Gas masks were issued in Kensington. Watching Auden and Isherwood's drama *On the Frontier* in Cambridge in mid-November, Tom confided to his host, Keynes, 'I am afraid that Hitler is not the simpleton that the authors made him out to be.'[14]

As his own new play neared completion, he and Browne dined at London's Reform Club with John Gielgud. Eager to play the part of Harry, and used to theatrical bohemianism, Gielgud was surprised the playwright was 'a rather sober-looking gentleman in a black coat and striped trousers'. He was even more nonplussed to hear later from Sybil Thorndike that Tom would not let him act Harry because Gielgud, having 'no Faith', could not understand Harry's motivation.[15] Tom had joked not long before that the 'perfect verse actor' must 'be something of a hero and an ascetic, if not a martyr'.[16] Gielgud failed to fit that bill. Besides, Tom was annoyed that the actor had gossiped about the nascent play to a journalist. However, Gielgud's perception that Tom's drama needed further 'clearing up' and that its Furies might provoke an unintentionally 'comic effect' was prescient.[17] In her diary Virginia Woolf recorded wryly how when the Munich 'crisis came' Tom's 'only thought was annoyance that now his play would not be acted. And he hurried up the revisions'.[18]

Frustrated, Emily was finding Smith College, where some found her snobbish, hard to settle into. Her favourite students admired this elegant, enthusiastic, and demanding teacher with her traditional Boston accent, sharp put-downs, and disciplined smoking habit: 'never more than five cigarettes a day'.[19] On occasion appearing more devoted to her strangely named elkhound than to her colleagues, she strode through Northampton beside Boerre. Tom encouraged her to be patient, and sought patience himself. Pound was in London that November, leading Tom to conclude 'his conceit is unbounded, and he can't be argued with'.[20] Repeatedly people canvassed Tom's public support for urgent causes. He remained temperamentally loath to commit. He owned up, self-mockingly, in another context, to having a 'costive kind of mind', not 'satisfied to say anything at all unless every possible shade and qualification demanded by the strictest criteria of scruple can be got down on paper'.[21] This made him a great poet, but sometimes an infuriating correspondent. When Sidney Dark, editor of the *Church Times*, asked him to sign a letter protesting against rising British antisemitism, Tom replied, 'I am naturally sympathetic with any protest against maltreatment of Jews, whether abroad or in this country. In other words, I take what seems to me the only possible Christian position.'[22]

Yet, while referring to a recent article about 'the tragic sufferings of the Jews today', Tom tried to explain why it was wrong for him to sign Dark's letter at this juncture. His reluctance is all the more striking because, shortly before, he had attempted to assist a German Jewish composer, Richard Fuchs, and had heard that Fuchs, though now free, had been 'imprisoned at Dachau'.[23] From the mid-1930s Dachau was mentioned in *The Times* not infrequently as the site of a 'concentration camp' for 'political prisoners'. By summer 1938 that newspaper was publishing pieces with such titles as 'Nazi Treatment of Viennese Jews: "Special Train" to Dachau'. By October and November there were stories entitled 'Threats to Vienna Jews: "Dachau, or Worse"' and 'German Jews Rounded Up'. The day after Tom refused to sign Dark's letter, in a piece entitled '600 Jewish Children Leave Vienna', *The Times* explained that 'In many cases the children's fathers are in Dachau concentration camp.'[24] Though his letter does not survive, Tom did write a personal note in December to his friend Philip Mairet, commending the *New English Weekly* for highlighting what that paper termed 'so-called "anti-Semitism" now spreading over the world'.[25] On 6 December, not mentioning any of this, he wrote to his German-born New York Jewish friend Horace Kallen, asking for help finding US speaking engagements for Louis MacNeice. A few weeks later, he expressed willingness to support a fund for refugees, but soon confided to Emily (who seems to have shared – or, at least, accepted – his prejudice), 'I am concerned about the refugees – if they are allowed to collect indefinitely in Britain there is great risk of eventual anti-semitism here: but where are they to go? And there is no denying that Jews in the mass are antipathetic!'[26]

He joked with the Tandy family; he socialised with Hope Mirrlees ('so tiring', he complained to Emily); on Christmas Day he dined alone with Hayward, who had moved flats.[27] He hoped proposals to send him to lecture in Mussolini's Italy might fizzle out. Several times he visited his and Vivien's old manservant, Janes, who was dying. Calling on the Woolfs, he displayed 'a humorous sardonic gift which mitigates his egotism', and seemed to Virginia 'a little mutton faced; sallow & shadowed', though she thought he 'has his grandeur'. When he told her his new play's 'flaws' were 'congenital' and 'Inalterable', he made them sound almost like hereditary family traits, but she confided to her diary that the 'flaws' were probably 'in the department of humour'.[28] Some days later, anxious as ever about the family name, he re-emphasised to Henry that *The Family Reunion* had 'nothing to do with the Eliot family, nor are there any characters which could possibly be supposed to resemble any Eliots'.[29] He hoped the play would appear in February or March.

By January 1939 he was deflecting *Criterion* submissions, letting people know the magazine was ending. Its final issue, published that month, carried material of interest to poetry readers – most notably MacDiarmid's 'Cornish Heroic Song for Valda Trevlyn'. There were also more arcane items that mattered to the editor, including (as a follow-up to the previous issue's review of *Nicholas Ferrar of Little Gidding*) a substantial critique of Blackstone's study of 'the community of Little Gidding', *The Ferrar Papers*.[30] Tom was gloomy. He wrote to Emily about 'the seriousness of the collapse of the civilization of the last four hundred years'.[31] Weariness shows in his magazine's ominously titled 'Last Words':

> With this number I terminate my editorship of *The Criterion*. I have been considering this decision for about two years: but I did not wish to come to a conclusion precipitately, because I knew that my retirement would bring *The Criterion* to an end. During the autumn, however, the prospect of war had involved me in hurried plans for suspending publication; and in the subsequent *détente* I became convinced that my enthusiasm for continuing the editorial work did not exist.
>
> Sixteen years is a long time for one man to remain editor of a review; for this review, I have sometimes wondered whether it has not been too long. A feeling of staleness has crept over me, and a suspicion that I ought to retire before I was aware that this feeling had communicated itself to the readers.[32]

The *Criterion* could claim to have published important writers from Auden to Woolf and from Proust to Valéry, but it seldom featured their finest work, and some readers had found it dull for years. Since relatively few of its subscribers were British, it had relied heavily on library subscriptions from America, Britain's colonies, and elsewhere abroad where it may (or may not) have been read intensively. Many contributors are remembered today principally because they were Englishmen friendly with the famous editor. Few articles were by women. In the final issue four out of thirty-six contributors were female, and three of those contributed only book reviews. In the penultimate *Criterion*, book reviewer Janet Adam Smith was the sole woman author.

To cheer himself up Tom dined with the Woolfs on 28 January, and accompanied Virginia to her brother Adrian Stephen's fancy-dress party. The author of the *Cats* poems had planned to go as 'Puss in Boots', wearing rubber boots, and had consulted with Woolf about how to ' "rig up" heads' ('Do you keep a store of fancy heads in the garret, or have you raided *two* productions of Mid. Night's Dream?'). In costume, though, he seemed to

Virginia to be wearing 'Lytton [Strachey]'s beard with a brown pop eye', and she thought he looked like the wife-murderer 'Crippin [*sic*]', a figure she had earlier linked to the Sweeney of *Sweeney Agonistes*. Young party-goers danced until 3 a.m., one woman 'almost naked'. Virginia felt 'a kind of liberation caused by wearing a mask, tipsiness & abandonment at not being one's usual self'. She sensed Tom 'expanding in the lights & stir, much as I do'.³³ Yet beneath the gaiety ran darker undercurrents. News had just reached Adrian, a psychoanalyst and anti-fascist campaigner, that Barcelona had fallen to Franco's forces. Virginia had been visiting Sigmund Freud, London's most famous Austrian Jewish refugee. Conversation had turned to 'Hitler' and how it might be a 'generation before the poison will be worked out'. 'What are *you* going to do?' Freud had asked her, talking of 'the English' and 'war'.³⁴

Though one could imagine Freud drawing unsettling conclusions about Tom's appearing disturbingly like Crippen at the psychoanalyst Adrian Stephen's party so soon after Vivien's removal from the scene, Tom had never admired Freud much. Now, though, at a time when he was reading in proof Christopher Dawson's *Beyond Politics* (which, amid rampant totalitarianism, lamented deteriorating relations between church and state), he shared at least some of Freud's anxieties about Europe. Looking back as he terminated the *Criterion*, he felt the 'seven years' after the Armistice ending the Great War had been 'rather the last efforts of an old world, than the first struggles of a new'. He regretted that recently 'The "European mind", which one had mistakenly thought might be renewed and fortified' had 'disappeared from view'. Having been 'the first periodical in England' to publish, for instance, Charles Maurras, the *Criterion* had not embraced fascism, but had appealed to a dispersed readership 'who are not Liberals by temperament' and who had little taste for 'practical politics'. Tom believed that 'perhaps for a long way ahead, the continuity of culture may have to be maintained by a very small number of people', but he had not given up hope. Still, conscious of impending war and deep 'demoralization of society', he expected 'It will perhaps need more severe affliction than anything we have yet experienced, before life can be renewed.'³⁵

He listened as efforts to advance ' "a new Christendom" ' and 'a new Christian order' (as advocated in Maritain's recently translated *True Humanism*) were discussed at the Moot that January. Karl Mannheim, who had 'worked' for some time with Nazi-supporting philosopher Martin 'Heidegger, whose position was entirely divorced from social reality', argued that 'this hour in this country was decisive' and that countering fascism 'involved us all inevitably in a kind of holy war'.³⁶ Tom had some sympathy with Mannheim, but his own sparse contributions to this Moot debate concerned philosophical principles, rather than suggestions about immediate combat. Arguing 'logical positivism' was 'the last stand of dogmatism for people who believed nothing', he sounded every inch the philosopher, rather than the poet.[37] It was as trained philosopher and committed reader of theology that he approached his forthcoming Cambridge lectures on relations between church and society.

Though the Boutwood Lectures' exact dates were not yet settled, he had agreed their outline with High Tory Anglo-Catholic educationalist Sir Will Spens, master of Corpus Christi College. In early 1939 Tom commended the 'important' review of England's school system known popularly as the Spens Report.[38] Spens would be in South Africa when Tom went to Cambridge, but both men were among the signatories to a January 1939 statement which, accepting such matters as 'the historical truth' of Christ's 'Virgin Birth' and the legitimacy of 'Catholic authority' but rejecting Catholic '"infallibility"', set out 'a Catholic interpretation of the Church of England'.[39] Tom had been chosen as Boutwood Lecturer not least because his views and those of the college master were closely aligned. At Corpus he was hosted by college president, *Criterion* contributor and Conservative politician Kenneth Pickthorn, an English historian. Geoffrey Faber found the 'whole ultra-Toryism of Corpus very repellent', but Tom fitted in well enough.[40]

His lectures acknowledged 'conversations with certain friends' at recent Moot discussions and elsewhere.[41] He told Emily that Oldham's October 1938 *Times* letter, which he had sent her, might serve as his lectures' 'text'.[42] Oldham had foregrounded the need 'to attempt to work out a Christian doctrine of modern society and to order our national life in accordance'.[43] Though at the Moot Tom maintained Maritain's *True Humanism* 'was written against the background of the French situation', he realised his own arguments were also 'deeply indebted' to Maritain, 'especially his *Humanisme integral*'.[44] Maritain, whose 'philosophical output' Tom found 'astonishing', had converted to Catholicism after experiencing both intense despair and temporary immersion in Bergsonism.[45] His work gained currency when, under the title 'Towards a Christian Society', Murry, drawing on Moot contributions, wrote at length in the 28 January *Times Literary Supplement* about Maritain's call for 'a vitally Christian lay State', and related *True Humanism* to recent European events:

> It must be possible, for instance, to pay the immense debt of spiritual obligation which the self-sacrifice of Czecho-Slovakia has imposed upon us – a debt of a kind that can never be satisfied by money alone, though we pour it out in millions: it can only be really satisfied by the

demonstration that Czecho-Slovakia has been sacrificed for the advent of a new Christian world-order – a new Christendom, as M. Maritain rightly calls it. Again, it must be possible, seeing how deep is the instinctive English and the French mistrust of them all, to bring into being some more human order of society than Communism, or Fascism, or National-Socialism. But we dare not any longer delude ourselves with the notion that we have – in our existing 'democracy' – such an order already.[46]

This was the immediate political, ideological, and theological context in which Tom delivered his Boutwood Lectures.

Drab in tone, and shorn of literary adornment, they mentioned work by Moot members including Dawson and Murry, and were demanding to listen to. Their immediate public impact was negligible. Having taken 'pains over them', Tom was 'not at all pleased' with the result.[47] After contending that 'a liberalised or negative condition of society must either proceed into a gradual decline of which we can see no end, or (whether as a result of catastrophe or not) reform itself into a positive shape which is likely to be effectively secular', he went on to argue for 'a positive Christian society'. This should be built on 'Christian education' and linked to 'the traditional unit of the Christian Community in England' – 'the parish'.[48] Tom was especially attracted to 'the rural parish' with its 'small and mostly self-contained group attached to the soil'. Englishness was a focus. He had consciously 'limited' his 'field to the possibility of a Christian society in England' and to 'the Anglican Church' as the 'only' way that 'the idea of a Christian society' could be 'realised, in England'.[49]

Still, alert to affairs in 'Germany', he sensed 'the danger that a National Church might become also a nationalistic Church'. He highlighted the value of a 'Universal Church' even as, seeking a society with '*respect* for the religious life, for the life of prayer and contemplation', he advocated living 'in conformity with nature'.[50] Though he did not use the word 'ecological', his focus on small rural communities accompanied denunciation of ' "soil erosion" – the exploitation of the earth, on a vast scale for two generations, for commercial profit: immediate benefits leading to dearth and desert'.[51] These interlinked aspects of his lectures connected with his work at Faber & Faber, where *The Rape of the Earth: A World Survey of Soil Erosion* was a new title, and where he would encourage *Criterion* contributor and denouncer of 'soil erosion', Kenneth Elliott Barlow.[52] Such elements also nourished poetry Tom would produce during the next few years.

To some listeners his lectures may have sounded quixotic. He half acknowledged this when, in a light-hearted letter to Hayward, he invoked

Walter Scott's poem 'Bonnie Dundee', spoken by a Tory Episcopalian battler who eventually led a failed rebellion: 'To the Lords of Convention
'twas Possum that spoke'. Tom exclaimed, 'Hurrah! Possum is up! So let
the forces of reaction, revolution, conservatism, liberalism, liberalism, conservatism, communism, fascism and everything else scurry back into their
holes!'[53] In his sombre, measured lectures, he pulled off no such trium-
phant rout, but did reach a ringing conclusion. Having stated, baldly and
provocatively, 'If you will not have God (and He is a jealous God) you
should pay your respects to Hitler or Stalin', he went on to describe his
reaction to 'the events of September 1938'. He voiced a sense of deep,
shared 'humiliation' not just in reaction to these events but also to an
awareness that something was rotten in national and European culture:

> The feeling which was new and unexpected was a feeling of humili-
> ation, which seemed to demand an act of personal contrition, of
> humility, repentance and amendment; what had happened was some-
> thing in which one was deeply implicated and responsible. It was not,
> I repeat, a criticism of the government, but a doubt of the validity of
> a civilisation. We could not match conviction with conviction, we
> had no ideas with which we could either meet or oppose the ideas
> that opposed us.[54]

Like Oldham and Maritain, Tom in these lectures sought to provide
arguments for a new Christendom. This was an aspiration he would seek to
articulate in poetry too, striving to further what, reading Maritain again
that spring, he called 'exploring "the frontiers of the spirit" ', attempting to
'regain, under very different conditions, what was known' to earlier ages –
part of 'this endless battle to regain civilisation'.[55] As he put it to Emily in
another context, one should refuse to 'surrender'. It was essential to 'go on
struggling'.[56]

Conscious he had authored no serious, publishable non-dramatic poetry
for two years, he hoped finishing his play might release him to make
poems. As had become habitual, he concentrated on his own projects at
home in Emperor's Gate, Kensington, most mornings, then did publishing
work at Russell Square in the afternoons. East Coker and Eliot genealogy
were still in his mind when he wrote to Henry in February 1939, but, with
his Cambridge lectures nearing conclusion, his focus turned again to completing the *Cats* book, and to *The Family Reunion*. The play was to be
published a day or two after its first performance. Presented by J. B. Priestley's London Mask Theatre Company, it opened at the Westminster
Theatre on 21 March with Michael Redgrave as Harry. By late February

Tom was attending rehearsals, juggling them with his visits to the Cambridge dons. Redgrave, he told Emily, was not as good as he should be; the actress playing Mary was 'only passable'.[57] Missing Emily, Tom thanked her for helping him modify the character of Mary, who might have married Harry but for whom it is now 'too late'. Mary tells Harry, 'You deceive yourself', and determines her focus will be college work instead.[58] While aspects of Tom's and Emily's psychodrama were acted out on stage, he continued with his day job. Book sales were slow. He kept an eye on Joyce's imminent *Finnegans Wake*, due for publication on 4 May. Additionally, he saw through the press MacNeice's *Autumn Journal*, a new collection by Spender, and other volumes.

On 8 March he was photographed for *Picture Post* at 'a kind of bogus dress rehearsal'.[59] Somewhat awkwardly, a confected photograph showed the seated Tom adjusting the trouser belt of Charles Victor who played 'the part of a police-sergeant'.[60] By the first night and Redgrave's ensuing party Tom had caught a bad cold which floored him for the next two days. The play was undeniably difficult to stage. Browne had decided the Eumenides, played by three women, should be masked, though the other characters acted naturalistically. Tom decided it was well enough performed, but expected 'very little in favour' from reviewers.[61] He was right. The *Times* critic judged Redgrave's 'performance of solid merit', but the play itself partly an 'arid essay' with 'not a great deal of narrative, and perhaps Mr Eliot has imperfectly realised how little there really is'. Intellectually intriguing, *The Family Reunion* lacked 'stage vividness'. Its dialogue 'partially fails to achieve that intensification of illusion which is the only purpose of any dramatic convention'.[62] Later, surveying the year's drama, the same newspaper considered Tom's play 'greatly inferior' to Priestley's most recent work.[63]

Reviews of performance and book came together. More than one reviewer located in Harry the same fault Tom had found in Hamlet: 'an emotion which is inexpressible, because it is in *excess* of the facts as they appear'.[64] Though some commentators, notably a *Church Times* critic and Tom's protégé MacNeice, found the play 'very moving' and perceived it concerned expiation and original sin, more found it puzzlingly problematic.[65] Still corresponding about Vivien (who wanted to maintain her access to a grand piano) and still having to emphasise he never wished to see her again, Tom had to accept that to many people his Harry was unfathomable or 'over the frontier of sanity'.[66] Virginia Woolf confided to her diary on 22 March that Tom was 'not a dramatist. A monologist.'[67] 'As you say,' he wrote to Emily, 'the play was something that I had to get rid of.' He realised its run would be short. Next time he hoped 'to choose a plot more objectively, and take one with practical advantages'.[68]

Resigned to this relative failure, he was photographed in colour at Russell Square on 13 April by German Jewish photographer Gisèle Freund. Tom had met Freund, a former student of Karl Mannheim, in Paris where she was in a relationship with Sylvia Beach's former partner Adrienne Monnier. Soon Freund would photograph Virginia Woolf, who was even less keen on the process than Tom. In brown jacket, greyish-green shirt and brown tie, his hair parted as if by a knife, he looked straight into Freund's camera. Hooded eyes intense but a little watery and with shadows under them, he appears shrewdly alert, but quizzical and rather tired. With his secretary 'ill for the last ten days', he had been doing much of his own typing.[69] *The Family Reunion* was about to end its run.

Occasionally people wondered about his state of health. On 2 May Louis MacNeice remarked in a letter that he had seen Tom at an Underground station the previous night: 'Surprisingly, he seemed to be blind drunk – rocking on his heels & staring at me vacantly.' When MacNeice saw him again a few weeks later, he was 'awfully tired & unwell-looking'.[70] Nevertheless, Tom kept going. On May 24 the New Criterion Limited was officially wound up. Adding hefty footnotes to fill out the volume, he revised his Boutwood Lectures for publication. Having digested the formidable Spens Report on English education as well as another recent report, *Doctrine in the Church of England*, he consulted Kenneth Bickersteth, headmaster of Felsted School, and other educationalists about the possibility of Fabers publishing a series of divinity primers aimed particularly at private-school pupils. Bickersteth, like the editor of *Picture Post*, was one of several people he encountered in 1939 who had seen the inside of a Nazi 'concentration camp'.[71] Bickersteth combined Tom's visit with the inauguration of the school's Literary Society: the poet came over as 'friendly', advising the boys to read their poems aloud to each other, seeking 'accurate use of words, and the accuracy of metaphors'. They were stuck that his 'own slow, precise speech was remarkable for its economy of words and its accuracy and clarity'. He commended 'translation from a foreign language as an "exercise" in writing poetry – for how else is the aspiring poet to practise writing verse when he is not sincerely moved to do so?'[72] Dispensing advice and inaugurating a literary society, however, were not the same as producing new poems. Still hoping he might visit America that year, he toyed with accepting a tentative invitation from Willard Thorp, husband of Emily's friend Margaret, to spend 'a spell' at Princeton teaching creative writing.[73] In theory at least, this would buy him free time. In the end, it was settled that Emily would come to England instead.

As usual, he acquired additional commitments. 1939 saw him elected an honorary fellow of Magdalene College, Cambridge, and nominated for a new 'preliminary group' to discuss 'Education'. Attending the Moot's April meeting, he had listened as colleagues formulated 'Steps to be taken in the event of war' – including a determination to urge the church towards 'a firm stand against hatred of enemies'.[74] With close friends he could be mischievous, sociable and jokey, but world events brought proliferating difficulties. He was doing his best for Franz Pfeiffer, a young German refugee whom Johanna Culpin had asked him to assist. At work he found it 'difficult to imagine what Faber & Faber will be without Morley', who was moving to New York to work for Harcourt, Brace and to bring up his children 'in America' with 'more settled prospects'.[75] Tom told Emily war might begin in September. Disregarding the threat, however, his sister Marion and niece Dodo planned to visit, while he hurried to finalise his lectures for publication. On 5 June, not long after a 'very happy' country weekend in the household of Hope Mirrlees's mother, Mappie, whom he liked greatly, he dined at London's Ivy restaurant with Mary Hutchinson.[76] She and Tom went on to *The Intruder*, an English version of François Mauriac's *Asmodée*, at Wyndham's Theatre. It was his first experience as a playgoer since *The Family Reunion*. Mauriac's successful country-house drama of demonic family passions had a disturbing English protagonist called Harry.

Welcome news was that Henri Fluchère, whose French translation of *Murder in the Cathedral* Tom admired, now wished to translate *The Family Reunion*. Though the *Criterion*'s internationalism was no more, maintaining links with France remained crucial to his intellectual life; not long before, he had helped host Maritain in England. Sustaining connections with Germany was more difficult. He had been surprised to hear of proposals for *Murder in the Cathedral* and others of his works to be published there. 'I wish that the Germans were not so unpleasant', he confided to Emily, worrying that a recent speech by Hitler sounded 'very able'.[77] Continuing to correspond with Ernst Robert Curtius, who was pursuing in Bonn his studies of pan-European Latin culture, Tom hoped to pay tribute to Munich-based Catholic philosopher Theodor Haecker whose 1933 *Was ist der Mensch?* had supplied the epigraph about conditions in '*kranken, chaotischen*' (sick, chaotic) times to *After Strange Gods*.[78] Tom knew Haecker's work well. Soon Haecker, a conservative Christian, would produce some of 'the most challenging examples of anti-Nazi Christian writing undertaken in Germany' as part of a group connected with the Munich magazine *Hochland* that brought together conservative Catholics opposed both to liberalism and to National Socialism.[79] Tom's own efforts at a conservative articulation of Christian resistance to liberalism, communism and fascism, pursued a related, albeit English-inflected, trajectory.

True to his continuing interest in small Christian parish communities, he signed up for Faber & Faber *Plays from St Hilary*, a series of modern nativity plays by eccentric Anglo-Catholic Father Bernard Walke. With his artist wife, Annie, Walke had turned his church into a celebrated shrine. Mixing vernacular English with tiny amounts of Latin, his plays had been performed by parishioners in Cornish fishing villages and broadcast 'repeatedly' by the BBC, demonstrating there was an appetite for fusing traditional High Church ritual with modern 'rural parish' life.[80] Tom's own religious life was, if anything, intensifying. When Morley's mother died, Tom quoted Dante's *Purgatorio* and assured Morley sombrely, 'The distress which is quite appropriate towards people in this world ceases to be applicable to souls in purgatory: the feeling of grief does not participate in our prayers for the dead.'[81]

The 'invaluable' Morley's departure did nothing to lessen Tom's workload and engagements.[82] During early July he headed north to receive an honorary degree from Leeds University, where he was hosted by Dobrée. When Emily arrived in England, though his contact with her was limited, once more they were together (with the Perkinses) at Stamford House and the adjoining Stanley Cottage. Tom made excuses for spending time with his sister Marion and niece Dodo at Southwold on the Suffolk coast. 'You have been very patient,' he assured Emily, 'but I did feel that they would feel defrauded unless they had a spell with me alone.'[83] Though they still enjoyed intimate trysts (he loved 'the moment under the yew tree'), and he signed his correspondence with her 'Lovingly and impatiently', he and Emily maintained independent lives.[84] In August she departed to stay at Barcaldine Castle, Argyllshire, with Lady Adam Smith, mother of Janet, while Tom went for his customary Welsh vacation with the Fabers. Throughout the summer he conducted business from several addresses, finalising the text for *Old Possum's Book of Practical Cats* (which his American publisher Donald Brace worried might be 'too English to appeal to American children') as well as for *The Idea of a Christian Society*; offering to meet Jewish and other refugees from Germany; supporting Browne by attending a pageant in Tewkesbury; and casting a mildly satirical eye on 'County' Cotswold folk.[85] On a visit with his Stamford House hosts to Middle Hill Park in Worcestershire, he surveyed at the home of elderly Miss Emily Georgina Hingley an interior that, as he told Hayward, 'would make Betjeman's eyes sparkle': 'a very fine collection of water buffalo heads, early muskets and assegais, oil paintings of Scotch lochs, and highbacked settles of the Ruskin period' along with 'a fireplace made of about fifteen old grandfather clock dials welded together symmetrically'.[86]

'If you remain keen on jew-baiting, that is your affair,' he wrote to Pound from Chipping Campden, 'but that name of Rothschild should be omitted.' Should Pound insist on his 'jew-baiting' note in the forthcoming instalment of his *Cantos* that Faber & Faber were due to publish, Tom offered to 'present' him with the name 'Bleistein' for use instead: 'almost of equal value METRICALLY'.[87] Though well aware of the plight of European Jews, Tom tolerated his old friend's rant, and was prepared to share a snide joke about Rothschild's 'value'. Wyndham Lewis, with whom Tom spent 'a quiet evening' around the end of August, had abandoned his earlier pro-Hitler stance.[88] With a nod towards humourist G. J. Renier's now forgotten *The English – Are They Human?*, Lewis had recently published his anti-fascist *The Jews – Are They Human?* and followed up later in 1939 with *The Hitler Cult*. Generally, Tom avoided polemic on what the *Times Literary Supplement* called 'the Jewish problem'.[89] Where Maritain, that thinker whom he so admired, directly addressed persecution of Jews in his 1939 *Antisemitism* (published in America as *A Christian Looks at the Jewish Question*), Tom made no published reference to this Maritain text. It does, however, appear to have helped condition his developing view that anti-semitism should be opposed by Christians as an attack on a religion bound up with their own. Nevertheless, he did not sign a manifesto against anti-semitism organised by Margaret Gardiner, honorary secretary of the London-based Academic Freedom Committee and the group For Intellectual Liberty. Tom argued on 18 July that

> I am more than doubtful about the value of such manifestoes as this, which merely reiterate what it should be assumed that every right-minded person feels. It is very easy to express sympathy with sufferers abroad, when what they want is practical help; and such statements may only exasperate the persecuted and irritate the persecutors. I also feel that the value of one's name on a manifesto is in inverse ratio to the number of manifestoes one signs. And I believe that the important moment for collective statements about anti-semitism will be later, if, as is possible, that mania is further exploited in this country.[90]

At the end of the summer Marion and Dodo sailed for America. Tom hoped to follow them in a couple of months, not least because Henry was expecting to undergo a serious ear operation. But nothing could be certain. Saying farewell to Emily, he assured her of the depth of their 'spiritual understanding', at the same time as treasuring her physical closeness. His wife might be institutionalised, but he still considered divorce impossible. He wanted Emily to understand how special, and delicate his relationship with her was. 'I don't think that it can be often that two people are able, in such a position, to preserve instinctively and without effort the right order of values and walk surefootedly and happy-heartedly along the edge of precipices and heights which most people would be unable to climb, or having climbed might fall from.'[91]

By the end of August 1939 the British government was considering how to respond to Hitler's 'third message to this country within a week' as the Nazis seemed ready to invade Poland. *The Times* reported Britain stood by 'our undertaking to help Poland in resisting any threat to her independence; and at the same time we, with the large bulk of world opinion, have not yet given up our hope that war need not be the only way out, if only reason and restraint could prevail'.[92] Photographs were published of the king being cheered while visiting the War Office; of anti-aircraft defences in Kent; of Jewish refugees filling sandbags outside University College Hospital, close to Russell Square. Vehicles marked 'ARP' – Air Raid Precautions – could be seen in the streets, as could lorries laden with sand. Anderson shelters were being built to protect against possible bomb damage; trenches scarred Hyde Park and Kensington Gardens. Evacuation plans were widely discussed, so that children might be moved out of larger conurbations, should bombing begin. 'If the children are evacuated tomorrow', Tom scribbled hastily to Emily at 6.15 p.m. on 31 August as she prepared to cross the Atlantic, 'it may be that ordinary passengers will not be taken.'[93]

On 1 September Hitler invaded Poland. That day's *Times* article, 'ARP Controllers Assume Duty', included advice about 'What To Do in An Air Raid': 'The best place inside the house is the basement.'[94] Two days later, after no reply came from Hitler to Britain's ultimatum demanding Nazi forces withdraw from Polish soil, Prime Minister Chamberlain broadcast on BBC radio at 11.15 a.m. on Sunday 3 September. Tom and Emily were in Chipping Campden when Chamberlain's words came over the wireless: 'I have to tell you now that no such undertaking has been received and consequently this country is at war with Germany.'[95] Tom helped Emily put up blackout materials on Stamford House's windows, to stop lights being seen at night if enemy bombers flew overhead. The couple also went into the garden, and picked flowers to bring inside. That evening, 'together', they stood 'looking out on the moonlight and the yew tree shadow more beautiful than ever before'. Signing himself 'Your adoring Tom' he assured Emily that 'those last minutes in the window are pictured in my mind with an intensity that can never disappear'. Everything seemed momentous. 'It will take me a long time to understand fully what has happened – there is a frightening kind of beauty.'[96]

On 5 September Emily and the Perkinses left for the States 'by a Dutch boat' from Southampton.[97] Tom had given Emily a ring dated 1810, assuring her he felt 'new happiness, which I think can never leave me'. In London he treasured a 'yew twig' from Chipping Campden.[98] But the world was shifting. 'Everybody is carrying gas masks now', he wrote the day before she sailed.[99] Air-raid rehearsals filled 24 Russell Square. From Salisbury Bruce Richmond had been suggesting to Tom, who, like Richmond, recognised war would bring particular publishing demands, an anthology on the theme of freedom. Tom went on reading manuscripts, and aimed to set aside a forty-five-minute weekly pause for 'meditation on the Gospel for the week'. His purpose was to 'realise' the passage of scripture 'as vividly and concretely as possible, and finally trying to draw out the symbolic meaning'.[100] He wanted to read St Augustine's *City of God*, 'and to get back to St John of the Cross, who is always grist for my little mill'.[101]

The outbreak of war showed his practical generosity. He knew Dobrée's daughter Georgina was studying in America (whose Neutrality Act of 5 September made its non-combatant position clear), and knew emergency currency regulations prevented her father from sending her money. So, having 'a small American income myself', Tom investigated how to divert to Georgina dollars from either a trust set up by his mother or from his US royalties.[102] Other reactions to hostilities were, he confessed to Hayward, more embarrassing. Waking at 6.30 a.m. on the Wednesday after war was declared, he experienced 'an unmistakable attack of emerods [haemmorhoids]', then 'was just dozing off again when I came to with a cramp in my leg. Fifteen minutes later came an air raid warning.' As quickly as possible he followed 'the Emperor's Gate drill' which involved making for 'the church, where there is a small hole in the bastion, possibly designed for the reception of lepers, which will just contain the vicar, Elizabeth [the vicar's housekeeper] and myself'. Apart from being very cramped, this bolthole afforded no easy access to toilets. With Kensington 'swarming with air raid wardens, with police whistles, and how they whistle', this became a pressing difficulty. Next time, Tom decided, 'I shall go in by way of the vestry, unlocking the door through into the church, as I think that what Elizabeth wants most at such moments of stress is a lavatory.'[103]

At work, where paper-rationing and wartime conditions would reduce the publishing list, there was topsy-turvydom. Only a week earlier, it had been business as usual. Now, suddenly the secretaries Miss Bradby, Miss Bland, and Miss Isaac were mucking in with Geoffrey Faber and their other bosses, including directors Charles Stewart and Morley Kennerley. They all taped up windows in case bombs shattered glass; prepared blackout arrangements; and assumed unaccustomed new roles. Just back from the 'surprisingly difficult' job of blackout in Chipping Campden, Tom adopted, not for the first time, a *de haut en bas* attitude, explaining to Hayward that in Gloucestershire 'if you leave a chink somewhere you may have the yokels brawling under your windows'. At 24 Russell Square he observed with impressed amusement,

Geoffrey buzzes between here and Wales. Miss Bradby is a first aid nurse, Bland is a Fire Fighter, the men in the packing department suddenly emerge in blue overalls, rubber boots and helmets, Stewart is busy trying to work out a lavatory system for the coal cellars, and everybody is useful but me. We had a rehearsal last week. The fashionable coal cellar is No. 4: it contains Stewart, myself, Miss Bradby and Miss Isaac, and when Geoffrey saw how select it was he insisted on joining it. The Russell Square air raids are ably conducted by Morley Kennerley, beating on a Woolworth saucepan.[104]

Outdoors at night blackout conditions meant that, while people could find their way around familiar streets, navigation became 'terrifying' in unfamiliar surroundings. Tom took to carrying a bicycle lamp in his overcoat pocket. He could cope with getting around 'Bloomsbury, some of Kensington' and 'Pall Mall', but felt unsure elsewhere. 'It is best only to dine at houses near tube stations, but you can't see a tube station until you are in it.'[105]

Plans to visit America were on hold. 'I shall be in London indefinitely', he told Virginia Woolf on 7 September.[106] Half-jokingly, in a note to Mappie Mirrlees next day, he referred to the outbreak of war as 'the catastrophe', and hoped he might visit if she kept on her house at Shamley Green in Surrey. Asking if she and Hope had plans 'for this dark season', he added, 'At this time one is eager for news of one's friends.'[107] Informing Pound that the new 'Cantoes' were 'on their way', although 'the question of a collected edition to date has had to be shelved', he hoped Pound would 'keep yr. head out of water in the turmoil of the maelstrom'.[108] Writing to Emily, he alerted her more than once to the fact their letters would be read by wartime censors. He sketched a lolling figure with feet up on a desk: 'Censor reading this letter.'[109]

'It is surely a mistake to suppose that a nation enters into war knowing quite clearly what it is fighting for', Tom wrote concerning 'Truth and Propaganda' in a letter to the editor of the *New English Weekly*. Addressing 'Englishmen' when it was clear that the 'uneasy interim *entre deux guerres*' was over, he urged profound scrutiny of what was happening: 'We cannot effectively denounce the enemy without understanding him; we cannot understand him unless we understand ourselves, and our own weaknesses and sins.'[110]

This was his position when the Moot met on 23–24 September for discussions and shared prayer at Annandale, headquarters of the Student Christian Movement, in London's North End Road. Activist, fundraiser and broadcaster Eleonora Iredale, one of only two female Moot members, was based there, but it was solely men who contributed to the opening discussion about 'the present situation'. With first-hand knowledge of the Nazis, Löwe argued Hitler would 'use every means conceivable' to win 'a long war' involving 'the terror of bombing'. Theologian Reinhold Niebuhr, whom Tom had met in 1936 and who was visiting from America, thought France would probably 'go Fascist'; 'Christendom' was 'disintegrating'. Various participants registered confusion. Tom shared this to some degree, though he sensed a moral deterioration extending beyond immediate events. 'We are involved', he said, 'in an enormous catastrophe which includes a war.' He then mentioned his Anglo-Catholic friend Vigo Auguste Demant's recent study *The Religious Prospect* as 'a book which had enormously helped' him 'in the clarification of issues', but it 'was terrifying in the magnitude of the task of Christianisation which it implied'.[111]

The Religious Prospect was emphatic: 'The Incarnation' that was 'known as the revelation of the Eternal Logos *to* man, provides the only Christian dogma upon which can be upheld the truth that man is not the creature or slave of history, but has the possibility of being in some sense its master and interpreter'. For Demant 'this truth is destroyed by the dogma of a one-dimensional temporal world common to the philosophies of historic Liberalism and Totalitarianism'.[112] Demant's was unlikely to be a book that either Winston Churchill, Chamberlain's recently appointed First Lord of the Admiralty, or the average person was likely to reach for. Even among the twenty-two people at this Moot meeting, half of them professional theologians, eyebrows were raised. Herbert Farmer, professor of systematic theology at Cambridge, insisted there would be problems if one were 'to speak on the basis of beliefs which are unintelligible to most people, e.g. the position held by Demant referred to by Eliot'.[113]

Tom held firm. Having already told Betjeman that Demant's was 'the best book written in England in the last year or two', he assured *New English Weekly* readers in October that it was of 'permanent value'. He admired how, instead of asking '*who* will win?' it focused on the question, '*what* will win?' Moving beyond arguments about 'Hitler and Stalin', Tom contended that 'ideas use men' and that 'In the sense in which war is something that starts with the fighting and ends when the fighting stops, we may quite well win this war without ideas. But in that event the statement "we won the war" must be countered with the question "who are we, now that we have won it?" '[114] In this spirit he would write what became the greatest English-language poems of the Second World War.

More immediately, he found himself on yet another working group: an 'Advisory Committee for the News Letter' that the Moot, guided by Oldham, planned for distribution to British churches.[115] Drawn from Moot members, this advisory committee comprised Tom, Oldham, former *Criterion* contributor Philip Mairet, Alec Vidler (editor of *Theology*, for which Tom had undertaken to write), and a supporter of 'the work of the Church at home', Lord Hambleden, chairman of retail chain W. H. Smith.[116] The committee grew into a larger group of 'collaborators', including Dawson, Mannheim, Murry, Niebuhr, Dorothy Sayers and others. The new weekly *Christian News-Letter* was small: two folded sheets, plus four-page 'supplements' addressing such issues as 'The Fate of the Jews'. Directed at opinion-formers, it would offer 'in a popular style yet without losing depth' religious 'interpretation of present events', practical suggestions (e.g., about evacuating children), and contributions to 'the formulation of war aims'.[117] With offices at 20 Balcombe Street, Marylebone, not far from Baker Street Tube station, it would become for Tom both a source of irritation and an important channel. Soon, it spawned a book series, and achieved a weekly circulation of 'over ten-thousand', making it by far the most widely read periodical he ever helped edit.[118] While the Moot's men debated theology, the practically minded Miss Iredale 'had the foresight to purchase thirty tons of paper'.[119]

The *News-Letter*'s focus was clear from the start: 'the big news rather than the latest news'. Its priority was 'The religious meaning of the experience through which we are passing'. It would balance 'identification with the nation' with showing how 'The Christian Church transcends the bounds of nationality', even when threatened by 'the black-out of mind'. The *News-Letter* was by no means pacifist, but, in the midst of 'breakdown of civilisations', it upheld the ideal of 'a dedicated brotherhood'. Clear that 'militarism destroys', it asked 'how can we create?'[120] This was the intellectual climate in which Tom, a non-combatant, desk-bound publisher in his early fifties, would write war poetry.

To start with he wrote no poetry at all. He told Emily the *News-Letter* was 'rather dull'. 'Everyone', he explained, 'feels a little uprooted', but it was hard to communicate the atmosphere of wartime England, especially with letters subject to censorship.[121] He did, though, send newsy notes to Hayward who had been helping translate documents for the French Embassy but felt 'very depressed' by his apparent 'uselessness'.[122] Wheelchair-bound Hayward had been evacuated to Cambridge. Tom visited him at his wartime refuge, Merton Hall, an Elizabethan house in St John's College grounds. It had been rented by Victor Rothschild for family and friends. Hayward helped run Merton Hall, but missed London companionship. He had taken with him his ever-growing archive of Tom's correspondence, drafts, and typescripts. Attempting to stay in touch, from 'exile' Hayward began sending friends, including Tom and Morley, fortnightly typed letters, 'Tarantula's Special News-Service'.[123]

Tom replied frequently. Writing sometimes in Sherlock Holmes style and on occasion as 'J. C. D. Duffin (Brig.-Genl. Retired, R.A.M.C.)' of '"The Rabbit Hutch", Nether Bottom, Little Piddlestone, Salop', he relayed details of parish quarrels amongst the 'war work of dusting hassocks and polishing the lectern' at St Stephen's Church.[124] When he could, he visited Hayward, which kept up spirits. In some ways corresponding with Hayward was easier than communicating with Emily. When she wrote about ' "basic fundamental principles" ' that were ' "common to all religions" ', Tom found her Unitarian ' "broadmindedness" ' problematic. His Christian belief was dogmatic: 'A "creed" in the strict sense, is not something which can be changed.' Rattled by her tenacious Unitarianism, he was at least as bothered by her continuing suggestions that he might divorce. 'It is very hard and very painful for me', he made clear to her, 'to have to mention a subject which, on two or three several occasions, I thought I had said all there was to say about.' There must be no 'illusory hopes'; they must 'submerge' their 'own griefs in those of the world'.[125] For him in wartime London the world's griefs were pressing; but across the Atlantic, Emily, whose country was not at war and who still hoped to marry the man whose ring she wore, saw things from a different perspective. From his standpoint, he was trying to console, guide, and sustain her spiritual life at the same time as he persisted in finding channels for his strong erotic feelings towards her and dependency on her – a profoundly problematic tangle whose amalgam of veneration, manipulation, and need cannot have been easy for her to accept, even though she loved him. As she had done for years, she went on accepting all this, but made repeated attempts to argue him round to divorcing Vivien and remarrying. Meanwhile, she pursued her precarious career in teaching and acting. He performed his more assured role as authoritative man of letters, albeit in the midst of war. She worried about him, and about herself.

He had written to Sir Robert Vansittart, chief diplomatic advisor to the British government, about possible war work. His letter had been shown to Stephen Gaselee, who counselled Tom to 'keep out of' the Ministry of Information, which had employed several writers to disseminate propaganda. Tom resolved to 'plod along at Fabers' where he went on generating his innumerable letters, and focused on poetry and theology.[126] In contrast with Auden, whose decision to leave Britain for America would be mentioned more than once in the wartime House of Commons, and in contrast with I. A. Richards (who, as Tom put it in September 1939, had 'been persuaded that his duty is to go to America'), he would not abandon his adopted country: 'I am here for the duration', he informed his old friend Aiken, 'or until the house collapses on me.'[127] Privately he feared ongoing warfare, interrupted by lulls, might last the rest of his lifetime, and 'very likely lead to defeat all round'.[128]

He thought it right to focus on 'immediate tasks', and on 'eternity', telling a friend, Meg Nason, in the Cotswolds during late September, 'the rest is not our business'.[129] As he put it when writing about language in 'East Coker', germs of which had been 'at the back of' his 'mind for a long time',

There is only the fight to recover what has been lost
And found and lost again and again: and now, under conditions
That seem unpropitious. But perhaps neither gain nor loss.
For us, there is only the trying. The rest is not our business.[130]

Browne was encouraging him to 'devise a play' suitable for performance by a small travelling company in villages – a bit like Walke's village dramas. Instead, Tom leafed through 'plots of Euripides', wondering if he could base a modern drama on *Alcestis*; for now, though, he opted to focus on 'a poem about the length of "Burnt Norton"'.[131] He was pondering this possibility in early October when Churchill (hardly his favourite orator) made a widely reported BBC broadcast on 'The first month of the war', impressing on Britons that 'Now we have begun', and emphasising that 'we are going on to the end'.[132] Though not quoting Churchill, Tom's new poem, which would open with the words 'In my beginning is my end', would be attuned to aspects of wartime rhetoric. No one knew exactly what war might entail, and the early months, while not without dread, were less traumatic than expected. Attending weekly *Christian News-Letter* committee meetings at Lord Hambleden's Belgrave Square mansion, Tom also tried to rendezvous with old friends. Arrangements were uncertain – would the bus service to the Woolfs at Rodmell be interrupted? – or else were haunted by undertones of farewell. He drank too much – 'recklessly out of boredom' – when dining with Morley Kennerley's family. In early October he suffered 'a sort of walking flu'.[133] When he went to dinner with the Kauffers and Hutchinsons, he was aware young Jeremy Hutchinson was off to join the Royal Navy (the newspapers were full of talk of convoys), and might or might not return.

On 11 October, under the headline, 'France Will Fight On', *The Times* reported French prime minister Daladier's broadcast to his people, 'Great Britain and France are mistresses of the sea, and, as you know, history shows that those who hold the seas are always victorious.'[134] The seas were many people's focus. Yet fears of aerial bombardment, which the Nazis had deployed effectively in Spain, persisted. Britain was experiencing the 'Phoney War' – the delay before the full onslaught hit. Tom met Bruce Richmond several times to discuss Richmond's planned anthology, *The Pattern of Freedom*. Its thematic sections would include 'The Free People', 'The Free Mind', and 'Refugees'. Tom's involvement encouraged the inclusion of Paul Elmer More's work, and he acclaimed Charles Williams's survey of Christian history, *The Descent of the Dove*, which emphasised the 'difficulty' of trying to 'know and endure' the 'Descent of the Dove' of the Holy Spirit.[135] However, even as he met literary friends including Alida Monro and Williams, he sensed changes beyond the covers of books. Prices were rising. Petrol was rationed. Some commodities, not least good whisky, were almost impossible to find. Tom missed old pals, especially Morley. Faber, now president of the Publishers Association, took to 'bicycling to the office every day', though to Tom in blackout London everyone felt 'cut off'. 'We communicate like moles in burrows'. If he did decide to start a new play, he would do so conscious that it 'may or may not ever be finished'.[136] Gradually, like everyone around him, he realised all plans were provisional.

Yet there was appetite for greater vision. After a sunny Dorset weekend with the Tandy family, whose recently adopted 'German Jewish child' he met (but referred to as 'it', informing Emily 'it' was 'a rather nice child, not at all objectionably Jewish to look at'), Tom went in late October for several days to Kelham.[137] Kelham mattered increasingly to his spiritual life. He involved several of its monks and their friends in work for Faber's theology list. With its riverside walks, Kelham's spacious rural setting offered peace after London's turmoil – even if the tranquility was disturbed by monks playing football against a Royal Air Force team. 'Football', Tom complained to Hayward, 'is the curse of the English monastic life.'[138]

The Idea of a Christian Society had just been published, three weeks after *Old Possum's Book of Practical Cats*. Whereas in the *Listener* Spender thought the latter 'charming', a review of the former cautioned that even sympathetic readers might find Tom's 'conception of a religiously inspired or conditioned society too much bound up within a traditional ecclesiastical framework'.[139] Leonard Woolf exchanged 'densely argued letters' with Tom, arguing that in a society in which most people were not thoroughly Christian, it would be authoritarian, if not wholly fascistic, to govern according to Christian dogma.[140] For many, not least in wartime, however,

Tom's Christian ideal was compelling. The *Cats* poems, selling 200 copies a week, cheered people up. *The Idea of a Christian Society* was more demanding, and less commercial, but triggered profound questions. 'We cannot afford to defer our constructive thinking to the conclusion of hostilities', Tom stressed in a short passage added after war had broken out.[141] *The Idea* offered believers not just an idea but an ideal, and, in certain weeks, sold 'more rapidly than the *Cats*'.[142]

Some issues he could not resolve. Again, Emily wanted to discuss divorce. Tom refused to do something that 'from the point of view of the Church was morally wrong'.[143] Knowing he was thinking about a new play, she wanted him to read Ibsen. He loathed Ibsen. Fastidiously, concerned lest letters miscarry, he recorded in his appointments diary when he wrote to her. Occasionally, he forgot. 'How is one to explain War to one's American friends', he mused.[144] As Hitler's forces advanced, he grew increasingly conscious of America as vitally important from an English perspective. He wondered if, after war was over, 'America and Russia' might 'pull the strings'. Surveying absurd goings-on at St Stephen's and elsewhere, he joked with Hayward about 'counter-counter-counter-counter-counter-espionage'.[145]

His own war experience so far involved constant invitations to spend time outside London – whether with Mappie Mirrlees at Shamley Green, or with the Richmonds in Salisbury, or the Fabers in Oxford where Tom endured an 'Old Bore' at All Souls, and watched his godson, young Tom, sing in a Gilbert and Sullivan comic opera at the Dragon School: 'painfully like a performance by trained poodles'. He visited the Woolfs in November: 'the 11.45 which Virginia told me to take had been cancelled, so I had to run my balls off to catch the 11.28 to Brighton'.[146] In Sussex he enjoyed 'hilarious small talk', and Virginia thought him 'more supple, less caked & rigid than of old. His teaching he told me, is that one improves with age.' Like Hayward she remained a determined non-believer, and noted Tom's customary sense of 'the working of the divine spirit which as usual he adored at 8 on Sunday morning, receiving communion from Mr Ebbs [the local vicar] – who did not impress him'.[147]

Tom's commitment to the Moot was as strong as his dedication to 8 a.m. services. He spent the weekend of 18–19 November in a Moot 'argle-bargle' at Jordans, a seventeenth-century Quaker meeting house in grounds near the Buckinghamshire village of Chalfont St Giles. The topic for discussion was education, but the location was arguably more impressive. Milton had finished *Paradise Lost* in a Chalfont St Giles cottage; Quaker William Penn, founder of Pennsylvania, was buried in the Jordans graveyard, and nearby was a Mayflower Barn, said to be built of timbers from that vessel which had carried Pilgrim Settlers to America. If Tom needed any further encouragement to contemplate English Civil War history and his family's Anglo-American lineage, Jordans was an appropriate place. Writing to Hayward soon afterwards, he adopted his usual jokey tone, presenting himself as an elusive, Sherlockian character, and recounting supposed St Stephen's parish gossip about him as someone 'of foreign origin'.[148]

In amongst epistolary attempts to cheer up Hayward with discussions of mock-invitations to Cambridge colleges, general gossip, and nonsense, sometimes, responding sympathetically to his friend's wartime low spirits, Tom revealed anxieties as he examined his own life. He recalled the 'smell of grapes' in his St Louis childhood home, and names of his earliest sweethearts. He looked back, too, over what he called that November 'the age of *l'entre deux guerres*'.

> Well, I think that I can understand, as well as could be expected, your feeling of 'having never expected or hoped for very much' etc. At least, I have no family, no career, and nothing particular to look forward to in this world. I doubt the permanent value of everything I have written; I never lay with a woman I liked, loved or even felt any strong physical attraction to; I no longer even regret this lack of experience; I no longer even feel acutely the desire for progeny which was very acute once; and since I became a Christian I feel that the only difficulty I should have in a monastic life – which is easy to say because I am not free to enter a monastery – would be the deprivation of French tobacco.

This was rather different from his telling Emily he liked the idea, at some stage, of 'a winter in America at a university', and his hope their 'mutual understanding and devotion' might go on growing.[149] He told Hayward, 'the last six years have been the only happy years of my life', but, even though discussing his own circumstances, he may have been presumptuous in suggesting to his disabled friend that 'the point is that one has to try to *tirer avantage* [benefit] from one's disabilities', which could confer a kind of 'peculiar detachment' useful to a writer.[150] In *The Descent of the Dove*, which Tom in December called 'a valuable book', Williams had written of Calvin and Ignatius of Loyola seeking to discover 'glorious manifestations of man's will' through 'supreme moments of self-destruction' in which 'they desired it to say "My Eros is crucified." '[151] While Tom, an admirer of Loyola's spiritual exercises (recommended to him by several priests), might not have put it that way, at a time when ideas of destruction were all around, he wrote to Hayward about having renounced his own erotic life. In these letters he did not discuss Emily. A few weeks later, concerning an unhappy

1. T. S. Eliot outside the Faber & Gwyer offices at 24 Russell Square, Bloomsbury. This photograph was taken by his brother Henry.

2. T. S. Eliot at his desk at Faber & Gwyer, 1926. This photograph was taken by his brother Henry, and seems to show a marionette hanging from the telephone.

3. A studio photograph of Vivien Eliot, inscribed by her
to her sister-in-law in 1930.

4. T. S. Eliot, Virginia Woolf and Vivien Eliot, photographed by
Leonard Woolf at Rodmell, Sussex, in September 1932.

5. T. S. Eliot and Vivien Eliot, photographed by Leonard Woolf
at Rodmell, Sussex, in September 1932.

6. Emily Hale (left) performing in a play put on by The Montebanks at Milwaukee-Downer College in 1924.

7. Emily Hale, circa 1926–1930.

8. Emily Hale at Abbot Academy in 1956.

9. One of a series of photographs taken on 4 July 1939 at Much Hadham Hall, Hertfordshire, on the occasion of a farewell party for the Morley family, who were leaving for the United States. Back row (from left): Richard de la Mare, Catherine de la Mare, Christina Morley, Frank Morley and Geoffrey Faber. Middle row (from left): the children Catherine de la Mare and Donald Morley. In front is T. S. Eliot.

10. Emily Hale with flowers in 1935, probably taken by T. S. Eliot, who called this photograph a 'masterpiece' when he sent it to Emily's friend Jeanette McPherrin.

11. T. S. Eliot and Emily Hale at Woods Hole, Massachusetts, in 1936.

12. The sloping rear garden of Stamford House, Chipping Campden. The yew tree (no longer present today) is visible at the top of this picture, which is taken roughly from the back door of the house, probably in the 1930s and possibly by Eleanor Malby, who was friendly with Emily Hale's aunt Edith Carroll Perkins.

13. The rear garden of Stamford House, Chipping Campden, looking towards the back door of the house, probably photographed in the 1930s and possibly by Eleanor Malby.

14. A group in the living room at Shamley Wood, Shamley Green, Surrey, around 1941. (From left) Constance Moncrieff, Mappie Mirrlees, Hettie James (with tray), Ellen James, Hope Mirrlees, T. S. Eliot.

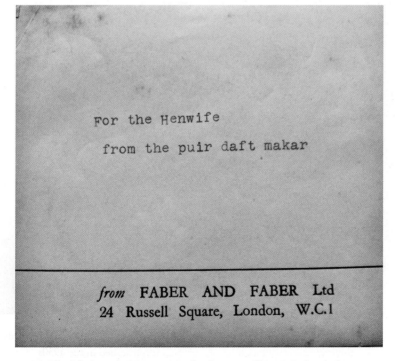

For the Henwife

from the puir daft makar

from FABER AND FABER Ltd
24 Russell Square, London, W.C.1

15. The label inside Mappie Mirrlees's copy of *For Lancelot Andrewes*.

16. Mary Trevelyan, photographed by Elliott & Fry, probably in the 1930s.

17. Shy, smoking and wearing his Order of Merit, T. S. Eliot, recipient of an honorary degree, talks with nineteen-year-old Schölin Andrade-Thompson after a rectorial ball at St Andrews University in April 1953.

18. Valerie Eliot photographed by Angus McBean in 1957.

19. T. S. and Valerie Eliot photographed by Angus McBean in 1957.

20. T. S. Eliot photographed in Brighton by Valerie Eliot, 1959–60.

couple, Tom, 'with his sly smile', remarked to Virginia Woolf, 'I never knew them in the moment of ecstasy.' Woolf was prompted to think 'the same of Tom and Vivienne'.[152] The poem he would soon write would emphasise having to 'go by a way wherein there is no ecstasy'.[153]

He told Emily again, 'I am naturally an emotional, rather than an intellectual person', and his correspondence with her remained an emotional lifeline.[154] Yet, though he could be loath to acknowledge it, he missed immediate female companionship. He enjoyed seeing Virginia Woolf and Mary Hutchinson, and had mentioned to Hayward in mid-November 'Miss Mary Trevelyan, the hearty Warden' of Student Movement House, an overseas students' hall of residence, then located at 103 Gower Street, close to Russell Square. This House had its own social club, and was a lively place. In late 1938 Mary Trevelyan had sat in its crowded clubroom, listening to the visiting celebrity Paul Robeson singing 'Ol' Man River'.[155] In November 1939 the musically gifted forty-two-year-old Warden, an extrovert vicar's daughter with a talent for organisation, had recently helped establish a temporary wartime chapel, and was planning a nativity play. Tom remembered meeting her three years earlier, when she had sent a teasing spoof of some lines of *The Waste Land*, and he had read to her students. Now, after reading at Student Movement House, he was amused to find she 'whisked me upstairs to her private study for a couple of glasses of bad sherry afterwards'.[156] As they drank, they heard something fall down the chimney – an alarming sound in wartime London – and felt relieved when the gas fire continued undisturbed. The ensuing years would see them grow closer.

Prayer was crucial. Approvingly, he read a 'very good note on "Prayer in War-time"' which Oldham would publish in his *News-Letter*, arguing prayers should be 'for the vindication of right', not for '*our* victory'. Since everyone belonged to God's 'human family', praying Christians were 'always in company with our "enemies"'.[157] To Edward Rich, an Anglo-Catholic vicar in Chiswick working with refugees and the poor, Tom emphasised the vital 'feeling of the reality of being baptised "into the death of Christ"', and signalled the intensity of his own prayer life:

It seems to me also that even the practising Christian fails to realise the meaning and importance of prayer. It is too liable to be thought of as something which is a praiseworthy habit, which has some spiritual efficacy in disciplining the mind like a kind of psychological physical jerks every morning and evening. If people could understand that it almost takes one's lifetime to learn how to pray; if they could understand that they need not only to practise prayer regularly, but also to reflect constantly on what it means to pray, they might be brought to understand that prayer in the liturgy is something more than people assembling to say their prayers or have them said for them – in short, the immense reality and gravity of corporate worship.[158]

Well able to convey gravitas, he remained the public man, but shared with Hayward, Emily, and other intimates his prejudices, treasured snobberies, and dandiacal touches. Presenting awards at a prize-giving in recently opened Raynes Park Boys' Grammar School in suburban Surrey, he surveyed a 'legion of the infant damned' – 'possible Nazis of the British future'. Then, for Christmas, as goods were getting scarcer, he treated himself to a fine 'spring suit': 'a nice small Glenurquhart Angola, with a thread of blue among the grey'.[159] He was growing used to weekending with out-of-town friends. The Fabers took him along on a family outing to *Black Velvet*, a 'rag' revue with a cast of over sixty. The king and queen had seen it, but Tom, who confessed to Hayward, 'when it comes to Jewish humour, I prefer either Max Miller or the Marx Brothers', found it 'about the dullest show I have ever seen'.[160] Feeling low, he took to bed for several days. To Mappie Mirrlees, whose home was an oasis of luxury, he sent thanks for further weekend hospitality, and, anticipating yet more in February, wished her 'as happy a Christmas as is possible for any of us'.[161] Hayward received 'doleful good wishes for 1940'.[162]

Pronouncing himself 'not a Neutral', Tom had sent his now committedly fascist friend Pound a 'Happy New Year' salutation, and would go on loyally publishing Pound's poems.[163] But he had set himself on a very different course. 'Is it old-fashioned of me to feel somewhat shocked by Auden's wanting to get naturalised in America at this time?' he asked Hayward, conscious his own commitment to remaining on British soil might demand much.[164] In late January, the king 'was inspecting the ARP control rooms in Kensington'; the queen listened to accounts of 'wounded seamen, victims of Nazi torpedoes, guns, and mines'.[165] Tom went for several weeks without hearing from Emily, though, as a hint, she had sent him an anthology of '20 Modern American Plays'. Wanting to maintain his bond, he assured her it would be 'a document in the genealogy of *our* next play'.[166] Yet he worried when there were pauses in their correspondence, and felt gloomy in mid-January: 'I allow time to think about creative writing, but nothing has come.'[167]

He distracted himself from war nerves by dining out, but something of the intensity of his feelings can be judged from the fact that even the experience of eating 'ginger prawns' on an unaccustomed visit to Chong Chu's Chinese restaurant in London's West India Dock Road for a farewell dinner with former *Criterion* contributor Montgomery Belgion (who was entering the military) had for him the most peculiar 'spiritual effect'. Its 'fascination' was 'mingled with' a kind of 'terror' Tom characterised as 'the terror of all quite alien or pre-Christian high civilisations'.[168] He was half-mocking himself, but, like the 'terror' in the stalled Tube train of 'East Coker', it was the sort of experience that could not be entirely joked away. A young Portuguese sculptor, Agostinho Rodrigues, making a bust of him in January, felt Tom 'moved like a shark'. The poet found the resulting sculpture made him appear both 'lecherous and rapacious'.[169] If he was disconcerted, so were some readers of 'East Coker', that poem of early 1940's unusually cold winter, with its 'chill' and 'fever' and its sense of Christian communion as a blood sacrifice: 'The bloody flesh our only food'.[170]

In February he spent 'four days in bed with a bronchitis'.[171] Water pipes at his Emperor's Gate flat had frozen, so he had been bathing at his club or at Russell Square, feeling depressed, and suffering (not for the first time) from low blood pressure. In bed he read the Psalms, composed occasional clerihews, doodled nonsense, and mulled over a more serious poetic project. He anticipated getting time very soon to put on paper the longer work taking shape in his imagination. He wanted, he explained to Hayward on 8 February,

> to get on with my new poem in succession to Burnt Norton – the second of the three quatuors – provisionally entitled East Coker; of which I have drafted the first two out of the five sections – it may be quite worthless, because most of it looks to me like an imitation of myself, and as for the rest, well, Blake and Clough kept getting into it, and I have been trying to rub them out – I *have* got rid of the line 'The Archer's bow and Taurus' ire,' which however did not look quite so silly as all that in its context.[172]

This, Tom's principal mention of 'East Coker' while he was writing the poem, indicates it was very much in his mind and partly composed at this time, and that he conceived of it as part of a continuing sequence.

On Shrove Tuesday, 6 February 1940, after perusing Yeats's play *Purgatory*, he had written to Emily about 'fiddling with a poem which may take some time to get right after I have finished it'. It was 'a year' since he had 'done any work in verse'; he felt 'a kind of stage-fright'. He complained, 'the writing of verse seems to require an unattainable intensity of feeling'.[173] Nonetheless, the poem had been in gestation for months. 'What profession is more trying than that of author?' he had written to Virginia Woolf in late December. 'After you finish a piece of work it only seems good to you for a few weeks; or if it seems good at all you are convinced that it is the last you will be able to write; and if it seems bad you wonder whether everything you have done isn't poor stuff really; and it is one kind of agony while you are writing, and another kind when you aren't.'[174]

That such musings accompanied fresh creativity is confirmed by his mentioning 'the *Almanach*' in a letter to Hayward on 10 January, not long after referring two days earlier to speculations about being 'buried'.[175] The third section of the new poem he would publish in the spring mentions 'the Almanach de Gotha' and a 'funeral' with 'no one to bury'. It takes the notion of blackout and, drawing on both Milton and James Thomson's *The City of Dreadful Night*, makes it powerfully metaphorical as the speaker contemplates the extinction of a society and its apparent social successes – 'O dark dark dark. They all go into the dark'. After its litany of apparently successful modern urban types (among whom Tom himself might be numbered), the poem involves meditation on emptiness and 'terror', using the image of 'an underground train, in the tube', that has stopped 'too long between stations'. Then the speaker addresses his own soul, telling it to 'wait without hope' until, eventually, 'the darkness shall be the light'.[176] This section concludes with a version of lines from St John of the Cross.

Written during the Phoney War, and drawing on blackout darkness, as well as on Tom's reviewing of his life's course ('Home is where one starts from') and his sense of 'years largely wasted, the years of *l'entre deux guerres*', 'East Coker' begins in his ancestral village. It develops into a sometimes bleak account of 'failure' offset by determination to 'fight'. Though the speaker's 'fight', conducted 'under conditions / That seem unpropitious', is a poet's struggle to articulate meaning, its deployment of expressions such as 'raid', 'shabby equipment' and 'Undisciplined squads' conjures up that other 'fight' going on in Europe. Tom the non-combatant had little to offer that struggle in physical terms, but his poem seeks a meaningful pattern 'Of dead and living', and urges, 'For us, there is only the trying'. Striving to 'be still and still moving' through 'empty desolation', it emerges from his reaction to a crisis in Western civilisation, yet strives, too, to see in this some possible redemption through the Christian story. Written when so many people were facing the possibility of sudden death, it ends with an English version of the French motto of Mary, Queen of Scots, who met her own violent death on the scaffold, yet whose Christian faith offered hope of resurrection: 'In my end is my beginning.'[177]

By February 1940, when Tom sniped in print that the prose idiom of sixty-five-year-old 'Mr Churchill' was 'like a court dress of rather tarnished grandeur from a theatrical costumier's', the 'Woolves' had returned temporarily to 37 Mecklenburgh Square, a short walk from Russell

Square.[178] The blackout meant 'no lighted windows', which 'depressed' Virginia. At her dinner party for Tom and other friends, conversation turned to 'Civilization'.[179] Most of the diners were pessimistic. Tom had grown concerned about whether it might be possible to maintain 'a common mind' between England and France as war pressures increased. He had been following debates, too, about American neutrality. The American ambassador in London, Joseph Kennedy (father of JFK), expected Britain would be defeated. Though the *Christian News-Letter* had just reported on a dissenting 'Declaration by American Christians', most American Episcopalians, like many other Americans, inclined towards neutrality. Tom's strong-willed US Episcopalian correspondent Dr Iddings Bell took this stance, describing the conflict as 'this *relatively insignificant* brawl going on in Europe'. Tom had written to the *Church Times* that January, stating he considered Bell 'grossly mistaken', yet declaring himself among Bell's 'English friends'.[180] Emily was hinting Tom should come to Princeton. 'If I had lived in America, and come to anything like my present position, I believe that it would have been the Church of Rome that I should have accepted and not the Episcopal Church', he mused, once again resisting her overtures.[181] This, he knew, was not what she wanted to hear.

With America reluctant to intervene and Germany so strong, Britain's situation looked unpromising. At the Woolfs' dinner party on 14 February the consensus seemed to be that 'the barbarian will gradually freeze our culture', with 'the light going out gradually.' Virginia watched Tom closely. A couple of weeks earlier, around the time he wrestled with the phrase 'Taurus' ire' (eventually expunged) in 'East Coker', he had been reading Rupert Gleadow's forthcoming Faber book *Astrology in Everyday Life*; his star sign was Libra and he had joked to Virginia glumly that he shared it 'with Hitler'.[182] Now, scrutinising his face, she observed

Tom's great yellow bronze mask all draped upon an iron framework. An inhibited, nerve drawn; dropped face – as if hung on a scaffold of heavy private brooding; & thought. A very serious face. & broken by the flicker of relief, when other people interrupt.[183]

Since just a few days later Tom sent Hayward a complete draft of 'East Coker', Woolf's pen-portrait depicts the poet during the period when that poem took its full form. What she saw on Tom's 'scaffold' face was a more profound version of what Tom in 'East Coker' noted on the faces of wartime London Underground passengers: 'you see behind every face the mental emptiness deepen'.[184] It was a look of blankness and worry – not an uncommon expression on British faces in the early months of 1940.

II

Puir Daft Makar

I N February 1940, having 'expelled' it after 'throes' of composition involving at least 'five' drafts, Tom showed 'East Coker' in draft to trusted readers
including Hayward and Herbert Read.[1] He made minor changes, sending
Emily a typescript only when 'ready for printing'.[2] Proudly, she read the
poem aloud to a select group of her students, as if, according to one account,
'it were a love letter from God'.[3] Tom's poetry emerged from a stratum of his
life which he kept suppressed – which is often how poetry arises. When
Betjeman took him to a private screening of *Ninotchka*, Tom liked how Greta
Garbo could convey emotion 'by suppression'.[4] He explained to Emily that
he avoided choosing 'as intimate friends, anybody who writes poetry', since
jealousy, even if concealed, was unavoidable.[5] She wanted him to consider
coming to live near Smith, but he resisted: 'facing a girls' college for so long'
put him off, and residing publicly so close to her would intensify the problems in their largely hidden extramarital relationship.[6]

In March he also declined an approach about a job at the College of the
City of New York, which intended to hire Bertrand Russell. Tom had no
wish to renew contact with Russell. He explained to Emily, 'that belongs
to a chapter of the past which I should prefer not to open again'.[7] In public
he could seem not just opaque, but increasingly sombre. He had concurred
with Cyril Connolly, editor of the new magazine, *Horizon*, that, as Connolly put it, 'Whatever happens in the war, America will be the gainer';
England would be 'poverty-stricken, even in victory'. Tom thought it
'more than probable that Britain, and the rest of Europe, will be beggared
and exhausted'. Nevertheless, he refused to see America as the future for
'"Civilisation"'. Such a 'hope' might be tenable in America, but in London
he maintained, 'To hold it here, at this stage, is only to accept the most
insidious form of defeatism.'[8]

Mulling over the idea of co-authoring with Pound and George Santayana 'a very queer book' about 'education', he soon abandoned that proposal, but did write an essay on education for the *Christian News-Letter*.[9] Partly it emerged from thinking about Christian society and the Spens Report. It aligned, too, with his emphasis on long-term thinking, even if his thoughts were sometimes bleak. Regarding his vision of a Christian society, to which a *News-Letter* supplement was devoted on 28 February, he wrote to Hayward, 'That anything like the condition I sketched will ever come to be, I have no expectation' – but the attempt mattered. He enjoyed a 'quiet weekend' with the Mirrlees family at their house, Shamley Wood in Shamley Green, 'playing chess, eating large meals and reading the works of Peter Cheyney', a crime novelist.[10] Growing attached to Shamley Wood's comforts, he found he could relax there, and as war intensified it became his principal place of refuge outside London.

Shamley Wood was home to a distinctive, large household. Its head was Mappie Mirrlees, whose brigadier son was serving in Libya. Wealthy, widely travelled, but now 'very frail', the widowed Mappie was 'a Christian Scientist, and of a very active temperament'. 'On the top of a hill' just outside the village, she lived with her 'also frail' younger sister, 'Miss [Constance] Moncrieff', a Roman Catholic, who, unlike Mappie (an enthusiast for homeopathy), 'believes in doctors'.[11] Tom described Mappie the following year as 'a very intelligent, though not intellectual, Scotch lady' with a large entourage.[12] He found her daughter Hope, the Cambridge-educated poet and novelist who had been in a long-term relationship with classicist Jane Harrison, trying at times as she fussed endlessly over her dachshund, but Hope had been a loyal friend. Tom played chess with her at 'the Shamblies' – when he was not playing poker or doing crosswords with other family members, who later (from autumn 1941) included Margaret Elizabeth Behrens, a humorous novelist in her mid-fifties whose devotion to her rabbit-hunting pekinese matched Hope's affection for her dachshund.[13] Margaret Behrens was the daughter of a distinguished Edinburgh surveyor, Sir James Inglis Davidson; her husband Richard (who died in 1940) had served in the Hussars regiment, and her brother was also a military man. Tom nicknamed her the Field Marshal, but she was observant, shrewd, warm-hearted, and he came to like her.

From its cooking and whisky to its conversation, Mappie Mirrlees's sometimes eccentric household had a markedly Scottish accent. Hints of its tenor can be gleaned from Margaret Behrens's light, middlebrow novel *Miss Mackay*, with its alertness to differences among members of the 'Established Church of Scotland', the 'Church of Rome', and a 'Christian Scientist', as well as its clear enjoyment in contrasting the *mores* of the Scots and the English.[14] Tom came to call the Mirrlees household at Shamley Wood 'Little Scotland', and recalled it as his ' "home": the nearest I have had since I was a boy'.[15] During his time there he sent Hayward verses in Scots dialect. In correspondence he mentioned, too, Robert Burns and 'Dunbar', the medieval Scots poet famous for his 'Lament for the Makars'.[16] Though the gift is undated, it was probably during this period that he presented Mappie – 'The Henwife' (a nickname from Hope's novel *Lud in the Mist*) – with a copy of *For Lancelot Andrewes*. Inside was a gummed printed Faber & Faber label on which was typed in Tom's best Scots:

For the Henwife
  from the puir daft makar[17]

'The puir daft makar' (poor foolish poet) may have been Mappie's nickname for him, but as war intensified there were times when Tom's situation could seem to him and others – not least, to some of his American correspondents – 'daft'. Still, even if the Mirrlees family might tease him or get on his nerves at times, he treasured their kind hospitality. Mappie became a favourite with this poet who had a fondness for distinguished old ladies. It was at Shamley Wood that he would work on a poem to follow 'East Coker'.

In early March, while the *News-Letter* was admitting 'Christian interest and effort in the refugee problem' had previously fallen short 'of that of the Jewish community', and was reporting 'shootings by the SS' near Lodz in Poland, 'numbering eighty to a hundred victims daily', *Murder in the Cathedral* was revived at the Mercury Theatre.[18] It was a play for murderous times. However, attending rehearsals, Tom decided that 'except perhaps in one or two spots I don't think it's very brilliant as poetry.'[19] Accustomed now to the blackout, he showed little desire to eat alone night after night in his small rooms at Emperor's Gate, and continued dining out. Wartime meant Faber's list now included such titles as *If Germany Attacks* and *Deadlock War*. Tom helped develop the Sesame Books series, offering inexpensive poetry volumes, including *The Waste Land and Other Poems*. This small selection of his work had appeared in February with a print run of 5,000 copies.

During the 'Phoney War' which lasted until April 1940, much of the fighting that directly affected Britain happened at sea, but caused nationwide alarm: the sinking of the *Royal Oak* battleship in Scapa Flow, Britain's largest naval base, cost 800 lives. British maritime supremacy could no longer be taken for granted, even if Faber titles including *The Navy at War* had a morale-boosting purpose. Several of Tom's literary friends, including

Betjeman, Kauffer, and former Faber director George Blake (novelist of *The Shipbuilders*), now worked at the Ministry of Information. Based in the new Senate House skyscraper off Russell Square, and soon to be headed by Duff Cooper, it was often disorganised. In 1939, it had printed over 2 million copies of the (today famous) 'Keep Calm and Carry On' posters, which were very rarely publicly displayed, and almost all pulped a year later. Muddle was part of war, but Tom and others were sceptical about 'MoI' operations. It was in Senate House that he sat with 'Informers' to watch the supposedly 'anti-bolshuvik [*sic*]' *Ninotchka* : odd sort of work.[20]

'Thank God I now can look at the world's affairs from a religious background, for without that, the stupidity and selfishness of mankind would be unbearable', he confided to Emily.[21] Still, he was horrified that spring by 'innumerable destitute sufferers in Poland, and the population of ruined Finland' after America had refused the Finns 'credits for munitions.'[22] Apart from his confessor, it was Hayward, still exiled in Cambridge, and Emily, much further off, whom he opened up to most. He recalled seaside days with Emily at Woods Hole, 'a bell-buoy tolling a little way off'.[23] Unlike Emily, however, Hayward had first-hand knowledge of wartime conditions, so some confidences were easier to share with him. He and Tom made an odd pair, but their joint bookishness, upper-middle-class waspishness, and sense of being isolated men in challenging circumstances made each value their rapport. Mutual concern was laced with irony, but deep. 'So will close', Tom Possum signed off his letter of 7 March, 'yr. faithful & devoted TP'.[24]

He asked Morley, who reported that Auden might write a book about America (an idea Tom liked), to help place 'East Coker' in a good American magazine. Tom sent the poem (regarded as the second of a planned 'trilogy') to Mairet for British publication in the *New English Weekly* around Easter.[25] It was, after all, a Christian poem, earthed in his English ancestral home-place, albeit related by implication to his American birth and, he explained to Emily in April, 'more affected by the events of the last seven months than immediately appears'.[26] At home his customary newspaper, *The Times*, reported regularly on American attitudes to the conflict. In February and March the same newspaper carried extended correspondence about Simonides' famous ancient Greek epitaph for the Spartan troops who had sacrificed their lives, obeying orders at Thermopylae, to withstand invaders. Tom did not join in the correspondence, but would draw on that Simonides poem a few months later, as invasion loomed.

After the hard winter, about a week before Easter he saw 'a faint indication of green on the trees in the Cromwell Road'.[27] On 'April Fool's Day' he watched an early-morning 'shaft of sunlight' – 'the first which has burst into my bedroom since last summer'. It lit up his worn black jacket, whose elbows and cuffs were so shiny that 'I could almost see my face in them, but did not want to.'[28] When he came to write it later that year, his next poem would include a 'distraction fit, lost in a shaft of sunlight'. This would represent the 'hints and guesses' which comprise most people's spiritual life, and need reinforcing through 'prayer, observance, discipline, thought and action'.[29] But, even if phrases and elements were beginning to constellate in his mind, he was not yet ready to write that poem. In fact, it seemed then 'several years' off.[30] Wartime pressures would accelerate its growth.

He was distracted, and let himself be distracted. Without taking a stance, he sent Pound an American complaint implying Pound had misleadingly presented Benjamin Franklin as antisemitic. Along with fellow Christian intellectuals including Philip Mairet, Maurice Reckitt and V. A. Demant, he attended meetings of the Chandos Group, linked to the *New English Weekly*. He participated in Oldham's editorial advisory board of the *Christian News-Letter*, which soon called attention to how 'Nazi authorities' were 'deliberately aiming at the total expulsion of all Jews and "non-Aryans" from Germany', with many 'frozen to death in their march'.[31] Sometimes glancingly, having declined the suggestion from the London publishing house Hutchinson that he write his 'memoirs', he thought about his upbringing, about America and Europe, and about ageing.[32] He joked to Hayward: 'I remember that when the electric telegraph was opened by submarine cable between America and Europe, old Mr Waldo Emerson (he was younger then, we all were) had some very apt remarks about the vista of peaceful understanding between nations which this invention made possible.'[33] That 'vista' seemed very far distant.

Tom came to feel in 1940 that 'In the Moot there takes place, in the course of time, a kind of personal relationship which is unique in my experience.'[34] During the 19–22 April Moot meeting at Jordans there was much discussion of Adolf Löwe's paper (soon published in the *Christian News-Letter*) on 'Social Transformation and the War'. This saw the war as 'the end of an epoch' of 'European leadership of the world'. Acknowledging 'the rise of the United States to the rank of first world power', Löwe wondered how to keep 'the path open to a European future' which might perhaps bring 'a "New Christendom" and in some respects even Federal Union' in Europe.[35] Tom, who had elsewhere expressed dislike of League of Nations-style European federation, said little, though he did assert that 'Power is a spiritual, not merely material, value' – a belief central to his wartime poetry.[36] Yet there was growing awareness of American neutrality as a crucial issue. 'American Christians and the War', an article in May's *News-Letter*, mentioned a United States 'manifesto' urging 'complete moral and material support for the Allies'; it had only 'thirty signatories'.[37]

In Britain during early May concern that the war was going badly led to Neville Chamberlain being replaced by Winston Churchill as prime minister. News of rapid Nazi advances through France that month spread alarm. A minority thought Britain should side with Italy (not yet allied with Germany) and seek an accommodation with the Germans. Whatever happened, Britain looked in need of help. It seemed as if the British Council would wish Tom to lecture at Italy's British Institutes in the early summer. Aware travel through France was increasingly dangerous, and that he might face Italian internment if Mussolini allied with Hitler, Tom was reluctantly manufacturing lectures for Italian audiences and planning perhaps to meet Pound in Rapallo. Pound, for his part, had sent him a reply for forwarding to J. V. Healy, the young American who had complained about his anti-semitism. When Healy cited the passage in *After Strange Gods* about 'free-thinking Jews' as evidencing a similar tendency in Tom himself, the poet responded, awkwardly,

By free-thinking Jews I mean Jews who have given up the practice and belief of their own religion, without having become Christians or attached themselves to any other dogmatic religion. It should be obvious that I think a large number of free-thinkers of any race to be undesirable, and the free-thinking Jews are only a special case. The Jewish religion is unfortunately not a very portable one, and shorn of its traditional practices, observances and Messianism, it tends to become a mild and colourless form of Unitarianism.

Going on to argue that 'The Jew who is separated from his religious faith is much more deracinated thereby than the descendant of Christians, and it is this deracination that I think dangerous and tending to irresponsibility', he asserted that 'my view does not imply any prejudice on the ground of race, but merely a recognition of what seems to me an historical social situation'.[38] Tenaciously, like the trained philosopher he was, he tried to argue his case. Healy retorted that Tom had indeed used the word 'race' in the offending *After Strange Gods* passage, and that it was 'unfortunate' to 'pick on Jews' in an era when they were being 'hounded and tortured'. Tom replied that 'the whole tone of *After Strange Gods* is of a violence that I now deprecate', but made it clear he did not now wish to qualify his statement about freethinking Jews. He felt he was being accused of 'insincerity'. Though disassociating himself from Pound's 'opinions about Jews', he found Healy's tone 'offensive'.[39] Evidently bound up with his commitment to dogma, and with his fervid reaction against his Unitarian past, his prickly intransigence was infuriatingly unconvincing. To Emily, whose Unitarianism was undiminished, he remained intransigent in a different way. 'Much as I long to come,' he assured her, 'I should not care to be out of England very long at the present time.'[40] He apologised if he seemed 'a little remote and unemotional', explaining he felt 'keenly, indeed as a kind of agony, the feeling for which "patriotism" is an inadequate term'. Using every night the rosary she had given him, he sensed his 'own life' as 'merely a small part of the life of a country' at war, and sent her his 'love & dependence'.[41]

Eventually, after inquiries to high-level Civil Service contacts, he was advised against travel to Italy. He was, he told Mappie Mirrlees on 16 May, 'half relieved and half sorry'. Britain and Italy might soon be at war. 'Meanwhile I am rather more apprehensive of the German air power against the troops in Belgium and France, than at home. It is Hitler's one strong weapon.'[42] Day by day, though, the threat was drawing closer. It was now over twenty years since he had tried to enlist in the US Navy in the Great War. A fifty-one-year-old, hernia-afflicted man prone to bronchial trouble and suffering from other minor ailments was hardly prime military material. What could he do? He often listened to BBC radio at 6 p.m. Each night the news was grim. On 23 May he wrote half-jokingly to a friend about a dinner invitation, 'I have a vision of coming back to my house to find it bombed and me with nothing to wear except evening clothes.'[43] That same week he dined 'with the Woolves' and poet William Plomer, then met John Lehmann, editor of *New Writing*. 'War talk' was 'wholly avoided', but insistently present.[44] Before her dinner guests arrived, Virginia had heard there was fierce fighting at Amiens and Arras. Churchill was in France, trying to bolster morale, but Woolf worried, 'The feeling is we're outwitted.' The oncoming Germans seemed 'youthful, fresh, inventive. We plod behind.' Observing Tom over dinner, she thought he was 'ossifying' into a 'curious writer's egotism'. She listened as he held forth: ' "Coleridge and I . . . people read only our best poems. They ignore all the rest of me. It is difficult, when lecturing, to leave out oneself . . ." ' 'Yet', she reflected in her diary afterwards, 'poor man if this complacency gives him a shell, no doubt it protects him from suffering. A very self centred, self torturing & self examining man'.[45] She had her own tormenting worries, though: 'Are we to be bombed, evacuated? Guns that shake the windows. Hospital ships sunk. So it comes our way.'[46]

'A period like this seems to have no private dates in it, and very little mental activity. It's rather a strain, what?' Tom wrote to Hayward after the Woolfs' dinner, adding, 'I have promised (if conditions permit) to go to Dublin to deliver that first Yeats Memorial Lecture: I reckoned that it would be an important event for the Irish, and one's going over for it might have some diplomatic value.'[47] Ireland, like America, was neutral. Britain needed any diplomatic leverage it could get. As British and French forces were pushed towards the Channel by German advances, over 400,000 troops faced death or capture on the beaches where they were now being bombed and bombarded. The king announced in late May, 'The decisive struggle' had begun. It would be 'life or death for us all'.[48]

Sunday 26 May was declared a national day of prayer. A few days later, *The Times* published the ancient Greek historian Herodotus' account of Spartan troops instructed 'to stay at their post and either win the victory or die'.[49] In late May and early June, the British made desperate attempts to evacuate British and French troops from Dunkirk. Tom worked on. He had been reading through the typescript of *The Testament of Immortality*, an anthology aimed at the newly bereaved. The anthologist was England-based Indian writer Nagendranath Gangulee, and Faber & Faber hoped to publish it. Conscious such books would be needed, Tom would write its foreword. Gangulee's 'fusion of Eastern and Western culture' impressed the poet-editor whose engagement with Sanskrit texts had gone considerably farther than that of Yeats.[50]

On 1 June in a piece which Tom and Richmond hoped might feature in future editions of *The Pattern of Freedom*, the *New York Times* devoted its editorial to Dunkirk: 'So long as the English tongue survives, the word Dunkirk will be spoken with reverence.'[51] On 2 June, Anthony Eden, Britain's Secretary of State for War, announced miraculous news on BBC radio. 'More than four-fifths of the British Expeditionary Force which the Germans claimed to have surrounded had been embarked at Dunkirk and saved.'[52] Under intense German bombardment, 335,000 troops had been evacuated by a huge flotilla of 'nearly 1,000 ships' of all kinds, both military and civilian, small and large. They had crossed the Channel after an emergency appeal to British sailors. This evacuation marked 'disaster, but no surrender'. Nazi invasion was now imminent. Churchill's speech to Parliament was widely reported on 5 June:

> The British Empire and the French Republic, linked together in their cause and in their need, will defend to the death their native soil, aiding each other like good comrades to the utmost of their strength. Even though large tracts of Europe and many old and famous States have fallen or may fall into the grip of the Gestapo, and all the odious apparatus of Nazi rule, we shall not flag or fail. We shall go on to the end; we shall fight in France; we shall fight on the seas and oceans; we shall fight with growing confidence and growing strength in the air;

we shall defend our island whatever the cost may be. We shall fight on the beaches; we shall fight on the landing grounds; we shall fight in the fields and in the streets; we shall fight in the hills. We shall never surrender. And even if – which I do not for a moment believe – this island or a large part of it were subjugated and starving, then our Empire beyond the seas, armed and guarded by the British Fleet, would carry on the struggle until in God's good time the New World with all its power and might steps forth to the rescue and liberation of the Old.[53]

Mention of the 'New World' clearly referred to British Empire territories including Canada, Australia and New Zealand, but was also an indication of hope that America would reject neutrality. With such considerations in mind, at the request of Kauffer at the Ministry of Information, Tom, whose 'East Coker' had been republished by the *New English Weekly* just three weeks earlier, wrote 'just after the evacuation of Dunkirk' lines entitled 'Defence of the Islands'. They were designed as linked captions to an exhibition 'to go round the walls of a room of war photographs for the New York [World's] Fair'.[54] As Britain and Germany jostled to influence Americans, the British Pavilion at the 1939–40 World's Fair was being updated. One addition would be a heroic mural by Charles Pears showing small boats at the Dunkirk evacuation. Drafted on 9 June and written to accompany images of 'Home Defence preparations' as well as naval, air, and military scenes, Tom's text speaks of fighters 'undefeated in defeat' and commemorates

the memory of those appointed to the grey
ships – battleship, merchantman, trawler –
contributing their share to the ages' pavement
of British bone on the sea floor

Its final words portrayed civilians in Britain's streets, who would be able to say to others 'of our kin and of our speech' (whether in America or elsewhere) that 'we took up / our positions, in obedience to instructions'.[55] The work ended, as he remarked to Hayward, with a 'resemblance' to Simonides' 'epitaph' for the Spartan dead at Thermopylae.[56]

With invasion and air raids imminent, Tom, like so many others, faced up to the possibility he might soon be killed. 'Flood-tides', wrote the young poet J. F. Hendry in 'London Before Invasion, 1940', 'may bring with them blood and fire'.[57] Tom mailed 'Defence of the Islands' to Emily on 14 June. Though he did not regard it as a poem, much later he came to include it in his *Complete Poems and Plays*. Just after Dunkirk, with his customary fastidiousness and a hint of that practical, ironic humour which endeared him to many English friends, he had written to Herbert Read, hoping Read and his wife might accept a packed suitcase when he visited them at their Buckinghamshire home.

> Thinking of raids, the only things I have that matter are my books and my clothes: the first because they cannot be replaced (such as they are) and the second because I should have to replace them. It would be very inconvenient to have this place destroyed and have to get all new clothes; so I want to pack up some essential winter clothes and stow them somewhere in the country. Then I shouldnt lose all my clothes at once. And if I was destroyed instead, then you would please consider the suitcase and contents as your own property (well preserved pre-war clothes will be valuable some day!) and keep this letter to show my executors.[58]

Such thoughts were encouraged by local activity in South Kensington where on 4 June the ARP director, monocled Major Lee, 'elderly and infirm but still active-as-a-cricket' and clad in a 'brown boiler suit', had arranged to have an 'experimental bonfire and incendiary bomb on our little green' set alight, so that civilians could be shown how to extinguish a blaze. Detailing this to Hayward, Tom slanted it towards farce. Major Lee was assisted 'by another elderly gent in a monocle and a blue boiler suit', Major Repington. 'Tumultuous' cheering arose when, during the demonstration, one of the majors 'hosed a stout lady in a print dress who in her excitement had imprudently ventured too close'.[59] The upshot of all this was that Tom was recruited by one of these majors to assist Kensington ARP activity. Tasked with visiting nearby properties, he had 'to talk to the people about stirrup pumps and incendiary bombs'.[60] As the summer advanced, he became more involved in ARP work, though he worried that in blackout streets he was most likely to 'be shot by mistake by a shortsighted L[ocal] D[efence] V[olunteer]'.[61]

Like many other Britons, he listened to Churchill's 18 June radio broadcast, widely reported next day. What Churchill called 'the Battle of Britain' was about to begin.

> Upon this battle depends the survival of Christian civilization. Upon it depends our own British life, and the long continuity of our institutions and our Empire. The whole fury and might of the enemy must very soon be turned on us. Hitler knows that he will have to

break us in this island or lose the war. If we can stand up to him all Europe may be free, and the life of the world may move forward into broad, sunlit uplands; but if we fall then the whole world, including the United States and all that we have known and cared for, will sink into the abyss of a new dark age, made more sinister and perhaps more prolonged by the lights of a perverted science. Let us therefore address ourselves to our duty, so bear ourselves that if the British Commonwealth and Empire lasts for a thousand years men will say, 'This was their finest hour.'[62]

With awkward, half-facetiously adopted tones of old-bufferish social snobbery, Tom, who in earlier years had never disguised his dislike of Churchillian rhetoric, asked Hayward in a letter typed the following day:

> Incidentally, did you listen to Winston's speech last night? the par-
> ticularly husky after dinner one? Whatever else one thinks, my dear
> John, you will agree that it is a pleasure to realise that we have, what
> has not happened in our time (mine or yours) – the typewriter is
> wobbling so I must turn over – a Prime Minister who is, as Henry
> James would have said, had he been one of us (for he was, as a matter
> of fact, the grandson of an Irishman) in some respects, and with cer-
> tain qualifications, what one might call roughly, in these days, a social
> equal: and a further pleasure (which I invite you to share with me) to
> reflect that the Churchill family, in earlier times, had an association
> with the county of Somerset.[63]

So, tortuously, the poet who had stressed his own bonds to East Coker in Somerset made a whimsical gesture of identification with the wartime prime minister. As the year developed, Tom's own poetry would share with Churchill's rhetoric an emphasis on endurance and resolve.

'East Coker', that poem focused on an English village which articulated both transience and enduring values while denouncing 'deceit' associated with 'quiet-voiced elders' and those 'old men' (who, the modern scholar Marina Mackay argues, can be seen as representing pro-appeasement voices), had particular wartime resonances as it spoke in 1940 of 'loss' and 'the fight'.[64] Those resonances were not confined to its occasionally explicit military terms. Years later, Tom's acquaintance the patrician Ministry of Information official Sir Kenneth Clark, wartime director of London's National Gallery and champion of high-cultural 'civilisation', recalled sitting in a May 1940 meeting about a poster campaign, 'This is What We are Fighting For'. Clark was sceptical of the rhetoric, and found his mind turning not to great abstractions such as 'democracy' and 'parliamentary institutions' but instead to

> a clear vision of a small English town – halfway between a town and a village – Tetbury or Long Melford. There it all was: the church, the three pubs, the inexplicable bend in the road, the house with the stone gate where the old lady lived . . . I used to think 'This is what we are fighting for.' The thought of the Germans marching in there . . . made me very angry.[65]

'East Coker', which Clark may have read around this time, resonated strongly with such sentiments, and, offering a 'sense of hope', was received with deep appreciation by many wartime readers.[66] As Clark had written in the *Listener* in his October 1939 piece 'The Artist in Wartime', 'There are certain things in life so serious that only a poet can tell the truth about them.'[67] For a lot of people in 1940 and after, Tom was just such a poet.

He hoped to find time soon 'to try to write poem III' of his sequence of quartets. Yet the poet who signed himself 'Gauleiter of Emperor's Gate' feared that 'the state of exhaustion which will follow our winning this war is hardly likely to favour the arts of civilisation in our time'.[68] In America Emily would have a 'change of scene and company' to help her 'build up her strength for another winter'.[69] She wondered whether Tom, in these desperate times, could still 'believe in the purposes of God'. His answer was that it was impossible to 'anticipate confidently how one will behave in a crisis of agony', but he hoped that even as nations suffered for the 'fault' of 'the decline of Christendom', it might be possible to 'try to see the suffering as a way back to God' and even to 'try to make oneself an instrument for God'.[70] In practical as well as spiritual terms, Tom's family were anxious for his well-being. Hoping Emily would not have 'too much time on her hands for brooding over Europe', he appreciated being 'in the minds of friends in America'.[71]

Eventually, after sustained engagement with Ministry of Information bureaucracy, and encouraged by high-level contacts such as Gaselee, he was preparing to fly to Dublin to deliver the first Yeats Memorial Lecture. Faber & Faber were about to publish Donal O'Sullivan's *The Irish Free State and its Senate*, and Tom fully realised that Eire, having fought against British colonial rule, was now a neutral country. Ministry of Information staff including Betjeman were working hard to counter wartime anti-British feeling there. Tom would conclude that, suffering from a 'kind of war nerves' Irish people could not really 'make up their minds what they think' about the conflict.[72] He knew that commemorating the great nationalist poet Yeats in Ireland's capital would have a diplomatic significance requiring both tact and stamina.

His own focus on what he called that summer 'The English Tradition' drew intensively on the relationship between the English nation and England's established church.[73] Yet at the end of June in Dublin's Abbey Theatre he spoke about the Irishman he termed 'the greatest poet of our time'. Having made the point that 'There are many aspects of his work – cultural, political, religious – which can be better treated by a compatriot', he proceeded to deliver a lecture which never used the word 'nationalism' or mentioned any other Irish poet. Instead, alluding more than once to Yeats's time in London, he set Yeats in a firmament including Shakespeare, Dickens, and Browning. Able to reinvent himself in terms of style, Tom's Yeats was 'pre-eminently the poet of middle age'. He was, too, one of 'those few whose history is the history of their own time'.[74] This Yeats was a version of the poet Tom sought to become. In a broadcast for Radio Eireann, 'Poetic Drama To-Day and To-Morrow', he again invoked Yeats while setting out his own vision of how 'The visible and intelligible plot of a verse play can be the corporal form of another and less understood reality.'[75] These lectures on a poet who 'had to wait for a later maturity to find expression of early experience' make lecturer and subject matter sound more alike than the audience might have expected.[76] At her request, Tom sent his Abbey Theatre typescript to Yeats's widow with whom he enjoyed a private lunch.

With a nod towards Eton-educated Lord Curzon, who epitomised English imperial hauteur, Tom joked to Emily and to Hayward that in Dublin he had dropped his customary role of 'Curzon-like aloofness' and assumed instead 'a mask of playful blarney' among the Irish; but 'theirs is a tiring society'. He was dined at Jammet's French restaurant, went to Mass at Donnybrook, drank at the Fox Rock Golf Club, was guest of honour at a lunch in the Dun Laoghaire Yacht Club that preceded 'a very large tea party', after which came his Abbey Theatre Lecture, followed by further celebrations.[77] On return to London he slept for eleven hours. Then he had to face the consequences of enlistment as an ARP warden. These involved a training course, including seven hard-to-hear 'intensive lectures' delivered in a strong cockney accent in the 'bad acoustics' of Kensington Town Hall. Tom learned how to report on houses ''it by a 'igh Hexplosive bomb', how to deal with the wounded, and how to liaise with the emergency services.[78] He took careful notes. Lectures and practice fire drills would be followed by an oral examination: 'if this is passed, I am inducted into a tin hat, Wellingtons, dungarees, and a superior gas mask, to report from time to time at the Belvedere Hotel', 6 Grenville Place.[79]

Aware of what war might bring, he was surprised but understanding when he heard the Kauffers had left for America. He suggested to Polly Tandy that his American relatives might help find sanctuary for her children there. He encouraged Mary Hutchinson to consider having her grandchildren evacuated to Canada. As well as supporting a 'Token of Freedom' scheme to provide extracts from Richmond's *Pattern of Freedom* Faber anthology to child evacuees sailing to the New World, he was soon helping Pamela Travers (author of *Mary Poppins*, and, like Tom a member of the *New English Weekly*'s advisory board) in her efforts to go to America to tell children there about 'Britain and the children of Britain, without direct propaganda'.[80] However, Tom still did not generally support the idea of granting writers special exemption from the risks of war. 'I wish that I might be in Maine with you,' he wrote to Emily on 6 July, 'yet nothing on earth (except some task of national importance) would make me want to leave England at present.'[81]

Crossing the Atlantic was dangerous, in any case, and not only for military personnel. That July British and American newspapers reported the torpedoing of the British liner *Arandora Star*, which had been transporting Italian and German civilian internees to Canada. Most of those on board were drowned, though a small number managed to survive in lifeboats or clinging to debris. Though there were widespread civilian fears about a looming air war, on an island which still thought of itself as a great sea power, the conflict, especially after Dunkirk, was also one involving civilian as well as military seamen.

Tom was prepared to die. Convinced America would join hostilities only if it seemed in American interests, he continued debating with American friends. Iddings Bell argued that 'resistance to Germany's theology cannot be carried out by dead men'. Tom countered that Bell's argument seemed 'very doubtful. St Thomas of Canterbury's resistance to the ideology of Henry II was far more operative after his death than before, and something might be said about the Lacedemonians after Thermopylae. Certainly, I would say that resistance to Germany's ideology cannot be carried out by men who are unwilling to die, or to sacrifice everything individually dear to them.'[82] Tom saw the immediate present and future as a life and death struggle. Mass bombing seemed imminent. Still, this did not stop him making light of the 'whirlwind' of air-raid 'Precautions'. One of his coping strategies was to send Hayward accounts of ARP daftness. Major Lee recounted tales of campaigning in 1890s Sudan and a Kensington 'Baroness' used a stirrup pump to spray nasturtiums, assisted by an elderly female friend: 'These women are the backbone of England,' Tom confided to Hayward, 'but don't say that I said so.'[83]

He watched another stalwart, 'dear Rose Macaulay' when, supporting Geoffrey Faber, he attended a meeting to protest against book taxation.[84] A few days later, soon after news of the loss of the *Arandora Star* and the sinking of many French naval vessels, he went on 12 July with Mary Hutchinson to see Michael Redgrave in American anti-appeasement dramatist Robert Ardrey's play *Thunder Rock*. Its protagonist, an American journalist who has covered European wartime horrors, shuts himself away in the Rock lighthouse. There he is haunted by ghosts of courageous drowned nineteenth-century transatlantic emigrants. The play did not hide its opposition to fascism, but presented themes of struggle and endurance more through the voices of civilians lost, long ago, at sea than through descriptions of modern combat. Tom praised it in a mid-July letter to Emily, even if he thought it intellectually underpowered. Aspects of it can be related to parts of the poem he would embark on.

In mid-July 1940 he was at Jordans again. At this Moot meeting Murry advocated 'a new united states of Anglo-Saxon peoples'. Other participants hoped for the 'failure of Hitler's invasion of Britain', speculated about possible 'civil war', and confronted the chance of being 'dead or in a concentration camp'.[85] In his short, philosophically measured paper circulated beforehand, Tom emphasised the need for the church as 'a visible and authoritative centre of allegiance outside of the nation', but feared 'little, except a constant assertion of right principles, can be accomplished until the disease of nationalism has run its course'.[86] An immigrant ready to die for his adopted country, he protested adherence to a supranational system of religious belief. Where others sought refuge in sex and wartime brief encounters, Tom, in another piece written around this time, hailed sociologist J. D. Unwin's *Sex and Culture* as a 'masterpiece' for its argument that 'restrictions upon sexual intercourse' led to 'social energy'. This energy found expression not just in 'war' but also in 'the higher religions and philosophy and the development of the arts'.[87] Such views matched his assertion to Emily that they should submerge their own feelings in the greater turmoil of the war. Tom's celibacy remained inviolate, though his desire for female companionship – whether epistolary or face-to-face – stayed strong. When Emily, on vacation, wrote from Maine, Tom remembered his own early days sailing up the Maine coast around Casco Bay. Again he recalled listening with her to that 'bell-buoy tolling lazily on a quiet summer day'.[88] She was, as so often, in his innermost thoughts, yet very far away. He missed hearing from his Hinkley cousins, but his Uncle Christopher and Aunt Susie as well as his siblings still wrote to him from Massachusetts. He relished their letters, though Emily's remained his most treasured.

On 15 July, amid 'preliminary encounters to the great air battles which lie ahead', *The Times* reported Churchill's 'Call to the Nation'. This stressed the need to 'strive without failing in faith or in duty' while 'keeping open our communications with the New World, from which, as the struggle deepens, increasing aid will come'.[89] Such words expressed urgent hope as Britain faced the continuing possibility, and even likelihood, of defeat. Rumours circulated in early August that President Roosevelt was seeking to make available a 'transfer of destroyers to Great Britain' to prevent potential British naval collapse.[90] Tom prayed. He carried out faithfully his churchwarden's duties at St Stephen's Church. He worked at home and in his Russell Square office, mulling over the poem he wanted to write. It, too, would keep open communications with the New World, particularly while, as the RAF and the Luftwaffe fought in the skies over southern England, the Battle of Britain began, and Britons waited to see if their navy might be reinforced.

At Faber & Faber preparations were underway to publish *Loss of Eden*, a propagandistic novel that imagined life under German occupation. Tom prevented British publication of American-based English writer Freda Utley's *The Dream We Lost*, which argued America should not enter hostilities and that, in certain circumstances, Britain should settle for 'negotiated peace' with Nazi Germany.[91] Like his colleagues, he felt the strain of war, but confided to Hayward with mixed pride and dismay, 'It is somewhat disturbing to me, to reflect that I have both the soundest constitution and the most phlegmatic temperament, in Faber & Faber's.'[92] His secretary there since 1936, the poet Anne Ridler (who found him 'a joy' to work for), was pregnant, and had left London to give birth; twenty-one-year-old Linda Melton became his secretary for the rest of the war and beyond, but life at 24 Russell Square was hardly dramatic compared with the aerial battles raging above.[93] The future depended on which side gained air supremacy. Due to invasion fears, the Anglo-Catholic Summer School of Sociology, which Maurice Reckitt had invited him to address, was postponed. The speech he had written shows him reflecting on 'the English situation against the background of the transatlantic world'.[94] American memories kept resurfacing too in his letters to Emily. Invasion fears notwithstanding, he went on attending meetings with 'my serious political-economic friends' in the Chandos Group. He enjoyed dining with the Hutchinsons. He even put up with his demandingly energetic *Christian News-Letter* colleague, Eleanora Iredale, about whom, sometimes with sexist venom, he liked to complain to Hayward: 'if I am Job, she is my Boil'.[95]

The start of August saw him preparing to sit his ARP exam. At least once a fortnight he would be on duty at the local Wardens' Post. It co-ordinated precautions and reporting of casualties and damage. ARP work was intensifying. Moreover, to give Joe Oldham a holiday, Tom had undertaken to oversee several August *News-Letters*: he assured readers this task 'can be hardly more unwelcome to you than the invitation was to myself'. Commenting on Churchill's 'authority', he remarked, 'I do not believe that any statesman to-day in this country could command popular success, whose mind and feelings were wholly detached from that obscure basis of Christian thought and emotion which is still integral with the people's ideals.' He went on to commend Portugal's Salazar as 'a Christian at the head of a Christian country'. In the next issue he wrote of how the readers' own nation was 'engaged in a vital struggle which revives the sense of community'.[96]

To the wealthy gay bibliophile Richard Jennings, a mutual pal to Tom and Hayward, with whom Tom dined from time to time and to whom he signed himself 'Your morose friend', he complained of having to smoke 'a kind of bogus American cigarette' in these days of rationing. The only whisky now available was 'undrinkable', but 'I might like a Nip of Gin before dinner: after that, I am as happy as anyone can be in these times, with Beer.'[97] With Jennings, as with Hayward, he indulged his taste for obscure aspects of the Sherlock Holmes 'Canon'. Typing Jennings a letter on the evening of 15 August, he began his last paragraph, 'Here I was interrupted for a few minutes by an air raid. No matter.' He hoped to visit, and 'bring a bottle of Gin (Plymouth)' later in the year, 'after the present pressure is ended', and after that when 'I have returned, if return I do, from Wales, about the middle of September'.[98] That phrase, 'if return I do', sounded whimsical; but it was the sort of thing many people said in Britain in 1940 when air-raid sirens blared and anti-aircraft guns pounded the skies.

'The first thing to do, when you hear the Syrens, or the gun fire preliminary', Tom wrote to Hayward on 23 August, 'is to have a good Piss: after that you are ready for the Jerry.' Woken abruptly and scrambling out of bed, he got used to donning as many layers of woollens as would fit under his blue ARP boiler suit, slinging his 'Civilian Duty Respirator' over his shoulder, making sure he had his torch, ARP card, whistle, and helmet with its large letter 'W' (denoting he was a warden), then heading for the Belvedere Hotel. Inside, he met guests in dressing gowns as well as the 'doughty boys of Post 26', his ARP group. Post 26 headquarters was at 14 Eldon Road, Kensington. Tom's Belvedere Hotel base, a few hundred yards away, was a sub-post. Though ARP personnel records do not survive and a 'snap' of Tom's 'Stirrup-Pump Squad' seems lost, a photograph of nearby Kensington 'Post 23', whose area was closer to Kensington High Street, shows eleven wardens, mostly middle-aged, and one a woman, with respirators, stirrup pumps and other equipment.[99] Tom's group patrolled the small, mainly residential area 'between Cornwall Gardens, Gloucester Road and Cromwell Road' which included St Stephen's Church. Among his fellow wardens were several former military men with experience of Britain's overseas empire, and 'a little dark fellow named Kholadi, described as the son of an Iraqui Carpet Merchant'. 'While patrolling in the moonlight' along with 'a brother warden', Major Festing, Tom had to listen to long accounts of 'Christian Missions in India. All the other wardens seem to have been seasoned in the East.' From time to time he had to blow his whistle, and enter buildings, climbing stairs to top-floor flats where he demanded lights be extinguished to preserve the blackout. Like Father Cheetham's housekeeper, he found these experiences took their toll. 'I have bought a ½ pint bottle of Jamaica Rum, with which I intend to dose Elizabeth and myself after the next nocturnal raid.'[100]

Uncertain how long he might live, he made plans to give away his childhood pocket watch. He had been given it for Christmas 1900, when he was twelve, and in August 1940 he wrote to Enid Faber, with whom over many years he enjoyed corresponding chattily, to say he would like to give the 'silver huntingcase watch' to twelve-year-old Tom, his godson, as a Christmas present. Conscious the watch now seemed old-fashioned, the adult Tom recalled that receiving it in 1900 had been 'a matter of some solemnity', and he made light of his wish to pass it on to his godson.[101] But the gift, as well as being an act of kindness, affection and trust, was also timely. It was a moment to pass on valuable possessions that could be handed down the generations – just in case anything calamitous happened. Aware in his new poem of 'a time / Older than the time of chronometers', Tom had a keen, quickened sense both of the solemn balance between 'Time the destroyer' and 'time the preserver', and he wanted to preserve what he could.[102]

In late August he wrote about French culture in the *Christian News-Letter*. He now portrayed Maurras, whose thinking had so influenced his sense of religious institutions fused to national identity, as 'a man of powerful but narrow mind'. Of late, Maurras had given support to France's collaborationist 'Pétain *régime*'. Tom called attention, too, to a recent English report, *The Church in Country Parishes*. Linking it to the need to regard 'agriculture' as 'a vocation, not merely as an industry', he argued that the 'values of our future society' must reflect such arguments.[103] 'Pretty tired,' he joined the Fabers for a Welsh holiday at the start of September, reassuring Emily he had 'seen no damage anywhere'. Even in London, he told her, 'I am in as safe a position as much the largest part of the population of the island', and, in any case, 'one's capacity of adaptation is remarkable'.[104]

Shortly before Tom left for Wales, as diplomatic efforts to woo America intensified, Churchill was reported to have spoken in Parliament about deepening ties between 'the British Empire and the United States'. Somewhat surprisingly, in the context of this 'process', the prime minister quoted the musical *Show Boat* whose song about the Mississippi, 'Ol' Man River', had been popularised by Paul Robeson: 'I do not view this process with any misgivings. (Cheers.) I could not stop it if I wished. No one could stop it. (Cheers.) Like the Missisippi, it just keeps rolling along. (Cheers.) Let it roll. (Cheers.) Let it roll in full flood, inexorable, irresistible, benignant, to broader lands and better days.'[105] Soon after Tom returned to London, Churchill announced 1,200 German planes had been shot down, and some 'transfer of American destroyers to the British flag' had been agreed.[106] Rumours about these '50 over-age destroyers' had circulated earlier. They were to be made available by America in return for US access to Caribbean British naval bases.[107] America remained neutral, but British requests to boost vital naval strength were bearing fruit.

In the wake of Hitler's determination that, before invading by sea, he would use bombing to raze British cities to the ground, Churchill invoked images of the Spanish Armada and of Admiral Lord Nelson's early nineteenth-century naval triumphs. People must not 'flinch or weary of the struggle', despite even 'these cruel, wanton, indiscriminate bombings of London'.[108] Though Tom's new poem was hardly the product of Churchillian rhetoric, or of Geoffrey Faber's September contention that publications were 'Britain's Ambassadors' abroad, these circumstances formed part of the volatile, charged atmosphere in which that poem would be written. Only some of the letters survive, but it is clear that from at least October 1940 until early 1941 Tom was engaged in lengthy correspondence with Henry in Massachusetts – and with others – about American reluctance to join the war.[109]

In June 1940 President Roosevelt's 'personal estimate of Britain's chances of survival' had fallen to 'as low as one-in-three'; by November, the British navy had lost 106 of its 176 destroyers.[110] The months leading up to the US presidential election of 5 November 1940 saw both the leading candidates, Roosevelt and his Republican rival Wendell Willkie, seeking to reassure a majority of voters who wanted to keep America out of the war. At the same time, Willkie, like Roosevelt (who would win an unprecedented third term of office) inclined towards supporting the British rather than the German side. Worried his president was 'greatly under the influence of foreign political and social philosophies, particularly that of Soviet Russia, or at least of Marxism', Henry contended that 'autocratic' Roosevelt was 'a consummate egoist, it seems to me even more so than Herr Hitler'. While he wrote to Tom on 14 November that 'You in England applauded his sending of fifty destroyers; and so did public opinion here', Henry complained Roosevelt's actions involved 'legal chicanery'.[111] From war-ravaged England, Tom rebutted his brother's arguments about US politics and transatlantic relations 'at length' in a way that made Henry rather prickly. Tom accused Henry of caricaturing Roosevelt as a 'Groton choir-boy'; anyway, there were more important issues at stake than the president's personality. To Tom it seemed Henry's underlying assumption was 'that the war does not concern America, and that help to Britain is pure generosity and not a matter of vital interest as well'. Ultimately, Henry came to accept 'that the risk of war should be faced if necessary to aid Britain'.[112] However, as both brothers knew, in this era of the America First movement by no means all Americans agreed.

Reprinted in June 1940 by *New English Weekly* after its initial publication by that same magazine in March, 'East Coker' had appeared as a Faber & Faber pamphlet on 12 September, five days after the start of the London Blitz, in an edition of over 9,000 copies. One sceptical reviewer heard its tone as 'sad' and 'disdainful'; Tom's correspondent Desmond Hawkins detected in it a 'majesty of address' which he linked to 'Yeats'. By the end of 1940 another reviewer connected it not to 'the outer war' but 'the inner war in our souls'.[113] Inevitably, though, outer war now preoccupied the poet, and Emily felt the strain of news reports. She wondered again why Tom had not come to America. Urging her to accept his situation, he sent occasional cables: 'ALL WELL'.[114] By mid-September air raids were so frequent that he had moved out of his vulnerable top-floor flat close to the railway line – an easy target – and had taken up residence at the wardens' base in the Belvedere Hotel. A bomb hit Kynance Mews in his ' "sector" '. Nearby, Lexham Gardens was bombed 'for the third time'. Exhausted by nightly bombing raids, he spent the weekend of 21–22 September at the Reads' Buckinghamshire home, sleeping from 11 p.m. on Saturday until 4.30 on the Sunday afternoon. When he got back, he was greeted on the steps of the Belvedere by fellow warden Captain Nigel Bellairs, who told him 'there was a [delayed fuse] time bomb at Russell Sq[uare]'. Though he did not think Fabers' premises 'totally destroyed by it' (in fact the bomb was removed, apparently unexploded, by the emergency services) the building was evacuated. Deprived of his office, and unsure about the safety of the room he had rented on the first floor of the Belvedere, Tom headed for the basement of the Oxford and Cambridge Club for a good night's sleep. By the eve of his fifty-second birthday he was due back at the Belvedere for two further nights' duties. 'I am not of the stuff of which heroes are made, and have no desire to qualify for a George Cross, and but for weekends should go dotty from lack of sleep.'[115]

Relying on a lift from Sir Philip Gibbs, a famous war correspondent now employed by the Ministry of Information, Tom hoped to spend the next weekend but one with the Mirrlees household at Shamley Green. He was trying to be out of London for as many nights as air-raid duties would allow. 'I am in less danger than most people', he reassured Emily once more.[116] Knowing she would be hearing and reading news of the Blitz, he cabled her on 28 September to let her know he was in London for only three days a week. He took solace in memorising Psalm 130. Beginning, 'Out of the depths have I cried unto thee, O Lord', its sixth and seventh verses read:

My soul waiteth for the Lord more than they that watch for the morning. I say, more than they that watch for the morning.

Signing himself 'Ever your very loving Tom', he hand-wrote Emily a letter assuring her that he carried with him her photograph inside his wallet, and had another in a gold frame in his hotel room. He found 'all the psalms especially helpful just now'.[117]

'Spoiling a moderately good poet and churchwarden to make an incompetent air warden', he wrote in pencil to Frank Morley in America on 9 October, trying to maintain a cheerful tone from the 'Tomb of Possum the Great' at the Oxford and Cambridge Club. 'I *want*', he revealed, 'to do another *quartet* – provisionally entitled *The Dry Salvages* (accent on the *vages* – see chart of Cape Ann).'[118] Clearly, though it would be 10 December before he confessed to John Hayward that he was actually 'working' at it, the poem was constellating in his head. Where 'East Coker' had begun with 'Earth' and 'Summer', he explained later, the new poem's initial cynosure would be 'Water' and 'Autumn'.[119] What seem his earliest notes show it as starting simply with a 'Sea picture'.[120] When developed fully, however, without naming the Mississippi, it would begin with a vision of that river, 'implacable' in its flow, a 'destroyer' as well as an abiding presence; but the poem's principal focus would shift to 'sea voices', anxious 'lying awake', 'living among the breakage', and relentless struggle, imaged not in terms of contemporary wartime endurance but as 'fishermen' in dangerous seas who persist in their efforts even though those may result in death and defeat.[121] 'The Dry Salvages' would draw on deep personal 'moments of agony', but be alert, also, to 'the agony of others': 'People change, and smile: but the agony abides.'[122] Written in the months after Tom had been pondering Gangulee's anthology and the career of Yeats whom Tom had encouraged to work with Shri Purohit Swami on the *Gita*, and drawing on his own earlier studies of Sanskrit, the poem fuses the world of Atlantic maritime struggle and drowning with the battlefields of ancient India as it universalises a need to go on, to persist, to 'fare forward'.

So Krishna, as when he admonished Arjuna
On the field of battle.
                              Not fare well,
But fare forward, voyagers.

This is the poem's sole use of the word 'battle': 'The Dry Salvages' mentions no Dunkirk, no Blitz. Yet, in its complexly refracted way it is attuned not just to faith, place, and the passage of time but also to the desperate struggle for 'freedom' present in the society in which it was written. In its 'prayer' it is alert to losses, to 'Women who have seen their sons or husbands / Setting forth, and not returning'. It comes closest to Churchillian rhetoric, perhaps, in lines about people 'Who are only undefeated / Because we have gone on trying'; but it is not Churchillian.[123] It is written, prayerfully and unmistakably, in its poet's own distinctive, struggling, and universalising middle-aged Anglo-American voice.

'ALL WELL LOVE ELIOT', he cabled Emily on 10 October.[124] She was taking communion at her local Episcopalian church again, which may have helped her feel closer to him, but bothered him because she remained Unitarian. Though Emily felt able to take Episcopalian communion while maintaining her Unitarian stance, this was a serious divergence from orthodox practice in ways that some modern observers may find hard to fathom. St Paul, in his first epistle to the Corinthians, had stipulated that the communicant had to 'examine himself' thoroughly before taking Christian communion. 'For he that eateth and drinketh unworthily, eateth and drinketh damnation to himself, not discerning the Lord's body.'[125] From an orthodox Catholic point of view, Emily might be endangering her soul if she took communion without believing fully in the meaning of Christ's crucifixion and resurrection. Tom worried about her apparently relaxed attitude towards Episcopalian communion, which could be seen as a risk to her as well as a challenge to the core beliefs of the church to which he was so profoundly attached. Such differences in belief and attitude remained a cause of strain between them.

Yet he longed for her letters. 'Reminders of normality' comforted him.[126] He cabled her again on 23 October, wishing her a happy birthday. As he lay in bed in the Belvedere Hotel, or kept watch on blackout Blitz nights, he found himself listening intently. Ordinary sounds could become disturbing. Haunted by a noise that would find its way into his final 'Quartet', 'I remember', he told her on 30 October,

on one of my first nights being bothered by a strange sound, going out to reconnoitre, and discovering after several minutes that it was merely dead leaves being swept along the street by the breeze. It is often difficult to distinguish whether what you hear is a small noise close by (even indoors) or a greater noise a long way off; and the sound of bombs can be very deceptive. Several times we have thought that a terrific report meant that something had fallen very near, and once or twice nearly ignored bombs that really were our business, because they sounded so far away.

He added that all this was simply 'an unavoidable duty' that got in the way of everything he wanted to do and was qualified to do. He was 'merely thankful to have had no occasion for the display of a heroism which I doubt whether I possess'.[127] Later he confessed to an English friend his sense of being persistently in an 'agony of apprehension of having to go out and deal with some half-mangled human being and probably do the wrong thing'.[128]

Keeping going against the odds, unflinchingly confronting potential defeat: that was part of the spirit of the time. Addressing his St Stephen's congregation, Tom's vicar, Father Cheetham, reflected not long afterwards on what he had seen at a major London railway station at 'the time of Dunkirk'. It had been 'a dark night indeed, and through the barriers there came soldiers, French, Belgian, British, more tired than any men I have ever seen, unforgettable men of undaunted endurance'.[129] During autumn 1940, completing his prose epic about the struggles of a Scottish Highland fishing community and heroism at sea, *The Silver Darlings*, Tom's friend Neil Gunn sent his typescript to Russell Square; this tale of maritime endurance was progressing through the publishing house while Tom worked on 'The Dry Salvages', and Gunn's sweeping historical novel of 'perilous living' was one which the Faber blurb-writer realised would connect directly with post-Dunkirk Britain. As a reviewer soon wrote, 'It is not merely that from this breed of seamen in the making, as the jacket puts it, come those who man our drifters, trawlers and minesweepers. From them, too, dispossessed and driven though they were, comes a heritage of endurance, daring and gaiety.'[130] Tom's poem of enduring 'fishermen' who are 'forever bailing', his account of a maritime-accented struggle that, with its 'drifting boat with a slow leakage', may not end well, accords fully with the spirit of its time, even if, conscious of 'drifting wreckage', it looks also towards eternity.[131]

Finished at the start of 1941, 'The Dry Salvages' emerged on paper in late 1940. Working on it took 'stubbornness'. He felt, he told Emily on 10 December, that 'the original impulse has eluded me like a dream on waking and the verse has not gained its own impetus. But there is only the trying.'[132] Such effortful 'trying' was part of the poem's meaning. By 17 December he had drafted 'the first two sections', and hoped to 'draft the last three during Christmas week'.[133] It was easiest to write at Shamley Wood where, even if the large household of women felt smothering at times, domestic comfort was welcome and he could shut himself away to concentrate. During the poem's development, Tom was conscious of his brother's being 'so nervous' about the Blitz, and found himself 'cabling' Henry 'frequently' to let him know he was unharmed.[134] The release of the short Ministry of Information film *London Can Take It* (sometimes re-edited for American audiences as *Britain Can Take It*) with its voice-over by American war correspondent Quentin Reynolds gave late 1940 audiences – and still gives modern audiences – a sense of what the Blitz meant to Londoners, and, along with newspaper and magazine reports and radio broadcasts such as 'London after Dark' by Ed Murrow on CBS, helped communicate widely and vividly to US citizens what civilians in London were going through. *London Can Take It* was designed to help win American support, and, like the Ministry of Information's US circulation of the '*Christian Newsletter*' and like 'The Dry Salvages', was part of a complex climate of transatlantic dialogue in late 1940 and 1941.[135] In December 1940 Tom and Henry were corresponding, too, not just about transatlantic relations, Willkie, Roosevelt and the fifty destroyers, but also about what was 'personal' in *The Family Reunion*, which Henry had seen in New York.[136] That same month Tom mentioned his 'favourite' Henry James ghost story, 'The Friends of the Friends', a tale of death, separation, 'unquenchable desire', and 'response to an irresistible call'.[137] Imaginatively, he accessed and reached out to his childhood and loved ones across the ocean. His sister Ada was undergoing surgery. Emily worried repeatedly about Tom, about her failing mother, about war. As well as including some sense of his ancestors who had participated in life beside the Mississippi and in the business of New England fishing, his poem touched on intimate family memories: the rhythm of the river in 'the nursery bedroom', or the 'smell of grapes on the autumn table' of his St Louis childhood home when he returned from summering on Cape Ann.[138]

Yet his use of the word 'autumn' rather than 'fall' to refer to that American experience marked out the distance he had travelled. He wrote his American-titled poem as a poet who, foolishly perhaps, had committed himself to England – a commitment some Americans resented, or regarded as wrong; a devotion that might herald death. English people found the poem's title strange. Many Americans found it hard to pronounce. When published, it came with a gloss on geography and pronunciation. The place-name title needed explanation. Yet Tom was a supreme poet of names and place names, and this one mattered in its particularity. Its precarious strangeness resonated between the English word 'salvage' and the French *sauvage*.

The Americans he cared about most – his siblings, Emily, other friends – were living in such different circumstances. It was not just hard to communicate to them what Blitz life was like, most of the time he wanted to spare them details. Though he told Virginia Woolf his only ARP 'Incident was without casualties', for most Londoners broken bodies and rubble-strewn streets were not uncommon sights.[139] Two fellow Post 26 wardens had 'crocked up', and one had fallen 'downstairs from extreme sleepiness'. A 'time bomb' had hit the Oxford and Cambridge Club's kitchen. Part of the 'United University' Club had been destroyed by 'a large bomb in Pall Mall'.[140] Emily's most dramatic news was that she had broken a tooth when her dog Boerre ran at her excitedly to welcome her back from a restorative vacation. Inevitably, there were disjunctions between Tom's experiences and those of his American correspondents. But 'The Dry Salvages' reached out to America. It was a reminder how much his native land still mattered to him, and that he knew American help was vital.

Yet, articulating solidarity with the 'we' who remain 'undefeated', the poem ends with an image of death and the 'yew tree' often found in English churchyards, as it marks 'The life of significant soil'.[141] The 'yew' had particular significance for Emily and Tom, who loved Stamford House's yew tree. However, the poem is not a love poem, and its 'significant soil' had a significance beyond the personal. While Tom and Henry had been discussing 'soil erosion and conservation' in their correspondence, Tom saw his new 'sea poem' as returning 'to Somerset', the county of East Coker, at its 'end'. Probably its concluding phrase was encouraged by the substantial impact made by Lord Northbourne's 1940 *Look to the Land*. Now seen as 'a manifesto of organic agriculture', linking soil science to Christianity, this book emerged out of England's wartime conditions and opened with pages devoted to the significance of soil. The topic was taken up, too, by Michael Graham's study of traditional farming, *Soil and Sense*, published by Faber & Faber in early 1941.[142] The poet treasured his deepening engagement with rural England and its parishes, even as London remained the centre of his working life.

Explaining that now he had to attend to his ARP duties during the night watches in Kensington, but spent most other nights out of London, Tom arranged to give another poetry reading for Mary Trevelyan's 'waifs' at Student Movement House, and assured her that October that he was keen to have news of her and her work. 'So much of London has been destroyed', Virginia Woolf wrote to him in mid-October. Mecklenburgh

Square, site of the Woolfs' London home, had been bombed: 'all our windows are out'. Their former residence in Tavistock Square was completely 'gone'. Virginia and Leonard were now mostly in Sussex. 'My dear Tom,' she wrote to him, wanting to check where and how he was; tired and shaken, she thanked him for a copy of 'East Coker' he had sent, and signed herself, 'your very grateful but not very articulate old crone'.[143]

At Shamley Wood he enjoyed meeting Hope Mirrlees's sister, Margot, 'Mrs Aubrey Coker of Bicester'. Intrigued by her surname, he discovered her husband was 'descended from a younger branch of the extinct Cokers of Coker'.[144] The poet of 'East Coker' relished the connection. Growing closer to the Mirrlees clan, he hoped to transfer his warden duties to the Shamley Green area. Bloomsbury around Russell Square was taking more hits: 'Every week produces a fresh deposit of time bombs or aerial torpedoes or land mines in the vicinity.' In Kensington he had got into the rather 'unreasonable' situation of 'paying board and lodging at the Belvedere' (where, since he was almost always on duty, he could not sleep), and so was 'paying out nearly the salary of a warden in order to be a warden', which made him feel foolish.[145] His clothes were distributed among several locations. Correspondence was going astray. With 'the battle in the tube at dusk', transport was increasingly difficult. Occasionally ('I can't bear shelters and cellars') his nerves showed. He wasn't 'getting enough sleep to be of any use in the day'.[146]

By November he had given up his accommodation at 3/11 Emperor's Gate and moved to Shamley Wood for most of the week. He took his work there, typed his own letters, and cadged weekly lifts to London with Philip Gibbs for Faber & Faber book committee meetings on Wednesdays. He stayed overnight in Hampstead with the Fabers, sleeping in their basement shelter. Occasionally, too, he travelled to Oxford, where the *Christian News-Letter* was now headquartered. While there, he met Charles Williams. Publishing, like so many other businesses, continued throughout the Blitz.

'My dear Virginia,' he wrote on 26 October 1940, 'it was indeed an elixir to hear from you.' Joking that Shamley offered 'the healthiest life that I have lived for years', he nonetheless matched her self-mockery and signed himself 'your toothless old crony'.[147] With formal embarrassment, 'affectionately and gratefully' he had explained to Mappie Mirrlees that he wanted to pay her four guineas a week for board and lodging.[148] Geoffrey Faber, convinced 'being an ARP warden in Kensington' was doing Tom 'no good', thought the Mirrlees household provided 'an excellent life for him: no contacts till lunch; privacy for writing ; and domestic comfort and peace from Air Raid Precautions'.[149] Certainly, Shamley Wood, where the 'puir daft makar', after watching sheep from his bedroom window, ambled to Sunday worship at the tranquil village church, was a different world from 'Post 26B'.[150] It was, Tom explained to Polly Tandy (to whom he sent a copy of the recently published new edition of *Old Possum's Book of Practical Cats* with illustrations – replacing Tom's original ones – by Nicholas Bentley),

> an establishment now housing eighteen women and children, including ladies, servants, and innumerable refugees, a decrepit but learned gardener and his wife, myself most [of] the week, a practical policeman from Barking (whose fambly are refuging here) at weekends: and an occasional Canadian soldier finds his way here by mistake at the end of the evening after leaving the Bricklayer's Arms or the Red Lion, but I hope that won't happen again. There is the regular German parade overhead every night, but so far no crumps nearer than a mile or so, and I hope there won't be, or any incendiaries either, as I haven't quite got the colony to master the stirrup pump yet.[151]

While all this was going on, he was much impressed by a typescript: James Hanley's novel, *The Ocean*, 'a grim masterpiece of the sea', encouraged his imaginings of endurance at sea.[152] In what one BBC official termed a 'rather pontifical drawl', Tom had made a late-November radio broadcast from London. 'A people and its language will advance or deteriorate together' and the writer's business was 'to preserve and extend the resources of the language'.[153] Then, as he worked on 'The Dry Salvages', his thoughts turned towards Christmas and sending gifts to family, friends, and godchildren. Given wartime conditions, Christmas at Shamley Wood was surprisingly luxurious. Among other things, Mappie presented Tom with La Corona Corona cigars. By the year's end he regarded his poem, drafts of which he sent to Hayward and Faber, as just about complete. He even had in mind a further, as yet unwritten, poem. It might be called 'Little Gidding'.[154]

12

Little Gidding

IN early January 1941 Tom told Mary Hutchinson he was finding time for both prose and verse, but had no immediate hopes of writing drama. Except for volumes in his Faber office, his books were stored in St Stephen's Church hall. Like so many other people, he realised everything might 'go up in smoke'; at least Bloomsbury was 'not quite so susceptible to incendiarism as the City'.[1] He focused on completing 'a set of four' poems, though other projects included assisting the *Christian News-Letter*. After its 1 January verse elaboration of the Lord's Prayer during 'the fury and cruelty of war', it directed attention towards needs for spiritual and societal 'reconstruction' – and to the importance of American practical support.[2] On 5 January Tom told Emily 'The Dry Salvages' was 'just finished', though he might 'tinker with' it. 'The fourth and last of the series' of poems would be set at 'Little Gidding'. When that was 'done', he might 'feel ripe to do another essay following up the Christian Society'.[3] Afterwards, he hoped conditions might let him work on drama. Even in the Blitz, he was making plans.

He travelled to Malvern College, a grand private school in Worcestershire, to address a January conference designed 'to consider how far the Christian faith and principles based upon it could afford guidance for action in the world today'.[4] With speakers including Murry, Demant, Kenneth Ingram, and Dorothy Sayers, it was presided over by William Temple, Archbishop of York. Two hundred delegates aimed to 'consider, from the Anglican point of view, what fundamental facts are directly relevant to a new order of society after the war, and how Christian thought can be mobilized to play a leading part to ensure the victory of the spirit'.[5] One line of argument, with an ecological dimension, encouraged Christian connections with farming and rural communities. Participants were encouraged to form 'cells' of 'common prayer, study and service'.[6] The following year, Murry would establish an experimental Christian community at Lodge Farm, Suffolk. Tom's contribution, soon revised for publication, was philosophical in tone. Characteristically suspicious of humanism's 'attempt to devise a philosophy of life without a metaphysic', he argued the 'need for a specifically Christian doctrine of education'. While recognising humanists had derived 'comfort from Buddhism and from Confucianism', he maintained, 'there is a sense in which wisdom that is not Christian turns to folly. Furthermore, wisdom is no substitute for faith.' Tom wanted 'hard thinking' about 'whether there are not permanent principles of what should be the goal of education'. Wary of aspects of the left-leaning Malvern Conference, he concluded that 'the task' he advocated was 'not to be accomplished by conferences and manifestoes, but by the patient toil of various minds in the humble and submissive hope of the direction of the Holy Ghost'[7]. His uncompromising contribution has struck some twenty-first-century commentators as 'medieval'.[8] With two fellow participants, he wrote to *The Times*, registering dissent from delegates' supposedly 'unanimously' adopted conclusions. However, as he brooded on the poem that would become 'Little Gidding', his thinking was nourished by this conference's emphases on small rural Christian communities, spiritual reconstruction, and accepting wartime conditions while looking beyond them.[9] At Malvern he may have sounded much more a theologically oriented social thinker than a poet, but intellectual and spiritual strivings had helped fuel much of his poetry to date, and would soon do so again.

While in Worcestershire he felt unwell, but travelled on to a Moot meeting in Berkshire. It featured considerable discussion of calls to form a new religious order. Tom argued such an order should not be linked too closely to the *Christian News-Letter*. Intergenerational tensions were also debated. Increasingly conscious that his work belonged to an older generation, he explained how in poetry 'since 1926 a new generation had arisen, now sharply divided' from his. Another participant highlighted 'general dissatisfaction and a call to remove the "old men"'. BBC assistant director of religious broadcasting Eric Fenn, a friend of Mary Trevelyan's, mentioned a feeling widespread among the military that an eventual 'reckoning with the "old men"' would be required. Anglican priest Gilbert Shaw detected convictions among 'younger people' that '"a certain crowd had to go"'. Having already cautioned against 'the wisdom of old men' in 'East Coker', Tom joined in the Moot's discussion of 'the perennial difference between a person of 60 and one of 30'.[10] Part of an older generation, he was coming to realise that 'last year's words belong to last year's language'.[11]

Suddenly, this was brought home. On 14 January, still feeling his age and 'ill with influenza', he scanned *The Times* for his co-signed letter about Malvern, and was shocked to read a report that 'Mr James Joyce, an Irishman whose book "Ulysses" gave rise to much controversy, died at Zurich yesterday.'[12] Tom noted 'with stupefaction' the obituary for this great Irish novelist. It struck him as slighting and patronising. He wrote immediately to assert that with *Ulysses* 'my friend Mr James Joyce' had produced 'the most considerable work of imagination in English in our time'; 'The Dead', which concludes Joyce's *Dubliners*, was 'one of the finest short stories in the language'. Angered when *The Times* decided not to print his letter, he sent it to Cyril Connolly's *Horizon*, with a stinging addition signalling displeasure at the 'abominably stupid' *Times* obituary.[13] His angry tone may have conveyed intellectual superiority, but, regarding Joyce as a commanding intellectual and an artistic equal, Tom, who became conscious of being 'the last living man of letters, of Joyce's generation, in England who was closely associated with him', wanted Joyce treated with fitting respect.[14] The novelist, whose company and correspondence he had relished for over twenty years, had died of a perforated ulcer. He was fifty-eight.

Expressing sympathy, Mary Hutchinson knew what this loss would mean to Tom. Fed up as his illness lingered, and as the blow of Joyce's death intensified a sense of wartime mortality, he circulated 'The Dry Salvages' among friends including Mairet and Faber. At times the poem drew on youthful memories of his father's summer home on the Massachusetts coast. The 'emotional charge' of these was all the more intense because Tom (who called himself to Enid Faber in February 1941 'Hal Eliot's little boy') had never revisited the house since 1915, when, in unhappy circumstances, he parted from his father, Henry, for the last time.[15] His fellow feeling for Joyce included their shared sense of never having achieved reconciliation with a father with whom each had argued and, for years, left unvisited, but whom each had loved profoundly. He cabled Emily on 29 January, sending his love and explaining he was recovering from a fortnight's influenza. By 9 February, 'The Dry Salvages' had reached 'draft no. 5'.[16]

His doctor advised him not to return to London until at least mid-February. Though he benefited from cosseting at Shamley Wood, some friends found his stay there amusing. 'Last time I heard from Tom, he was domesticating with Hope Mirrlees: spiritually, of course', Virginia Woolf wrote to Mary Hutchinson.[17] Struggling with correspondence, he hired a local typist, and turned his mind to a BBC talk. He had agreed with Eric Fenn to broadcast in a radio series about the Anglican Church and post-war reconstruction. Other contributors would include Oldham, Mairet, Maurice Reckitt, and further Malvern or Moot speakers. Tom recast his piece several times, highlighting 'sacrifice', prayer, family Christian education, and the need to 'know the dogmas of our faith'. His talk, broadcast on 2 April, concluded with an account of French priest Charles de Foucauld, killed at prayer in 1916 in North Africa. Foucauld's life, 'as the world judges', was not one 'of striking success'. Yet, 'through the mysterious power of holiness', it had become exemplary and remarkable: 'there is no higher glory of a Christian empire than that which was here brought into being by a death in the desert'.[18] That last, resonantly alliterative phrase might have been taken by radio listeners as referring obliquely to intense ongoing fighting in North Africa, but it is also the title of a philosophical poem by Robert Browning that deals with death, love, fire, Christian faith, and the meaning of art. In 'Little Gidding' Tom would embark on his own, very different philosophical poem addressing these themes.

On 20 February Faber & Faber published 'Burnt Norton' as a sixteen-page booklet in the same format as their now five-month-old edition of 'East Coker'. After initial magazine publication, 'The Dry Salvages' would be published similarly on 4 September. During early 1941, though, as elements of 'Little Gidding' began to constellate, Tom was seeing through the press a new long poem by Auden, the younger generation's leading poet. In America this work would be called *The Double Man*, though Faber's edition was titled *New Year Letter*. It concluded, as Edward Mendelson points out, with a passage filled with 'names and thoughts' derived 'mainly from a single book, *The Descent of the Dove: A History of the Holy Spirit in the Church*, by Charles Williams'.[19] While Tom, involved in considerable discussions over the 'invisible twin' in Auden's *Double Man* title, had long been familiar with ideas of *dédoublement* and with Williams's work, their deployment in Auden's poem brought them again to the older poet's attention.[20] In his own way, assuming 'a double part' and writing of how 'The dove descending breaks the air', he would deploy them in 'Little Gidding'.[21]

'I tire very quickly,' he complained to Hayward on 14 February.[22] Nevertheless, he agreed to deliver the W. P. Ker Lecture at Glasgow University either later that year or early next, and set to correcting proofs of 'The Dry Salvages' for the *New English Weekly* of 27 February. He made sure to ask Mairet to have copies sent not just to English friends including Faber, Richmond, Virginia Woolf, and Hugh Stewart who had taken him to Little Gidding, but also to Emily, Henry, Morley, and Ted Spencer. American connections were much on his mind, not least because his first cousin, Martha, head of the Washington-based Child Welfare Bureau, was then visiting England as the only woman member of a US government commission to 'investigate civil defence'. Martha May Eliot, a distinguished paediatrician, had taught at Yale. She lived with a lesbian partner; though this was not something the family discussed publicly, Tom's discreet acceptance of it matched his attitude to lesbianism elsewhere. He described Dr Eliot rather patronisingly as 'a good specimen of the family' and 'perfectly efficient in her line'. She gave her sickly-looking anglicised cousin 'a box of concentrated vitamins'.[23]

He was now quite clear about aiming to have four substantial poems that would form a book. Readers, he explained to Emily, would 'perceive that I have been struggling to create a new form. The four poems (which may be considered as one poem, though the *form* is in the separate parts) may be considered as related to the four seasons and the four elements.'[24] He thought he had never before begun a new poem 'so soon after' its predecessor, but registered that his 'going on with verse in war time' might make 'a deeper impression on people, and give them more encouragement, than any prose I could do'. He liked keeping 'alive the idea of culture by creative work if one can'.[25] Sustaining culture was crucial, but so was maintaining hope in the face of loss. He pondered Joyce's death. His cousin Marguerite's son had been killed in Albania. From America his sister Ada wrote little about her cancer, but he knew it was progressing. On a morning walk at Shamley Green where, wearing a cap and carrying a walking stick, he sometimes took extended rambles, Tom saw signs of spring, but also a dead fox lying in a pool. He made a grim joke to a Faber secretary about publishing his 'Last Poems', then his 'Posthumous Poems'.[26]

'There is a lovely word I found in the *OED* and want to use as soon as I can', he confided to Hayward on 3 March.[27] The *Oxford English Dictionary* defined 'antelucan' as 'of or pertaining to the hours just before dawn'. Tom the ARP warden who mentions 'the morning watch' in 'The Dry Salvages' had become all too familiar with such hours, but 'antelucan' (like 'the morning watch') also had religious overtones. The *OED* cites a seventeenth-century bishop's 'antelucan devotion' and Thomas De Quincey's mention of 'crepuscular antelucan worship, possibly having reference to the ineffable mystery of the resurrection'. As poets often do, Tom carried this treasured word around with him for some time before using it in a draft of the new poem which would fuse his ARP activities with his religious life. In line with his customary habits of mind, though, this poem would not be presented as directly autobiographical: it amazed him 'how people can write an autobiography', he confessed, 'but it is probably because they have less to suppress than I have'.[28]

By early March he was back into the Wednesday-morning routine of travelling from Shamley Wood to London 'in a Small Austin' with several older men: 'Sir Philip Gibbs, Major Ibbetson', and former soldier Sir William Pulteney, who held the ceremonial position of Black Rod in the

House of Commons. In London Geoffrey Faber (whose collected poems joined his firm's 1941 poetry list alongside 'The Dry Salvages') played Tom a gramophone record. With its profoundly affirmatory ringing conclusion, Sibelius's Fifth Symphony left him 'in a state of excitement: I wish I could write like that'.[29] Young poets, including twenty-year-old trainee soldier Keith Douglas and twenty-one-year-old recently conscripted Glasgow undergraduate Edwin Morgan, hoped to join his poetry list, but did not. As ever, he accepted work sparingly, monitoring emerging talents, including Welshman Vernon Watkins whose first, 1941 Faber volume includes a dialogue between the dead and the living; and thirty-year-old Henry Treece whose 'New Apocalyptic' writing was encouraged by Tom's friends Roberts and Read. Despite considerable 'admiration', Tom rejected a version of what became MacDiarmid's *In Memoriam James Joyce*.[30] Not all work added to the poetry list has lasted well. Few today read A. L. Rowse's 1941 *Poems of a Decade*, or *Verses of a Fighter Pilot* by the late A. N. C. Weir, a young Battle of Britain pilot whose family knew Geoffrey Faber. Weir's 'Sick City' presented a flight over vulnerable London. Tom would deploy with greater assurance imagery drawn from the air war and Blitz – phenomena all too obvious from Faber's 1941 publishing list whose titles included *Democracy's Last Battle* and *Blitzkrieg*.

Emily was concerned about his health, but his life and hers were so different. She had been 'skating – and skiing'. Tom told her he was glad to hear it, and to think of her as a 'very sporting person'; but he pondered how the passage of time had brought Joyce's death and old friends' dispersal: 'My little group of writers of the early days is well broken up: Lewis is in America, and Pound (with whose political opinions I of course have no sympathy whatever) is I believe still in Italy.'[31] Oddly, Emily, who thought frequently about their times at Chipping Campden, asked why he 'had never written a poem about the Cotswolds'. 'Perhaps you forgot Burnt Norton,' he replied, 'or perhaps you consider it geographically out of the area – but certainly not out of it emotionally.'[32] However much they might sign letters with love, and treasure one another's photographs, their lives' divergence increased. Despite hidden personal references, the focus of Tom's recent poems was not principally on their relationship. With his own recent poems in mind, he confided to Geoffrey Faber in late March,

Possibly the need to build up this imagined scheme of the operation of poetry, to put into the front of consciousness the difficulties and delights of the technical problem (to see, for instance, the sort of thing I have been doing lately simply as experiments in putting together three or four unelated things, as one would fiddle with chemicals, just to see what happens when you put 'em together) is due (as perhaps with Henry James) to an inner necessity to get my mind off my feelings in order to get them out [. . .][33]

Nevertheless, his emotional life was insistently unsettling. Around the time when he confessed to Emily in early April that 'Little Gidding' was still 'sticking somewhere inside me', she continued to ask about possible marriage, checking if for Tom their religious differences constituted an 'impediment'. He responded, 'If I had been conscious of any impediment on the ground of religious difference I should have made it clear to you long ago.'[34] This was unambiguous, but hardly suggests the tone of a lover. She continued worrying in case, as regards religion (and perhaps otherwise), he saw her as ' "lost" '.[35]

Keeping up not just with Emily but with old friends was something he strove to do, but wartime conditions made everything difficult. Despite water coming through her kitchen ceiling, and feeling 'at sea' in other ways, Virginia Woolf invited him to Monk's House, her Sussex home, for 5 April. Committed to speak at a conference, he had to decline ('will you repeat the invitation later?'), sending her – in his 'Tom Possum' guise – 'the undying affection of TP'. His words both echoed and surpassed her invitation's sign-off, 'Yr aff Virginia'.[36] Still under the weather, he concluded that his earlier 'influenza' had been bronchitis, and, fearing its return, he paid for a lung X-ray, which suggested no lasting problems. Illness, however, made him tetchy. He was annoyed at the 'Common Man Racket' represented by socialist J. B. Priestley's popular wartime broadcasts. Tom considered it time 'someone said a helpful word for the Upper Middle Classes – and even for the Aristocracy, if there was any'. Shamley Wood, for all its upper-middle-class charms, sometimes vexed him: too overheated and female-dominated. 'Such a long spell of solely female society has had a very depressing effect upon me', he complained on 25 March to Hayward. The two men conducted a protracted correspondence about shaving. Tom signed himself, with knowing self-mockery, 'Yr. hypochondriac, misanthropical, mysogynistical TP'.[37]

'Eclipse of the Highbrow', a piece in that day's *Times* attacking cerebral 'poetry' and other arts 'unintelligible outside a Bloomsbury drawing-room', while suggesting a 'drop' in poetry sales, did nothing to lessen his misanthropic mood. He could savour a *Times* retort published above the name of Geoffrey Faber: 'The age you so much dislike is in fact by no means past, and its protagonists are by no means ghosts haunting the ruins of a decadent and mythical Bloomsbury.'[38] Yet in the actual Bloomsbury, as in Kensington, ruins and haunted survivors were all too evident.

'London, 1941', as Mervyn Peake put it, was 'Half masonry, half pain'.[39] In St Stephen's parish Father Cheetham ministered to frightened families seeking shelter on the platforms of Gloucester Road Underground station as sirens sounded and bombing continued. After making a Home Service broadcast in late March Tom thought sleeping at the BBC 'better than a tube shelter but similar'.[40] 'I don't know how much safer one is in a basement,' he confided to Dobrée, 'but I know that it is far less noisy; you don't notice the house shaking so much, and you sleep better.'[41] Blitzed out of Bloomsbury and depressed in Sussex, Virginia Woolf wrote to another friend that month about 'being a good deal bombed at the moment. Rows of incendiaries fell on the farm two nights ago and burnt haystacks.'[42] Still thinking about the 'fairy gold' of Priestley's broadcasts as well as his own 'Towards a Christian Britain', Tom remarked to Hayward, 'people are ready to lap up blood & sweat from Churchill, yet they want to be told that their "Christian Britain" is just around the corner'.[43] His 'Little Gidding' needed to manifest more than 'fairy gold'.

In London on 3 April he received news that shocked him at least as much as the loss of Joyce. 'The death of Mrs Virginia Woolf' was reported in *The Times*.[44] 'For myself and others,' Tom wrote to Leonard next day from Shamley Wood, 'it is the end of a world.' He felt 'numb'.[45] Woolf had gone for a walk by the River Ouse on 28 March, leaving behind a note telling Leonard she feared the onset of another episode of 'madness'; her body was not found until 18 April.[46] An inquest produced a verdict of 'Suicide while the balance of her mind was disturbed.'[47]

In the wake of the Pope's Easter appeal denouncing 'atrocious' wartime targeting of civilians, and after Bishop Bell had argued controversially in *The Times* that Britain should try to negotiate with Germany a mutual cessation of 'night bombing', Tom confessed that German successes 'in the Mediterranean, the bombing of London, and Virginia's death have combined to depress me – the last perhaps more than I was aware of at the time.' He realised he had come to regard Woolf 'like a kind of member of my own family'. Even though, he confessed, he 'did not know her work very well', and his interest was 'entirely personal', he had 'felt at ease with her' in some ways even more than with his kith and kin.[48] He found it hard to express how intensely he missed her. And, though Tom would not have seen the letter, Woolf had written to her sister about five years earlier, rather wistfully making clear how close she felt to her sometimes infuriating friend: 'I had a visit, long long ago from Tom Eliot, whom I love, or could have loved, had we both been in the prime and not in the sere; how necessary do you think copulation is to friendship?'[49] Their closeness is affirmed by the body language of a telling photograph, taken in the late summer of 1932. Tom is smiling, standing very close to Virginia. They look every inch a couple. Also in the picture is Vivien, but she stands apart from them, as if an interloper. Now Virginia was gone.

Despite his scepticism towards any supposed Bloomsbury group, he had relished her letters, her company; she had been his publisher and confidante, sharing, not least, knowledge of what it meant to live with breakdowns. They had in common, too, a certain, sometimes cutting, patrician tone. He realised his generation was passing. Her death meant, for him and others, that 'a kind of pin has gone which held a lot of people together, and gave their belonging together a pattern and a meaning which has gone'. He sensed now 'a mood of social isolation, with the prospect of becoming a ghost in an alien, plebeian and formless society'. Having unburdened himself of some of this to Hayward, he continued their epistolary debate about shaving – but signed himself 'Your futile Tp'.[50]

His sense of ailing was not helped when a laryngological examination subjected him to a cocaine spray: 'I am one of a minority for whom cocaine is undesirable', he wrote in May 1941.[51] Now, invited by his influential Oxford crony Richard Livingstone, he became president of the Classical Association; but that did not dispel a mournfulness that owed something to Woolf's death, and something (he confessed to Hayward) to the apparently endless wartime 'General Situation, the feeling that this must go on and on, that we shall be sold to America, that civilisation is going to pot whatever happens, though nothing could be worse than a world ruled by Germans.'[52] Not everyone agreed. In Italy, Pound, enthusiastically broadcasting on Mussolini's state-sponsored radio, was corresponding sympathetically with pro-Nazi propagandist William Joyce, 'Lord Haw-Haw'. Pound had realised during April that in sections of the American media he was ' "charged with fascism" '.[53] Commenting in print on Pound's 'sillier sallies' a few months earlier, Tom had written, 'I only fear the apparition of Mr Pound's imaginary hero, the Strong Man.'[54] Wartime censorship added to the distance between the two poets, but each kept an eye on the other's course. Harshly tested, their friendship endured.

Tom knew he should pay public tribute to Virginia Woolf, but the right words remained elusive; sending Leonard an 'uncorrected text' on 10 May, he feared it exhibited 'a kind of pomposity' that was 'abhorrent'.[55] In *Horizon* his piece called her 'a great writer' and expressed 'desolation at the loss of a friend'. Saluting her 'qualities of personal charm and distinction, of kindness and wit', it stated, 'Virginia Woolf was the centre, not merely of an esoteric group, but of the literary life of London.' With her death 'a whole pattern of culture' was 'broken'; but there was also a profoundly personal and more-than-personal 'damage' that 'cannot be communicated'.[56] Loss, damage, and the struggle to communicate would also form part of 'Little Gidding'.

Late spring and early summer saw him still dividing his time between Shamley Wood, Oxford, and London where he lunched with Dobrée at the Oxford and Cambridge Club. Tom was trying, yet again, to find work for ailing psychologist Nikolai Iovetz-Tereshchenko. Encouraged by Faber and Read, he decided to publish Henry Treece's poetry collection. He met people well informed about the war, including Sir Robert Vansittart. He wrote to the usual range of authors, would-be authors, and never-to-be authors, while trying to convince Rowse not to make too much trouble about a book cover. Faber director Richard de la Mare was, Tom cautioned Rowse, 'the greatest living producer of books'.[57] It was now over fifteen years since Geoffrey Faber had hired Tom, whose loyalty to the firm was hard to overstate. The Blitz and associated struggles brought them closer as, like so many others working in London, they struggled to maintain their business amid devastation. In a sonnet, 'To T. S. Eliot', George Barker (then in America) imagined Tom as 'a living martyr', who sat, writing, 'Expecting a bomb or angel through the roof / Cold as a saint in Canterbury Cathedral'.[58]

Enid Faber had gone with her son, 'small Tom', to see the blitzed City district earlier that year, surveying 'the extinction of Paternoster Row'. Geoffrey was impressed by her account of the 'sad, yet impressive sight' of 'St Paul's barely touched – a bit of window gone, no more – and standing magnificent, majestic, in a sea of almost utter desolation.' Suddenly, the buildings where Faber had learned the rudiments of the publishing trade, 'Amen Corner', were 'no more'.[59] There were times, Tom explained to Emily that April, 'when the war submerges everything', and he thought his new poem would 'bear some traces of the experiences of the last eight months'.[60] In early May the Faber offices came close to being destroyed during a raid in which, as Geoffrey Faber told Morley, 'the 2 houses opposite us on the other side of Thornhaugh Street were burned out'. Shocking and deadly, the carnage was also spectacular. From his home, Faber had been looking out 'from the top floor windows, which give a pretty wide view over London'. He saw 'a sort of sea of fire beyond the trees and the church spire, with a gigantic cloud of smoke billowing up into the clear sky in brilliant moonlight. And somehow so beautiful that it was quite hard to realize what it meant or to feel unhappy.'[61] A few days later, Tom wrote to Emily, uncertain about the future, but sure he wanted 'to see the horror through', and not 'be absent from London altogether'.

I want to share something of what London and my friends there experience. The one thing that would be unendurable would be to be wholly outside of things: and I don't imagine for a moment that there is any heroism about this. I miss you very much – but I don't want to be in America, and I don't want you here – I want you and peace, with a world in which it is still possible to do some good and to enjoy simple things. And I want to finish my poem.

Your loving
Tom[62]

His earliest surviving notes towards 'Little Gidding' are undated, but by 20 May he had a draft of 'the first part', then was 'stuck'.[63] By the time he spent the long weekend of Sunday 1 June 1941 with Hayward in Cambridge, looking 'very haggard and washed-out and dispirited', with a 'feverish cold', he had 'got as far as making a rough, preliminary draft'.[64] He told Emily on 29 June he had been looking up 'something in Dante', and had 'toilsomely drafted a section II'.[65] On 4 July he wrote to Browne about 'struggling to get on paper the fourth of my series of poems'.[66] He sent Hayward (then editing a selection of Tom's prose) a substantial draft 'fragment', though not the 'whole', on 7 July; and that same day he informed Emily the poem was 'now about 4/5 drafted'.[67] Scribbled on a sheet torn from a pad used for drafting 'The Dry Salvages', the earliest jottings had made it clear that Dante, the dead, and the invocation of God were very much in Tom's mind, and that, moving beyond the elements of his three recent long poems, the new work would focus on fire.

Winter scene. May.

Lyric – air earth water end & &
daemonic fire. The Inferno.
They vanish, the individuals, and
our feeling for them sinks into the
flame which refines. They emerge
in another pattern & recreated &
reconciled
redeemed, having their meaning together not apart, in a unison
which is of beams from the central
fire. And the others with them
contemporaneous.
Invocation to the Holy Spirit.[68]

These notes' first two sections clearly relate to part one and the beginning of part two of the eventual poem. They indicate that it will move from infernal, through purgatorial, to a sort of paradisal, unifying fire. Though he professed himself 'worried and diffident and depressed', even the way Tom wrote about his efforts on 'Little Gidding' as an attempt to 'wring victory out of defeat' indicates its overall trajectory.[69] Written at a point when, in mid-1941, defeat seemed possible – and perhaps probable – and when Dantescan 'daemonic fire' had ravaged London, the poem moves towards a spiritual unity representing victory over the sunderings of death and conflict. He envisaged it as the culmination of his 'Kensington Quartets'.[70] Later, perhaps because it sounded too restrictively upper class, he abandoned that title; but it came from the place where as churchwarden and ARP warden, he had known worship, destructive fires, and threats of fire.

'I have finished the poem', he told Emily on 14 July, 'but am very doubtful about it.'[71] He would consult Hayward. Needing to write blurbs, to draft a preface for Anne Ridler's *Little Book of Modern Verse*, and to choose Kipling poems for a new selection: all these things had slowed him down, as had a visit from Robert Sencourt, who arrived in a borrowed car and 'whisked' him off to tea at the grand country house where Sencourt was staying with aristocratic hosts.[72] By 21 July, in a letter to Ted Spencer, Tom was describing the 'fourth, I hope final, quartet' as 'just written'; he was also about to have 'most of' his teeth extracted under general anaesthetic and replaced with dentures.[73] Less alarming was Disney's *Fantasia* in the cinema; he told Emily he liked parts, but the use of Beethoven's Sixth Symphony was 'cheap and vulgar'. Overall, 'Disney, or the Disney Corporation, has a very remarkable imagination, but it is not the imagination of an adult.'[74] Very soon afterwards, having missed an April Moot meeting through illness, he participated committedly in an Oxford Moot on 1–3 August. Discussions ranged from 'Christian archetypes' to education, 'division of consciousness', and the role of Christian imagination. Tom championed the need not just to 'establish the primary virtues but to give them a significant pattern for a particular people as an aim and centre of belief'. He listened as Mannheim contended that a crucial 'difficulty was that Christian values were based on withdrawal from society whereas the problem of the modern man was the use of power'. In response to another paper, Tom cautioned against 'expecting too much' from 'poets and philosophers' whose 'illumination' could take 'peculiar and perverse forms'. Nevertheless, for the following Moot he agreed 'to write a paper on the "Revival of Christian Imagination"'.[75]

In some senses 'Little Gidding' was the apogee of his effort to bring new life to Christian imagination. Unifying divided elements to provide a 'significant pattern', it balanced withdrawal from society (as Nicholas Ferrar's family had withdrawn to their rural Christian community) with participation in contemporary events – most obviously the London Blitz. It asserted the importance both of historical patterns and of belief for a particular people. In summer 1941 as he passed from Oxford to Shamley Wood, then to London (staying with the Fabers in Hampstead), then to 'the Hertfordshire seat of R. de la Mare Esq' at Much Hadham, and then, in late August, to the Fabers' Welsh house at Tyglyn, Tom worked on small changes to his poem.[76] He sought to bring together not just themes but symbols which had recurred throughout the earlier quartets. So, for instance, he explained to Dobrée on 6 August, 'There are really three roses in the set of poems: the sensuous rose, the socio-political Rose (always appearing with a capital letter) and the spiritual rose: and the three have got to be in some way identified as one.'[77]

Not all readers read the poems so diagrammatically, but Tom's ability to combine intuitive word-music and imagery with his powerful analytical imagination's architectonic power remained a strength. Few would disagree that his poem's final rose emblematises remarkable unification. Working on the poem, he remained attentive to practical matters: hoping to have his Kipling selection published in time for Christmas purchasing, he advanced its introduction. Kipling was 'patriotic', an unusual sort of 'Tory', an 'alien' whose 'foreignness . . . gave him an understanding of the English countryside'. Kipling's 'pagan vision' offered, too, 'insight into a harmony with nature which must be re-established if the truly Christian imagination is to be recovered by Christians'. Putting much of himself into it, Tom completed this essay, adding to it the date of his own fifty-third birthday.[78] None of this distracted him unduly from seeking work for the hard-up Dylan Thomas as well as for the young Ceylonese Tamil editor of *Poetry London*, Meary James Thurairajah Tambimuttu, whose planned anthology, *Poetry in Wartime*, Tom was encouraging – and which Faber & Faber published in 1942. That volume contained none of Tom's own work. 'I don't write about the war' he would maintain in 1943, though he backtracked somewhat: 'if feelings and emotions due to the war come into my verse of themselves, that is all right.'[79] Thinking Mary Trevelyan's knowledge of Ceylon and of London's overseas students might be of use to Tambimuttu, Tom put him in touch with her.

September 1941 also saw him composing a *Christian News-Letter* while Oldham was on holiday. Tom wrote about Christian education in Britain and Christian virtues, and set out *'patriotism'* as 'fundamentally a virtue', but his opening section featured 'The Christian Education of France'. As 'one who has never been an admirer of Republican government in France', he showed some sympathy with the right-wing Vichy slogan *'Famille,*

Travail, Patrie' which sought to replace *'Liberté, Egalité, Fraternité'*, but generally he thought Vichy ideology represented something 'worse than that from which it reacts'. Pointedly, responding to a *Times* piece on 'A "New Order" for France' which had dealt with 'The Vichy Substitute for Democracy', Tom stated that

> What gives us the gravest anxiety, is the statement (in the *Times* article cited) that 'Jews have been given a special status, based on the laws of Nuremberg, which makes their condition little better than that of bondsmen.' Anti-semitism there has always been, among the parties of the extreme Right: but it was a very different thing, as a symptom of the disorder of French society and politics for the last hundred and fifty years, from what it is when it takes its place as a principle of reconstruction.[80]

He hoped the 'French ecclesiastical hierarchy' would organise 'protest against such injustice' and that, if France threw off German rule, these measures should be abandoned.

In March the *Christian News-Letter* had reported that while French 'Protestant Churches' might 'collaborate with the Vichy Government', nevertheless several courageous pastors 'have declared themselves opposed to anti-Semitic activities, and have given strong support to relief measures in aid of non-Aryan refugees from Germany in internment camps in southern France'.[81] More recently, the *News-Letter* of 30 July had run a front-page piece on 'Anti-Jewish Feeling', though its defence of the Jews (who *'qua* Jews' could 'be exceedingly irritating') was backhanded, and it regarded 'Christianity ' as 'the achievement' of Jewish 'pioneer spiritual pilgrimage'.[82] In a 'correction' to Tom's Vichy France piece, the scholar Alfred Zimmern pointed out that French Protestants had already protested against Vichy antisemitic laws.[83]

'10,000 JEWS ARRESTED IN PARIS', *The Times* reported on 22 August. In two days '10,000 persons who could not prove they were Aryans were arrested and sent to concentration camps'. On 11 September the same paper described 'the preventive arrest of about 120 Jews belonging to the liberal professions' in Paris. They were to 'be detained in a concentration camp'.[84] Nevertheless, when the Reverend James Parkes, a leading British Anglican expert on antisemitism, submitted a supplement on 'The Jewish Question To-Day' to *The Christian News-Letter*, Tom told Oldham, 'I do not feel happy about it, because it seems to me better to leave the Jewish problem alone than to deal with it unsatisfactorily.'[85] Parkes's clear-minded piece summarised logical arguments against antisemitism, scrutinising illusory ideas of 'The Jewish Problem' and practical difficulties; most pointedly, it stated,

> No man knows what Jewish casualties as a result of the Nazi occupa-tion of Europe may have risen to be before the domination is destroyed. To say that the figures have passed the million mark already is only speculation.[86]

The Nazis' Wannsee Conference, formalising a masterplan for mass extermination of Jews, was still some months off; smaller-scale extermina-tions were already underway in eastern Europe and Russia, but *The Times* published no news of these, and it is unlikely Tom knew about them. Yet, like so many contemporaries, he knew Jews were at extreme risk: 'Die the soldiers, die the Jews', as MacNeice had put it in a poem dated 'July 1940'.[87] Moreover, as Tom's letter to Oldham indicates, he perceived 'popular anti-semitism' was a domestic as well as a foreign problem. His maintaining in September 1941 with regard to Parkes's paper that 'This is primarily a reli-gious, not a racial problem' was wrong-headed. His assertion that 'the problem' pertained not to 'true Jews' but to 'half-Europeanised Jews who have lost their faith without adopting any other' hints he was still stuck in the frame of mind of *After Strange Gods*. Trying to be penetrating and sub-tle in his analysis, he missed the point; or, more invidiously, he revealed that underneath his arguments there remained, despite denials, a deep-seated antisemitism he had harboured since childhood:

> To suggest that the Jewish problem may be simplified because so many will have been killed off is trifling: a few generations of secu-rity and they will be as numerous as ever.[88]

Tom's objections to publishing Parkes's paper were over-ruled by Old-ham and other members of the *Christian News-Letter*'s editorial committee. The piece appeared on 10 October.

Mary Hutchinson's husband had been ill. Her son had narrowly missed drowning in the war at sea. She reproached Tom for not keeping in touch. Tom assured her she was 'as firmly fixed' in his 'affection and regard as ever', protesting he had 'no social life' of his own beyond professional con-tacts, and, with, 'no place of my own', spent his time shuttling between the Mirrlees, Faber, and de la Mare households. In late September he had been at Oxford for meetings, then in London, then lecturing in Bristol with a 'Sunday at Wells' with the Underhills, and, afterwards, at Shamley Wood, preparing for forthcoming Durham and Newcastle trips; on his northern excursion he 'was treated to a blizzard: snow, hail, rain, sleet and wind: however, about 25 clergy turned up to hear me talk about Christian Education'.[89] His protested busyness rang characteristically true, but just as typical was his determination to refine his new poem, even if sometimes he felt guilty to be so engaged in the middle of a war.

In May the US government had established an Office of Civilian Defense, preparing for wartime emergencies. Emily hoped to enrol in such work. She was trying again to encourage Tom to visit the States. Citing wartime restrictions, he reminded her 'how difficult that is'.[90] That October he failed to cable her on her birthday, having forgotten his pocketbook when he went out; but he recalled fondly earlier times when they had celebrated her birthday in England. His life of meetings, editorial work, and other commitments did not let up. He was conscious, too, he had agreed to discuss *The Duchess of Malfi* – a drama of 'spiritual terror' – on the BBC's Indian Service ('blackchat', he called it to Hayward), and in November to address overseas students at Student Movement House 'for Mary Trevelyan'.[91] At her instigation, he wrote to Horace Kallen in the States, requesting help for a Viennese Jewish refugee, John Amon. Tom enjoyed seeing 'Mary' (he no longer called her Miss Trevelyan) several times in late 1941, and engaged readily in more 'blackchat' with her 'Gold Coast Students'.[92] He mentioned to Emily that he would talk to them 'on Culture'.[93]

Early December brought an 'all-day meeting' in Surrey with Maurice Reckitt, editor of *Christendom*, and other members of the Chandos Group associated with Mairet's *New English Weekly*.[94] In advance, Tom drafted notes on 'culture', which he copied to Mary Trevelyan as a gift. She had been collecting his work, but some of her collection had been stolen. 'Culture', he argued, did not belong to 'a privileged class', yet neither was it 'shared equally by all'; 'the problem of culture is at bottom a religious one, only it is the problem of a universal religion in a particular place'.[95] Attempts to theorise both 'culture' and 'education' increasingly preoccupied him. Richard Livingstone, who sometimes hosted his Oxford visits, had recently published *The Future of Education*, as Tom acknowledged in a December letter to *The Times* championing an 'Education' that included ancient Greek.[96] Preparing his paper for a Moot in Oxford on 19–22 December, he apologised for a contribution less substantial than others; his 'Letter' to Oldham argued 'that the Imagination is essentially religious' and that 'as the religious imagination atrophies, the imagination *tout court* disappears also'.[97] His vision of fusing imaginative and religious life was nowhere more manifest than in 'Little Gidding'. The emphases of the Moot and *Christian News-Letter* on developing small Christian groups, seeking religious unity even with the faithful in enemy countries, and sustaining faith throughout difficult times all accord with that summative poem.

However, before 'Little Gidding' was refined to his satisfaction, the international power-balance shifted. Having attacked Russia that summer, in violation of Hitler's non-aggression pact with Stalin, Nazi forces were besieging Moscow and Leningrad despite heroic Soviet resistance throughout the bone-chilling Russian winter. More immediately apparent to Britons was news of 7 December's Japanese attack on Pearl Harbor. The United States was suddenly at war. Tom heard about blackout preparations on America's Pacific and Atlantic coasts. 'I fear too', he wrote to Emily on 8 December, 'that the Japanese will prove free from even such scruples in the conduct of warfare as the Germans possess.'[98] On Christmas day news reached Shamley Wood of 'the (not unexpected) collapse of Hong Kong' to invading Japanese forces.[99] The expanding war, already more than two years old, would be protracted. Tom feared it might last another 'five years'.[100]

Not for the first time, though, over the Christmas period the Mirrlees household provided insulation from world affairs. Having relished his share of 'a fine turkey', Tom recounted to Hayward a catalogue of his Christmas presents. These included 'a box of Caledonia oatcakes and a bit of Dunlop cheese; a box of cigars; from two different sources, 700 cigarettes; three boxes of Chilean matches; a blotter; a honeycomb and also a pot of honey; and three neckties'. Where once he had tallied up his activities to his mother, impressing her with his industry, now he did so with proud weariness to Hayward, Emily, Mary Hutchinson, and other intimate correspondents, partly to excuse his seeing them infrequently or not at all. He wrote to Hayward in Cambridge just after Christmas:

> I am now faced with (1) a translation prize for *Message*, the Belgian periodical (translations from Verhaeren, Michael Roberts and myself and a Belgian being the judges); (2) making selections from Saroyan; (3) writing an article; (4) reading manuscripts. I am afraid that owing to (1) the W. P. Ker Lecture in Glasgow in February (2) writing the Classical Association address, I shall not get to Cambridge until the middle of April [. . .][101]

Such listings concealed the life he suppressed. Vivien, still cared for in her private asylum and reported by her brother in early 1941 as 'extremely wretched & tottery, but otherwise sensible & normal', goes unmentioned, though Enid Faber seems to have continued to visit her, and after Vivien's mother died in April 1941 Tom liaised with Maurice Haigh-Wood and lawyers about matters of 'probate'.[102] Thoughts of Emily he kept largely to himself except in correspondence with her; he suggested that now their letters might be subject to American as well as British censors, 'so that you will have to be careful'.[103] Determinedly, she had indicated to him again that he should not 'interfere' with her religion, and he acknowledged that.[104] Sometimes seen as sharp and stand-offish, she was finding the institutional politics at Smith hard to cope with. Her most loyal students (at least one of whom, supervised by Emily, wrote a dissertation on Tom's work) loved to recall how at a Valentine's Day party in Smith's Laura Scales House when guests were invited to come 'as a book', Emily (wearing a pale-green dress and looking 'imperiously' into a hand-held silver mirror) had made a dramatic entrance dressed as Edith Wharton's 1934 autobiographical account of bygone sophistication, *A Backward Glance*; but the dining table in Laura Scales House at which Emily habitually ate was one that many people avoided, put off by her fastidiousness over food, and by what some students and colleagues perceived as her disdain.[105] Not everyone appreciated her allusions to her special poet friend. Like Emily, who had grown used to living alone, Tom found it challenging to fit into other people's routines. His lack of a permanent home, though he could make a joke of it, contrasted markedly with the position of work colleagues such as de la Mare and Faber (whose families were constantly kind to him), while it heightened his fellow feeling for that displaced person, Hayward, and, to a degree, for Emily. However nice friends or relatives were, Tom grew irritable if deprived of privacy, and was pleased to think she felt likewise.

At work he signed up Edwin Muir, whose poems he had long appreciated, for the poetry list. Tom was doing further broadcasting, had been recruited to yet another group (the Sword of the Spirit) 'to maintain the Christian tradition', and was considering trying to join the Garrick Club, an exclusive all-male establishment bastion in London.[106] He warmed towards proposals from George Hoellering, 'a plausible Austrian refugee', to film *Murder in the Cathedral*, and had accepted a British Council invitation to lecture in neutral Sweden that spring.[107] By early 1942 the height of London's Blitz had passed; cultural life continued defiantly among the ruins. Tom lunched with Faber agricultural writer Lord Lymington; with Kenneth Clark and his wife Elizabeth; and with Henry Moore whose remarkable Blitz drawings of people sheltering in London Underground stations had been exhibited the previous year. Exiled Czech composer Vilem Tausky was commissioned by the PEN Club to produce incidental music for a setting of 'East Coker'. Around the time Tom was seeing through the press Tambimuttu's *Poetry in Wartime*, at the urging of remarkable Indian barrister Cornelia Sorabji, he wrote in February his 'short epigrammatic poem', 'To the Indians who Died in Africa', for a Red Cross anthology to aid 'the Indian Troops Comfort Fund'. Though Tom the admirer of Kipling and sympathiser with British imperialism might use casually racist language in private, in this public work he consulted fastidiously lest mention of such things as a 'graveyard' might offend 'devout Moslems, or others'.[108] The piece – which he regarded as verse, rather than poetry – comes from his lifelong interest in India, but draws, too, on his Kiplingesque awareness of displacement: 'Every country is home to one man / And exile to another.'[109]

In late February, fortified (he explained to Hayward) with 'sandwiches and a small flask containing some rum, which was useful and cordial for an unheated carriage', and clad in 'my overcoat, gloves, and a small skull cap called I believe a beret', he took a train north to lecture at Glasgow University. He lodged there with his host, fellow Moot member, Sir Hector Hetherington, in the Principal's House in Professors' Square, Gilmorehill, and was conducted around the soaring Victorian Gothic campus by the formidable 'Professor Fordyce (Professor of Humanity, that is, Latin)'. Glasgow and, particularly, nearby Clydebank and Greenock had been bombed intensively in 1941; but, as in London, wartime sufferings intensified hunger for cultural nourishment. Tom was to speak in the historic Humanity Classroom, which held 200 people, but such was demand for his lecture on 'The Music of Poetry' that its venue became 'the Chemistry Lecture Room (capacity 500)'.[110] His audience included Hugh MacDiarmid, who was then working in a Clyde shipyard. Tom began by acknowledging that wartime made it 'almost impertinent, even as a man of letters, to concern oneself with a purely literary subject', but his focus on poetic music was intense. Admitting that a poet 'is always trying to defend the kind of poetry he is writing', he hinted – in his mentions of listening to Yeats's voice, of poetic idioms going 'out of date', of the need to vary 'intensity' in 'a poem of any length', and in other ways – at his own recent work. 'There are possibilities of transitions in a poem comparable to the different movements of a symphony or a quartet.' He confessed inability 'to retain the names of feet and metres', and serious reservations about the usefulness to a poet of 'the analytical study of metric', but the heart of his lecture emphasised shifting relationships – across history and within poems – between 'musical elaboration' and 'speech'.[111]

After his Glasgow lecture, he stayed for a short time with George Blake in Dollar, 'a comely and dignified little Scotch town, centred about the Academy, with a Burn purling down the high street'.[112] Soon, liking the Blakes and their surroundings, the poet who had grown used to the

Mirrlees family reflected, 'I have a peculiar *tendre* for everything Scotch which psychology may be able to explain but I can't.'[113] Blake had prepared his eight-year-old daughter Sally for the visit of this 'important man', who presented her with *Old Possum's Book of Practical Cats*, inscribing it from 'Tom Possum'. As a treat, he read aloud to Sally – not from the *Cats* poems but from Uncle Remus stories, putting on a Southern American accent. Disliking this, she began to cry. Decades later, she reflected he had 'put the enjoyment of his own performance above the sensibilities of his young listener'.[114] When he read to the children of Michael Roberts and Janet Adam Smith, his performances had an almost 'ritual' quality; he would be assigned a special chair as the children clustered round.[115] Other godchildren, including the young Morleys to whose family magazine he contributed, adored him; young Susanna Morley regarded him as 'a big brother'.[116] In characteristic acts of private generosity, he helped pay school fees for Polly Tandy's daughter Alison, and offered help to 'the Waif' Omar Pound, whose 'mischievous parent' was the supporter of an enemy regime.[117] But Tom's sense of how to behave with the young was not infallible.

When alone, he felt 'heavy sadness' as he pondered 'the present state of affairs, especially in the Pacific'. He worried 'mental tension' was affecting his writing, including letters to Emily, whom he cautioned against too much war work.[118] As he aged and his fame preceded him everywhere, his prose style grew more ponderous. Many of his early essays had been book reviews and other journalism, but for years now he had been asked for set-piece lectures; increasingly he could sound like a grandee addressing grandees. In April, defending the civilising power of Latin and Greek, he confessed at Cambridge in his Classical Association presidential address – 'The Classics and the Man of Letters' – that he could not provide the exact source for one of his references: 'I read this in one of the periodicals which are found in the waiting-rooms of certain experts in applied science; and having neglected to make a note of the passage before being summoned to my professional appointment, I cannot quote chapter and verse.'[119] Perhaps his hearers smiled when they realised he meant a dentist's waiting room.

His celebrity and acumen, however, were clearly valued by the British Council. Following publication of his poems in Swedish translation, they had him travel in 'flying suit and harness' from Scotland to Sweden in late April for a five-week tour. His base was Stockholm's Grand Hotel where, traditionally, Nobel Prize-winners were entertained. Then, heading for Uppsala, Lund, Strängnäs and elsewhere for readings and lectures, he met writers, journalists, royalty, clerics, publishers. Highlights included a theatre visit to see *Gustav Vasa*; Tom 'sat next to a newspaper editor who is notoriously in the pay of the Nazis' as together they watched this 'historical play by Strindberg which seems to be modelled on Shakespeare's historical plays but also contains several neurotic Swedish characters who are not very Shakespearian'.[120] By the time he returned to London, 'exhausted but not wrecked', in late May, he had been widely interviewed in the Swedish media, and had encountered British and American diplomats, one of whom gave him a letter of introduction to J. G. Winant, the recently appointed American ambassador in London. Recasting his Glasgow lecture, Tom had told the Swedes 'language' was the 'instrument' of 'civilization'. In a gesture of homage, he pointed out, 'When most poets, even great ones, would have been repeating themselves, or silent, Yeats was still inventing and exploring.'[121] Reflecting on his Swedish exploits, he wrote to Henry, 'What is accomplished by this sort of cultural warfare is impossible to say: but it [is] a part of total warfare which one must, as an individual, accept one's part in.'[122] He was not cheered by having to 'grind out' a July '*Christian News Letter* for Oldham', in which he turned again to 'education'.[123]

Gradually, he drew closer to Mary Trevelyan. The previous year, with his support, Faber & Faber had signed up her account of work at Student Movement House and her 1937 'journey round the world'.[124] Her short book *From the Ends of the Earth* communicates her intrepid spirit, religious commitment, and organisational zest. By the time it had appeared on 2 April, Tom and its author were already engaged in occasional warily flirtatious exchanges. On his side, he clearly welcomed a certain closeness, but not, evidently, a sexual relationship. Had he really not noticed the possibility of double entendres when, in February, countering her accusation of formality, he sent an oddly worded reply?

The stiffness, perhaps, is native Calvinism: it is a handicap which I cannot overcome. I subscribe myself, in the most limp and flaccid tones of which I am capable, and in a melancholy voice,

Your respectful
T.S.E.[125]

By March he was telling her he 'would ring up to suggest an evening', though he 'could not permit myself anything so pleasant during Holy Week'.[126] By late June, as 'your faithful and humble friend Tp', he was giving her a litany of his engagements. Tired out, he was 'going to the New Forest to recuperate', but hoped to 'induce' her 'to have lunch or dinner' thereafter.[127] In the New Forest he dutifully produced verses for a forthcoming American anthology, *London Calling*. 'A Note on War Poetry' is, in effect, about his inability to compose 'war poetry' to order.[128] By late July, writing to Hayward, he mentioned Mary in a postscript as 'this indefatigable woman' whom he would 'have to take to dine' before, 'still pottering with *Little Gidding*', he headed north for an August holiday with the Blakes in Dollar and a visit to Janet Adam Smith's family in Penrith.[129]

Mary Trevelyan found him fascinating, and (though partly she concealed the fact) was falling in love with him. Before long, he would become a 'Vice-President' of her Student Movement House.[130] She had heard stories about his life with Vivien. He informed her he had experienced 'close and confined association with the demented', but maintained a reticence and kept at a certain emotional distance.[131] On occasion, with jocularity, he sought her assistance in dealing with difficult people, but behind her back he joked about her tenacious interest in him. Emily remained his principal female correspondent. With her (ostensibly thinking of her ageing Uncle John) he had been discussing how 'one has to keep in mind that the person one knew in the past is the real person, and now, at best, only partly present'.[132] He still told Emily how much he thought about her, treasuring her letters and photographs. Yet when Mary (to whom he did not mention Emily) was out of touch, he missed hearing from her. In early September he sent her 'a nice sheet of paper & a good envelope' to encourage correspondence; and by the middle of that month, conspiring with her to help an Indian academic, he was infusing his practical-minded prose with doggerel verse, struggling to find rhymes for 'Trevelyan'.[133]

By this time, 'Little Gidding' was nearing publication. Sharing drafts with Hayward, Faber, and others, Tom was unusually uncertain about its worth. He might 're-write' it again, he had told Emily on 1 June.[134] The section causing most trouble was the second, largely in Dantescan terza rima. He had been reading Laurence Binyon's ongoing translation of Dante into an English variation of terza rima, and had offered 'minor suggestions' about Binyon's *Paradiso*; but he had worried his own poem lacked 'some acute personal reminiscence' which, though 'never to be explicated', might 'give power from well below the surface'. Similar anxieties underlie his 'Note on War Poetry' which ponders how 'private experience at its greatest intensity' may become 'universal'.[135] He sent Hayward a 'rescension of Part II' of 'Little Gidding' on 17 August, but ten days later was still unhappy. He was anxious that 'the visionary figure' who 'will no doubt be identified by some readers with Yeats though I do not mean anything so precise as that' was not to be thought of as in 'Hell', but rather to be associated with the poets in Dante's 'Purgatorio'.[136] He also explained that the source of the lines including 'All shall be well' (apparently pointing towards a sense of paradise) was medieval mystic Julian of Norwich.[137] That phrase also resembles some of Tom's 'ALL WELL' wartime telegrams to Emily. Christopher Ricks and Jim McCue tellingly point out, too, that it is very close to 'a habitual phrase of Winston Churchill's, occurring dozens of times in his wartime speeches', and which both Tom and Hayward used in this period.[138]

As he completed 'Little Gidding', he worried not just about war but also about Emily's health; ill with an as yet undiagnosed ailment, she faced possible hospitalisation, and was feeling the strain as Smith College proposed asking external assessors to evaluate staff. Might she lose her job? Like him, she was tired. She decided to take a sabbatical. His way to recharge was a 'week of almost complete silence' in the New Forest near the Beaulieu River.[139] By September, though, his poem was ready, he thought, to join the others in due course. He accepted Hayward's advice that having 'Kensington' in the sequence's title would be too private a reference, but Tom was attached to the term 'quartet'. 'It suggests to me the notion of making a poem by weaving in together three or four superficially unrelated themes: the "poem" being the degree of success in making a new whole out of them.'[140] As the culmination of his series, 'Little Gidding' was also the poem whose music most directly articulated wartime experience, even though it looked also towards Dante and towards the English Civil War so closely linked to Ferrar's Little Gidding community.

Freighted with awareness of 'the dead' and the Blitz atmosphere of 'Dust in the air suspended', 'Little Gidding' presents in its second part a pre-dawn (Tom had reluctantly relinquished the word 'antelucan') patrol through urban streets.[141] Blending Dante's tone and imagery with a memory of Herbert Read's poem 'To a Conscript of 1940' which features dialogue between living and dead speakers, this extended passage draws on Tom's own experience of nocturnal ARP patrols and on a feeling, not uncommon in wartime London, that (as Kathleen Raine put it) 'we ourselves are ghosts'.[142] So, after a warplane ('the dark dove with the flickering tongue') passes over, the speaker meets a 'familiar compound ghost' reminiscent of 'some dead master'. As the speaker assumes 'a double part', this ghost seems to speak through him, revealing that 'Last year's words belong to last year's language / And next year's words await another voice.' Instead of revealing a glorious future, in disclosing 'the gifts reserved for age', this voice reveals that ahead lies suffering that will include

> the rending pain of re-enactment
> Of all that you have done, and been; the shame
> Of motives late revealed, and the awareness

Of things ill done and done to others' harm
Which once you took for exercise of virtue.[143]

This deep personal shame can only be worked through by immersion in 'refining fire', and the poem's fourth part, in which 'The dove descending breaks the air / With flame of incandescent terror', fuses the Christian Pentecostal dove with Blitz imagery, maintaining that the ultimate source of this 'torment' is 'Love'.[144] As the poem nears conclusion, maintaining that 'Every poem' is 'an epitaph', and that 'History is now and England', notes of personal shame and deeply held patriotism are transcended in a vision of how the whole course of a life from childhood onwards might be reinterpreted in an arduous process to achieve a final sense of 'complete simplicity / (Costing not less than everything)'. This leads ultimately to a moment both apocalyptic and paradisal

When the tongues of flame are in-folded
Into the crowned knot of fire
And the fire and the rose are one.[145]

If Tom had worried his poem lacked deep personal underpinning, his worry was unnecessary. Though transfigured, his sense of his life's mistakes, of hurts he had inflicted, of struggles to articulate poetry, and of his wartime experience in a fire-ravaged city nourish the poem. Its title, directing readers to that small community whose own church had been ravaged in a centuries-old fire, helped set 'Little Gidding' apart from personal revelations; but the poet who honoured the small group at Little Gidding was also the contributor to the Christian 'cell' of the Moot, and churchwarden at St Stephen's, Gloucester Road, Kensington. Ultimately the poem's Christianity points towards his belief, even at wartime's height, in a deep, unifying faith. The work's specific origins in his experience serve as reminders that its roots lie not in any sense of impending victory that emerged during later stages of the war, but rather in that earlier awareness that victory was very uncertain. What mattered was facing up to whatever the ultimate meaning of life and love might be. When Tom had written 'Little Gidding', he had stared, like so many others, into the face of extinction.

13

Deaths

IN some senses 'Little Gidding' was what he called in October 1942 'patriotic poetry'.[1] Neither British nor American, its patriotism is particularly
English: 'History is now and England'.[2] Those words, like the imperial
speech of Shakespeare's John of Gaunt equating 'this scepter'd isle' with
'England', and like Rupert Brooke's Great War lines 'there's some corner of
a foreign field / That is for ever England', articulate an English identity politics that resonates across centuries.[3] 'I belong to England', Tom wrote to
Emily that August. His 1942 Scottish holiday heightened that awareness;
even then, he added, 'I don't feel at home in northern England: I regard the
west and East Anglia as my parts, and for something alien prefer to cross
the border, as I really like Scotland and the Scotch very much.'[4] 'Little Gidding' was, too, for many readers, 'poetry arising out of their experience of
war'.[5] Yet its final lines move beyond national identity and conflict to that
transcendent Christian unity which, even during all-out war, remained the
goal of the poet and many of his friends.

After 'Little Gidding' appeared in 15 October's *New English Weekly*, Robert Speaight wrote in the Catholic periodical the *Tablet* that 'only those who
are prepared to accept the fundamental doctrines of Christian asceticism at
a moment when they have never been more unpopular, will receive the profound thought to which the poetry so rigorously conforms'.[6] Yet the work's
appeal was much wider than that. In the literary journal *Scrutiny*, which
Tom had been trying to bolster throughout times of paper shortage, D. W.
Harding, who edited *Scrutiny* alongside F. R. Leavis, concluded his 'Little
Gidding' review by stating that 'it ranks among the major good fortunes of
our time that so superb a poet is writing'.[7] If several reviews were by Tom's
supporters, his poem was also a commercial success: the initial print run of
its Faber pamphlet edition, published on 1 December, ran to 16,775 copies.

Publication of 'Little Gidding' made possible the assembling of Tom's four 'quartets' in book form. Eventually, as *Four Quartets* the poems would appear together in New York from Harcourt, Brace in May 1943, with Faber's British edition following in 1944. So, in publishing terms, the work's reverberations continued throughout the war. As Mary Lee Settle, a young American in 1940s London, recalled, Tom 'had somehow refined what he had to tell us, beyond the banality of disappointment and hopelessness, into a promise like steel. The accepted premise is that little poetry truly reflects World War II. But there is "Little Gidding".'[8] More than ever, too, his work was receiving critical appraisal. A 1942 article about his recent poetry by a young Oxford don, Helen Gardner, gave him 'great pleasure'.[9] Yet with the completion of 'Little Gidding', despite continuing to write verse for the stage and for the page over succeeding years, he ceased in effect to write poetry.

The fate of Yeats – who had created astonishing poetry in old age – would not be his. Instead, that in-folding of 'tongues of flame' at the end of 'Little Gidding' marked a closing up of access to the deepest sources within himself which had powered, profoundly but infrequently, his greatest work.[10] Even while finishing 'Little Gidding', he had worried to Emily in July 1942 that 'war' had 'precipitated' in him 'a phase of middle age' accompanied by 'spiritual aridity' and 'suspension of other feelings'.[11] He hoped to live through this, and move beyond it; but his poetry did not do so. As verse dramatist, writer of measured, thoughtful prose, and as publisher, and lauded, internationally celebrated public man, he would continue to flourish. Yet as poet, except for the readers of some private verses and for the few who cherish 'The Cultivation of Christmas Trees' (his early 1950s 'pot boiler'), his work was done.[12]

The ongoing war allowed little time to take stock, but produced much anxiety. Worried about her job, beliefs, health, and relationships with Tom and her family, Emily was experiencing 'great strain'. Recounting some of his early memories of her, on 27 August, with just the last seven lines of 'Little Gidding' to write, Tom regretted 'there is nothing I can do'. Wartime regulations about sending money abroad meant he could not even help pay for medical 'specialists' Emily needed.[13] Teetering on the edge of breakdown, she accused him of 'deception' in their relationship. He denied this, and grew 'ill' himself. He was concerned, too, that Henry was 'very frail', and Ada, facing a second cancer operation, might require 'a third that will be the end'. He hoped, he assured Emily, 'to come in the autumn of 1943 if an opportunity offers', but 'without any public reason' he could not visit America 'before the end of the war'.[14]

He feared Emily might be showing his letters to other people, particularly her old friends the Thorps: 'I want to continue to feel that I am writing to you alone.' Yet he realised that, eventually, she might dispose of his correspondence; Tom wished none of his 'really private' letters be published 'or made use of in any way for 50 years after my death'. He hated the idea that fears about publication might introduce 'a kind of invisible censorship' into their exchanges.[15] Their correspondence helped bind them together, yet spoke too of isolation and an ongoing impasse. 'I was certainly not repudiating the past or anything that I have felt', he wrote on 13 October, making clear his 'gratitude' to her was 'endless'. 'But when this cannot take its natural conclusion, and at a certain point an absolute moral law comes between, then even that is a quickening which cannot be borne continuously.' Accusing him of being 'self-centered', she had been pressing him again about marriage and divorce. For at least the third time, he explained at length his understanding of his church's position, expressing resentment that she was putting him 'in the strange position of an unwilling lover, whose slowness and hesitancy, perhaps whose cowardice, make it necessary to force a decision!' If Emily still saw him as Prufrockian, he viewed himself as committed to his religion's demands, but felt 'an intolerable and terrifying sense of guilt', worrying he had created 'misunderstanding' between them. 'I am quite ready to agree', he replied, 'that if I could live with you I might become a finer man; but that could hardly happen, alas, if in order to live with you I had to do what I believed wrong.' Conscious of both his 'pain' and hers, he signed his letter 'Your loving and devoted Tom.'[16]

Emily had, her friend and protégée Jeanette McPherrin recalled, a 'most earnest desire to be a good woman'. While she could be captivating on stage and off, she was also prone to 'introspection that led to an increasing preoccupation with her inner world'.[17] Intense introspection was something she shared with Tom; it brought them close, but also created strains, and sometimes they fed off each other's troubles. 'I am very depressed and unhappy', he told her on 20 October, worrying the 'unhappiness' might be long-lasting.[18] Overcome with her own anxiety, Emily had gone to stay with a friend, Lucia Briggs, on Grand Manan island, New Brunswick, Canada. From her seclusion she sent Tom a 'lovely letter', though it took several weeks to reach him.[19] Reading it, he assured her 'my feelings remain always unchanged'. He emphasised, 'you must be sure of my love which no change of aging or maturing can alter'. Yet he also admitted fears about times when 'flowers fade and one suspects that it has all been an illusion'.[20] Earlier, pondering his feeling of being 'homeless', even as he enjoyed visiting the Fabers (who had taken on a substantial country property at Minsted, Sussex) and relished the comforts of life among 'the Scotch Ladies' at Shamley Wood, he confessed to Hayward, 'I seem to be dependent upon a place where I can go and be ill from time to time.'[21] Struggling with ailments and badly fitting dentures, he professed himself 'a wambling old codger'.[22]

His bronchial troubles recurred in the unusually cold winter of 1942–3, and plans for a British Council trip to Reykjavik had to be cancelled. Signing off 'Yours with love, Tom', he explained to 'Darling Djuna' Barnes in America, 'I don't expect to do much brain work of any use this winter, because most of one's energy may go into trying to keep warm.'[23] Nevertheless, as man of letters he edited and introduced a selection of Joyce's prose. In addition to generating innumerable business missives, he corresponded with several family members, and went on writing to Emily (whose health remained uncertain) on average more than once a fortnight for the rest of the war. Worshipping regularly and going to confession with London priest Father Philip Bacon (to whom he inscribed a copy of *The Classics and the Man of Letters*), Tom mulled over the future of Christian education and society, not just at further Moots and similar gatherings, but also in many articles. More mundanely, as one of the few males at Shamley Wood he was called on to climb up a ladder when Mappie Mirrlees locked herself in the bathroom. As he said in another context to Emily that year, 'We all have to present different sides of ourselves to different people'.[24] Yet his tastes in poetry increasingly diverged from those of younger contemporaries: 'I do fear that Dylan Thomas has been up a blind alley, an alley choked with rather rank vegetation of verbiage'. In one mood at least, Tom had 'to go back to the dead to find poetry that I enjoy reading.'[25] Still, receiving a salary increase at Fabers was 'very gratifying'.[26] Writing to Polly Tandy in Dorset, he sent 'Love from Possum who isn't quite dead yet.'[27]

More and more friends were dead, however: not only great contemporaries including Woolf and Joyce, but also less celebrated folk. The fiancé of Faber's daughter Ann was killed in Egypt. Mary Hutchinson's husband, Jack, died in October. Alert to Mary's 'loveableness', Tom worried she might struggle without Jack. Harshly he confided to Hayward 'she has never struck me as a very intelligent woman'.[28] In late 1942 Miss Sunderland-Taylor, owner of Stamford House, died; that Chipping Campden property would pass into other hands, and Tom and Emily might never go back there. He had liked to think of patrician Emily as a Campden 'lady of the Manor'.[29] However, he counselled 'Beloved Emily', 'Only by accepting the past as past is there hope of a future'. Sympathising with her 'struggles', he quoted to her Christina Rossetti's poem 'Uphill': 'the road winds uphill to the very end'.[30] There seemed no let-up. Every day *The Times* reported further wartime losses; each night fire-watchers were on the roof of 24 Russell Square. In the latter part of 1942 a flat next door, into which Faber & Faber had expanded, was refurbished for the use of the company's chairman when in London. Tom was encouraged to use it when he could. By 1943 he was making regular stays there, and, after respite at Shamley Wood and elsewhere, he returned to London fire-watching, often (though he suffered from vertigo) on the roof of the Faber building.

'Is a Christian Society Possible?' was the title of a piece he completed in January 1943. Arguing that 'every culture of the past had had a religious basis' and that 'if our society in the future was to have any cultural pattern at all, it must be a religious pattern', he warned, nevertheless, against 'premature unification of various Christian bodies' since 'unification by minimal belief' would lead simply to 'secularisation'.[31] His article was rejected as insufficiently 'positive' by the American editor of the *Christian Century*, but its argument aligned with his 'Notes towards a Definition of Culture', planned in late 1941 and early 1942 but not published until early 1943 in the *New English Weekly*. Here, alert to tensions between 'modern civilisation' and 'true culture', Tom, still stung by that 1941 *Times* 'leading article' on the 'Eclipse of the Highbrow', wrote about the 'elites' discussed by Karl Mannheim at the Moot and in print, contending 'there is no total culture without a religion'.[32] Elites also interested his sister Ada. 'Who are the true elite?' she asked him in an April 1943 letter; 'I'd like to discuss that with you.'[33] Co-authored with her husband who drew on and updated her 'unpublished papers and notes', Ada's final book would have a section on 'Elites'. Like her brother, she had an Eliot's sense of maintaining cultural 'leadership'.[34]

Early in 1943, broadcasting on Poe – 'very hard to place' and 'not a *typical* American writer' – Tom emphasised that poet's 'power of *incantation*' and how 'strange names he invents take on meaning'. He saluted Poe's unforgettable work in poetry, prose, and 'poetic theory'.[35] Though Tom did not say so, Poe's great theme was death. Having read Poe since childhood, he, too, was brooding on that topic. He attended a requiem Mass for Philip Morrell, who had died on 5 February, five years after Ottoline: 'Ottoline got the kind of Memorial Service that Philip liked, and Philip got the kind Ottoline would have liked', he reflected to Hayward, who had sent a 'kind and sympathetic letter' about Ada. Tom tried to explain how much this sister, whom Hayward had never met, meant to him.

Being nearly twenty years older than I, and having no children of her own, she came to occupy a quasi-parental relation with me (my mother would be 100 this year!) Also she and I have always had more in common than with the rest of our family. She has far more brains than any of the others, and with my grandfather's organising and executive ability combined a more reflective mind, and a capacity of abstraction, coming from the other side of the family. Without being 'masculine' in any way to suggest psychological distortion, she has a capacity for impersonal thought, and for detaching herself from emotion and prejudice, which I have never found in any other member of her sex. So I have always felt a tacit understanding with her, and a more satisfactory relationship, than I have ever found in those of either excitement or friendship with women – in the long run.[36]

As her illness worsened, this sister to whom he felt so attached (and who had often sent weekly letters) signalled she too felt their closeness. 'Dearest Tom', she wrote, not hiding she was dying. She recalled how they had sat together when he was an infant in St Louis, mouthing sounds and rhythms to one another before he learned to talk. Knowing that the war meant they would never meet again, she told him, 'It has been a great stimulus and comfort to me all these years to write and receive letters from the one member of the family who I have believed really respected the sort of life I have chosen to lead.' Then she quoted Tennyson (' "That which drew from out the boundless deep turns again home" '), and signed off 'With the deepest affection'.[37]

He was very grateful to Emily for visiting Ada. Not long before he had heard from his Harvard contemporary Leon Little that Harold Peters ('my oldest friend', he explained to Emily) had died after falling from a dock.[38] Tom found thinking about Ada 'almost too painful'.[39] Writing a lengthy pamphlet directed against the 'fundamentally unsound' unification of churches in India helped occupy his mind, but brought scant emotional consolation.[40] When he travelled north in mid-April to address wartime exiles in Edinburgh's Czech House, one Czech thought Tom resembled 'a stock-broker', reading his lecture 'in a monotonous, emotionless voice, as if it were a balance sheet or financial report to a shareholders' meeting, never lifting his eyes from his notes'.[41] Just a few days earlier in London he read with eleven other poets 'in aid of the French in Great Britain Fund'.[42] Sitting in the front row at the Aeolian Hall were the queen and teenage princesses Elizabeth and Margaret. The girls found it hard to keep straight faces as Tom intoned his work. He confessed to Emily he had wanted to tell Princess Elizabeth 'I was as bored as she was.'[43] The princess's mother recalled him as 'rather lugubrious'. 'Such a gloomy man.'[44]

In the midst of private sorrows he fulfilled his public duties. St Anne's Church in Soho had been substantially destroyed in the Blitz, but the adjoining St Anne's Church House was being set up as a 'centre of evangelization'.[45] Tom joined in the efforts to establish this new centre, with which several writers became involved. Participating in an event there on 6 May 1943, he co-organised, too, at Church House what Philip Mairet, his fellow organiser, recalled as 'a series of conversational classes on the nature of culture'.[46] These helped form the germ of a future book. He also agreed to become English president of a new transatlantic association, Books across the Sea, and president of the recently founded Virgil Society. He lectured to London's Norwegian Institute. He proofed the first British edition of *Four Quartets*. After earlier declining to join the left-wing 1941 Committee, he now joined the Burke Dinner Club, a Conservative dining group, having described Edmund Burke to Hayward in late May as 'an admirable writer' – unlike Matthew Arnold whose 'smug superiority' marked him 'as a plebeian'.[47] Bringing together right-leaning authors and journalists (including Osbert Sitwell and crime-writing journalist Collin Brooks) along with Conservative MPs such as the club's founder Pierse Creagh Loftus and future Attorney General Reginald Manningham-Buller, the Burke Club met initially in private rooms at the Trocadero. Generally, it opposed pressures for nationalisation and a welfare state. Its parliamentarians championed such institutions as private schools, and in succeeding years it was addressed by visiting speakers including Lord Rothermere and Harold Macmillan. Tom's instincts had long tended towards the independent-minded right. He distrusted pressures towards government-controlled centralisation. Joining the Burke Club brought him closer to England's Conservative establishment.

Yet he remained more committed to fundamental principles than to minutiae of party politics. 'Something beyond justice was necessary as a criterion of justice,' he argued at that June's Moot.[48] First principles and correct doctrine mattered most, which was why he opposed any doctrinal fudging that would dilute the identity of a merged South Indian church conglomerating 'Anglicans, Presbyterians, Congregationalists and Methodists'.[49] This was also why he disliked plans for large post-war cultural bureaucracies homogenising the work of individual artists, cultures, and nations. He advocated instead post-war European reconstruction that brought cultures into dialogue, without threatening excellence and distinctiveness. Drawing on his philosophical training and anthropological, sociological, and theological reading, he sought to theorise what 'culture' fundamentally meant. For him, it necessitated a religious basis. Such thoughts would lead in due course to his opposing the concept of UNESCO. More immediately, in the midst of the war, thinking about differences between Scotland, England, and other British Isles cultures, and pondering global cultural differences, he maintained 'No art is more stubbornly national than poetry,' even as he strove to sustain 'some degree of unity in European literature' and a sense of Europe's religio-cultural unity.[50] His conservative attachment to England accompanied, and in part reinforced, his commitment to Catholic Christian ideals.

So, in late summer and autumn 1943, he sent messages of support to magazines and communities seeking to preserve values his *Criterion* had championed. Telling Francophone readers he looked forward to writers participating in the work of restoring '*la culture européenne*', he also assured Portuguese journal *Aventura* that 'no European literature, I am convinced, can long flourish in isolation from the others'; instead, 'the ultimate unity of Europe cannot come through identity of political organisation', but 'from the unity of the Christian Faith'.[51] Repeating this message internationally and locally, he also strove to support Father Cheetham's 'devotion, toil, and courage' at St Stephen's, 'throughout the most difficult period of the war'.[52] And he hoped that poetry, however much developed by 'an *élite*', might come to be treasured by 'the main, and more passive body of readers not lagging more than a generation or so behind', and might have a 'social function'.[53] Something similar had happened to his own earlier poems.

While, in the context of the Indian church, he wrote of needing 'a stern conscience and a sound head' to face 'The peace of death', his sister Ada, who epitomised such qualities, lay unable to 'move without agony' and 'only kept going by strong sedatives'. When she died on 2 October, Tom was left lonelier than ever; he thought it 'hardly a blow', but it marked 'the end of another chapter'.[54] 'The immediate effect', he wrote to Emily on 16 October, 'is simply to make the barrier between life and death seem much thinner than before.'[55] Dutifully, he outlined the part played by 'A healthy ruling class' in the context of 'social responsibility' for Oldham's *Christian News-Letter*, and defended Kipling against charges of antisemitism, but by late 1943 he was complaining to Mary Trevelyan about feeling ill again. After a December week in a nursing home, he confessed to Hayward being 'not altogether sorry' to miss Student Movement House's nativity play performed by Trevelyan along with her 'coons and refugees'.[56]

He might joke about her and her charges, but he liked capable, sympathetic, tenacious Mary. Emily, however, was someone to whom he had felt close for decades, and who had known him long before he became famous. Their shared history had shaped each of them. By now, having left Smith, she had taken a job at Bennett Junior College, a private two-year undergraduate college for women that was attached to a high school in Millbrook, New York; but before long she would transfer to a poorly paid short-term teaching position at Concord Academy. With tender concern she sent an account of Ada's funeral, which she had attended with Henry and Theresa. Tom responded with gratitude and sadness. He was concerned, too, about his sister Margaret, who had been living eccentrically as a recluse in the Hotel Commander, Cambridge, Massachusetts, for the last three years, and who had not visited Ada. Tom informed Emily he thought it best for Margaret to move, eventually, 'voluntarily to some sanatorium (not a mental home)'.[57] He continued to avoid any contact with Vivien, who remained at Northumberland House – an institution that survived unscathed.

Mulling over mortality and wartime, Emily had been arranging what might happen in the event of her own death, and seeking homes for treasured possessions. Following conversations with Willard and Margaret Thorp, she had contacted Princeton University's librarian about placing Tom's letters to her there 'in a safe repository' before their eventual transmission to a 'permanent home', perhaps 'the Bodleian Library'.[58] A friend heard from Theresa that during the war Emily 'would dutifully kiss the members of the Eliot family', behaving 'almost as if she were already an in-law'. Unsettled, Henry wrote to Tom, asking if there were any basis for Emily's behaviour. Henry was taken aback to receive Tom's reply that there was. Angry, Henry tore up this letter, remarking to Theresa, 'Tom has made one mistake, and if he marries Emily he will make another.'[59] Tom felt vexed at Henry, and uneasy, too, about his brother's determined extending of their mother's collection of Eliot manuscripts. To Emily Tom compared this collection to that of Harvard's 'glass flowers'.[60] Its development seemed to him compensation for Henry's career disappointments. At his long-established transatlantic distance, Tom found family relationships hard-going.

As 1944 began Emily had her own disappointments. Unsettled at Bennett Junior College, she would shift now from undergraduate teaching to full-time high-school teaching at Concord Academy. Tom worried about her stamina; but, like others, he wondered, too, if war might end within the year. Though he thought Churchill had 'just the right balance of aristocracy and vulgarity to be a leader of the present age', mass bombing of enemy cities, including Berlin, horrified him.[61] An end to war would permit his long-term return to London (probably to flat-share with Hayward), and let him visit America. Meanwhile, overnighting regularly in Faber's Russell Square apartment, he played his part in fire-watching: 'Geoffrey always gets up and makes cocoa in the raids. We occasionally put on a helmet and peer out through the roof door.'[62] Often the caretaker, Mr Lister, was there to assist, as was a feline companion, Cat Morgan, who had adopted the building as his residence. Tom's impression of early 1944's air raids was that, though 'a strain', 'So far, they have not given me the

impression of severity which the facts seem to justify: but they have tended
to pass to the west – over Kensington and Paddington.'[63] In private, he
reread Emily's letters and went over memories of their time together. He
had destroyed '*other people's* letters' so as to free up a second deed box to
hold those from Emily, though, at her request, he burned some. He assured
her their times in Chipping Campden had been 'the happiest days I have
ever had'; 'since the summer of 1940' the signet ring she had given him had
'not been off my finger'.[64] Each still prized their relationship, but sought to
ensure their affairs were in order in case death came suddenly. When Emily
decided to part with her elkhound Boerre (who died later that year), Tom
felt a 'pang'.[65]

   In public, going about London, he noted damage to the Oxford and
Cambridge Club, and shattered windows at the London Library. Both
were 'out of action' in early March, causing him problems as he worked on
a lecture about Samuel Johnson to deliver in Bangor, Wales.[66] Still, 'the
modern fashion', he told Emily, was 'not for all-night raids, so, if they
come early enough, one can usually get a night's sleep afterwards'.[67] When
in town, he was invited to social events, and felt obliged to take on 'one
small war job after another – I call a "war job" any job which one only
undertakes because of the war – little articles for Allied periodicals, talking
to soldiers (American and Allies), presiding over "Books Across the Sea"',
British Council engagements and other commitments – including literary
and ecclesiastical ones beyond the usual remit of a publisher.[68] Obligingly,
he agreed to talk on Walt Whitman and modern poetry to US soldiers and
others at London's Churchill Club whose lecture programme was co-
directed by Elizabeth Clark, and to defend Kipling against further charges
of 'anti-Semitic feelings', though he signalled concern about involving a
'Jewish representative' in plans for a new national syllabus of religious
instruction.[69] All this impeded his regular commitments: he missed Moot
and Chandos Group meetings, but his participation in the *Christian News-
Letter* and his religious life remained strong. To Mary Trevelyan he wrote
about having 'had in the back of my mind for some time to try to write out
(for myself only) a meditation on the Passion, which I have sort-of framed
in relation to the Rosary'.[70]

   Fed up with being unable 'to stop' for long 'in one place', he still hoped
to share a London flat with Hayward when hostilities ended; but, despite
Russian headway on the eastern front and increasing Allied pressure on
Italy, victory seemed some way off.[71] Southern England saw growing
numbers of American troops readying for possible invasion of France or
Belgium, but success would depend on strategy and weather. Meanwhile,
struggling with his correspondence, Tom grew reproachful sometimes,

'writing into the dark'.[72] He made himself complete an overdue Kipling piece for publication in Russia, as well as (he girned to Hayward in a self-typed letter) 'stuff for the Factious Fogs Frogs I mean', and material for Czech, Norwegian, and other audiences.[73] Constant themes were Europe's cultural unity, underpinned by shared Christian heritage, and the importance of national and regional distinctiveness. With affection, he also conveyed to Hayward news about Geoffrey Faber, 'The Chairman', who, having 'retired to Minsted' for a spell 'with three bottles of whisky and six of gin', was focusing on how 'to continue the educational programme of the Conservative Party'.[74] Tom, enjoying his association with the Burke Club and writing a prickly, penetrating letter to *The Times* about the word 'aristocracy', was often on the chairman's wavelength.[75]

'Nobody realises that I HATE poetry', he complained to 'Dearest Djuna' Barnes that May, after being deluged with poems by English-based American servicemen.[76] The same day he wrote flirtatiously to Mary Trevelyan, asking her not to address him as 'Dear Poet', but instead, perhaps, call him 'Tom Possum' (as 'juvenile friends' did); and he explained to Morley that American librarian-poet Archibald MacLeish ('a douce wee body and very serious') was encouraging him to become Library of Congress 'Consultant in English Poetry' which could involve spending 1945–6 in America.[77] The British edition of *Four Quartets* was scheduled for autumn publication, but Tom was conscious he had nothing to follow 'Little Gidding'. He considered 'trying to write a new play', but was distracted by preparing a 'Virgil Society Address'.[78] Always there were distractions, obligations, worries. MacLeish, who had read transcripts of some of Pound's broadcasts, knew Pound could face 'Treason' charges, and did not keep the knowledge to himself.[79]

'In America, perhaps', Tom mused to Emily, 'this war still seems just a war; but in Europe it is more like going through a long earthquake: you shut your eyes in order to bear it, and wonder how far the world, when you open your eyes on it again, will look like the same place.'[80] Early June 1944 brought commotion. In cloudy London, having just recorded a message about Virgil, Europe, and the 'spiritual kinship, which is Christendom' (broadcast on the BBC's European Service on 5 June to coincide with Allied forces entering Rome), Tom found there were no trains to Shamley Green.[81] Next day brought a lull in the cloudy weather, and the Normandy invasion was launched. 'To celebrate D Day' Tom sent a message to Hope Mirrlees's sister Margot, who liked to collect mementoes of important moments; then, like so many, he awaited news.[82] The king broadcast on the BBC, linking the invasion to 'the will of God'. Exhortations by General Eisenhower and other leaders filled the airwaves. Photographs appeared of

Churchill and the king visiting air headquarters of the Allied Expeditionary Force. Under a one-word headline, 'Attack', 7 June's *Times* reported that, 'Four years after the rescue at Dunkirk of that gallant defeated army without which as nucleus the forces of liberation could never have been rebuilt, the United Nations returned yesterday with power to the soil of France.' On another page, a story headed '"France Stands Up"' quoted General de Gaulle's broadcast of the previous day: 'The supreme battle has begun!' Soon afterwards *La France libre*, a London-based Free French periodical, published Tom's 'What France Means to You'. Written weeks earlier, it recalled how 'the first time I set foot in Europe was on the quay of Cherbourg'. Hymning 'perfect' Paris, it concluded *'je ne puis envisager qu'avec confiance l'avenir de la France'* (I can only contemplate with confidence the future of France).[83]

In the ensuing days, adding contributions to the war effort while pursuing his normal publishing business, he typed a tribute to Chekhov for publication in Russian, and wrote on 'The Responsibility of the Man of Letters in the Cultural Restoration of Europe' for the Norwegian *Norseman* magazine. Tom realised 'the date' of D-Day marked 'an epoch'.[84] His mind, he told Emily, was 'a blank'.[85] Nonetheless, checking proofs of *Four Quartets*, he thought the series improved towards the end. He missed June's Moot because he did not want to leave the Shamley Wood ladies without a male protector while bombing nearby in the wake of D-Day brought a 'close shave' and was 'very rough' – 'like a naval bombardment' he wrote to Mary Trevelyan, hoping she was all right in London and assuring her, though he hated the telephone, 'I'll ring you up.'[86]

'A bomb' in Russell Square 'blasted' the flat at number 23. Tom's wartime secretary, Linda Melton, and his fellow director Morley Kennerley had been at their desks. 'The office can keep going. We have no windows,' Tom wrote to Read from Shamley Wood, 'and they tell me most of the ceilings are down and the doors off, and everything is in a mess. My books are all knocked about and mixed up with plaster.'[87] Nevertheless, he soon returned there to fire-watch with Faber, arriving 'just in time for two fly-bombs [German V1 explosive rockets] to pass over us simultaneously with a thunder storm and a torrent of rain'.[88] Usually Tom was in a three-man fire-watching team; they divided the night into two-and-a-half-hour watches. Still troubled by his congenital hernia, he slept (he explained to Hayward that summer) 'in my truss, in case of sudden blasting, which is not very comfortable'.[89] He was worried, too, lest Mary Trevelyan, whose quarters nearby had large expanses of glass, might be injured. Wartime anxieties brought him closer to her and he confided aspects of his marriage, letting her know that he had written to his solicitors to ask them to find out whether Vivien had not better be moved out of London. Though persisting in his determination to avoid direct contact, he kept in touch with lawyers and others (including Enid Faber, who continued visiting Vivien occasionally), making sure his wife was looked after; in the event, she was not removed from London, and the dangers passed.

In her different way, Mary Trevelyan was as preoccupied as Tom with post-war reconstruction. Frustrated by bureaucratic aspects of her Student Movement House job, she had decided to resign, committing herself to YMCA war work in France and Belgium after the summer, in the wake of Paris's liberation. Tom was eager to see her before she left. Partly at her suggestion, they exchanged watches. She received an advance copy of the Faber *Four Quartets*. She wanted him to meet her mother. To her these were significant actions; and to him also, but not quite in the same way. While this was going on, he made his most notorious publishing decision, rejecting George Orwell's *Animal Farm*. He had been working with Orwell, who was employed by the BBC, on broadcasts. After Cape (advised by the Ministry of Information) had declined the book, Orwell asked Tom for a quick decision. Tom recognised *Animal Farm* as 'distinguished'; it constituted, he told Orwell, 'something very few authors have achieved since *Gulliver*'. However, having so recently and dutifully written for Britain's Soviet allies, and being well connected with the Ministry of Information, Tom doubted whether 'this is the right point of view from which to criticise the political situation at the present time'.[90]

Nazi 'flying bombs' (nicknamed 'buzz bombs') were a 'nuisance' that July: 'more windows broken but fewer houses demolished', he informed Emily.[91] Fire-watching each Tuesday night, he was ashamed to feel 'relief when the sound indicates that the bomb is going to hit somebody else'.[92] By August he was hoping for a holiday, 'as my blood pressure, always low, is now 104, and the brain is not working too rapidly'. However, he had managed to 'grind out my screed on "what is minor poetry?"' – a lecture for Swansea the following month.[93] In early September he claimed to Hayward he had spent a week writing 'no letters' and enjoying 'the *3 Mousquetaires* of Dumas, which I had never read before'.[94] With fighting in France going well, he decided that, once hostilities ceased, he would like to go to America for more than one short visit, but could not commit to the long-term position of poetry consultant in Washington. He told Hayward in late September, 'I think I shall be content to pass another winter at Shamley; and I should certainly prefer to move to London in the early spring than in the winter. The news that there are 900,000 houses in London in need of immediate repair is not encouraging.' Encouraged by Geoffrey Faber, he had 'started a course of massage with his masseuse, the blind lady', and felt it was alleviating his increasingly severe 'writer's cramp'. As well as giving him occasional messages from the spirit world, the eccentric Orcadian masseuse Mrs Millington maintained Tom had 'been starved of sugar for a lifetime – which makes me feel important'; she prescribed 'Sanatogen mixed with glucose.'[95] 'I do believe that these five years have had a withering effect,' he confessed to Emily, 'as well as aging one more rapidly.'[96]

Throughout winter 1944, in addition to his publishing work, he continued delivering BBC 'cultural propaganda', corresponding widely, and giving talks – with regard to Milton he told American soldiers, 'Very few poets have been nice men.'[97] Living at 54 Main Street, Concord, and teaching at Concord Academy, Emily visited Tom's cousin Eleanor from whom he had not heard for five years. Tom sent 'Love and kisses' on Emily's birthday, and made it clear to Mary Trevelyan that he was eager to hear her news.[98] Having driven a Ford V8 off a Normandy landing craft, then progressed through bombed France to Brussels where the intrepid Mary was used now to 'a mass of human suffering', she was helping with 'mental rehabilitation' of troops at a YMCA centre, and sending Tom regular wartime dispatches.[99] He urged her to take care. Admiring her composure and spirit, he agreed to look after some of her belongings while she was abroad, and asked for 'an option on your eventual memoirs'. Yet there remained awkwardness between them. She accused of him of being 'curt'. Ill in December with further respiratory problems, saddened by the deaths of his old friends Sydney Schiff and Sydney Waterlow, and unable to attend a Moot for which he had prepared, he signed himself to Mary 'your affectionate and wellmeaning friend', but explained half-jokingly that Christmas was a time he 'should like to spend always in a monastery'.[100] She, on the other hand, cherished memories of sharing her nativity plays with him.

His gloom deepened. To Hayward he confessed, 'I see nothing to relieve my depression about the future: Europe unsettled and factious for the rest of our lifetime, America and Russia likely to behave according to one's worst fears; and one's private life in uncertainty, penury and discomfort.'[101] Hayward might have queried the accuracy of that word 'penury', but Tom was disinclined to be cheered up. Though he avoided mentioning Emily to Mary, he told Emily of Mary's October letter about 'quite appalling conditions of demoralization and starvation' in Europe.[102] In December Mary mentioned to him Belgium's 'terrible concentration camp of Breendonck' in the context of 'persecution of the Jews'.[103] Surveying conditions at home in England, Tom sensed old 'animosities' of 'class'; and in America persistent 'animosities of race'.[104] Darkening his mood further, he had agreed to a grim war job. Perhaps aware that in 1940 Tom had helped edit and publish a 'most moving' account of Polish sufferings, *My Name is Million*, representatives of London's Polish Research Centre had asked if now, 'as a Christian and a man of letters', he would preface the English translation of a short, anonymous, fictionalised 'ghastly record' of conditions in the concentration camp at Oświęcim, notorious today as Auschwitz. Smuggled out of Poland, the story 'Roll Call' seems to have been based on an actual 1940 Oświęcim event involving torture when a prisoner went missing. Tom wrote of how its author communicated 'the degree to which suffering isolates men each in his private hell'. 'Sympathy and compassion' managed 'to unite the characters in a communion of misery', presenting an 'abomination' where 'torturers and tortured all exist in one hell together'.[105]

Unpublished, the 'Roll Call' translation seems to have been lost. Its account predated the Auschwitz mass murder of Jews, but Tom's use of the word 'notorious' to describe the camp in his preface (completed in early 1945) suggests knowledge of Auschwitz from other sources too. As early as May 1941, reporting 'German Atrocities in Poland', *The Times* had named 'the concentration camp at Oswiecim' where 'hundreds of Poles have died'; a month later it had described conditions in 'this notorious detention camp'.[106] By 1943 a short article, 'Poles' Martyrdom', mentioned 'Oswiecim' and (probably for the first time in *The Times*) 'gas-chambers' at another Polish site.[107] A longer, June 1943 *Times* piece, 'Nazi Brutality to Jews', mentioned killings of Cracow's Jews, with 'others taken off to the Oswiecim concentration camp', and in October 1943 *Horizon* (a magazine Tom read often) occasioned considerable discussion when it published Arthur Koestler's fictionalised account of 'useless Jews' being gassed at Chelmno in Poland.[108] However, in September 1943 a major *Times* article, 'Poland's Martyrdom' (subtitled 'A Policy of Extermination'), made no mention of Jews, but stated, 'Wives, mothers, or daughters of men reported to have deserted were taken to a camp at Oswiecim and there murdered in gas chambers.'[109] On 8 July 1944 a brief *Times* piece, 'Hungarian Jews' Fate', subtitled 'Murder in Gas Chambers', presented a Polish Ministry of Information statement which concluded, 'When the Germans, in the second half of 1942, started their extermination of Polish Jewry the gas chambers of Oswiecim could not cope with all the victims, so two more death camps were erected – Tremblinka [*sic*] and Rawa Ruska, near Lwow. In these camps more than 2,000,000 Polish Jews have been murdered since 1939.'[110] A further short piece, ' "Mass Executions" of Poles', made no mention of Jews but reported that 'On October 7 the Germans began mass executions of Polish prisoners in Oswiecim by means of poison gas.' At this distance, it is impossible to know exactly what in early 1945 Tom knew about

Auschwitz. It seems improbable he had read every *Times* article; yet clearly he had links to the Polish community, and knew enough to call Auschwitz 'notorious' and highlight 'the evil' that 'lies in treating any group of human beings, whether foreign foes or domestic factionaries, whether a nation or a class, as something less than human'.[111]

He knew, too, that other 'concentration camps' existed both 'on Polish soil' and 'in Germany itself'. Prefacing 'Roll Call' which (as the modern scholar Joanna Rzepa makes clear) did 'not mention Jews', Tom saw the deaths of 'Poles at Oswiecim' as indicative of 'demonic forces which are prowling about like influenza or the plague' and which had a 'terrible *congruity* to the modern world'.[112] Not long after he wrote this piece, *The Times* in May summarised results of a Soviet-led inquiry into Auschwitz. This short article was headed '4,000,000 Deaths at Oswiecim Camp'. It, too, gave no account of Jews, but its mention of 'documentary film' hinted at footage that would soon shock the world.[113] Though by April 1945 Tom was conscious British newspapers were running stories about concentration-camp atrocities, and he wrote to Emily that month that 'the nightmare of the concentration camps (and this has been going on for ten years) is in everyone's mind', nowhere in his public prose did he make further mention of Auschwitz.[114] When Herbert Read implied there was antisemitism in a February 1945 article by Tom's friend Montgomery Belgion, Tom would have none of it. He dismissed as a 'quibble' Read's point that Tom's fellow Moot member Karl Mannheim (whom Belgion had linked to 'Germanization of Britain') was 'not a German but a Hungarian Jew'.[115]

By January 1945 Tom still had no permanent home. Friends' houses remained his refuges. Lying in the bath, daydreaming about pictures in T. A. Stephenson's *Seashore Life and Pattern* – one of his Christmas presents – it suddenly struck him there was a mistake in 'The Dry Salvages': '"hermit crab"' should be '"horse-shoe crab"'.[116] The error annoyed him. 'How could one find the remains of a hermit crab on a beach. All there could be would be the shell of some other crustacean.'[117] Why had no reader pointed this out? He even notified the *New English Weekly* about this 'alteration'.[118] His unease was intensified, surely, by having been for so long a sort of hermit crab, adapting himself to other people's homes.

War still raged. For Christmas the courageous Mary Trevelyan had sent him a Belgian appointments diary, encouraging him to think of her daily. She sent, too, vivid bulletins, chronicling 'a German raid with bullets flying about'. After reading this material (and often sharing it with the Mirrlees household), Tom was asked to forward it to her mother. Quite apart from concerns about being drawn into the Trevelyan family, Tom feared Mrs

Trevelyan might be upset by thoughts of her forty-seven-year-old daughter dodging bullets.[119] Regularly now, he addressed her as 'My dear Mary'. Signing himself 'yours ever, Tp', he gossiped about conditions at Shamley Wood, mentioning he was making recordings for George Hoellering in connection with the planned *Murder in the Cathedral* film.[120] To Hayward, styling himself 'Your faithful Tp', he revealed that Theodore Spencer wanted him to apply for a Harvard professorship. 'If a dictatorship were established here, and I had to flee for my life, I might be very glad of such a post: but I cannot think of any other circumstances under which it would be tolerable.'[121] To Spencer ('My dear Ted') he sent a tactful refusal.[122]

At Russell Square, work was interesting. Robert Graves had sent a first draft of *The White Goddess*. *Four Quartets*, published a few months earlier with a print run of 6,000, had been well received. Tom signed himself 'METOIKOS' (resident alien) in response to a *New English Weekly* piece by 'CIVIS' (citizen) advocating a government-controlled 'Full Employment Scheme'. He opposed such 'totalitarian bureaucracy'.[123] As spring approached, he felt deeply tired, wrestling with ideas of what culture, not least post-war culture, might look like. Bemoaning 'decline of culture in Britain', and emphasising how religion 'gives a meaning to life, and preserves the mass of humanity from that boredom which ends in despair,' he sounded solemnly prophetic, writing in the wake of 'Matthew Arnold's *Culture and Anarchy*'.[124] He hoped, he told Allen Tate, to produce 'a more up-to-date affair than *Culture and Anarchy*', but the very phrase 'social criticism' which Tom applied to his writings on society came from Arnold's subtitle to *Culture and Anarchy*. Like Arnold, Tom turned increasingly to 'social criticism' as his poetry dried up: 'When I shall write a poem, heaven knows', he complained to Tate. '"Cultural relations" jobs' kept getting in the way.[125]

So did other matters. There was consternation in April when his fellow Faber director C. W. Stewart died after falling 'in front of a train'.[126] Less publicly obvious was turmoil in his relationship with Emily. Though very few of her letters to him survive, she kept a copy of her 26 April attempt 'to re-align relations between us once again, after now nearly six years separation'. Admitting 'we have both changed', and referring to a period of breakdown, she explained how, 'After my illness, I wanted most strongly to feel I could marry you and so wrote you.' Since Tom had made clear again this was 'impossible under existing conditions', Emily 'wondered whether I might not be happy with someone else'. It might be that 'our love for each other would remain always a rare thing to hold close, but of a nature to be unfulfilled'. She felt, as she had felt before, that their association was not 'normal', and, after pondering matters 'for these two years past', suspected he too 'may have sensed this'. His letters seemed 'usually so very undemonstrative and impersonal'. Asking, 'Do you still feel that if you *were* free you wish to marry me?', she reminded him of 'the unusual, very complimentary, rather grave responsibility you have placed upon me – and which I have always consented to accept – since 1934'. She added that 'if you do wish to marry me ever, I shall keep myself always waiting and ready for you'.[127]

Though, as requested, Tom destroyed the original of this letter, in May he clarified that 'nothing' could change his attitude to divorce except 'complete loss of Christian faith'. Only 'a death' could alter their situation. Not naming Vivien directly, Tom made it clear that 'thought' of her 'death' he 'considered sinful and to be put away from me with constant effort'. Emily, he emphasised, must make her own choice without taking his feelings into account. 'Nothing could give me more, or more enduring pain, than the thought that you should deliberately sacrifice a genuine chance of happiness in this world, out of loyalty, or fear of giving pain, or for the shadow which is all I am in a position to give as a substitute for substance. The pain of that thought would come between us more effectually than any decision you could make.' He admitted war had changed them both, but stated he was 'not aware of any fundamental change in my feelings, except the change that takes place in everybody according to their time of life'. He acknowledged theirs was 'not a relationship such as the world understands', but felt this kept it 'uncontaminated', even if he would prefer it to be 'both lawful and permanent'. 'In plain words,' he added, 'I should never want to marry anyone else.'[128]

Combining the tones of frustrated lover with those of a philosopher, Tom mixed scruple with implied moral blackmail. Clearly, each of them was considering how war and prolonged separation had changed them; and each (though Emily stated 'There was no one actually asking me') was wondering whether they might find other partners.[129] Yet they shared such a long, intense history that neither could renounce the other, even though such thoughts haunted their protestations. He had been rereading her letters; she had been looking over his poetry, and told him it expressed 'futility'. He replied he could 'not understand this at all'; but such an interpretation of his poems was surely linked to her worry about their relationship.[130] At the height of this emotional tussle, Emily cracked a bone in her wrist. She also had a row with her new employers. Life was a struggle for her. Sometimes it seemed she was still re-enacting one of her finest roles – in J. M. Barrie's *Dear Brutus*, that sad comedy of misaligned couples, lost chances, might-have-beens.

While all this was going on, Tom's public life burgeoned. Following powerful Allied advances in Europe, the British Council wanted him to go to Paris. By April, his fire-watching duties were over. He suggested to Edmund Wilson they might meet 'in Paris' in early May.[131] Setting off by boat on 5 May, he reached Paris at 6 a.m. next morning, anticipating lunch at the British Embassy, followed by lecturing in French in the presence of the frail Paul Valéry, and 'five "receptions" in five days'; 'It's a nightmare', he confessed to Hayward, telling Emily he was 'dreading' it.[132] In retrospect, though, it appeared more fun, with a visit to Versailles, 'a ride in a jeep with two Americans and a Chinese diplomat', media interviews, and crowded lectures: 'I saw everybody in the literary world except Claudel and Sartre.'[133] Tom was in Paris for VE (Victory in Europe) Day which followed Germany's official surrender. As requested, he lectured on *'le rôle social des poètes'*; he quoted no poetry, but, introduced by Valéry, prefaced his disquisition with heartfelt remarks about 'inviolably beautiful' Paris.[134]

Returning to London, he soon had bad news. Charles Williams, his 'loved friend', died on 15 May. 'Still dazed by the shock', Tom was telephoned by *The Times* and spent several hours writing Williams's obituary.[135] He was coming to terms, too, with other news, reported briefly in *The Times* while he was abroad: 'Ezra Pound, the American poet, who broadcast from Rome under the Fascist regime', had 'been arrested near Genoa' and 'would be brought to trial' for 'treason'.[136] Eager to help his old friend, Tom was soon in touch with MacLeish; but by late May Pound, who when interviewed had described Hitler as 'a saint', was being held by the Americans in a concentration camp near Pisa, and Tom, after a brief Cambridge visit, was having to plan a return to Paris.[137] He had been invited to rehearsals of *Meurtre dans la cathédrale*. Henri Fluchère's French translation was to be performed at the Théâtre du Vieux-Colombier. Tom met old friends including Sylvia Beach, much aged after 'five months in a gestapo prison', and relished seeing *Meurtre*: 'when it comes to matters of art, the French are the most thorough and precise people in the world'.[138] Directed by Jean Vilar, who starred as Becket, this play about a man resisting oppressive state power was a hit in the newly liberated French capital. It ran for 150 performances. Tom, addressed as *'maître'*, was a literary hero, but told Emily he felt more like 'a returning ghost, or that I had come to a city of ghosts'. Paris seemed an 'unreal' city.[139] Meanwhile, Pound, who had helped edit *The Waste Land* there just over two decades earlier, was now imprisoned in a concrete-floored, six-foot-by-six-foot floodlit steel cage. Undergoing psychiatric evaluations, he faced a possible death sentence.

For now, offering support to Omar Pound and liaising with Dorothy Pound's London solicitors as well as with MacLeish and other Americans, Tom could do little but wait. 'None of us here know what he said in his wireless talks', he explained to Morley, hoping Pound, who needed a good lawyer, would not 'take some crazy theatrical pose'.[140] In London, provided an apartment could be modified to accommodate his wheelchair-bound friend, Tom was arranging to rent a large, high-ceilinged third-floor flat with Hayward at 19 Carlyle Mansions in Cheyne Walk, Chelsea, overlooking the Thames. Confident in the building's lift, and enthused by offers of furniture from Shamley Wood, he grew immersed in domestic arrangements.

Hoellering urged him to act Becket in the proposed film of *Murder in the Cathedral*, but Tom, though supportive, resisted being drawn back into earlier work instead of focusing on writing a new play. While the Carlyle Mansions flat was being prepared, he lodged temporarily at 14 Elvaston Place, just off Queen's Gate, Kensington; his books remained at Shamley Wood. Life still seemed nomadic and unsettled, yet he confessed to Emily a 'pang' at the thought that sharing with Hayward represented 'a future *nothing better than which* can happen'. 'I am sure, my dear, that you will understand.' This was another indication he was not envisaging marrying her. He told her that in recent years he had struggled to find 'the right tone' in which to write to her about their ' "friendship" '. He put that word 'in inverted commas because it has to be a very peculiar kind of friendship (for which the word is inadequate) to be anything'. He wanted her both 'to feel *free* and to feel quite certain of my love'. He shrank from the thought of others reading her letters, yet if his letters to her were preserved, then 'I want the world to know and remember something about you.' Again, this phrasing might suggest he did not envisage the public acknowledgement of their relationship that marriage would entail, even though he wished 'I could really cherish and comfort you.' He signed off, 'Lovingly / Tom'.[141]

To some extent he had always wanted their relationship to be a love match, yet also a covert friendship that was kept within limits. He had gone on trying to have things both ways, and she had accepted that. But the strains were becoming overwhelming. Mid-July brought news from Emily of the death of Tom's last surviving uncle, Christopher Rhodes Eliot, at whose summer camp fifteen-year-old Tom had heard the water-dripping song of the hermit thrush that features in *The Waste Land*. Just days later came news of another death, that of Valéry 'who', as Tom put it in a telegram to Paris on 26 July, 'more than any poet in Europe was the poetic consciousness of his time'.[142] All this added to what he described to Emily as 'the end of a chapter'.[143]

In August he felt repugnance at London's 'hollow gaiety' following the dropping of atomic bombs on Hiroshima and Nagasaki – events prefacing Japan's surrender on 2 September.[144] He was still 'depressed' at Britain's July 1945 election, which had seen Churchill's Conservatives defeated by

Labour under Clement Attlee, who would introduce a welfare state.[145] As Tom explained to young poet Robert Waller, 'My normal preference for the Conservative Party is partly due, I think, to the fact that the element I dislike in the Labour Party is the element I happen to come across most often: the half-baked intellectuals and publicists; and that the element I dislike in the Conservative Party is the element with which I have the least acquaintance – that represented for the public by Beaverbrook, Bracken, etc.'[146] Instead of meeting newspaper tycoon Lord Beaverbrook or wartime Minister of Information, Brendan Bracken, Tom socialised with Burke Club Tories. His Conservative Englishness distanced him from Emily, however patrician her Bostonian instincts. She suspected he disliked change; he admitted that. 'America is not a good place for me to work and think in,' he explained, 'but ideal for a holiday.' He hoped to 'visit', but there was no suggestion his long-term future could be with her in his native land.[147] She reproached him for seeming to ' "withdraw from life" '.[148] He denied doing so, and imagined holidaying with her again in the Cotswolds, but, however much he might treasure photographs of her in her youth, he may have been withdrawing from long-term possibilities with Emily. He still wore her ring.

Weekending at Shamley Wood in early September, Tom and the Mirrlees' gardener lowered a substantial box into a specially dug grave 'filled with rosemary under the oak tree'. They were burying Hope's 'horrible old dachshund'.[149] The house was to be closed up soon. The family were moving to Lee, near Ilfracombe in Devon. 'It is a real pang to be leaving', he wrote to 'Dearest Mappie'. 'I do not believe there is another household anywhere in which I could have felt so much at home.'[150] Unsettled and ill (he had just endured further dental work on a poisoned tooth), he spent the second half of September holidaying at Lee. Returning, he found a moving letter from thirty-four-year-old poet Czesław Miłosz, a friend of the author of 'Roll Call'. While with the resistance in wartime Warsaw, Miłosz had translated *The Waste Land* into Polish; out of 'admiration and respect for Poland', Tom wished to accept no royalties for its initial publication.[151]

Expanding post-war communications brought increasing demands for publication of his work in other languages. His business correspondence proliferated. On 19 October, aware Pound was still incarcerated near Pisa and that incoming mail would be read by censors, Tom wrote to him, indicating Faber & Faber remained committed to publishing further *Cantos*. Less enthusiastically, he invited Pound to send his ongoing translations from Chinese. Principally, Tom urged, 'the great thing is that you should get the best possible counsel in America'. He advised, 'do exactly what your lawyer tells you to, and only talk when he wants you to talk'. Aware his letter would be read by other eyes, he sent 'Ez' his 'Fraternal greetings, and on this occasion I shall subscribe, probably for the first time in our correspondence of many years, my public signature, T. S. Eliot'.[152] He hoped his friend might be shown leniency, if only for his worth as a poet and mentor of poets. Pound's troubles, though, were far from over.

As socialist pressures intensified in Britain, Tom published an October 1945 essay, 'The Class and the Elite', and continued work on his study of what 'culture' meant. Where others championed post-war institutions – the welfare state, the United Nations, UNESCO – Tom in such pieces as 'What is a Classic?' emphasised a need for philosophical depth and lasting foundations for post-war civilisation. 'The first task of a cultural organization should be to consider how far "culture" is susceptible of "organization"', he argued in a November 1945 letter to the press about UNESCO: 'The opportunities for getting lost in a verbal labyrinth without issue, when the representatives of 37 nations have assembled to draw conclusions from unexamined premises, are unlimited.'[153] To Tom UNESCO continued to represent a managerial bureaucratisation of culture with which he was 'at odds', as well as a challenge to his own long-standing vision of an international fraternity of creative writers centred on European traditions.[154] His absolutism ('There is no classic in English') could make him sound eccentric, but his reputation ensured his voice was heard, and invitations to lecture – in Chicago, Geneva, London – came thick and fast.[155] Mostly, though, he eluded capture. 'My chief function is to write verse, and verse plays, and to publish the poetry of other writers', he explained that year; using the word 'poetry' for other writers' work, but 'verse' for his own, constitutes a formal modesty, but hints too at possibilities he might continue writing 'verse' – principally for the stage – rather than 'poetry'. In the same piece, addressed to a French audience, Tom presented himself as increasingly interested in 'recent years' in 'political philosophy', and as having 'returned to the reading of Edmund Burke'.[156] Like his turn from poetry to verse, his Burke Club conservatism and commitment to expounding a related cultural politics would become increasingly obvious.

In November he signed the lease on the Cheyne Walk flat. Though Vivien was still at Northumberland House, Tom's instinct for domestic concealment remained strong. He told Hayward he would like any telephone in the flat to be registered in Hayward's name. The two men corresponded about hiring a housekeeper (best to avoid one 'who may fly off the handle because she is going through the menopause'), cooking ('Do cooks like gas or electric best?'), curtains and flooring.[157] Removal preparations were tiring – cold weather and a gas strike hardly helped. Tom's doctor advised him to take things easy. At Morley College, Lambeth, in late November he attended a recitation of MacNeice's *Agamemnon*. But, as Christmas approached, his Cheyne Walk removal risked slipping into 1946. More alarming news was that Pound, after being transported to Washington in mid-November, might need to plead insanity to avoid being found guilty of treason. Tom wrote to E. E. Cummings, 'in the faint hope that you might be able to visit him' in detention, and asked Cummings to cable 'what the sentence is'.[158] Over the next few months Tom strove to rally support, but several writers thought Pound should be put to death.

Tom spent Christmas with 'most lovable' Mappie Mirrlees's household at Lee.[159] Enjoying Mappie's peerless cuisine as always, he was still seeking a housekeeper-cook, and did not mince words to Hayward: 'in my opinion all women are difficult until they are over 50, and often until 90.'[160] Emily was then aged 54, but Tom still wrote to her as his 'Dearest Girl', and had tried to console her when her mother died: 'I feel for you very much', he assured her, and had 'always mentioned your mother in my prayers.'[161] He and Emily shared gossip and mutual friends. Their transatlantic 'friendship' continued, but Tom needed immediate female support. In London, he interviewed a former nursery governess, Madame Frenay, on 8 January 'and was very well impressed'. 'Middleaged, portly, and pleasant', she was reputedly a fine cook, and willing to sew too.[162] Tom asked his secretary at Fabers to pursue references. As well as typing his letters, Miss Melton was used to looking after her boss, but he was clearly unwell, suffering from coughing, spasms, and a high temperature. After a spell in hospital, it was decided he should have an operation later in the year. Tom maintained he had a bad cold, but his respiratory problems were hardly new; nor was discomfort from his hernia. He was acutely conscious, too, that in America Henry had endured pneumonia. It might be some time before Tom could see his elder brother, his two ageing sisters, and Emily in Massachusetts – or visit Pound, who had avoided further court proceedings after being declared insane by psychiatrists. Pound's American publisher, James Laughlin, told Tom the diagnosis might be 'medically correct'.[163]

In late February, a fortnight or so after Tom rejected MacDiarmid's *In Memoriam James Joyce*, calling it 'a magnificent tribute to language' but one 'very few people would read', he was ensconced in the Cheyne Walk apartment, though he still went regularly to nearby Kensington to perform his churchwarden duties at St Stephen's.[164] 'Collecting all the newspaper cuttings I can get from America about Pound', and preparing to publish the *Pisan Cantos*, he informed Allen Tate that he was marshalling Pound's support among English poets.[165] More immediately, though, he worked with Madame Frenay and others to ensure all was ready for Hayward to move into the apartment during March. In an era of rationing he consulted Hayward about a shirtmaker to make 'some spring shirts'; Tom's 'wool shirts may hang out for another winter'. Madame Frenay showed 'enterprise and resourcefulness'. Her 'cooking' was 'good, especially the soups', and her housekeeping assisted by many gift parcels, containing everything from soap to cheese, which arrived from Tom's American correspondents.[166] Tom hoped to visit the States in May, excursing as far south as Washington to visit Pound at St Elizabeths psychiatric hospital. He made clear to friends that he strongly disagreed with Pound's antisemitism and politics, but would stand by him. In late April he wrote a substantial paean to Pound's 'example of devotion to "the art of poetry"', for publication in September's *Poetry*.[167]

Much of his time during early spring 1946 was occupied with 'Cultural Relations': dining with Nobel Prize-winning Chilean poet Gabriela Mistral; reading alongside French poet Pierre Jean Jouve, William Empson, and Dylan Thomas; attending council meetings of the Fédération Britannique des Comités de L'Alliance Française; adding his name to a telegram to President Truman, requesting release of 'three thousand conscientious objectors' imprisoned 'in your country'.[168] More demanding was his promise to provide 'notes' on culture and Christian unity for discussion by an Anglo-Catholic group in Oxford in April (Tom deprecated 'the unreligious pseudo-culture amongst which we live'), and the March radio addresses he wrote for broadcast to Germany as 'Der Einheit der europäischen Kultur' ('The Unity of European Culture'). Retreading familiar ground, with additional nods to Rilke, Goethe and others, he emphasised that 'The frontiers of culture are not, and should not be, closed.' A 'common *tradition* of Christianity' had 'made Europe what it is'.[169]

At home, through Faber poet Ronald Duncan he had met Benjamin Britten, and hoped Fabers might publish Duncan's libretto for Britten's opera *The Rape of Lucretia*, soon to be premiered at Glyndebourne. Still interested in modern music, Tom was friendly, too, with Michael Tippett who had sought his advice when composing his 1944 oratorio about Jewish persecution, *A Child of Our Time*. Tom had taken Mary Trevelyan to a performance of Tippett's oratorio in February; in March, inviting Tom for gin, she gave him eight eggs and her book, *I'll Walk Beside You*. Newly published by Longmans, it did not name him, but consisted largely of letters she had written him from Europe towards the war's end. Signing himself, 'Yours in haste P', he thanked her for the volume ('very odd to read in a book what had been letters to oneself'), and the eggs ('8 is too many, and if you go on like this I shall write to your mother about it'), and the suggestion of gin ('I didn't read your message about the gin in time to act upon it'), but signalled he was very busy and just off to speak in Salisbury.[170] The High Anglican Mary, who came to worship at Tom's church, was persistent. They continued to meet, but Emily remained his 'Dearest Girl'.

By Easter week, during which he wrote an obituary for his 'genius' friend Keynes who had died 'suddenly – and unexpectedly', he was about to receive a visa for travel to America.[171] After the ten-day crossing in late May 1946, he stayed in New York with Morley, before paying a private visit to Cambridge where Henry, 'ill enough to give anxiety', had been diagnosed with incurable leukemia.[172] Tom planned to divide the rest of the visit between New York, Woods Hole, seeing Pound in Washington, holidaying with Henry in Dublin, New Hampshire, and spending time with Emily in Dorset, Vermont, where she was taking a leading role in Noël Coward's *Blithe Spirit*. He would pay his way by fitting in, too, various academic commitments before sailing back to Britain in late July. Among those with whom he renewed contact in hot, humid New York were Djuna Barnes, Donald Brace, the Morleys, Auden, Marianne Moore, Kauffer and Marion Dorn, Allen Tate (now working for publishing house Henry Holt), and Laughlin with whom he seemed to concur that Pound might be 'incurable but harmless'.[173] In Washington in early July he stayed with his cousin Martha, who knew Dr Winfred Overholser, responsible for Pound's care at St Elizabeths. Tom would visit Pound, too, whose new cantos, drawing on experiences in the Italian detention camp as well as recalling earlier times, moved him deeply. Officially, the North American trip was a business one. Tom liaised with Faber authors, academic contacts, and US publishers. He recorded several of his poems on gramophone records. Yet the visit's greatest importance was private.

In New England he was eagerly anticipated, not least by Emily and her relations. 'Uncle' John Perkins wrote from 90 Commonwealth Avenue, Boston, to Meg Nason in Chipping Campden, describing celebrations for his eighty-fourth birthday on 6 June, when Emily had come to dinner:

> We had hoped that Mr T. S. Eliot could be with us. For his ship arrived in Montreal on June 2; but he had to go directly to New York. It is a business trip in behalf of his company, Faber & Faber. However on the Saturday following, June 8, Mr Eliot did come to us and Emily came from Concord. You can imagine what a happy reunion we had after several years. He will be in America until late July, I believe; and we hope to see more of him. He looks & appears well, but thin, not older.[174]

After seven years' separation, suddenly Tom saw again not just Emily and the Perkinses, but also, in different circumstances, Henry, Theresa and other close friends, including Pound. He noticed how worried Theresa was ('she had carried so much responsibility alone'), and realised this might be his last opportunity to spend time with Henry, who rallied in his company.[175] Full of affection for Emily, he soon travelled to Vermont where he admired her in *Blithe Spirit* – a play about a writer haunted by competing ghosts of two dead wives. If a realisation was growing in him that, despite their long-standing understanding that he might marry her in the event of Vivien's death, he could not do so, then at this stage he could not bring himself to tell her. He was conscious she looked thinner than he remembered, and had so recently lost her mother.

For a time at least, he presented himself as genial, playful, and in holiday mood. Twenty-two-year-old Sally Foss, daughter of Emily's old schoolfriend Mary Foss (née Parker), drove him from Massachusetts to Vermont in July 1946 and found him charming. She recalled much later how Emily had told her he 'loved to stop in brooks and to wade in the water'. Sally Foss broke the journey beside a rural stream, and Tom waded in, having 'rolled up his pants up to his knees and then he said, "Oh, this is perfect."' During the drive he recited some of his *Cats* poems, and on arrival in Dorset he joined in some children's games on the lawn behind the Dorset Inn. Over dinner, he, Emily, and the Fosses discussed the play, and the attractions of Chipping Campden with much laughter. It struck Sally Foss that Tom and Emily 'were obviously very, very close friends', rather than lovers. 'They were obviously very comfortable with each other and having a good time.'[176] The Fosses were Emily's trusted friends; she and Tom relaxed in their company. Yet deeper tensions between them remained.

The Vermont interlude was a welcome break, but other meetings were more difficult. In Washington he met Pound and one of Pound's doctors, though both Dorothy Pound and Dr Overholser were away. The doctor was tight-lipped. All Tom perceived, however, was 'exaggeration' of Pound's 'well known characteristics.' Anxious to say as much as he could manage, the 'babbling' Pound delivered an intense 'monologue', passing rapidly from topic to topic. 'I am sure', Tom wrote to Allen Tate afterwards, 'Ezra ought to be removed to a private sanatorium as quickly as possible.'[177]

In August, having sailed back across the Atlantic on the *Queen Mary*, taking 'a cocktail every evening' with upper-class fellow passengers who gossiped about divorce, he was ready to catch up with correspondence, disperse presents to Hayward, Mary Trevelyan and others, and retire from the *Christian News-Letter* editorial advisory group, hoping to make time for new work.[178] He sent slight, occasional verses to Spender and Hope Mirrlees; then, having declined Ronald Bottrall's invitation to an early

September 'cocktail party', he anticipated a short holiday.[179] Browne was encouraging him to improve *The Family Reunion* for a new production, but Tom preferred finishing substantial prose work (his nascent *Notes towards the Definition of Culture*) and starting 'a new play' – which would become *The Cocktail Party*. Drawing partly on Euripides' ancient Greek tragedy *Alcestis*, whose story had been turned into a comedy – *The Thracian Horses* – performed at the Lyric Theatre, Hammersmith, in May 1946, Tom's new drama would also offer comedy, while incorporating some tragic elements. As for rewriting *The Family Reunion*, he concluded, 'I feel that it would be healthier for *me* to leave it alone.'[180]

Yet again, he was reviewing his life. To Polly Tandy, whose errant husband had started a new relationship, he wrote about his own past, explaining how in youth he had rebelled against becoming a philosophy professor and had felt

a maddening feeling of failure and inferiority. To escape from *that*, I had to make a complete mess of my personal life and marry the wrong woman, for the wrong reason or very nearly for no reason at all. I didn't know why I was doing all this.[181]

If his past emotional life seemed a mess, his present was no less complicated. He stayed in regular epistolary contact with Emily, but, however affectionate, their relationship had reached an impasse. He went on seeing Mary Trevelyan, but attempted to maintain a friendly distance. No matter how little he mentioned it, he remained conscious of Vivien's plight. Expressing deep sympathy to Treece and his wife, whose infant son had died, he wrote of 'desolation' that accompanied 'loss of a parent or brother, sister or friend', involving a sense of the 'past' being 'injured'. He carried such a sense within him, though he understood that 'with the loss of a little child it is the loss also of a part of the future'.[182] As publisher he could be hard-nosed, tenacious, unyieldingly precisian; yet his private acts of generosity, sensitivity, and kindness were outstanding. Having spent years backing the refugee author Nikolai Iovetz-Tereshchenko, who was seriously ill in 1946, Tom visited him in hospital on several occasions, paying his medical bills.

Strangers could be overawed by him, but, realising this, he tried to put them at their ease. Meeting him with Hayward over martinis at the home of Morley Kennerley that year, twenty-eight-year old Mary Lee Settle realised he knew she was 'terrified'; but, she recalled, he recounted anecdotes from his past, and 'comforted, instinctively, without a question or a hint of condescension'.

He was playful. He told about trying to learn the ukulele by correspondence, 'to impress the girls'. He practiced with a flashlight, tented
under the covers in a London boardinghouse so his landlady wouldn't
hear him. I see now he was being a little flirtatious. I would not have
dared to recognize it then.[183]

That same year Collin Brooks, the Conservative writer and fellow
member of the Burke Club, acting on behalf of a family friend, asked Tom
to sign a book for a young admirer, Valerie Fletcher. Tom did so. Miss
Fletcher also sent good wishes for his birthday on 26 September, for which
she received a brief note of thanks, dictated by Tom to his secretary.
Twenty-year-old Esmé Valerie Fletcher had been born and brought up in a
middle-class, mock-Tudor semi-detached home at 20 Ancaster Road in
leafily suburban Headingley, Leeds, and privately educated at Queen
Anne's School, Caversham, a sporty, all-female boarding establishment
near Reading – Betjeman's muse Joan Hunter Dunn was a former head girl.
The school had an inspirational English teacher, Dorothy Bartholomew, a
committed Anglican fond of metaphysical poetry, who taught Valerie
some modern verse. Listening to a gramophone record, 'The Voice of
Poetry', at school during the war, the girl had heard John Gielgud's
thoughtful 1939 reading of 'Journey of the Magi'. Miss Bartholomew
remembered fourteen-year-old Valerie asking, 'Who wrote that poem?'
When told, the girl said, 'I shall marry that man,' then paused: 'But how
shall I meet him?' According to Bartholomew's later account, she suggested Valerie 'could become his secretary, I suppose'.[184]
Whether or not this tale grew embellished over time, Valerie certainly
liked to recall listening to the poem. 'I was overwhelmed by it', she stated
later. 'I remember intense excitement, as though a bomb had exploded
under me. I knew something had happened. I knew this was different.'[185]
She began to investigate her new poetic favourite, and soon came across his
introduction to Harold Monro's 1933 *Collected Poems* where Tom had written, 'There is no way out. There never is. The compensations for being a
poet are grossly exaggerated; and they dwindle as one becomes older, and
the shadows lengthen and the solitude becomes harder to endure.' That
expression of pained loneliness 'haunted' the teenage girl; she knew she
'just *had* to get to' the author.[186] Her preoccupation became a family joke in
her native Leeds. Then, when, thanks to her parents' friend Collin Brooks,
Tom signed her book and answered her letter, she set her heart on meeting
him. After library work at Leeds University, this resourceful young woman
relocated to London, securing work as secretary to impoverished novelist
Paul Capon, then to the writer Charles Morgan (whose work Tom and

Hayward disliked). Soon she took on occasional work for Dylan Thomas who was working on screenplays. What she really wanted, though, was 'to get to Tom'.[187] Amused, Dylan Thomas, well aware of this, and about to call on Tom, asked Valerie to go round some film studios and borrow appropriate clothes for him to wear since his own were 'terrible'. After she had done this, and just as he was setting off for Tom's upper-storey Russell Square office, Thomas asked her, 'What is it worth to you if I push his present secretary downstairs?'[188]

Wholly unaware of such designs, Tom focused on his 'culture book' — 'creeping ahead' — and hoped to visit America again in summer 1947.[189] Though he kept up his clubs and discussion groups — the All Souls, the Burke, the Chandos, the Moot — and worked on lectures (preparing one on Milton for the British Academy in early 1947, and revising for publication his 1944 Bangor lectures on Johnson), he declined many British invitations. Conscious of post-war restrictions which strictly curtailed how much money Britons could take abroad, he accepted only the most prestigious, lucrative, and convenient invitations for America in the spring. Before that, he had a hernia operation scheduled at the private wing of London's University College Hospital for early January, and had been warned against developing a cough — which made him reconsider winter excursions, though not his habitual cigarettes. In America Henry was expected to live only 'a matter of months'.[190] Feeling the strain of all this, nonetheless Tom completed a draft of his 'Culture book' by early December, passing it to Faber and Mairet — then later Hayward — for comments.[191] He agreed to go once again to Mary Trevelyan's Student Movement House nativity play; wrote to the *Catholic Herald* supporting an amnesty for remaining 'prisoners of war'; and hoped his hernia operation would set him up for 1947.[192]

Instead, he fell ill over Christmas. Ten days in hospital with respiratory problems meant the hernia operation was postponed. When he came home to Carlyle Mansions, still weak, he was shaken to learn Karl Mannheim had died, and paid tribute to Mannheim's 'talk' which 'was always a stimulant'.[193] Soon afterwards, he got a much worse shock. Hayward answered the telephone early one morning. It was Maurice Haigh-Wood. Vivien, after suffering from 'high blood pressure', had died unexpectedly of 'syncope' and 'cardiovascular degeneration'.[194] Tom wept. Burying his face in his hands, he exclaimed, 'Oh God! Oh God!'[195] He wrote that same day to Emily,

> One's reactions are never simple, unless one is quite insensitive. At the
> moment I feel quite dazed, and at the same time all the nightmare of

the past flows back. The thought of this unhappy, useless, tormented and tormenting life appals me. May she rest in peace.

I shall wear half mourning for six months. So far as all but a few friends know (and they do not know a great deal) there was normal affection until increasing dementia caused inevitable alienation and inevitable separation when co-habitation finally made my life impossible. I wish to preserve decorum for the sake of the dead, and also for the sake of the living. So I think that for the present our own plans and deliberations should be kept to ourselves. I am thankful that I shall see you in April (for it seems pretty certain that I shall not be summoned to Henry before then) so that we can talk about the future, for a year hence. We have many practical problems to solve.

I must get over the next few days before I write more.

Lovingly,
Tom[196]

He dined with Geoffrey and Enid Faber that night – to them he could speak openly – but the following day, still in 'great shock', he was 'completely dazed and somewhat paralysed'.[197] Maurice, Maurice's wife, and Enid had been, Tom believed, Vivien's only regular visitors. Maurice handled all the funeral arrangements. In her will, made over a decade earlier, Vivien had asked to be buried at Eastbourne where her father was interred, but Eastbourne's cemetery was only for local residents, so she was buried at Pinner in Middlesex, where her mother's body lay. 'I am going through an infernal passage which, like all infernos, is incommunicable, though perhaps some of it may be explainable at a later time', Tom wrote to Enid on 24 January.[198] Four days later, to Mappie Mirrlees who, like Hope, had sent a consoling letter, he wrote:

I cannot tell you what a shock this has been, and how it makes me feel that my whole life has been to pieces and must be put together again. It is very difficult to express what I feel; and to nearly everyone I should not say even this much. It is entirely different from the sorrow that one feels when somebody one has loved very much has died: and to me at the moment it seems very much harder to bear than simple grief. When I think of her, I am only glad for her and everyone's sake that this has happened: so my feelings have not even the dignity of being affectionate or altruistic.[199]

The funeral at Pinner on 29 January was private. It was the coldest weather for several years. The previous day's snowstorms had disrupted transport, and Enid Faber recalled that 'The Haigh Woods, Tom and I were the only mourners in a funeral chapel with blasted windows on a freezing day, and Tom's flowers were missing.'[200] He stood with the tiny cluster of mourners, at the grave of his fifty-eight-year-old wife.

A few days afterwards he wrote to Frank and Christina Morley about feeling 'as if I had descended into depths such that there was a great gulf fixed'. He was still in shock: 'The shock of looking at a rather unpleasant stranger, and finding that it is oneself in a mirror; the shock of finding, at 58, the greatest crisis of one's life.'[201] Not wanting to let the director and actors down, he attended a performance of *The Family Reunion* which had been revived by Browne at the Mercury Theatre. As soon as the curtain fell after the last words about 'the departed – / May they rest in peace', Tom left the theatre.[202]

In response to a telegram from Emily, he told her, guiltily, 'as you cannot share my present sufferings, all I do by mentioning them is to inflict suffering, as I have always done in my life'. Yet he tried to explain his 'crisis'. Vivien's death had precipitated in him a biting sense of 'conscience, and the horror, with an intense dislike of sex in any form'. It was not, he made clear, 'a recrudescence of any past affection'.[203] His phrasing here echoes his account, written eighteen years earlier, of 'recrudescence of an ancient passion' in Dante's *Purgatorio* where such 'recrudescence' led to 'passionate conflict of the old feelings with the new' in the context of 'renunciation'.[204] Though Tom's echoing of his earlier account may have been unconscious, he was again in the midst of a clash between old feelings and new as he tried to reconcile his sudden sense of Vivien's death and the awareness of his own late middle age which it had precipitated with the love for Emily he had felt in his youth and which, in partly transmuted form, he had continued to feel.

Instead of quickening that love, and encouraging marriage to Emily, it was as if Vivien's death pointed him all the more definitely towards renunciation. It made him confront fully an awareness his love for Emily now was so different from what he had felt in his youth that pressing ahead with marriage would be impossible. Surveying the 'agony' of life with Vivien, and those 'summers, the happiest of my life' with Emily in Chipping Campden, when 'I was escaping from my life and getting through the little door, and while I was in the garden I became a young man again', he felt 'there were still two lives alternating, of youth and of age'. Vivien's death had forced a sudden recognition:

I had no idea until the moment came, of the way in which a death – the death of someone never loved or desired – would make me see myself. For her I felt only a detached relief from a life which was hardly worth living, since it was very improbable that more years would have brought her any greater understanding or progress on the road to eternity: for the rights and wrongs, for my own share of culpability, or for any harm that I may have done her, I felt merely that the balance had been struck, whatever it was, and that there was no use thinking of that more. I should never know – and on that plane, the chapter was indeed closed. But when the coffin was settled in the grave, and I turned away, I felt – without emotion, in the usual sense – that a great deal that was myself was dead. I have no knowledge whether the old story is true, that an Egyptian mummy is preserved in its wrappings exactly as it was at the moment of embalming, and that when it is exposed and unwrapped, we see it for a moment as it was 4000 years ago – and that then it crumbles into dust in a few moments until nothing is left but the bones. But I felt as if something of the sort had happened to me. Suddenly I felt as if I had been preserved in a mummified youth, and at that moment I became my chronological age – not a young man to whom opportunities are open, but a senior who had lived his life, such as it was, a man getting on for 59, with limited possibilities for the remaining years, and no resiliency or capacity for fresh adaptation. And up to this moment, I have felt like that steadily. That, in fact, was the real shock. That I am my past, and the whole of it, whether I like it or not; and that I meet myself face to face as a stranger whom I have got to live with, and make the best of, whether I like him or not; and while I still love you, and all those whom I love in various relations and degrees, as much as ever, it is this previously unknown man whom I, and they, will have to get to know.[205]

This he mailed Emily on 14 February. She sent a 'very sweet and kind' letter six days later, thanking him for his 'clear' and 'comprehensive' account, and expressing sympathy with his sense of 'duality'. But he felt she did not fully understand. He was dreading meeting his dying brother, whose 'intense devotion to my bibliography' seemed 'morbid'. 'It makes me feel all the lonelier with him – for I do feel very lonely in his company – because it reminds me that it is my reputation, rather than any enjoyment of what I write for its own sake, or any sympathy of thought and sensibility, that he has to find his satisfaction in.' Alluding to changes in himself, he told Emily:

At present, I no longer want anything in this world except to do the best writing I can in the ten or twelve years of some degree of

creativity that I may hope for, to meet all coming external vicissi-
tudes in a spirit of Christian fortitude and faith in the Christian hope
of eternity, and I no longer feel any vitality over and above that
needed to carry out those duties. I am so shaken that the thought of
any life beyond that terrifies me: sometimes one has just the strength
to go on the same course, whereas if one stopped for a moment, or
tried to change the course, one would drop.

To the woman who read these words, and who had treasured for years
the hope that Tom would marry her, this promised disturbingly little.
Clearly, Tom felt trepidation at encountering her in these new circumstances: 'it will be as if I was meeting you, and my family, for the first time:
I hope I shall not feel simply a ghost, a temporary visitant from another
world'.[206]
He numbed himself with work, with meetings, and with dictating letters in which he showed himself meticulously businesslike as ever, but the
weather numbed him too. Ever since the beginning of the year, he had
been huddling over an electric fire (the only source of heat in his Russell
Square office) at a time of electricity cuts. The new flat, also, relied on electric heating. 'At the moment, our attention is fixed on the problem of
survival', he told Frank Morley, likening conditions to those of 1940–1
when he had to think about how to stay alive for 'the next twenty four
hours'.[207] The weather had been 'the severest ever known'. Even if this was
an exaggeration, Tom's complaint reflected his depressed mood, as well as
determination to persevere. He was planning how to manage his trip to
America before Henry succumbed to his fight with leukaemia. Staring into
the mirror each morning, he resolved to get time for creative work beyond
letters, lectures, and articles. His comment to Morley aligns with some of
what he told Emily: 'at 58 I want to get at least one more major work done,
while I have the vigour for it. I am aware now of having no energy to
waste.'[208] In mid-February he was still convalescing from what he called 'a
second round of bronchitis', and conditions did not improve: soon he
found the heat shut off for five hours a day, and no water in the flat.[209] He
blamed 'a weak and distracted government. No brains, and not much character, wherever you look.'[210] To Emily, who worried repeatedly that he
was too self-preoccupied, he wrote on 10 March that he was 'still in a very
dark passage', and that 'self-understanding is a process which has no end in
this life, and probably is consummated only in purgatory'.[211]
Sitting in his office on March afternoons he wore 'two undervests, a
couple of pullovers' and an 'overcoat'. As the post-war fuel crisis intensified, he was struck by a story in London's *Evening Standard* which claimed

an eighty-four-year-old man had hanged himself 'because he couldn't stand the sight of snow any longer'.[212] Sitting that month for the artist Patrick Heron (whose father, Tom, he had known for some years), he wore a thick dark blue overcoat and looked solemn. He had taken two weeks to reply to a letter from young Jewish poet Edward Field accusing him of antisemitism; when he did so, his retort was forthright:

> I am afraid that you are over-sensitive and like some other people inclined to find anti-semitism wherever the word Jew is used in connection with an individual who is not depicted as one of the finer types of his people. There is no anti-semitism in my poetry whatever.[213]

Tom was determined not to allow that his writings could be seen to reflect any of the antisemitism which had been accepted within his family. In what seems at best a striking failure of imagination and empathy, his apparently uncomprehending attitude appeared to be that in these years after the Nazi horrors Jews were behaving somewhat hysterically, and were hallucinating antisemitism where there could not possibly be any. 'I am no more anti-semitic', he insisted, 'than I am anti-Welsh or anti-Eskimo.'[214]

His annoyance on this point overlay a deeper disquiet. He feared that to Emily he seemed 'very self-absorbed', but worried more that he had to communicate to her that 'ultimately' the subject which absorbed him was 'myself and you, or myself in relation to you'. She might think him 'callously indifferent' to her 'feelings', but a sense of his own 'failure towards other human beings' (including his family) afflicted him. However much it might appear sheer 'egotism', this sense led him to a conviction that he could not marry.

> You will see perhaps a little, how Vivienne's sudden death brought about a new awareness. I am far from sure that I yet know the truth about myself, but I am sure that no one else can. The feeling which took possession of me – and I was so surprised by it that I did not recognize it at first for what it was – was that I was wholly unfitted for married life; that I had made one appalling mistake which had brought much misery to others (I am not pretending to be wholly altruistic about this!) But my re-living of my own sufferings is criticized by a voice within me which whispers that without that wretchedness I could not risk it again. There is in this an element of rationality: recognition of having grown in to one relatively satisfactory way of life, in which I found myself, as a man alone, able to reach out to a

number and variety of people in human affection and friendliness, in contrast to the complete isolation of married misery; recognition of inability now to carry out the continuous self-adaptation to another personality, and memory of the strain and the complete failure of purely external adaptation against which one's nature rebels. And I also ought to know by experience that it is impossible to make another person happy unless one is happy oneself.

He tried to cushion the blow to Emily by adding that he knew he was 'not very well at present' and that 'I never have, and never could, love any woman but yourself', but he made it clear that he did not expect meeting her again in America would change his mind.[215]

At Easter (6 April) 1947 he wrote again: 'A woman usually wants a husband: some men want a kind of divinity, a sort of human surrogate for the B[lessed] V[irgin] M[ary]. I have had this.' He explained that if he could have married Emily when younger, 'I certainly should have done so wholeheartedly, exchanged the one relationship for the other, and adapted myself to it. But no one but you!' However, it was now too late. He had been shocked 'to discover that I recoiled violently from the prospect of marriage', now that marriage seemed a possibility. He had wrestled with the issue for three months, but his mind was made up: 'I cannot, cannot, start life again, and adapt myself (which means not merely one moment, but a perpetual adaptation for the rest of life) to any other person. I do not think that I could survive it, as a person; I cannot bear the company of any one person for very long without extreme irritation and suppression.' This sounded selfish, old-bufferish, self-protecting. Yet it was what he felt.

This is what we have to face. I am afraid, my dear, that the cataclysm is a much greater upheaval than your kind and patient and sympathetic words show any realization of. Physical intimacy without entire spiritual intimacy would be a nightmare (I know a little of that, as you may imagine: but it isn't now just a question of exorcising the demons of the past). And in writing every word I have the terror thinking that what I say will impress you simply as perverse, or insane, or dishonest, or as cobwebs to be swept away; and I feel in a state of utter destitution.[216]

Unsigned, this letter brought destitution to Emily too. If she thought he would change his mind, she was wrong. His trip to America would bring several painful encounters.

Preparing for it, he dealt with an assortment of work commitments. He assured poet and Scottish nationalist Douglas Young in April that 'as an English regionalist (I sometimes wonder whether I am the only one) I have a warm sympathy with the aims and aspirations of the Scottish movement'. He professed 'warm admiration' for 'the Scots language', but could 'not pretend an adequate knowledge' of it, lacking 'the finer discrimination, the appreciation of the right or the wrong word'.[217] In this way he excused himself from writing a preface to Young's poems. Tom could sound less enthusiastic about Scots verse elsewhere, but had several times attempted it. In doing so, he showed the limitations of his ear; astutely attuned to verse in English, he could err when it came to Scots rhymes. Still, none of that got in the way of his maintaining in the wake of the 'Master Minds' lecture he delivered on Milton at the British Academy in late March 1947 that Milton's 'genius' in *Paradise Lost* had its 'limitations' – most obviously in 'visual observation'.[218] If Tom was the most ambitiously learned religious poet of modern times, he remained awkward about this most commanding of his seventeenth-century predecessors.

He had his Milton lecture with him when he flew into New York on 23 April, since he was contracted to deliver it at the Frick Collection in Manhattan ten days later. In between, he spent most of his time in Cambridge where Henry, now bedridden, was extremely ill. Tom paid him repeated visits. Though Henry, 'my dear brother', spent much of the time dozing, 'he was able to sit up, for at least half an hour at a time, and talk'.[219] On 5 May he was taken to hospital. Tom was reading at Wellesley College that afternoon. He was contacted, but could not get back before his brother passed away. The funeral was conducted by the Society of St John the Evangelist. Theresa, who had done 'everything for him', took Henry's ashes to Louisville, Kentucky, where her family had a tomb; 'and while', Tom wrote to Mappie Mirrlees, 'we should have preferred an Eliot to be interred on the right side of the Ohio River, we have such affection and esteem for her that we are happy that she should have her wish'.[220]

According to a friend who spoke to Theresa later, it was around this time that Tom went out one day, telling her, 'I've got to get something over with.'[221] The crisis of Henry's death had made Tom resolved that he must tell Emily face-to-face that he could not marry her. Tom knew Henry had been convinced marriage to Emily after all these years would be a mistake. Exactly what the brothers spoke about when Henry was dying is not known, but Tom now nerved himself to confront Emily. Theresa perceived relations between Tom and Emily as not always easy. She 'described occasions when the two "got across" each other in conversation, so that when Emily left', Tom was seen to 'frown theatrically and clench his fists in mock irritation, conveying by exaggeration the very real exasperation he felt'. At one point, Tom told Theresa 'he would be prepared to "kill himself'" (those were his words) if Emily insisted on marriage'. Now, after so much anxiety and delay, he spoke to Emily one-to-one, telling her 'all thought of marriage between them must be forgotten'. When Theresa asked her brother-in-law how Emily had reacted, Tom replied that 'on the whole she had taken it very well'.[222]

The words Tom spoke to Emily are unrecorded, but were surely aligned with his letters. The two met repeatedly. Recounting events years later, Theresa telescoped what happened. In summer 1947 Emily (who had tendered her resignation from Concord Academy) wrote about her long-standing 'mutual affection' with Tom to her friend from Scripps College days, Lorraine Havens, saying that it had 'come to a strange impasse whether permanent or not, I do not know'. After Vivien's death,

> I supposed he would then feel free to marry me as I believed he always intended to do. But such proves not to be the case. We met privately two or three times to try to sift the situation as thoroughly as possible – he loves me – I believe this wholly – but apparently not in the way usual to men less gifted i.e. with complete love thro' a married relationship. I have not completely given up hope that he may yet recover from this – to me – abnormal reaction, but on the other hand I cannot allow myself to hold on to anything so delicately uncertain.[223]

Their meetings in May and June 1947 cannot have been easy for either of them. For their parting encounter, Tom travelled to see Emily in Concord, and went over in his mind repeatedly afterwards his final picture of her 'framed in the doorway' of a house in Hubbard Street.[224] Partings, pain, and worry filled his American visit, but, as ever, there were also official engagements. Just nine days after Henry's death, having had to cancel the appointment the previous week, Tom gave an hour-long reading to 'an overflow audience of about 1700' in Harvard's Sanders Theatre. Introduced as 'the first poet of our time', he spoke afterwards about literary plans: 'I'd like to do a play next', he explained, a 'sort of successor' to *The Family Reunion*. Surveying student life, he contrasted the leisured atmosphere of his own student days with modern Harvard's tenseness and worry. He saw a 'Worried Generation'. 'I don't mean to suggest', he added with a smile, 'that there isn't plenty to worry about.'[225]

Well aware of Tom's tendency towards worry, elusiveness, and emotional indecision, later, when they were together at Yale (where he reheated his 1944 lectures on Johnson) on 26 May Emily set in front of him her copy of *Prufrock and Other Observations* which he dutifully inscribed 'for Miss Emily Hale'; again dutifully, on his return from visiting Pound at St Elizabeths and reading at the National Gallery in Washington, he came to give the graduation address at Concord Academy, where Emily was finishing up teaching, on 3 June. In his revealing speech he addressed himself, and surely Emily, as well as his wider audience. He joked at the start about 'two people' who might have 'made a mistake'. Later he contended that, though 'nobody is altogether "a success" in life' and 'everybody is more or less a "failure"', a poet 'is not a successful man', and 'in the eyes of God all of us are weak and sinful'; he was 'haunted' by 'doubts' about the value of his work, and 'wrote *The Waste Land* simply to relieve my own feelings'. Poetry could help one distinguish between 'an appeal to our reason' and 'an appeal to our emotions'. In a passage dropped from the printed version of this Concord Academy address he linked the writing of poetry 'to the greatest and most general profession of all – that of marriage', contending that 'married people must always regard each other as a mysterious person whom they are gradually getting to know, in a process which must go on to the end of the life of one or the other'. He went on, 'Every moment is a new problem, and you cannot succeed, in the best meaning of "success", unless you approach the new poem, or the familiar husband or wife, with the feeling that there is a great deal for you to learn.'[226] If these words drew on his relationship with Vivien, then, like his private words to Emily, his view of marriage as bringing 'every moment' a 'new problem' suggested no appetite to re-enter the married state.

After speaking at Concord he returned to Cambridge where at Harvard, along with I. A. Richards, Secretary of State George Marshall, Robert Oppenheimer (father of the atom bomb), and others on 5 June he was awarded an honorary doctorate from his alma mater. Harvard's President Conant called him 'a religious and learned poet whose words the world will not willingly let die'.[227] At the Commencement ceremony, Tom, who had encountered President Truman on his visit to Washington, was impressed to hear George Marshall outline what became known as the Marshall Plan for Europe's economic regeneration. Here was a proposal that was practical in its efforts to revive farming and business, not a bureaucratic scheme to take control of 'culture'. Tom's American visit concluded with a visit to his old high school, Milton Academy, then the conferment of honorary degrees at Yale and Princeton before he flew back to London on 19 June.

He disliked transatlantic flying: 'the body does not respond favourably, nor does the soul, to being transported so quickly from place to place'. His time in America, he confessed to Morley, had been 'very strange. I don't think that I have been through such a bad patch since 1915.'[228] Back in London he had to come to terms not just with the death of his brother but also with the death of the dream he might marry Emily. Though she found this very, very hard to accept and they went on corresponding for almost another decade, gradually their exchanges of letters grew less frequent as it became apparent a key aspect of their relationship had gone. 'My thoughts will follow you from place to place', he wrote to her on 25 June, and they did. Giving up her rented house, and longing for a home of her own, before long she began teaching at another private girls' high school, Abbot Academy in Andover, Massachusetts. But his life moved increasingly further away from hers. He would never forget her, and she seemed unable to renounce him. He assured her, 'Whether it brings you pain or comfort, or whether it means less than either, you have all my love and devotion always, and this I must tell you.'[229] But what followed was a tense, long, painful dwindling, and an awareness that something had died.

14

Honours

H E went on writing to Emily, 'wondering how you have been'.[1] They exchanged news, tussled emotionally, and discussed what might eventually befall their letters. But their correspondence lacked its earlier ardour, and as this aspect of his private life slowly wound down over succeeding years, his public life showed no signs of let-up. Summer 1947 saw him revising 'the culture book' which 'has now gone rather sour on me'.[2] In mid-July he had his postponed hernia operation, at the private London Clinic near Harley Street; successful, 'for fear of coughing' it stopped him smoking only briefly, but sorted at least one lifelong discomfort.[3] Friends and his secretary visited him as he convalesced, but it was September before he returned to Russell Square. Looking a little thin, he was snapped for that month's *Vogue* by American photographer George Platt Lynes. Tom thought the images 'very good indeed': 'I look like a moderately good film actor in a variety of parts.'[4] In several pictures, carrying raincoat and rolled black umbrella, he wears a dark three-piece suit (white handkerchief in breast pocket) and fedora hat. In at least one he is seated indoors, relishing a cigarette.

October brought dental surgery, leaving him with false teeth, no teeth of his own, and, for a time, difficulties in chewing. Though his operations took him away from work, he found time to correspond in private and public about the 'obscure', linguistically inept activities of UNESCO, and to fight a relentless epistolary duel with bibliophile E. H. W. Meyerstein over Milton's use of the word 'prone'.[5] His tenacity on these topics sprang from his meticulousness as a philosophically trained poet. Now, though, instead of creating poems, he attempted (in ways Mary Trevelyan's new employer, UNESCO, may have found trying) to 'deprecate grandiose and cloudy schemes for "producing international understanding"', and to define 'culture' in his new prose book.[6] Meanwhile, still aspiring to write another play, he heard from Hayward that the restless American writer and socialite Emily Holmes Coleman had left her rancher husband and would 'crown her career by entering a convent'.[7] Though this story may have been inaccurate, a woman whose life leads unexpectedly towards religious commitment would be at the heart of his next drama.

Given his recent experiences, his choice of several poems about death and dying for a 'personal anthology' broadcast by BBC radio in November was unsurprising.[8] Late that month he learned the king wished to bestow on him one of Britain's highest honours, the Order of Merit. Tom accepted, expressing with formal precision an 'earnest desire to augment my worthiness of it'.[9] Soon, Pound, corresponding with Wyndham Lewis, nicknamed Tom 'O.M.'[10] On 7 December he flew to Rome, staying with the Bassianos, meeting Italian poets (including Giuseppe Ungaretti and Eugenio Montale), accepting membership of the Accademia dei Lincei, and having an audience with the Pope, who gave him two rosaries. In Italy he lectured for the British Council on 'Poetry in the Theatre' and on Poe's European influence. Contending that a new poetic drama was possible, he stressed theatre as a collaborative activity, different from poetry. Verse drama could access a deeper level of life than prose theatre. He may have been going over old ground, but he was also preparing for another play.

January brought many letters congratulating him on his Order of Merit, including one from Leonard Woolf. Thanking him, Tom recalled discussing with the Woolfs the unacceptability of honours in general; on that occasion, when Leonard had asked whether Tom would make an exception for the OM, he had replied he 'did not know'.[11] To Murry he expressed 'doubts and qualms', but mainly pleasure, confessing with regard to their long-standing, sometimes disrupted friendship, 'I have always had a sense that we should never get away from each other, so long as we each obeyed our own daemon.'[12] Feeling his daemon stirring, he was discussing with Martin Browne the 'new play' advancing towards 'mental formulation'. Tom expected it 'to be born this year', though 'I do not know how long it will be before it learns to walk, to say nothing of an acrobatic turn worthy of the theatre.'[13] The previous summer, Browne had enjoyed success at the first ever Edinburgh Festival where he had been invited to direct both *Murder in the Cathedral* (with Speaight reprising the role of Becket) and *The Family Reunion* as a 'Festival Season' of 'T. S. Eliot Plays' at the Church of Scotland's Gateway Theatre.[14] Now Edinburgh wanted more, but Tom, whose 'engine' had been 'out of action for so long', knew a summer 1948 deadline would throw him into a 'panic'. Mixing his metaphors, he suggested instead a 1949 premiere, provided he could 'break the back of the new born infant during the summer'. He hoped to start 'in two or three weeks' and to polish the play at Princeton where he had accepted a visiting fellowship later in the year.[15] Emily's friends the Thorps had helped arrange the Princeton appointment. If at one time she had hoped that such an arrangement might lead him to change his mind about marriage, she realised now that this was very unlikely, and suggested to him that he limit his correspondence with her to a monthly letter. He obliged.

He was more confident about embarking on the play because around this time he completed revising *Notes towards the Definition of Culture*. Continuing to exchange letters with Emily, albeit less frequently, he also kept in touch with Mary Trevelyan, who had written to him from Rangoon, having gone from UNESCO in Paris to work in Burma among (as Tom called them in a letter to her) 'these touching little Burmen and Burwomen'. As she had done from wartime Belgium, so now from Burma she sent newsy letters about her activities; he joked with her that she was 'beginning to take everything too seriously', and offered her one of the rosaries the Pope had given him.[16] Chain-smoking, hearty Mary enjoyed exchanging churchy gossip with him, but had always been alert to a deeper 'sense of mission' and efforts towards 'the redemption of the world'.[17] In some ways she would be a muse for his play.

On 12 February 1948 at Buckingham Palace 'Mr T. S. Eliot had the honour of being received by His Majesty, when The King invested him with the Insignia of a Member of the Order of Merit.'[18] A week later, around the time Tom was elected to the Garrick Club, the king and queen met him again at the Mercury Theatre when they saw *Murder in the Cathedral*. They witnessed 'a very bad performance, between ourselves', he reported to I. A. Richards, adding in postscript, 'Trying to start a play – but it's agony after nearly ten years out of practice; and it makes me realise how many more interruptions I have than ten years ago. The next ten years, no doubt, are the worst.'[19] Having sat through a performance of his best-known drama, Tom wrote some words about it for a BBC broadcast of *Murder* in Hindustani, summing up its 'essential theme' as 'the perpetual conflict between the eternal and divine order, and the temporal and worldly order. To those who live only in and for the latter, the former will always seem folly.'[20] Such themes would be important in his new play also.

Though guilt, affection, and exasperation were mingled in his attitude towards Emily, he wished to do all he could for her and those dear to her. In March, at Edith Perkins's request, he made a formal presentation of Emily's aunt's 465 colour slides of British gardens (including several in and around Chipping Campden) to the Royal Horticultural Society. He spoke of how sad it was that Mrs Perkins, who had loved gazing at flowers, was now blind.

If the Perkinses were linked to Emily and the Boston Unitarianism from which he had converted, then 'conversion' was in his mind as, around that time, he wrote the only sermon he ever delivered. Recalling childhood and his own conversion ('One may become a Christian partly by pursuing scepticism to the utmost limit'), he pondered what conversion might mean in the context of Christians undergoing 'persecution'. Should Christianity become a minority faith in the West, would there be 'compromise' with secularism? These issues would surface in his play; but he stated again, 'I have never made any direct attempt to convert anyone', emphasising 'penitence and humility' as 'the foundations of the Christian life'.[21]

Worried about his old friend's plight, he had been shown some typescripts of Pound's Italian broadcasts. 'I fear your father does not want to accept freedom on any terms that are possible', he remarked to Pound's daughter in London that April.[22] To Pound's mistress, Olga Rudge, he confided that, though he believed Pound – whom he came to regard as 'insane' – was neither antisemitic nor anti-British, his radio talks contained material that 'to the semite' was 'certainly anti-semitism. It might not have been, 20 years ago; but in the state of self-consciousness and hysteria of the last few years this would set American Jewry howling, and very few Jews would speak up for him.'[23] Tom's alertness to post-Auschwitz Jewish sensitivities does not sound unduly sympathetic. His loyalties to former mentors accused of antisemitism and war crimes remained strong. In an invited tribute for Maurras's eightieth birthday, he concentrated deliberately on literary, rather than political aspects of that 'master', who had been sentenced to life imprisonment as a wartime collaborator.[24]

As he worked on his new play, his imagination quickened. Anxious about possible crises in the Mirrlees household where Mappie was ill, he wrote to Hope about a strange 'dream in which I engaged in devising stratagems, with a ball of twine and a hammer, to rescue Mouse from a camel which had strayed into the garden, and eventually clambered into a tree, with Mouse in my pocket, to escape from a wart-hog, which, oddly enough, became smaller and smaller as it approached'.[25] If his dream-life could race, the intensity of his religious commitment showed no sign of diminution. Still, even as he went about his duties at St Stephen's, he admitted his faith was complex and unsettled. Murry's new book *The Free Society* aligned Christianity with British and American values, holding open the possibility of a just war against communist Russia. After reading it, Tom wrote to Murry:

> I do not know how far I am lacking in mystical sense, and how far it
> may be that I am anxious to display myself as an intellectual (which I

am not) instead of an *emotif*. The insistence upon dogma, doctrine, authority, may be simply part of my general anti-romanticism, which again may be the anti-romanticism of a romantic who has always been powerfully attracted to Indian types of speculation. But I do believe that it is hardly possible for any individual to be wholly orthodox – that is to say, perfectly balanced. The fact that to be wholly orthodox one must be constantly maintaining points of view which are logically contradictory, makes Christianity the most diffi-cult of all religions, and at the same time is to me a guarantee of its truth.[26]

Such thoughts accompanied him everywhere, and religious observances permeated his life at home, work, and further afield. Persuaded by Henri Fluchère, he travelled to Marseilles and Aix-en-Provence in mid-April. Lecturing in English, and (thanks to Fluchère's translation) in French on Poe, he received an honorary degree – commitments postponed from the previous year. Interviewed by French reporters and feted by academics, he relished staying for several quiet days with Fluchère's eighty-seven-year-old mother who lived alone in the village of Sainte-Tulle, proud of the wine, raisins, and almonds 'grown on her own acre'. His time there reminded him of one of the many reasons he loved French culture. She 'cooked a delicious leg of lamb with garlic'.[27]

Convinced that meaningful cultural relations flourished between indi-vidual artists and that 'a relation between countries which is a relation only between governments is a totalitarian one', he continued what he described to Pound as his 'campaign against UNESCO'.[28] But he rejected Pound's criticisms of his native land: 'If America hadn't come into the war where should I be?'[29] Death and the possibility of death were still on his mind that spring. Mappie Mirrlees, of whom he was so 'very fond', was dying.[30] Tom visited her just before going to Marseilles, finding her very weak, though he thought she still recognised him. She died soon afterwards: 'one of the most wonderful and endearing old ladies I have ever known,' he wrote to his niece, 'and endlessly kind to me'.[31] Tom's admiration of her (and her household's celebrated cuisine) led Faber & Faber to add to its cookery list *Wishful Cooking*, a book of recipes Mappie had assembled with her daugh-ter Margot. Featuring such triumphs as 'aubergines montelimar', 'hare with cherries', and 'radish rhapsody', it represented, according to its blurb (which Tom oversaw), 'the best traditions of English country-house cook-ing', and was a fitting tribute to the old Scots lady who had travelled the globe in some style, collecting recipes, shrewdly hiring fine cooks, and nurturing her 'puir daft makar' throughout the war.[32]

Opposed to Britain's Labour government, to UNESCO, and to increasing European secularisation, he knew that to some 'my thinking is "reactionary"'.[33] Nevertheless, he pressed ahead with publication of *Notes towards the Definition of Culture*, and supported new developments of which he approved. In early June he went to Oxford for the opening of the Maison Française there, at which he was awarded the Légion d'honneur. He returned later that month to accept an honorary degree from Oxford University, a doctorate to match one awarded *in absentia* by the University of Munich. Hayward grew increasingly proud of his flatmate's many distinctions, and correspondingly protective. They were an odd couple: Hayward a gossip and a committed atheist, Tom generally discreet and devoutly religious. Yet it suited each to live with the other. Considerate of his wheelchair-bound flatmate's needs, Tom went out of his way to keep the prodigiously well-read Hayward in touch with friends and colleagues, including those at Faber. Hayward was not just Tom's domestic gatekeeper, but also expert on his writings: following the success of a Penguin edition of Tom's *Selected Poems* (50,000 copies published in July 1948), Hayward went on to edit a Penguin selection of his prose. Both men knew what it was to cope with emotional loneliness and a difficult private life. They cared for one another, each respecting the other professionally. As well as publishing Graves's *The White Goddess*, Tom now added W. S. Graham to Faber's poetry list, supplementing his ongoing publishing of Pound (whose *Pisan Cantos* with their 'new poignancy of personal speech' appeared that year), Auden, MacNeice, Spender, and others.[34] Though most famous for his own work, he had become, too, the most respected poetry editor in the world. Several poets, including Auden, Kathleen Raine, Barker, Mac-Neice, Muir, Marianne Moore, Montale, George Seferis, and Spender were contributing to a Festschrift being assembled by Tambimuttu and Richard March for his sixtieth birthday. When one contributor, Empson, quarrelled with him that summer, Tom, while continuing to champion Empson's poetry, suggested tartly that Empson deal in future with his recently hired Faber junior colleague Peter du Sautoy.

Tom sent Browne 'the first draft of three scenes' of his new play on 1 June, mentioning also that he was now 'on the Council' of the 'curious' Festival of Britain planned for 1951.[35] As he had told Harvard students the previous summer, 'There are, after all, things one must do.'[36] Though he had drafted only the first act, Tom was, Browne recorded in his diary, 'in gay mood' over dinner on 15 June.[37] They discussed what, drawing on a bawdy Irish-American song familiar in late-nineteenth-century America, he had provisionally entitled *One-Eyed Riley: A Comedy*. Six weeks later, much of the work (which he then regarded as a four-act play) was in draft.

He decided 'a better title would be THE COCKTAIL PARTY. A cocktail party of guests whom the host didn't want, corresponds very well to a family reunion from which part of the family was absent.'[38] Working quickly on this play which he hoped to finish later in the year at Princeton, he was relishing the challenge, even if Browne found the drama too 'static'.[39] As Tom wrote to his author Lawrence Durrell, with whom he enjoyed corresponding, the modern dramatist lacked Shakespeare's advantages: 'We have got to make plays in which the mental movements cannot find physical equivalents. But when one comes to the big moment (and if we can't get it we can't do drama) there must be some simple fundamental emotion (expressed, of course, in deathless verse) which EVERYBODY can understand.'[40]

During this period, though he wrote to Emily about twice a month, he was reproached by Mary Trevelyan for not staying in regular touch. A little stiffly, he told her he sometimes envied men in public life whose jobs were 'considered to be of "national importance"', and so were not expected to have time for anything else.

But a man in my sort of private position is expected to have time for everything: everybody tells me that I ought to concentrate on one thing but I observe that what they want me to concentrate on is always the thing in which they happen to be interested. The effect is, that I neglect things indiscriminately, and relax only into torpor.

I will only ask you to believe that I value your friendship; and that if at any time I am invisible or inaudible, that is no indication of disloyalty.

Yours ever
Tom[41]

Before he left for America that autumn he sent a tribute for MacDiarmid (about whose work he felt some ambivalence) to be read aloud at a Scottish celebration, and corrected the proofs of *Notes towards the Definition of Culture*. Due for Faber publication in November, it reaffirmed links between culture and religion, championing 'the region' as a key unit in a society of 'unity and diversity'. Tom maintained 'culture will have to grow again from the soil' in the 'new civilisation' which was 'always being made'.[42] Drawing on articles written since 'Little Gidding', *Notes* constituted his most sustained mature contribution to cultural theory. Engaging with thinkers from Trotsky to Karl Mannheim, its intellectual ambition was obvious and it established him all the more firmly as a conservative social thinker. Yet it was also a tombstone in terms of his poetry, reinforcing his transition to cultural commentator, literary critic, and verse dramatist. In many ways, it ran against the grain of the times, and could be unconvincing. He might contend that 'The Englishman, for instance, does not ordinarily think of England as a "region" in the way that a Scottish or Welsh national can think of Scotland or Wales', but his use of the word 'national' in that sentence undermines it: for most Scots 'the Borders' or 'the Hebrides' might be a 'region', but 'Scotland' remains a 'nation' just as much as 'England' does to the English.[43] Still with UNESCO in his sights, in the context of 'the unimaginable world culture', Tom attempted ambitiously to consider such issues as 'the colonial problem'. His language of 'higher' and 'lower' cultures has not worn well, but his vision of 'a healthily *stratified* society' and his patrician tone might have raised few eyebrows at the Burke Club.[44]

About ten days before sailing to America, he asked the patient and obliging Mary Trevelyan if, after he returned, he could sing to her '(repeatedly if necessary) two stanzas of a simple song called "One Eyed Riley"'. If she would 'write out the score', then he could use the 'perfectly proper' part of it in his play, supplying Browne with the appropriate music.[45] Then, just after the publication of Tambimuttu and March's Festschrift, and a couple of days before his sixtieth birthday, he boarded ship. He was leaving, he told Polly Tandy in a jokey letter (with a wink to Edward Lear) 'in a state of the most extreme melancholy, umbrageousness, diffidence, misery, peakiness, wishfulness and blanc mange', but he hoped to return 'in a state of satisfaction, contemplation, misery, cosiness, and hot-pot'. He looked forward to being at 'The Institute of Advanced Study (golly what a name) Princeton'.[46] Though he did not say so, he was also anticipating with some trepidation meeting Emily, the Perkinses, family members and others in a series of side trips. In his luggage was the typescript of *The Cocktail Party* – his pretext for 'advanced study'. Tom enjoyed his transatlantic crossing without being pestered: 'not a soul to identify Old Possum', he confided in a letter to Hayward from on board the SS *America*. 'I eat and sleep, take two martinis at 6 p.m. and two bourbons at bedtime.'[47]

After a brief stopover with the Kauffers in New York where he saw Marianne Moore, he proceeded to Princeton. From there, signing himself 'Tp / Advanced Student', he wrote to Mary Trevelyan.[48] The Institute for Advanced Study was, he explained to Mary Hutchinson, 'a Jamesian Great Good Place for elderly celebrities'.[49] Among those he met were Jacques Maritain and Reinhold Niebuhr; also in the vicinity were Robert Oppenheimer and other 'atom-bombers', as well as Albert Einstein, Paul Dirac, and a group 'working on a Thinking Machine'.[50] Unimpressed by this computer, Tom *was* impressed to have use of a blackboard, with a sign one side of which 'says ERASE and the other DO NOT ERASE, so I must get to work on that'.[51]

Close to old friends and acquaintances including the Thorps, he rather enjoyed Princeton, though contact with Emily brought pain as well as pleasure. He visited her at Abbot Academy in Andover, where she would work for almost a decade, and later she received from him a typescript of *The Cocktail Party*. Both of them wished their relationship to remain affectionate, but it could not be as before, and Tom, sensing face-to-face meetings were awkward now, was prepared to reduce direct contact. Accepting that, but continuing to correspond with him, Emily became a much appreciated teacher of drama at her school, where she spoke on occasion to pupils about her special friend, and staged a range of dramatic productions, including, yet again, one of her favourite plays, Barrie's *Dear Brutus*, that tragicomedy of love's might-have-beens.

Eager to fund what he hoped would be one of many annual returns to America, Tom agreed to lecture at the University of Chicago in two years' time. He also made several side trips. As well as seeing Emily, he visited Henry's widow Theresa and renewed many other Massachusetts contacts. He went to Washington for official engagements (including a Library of Congress lecture, 'From Poe to Valéry'), and to stay with his old Harvard friend, distinguished American public servant William R. Castle. He met Ezra and Dorothy Pound. At his old high school, Milton Academy in Massachusetts, he delivered the 'War Memorial Address' on 3 November. As requested, he spoke there on leadership, and, concentrating on literature, described (without naming him) Pound's mentoring work. His characteristically thoughtful talk to Milton's schoolboys and teachers was shot through with revealing asides: 'It is, to me, wholly unintelligible that any man should *want* to be a leader. But then, I cannot understand anyone wanting to be a poet.' Commending Edmund Burke 'for political insights and statements of permanent value', he also warned against 'a totalitarian society in which both art and science are expected to be of immediate utility'.[52]

While he was at Milton unsettling news reached him: he had been awarded the Nobel Prize in Literature. A telegram from Stockholm had been sent to him at the Institute for Advanced Study on the morning of 4 November, and someone there phoned the Milton school office. If this brought him wild schoolboy cheers, and a certain inner satisfaction, it also complicated his schedule. 'My plans', he complained to Marianne Moore, 'have been completely disarranged by this misfortune, which is going to send me off to Stockholm, if I can get there by December 10.'[53] To John Berryman, whom he met soon afterwards, Tom remarked, 'The Nobel is a ticket to one's funeral. No one has ever done anything after he got it.'[54]

In Princeton, arrangements grew hectic. A *Life* magazine photographer arrived, and Tom posed by his blackboard. Clad in dark suit, white shirt and tie, he had chalked up lines of lettered squares, apparently graphing aspects of his new play. Glancing back at the camera with raised eyebrow, he produced a look of intense Advanced Study. Cataloguing his burgeoning commitments, he wrote to Hayward, arranging, en route to Stockholm, 'to collect my dress clothes' from the Chelsea flat.[55]

On 10 December, after a trumpet fanfare and the arrival of the crown prince and Swedish royal family, Tom, in white tie and formal dress, and wearing his Order of Merit, sat on stage at a splendid ceremony in Stockholm's City Hall. Around him were 1948's other Nobel Laureates – to several of whom he took a dislike. As the prizes were awarded, he was fourth in line. Called forward, he heard a long presentation speech by Anders Osterling, permanent secretary of the Swedish Academy, who spoke of him as a poet who 'from an extremely exclusive and consciously isolated position' had 'gradually come to exercise a very far-reaching influence'. His verse and prose had 'a capacity to cut into the consciousness of our generation with the sharpness of a diamond'. Osterling ended by pointing out that, 'Exactly twenty-five years ago, there stood where you are now standing another famous poet who wrote in the English tongue, William Butler Yeats. The honour now passes to you as being a leader and a champion of a new period in the long history of the world's poetry.'[56] Replying to one of many toasts at the ensuing banquet, Tom spoke with elegance, humour, and dignity. He stated that on first hearing news of the award, he had experienced 'all the normal emotions of exaltation and vanity that any human being might be expected to feel at such a moment, with enjoyment of the flattery, and exasperation at the inconvenience, of being turned overnight into a public figure'. Addressing the assembled dignitaries, he concluded, 'I stand before you, not on my own merits, but as a symbol, for a time, of the significance of poetry.'[57]

After 'a small party of not more than a hundred or two guests' given by the Nobel family from midnight onwards, there was dinner at the royal palace with government and other grandees the following evening. Next came a performance of *The Family Reunion* in Swedish at the National Theatre; then a further dinner party; and explaining to a fellow laureate the importance of Edward Lear; and being serenaded while shaving at 6.45 a.m. by 'six comely young chambermaids' with 'cardboard crowns on their heads with lighted candles in them' in celebration of St Lucy's Day. After all that, he returned to London with his Nobel Prize cheque – worth, he confided to his sister Marion, just over '£11,016'.[58] As soon as he was back he 'was busy for three days and then took to bed and slept for a day and a half'.[59] Christmas, in the wake of all this, was comparatively restful, though he received so many congratulatory letters that he struggled to answer them, and began to fear that, even with secretarial assistance, he would never again in life feel up-to-date with correspondence.

If at Princeton he had not done as much to his play as he had hoped, by mid-January he was back at it, working in the flat each morning, before going into his office in afternoons. 'Trying to write a play' was, he confessed to Violet Schiff, 'work for which I have no native gift', but he had done it before and would do so again.[60] Aiming to focus, he was, as always, distracted. In addition to responding at length to an Anglican report on education, he travelled to Oxford to address an Alliance Française dinner on 19 January, invoking Scotland's 'Auld Alliance' with France and emphasising that 'the consciousness that Britain is a part of Europe is more and more widespread'.[61] Other obligatory dinners followed, but underneath his sense of busyness he felt saddened by the death of two younger contemporaries: in England Michael Roberts, whose 'aptitude for wisdom' Tom valued highly, had died in December; then Ted Spencer at Harvard died in January.[62] Tom worked on. With characteristic generosity, he offered financial assistance to Roberts's widow, Janet, who was left to bring up her young family.

By February 1949 he was confident he had *The Cocktail Party*'s first act completed to Browne's satisfaction, and had finished a second draft of act two, with the remainder of the play still to be revised. He was hoping his sister Marion and niece Theodora could attend its opening run in Edinburgh that summer, and he went to see Ibsen's domestic tragedy of self-delusion *The Wild Duck* at the St Martin's Theatre. Between the Burke Club, his other dining or discussion groups, and his membership of the Garrick, he was a grandee whose patronage was constantly requested: 'I always seem to be the only Elder Man of Letters on duty in London', he complained to Mary Hutchinson.[63] Yet if age, a certain assumed grandeur, and obligations sometimes went together, he remained alert to younger talent, including that of Robert Lowell, whom he had met on several occasions in the States and with whom he developed an affectionate working relationship. In 1949 Faber & Faber became Lowell's British publisher.

Browne had expected the Old Vic Theatre Company might premiere Tom's new play, but, after tensions arose, Rudolf Bing, director of the Edinburgh Festival, put Browne in touch with impresario Henry Sherek. This 'real commercial showman' agreed to take on Tom as a client and bring the new play to Edinburgh. Browne, who saw the playwright as an 'austere, quiet poet' with an 'academic manner and reputation', was amused when he and his wife asked Sherek and Tom to an initial meeting over lunch: 'acute embarrassment all round'.[64] The ebullient Sherek knew relatively little about Tom but had heard that he was 'something of a recluse'. He recalled:

When I was introduced, horrified distress was plainly visible on T. S. Eliot's face. He had probably never seen a theatrical producer or met anybody looking remotely like me before, and his expression showed clearly that he hoped fervently that he would never have to again.

Conversation seemed impossible. Sherek tried to break the ice by suggesting Tom must be proud that a fellow Missourian, Harry S. Truman, was president of the United States. There was a very long silence, during which the Brownes sat 'bolt upright, petrified with anxiety'. Eventually, Tom glanced at Sherek with what the impresario thought was 'something approaching loathing and prepared to speak'. Sherek had been expecting a 'rich Missourian twang'; instead, to his 'astonishment', he heard, eventually, 'a slow drawl' and 'an accent which was irrefutably English': '"We who were born in the State of Missouri are rather prouder of having produced Mark Twain."'

No further conversation ensued. When the meal was over, Tom 'fled'.[65]

Yet, gradually, after some further encounters each of these contrasting characters came to appreciate the other's strengths. Browne realised Sherek gave Tom 'the opportunity he had always wanted, to offer his play-writing talent to the theatre-public on equal terms with other dramatists'.[66] Just as Tom had remained loyal to Browne, so now they both realised that they had a staunch ally in Sherek. The Sherek Players Ltd would produce Tom's new play at Edinburgh in association with the recently founded Arts Council of Great Britain. Tom's own theatre-going continued – some of it done out of obligation, some for pleasure and research. He saw a production of Jean Anouilh's *Antigone* produced by Henri Fluchère at London's Institut Français in March. Though *The Cocktail Party* was very different, it shared with Anouilh's play the desire to bring contemporary issues into productive dialogue with ancient Greek forms. Where his previous play had included the Eumenides, the new drama included three mysterious 'guardians'. They seem at once part of contemporary life and participants in a timeless libation ritual. Browne linked their presence to the figuring of supernatural 'guardianship' in James Bridie's 1930 play *Tobias and the Angel*, but parallels with Greek drama are more striking.[67] One of the characters, Edward Chamberlayne, speaks to Celia Coplestone in a draft version about the inner '*daemon*', but Browne persuaded Tom to cut this Greek word from the final text.[68]

Dining out with cronies at the All Souls Club, Chandos group and Burke Club, and wheeling his flatmate around town to various engagements, Tom also enjoyed the company of Mary Hutchinson and Mary Trevelyan. To the latter he complained in mid-March of being 'heartily sick' of being 'hermetically sealed up with my seven imaginary characters', though this did not stop him asking her for 'tips about my East Indian island: are there monkeys, and do people tie their victims up in the jungle and smear them with sticky stuff to attract insects[?]' His complaint that 'There is no information on these points in any of your reports' indicates how much the situation of Celia in the play he was writing was linked to the long, newsy letters she sent him from her travels on behalf of UNESCO to Burma, Malaya, and neighbouring countries.[69] Tom liked Mary to think she had made a 'contribution to the character of Julia' in his new drama, and sometimes, playfully, he called her 'Julia'; but aspects of her can be seen in Celia, whose fate is the most shocking in the play.[70] Just as he drew on contact with Hoellering (still working on filming *Murder in the Cathedral*) for a sense of the film industry in his play, so he drew, too, on Mary's experiences. He found her useful, inspiring, and sympathetic; yet, though she suggested he was not keeping in touch as often as she would like, he continued in his warm, sometimes flirtatiously friendly letters to make it clear that he had to ration his time. He maintained a certain distance between them. Attentively, she began to record his behaviour, reminiscences, and foibles in her private memoir entitled 'The Pope of Russell Square'.

His play was now in four acts. 'Not confident about anything', he tried to rework act four for Browne in mid-March.[71] Around the same time news broke that a Library of Congress committee, whose fourteen members included Tom, had decided to award Pound the $10,000 Bollingen Prize. The award was for the *Pisan Cantos*, just published in America and due from Fabers in London later that year. This generated a great, long-lasting furore, particularly in the States where some commentators saw the prize as rewarding treason, fascism, and antisemitism. Tom had written some years before that the *Cantos* were 'the only important long poem of our time', and had been hoping publication of a carefully edited selection of Pound's letters as well as the new *Pisan Cantos* might help Pound's case.[72] Now he, his old friend, and the Bollingen Prize committee were denounced. Soon, under political pressure, the Library of Congress decided to withdraw from awarding future prizes, but arguments over the Bollingen, and, more generally, the rights and wrongs of Pound's situation would reverberate loudly for years. Tom's ongoing defence of Pound was accompanied by news that 'Cal' – Robert Lowell – had been institutionalised after a mental breakdown; when he heard this, Tom felt 'profoundly distressed'.[73] His own experience of breakdown and mental illness shaped his understanding of others' plight.

As his play advanced, he heard Alec Guinness wanted to act in it. This pleased him, but while, continuing to correspond with Emily, he worked on revisions to his drama about marriage, love, self-delusion, 'The experience of loneliness / Living with another person', humiliation, betrayal and religious commitment, Mary Trevelyan asked him to marry her.[74] Having felt herself in love with him since 1942, and treasuring moments such as an incident when he had held her 'hand for an unusually long time on parting', she wrote before going to Paris for several days, giving him time to reflect on her proposal.[75] His reply, whose first sentence included the word 'catastrophe', was difficult for both of them. He did not name Emily, but stated there was 'another person' with whom he had been involved and that he had 'realised – with a shock – several years ago and in quite another context, that I was burnt out, and that I could no longer feel towards anyone as I once had, and up to that moment believed I still did'. This 'tragedy' had left him 'ever since, a haunted man', convinced 'the thought of trying to share my life with anyone had become a nightmare'. Now, after 'a kind of psychological change of life', he felt he was simply trying to accomplish what he could 'in creative work' before his time ran out. What he told Mary substantially echoed what he had told Emily. His state of mind might 'be just a somewhat premature ageing; it may be party [sic] that what I went through in a good many years of agony had exhausted and crippled me more than, during the five or six years before the war, I had recognised'.[76]

Tom's mistyping 'party' instead of 'partly' in that last, confessional sentence is a further hint that at some level *The Cocktail Party* was bound up with his relationship with Mary. In his play, the character of Celia, who shares Mary's globe-trotting intrepidity as well as her religious commitment, ends up being martyred. In art, staging aspects of his psychodrama, he found in Celia's martyrdom a dramatic solution. In life, he sought to maintain his friendship with Mary even as (with the unnamed Emily, as well as his marriage to Vivien in the background) he made it clear they could not marry or be more than friends.

Well, one so easily falls into assuming that another person understand [sic] what one feels, without facing the fact that they can't do that in ignorance of things one has not told them, and which reticence makes it impossible to tell. Which, even when it comes to a show down, one can only hint at. As for yourself and me, I honestly didn't know that it was anything like that. Not that it had not crossed my mind, some time ago, that something might have developed if other things that had happened to me in the past had not made it impossible for me – but that's all, and I did think we had arrived at a stable friendship. I should hate to lose that, because you have become an important part of my life, though I have to parcel out my time in such ways that I cannot ever see a great deal of any one person. It is always a long time before I can convince myself that anyone (of either sex) really likes me very much and wants my friendship, and I am always surprised and grateful when I believe someone does. But even in the curious life I lead, it would mean a great gap if you were not there at all.[77]

In his way, he tried as hard as he could to make it easy for her to accept his refusal without humiliating her. Typing 'PRIVATE' on his letter's envelope, and signing himself 'your affectionate and appreciative friend', he suggested he destroy her letter – and sent her a copy of a note from an Indian correspondent which he thought would amuse her. But Mary was not so easy for Tom to control as was the fictional Celia, and, even when she accepted what he told her, she went on thinking, as Emily had, that somehow he might come around. They continued to meet, and correspond. She was keen to go on seeing him. He liked her very much, and felt wary.

While all this was going on, he was still sitting, very intermittently, for the artist Patrick Heron. Eventually, viewing Heron's work as it developed, Tom, was struck by the painter's depiction of him. He told Heron, 'It's a cruel face, a cruel face: a very cruel face! But of course you can have a cruel face without being a cruel person!'[78] Heron's oil portrait, dated 1949 and now in London's National Portrait Gallery, shows Tom simultaneously full-face and in profile. It could be interpreted as suggesting he was two-faced, but, more accurately, it captures psychological complexity. Tom did his best not to be cruel to Mary Trevelyan or to Emily, and continued to write to both with affection. Yet, as in the play he was writing, he was troubled by worries about possible cruelty and self-delusion. At the same time, he did not allow emotional crisis to stop him working on his drama, his other commitments, or his job. As he put it to Allen Tate that May in a thoughtful letter about Robert Lowell, 'a regular job, however boring (all jobs are boring) is desirable to steady the nerves'.[79] On the same day he wrote to Mary, telling her he was very busy, 'very tired', and that, though he would telephone 'if there is a chance of a quick lunch', it looked as if he might not be free for dinner for at least three weeks.[80]

Three weeks later, on his return from engagements in Oxford, he did take her to dinner, as his guest at the Garrick Club. Hoping all would be well between them, he was soon sending her his customary newsy, busyness-filled, gossipy letters. As far as his play went, he grew more confident. Determined to avoid 'making up with nice poetry what is lacking in dramatic quality', he was pleased to have written, for the first time, 'a play in verse with no chorus whatever' that dealt with '*contemporary* life'. If audiences expected poetry, then for much of the play they 'should not be conscious of the difference from prose'.[81] Though he elaborated on this, and did not wish to eschew poetry entirely, it's hard to imagine Racine or Shakespeare taking such an attitude. Tom's attention to language – whether in revising his play, editing others' work, or critiquing a new '*easy* to understand' translation of the Bible – remained exact and exacting.[82] Yet the unmemorable verse he was writing fell far short of his earlier poetry. Seeking a drama that was 'superficially at least purely realistic', he wanted sets appropriate to a 'perfectly naturalistic play', rather than anything suggesting ' "experimental" theatre'.[83] Taking care to read his play's verse aloud to Browne, so the actors might be helped in mastering its rhythms, he tried to balance delicately between the acoustics of verse, and audiences' expectations of realism.

He had other expectations to cope with too, including those of people aware of his substantial royalties and post-Nobel wealth. Magdalene College, Cambridge, where he enjoyed being an honorary fellow, wanted a portrait of him for their hall. They suggested he might pay for it himself. Relaying this to Lewis with a certain resigned amusement, Tom suggested buying the recent portrait by Lewis available at London's Redfern Gallery. Tom recalled that, painting it, Lewis, had been 'obliged to peer closely at me every few minutes, as it was the last picture he was able to paint before complete blindness put an end to the practice of this art'.[84] For Tom, purchasing this picture would benefit one of his oldest artist friends, and keep the Magdalene fellows happy; but it wasn't cheap. 'It seems to me,' he added to Lewis, 'they might pay for the frame themselves.'[85]

By the time Marion and his niece – 'my family', as he called them to Polly Tandy in July – arrived, his thoughts were turning to Edinburgh.[86] His play would be staged there at the Royal Lyceum Theatre from 22 August. Angry at the Bollingen furore, which had led to his being linked with fascism and antisemitism by commentators including Robert S. Hillyer whose *Saturday Review of Literature* articles – 'Treason's Strange Fruit' and 'Poetry's New Priesthood' – circulated widely, Tom grew anxious lest the debacle further harm Pound. Before leaving for Scotland he sent a letter to the *New Alliance and Scots Review* (where correspondence attacking Pound had appeared), making it clear the author of the *Pisan*

Cantos was no ' "self-convicted" traitor', but had been found by 'the Federal Court' to be 'of unsound mind and therefore unfit to be tried'.[87] He worried, though, about Pound's future.

When he reached Edinburgh after attending London rehearsals, he told journalists just before the final dress rehearsal that he had been working on the play for fifteen months. 'Even now I am not sure that I have finished it.' Tom was reported telling an American commentator who asked why the play was in verse, 'some things' could 'be better said in verse than in prose', and 'Besides, verse came easier to him than prose.'[88] Sitting just behind Browne who was in the front row of the Lyceum's dress circle for the last rehearsal, at the line, 'Hell is oneself', Tom leaned forward 'and whispered: "Contre Sartre" '.[89] From the start, *The Cocktail Party* let audiences hear in its party guests' chatter distinctively witty verbal clinks and rhythms appropriate to the title:

> PETER.   I like that story.
> CELIA.   I love that story.
> ALEX.   *I'm* never tired of hearing that story.
> JULIA. Well, you all seem to know it.
> CELIA.   Do we all know it?[90]

Tom thought the performance 'a triumph'.[91] What he and audiences saw staged was a 'comedy' in which he had taken aspects of his own experience – a middle-aged man's relationship with two women (one of them younger), time spent in sanatoria from the Malmaison to Harley Street, society parties, reports of life in the Far East, loneliness, marital failure, humiliation, feelings of guilt at having hurt other people, worry about self-delusion, religious commitment – and distributed these deftly among characters from upper-middle-class London life.[92] This play, like so much of his other poetry and drama, deployed the idea that there was a 'real reality' deeper and more disturbing than everyday 'reality'.[93] Headed by Sir Henry Harcourt-Reilly, the play's 'guardians' operate like spiritual directors, guiding other characters' lives according to what can appear a preordained pattern, saving them from being 'self-deceivers'.[94]

In an amusingly complicated geometry of relationships, this playwright who thought he could have been a lawyer lets audiences observe a middle-aged lawyer, Edward Chamberlayne. Plagued by 'indecision', Chamberlayne is conscious 'what it is to feel old' and to 'feel that you have lost / The desire for all that was most desirable'.[95] He and his taken-for-granted wife, Lavinia, are led to perceive truths about each other which let them begin to renew their marriage after each has had an affair. Celia Coplestone, with whom Edward had thought himself in love, is told, 'If I have ever been in love – and I think that I have – / I have never been in love with anyone but you, / And perhaps I still am.'[96] Emily came to believe that this play contained a 'hidden meaning' that was important to her; but for assistance it is 'Miss Mary Trevelyan' who is acknowledged in the published text, and Mary believed that the drama encoded a special meaning for *her*.[97] The play's Celia discovers her passion is for religious commitment in a nursing order, rather than love for a man. Echoing the final utterance of the Buddha, Celia is told by Reilly, 'Work out your salvation with diligence.' Reilly's next words, spoken into a telephone, are the last words of Christ on the cross, 'It is finished.'[98] Later, we learn Celia has been crucified. On stage, once again in a play featuring a woman's death, Tom was working out issues that could be more neatly reconciled than in his life where, even after Vivien's death, he felt unable, despite their wishes, to commit himself either to Emily or to Mary – neither of whom seemed to be heading for crucifixion.

This drama whose mysterious Reilly speaks of 'shuffling memories and desires', contained clear echoes of Tom's earlier poetry, though not all theatregoers noticed or were troubled by them.[99] The eight-day Edinburgh run was completely sold out in advance. 'All-day queues' formed 'for returned tickets'. Yet the *Scotsman*'s reviewer, while relishing a 'wit' that 'sparkles throughout', wondered if the poetry required 'greater power of emotional expression'; and drama critic Ivor Brown (who generally disliked Tom's work) damned with faint praise the play's 'certain amount of crossword-puzzle appeal'.[100] The *Times* drama critic perceived true 'distinction', however, commending 'lucid, unallusive verse which endows everyday speech with a delicate precision and a strictly occasional poetic intensity'. *The Cocktail Party* presented 'in the shape of a fashionable West End comedy a story highly ingenious in its construction, witty in its repartee, and impregnated with Christian feeling'.[101] A comparable range of views came from reviewers and audiences who saw the play later, briefly in Brighton in late 1949, then in New York in early 1950, and afterwards in London and elsewhere. It became a hit, but, despite Tom's small additional revisions, and despite reviews (several by people linked to the dramatist) praising the wit, there were persistent concerns about lack of poetic intensity. Some thought the work manipulative and unconvincing; others a masterpiece. Either way, it was widely discussed, commercially successful, and made its author even more of a household name. Buoyed up by his time in Edinburgh, where he lunched with Scottish dramatists including James Bridie and Joe Corrie, and dined with fellow poets MacDiarmid, Sydney Goodsir Smith and Norman MacCaig, Tom was already contemplating his next play – another contemporary drama patterned after a Greek original, Euripides' *Ion*.

Back in London, the main change was that he had a new secretary. Encouraged by Collin Brooks, Valerie Fletcher had applied for a job at Faber & Faber. Like most secretaries at the time, she had no degree, but her experience of library work and assisting writers made her well qualified. Tom was amused to hear she had left her job with Charles Morgan 'because she did not like cooking'; much later she suggested her departure had been precipitated by Morgan's wish 'to be beaten, in the nude, with the flat of a sword'.[102] She did not confess she had been obsessed for years with the idea of becoming Tom's secretary. Before submitting her application, she 'walked up and down outside Faber's for nearly two hours', summoning 'the courage' to hand it in.[103] Years later, she still recalled vividly her interview with Tom in his 'little Dickensian office':

He was as terrified as I was. He smoked and smoked. I had been so nervous I had cut my hand the night before on a tin and it was all wrapped up.

We talked about 17th-century poetry and so on and, as I was leaving, he put his chin round the edge of the door and told me that he had to see all of the applicants before he made a decision. I knew there were a lot of other girls – one of them had a double first at Oxford. But then he paused, looked at my hand and said: 'But I hope you'll be able to type in about 10 days' time.'[104]

Receiving a letter two days later, she started work on 12 September. In another account of her job interview with Tom, she recalled her sense of how nervous he had been, and how 'Much to his relief, she quickwittedly began to interview herself and got the job.'[105] She was twenty-three, poised, and efficient. Tom soon referred to her in letters to Janet Adam Smith, Mary Trevelyan, and Mary Hutchinson. He advised Mary Hutchinson not to 'mention' Charles Morgan to her.[106]

By late October, with his diary engagements now co-ordinated by Miss Fletcher, he was off to Germany for several weeks. Lecturing and reading for the British Council, he toured Hamburg, Berlin, Hanover, Göttingen, Munster, Bonn, Cologne, Heidelberg, and Munich. Throughout, he emphasised that 'the culture of every people arises from their religion', and stressed the cultural bonds forming 'the organism of Europe'.[107] He spoke in English variously on 'The Aims of Poetic Drama' (general audiences 'should be affected by the poetry without knowing it'), on 'The Idea of a European Society', and, reworking older material, on Shakespeare's verse.[108] The tour represented his determined commitment to post-war reconciliation. It left him very tired, but he pressed on. With Robert

Speaight he visited Brussels in early December to speak as 'guest of honour' at 'Les Grandes Conférences catholiques'.[109] Then he attended *The Cocktail Party* at Brighton, a warm-up for January's New York production. After Christmas, urged by his doctor, he took a substantial holiday, sailing with the Fabers on a long voyage to South Africa where, at the start of a new decade, he soaked up the sun. He was pleased to see Hope Mirrlees, who had moved to South Africa following her mother's death. He enjoyed a different, more relaxed, lifestyle far from London's winter cold and fog. On its own journey to distant New York, *The Cocktail Party* went on without him.

15

Alone

*T*HE *Times* called Tom's 1950 South African cruise a 'rest cure' – a phrase that, later, he considered as the title for a play.[1] Misleadingly, his fortieth anniversary report to Harvard's 'Class of 1910' claimed he had had 'No vacations. No ideas'.[2] Certainly, the Fabers, his travelling companions, saw he needed rest. If, occasionally, he thought of work and 'Miss Fletcher', then undoubtedly, 'looked after and valeted as in the old days', he enjoyed the comforts of his ocean voyage.[3] Smoking and drinking pleasurably, he attended the ship's fancy-dress party dressed as Sherlock Holmes. Disembarking in Cape Town, he looked more relaxed, but still strained. 'Interminable drives' to sights including historic Simon's Town seem to have bored him, but he saw Hope Mirrlees at Stellenbosch, relished 'good steaks', and visited the Groot Constantia wine estate. To Hayward he reported meeting local luminaries, including 'famous author Stuart Cloete' and General Smuts.[4] Politically 'very depressing', South Africa struck Tom as 'beautiful but melancholy'. Lunching at 'the Follies' in Cape Town's Hout Bay, he thought of Conrad's colonial fiction of racial tensions, *Almayer's Folly*. Undeniably, though, the Cape offered well-off visitors fine eating and drinking. Sailing home, he amused himself by writing a letter, ostensibly from 'the Rev. John McHaigh LL.D., B.Sc.', exhorting Faber to 'TEMPERANCE' and bemoaning a life 'ruined because of excessive indulgence in beer, whisky, gin, rum and other strong drink'.[5]

He was cheered to hear that *The Cocktail Party*, initially starring Alec Guinness and Irene Worth, was successful in New York. In London, however, work recaptured him. Serving on the Festival of Britain advisory board, he resumed publishing duties, and turned his mind to 'The Aims of Education', on which he had agreed to lecture in Chicago that year. He was distressed to hear that his friend F. O. Matthiessen, after increasing

isolation at Harvard, had killed himself. Discreetly homosexual (his partner had died in 1945), and a self-proclaimed socialist in McCarthyite
America, Matthiessen had identified, too, as Christian. 'I always thought
him', Tom wrote on 5 April, 'a person of a kind of repressed excessive
intensity' and 'a very religious man. Perhaps that was part of the trouble – I
mean that he had a capacity for religious fanaticism, without the discipline
and control of a dogma or a church.'⁶ The day after writing about 'discipline and control', he had Mary Trevelyan in mind as he wrote to *The Times*
supporting 'students of Asiatic and African races' at London University.⁷
Yet while involvement with Mary's Student Movement House had
brought him closer to her, he knew he would not marry her. His scribbled
note to her on 15 March stated it was 'against my rules to see *anyone*
more than once a 4tnight & stricter in Lent', though they did meet in late
March. Pleased she too was a heavy smoker, he saved her 'a nice Benson &
Hedges tin'.⁸

Mary's persistent feelings, however, brought him 'embarrassment and
unease'.⁹ On Monday 29 May, she again proposed marriage. She loved him,
admired him, was good for him; they shared so much. He replied that Friday: 'I am afraid I must try to expose (as I have done to no one so far) the
most agonising experience of my life.'¹⁰ For many years, he explained,
he had been deeply in love with someone else, 'and would willingly have
sacrificed everything for the possibility of marrying her'. He named neither Emily, nor Vivien, but recapitulated to Mary what Emily already
knew:

Then, when finally I was free, I realised quite suddenly that I was
deluding myself with emotions I had felt in the past, that I had
changed much more, and in ways unsuspected, than I had thought. I
found that I actually could not bear the thought of it. You will of
course infer at once that this was merely a particular relationship
which, when it reached the possibility of completion, was found no
longer to exist. But it is much more than that, and that is what cannot
be expressed in any words I can find. I take it to mean that I am still,
in a way, in love with her, even though I prefer not to see her, feel
embarrassed and unhappy when I do, seem to have very little in common now. There is also of course the feeling, which only a man can
understand, that a man, in all these situations, is somehow always in
the wrong. Anyway, I do care enough about her to be unable to contemplate except with horror the thought of marrying anyone else, or
of any other relationship except that of friendship. And I have never
wanted to marry anyone except this one person.

Clearly these words were wrung out of him. Having tried to explain matters to Mary before, he had done so, he realised, in a way that might be interpreted as relating to Vivien, rather than to this unnamed other person. He told Mary his sense of secret, innermost agony was something from which he would never be released, 'except, I hope, at the moment of death'.[11]

He signed himself 'Affectionately, Tom', but Mary found his letter hurtful and intensely annoying. In her private memoir, she wrote that he was in a prison mainly of his own creation. Why would he not let her release him? At one level, Mary was deeply perceptive, and minutely attentive to everything Tom said. She treasured the way, as they strolled together after dinner, he sometimes sang in a low, tuneless voice music-hall songs from his youth and Negro spirituals. She tried to sum up his stubborn emotional imprisonment. She observed his rages, and listened as he inveighed against modern depravities. Telling him that the characters in his plays were too like puppets, she chronicled his sharp remarks on contemporaries: 'Aldous [Huxley] is not interested in people except in so far as they can be used by him.'[12] Nonetheless, questions remained about whether Tom was exploiting her, and whether, whatever he maintained, he might change his mind about marriage. Listening to records, he relaxed with her in her flat. Making use of her as a driver, he was a fine raconteur. With his sometimes booming laugh, he told her further anecdotes about his life as they sped through London in her car. Spirited and shrewd, she looked after his interests, but sometimes considered him devious. Like Emily, Mary did not want their relationship to end, but hoped he might realise their closeness more fully. She sent him cigarettes and an expensive cigarette case. In one of their arguments he described himself to her as an unsatisfactory friend.

In public his carapace remained impermeable. Yet, lecturing on 'What Dante Means to Me' at London's Italian Institute on 4 July, and in completing an introduction to *Huckleberry Finn*, he reviewed and revisited aspects of his life. By far the longest quotation in his Dante lecture comes from Shelley's portrayal of Rousseau – presented in terza rima as epitomising weary 'wretchedness'; 'Huck', Tom states in an essay recalling his long-dead parents and his childhood, 'is alone: there is no more solitary character in fiction.' Mark Twain is presented as longing for a 'happy domestic life of a conventional kind', yet resenting 'violation of his integrity'.[13] Visiting Hayward around this time, an American noted the lonely bleakness of Tom's bedroom, its domestic wretchedness contrasting with the fine clothes hanging there:

Its walls looked as if they'd been uniformly stained with nicotine. There was one bare bulb on a chain, an ebony crucifix over the single bed. The wardrobe closet was open: crow-black silk ties on a rod, a scarlet water-silk sash, three glen plaid suits, others in shades of gray and black; a Prince Albert hanging by itself. 'The confessional,' said Hayward, 'here we have our bedtime chats. He tells me everything.'[14]

Around this time Mary Trevelyan came to realise that the woman with whom Tom had been in love was his American friend Emily Hale, but he did not discuss Emily, who remained substantially a mystery. Mary Hutchinson also thought Tom's relationship with Hayward 'hard to understand'. She decided the poet valued Hayward's 'criticism and proofreading', and maybe 'was moved by pity' for his friend 'in his pathetic illness and wanted to expiate his guilt by shouldering a burden; perhaps the pain of living with an often irritable [Hayward] (almost as painful as living with a hysterical wife) came from a masochistic need. They did try not to meet too often though they lived in the same flat, a French housekeeper bringing meals to each one in his own room.' She noted, too, Tom's deliberate choice of 'a cell looking on to a narrow well of walls, preferring this, perhaps wisely, to a room with a splendid view of the Thames'. On Sunday afternoons, she recorded, the two men would go for 'a walk'. 'Often', they would excurse to 'a cemetery'.[15] Stephen Spender recorded that when Auden visited the Carlyle Mansions flat one day, he found Tom 'playing Patience'. When Auden asked him why he liked playing this card game so much, Tom reflected gravely for a few moments and then replied, 'Well, I suppose it's because it's the nearest thing to being dead.'[16]

One way to deal with a bleak private life was to accept distractions. He spent much of the latter part of 1950 in America. His sometimes rambling lectures on education, delivered in October and November under the auspices of the University of Chicago's Committee on Social Thought, showed tiredness, and hinted at isolation: 'What education would we design, for instance, for an individual destined to become a permanent Robinson Crusoe?'[17] His second lecture started by maintaining that 'for good and loving parents a poet is almost the last thing they could want their child to be, unless they thought it was the only way of saving him from becoming a criminal'. It concluded by quoting the young French mystic Simone Weil, who had starved herself to death seven years earlier and whose work Tom selected as a 1950 book of the year. He read aloud to his Chicago audience a passage where Weil stressed life as 'impossibility', 'absurdity', and 'contradiction', asserting that 'This contradiction, the mark of our wretchedness and our greatness, is something that we must accept in all its bitterness.'[18] That autumn in Chicago he circulated, lectured, and socialised with intellectual luminaries, who ranged from Julian

Huxley to self-important university leaders. Yet a graduate student working as a faculty dining-club waiter recalled him, looking lonely among grandees at lunch, sitting 'through the entire meal in silence, hunched over his various plates, and in particular with his striking profile dangerously close to immersion in the soup, ignoring even my *sotto voce* request if I might give him more coffee'.[19]

Opposing totalitarianism and defending individual freedoms, Tom the public lecturer turned, predictably enough, to 'The Issue of Religion'; but he also pondered his sense of isolation and his writerly dilemmas:

> If I feel ready to write a poem, and I therefore decline to address a meeting on behalf of some good cause, or prepare a paper for an important week-end conference, what is the outcome? If the poem turns out a good one, I feel justified; if it is a failure, I feel guilty. The success is always uncertain; and as for the failure, I am thinking of instances in which one could have been certain, in sacrificing the writing of the poem, of being engaged otherwise in doing something at least moderately useful. And if it is difficult to decide for ourselves, it is often impossible to judge for others. Was Thoreau a good citizen when he retired to Walden?[20]

From Chicago, where he recorded poems for NBC broadcast and, in constant demand, felt tired 'seeing people and recovering from them', Tom proceeded not to Thoreauvian seclusion at Walden Pond but to Harvard, where, having just finished writing it, he delivered in November the first Theodore Spencer Memorial Lecture.[21] Recalling Spencer's 'fundamental goodness', he spoke on 'Poetry and Drama', indicating, among other things, that 'the source' of his 'story' in *The Cocktail Party* lay 'in the *Alcestis*', Euripides' tragedy about the resurrection of a self-sacrificing wife.[22] Privately, he went on pondering his new play. Its characters would attempt to resolve emotional confusions arising from long-concealed secrets.

More and more he found himself surveying his earlier writings and actions, sometimes dropping public hints about how his work might be read, while in correspondence with Emily, Mary Trevelyan and others he sought to maintain difficult but emotionally important, largely hidden relationships. He was not alone in remembering things past. Trying to do justice to Vivien and Tom, Enid Faber wrote that November 'Recollections of Vivienne Eliot', recalling Vivien as sometimes vivacious but also difficult, not least in her feelings about passing on her personality to any 'children'.[23] Reconciled to a childless, solitary future, and used to separating his work from his private life, Tom was momentarily disconcerted when he heard from Mary in London that Miss Fletcher had attempted to help one of Mary and Tom's more problematic acquaintances, a Bengali called Ghosh, by having dinner with him. 'I don't like my secretaries chumming up with my waifs & strays, and anyway young ladies from Leeds should not be dining with Bengalis, no lady under 45 ought to think of such a thing', Tom told Mary, mixing prejudice with affectionate banter: 'P.S. I hope you boxed Miss Fletcher's ears.'[24]

From London, however, Hayward assured him, 'Miss Fletcher is as efficient as ever.' Tom's correspondence was being kept in order, and at the flat, 'Madame', the housekeeper, was preparing Christmas puddings.[25] Tom concentrated on Harvard duties. Ageing, and shy with new acquaintances, he amused student poet and editor Donald Hall. Having been reprimanded for letting the *Harvard Advocate* reprint some of Tom's earliest poems without permission, Hall was now tasked with driving Tom the 500 yards or so between his lodgings and an *Advocate* party. As Tom stooped to get into the front passenger seat of Hall's car, Hall realised his guest had not noticed there were already two young women in the back seat. 'Mr Eliot,' Hall blurted out, 'I'd like you to meet . . .' Nonplussed, in an era when it remained customary for older gentlemen to doff their hats to ladies, Tom 'twisted and jumped . . . reaching for his hat, and rising all at the same moment, so that with an abrupt jerk upward he hit his head on the doorframe of the car and knocked his hat off'.[26]

From Cambridge, where the proximity of Theresa, Emily, Eleanor Hinkley and others let him feel at home, he proceeded to New York, staying at Ted Kauffer's apartment overlooking Central Park. He was visited there by a young American protégé, William Turner Levy. They chatted, smoked, and drank bourbon. Levy recalled the telephone and doorbell ringing 'almost continuously'. Complaining that everyone wanted him to meet their friends, Tom ignored this din. Characteristically 'hunched over in a meditative attitude', he spoke and listened with concentration.[27] A wealthy intellectual who became a New York priest, Levy wrote a detailed memoir, giving a good sense of the older poet.

The young – particularly men – continued, sometimes diffidently, to seek Tom's advice. Where it seemed worthwhile, he might become, as he had done for decades, an occasional mentor. Inexorably, old friends who had known him before his celebrity, passed away. In late 1950 he wrote to Emily's now blind Aunt Edith, sending consolations on the loss of her husband. Edith Perkins's frailty made those who cared for her anxious. If Tom's meetings with Emily were now more difficult, she and her circle remained important to him; and in Cambridge he had been glad to find his cousin Eleanor 'lively and intelligent' as ever.[28] His relationship with Emily became one of mutual affection and occasional encounters; both sides knew it was dwindling. Whereas in the early 1930s they had exchanged on average almost two letters a week, by the 1950s, adhering to the regime Emily had initiated, each wrote little more than once a month. Though Emily continued to keep his letters, she had begun to give away some of the books he had inscribed to her. They wondered what would be the long-term fate of their correspondence.

The Cocktail Party's year-long New York and London runs ended in early 1951, and Tom was not long back in London before becoming embroiled in controversies. On 16 February the *Daily Mail* reported 'Britain's shyest and richest poet' had 'issued a statement last night refuting allegations that some of his poetry voices anti-Semitic sentiments'. In America, six girls at a 'Boston finishing school' had complained after a teacher read them poems by Eliot and Pound, a Twain letter, and 'a medieval poem'. Around the same time, at London's Institute of Contemporary Arts Tom had 'walked into the room just as Mr Emanuel Litvinoff, a Zionist from Hampstead, had begun to read a poem which attacked Mr Eliot for his alleged views on Jews'. Alerted by Herbert Read to Tom's presence, Litvinoff continued reading his poem, 'To T. S. Eliot', which asserted, 'Bleistein is my relation', and complained about not being 'accepted in your parish'. Interviewed at the *Zionist Review*'s London offices, Litvinoff cited 'Gerontion', 'Sweeney among the Nightingales' and other early poems, telling a *Mail* reporter he had gone on reading his 'trenchant attack' on 'Mr Eliot for his attitude to Jews', even as the poem's addressee arrived. After Litvinoff's reading, Spender had 'jumped up and said the poem should never have been read'. Others demanded explanations. 'There was some heat,' Litvinoff recalled, 'Mr Eliot stood quite silent. I did not hear him say anything, but as I left I heard him turn to a friend and say he thought it was a good poem.' To the same *Mail* reporter Spender objected to Litvinoff's poem: 'I felt he was classing Mr Eliot with the people who committed atrocities on Jews in concentration camps, whereas I believe that anything Mr Eliot has written about Jews comes under the heading of criticism. I hope that if ever I criticise the French I will not be regarded as anti-French.'[29]

Not wishing to encourage this controversy, which went unreported elsewhere, Tom, awaiting hospitalisation for a minor operation, kept a low profile; but, perhaps as a result of contacting Faber & Faber, the reporter commented,

Speaking for Mr Eliot at his publishers' office in Russell-square, his secretary said: 'Many Jewish people have written to him accusing

him of anti-Semitism. It is not true. Mr Eliot has no bias against Jewish people and is not anti-Semitic. If that impression has gained
ground it is because his poetry has been misinterpreted.'[30]

For the moment, this statement seemed to quieten interest, but accounts
of the reading circulated. Tom continued insisting he was not and had not
been antisemitic; his early poems 'were not regarded at that time as anti-
semitic'.[31] By early September he had completed his preface to a translation
of Simone Weil's *The Need for Roots*, and had discussed Weil on a recent
Paris visit. 'She was intensely Jewish, suffering torments in the affliction of
the Jews in Germany; yet she castigated Israel with all the severity of a
Hebrew Prophet'. Tom explained he used 'the term "Israel" as she used it,
and not, of course, with reference to the modern State'. He felt powerfully
attracted to the work of this 'woman of genius, of a kind of genius akin to
that of the saints'.[32]

Far from Tom's busy London life, in Andover Emily had established
herself yet again as an ambitious, exacting teacher of speech and drama.
She retained her idealism, but, writing for the *Abbot Academy Bulletin* in
early 1951 as a 'Teacher of Dramatic Interpretation', she hinted that dramatic performance might involve a need to avoid personal problems:

> each individual who can do so loves to escape from his or her personal
> world into a happy land of 'make-believe'; loves to be someone else,
> to enjoy the illusion of becoming another personality than the one
> familiar to himself, enjoys 'dressing up' and 'pretending' as do boys
> and girls in childhood [. . .] The urge to 'play act' becomes, in the
> terms of modern psychology, a need for 'self-expression,' a desirable
> form of 'escapism,' or 'release.'

For Emily preparing a play taught all its participants to be 'persistent and
cheerful in the face of all discouragements and difficulties'. She saw her
times as an era 'of stress' and 'tense emotional backgrounds'.[33] Still impressing her chosen pupils, she maintained her patrician style and dignity,
reprimanding disrespectful girls from another school by telling them forthrightly, 'I teach at a school called Abbot Academy. The oldest girls' school
in the United States.'[34] Such a tone did not always win friends, but it was
one that Tom knew and understood.

In London, Miss Fletcher's situation was very different. Like other Faber
colleagues, even if, later, she recalled the Russell Square atmosphere as
' "feudal", in the sense that women were useful for typing, that's about all',
she felt intensely loyal towards her boss, though her interest in him went

further.[35] She soon learned about some of his oldest friends, informing Violet Schiff in March 1951, for instance, that his minor operation had left him 'better than he has looked for a long time'.[36] As their working relationship developed, she noted in her diary what he wore on particular days; she moved lodgings to Kensington, and, like Mary Trevelyan, attended St Stephen's Church; her preoccupation with him remained a family joke, mentioned in letters home to her mother in Leeds. But in all her dealings with him she remained formal, her meticulousness seeking to match his own. She knew he admired what he called in 1951 with regard to Virgil a 'civilized world of dignity, reason and order', though it was striking how he apparently identified with the Aeneas who felt 'very decidedly a worm' in determinedly but 'shamefully' abandoning Dido.[37] 'Mr Eliot', in turn, was circumspect and rather shy towards 'Miss Fletcher' as he prepared his preface to *Murder in the Cathedral: A Screenplay* (which would accompany screenings of Hoellering's film that autumn) and prefaced also a forthcoming translation of Josef Pieper's *Leisure the Basis of Culture*. There seemed little leisure as Valerie Fletcher carefully oversaw cultural appointments in his diary: speaking at a Festival of Britain celebration in Chichester after his return from a short Spanish holiday; unveiling a plaque to Yeats in London in May; or in early June proceeding from his oration at Brighton's Alliance Française meeting ('to be a "good European" does not seem to me to require any diminution of local and national loyalties') to speak soon afterwards at a gathering to back 'the setting up of a residential house for elderly women'.[38] At this last event, though he had told Mary Trevelyan shortly before that he would never write his memoirs, he spoke about old people 'who primarily need privacy' and those 'whose primary need is company', and reminisced about visiting an old lady in 'a public institution' – a widow 'for sixty odd years', who was treated as if she had never been married, since 'The synagogue at which she had been married a great many years before had been destroyed in the blitz, together with all its records.'[39] His speech, even in the crowded hall, involved yet another image of complete isolation and signalled how relief of loneliness was a compelling human need.

Though he holidayed by himself in Switzerland that year, he kept up with several female friends, not just with Emily and Mary Trevelyan. After weekending in July at the home of Hope Mirrlees' sister Margot, he sent a note of thanks, contrasting his imperfect typing with that of Miss Fletcher. He enjoyed Enid and Geoffrey Faber's hospitality at Minsted. Yet when Donald Hall visited him at his Faber office that autumn, Tom's 'face was pale as baker's bread'. He looked '*cadaverous*', walking with a slouch, then sitting stooped at his desk.

His head shook forward slightly, from time to time, almost as if he nodded toward sleep. He smoked, and between inhalations he hacked a dry, deathly, smoker's hack. His speech – while precise, exact, perfect – was slow to move, as if he stood behind the boulder of each word, pushing it into view.

At sixty-three, Tom looked 'at least seventy-five'.[40]

Seeking light relief, he published further feline verse, though 'Cat Morgan Introduces Himself' appears a revival of an older piece. By 1951 the black cat who had attached himself to the Faber premises and who, smelling of fish, had been Tom's occasional companion there in 1944, was also ageing. Admitting 'retired' status, the poem's cat speaks as publishing-house 'com-mission-aire', guarding the Faber portals in old age, but still pleased 'some of the gals is dead keen' on him.[41] These verses' publication in October 1951 seemed to signal there was life in the old cat yet; but soon Cat Morgan died of old age.

Though he had nothing yet ready to show Browne, Tom was pleased to have another play in gestation. Progress seemed slow and painful. 'I hope the new play has been moving along as you want it to, and *greatly* look forward to seeing a draft,' Browne wrote in October.[42] No draft arrived. Instead, suffering from a heavy cold and looking 'excessively tired', but deploying 'his best courtly manner', Tom went to Paris the next month to open a large British book exhibition at the Bibliothèque Nationale; his short speech, listened to by the French President, the British Ambassador, and other dignatories, maintained that writers 'should work in privacy and silence.' Those could be hard to find. At the start of December, awarded a Sorbonne honorary degree, he was wined and dined. Offered oysters, he declined, saying, 'I have problems', then giving a 'jerky laugh which repeated itself in four or five implosions'.[43] Annually now, he came to feel ill in the London winter. Fulfilling public obligations, which included on 12 December laying a wreath on Browning's Westminster Abbey memorial, and joining Harold Macmillan, Spender and others for a prizegiving 'luncheon at the Dorchester Hotel', his mood was hardly lightened when he drafted, at *The Times*'s request in early 1952, an obituary for Geoffrey Faber so that it might be ready if needed.[44] The Faber chairman was a year younger than Tom. It was odd discussing with Faber the progress of his lecture on the making of poetry, 'Scylla and Charybdis' (which Miss Fletcher was about to type up), while simultaneously pondering Faber's obituary.

Still, soon after Miss Fletcher had typed his words, 'in few human beings do we find a complete consistency of belief and behaviour', Tom, recently elected vice president of the Royal Literary Fund and president of the London Library, was writing to *The Times*, quoting from memory eight lines of a 1906 Broadway song, beginning 'Always go while the goin' is good'.[45] Revered as a great man, and with his *oeuvre* tabulated in Yale librarian Donald Gallup's *T. S. Eliot: A Bibliography*, due in 1952 from Faber & Faber, he continued liking to complicate his solemn image. Miss Fletcher treasured that, even as Mary Trevelyan shaped her rather different account of 'The Pope of Russell Square'. Meanwhile, Britain's elderly Queen Mary listened to his voice in the cinema when, without appearing, he spoke the Fourth Tempter's words in the film of *Murder in the Cathedral*. Tom thought his was 'the first contemporary verse play to be adapted to the screen'. Its 1952 'gala première' was at London's Academy Cinema in Oxford Street on 28 February.[46]

Everyone wanted a part of him. Late March brought his 'Scylla and Charybdis' lecture in Nice; in April, looking gaunt, he received an honorary degree from the University of Rennes; in May he was in Massachusetts, visiting relatives in Cambridge – and Emily at Andover – then reading in New York to a large audience at the Young Men's Hebrew Association before going to church, then to Central Park Zoo, with Levy. No sooner had he returned to England on 1 June than as recently appointed president of the Alliance Française he went to Edinburgh to address the Alliance's annual gathering, stressing the need to believe in 'a community of the living and the dead and the unborn' who affirmed 'an historical identity of culture'.[47] Late June saw him chairing a National Book League meeting in London and speaking about Braille (he confessed 'possible blindness' had 'always haunted' him), while in July he opened a library named after an American ambassador, then delivered his presidential address to the London Library, hymning its 'service to English civilisation'.[48] In Britain, America, and continental Europe he was regarded as the living embodiment of literary culture. His stamina, sheer intelligence, and studied care let him perform this role with aplomb; but it scarcely lessened his sense of private loneliness.

He reacted with consternation on discovering in the journal *Essays in Criticism* for July 1952 an article by a young University of Manitoba academic. John Peter's 'A New Interpretation of *The Waste Land*' argued that the poem expressed intense love for 'a young man who soon afterwards met his death, it would seem by drowning'.[49] In an era when homosexual practices remained an offence under English law, Tom sought legal advice. Corresponding with Peter and with the magazine's editor, F. W. Bateson, he contended that any attempt 'to demonstrate that the poem is essentially concerned with homosexual passion' was 'not merely wholly mistaken, but highly offensive'. Alert to the law, he pointed out that 'Some readers may infer that the author of a poem on an homosexual theme must himself be a person of homosexual temperament, if not actually of homosexual practices.'[50] Tom had many gay and bisexual friends, but did not wish to be thought homosexual, or criminalised. Peter and Bateson backed down after warnings from Tom's solicitors, who demanded the article be disseminated no further. In later decades, Bateson and others returned to this topic, linking *The Waste Land*'s perceived homoeroticism to Tom's early friendship with Jean Verdenal. Discussing Peter's article with his friend Frederick Tomlin, Tom 'shook his head sadly, and merely exclaimed "Good Gracious!" '[51]

Meanwhile, Faber & Faber had been losing money. In summer 1952 Tom bought enough shares to help keep the firm afloat. For additional short-term financing, Geoffrey Faber drew on his own funds, but Tom remained anxious. Conscious of a changing post-war world yet wishing to maintain old alliances, he wrote in August, warmly thanking the ailing '*maître*' Maurras for his poetry collection *La Balance intérieure*. Lamenting the modern era's lack of '*l'esprit de finesse*', Tom assured Maurras of his '*admiration soutenue*' (sustained admiration).[52] Then, after a summer which had included seeing *Macbeth* at Stratford with Margot Coker, a further Swiss holiday, and some determined deferral of dining with Mary Trevelyan, he wrote confidentially to Faber in October, encouraging him to think about restructuring the publishing house.

> Now, if we survive the next two or three years, what of the future? You and I will both be ready to retire. When I say 'retire' for myself, I mean that, if my next play is reasonably successful, I should consider surrendering my salary, and asking (for a few further years) only for a room and a secretary.[53]

Faber, however, was not ready to retire, and Tom, conscious he owed him 'more than you have ever known', indicated he might be prepared to provide further financial support. In his personal life, he wrote to Faber, 'I have a great deal to look back upon, and to look inside at, which is anything but reassuring to a gloomy Calvinistic temperament like mine.' From a practical publishing standpoint, though,

> I often feel that any usefulness I have had for F. & F. is a thing of the past. I am no longer in a position to undertake more work: the increasing pressure of outside burdens means a constant fight to get enough time either for F. & F. or for my own writing (when I say 'my own writing' I mean of course the writing I want to do).[54]

433

For now, Tom volunteered to take a salary cut, and helped Faber recruit a new, younger colleague from All Souls, Charles Monteith. Yet, when Tom as 'Old Publisher' addressed the Society of Young Publishers in London during November, he showed himself astute as ever, counselling listeners that 'the most important difference between poetry and any other department of publishing is, that whereas with most categories of books you are aiming to make as much money as possible, with poetry you are aiming to lose as little as possible', then going on to offer something of a masterclass on his job's obligations, expectations, and economics.[55] Thoughtfully, in early 1952 he had sent a careful, kindly letter to an American schoolgirl who had asked him about how to start writing; 'don't write at first for anyone but yourself', Tom advised Alice Quinn, who in later life became poetry editor at the *New Yorker* and executive director of the Poetry Society of America.[56] In age, as in youth, Tom combined remarkably the instincts of poet, editor, mentor and publisher. Cannily, confident that within a year he would have a further play to publish, he let Harcourt, Brace bring out in November 1952 an edition of his *Complete Poems and Plays*.

An ageing businessman, initially called simply 'The Company Director', lay at the heart of his new verse play. To some degree it involved transfer of power from one generation to the next, while engaging again with how people face up to secrets hidden in their past. Early notes show Tom identifying characters mainly by roles – 'The Company Director', 'The Young Secretary' – and calculating their relative ages. Twenty-five years would separate two central characters: the Company Director had 'Married at 55 when his wife was 30.' As the play developed, Miss Fletcher played her part in retyping drafts, neatly inking in minor changes. As often, Tom introduced many alterations. The character originally called 'Lucasta Windibank' whose flirtatious dialogue about mutual attraction, shyness, romantic misunderstandings and the danger of hurt feelings is significant, was renamed 'Lucasta Angel', a name suggestive of blessed radiance. As the play matured, Miss Fletcher, always observant of her boss, became along with Hayward and Mary Trevelyan one of its first readers. The playwright could not avoid being conscious of his secretary's benign scrutiny. Issues of succession, staff interviews, upper-class and upper-middle-class English life: all these Tom knew well. He sought to demonstrate, too, some understanding of young women. Not always convincingly adapting elements of Euripides' *Ion* and motifs from Victorian melodrama, he wove a convoluted plot, which he carefully summarised in prose. It involved lost twins, reconciliations, and an ending in which 'everyone is happy'.[57]

By late 1952 he had an advanced draft of two acts, sent to Browne around early December. Despite the comic scenarios and banter, Browne came to detect in the play's 'most powerful' scene a 'mutual loneliness'.[58] Awareness of the hurt of childlessness, longing for reconciliation, and the theme of a guilt-ridden older man with a complicated past who has fallen for a younger woman – all these elements give the play emotional resonance; but its tangled, over-contrived plot, and sub-Wildean wit can be seen as drawbacks. Nevertheless, as it took shape, Tom felt some renewal of creative energies. With plans afoot to revive Faber's 'Ariel Poems' series, in late 1952 he wrote 'The Cultivation of Christmas Trees'. Surviving notes for this poem suggest his awareness he was writing out of a sense of duty:

I am again bidden to write a poem
for this season
It is over 20 yrs since I have attempted
such a task.[59]

Though he did not release the much-revised 'F. & F. pot boiler' for publication until 1954, its tone stayed rather stiff; like much of his plays' verse, it lacks poetic intensity.[60] The new play brought his poetry no profound refreshment, but developed its own interest – for Tom, for large 1950s theatre audiences, and, not least, for Miss Fletcher.

Encouraged by Browne and Hayward, Tom made considerable revisions until he and his advisors were confident *The Confidential Clerk* could premiere at the August 1953 Edinburgh Festival. For his title character, Tom sometimes drew on Lloyds Bank memories. His clerk, Eggerson, whom he thought the play's 'only real Christian', was presented in 'dark grey suit' and 'Antiquated bowler' hat; like 'Company Director' Sir Claude Mulhammer, whose 'grey suit' was elegantly 'well pressed', he revealed aspects of his creator.[61]

Tom's international celebrity brought dizzying expectations. Browne recalled how 'On the front page of the *Sunday Times* for 21 December 1952 appeared the announcement that *The Cocktail Party* had played to close on a million and a half spectators, and that five theatres in New York had offered a home to the new play after its Edinburgh opening.'[62] Such bidding wars excited Sherek, would boost Tom's earnings, and increased the pressure. Still, insisting his play should go to London before New York, and accustomed to pressure of all sorts, he was stubborn as well as principled. January 1953 saw him continuing to defend Maurras, who had died in November – 'a great prose writer' whom, since 'if I am not mistaken, Fascism and Royalism are fundamentally incompatible', it was 'misleading' to term 'a "Fascist"'.[63] Around the same time he spoke vividly to Mary Trevelyan about the intensity of his belief in 'hell', and his 'constant fear of it'; he said he had always had a sense of hell, and worried that in this he might be abnormal.[64] Feeling 'rushed', he tried to get *The Confidential Clerk*'s third act 'into generally acceptable shape', and sat 'one morning a week' for the elderly Jewish sculptor Jacob Epstein, who was making a portrait bust.[65]

Much of early 1953 was spent revising the play, but, as always, he tried to juggle other commitments too. On 17 February he wrote at length to Dr William Kolodney, director of New York's 92nd Street Young Men's and Young Women's Hebrew Association, at whose Poetry Center he had read in 1952. Encouraged by writer John Malcolm Brinnin, who thought Tom was not antisemitic, Kolodney (less convinced) had requested a statement supporting 'a public stand against the present anti-semitic policy of the Soviet Government'. Responding, Tom wished to say more:

> The only striking difference between the present anti-Semitism in Russia, and the anti-Semitism of Hitler's Germany, seems to me this: that the Russians have learned from the mistakes of the Germans, and are much shrewder propagandists. The Nazis persecuted Jews for being Jews, and thereby incurred at once the antipathy of all civilized people. The Russians refrain from any overt doctrine of racial superiority, which would too flatly contradict their supposed principles, and interfere with their foreign policy.

This letter went on to analyse the 'pattern of *policy* and *hysteria*' common to 'all anti-Semitic movements', and expressed clear opposition to the regimes of Nazi Germany and communist Russia, as well as to antisemitism.[66] Perhaps unfortunately, it was not published until 1963, and in the shorter term Tom's support for Pound (whose *Literary Essays* he was readying for publication) exacerbated suspicions that even after the horrors of the Second World War he was ready to side with antisemites.

He had grown used to eminence – whether it involved dining at the Garrick Club with Mary Trevelyan or his friend Tomlin as his guest; or helping found, as he did in 1953, the Poetry Book Society; or travelling to St Andrews that April for an honorary degree. Yet Tomlin, recognising Tom seemed relatively 'at home' in the Garrick, suspected this was because 'his privacy was more respected'; there were 'no nudging whispers – "That's T. S. Eliot." '[67] At St Andrews, invited to a ball after the degree ceremony, Tom 'retired to a private room'. Nineteen-year-old student Schölin Andrade-Thompson, whose dancing partner insisted she must be taken to meet the poet, was tongue-tied, and remembered 'a very shy man who was equally discomfited'.[68] His private shyness, evident not least to young women, offset his polished professional self. Soon after returning from Scotland, he was due to attend the annual Royal Academy banquet. Other guests would include the Archbishop of Canterbury. Prime Minister Winston Churchill, an amateur painter, would speak on tradition and innovation in art.

Nineteen fifty-three was the year Penguin published 40,000 copies of his *Selected Prose*, edited by Hayward. By summer Tom was back in America, introduced by the University of Illinois president as 'a man long claimed by the two great English-speaking peoples of the world and increasingly by all the other civilized nations'. So daunting was the poet's fame that this academic felt obliged to remind the audience, 'Mr Eliot is a human being.'[69] Tom could be proud of his international distinction, but it could make him appear (especially to the young) a venerable monument, rather than a person. In London, *The Times* hailed Epstein's 'vivid' bronze bust of him. Exhibited that June, it suggested, perhaps, 'the questioning and intensely serious critic rather than the poet'.[70]

His American tour included St Louis, Cambridge (where he stayed with his sister-in-law), Washington, and New York. In almost all of these places his hosts were friends or relatives who had known him prior to his global celebrity, and to whom he need not explain himself. At St Louis, distracted by 'so many memories of my early years', he lectured to an audience including his sister Marion and Emily (who had travelled with Dorothy Elsmith especially to hear him) on 'American Literature and the American Language', and stayed first with Leonard C. Martin (who had married Alice, granddaughter of William Greenleaf Eliot) in a fine shingle house at 22 Joy Avenue, Webster Groves; then Tom was hosted at 44 Portland Place, the equally commodious suburban home of Lawrence T. Post, his erstwhile Smith Academy schoolfellow.[71] In Washington, where he visited Pound, he stayed with Bill Castle at 2200 S. Street NW, in the Kalorama district favoured by several presidents; and in Cambridge he enjoyed his sister-in-law's home at 84 Prescott Street, near Harvard Yard. All these elegant buildings still exist, and give a good idea of the well-appointed milieu Tom and his circle took for granted. With familiar Americans of his generation in discreet surroundings, he could relax; but outside such environments he could appear dauntingly alien. His acolyte, Levy, saw him in New York, where Tom stayed with his publisher friend Bob Giroux in Giroux's 115 E. 69th Street apartment. Though Tom became Levy's generous mentor, the young man saw him as not quite human. With his large hands, Tom

handled all objects in a clumsy way – even, oddly enough, his own fountain pen and pocket watch. His slow and careful use of objects

was not methodical, as I originally had thought, but, instead, pains-
taking. All physical chores, even the putting on and taking off of an
overcoat, seemed to Eliot to offer a resistance which he had to combat. It was for this reason, in part, that I thought of him as a man not
associated with objects or possessions. His mind was his sole possession, and I always thought of him as cerebral rather than physical. His
body was almost an encumbrance.[72]

If in London Hayward manifested physical awkwardness, this only
increased Tom's fellow feeling. Making sure to keep him up to speed with
his travels, when Tom returned by plane in June 1953, he valued the privacy of their shared Chelsea apartment. July visits to 'Cousin Tom' from
his young cousin Barbara and niece Theodora kept him in touch with
American kinsfolk, though it was difficult to fit in with their schedules. He
suggested Barbara confirm arrangements by telephoning Miss Fletcher.[73]
She acted, like Hayward, as his gatekeeper, observing his life's complexi-
ties, which included his relationships with women. When Emily visited
London in August, Tom had to cancel a planned outing with Mary Trevelyan, so that he could meet Emily's train.

The Confidential Clerk opened in Edinburgh that month with a cast
including star performers Denholm Elliott and Margaret Leighton. After
reshaping passages during rehearsals, Tom attended the final dress rehearsal
at Edinburgh's Royal Lyceum Theatre on 24 August. Friends including
Margot Coker ('much amused & impressed') and his German translator
Nora Wydenbruck came north too. Emily was there – a mistake, thought
Tom's niece, whose remark about Emily looking a 'pale shadow of her former self' was recorded by Mary Trevelyan, herself among Tom's Edinburgh
entourage.[74] For the following night's official world premiere, the dramatist, who had given lengthy interviews and seemed more relaxed than at his
previous Edinburgh opening, sat with his niece and Sherek in one of the
Lyceum's boxes. As the performance got underway, he 'even managed to
laugh at his own jokes', particularly when (in what Sherek thought Tom's
'funniest joke') his character Lady Elizabeth Mulhammer, with perfect
comic timing, uttered the lines, 'He was run over. By a rhinoceros / In
Tanganyika.'[75] The play, a *Times* critic decided, was 'likely to be found brilliantly entertaining even by those who are left wondering what it is all
really about'.[76]

After the premiere, sure Tom would not wish to dine in public, Sherek
arranged 'supper for the company in a private room' at the Caledonian
Hotel. He and Tom strolled down Lothian Road, arriving early, and spent
time opening congratulatory telegrams, including those they had sent each

other. 'Really, Tom, the ego of some people!' exclaimed Sherek, complaining about telegrams signed only with a first name. Tom, Sherek recalled,

> peered at me over his spectacles and said slowly, with an absolutely impassive expression:
> 'I say, Henry. I wonder who this telegram is from? It's simply signed "Henry".'[77]

BBC Television broadcast the play's second act at the end of August, massively increasing ticket sales for its September run at London's Lyric Theatre. 'With *The Confidential Clerk*, Mr Eliot has done it again', pronounced the *New Statesman*.[78] After the London first night Tom hosted a party for the cast at the Savoy Hotel, and sat between Margaret Leighton and Isabel Jeans, the play's leading ladies in their 'ravishingly glamorous' dresses. Sherek whispered, 'The fruits of victory, eh Tom?' and noted that the dramatist 'did not seem displeased'.[79] Soon young Queen Elizabeth and her sister were spotted in the dress circle's front row, having gone 'informally' to see this play whose success seemed assured.[80] Like most of Tom's plays, it involved the consequences of long-concealed personal secrets. At Russell Square, Miss Fletcher was inserting last-minute alterations on a typescript so that *The Confidential Clerk* might be published almost simultaneously in London and New York the following March.

Tom, who had joked to Enid Faber that the play might be received as 'a "mirthquake"', enjoyed the success, even if some reviewers detected confusions in the plot.[81] But he was shocked to hear that 'poetic genius' Dylan Thomas had died in New York on 9 November, aged thirty-nine.[82] Tom's name headed the signatories supporting a Dylan Thomas Memorial Fund; and Valerie Fletcher, who had liked Thomas, shared his sadness. About to lecture on 'The Three Voices of Poetry' for the National Book League in London, Tom found himself concluding that 'the proper language of love – that is, of communication to the beloved and to no one else – is prose', rather than verse, and that poets are often 'haunted by a demon'.[83] He sent a copy of this lecture to Emily, who, billed as 'a lifelong friend of Mr Eliot', gave her own lecture in Boston that November on *The Confidential Clerk*.[84] In London, lunching with Tomlin in December, Tom requested they sit in the restaurant 'as much out of sight as possible'. Conversation ranged from occult experience to his having been warned to 'cut down on smoking'. Suddenly, Tomlin was 'nonplussed' when Tom (who had described himself in a goodwill message to the *London Magazine* as 'an elderly man of letters') asked unexpectedly, 'How does one set about *dying?'* Tomlin thought the man who asked the question was 'intensely – even wretchedly – lonely'.[85]

Realising he needed rest, the Fabers had invited him on another winter cruise to South Africa. They sailed on 30 December 1953, spending the second half of January in and around Cape Town. Tom viewed his portrait by Lewis in Durban's Art Gallery, made a recording for the South African Broadcasting Corporation, visited Hope Mirrlees once more, and spoke about poetry and drama at a 'Foyle's Literary Luncheon'.[86] He also read the recently published first volume of *Systematic Theology* by German Lutheran Paul Tillich, an anti-Nazi Christian existentialist who had been a New York colleague of Tom's friend Reinhold Niebuhr. From London Miss Fletcher forwarded press cuttings, and helped renew Tom's radio licence; as usual, Hayward sent literary gossip. It was March before Tom returned to England. He started catching up with correspondence, and produced two sets of Augustan occasional verses honouring newly knighted Sir Geoffrey Faber, but almost immediately was admitted to the London Clinic suffering from tachycardia. Urging her to keep this news secret from the press, Hayward explained to Helen Gardner, whose Faber-published 1949 *The Art of T. S. Eliot* Tom now thought the best account of his work, that 'The Bard' had been 'overexerting himself' in South Africa and was 'under strict doctor's orders to rest'.[87] The *Daily Mail* soon reported he was 'exhausted'; in America rumours spread he had had a heart attack.[88] Visiting him in hospital, Hayward, who (like Mary Trevelyan) sometimes thought Tom maddeningly hypochondriac, was disconcerted by his striking cheerfulness. Propped up on pillows, he looked 'like a cat which has eaten several canaries and surrounded by a large part of the Chelsea Flower Show'.[89] 'The tachycardia was something purely nervous', Tom maintained that May.[90] By then he was back in the flat, but still under doctor's orders.

Heartening news came from America. Remarkably for a modern verse play, *The Confidential Clerk* had become a *New York Times* bestseller; in England, with a print run of 20,000, it was also selling well, though, after eight months of performances, its theatrical run had ended. Around the end of May Faber's production manager scribbled on galley proofs of 'The Cultivation of Christmas Trees', 'Miss Fletcher Will you please show to Mr Eliot'. She did so, and he marked it 'Corrected' on 3 June, a couple of days before writing to Sir Geoffrey about celebratory occasional verses now inscribed on presentation glassware.[91] But Tom, though managing correspondence with Valerie Fletcher's help (she visited the flat, sometimes four times a week), was still taking things easy, and planned three weeks off in July.

As ever, he remained loyal to friends. In a short *Times* letter he backed Robert Oppenheimer, the atomic scientist who had directed Princeton's

Institute for Advanced Study during Tom's stay, and was now under suspicion for apparent left-wing leanings. Privately, Tom described Oppenheimer to Willard Thorp that June as 'a combination of genius and simpleton'.[92] More troublesome was Tom's long-standing friendship with Pound. His edition of Pound's 1954 *Literary Essays*, whose laudatory, formal preface makes no reference to Pound's confinement, was a carefully planned project. That August, provoked by what he saw as Pound's stubborn folly, Tom reproached him: 'I do not see why I should continue to accept from you insults to my nationality or to my religion. The latter includes the Jewish religion.'[93] Pound remained cussed as ever. Yet Tom's loyalty persisted, and extended to the dead. Stanislaus Joyce, the late novelist's brother, visited him in London that summer and showed him a memoir he was writing about Joyce; Tom ensured *My Brother's Keeper* would become a Faber book.

Some loyalties seemed markedly eccentric. Years afterwards, Hope Mirrlees recalled how he liked to wear an appropriate rose on the 22 August anniversary of the 1485 Battle of Bosworth, which ended England's Wars of the Roses. In July 1954 he explained to Sherek, 'I have always been a stout supporter of the Yorkist cause in general and of Richard III in particular, and for some years have made a point of hearing Mass on the anniversary of the Battle of Bosworth.'[94] The attentive Valerie Fletcher, a Yorkshirewoman, might scarcely disagree, but she, like others, worried about his persistent ill health. To him illness was 'penance', 'a reminder that after one has passed middle age one must be, in one sense, a little "retired" from life', though one must not '*waste* any of the time that is left'.[95] His elderly sister Marion visited him late that summer, and Tom thanked Mary Trevelyan (with whom he continued to dine and exchange gifts) for driving them around. After a fortnight's Genevan holiday in September, he was back in London in time for October's publication of 'The Cultivation of Christmas Trees'; 'perhaps not poetry', he feared, though he sent it to friends, including Emily.[96] Bad news came from America. Ted Kauffer had died: 'a sad and very loveable soul, who had lost attachment to this life.'[97] Not long afterwards, recording in November a BBC radio tribute to David Jones (whose work he published and continued to champion) Tom turned again to thoughts of 'old age', and longing for 'surcease of solitude'.[98]

He still had 'hopes', he told Rupert Doone that November, 'of writing another play', but his energy levels were not high.[99] He tried to limit his nights out to Tuesdays and Thursdays. Having formally withdrawn from the Faber book committee in 1953, then ceased to be 'a "working director"' in 1954, he retained his office and secretary. He read typescripts in areas including poetry, theology, and political philosophy, but his regular involvement diminished.[100] He felt close to Geoffrey Faber and colleagues, but trusted the business might develop with considerably less input from its most famous employee. More difficult to cope with – and to believe – was that, temporarily, he had 'given up smoking'. As a result, he confessed to Levy's mother, who sent 'a beautiful box of candy' which he opened on Christmas Day, 'I eat more of everything, including candy.'[101]

Though London's worst 1950s smog occurred in December 1952, killing several thousand people, air pollution remained bad, particularly before the 1956 Clean Air Act. Tom had long suffered from what he considered heavy colds, bronchial problems, and a smoker's cough, but it had become evident he was emphysemic. Mid-January 1955 saw him admitted again for a London Clinic rest cure. His pulse rate was troubling. Though it steadied, after he was released he described himself in a note to Mary Trevelyan on 26 February as 'left in a state of severe depression & a conviction that I have lost the last flicker of intelligence and energy'.[102] Miss Fletcher, visiting him at home at 5 p.m. on several days, did what she could to help. Mary, anxious to cheer him up, drove him around London, visiting places mentioned in *The Waste Land* as he regaled her with memories from the time of its composition – not all anecdotes conducive to happiness. As they passed Trafalgar Square, he remembered how Vivien had once thrown her nightdress out of a nearby upstairs window – perhaps at the flat in Burleigh Mansions.

His mood was hardly helped by what he described to Allen Tate in February as Pound's 'increasing megalomania'.[103] Until March, when poet and translator Robert Fitzgerald sent extracts, Tom had 'never seen' extensive transcripts of Pound's 'notorious' wartime Italian radio broadcasts with their antisemitic and anti-Allied propaganda. Now, after asking to see them, Tom thought 'nobody could read these outpourings and regard the writer as sane'.[104] Exasperation compounded his dejection. Mary Trevelyan, who discussed Tom in detail with Hayward that April, worried he was becoming immensely indignant towards anyone who disagreed with him. She thought he was suffering from the 'strain' of having become a 'Classic' in his own lifetime, and needed close friends who were not simply acolytes.[105] He seemed unsettled, prone to tetchiness, even sometimes reclusive. Growing annoyed when, increasingly, he took to shutting himself in his room and not communicating, Hayward dared not intrude. Though Tom fought it, Hayward thought he had 'a streak of sadism'. After discussing these domestic tensions with Mary, Hayward asked Tom why he was angry. Tom replied that Hayward was spreading gossip about his health. They had quarrelled, too, the previous week, when Tom complained about the '*tone*' in which Hayward criticised some of his remarks. Tom tried to sidestep the problem, explaining he was slow to react, but that his anger tended to linger. Trevelyan in her account of this period complained he could be furious, cutting, self-important, snobbish: 'WHY should I have been cursed with such mediocre contemporaries?'[106]

Stubborn or not, he mustered his strength. Having returned to his working routine, he was assured by doctors he could travel abroad, as he planned to do in late spring and summer. 'Author and Critic', his talk to London's Authors Club on 13 April 1955, noted wryly how critics liked to detect 'the certain decline of the author's powers'; the artist's 'privacy' must resist intrusive 'biography'.[107] Less than a week later, he lectured at a London Conservative Union Literary Luncheon at the Overseas League in St James's Street. Here Tom the Burke Club member praised Burke ('certainly a Christian thinker'), along with Bolingbroke and Disraeli, commending also 'that admirable little book *Conservatism* written by Lord Hugh Cecil' and volumes by Frederick Scott Oliver, who, years before, had supported the *Criterion*. Though he sided happily with Tory intellectual traditions, some of his discourse, as when he aligned himself with the 'political theory' (as distinct from 'political party' or '*movement*') of Maurras – 'a man whom I held in respect and admiration, although some of his views were exasperating and some deplorable' – involved terrain unfamiliar to most Tory voters.[108] As was clear in his 1954 Faber reader's report on his American admirer Russell Kirk's *The Conservative Mind*, while Tom was attracted by conservative political philosophy, many actual conservatives seemed not always 'concerned with conserving the right things', and he was wary of appearing too narrowly party-political.[109] After his Conservative Union speech was published with an introduction by Tory prime minister Anthony Eden, Tom indicated to Pound that Eden's preface was not his idea, and, indeed, his speech 'implied criticism' of Eden.[110] Yet his correspondence leaves little doubt of his rightist leanings, including his Tory-inclined hostility towards American disapproval of 'the existence of the (now almost inexistent) British Empire'.[111] One keen listener to his Conservative Union talk recalled Tom styling himself 'a detached contemplative'. Nonetheless, when afterwards a young man remarked, 'from what you have been saying, I get the impression that you vote Conservative', Tom 'replied, with the slightest smile and the usual measured tempo: "I should be quite content . . . for that inference . . . to be drawn." '[112]

He felt well enough – and obligated enough – to fly to Hamburg in May to receive the Hanseatic Goethe Prize and give an address ('Goethe as the Sage') at Hamburg University. While he spoke movingly about a drawing of 'Goethe in old age' which he had kept on his office mantelpiece since the early war years, his 'Discourse in Praise of Wisdom' quoted not one line of Goethe, whose work he knew only patchily. If his mention of 'pointing a pistol at my own head' was an allusion to the fate of Goethe's depressive, suicidal Young Werther, it was uncharacteristic, as was Tom's emphasis on wisdom as 'a native gift of intuition' and on desire to understand 'the human heart'.[113]

One heart he wished he could understand was Miss Fletcher's. In March, not long before his tetchiness reached its height, he had complained to Mary Trevelyan that he could not get to know his secretary at all; when he tried to, she seemed to shut up like a clam. Yet she visited him at home, attended his church, and knew all about him and his friends. Liking her, he wondered just how much she liked him. At least one other Faber secretary noticed that, although usually the secretarial staff wore slippers or casual shoes at work, Miss Fletcher always changed 'into high heels' when going to Mr Eliot's office.[114] Tom's new play, initially titled *The Rest Cure*, would deal with an ailing retired grandee's relationship with a young woman – his daughter Monica – to whom, eventually, he reveals secrets from his past, including his long-lasting, frustrated love for a woman he never married. The drama would also involve Monica's romance. Once again, Tom reconfigured aspects of his past and present experience in a drama of intergenerational relationships. As the play developed, Miss Fletcher grew closely involved in adjusting and overseeing its revised typescripts; neatly, she entered changes. She became Tom's most important reader.

In May 1955 he flew to America: more family visits to Eleanor Hinkley and others in New England, meals with Bob Giroux and Djuna Barnes in New York, a call on Pound in St Elizabeths which, Tom told Hayward, 'passed off well enough', and several readings at Harvard, in New York, and Washington. By late May he thought himself 'in excellent health', boasting that his reading for the *Harvard Advocate* had made him 'feel like Frank Sinatra for a few minutes'; but such elation could soon wear off.[115] A young Harvard academic, observing him in company around this time, reflected how 'painfully shy', 'hard to talk to' and 'lonely' he seemed.[116] On returning to London, he was spotted by Tomlin 'walking with meditative slowness, no doubt complicated by the arthritis from which he had begun to suffer, and aided by the now indispensable walking stick'.[117] This did not stop him holidaying in Geneva in August. He sent Mary Trevelyan several postcards, then made sure Miss Fletcher too had a vacation: just as, on another occasion, he gave her an introduction to Max Beerbohm when she holidayed at Rapallo, so now he helped arrange her stay with his friend from the Mirrlees household, writer Margaret Behrens, who was living in Menton on the Côte d'Azur. For two summers she vacationed in the house of Mrs Behrens, who had known Tom since Miss Fletcher was a girl.

He spent his sixty-seventh birthday recording his poems for Caedmon Records, and soon afterwards sent glass engraver Laurence Whistler verses to celebrate Geoffrey and Enid Faber's forthcoming thirty-fifth wedding anniversary in December. But he was finding walking increasingly difficult, and, very soon after being filmed (nervously) for BBC Television's *Panorama* tribute to Kauffer, he was admitted to the London Clinic with a foot infection. He spent two weeks there.

30 October 1955 was Pound's seventieth birthday. Tom had sent Berkeley's fledgling *Pound Newsletter* a salute to 'a great poet'; but in mid-November he avoided another invitation to discuss Pound's work, declining to repeat what he had said elsewhere, and avoiding discussion of 'matters on which I disagree very strongly with Pound's views'.[118] He restated his commitment to 'the awakening of the religious life' at an All Souls Club meeting at the Garrick on 16 November, not long before he saw Philip Larkin's 'Church Going' and other poems in Larkin's *The Less Deceived*.[119] At this time Faber & Faber published Larkin's fiction, but not his poetry. Charles Monteith had passed *The Less Deceived* to Tom, who returned it with a scribbled comment: 'Yes – he often makes words do what he wants. Certainly worth encouraging.'[120]

By late November, Tom was walking better, and thinking about Lewis. Blind and ailing, the artist occupied a condemned London building which he refused to leave. Tom sent his theatrical friend Ashley Dukes a cheque to buy Lewis his favourite tipple, champagne. Compared with Lewis's and Pound's situations, his own was luxurious. That December he lunched with Margot Coker, and met again with Mary Trevelyan, giving her one of his favourite books, *The Pickwick Papers*, as a Christmas present. The redoubtable High Anglican Mary remained a close companion, but he was determined she understand the nature of their relationship; he sent her in January 1956 his recent talk about the dangers of Billy Graham and the evangelical Christian movement, Moral Rearmament.

It was Mary whom Hayward telephoned on 24 January 1956 when Tom was taken by ambulance to the London Clinic, but hearing he was ill alarmed Emily too. Hayward wondered if some attention-seeking was involved. Sometimes, as if joking he was a child who needed nurturing, Tom would sign himself to Mary as 'Bunsir', her 'Godson (adoptive)'; but in February Mary – hardly emotionally invulnerable, and still in love with him – felt slighted by one of his clumsy remarks.[121] It was as if he had turned against her and Hayward, despite their best attempts to sustain him. Emily, an ocean away, still teaching at Abbot Academy and an increasingly occasional correspondent, could do little. She was pondering arrangements to have her letters to Tom deposited in an archive, and had her own concerns about mortality. What on earth did Tom want? He could not, or would not, say. Locked in his own anxious speculations, he sensed time passing, and, however much (as he told her later) he felt his life enhanced by Valerie Fletcher's presence, he could not bring himself to tell her. In late February Father Cheetham retired 'in the sixty-fourth year of his age' (as Tom put it with a biblical inflection), after 'a peremptory ultimatum from medical advisers'.[122] Paying fulsome tribute to his vicar and friend, who had only months to live, Tom was all too aware of being older than Cheetham, of having poor health, and of possessing strong feelings for a woman less than half his age who might consider them absurd. Perhaps for him, too, death would resolve things. Lacing gloom with banter, he corresponded with a friend on 5 April about what sort of wine Keats, who might not have known 'what he was drinking', intended in his 'Ode to a Nightingale', that poem about being 'half in love with easeful Death'.[123] Tom's forebodings persisted. On 13 April he wrote to Mary Trevelyan, telling her he had authorised his physician to inform her (as 'a friend of my sister') about his health should he become suddenly unwell and unable to communicate.[124] The doctor already had permission to tell Hayward, and Tom was confident Mary would contact his sister Marion in an emergency.

Before Hayward, Trevelyan, or others could discern his emotional state, he was off to America next day. At the end of April, reviewing his achievements and those of others, he lectured on 'The Frontiers of Criticism' to 13,523 people in America's largest college basketball arena at the University of Minnesota. There he speculated about how far biographers might investigate a poet's 'inner experience'. Unusually, the final poet he mentioned was Sappho, author of 'poetry, the spark which can leap across those 2,500 years'.[125] Sappho, though he did not say so, was one of the greatest articulators of the disturbing intensity of erotic love, and a poet whose words about the child–mother bond meant much to him. His mentioning her at this time seems revealing.

New York, Minnesota, Chicago, New York, Washington, Cambridge, Connecticut, New York, then back on the liner *Queen Mary* to Southampton: Tom's itinerary for the six weeks up to June 11 was exhausting, even for Hayward to read. For Tom it was worse, but, after he had cabled from New York (where he enjoyed the new Lerner and Loewe musical *My Fair Lady*), to say he had arrived 'sound and sane', he and Hayward corresponded amicably.[126] Appreciating, too, Tom's 'saucy postcard' about the Minnesota lecture, Hayward reassured him that Miss Fletcher had dealt effectively with a 'Scotch lunatic' who had bombarded Tom with poetry, fiction, and musical compositions.[127] During his return voyage, however, Tom suffered severe tachycardia. Stretchered off at Southampton, he was taken to London's French Hospital, but released after a week. News came that his reclusive sister Margaret had died in Massachusetts, aged eighty-five. The superintendent of her Cambridge apartment block had noticed deliveries accumulating outside her door; she was 'found dead' inside.[128] Just a month or so earlier Tom had complained to Mary Trevelyan that Margaret, suffering from mental confusion, was being 'tiresome'; now he realised she had been approaching death, and he was too frail to travel to her funeral.[129]

With death on his mind, on 29 June he reconfirmed his own funeral arrangements: he wanted his body taken 'at the earliest possible moment' to St Stephen's; on the eve of burial the Vespers of the Dead were to be sung; the morning of burial was to have a sung Mass of Requiem followed by the Absolutions.[130] Years earlier, he had already told Mary he wanted 'the Allegretto from the Seventh Symphony [of Beethoven] for my funeral march'.[131] If Cheetham was able, Tom hoped he would participate in the service. In preparation, Tom had purchased a plot in the St Stephen's Burial Ground at London Necropolis, Surrey. Yet though prepared for death, as the scare of tachycardia receded, he realised he wanted to live. Telephoning him, friends sometimes noticed 'gasps and sighs' reaching 'almost stethoscopic volume' – indications of emphysema.[132] However, in early July he pronounced himself 'almost fully active again' and, though intuiting that the Cold War world was heading 'towards the Dark Ages', he anticipated attending the London revival of a play that remained close to his heart: *The Family Reunion*.[133] Soon he was joking in a letter to his old Harvard classmate 'Nick' Brooks, about 'letters of condolence' received 'on my approaching demise'. He pronounced himself as resilient as King Bolo's big 'Black Queen' who was, he reminded Brooks, 'always Bright and full of Beans'.[134]

A month's Swiss holiday intensified his zest, and Tomlin, with whom he lunched at the Athenaeum around this time, was struck by how their conversation turned to the topic of women. Alluding to regrets in general, Tom bent his head, remarking, '*I* can never forget anything.' Then, 'looking hard at the table', he 'agreed that whereas a man could enjoy a woman's company up to a point yet remain unwilling to push the friendship any further, a woman *tended* to demand one's full and exclusive attention. He then made the remark, on which he seemed to have been ruminating for some time: "Some women think that if they want a thing hard enough, it must be right." '[135] He mentioned neither Emily nor Mary nor anyone else; but when the topic became celibacy he laid his hands 'flat on the table, as he often did when stressing a capital point: "Well, it *can* be done, as I know." '[136]

Some Faber colleagues had observed him occasionally after work sitting having a drink with Miss Fletcher in the Hotel Russell. Most Faber secretaries found him daunting. Rosemary Goad, who became a secretary at Russell Square in 1953, 'couldn't really believe it coming up in the lift with him'. He was 'a very elegant figure. Smart suits, beautifully polished shoes.' But, while always polite, he quickly grew exasperated if, for instance, he heard a secretary swearing. 'He was quite austere. He could be quite alarming.' In the general atmosphere which Goad (who later became a Faber director) recalled as 'terribly misogynist in many ways', the secretaries 'were all greatly in awe of him'. Yet they also saw his 'very, very dry sense of humour. He could be very funny. He would say things like "Grave news from Cornwall." And you'd wait. "A. L. Rowse is writing his memoirs." He was very good at one-liners.'[137]

By this time, Miss Fletcher, who loved his wit, knew him better than any woman of her generation. He was keen she understand the background underlying his public persona – he had inscribed 'for Miss Valerie Fletcher from T. S. Eliot' a copy of the 1953 printed version of *American Literature and the American Language*, containing an appendix on 'the Eliot family and St Louis' – but he was uncertain how much to reveal to her.[138] If Tomlin, watching him hail a taxi with 'the usual liberal flourish of his stick', thought him 'one of the most unhurried of men', and later reflected how 'Unhurried men (and women) are reassuring', then Tom had a reputation for being utterly tardy in expressing his deepest emotions, while Miss Fletcher, though the other secretaries 'used to tease her mercilessly about her devotion' to her boss, had hidden hers from him for years.[139] Nevertheless, it became obvious to each of them, and to some around them that they were growing close, even if Rosemary Goad recalled how among the secretaries 'None of us suspected any romance. It was so unlikely, it never occurred to us.'[140]

Away from Russell Square, the sharp-tongued, sharp-eyed Hayward had signalled to his aggrieved flatmate that he disliked the new play. Its elder-statesman figure attempts to unburden himself to his daughter, and struggles to articulate love. Hayward was proud of his closeness to his famous friend, and jealous of Miss Fletcher – a rival presence. In late August or early September Hayward gossiped to John Malcolm Brinnin, who had met Valerie Fletcher several times and was then visiting from America:

'Tom's now developed something called emphysema,' he said. 'It's rapidly become apparent he needs a nurse more than I do. And I have an informed suspicion that the ever-adoring Miss Fletcher is ready to assume the role. You know her?'

'The young woman in his office?'

'There's something more to that flower of the Yorkshire marshes than meets the eye,' he said. 'The perfect secretary has begun to see herself as the lady with the lamp.'[141]

Hayward's phrase 'the lady with the lamp' indicates he perceived Miss Fletcher might assume a devoted, Florence Nightingale-like role, but even Hayward did not realise how close she and Tom had grown.

As his attraction towards Miss Fletcher deepened, his relationship with Emily grew more problematic. It was not simply that they corresponded much less frequently; it was also that, setting her affairs in order, Emily, encouraged by the Thorps and eager librarians, was determined that Tom's letters to her should pass now to Princeton University Library. Sickened by the prospect that their contents might soon become public, Tom could not prevent this. He pointed out to Emily that many contained 'comments on living people', whose 'feelings could be hurt'. Consulting his lawyers, whom he had ensured would be among his literary executors, he wanted the standard delay of fifty years on the letters' publication, but worried that, even if unpublished, the letters might be consulted by 'students' in the library, and 'a great deal would get out'.[142] Emily, however, was undeflectable: Tom's letters up to 1947 – the year he had made clear they would never marry – should now be deposited at Princeton. Asserting her strong will after decades of acceding to Tom's wishes, she handed over the letters. In mid-October, he informed her, 'it makes me feel as if I was already dead, or ought to be', and asked, 'are they being read by the Thorps and perhaps others, or are they sealed up?' He assured her he would continue corresponding, but wrote waspishly, 'If my current letters are to be added year by year, I shall have to think of things to say which might interest future researchers.'[143]

Her action brought home to him how far their relationship had changed. 'But what do you mean', he wrote to 'Dearest Emily' on 27 October 1956 – her sixty-fifth birthday – 'by saying that long ago I made you feel the necessity of regarding me as a Public Figure? I certainly hope that I do not see myself as a Public Figure!' It was her way, though, of acknowledging an emotional distance, an intimacy irrevocably altered. Tom tried to justify his attitude:

I hope you will not think I am being fussy, and I do not want to say this (and whatever eye looks at the letters first, at some future date, I should like to fall on *this* letter first, if you will add it): It isn't the intimate and personal things that I would wish to conceal from the curious reader, when we are all gone – let the whole world see that. One is not ashamed of one's intense and passionate moments, but of the petty gossip, the exhibition of vanity, boastfulness, peevishness, perhaps even malice unconscious – and of all the callow and mistaken judgments upon people that one has made in the past. But a correspondence should not be edited to show the writer in the most favourable light! And the great reason for delay is the avoidance of pain to anyone still living.[144]

Emily was trusting in the verdict of posterity. Tom, too, had his eye on that, as well as on the judgement of God. His wish not to have the living hurt was reasonable, as was his desire for privacy; but what Emily had done clarified his attitude not only to her but also to his conduct towards Valerie Fletcher. Emily had been hurt by Tom's long-term treatment of her. Now Tom was stung by what Emily had done, and he too would act decisively.

His typed correspondence around this time contains occasional signs that his secretary found it hard to maintain perfect concentration on her boss's dictation. On 29 October 1956, for instance, Tom had to alter in ink the typed words 'an agnostic' to 'a Gnostic' – an understandable secretarial slip, but not the sort Miss Fletcher was accustomed to make.[145] Not long afterwards, hoping his intuition was right, yet striving to minimise mutual awkwardness if he was wrong, Tom wrote a letter ('Dear Miss Fletcher') which he gave her as if it were official business.[146] It was his marriage proposal. He was concerned lest it be unwelcome. Might Miss Fletcher have some other admirer of whom he knew nothing? Somewhat unrealistically, he asserted that if she did not wish to accept it they need never speak of the matter again. He sought to avoid hurt and embarrassment by putting all this in a letter. He thought her a splendid secretary.

As she soon revealed, he need not have worried. When she disclosed she had loved him for years, he felt huge relief and elation. She recalled:

After he proposed, he suddenly said, 'Do you know my Christian name?' I said yes. 'I just wondered,' he said, 'because I've never heard you call me by it.' He told me he wasn't sure I liked him. I'd been so formal with him, and that if he'd known what I felt he would have acted more quickly.[147]

They would marry soon. She 'was frightened he might waver and have doubts at the last minute'.[148] Like him, she saw life as a pattern, even if one clarified only in retrospect. In time, she made him and others aware her relationship with him had been her life's goal, but initially she kept her own counsel. To each of them marriage would fulfil their deepest wishes; but, during their short engagement, their relationship would remain secret. Tom bought a large, expensive engagement ring. Valerie wore it under a finger stall, but her fellow secretaries spotted it – a 'socking great emerald'. 'We asked her many times who'd given her the ring, but she never told us,' Rosemary Goad recalled.[149] Tom mentioned their engagement neither to

Hayward nor to Mary nor to Emily or other confidants. He and Valerie knew that as soon as news of this liaison between a sixty-eight-year-old Nobel Prize-winner and his thirty-year-old secretary became public, it would be uncontainable. Probingly, both Hayward and Mary Trevelyan asked Tom if he was getting Miss Fletcher a Christmas present. He answered in the negative. Hayward accused him of meanness, suggesting Tom should get 'the biggest bottle of scent you can possibly buy'; to Mary Tom replied austerely that it was not appropriate to give presents to one's secretary.[150]

The engaged couple planned their future. Valerie's parents, who had given their blessing, would attend the London ceremony in January; Tom's solicitor would be best man. There would be no other guests. They would get a special dispensation for a 6.15 a.m. ceremony, which would help avoid press intrusion. Collin Brooks and his wife Lil were taken into their confidence, and offered accommodation, if required. Tom scrutinised the rental agreement he and Hayward had signed; he did not want Hayward forced to move after losing his rent-sharing flatmate. In strict confidence, Margaret Behrens in Menton (where they planned to honeymoon) was contacted about arrangements. Occasionally, as in a late December letter to writer Dwight Macdonald, Tom mentioned he might be heading 'South for a few weeks'; Valerie helped him clear his diary.[151] Now sharing with each other aspects of their earlier lives, Tom told her his existence had been 'like a bad Dostoyevsky novel written by Middleton Murry'. Quoting 'with some bitterness' from Elizabeth Barrett Browning's poem 'A Musical Instrument', he was all too conscious of 'the cost and pain' that formed 'a poet'.[152] For him, as for Valerie, though in different ways, this late marriage would be a risk. Shortly before the wedding, he had been told by doctors that 'his chances of surviving much longer were fifty-fifty'.[153]

On Christmas Eve 1956 he wrote a difficult letter, confident it would not arrive until around New Year. 'My Dear Emily', it began, breaking to his old love news of his forthcoming nuptials. He promised to write 'soon, about other matters', and signed himself 'with constant affection, Tom'.[154] When Emily received this letter, she responded with dignity, and Tom thanked her the following February for her 'fine letters', mentioning also that 'Valerie was very much pleased by your writing to her.' He hoped Emily would 'be able to come to England to meet her'.[155] Yet, as realisation sank in, Emily felt increasingly devastated. After all her years of waiting, how could their relationship have come to this? She faced the possibility they might never meet again, and the archive of their correspondence at Princeton ends with his letter of 10 February 1957, signed 'With much love, Tom'.[156] Those letters would prove to posterity how he had treated her, and how important she had been to his poetry. It was almost too much to bear. A few months later she retired from Abbot Academy and suffered a breakdown; she returned to Woods Hole, then later to Chipping Campden, places where she had friends and which she associated with past happiness and with Tom. Briefly, she resumed teaching, but soon resigned for good, living on in Massachusetts, latterly at Concord, and using a bequest from her aunt to fund foreign holidays. Eleanor Hinkley sent her news of Tom, and she began a memoir about her relationship with him. Much revised with help from the Thorps, and sometimes showing confusion, eventually this became a short introduction to the correspondence at Princeton, deposited there alongside it. Though she regained some considerable spirit in her final years, in the late 1950s friends thought Emily's life seemed to have drained out of her. It had.

Having proposed to Valerie by letter, and written to Emily, Tom, with a horror of face-to-face emotional confrontations, turned to a further separation. In early January 1957, asking him to read it in his presence, he handed Hayward a small white envelope on which was typed simply 'John Hayward Esqre'. Inside, typed on Faber & Faber notepaper, was a letter dated 7 January explaining that Tom would be leaving the following morning because 'Valerie Fletcher and I are getting married.' It stated that, apart from those involved in wedding arrangements, Hayward was the first to be told; that after the ceremony the couple would honeymoon in Menton, and then return to a London hotel while seeking a long-term home. Tom's letter explained he had thought 'a great deal' about Hayward's position, and would continue paying rent until the flat's rental agreement expired in 1960. Signed 'Affectionately yours, Tom', the letter requested Hayward 'avoid discussion, particularly retrospective discussion' at this time.[157] Hayward, realising his suspicions about the 'flower of the Yorkshire marshes' had been right, tried to put the best face on things. Tom left next morning to start his new life. Not invited to the small, private, early-morning ceremony on 10 January at St Barnabas Church, Hayward felt 'as if', he confessed, 'Tom had suddenly died'.[158] Soon, almost as devastated as Emily, and as unsettled as Mary Trevelyan (to whom Tom had written similarly, and who also felt bereft) Hayward took to describing himself bitterly as 'the Widow'.[159] He stayed on in the apartment, alone.

16

Together

'WE love each other very much and are both sure that we are doing the right thing', Tom wrote on 9 January, mindful of 'the disparity of age and the obnoxiousness of most of the press'.[1] He rose very early next morning, hoping all would go to plan. Valerie and her parents had spent the night at Bailey's Hotel, Kensington, opposite Gloucester Road Underground station. Then, in Tom's words, 'at 6.15 in the morning by special license from the Archbishop of Canterbury in order to evade the Press', the private ceremony was conducted at Kensington's St Barnabas Church by the Reverend C. P. Wright, a trusted acquaintance.[2] It was, Valerie recalled, 'a beautiful clear morning'.[3] Tom's lawyer, Higginson, was present. The only other guests were the bride's parents. Later, Tom discovered Jules Laforgue had been married at St Barnabas in 1886, but on 10 January 1957 the newly married couple sped away to honeymoon in Menton. As scheduled, a brief announcement appeared in next day's *Times*:

> The marriage took place quietly yesterday, at St Barnabas', Addison Road, Kensington, of Mr Thomas Stearns Eliot, OM, younger son of the late Mr and Mrs Henry Ware Eliot, of St Louis, Missouri, United States, and Miss Esmé Valerie Fletcher, only daughter of Mr and Mrs James Fletcher, of Headingley, Leeds, and grand-daughter of the late Mr James Bruce.[4]

The Times said no more, but other journalists were less discreet. 'T. S. Eliot weds his secretary' proclaimed a *Daily Mail* front-page headline on 11 January, highlighting the 'secret' wedding and the couple's ages. The *Mail*'s reporter had contacted Geoffrey Faber, to whom Tom had written in advance. 'I knew about it, but I am not in the habit of getting up at five in the morning to attend wedding ceremonies', Faber stated, adding loyally, 'I think it is a very sensible and excellent marriage. They have known each other for seven years and they have been engaged for some time.'[5]

Margaret Behrens met them at Menton, where, if the weather was hardly hot, '*nearly* every day' was 'sunny', and markedly warmer than London.[6] The Eliots stayed for three weeks, keeping a low profile, but calling on a few friends including Dorothy Bussy's family, and visiting French Riviera beauty spots. At Roquebrune where Yeats had died in 1940 and where Tom's old friends the Schiffs had had a house, they honeymooned 'in a ramshackle villa perched 800 feet up a mountainside outside the medieval walled town', according to one report which quoted Valerie's admission she had long ' "hero-worshipped" her husband'.[7] With the words 'Here we go again', Tom soon sent this report to his old Harvard pal 'Nick' Brooks.[8] The newly-weds mailed postcards home, and Tom made sure to thank Hayward for a telegram – 'a masterpiece of J. H. wit & gallantry which gave immense pleasure'.[9] Towards the end of their honeymoon they were photographed by a *Daily Express* journalist, in 'the red-carpeted salon of an inconspicuous old people's hotel'. The reporter described Tom's 'delighted roar of laughter' as the world's most photographed poet exclaimed, 'You are the first to get a picture of the bride.' The honeymoon, Tom explained, was 'Just the way we wanted it', both 'quiet and peaceful'.[10]

'I am madly happy in being her husband', he told Violet Schiff on their return; Valerie informed her former secretarial colleagues it had been 'A wonderful honeymoon apart from TSE catching flu, and cracking a tooth.'[11] If their glee was evident, clearly, too, Tom would need looking after. 'Valerie had to nurse me through bronchitis', he confided to Violet Schiff.[12] A press photograph of the returned honeymooners at the airport shows Tom wrapped up in a heavy dark double-breasted coat and dark headgear; beside him Valerie in her veiled pillbox hat looks prepared and watchful. The *Daily Mail* chronicled how Tom 'limped into London airport on his two sticks, a married man at 68', describing himself as 'a shy man' who had 'fled from publicity'; but the poet also 'chuckled delightedly': 'Funny thing now is that far more people want to see my wife than want to look at me.'[13]

Valerie explained that before the wedding 'We could not be seen together outside the office, so it was frightfully difficult choosing rings and things.'[14] She had been active in finding their marital home, a spacious ground-floor apartment at 3 Kensington Court Gardens. Near Kensington High Street, this discreet, upmarket block of flats had been built the year after Tom was born. Its well-off residents included military men, doctors, and figures connected with royal affairs. Valerie supervised redecoration and purchase of furniture, while training a new secretary to work with Tom at Russell Square. Tom wrote to his cousin Eleanor, assuring her that Valerie had 'a keen interest and amused curiosity about human beings, and a great sense of humour'. Just as he was trying to give Valerie a clear notion 'of what is the "Eliot clan" and that one of the facts of life is that the world is divided into Eliots and non-Eliots', a congratulatory letter arrived from his cousin Frederick, welcoming an addition to 'the Eliot clan'.[15] On 9 February Tom took hold of the copy of *American Literature and the American Language* which he had earlier inscribed 'for Miss Fletcher'; now he inked in words 'for the newest recruit' to 'the Clan of Eliot' from 'her loving husband'.[16]

When he felt better, the couple were photographed by celebrated theatrical photographer Angus McBean. He posed them side by side, their profiles closely aligned, echoing each another. They began to be seen at public events, including an 'Anglo-German Society' dinner at Hyde Park Hotel on 11 February.[17] Back at work, Tom was amused when Djuna Barnes rejected his blurb for her new book *The Antiphon*; accepting this rejection gracefully, he promised her on 7 February 'something briefer and more conventional', but scribbled on the rejected wording 'to be preserved'.[18] He was in excellent spirits. 'It is a wonderful thing', he wrote to Levy, 'to be happily married, and a very blessed state for those who are called to it, even at my age. I have a very beautiful and good and sensitive wife, with a very good mind as well and a passionate love of poetry – she has everything to make me happy, and I am humbly thankful.'[19] His sense of gratitude was quickened by news of Lewis's death on 7 March; Lewis had 'genius', Tom wrote later that month.[20] Yet there was a striking contrast between the grim demise of the 'very sick' Lewis with whom Tom had dined in December and his own new-found happiness.[21] He crafted several public homages to this 'great artist', calling him 'one of the most intelligent men of my age'.[22]

Valerie, with whom he was assembling a wedding album including their letters of congratulation, was now the centre of his life, but he did not withdraw from all other concerns. On 9 April Charles Monteith sent on to him a prize-winning collection by 'a young Englishman whose poems have been published chiefly in America.' Monteith suggested it was premature to 'take him on yet', but after Tom read the work, he scribbled, 'I'm inclined to think we ought to take this man now. Let's discuss him.'[23] The poet was Ted Hughes, whose collection *The Hawk in the Rain*, Faber & Faber went on to publish that year.

By 12 April they were 'now at home' in Kensington. Tom's desk was delivered that afternoon. He typed a letter on it, hymning his wife ('Of course Valerie is beautiful'), and assuring Eleanor that Valerie admired Hawthorne's fiction.[24] As their belongings were arranged in the flat, he delighted Valerie by inscribing many of his works to her, celebrating his sense of the 'ecstatic' in their marriage. These private dedications, the adoring letters that he loved to write her each week even as they shared the same apartment, and the verses he addressed to her (usually for her eyes only) reveal an older man giddy at his younger wife's erotic attractiveness. He revelled in telling her how he felt. On 10 April he inscribed his *Dante* to her 'in the humility of Love'; more friskily, along with both their names, he added to the title page of her copy of *Sweeney Agonistes* that this book was inscribed by 'Tom, for his beloved bedfellow Valerie, for her upon whom he relies and lies, touching her from mouth to toes'.[25] She was 'my dear, very dear wife' – 'my beloved Valerie'; she was (as he put it a year later 'in adoration') 'my lilywhite doe'.[26] Throughout their marriage he continued writing to her in such doting terms, celebrating their emotional, intellectual, spiritual, and, not least, physical union when 'with nothing on' (or, rather, 'She in high heels' and he 'in bare feet') they touched 'nipple to nipple', enjoying 'Tingling and burning'. Where once he had used the same nickname to Emily, now Valerie was his 'tall girl'; but where his sexual conduct towards Emily had been curbed and often sublimated, with Valerie he behaved – and was encouraged to behave – very differently. He celebrated in verse the time 'When the tall girl sits astraddle on my lap', and 'I can stroke her back and her long white legs'. Valerie treasured these intimately private writings, hoarding them along with all other mementos of their married life – menus, theatre programmes, photographs. Yet his erotic writings for her contain elements of awkwardness, as when he writes clunkily of how 'our middle parts are about their business'.[27]

For Valerie he wanted to create a secret, shared world of love expressed in writing, one which might heighten their mutual excitement but also serve as record and resource: neither of them knew how long they might have together. So, describing how his beloved's 'nipple / Pushes into the very centre of my palm', and of how his 'fingers' came 'to rest on the hair between her thighs', he created a private erotic treasury that was excitingly important to their marriage.[28] It was for sharing, but only between themselves. He wrote of her breasts, his erection, their bed. Into 'Valerie's Own Book', a manuscript collection kept in their flat, he copied out his poems, from the ribald 'Bolo' sequence to the terza rima of 'Little Gidding', keeping nothing back. Writing her love letters, love poems, and communicating as intimately as he knew how, he was Valerie's own writer now, telling repeatedly his 'Love   adoration   desire'.[29] They relished that intense, secret sharing.[30]

Though the outside world knew nothing of these private writings, Tom did appear, as Rosemary Goad put it, 'completely rejuvenated'.[31] He wrote to Sherek on 3 May, remarking that the George Bernard Shaw-derived musicals *The Chocolate Soldier* and *My Fair Lady* were (unlike Shaw's non-musical *oeuvre*) works 'I should like to see again and again'.[32] Later that month he was seen 'laughing aloud' at Robert Frost's jokes when that poet – hardly Tom's favourite – read in London; privately, he and Frost discussed Pound's plight and what, if anything, could be done to help free him.[33] Tom and Valerie met her former employer Charles Morgan at an Anglo-Swedish Society dinner in Claridge's Hotel on 30 May. The new husband and wife seemed fully at ease. Seeing 'Valerie' looking 'very happy', people remarked particularly on Tom's metamorphosis: 'His whole deportment, expression, spirits, were transformed, as if a great weight had been lifted from his shoulders.'[34] Whether protesting against communist repression in Hungary or pronouncing himself 'very unhappy about the Nuremberg trials' since they were 'trials of the vanquished by the victors' and ignored such matters as the Russians' 'Katyn massacre of Polish officers', Tom had not lost his solemnity.[35] He contested with tenacious annoyance any continuing 'accusation of Fascism and anti-semitism', though that did not curb his private jokes about photographs where he appeared to have 'a villainous squint or a Jewish physiognomy'.[36] He defended the BBC's highbrow radio *Third Programme*. He prepared for September publication his new essay collection, *On Poetry and Poets*, dedicated to Valerie and assembled with his customary editorial clarity, though *The Times* termed it 'Mr T. S. Eliot's Foie-Gras Sandwich'.[37] But he was prepared, much more than before, to undercut the solemnity expected of him. For Valerie, it seemed, he would do anything. On 28 May they danced at the May Fair Hotel's New Bridge Ball: Tom, 'immaculate in evening dress', told reporters, 'This is my "coming-out" tonight. I haven't danced for years . . . I'm not telling you how many.' Valerie explained, 'This is the first time we've danced together in public.' She had waited for a waltz – 'which I know he prefers'.[38] Before long she bought a cine camera, filming him strolling up and down the pavement near their flat: he paraded mischievously, swinging his walking stick like Charlie Chaplin.

Revelling in each other's company, they summered privately, holidaying on the Isle of Wight with Tom's sole surviving sister, sharing memories. Tom and Valerie enjoyed reading to one another. He read her a lot of Dickens (a favourite was *Martin Chuzzlewit*) and other Victorian literature; she often read him poets' letters. In September they holidayed in Scarborough, Yorkshire, seeing her parents in nearby Headingley. Visits to Valerie's parents became an established pattern. A local butcher's wife saw Tom walking with

Valerie's mother. 'Tall, elderly, very refined-looking', he wore 'a beautiful overcoat'. Valerie's mother was about six years younger than Tom. She liked him, detecting a 'virginal' quality.[39] The newly-weds were photographed leaning on a Leeds garden gate. As autumn set in and turned to winter, Tom's health grew uncertain again, but Valerie nursed him. Selecting metaphysical poems for a late-1957 radio broadcast, he chose verse illustrating 'conjugal love at its highest', but also lines where Aurelian Townshend has Fate intertwining the 'threads' of two lovers' lives – 'hers the longer'.[40]

He ceased seeing Mary Trevelyan, whose initial reaction to his marriage was to think 'he had gone out of his mind'.[41] She had written to him, signalling that her affection would continue. Thinking this 'gross impertinence', he wrote to tell her so, though later she received an invitation to dinner. Mary 'pleaded a previous engagement', and they never met again.[42] Shocked by a rejection that she never fully got over, she sympathised with the 'Widow' Hayward, and finished assembling material for her substantial memoir, 'The Pope of Russell Square', in which she recorded revealing details: Tom's angry slamming of her car door; how before he married Valerie he had liked to wear over his expensive suit an over-large coat inherited from his brother; the way he wore a red tie to commemorate the execution of Charles, King and Martyr. Neither Mary nor her heirs could publish this memoir in full, since it drew extensively on his letters, whose copyright belonged to Tom and his executors.

He faced greater difficulty as regards Emily. By October 1957, having consigned many of his letters to Princeton, she had travelled to England, renting a cottage at Chipping Campden. She wrote to Tom, and he replied. In response, she confessed, 'Nothing seems natural these days, but if you care for me to meet Valerie and continue a long friendship normally, I think the moment has come perhaps.' Mentioning she would soon be returning to Boston via London, but not giving him an address for correspondence, she signed herself 'Emily Hale'. 'Apprehensive about her state' and what he saw as her 'very strange behaviour', he wrote to Eleanor Hinkley to ask what was going on.[43] He and Emily did not meet. She returned to the States and lived from 1958 until 1963 close to Smith College in Northampton, Connecticut. She and Tom never met again.

Though they would hear news of her, particularly from Eleanor, Tom and Valerie judged it best to keep their distance. Tom told Eleanor he found Emily's situation 'distressing'. He worried she might lack 'the mental resources or interests necessary in retirement' after the 'intensity' of her theatre work.[44] After seeking Eleanor's advice, he was about to send Emily a letter, but decided it was wisest to leave her alone. He feared she had wasted resources on 'this *recherche du temps perdu*' in the form of the

Princeton letters, memoirs, and recordings of herself.[45] Around the time Emily left England in October 1957, and while Tom was still recovering from Asian flu, Valerie's father, James, an insurance manager in his early sixties, died. Tom was too ill to attend the funeral, and Valerie asked Collin and Lillian Brooks to visit him while she was away, since 'Left to himself he may give way to depression.' Dealing with marriage, with her frail husband's long-standing admirers, and with the loss of her father (which left her feeling 'as though an amputation has taken place') all in one year, Valerie coped with a resilient grace which was, as Tom, Eleanor, and others came to realise, her signature strength.[46]

While all this unfolded, he finished his new play. By January 1958 Valerie was rapidly typing it up. It would premiere at that summer's Edinburgh Festival. She telephoned Sherek, telling him there was only one copy, and that Tom was ill in bed; Sherek must come to their apartment to read it. He did so, and told Valerie it seemed disappointing. He recalled her response:

'It's the first draft and you can't take it with you. Anyway, Tom is terribly nervous and you simply must go in and tell him that you like it, or it may affect his health.'

So, with mixed feelings, I sat on his bed (he was looking very ill) and told him that I thought it was splendid.

At these words, Tom 'looked better at once'. Sherek would not have been surprised 'if he had jumped out of bed there and then and danced a fandango'.[47] Valerie knew what her husband needed to hear in order to finish this play whose drafting had formed part of their courtship. He saw Sophocles' *Oedipus at Colonus* as in its 'background', but was anxious about it.[48] Soon, with guidance from Browne and Sherek, *The Elder Statesman* was reshaped and ready for Edinburgh.

Making clear he had 'no sympathy with Pound's racial prejudices', Tom reiterated in a message published in February that it would be 'appalling' for 'perhaps the greatest poet of his generation' to 'end his life as an inmate of St Elizabeths Hospital'. Concerted campaigning by Pound's friends and supporters (including Frost and Archibald MacLeish) led to the eventual dismissal of the indictment against him, and to his release, after psychological re-examination, in April 1958.[49] Pound's vertiginous charisma continued to win admirers. He sailed for Italy with his twenty-six-year-old muse and collaborator Marcella Spann, as well as his long-suffering wife Dorothy. Arriving in Naples, en route to his daughter Mary's castle home at Brunnenburg, northern Italy, the old poet, who from time to time denied antisemitism, gave what looked like a 'fascist salute'.[50]

About two months before Pound returned to Italy, Tom and Valerie went there. Celebrating Tom's honorary degree from the University of Rome, they stayed for over two weeks, relishing the food and sunshine. Then, not long back in London, they set out again, crossing the Atlantic in April on a tour that included Texas. Opening a library exhibition of his work, Tom inscribed 'to my darling, my Valerie, in Austin' a first edition of *Prufrock and Other Observations* with which he was presented.[51] In Dallas, he was made an honorary deputy sheriff. Then came Manhattan. Tom's friend and New York publisher Donald Brace had died in 1955, and Robert Giroux, who had worked with Frank Morley and whom Tom liked, had moved from Harcourt, Brace to Farrar, Straus & Cudahy (later Farrar, Straus & Giroux) that same year. At his new firm, Giroux, now established as one of America's leading publishers, went on being Tom's US editor. Making hotel arrangements for the Eliots' 1958 visit, Giroux remembered Tom telephoning: 'The hotel was just fine, but they would like a double bed.'[52] Walking out in Manhattan, Tom sported a Texan ten-gallon hat to go to church. He gave a reading at Columbia University. In private, prompted by Valerie and after they had all downed several martinis, he recounted to Levy a 'blackface' vaudeville sketch heard in his youth.[53] Levy noted how proudly Valerie wore 'a gold charm bracelet which Tom had given her. It consisted of miniature books, each bearing the title of one of Tom's major works.' To Levy Tom confided, 'This last part of my life is the best, in excess of anything I could have deserved.'[54] Throughout the trip, both the Eliots photographed each other repeatedly. In New York they also visited Marianne Moore, whom some people thought 'had a crush on Tom'. Valerie photographed the two poets, asking him to put his arm around Moore. Later, when Elizabeth Bishop asked, 'Was it a real hug? Marianne said, No, it was *gingerly*.'[55]

From New York they headed to Boston and Cambridge. On this, her first visit to the States, Tom wanted to introduce Valerie to scenes of his youth, and to relations and friends she had never met. 'One of the things I like most about Cambridge is it doesn't change so fast', he told a *Boston Globe* reporter for a story about 'Introducing Valerie to US'.[56] They visited Tom's sister Marion (now looked after by a carer), his cousin Eleanor, sister-in-law Theresa, and old friends. Valerie photographed Tom and Theresa aboard a 'swanboat' in the Boston Public Garden, and snapped Tom with Marion, his cousin Martha, and other Eliots at 83 Brattle Street, Cambridge.[57] At Harvard he was honoured with a Signet Society reception, and at Eliot House on 12 May Valerie listened as he delivered an after-dinner address. Harry Levin spoke warmly of him there, and I. A. Richards recalled scenes from Lloyds Bank days, as well as Tom's remarking once of

China that he did 'not care to visit any land which has no native cheese'.[58]
An incident at the Levins' house involved their large dog. Approaching
Valerie, who was wearing a strapless dress, the creature licked her bare
back; her horrified hosts did not know what to say, but Tom retrieved the
situation, remarking, 'I know just how he feels.'[59] As their American visit
neared its end, at Boston College, where he read his poems with commentary, he sounded buoyant, telling an audience of students and clergy that
every poet thought his most recent poems the best, 'though not', one
reporter recorded, 'as good as the ones he is going to write'.[60]

Back in England for the summer, 'the inseparable Eliots' took things
easy for a time, then travelled to Edinburgh for the opening of *The Elder
Statesman* at which they sat, as so often, 'holding hands'.[61] As first performed, the play's third act, written after the Eliots' marriage, may have
had a special resonance for Valerie, who listened appreciatively in Edinburgh as Anna Massey, playing the part of the young Monica, told her
onstage beloved, Charles, 'You've no idea how long I've been in love with
you.'[62] After the performance, and prompted by Valerie, Tom 'strolled'
onstage to address a cheering crowd after the performance, yet stood mute
for some seconds, searching for her face 'in the audience'. As soon as he saw
her, he gave 'a short and well-phrased speech'. Next morning, he coped
'with his usual sagacity' at a press conference, and impressed Sherek by cutting 'nine and a half minutes from the play'. Eventually, he removed 'a
further four', making the English first night a crisper affair. At London's
Cambridge Theatre, where Tom had arranged a box for Hayward, 'ambassadors' and 'peers of the realm' mixed with Mr and Mrs Douglas Fairbanks,
a Hollywood producer, and Sir Jacob and Lady Epstein. The curtain was
held for nearly five minutes to accommodate Tom and Valerie's late arrival.
They sat with the Shereks in the royal box. Afterwards, they joined the cast
for a private party at À L'Ecu de France in Jermyn Street, where, at midnight, a cake topped with 'a pen in hard sugar' and a single candle was
carried in: it was 26 September – Tom's seventieth birthday. The diners had
'clubbed together to give him a leather-bound case to hold a playscript'.
Presenting it, Sherek hoped he would 'write another lovely play soon'.[63]
Tom was preparing to go to Paris in October, to speak about Kipling and
to take Kipling's place as the British member of the distinguished Académie
Septentrionale. Meanwhile, arrangements were in place for *The Elder
Statesman* to open in New York.

'Love reciprocated is always rejuvenating', Tom had told an Edinburgh
interviewer, 'Now I feel younger at seventy than I did at sixty.' Yeats was
in his mind, and he expressed hopes he *might* write a further play. 'I'm curious', he added, 'to see if I shan't also want to write a few more poems in a

rather different style. I feel I reached the end of something with *Four Quartets*, and that anything new will have to be expressed in a different idiom.'[64] The one new poem he released for publication was 'A Dedication to my Wife'. Its account of 'lovers whose bodies smell of each other' represented 'private words' addressed to Valerie 'in public'. Mediating between his erotic texts written exclusively for her, and his widely circulated published work, this poem links to *The Elder Statesman* and to an inscription he added to her copy of *The Sacred Wood*: 'for my Valerie the touch and smell of whom intoxicates her husband'. On the play's publication in April 1959, he added a version of the poem as a formal dedication.[65]

Yet if he hoped for a late burst of erotically charged poetic creativity akin to that of Yeats, it was not to be. Tom had never written as nakedly in the first person before, and had never produced poems as closely familial as those of Robert Lowell, whose 1959 *Life Studies* he liked 'very much indeed'.[66] Now, though he could write private letters to Valerie and Eleanor, making clear how 'good & beautiful & intelligent & congenial' Valerie was, his verse celebrations of her failed to ignite.[67] What he wrote remained private accounts, rather than fully achieved poetry. Similarly, the verse of *The Elder Statesman* articulates a mellow glow, but lacks sufficient linguistic life to be truly memorable. In the wake of *Waiting for Godot* and *Look Back in Anger*, *The Elder Statesman* seemed staid and old-fashioned. *Time* magazine reported 'British critics' had reacted with 'mostly middle-drawer adjectives – "entertaining", "touching", "his most human" – while the *Observer*'s Kenneth Tynan crashed through with "banal" '.[68] By the end of November, it was being announced that Tom's drama was playing to half-full audiences and, having 'failed to repeat his earlier successes', would end its London run after eleven weeks.[69] Its planned New York run evaporated.

His young wife cheered him, but his contemporaries grew fewer. Dame Rose Macaulay, whom Tom and others joined in protesting in October 1958 against Soviet treatment of Boris Pasternak, died that month. Macaulay, spirited Anglo-Catholic novelist of *The Towers of Trebizond*, had been a notoriously bad driver: Valerie recalled sitting beside Tom in the back seat while Rose, steering, chatted to them both, constantly glancing back, until Tom could stand no more and pleaded, 'For God's sake, Rose, keep your eyes on the road!'[70] George Bell, Tom's old ecclesiastical supporter, was another, closer loss. In London on 30 December Tom recorded a BBC radio tribute to him, recalling Bell's 1930s 'protests against the religious and racial persecution' in Germany, and calling him 'a "lovable man"'; he used a very similar phrase when dedicating a statue in St Stephen's to the memory of Eric Cheetham.[71] On New Year's Day, Tom wrote to the Royal Literary Fund on behalf of Edwin Muir, another 'lovable' man whose work he admired increasingly; but Muir, whom he would memorialise that April and whose *Selected Poems* he would later edit, died on 3 January.[72] Registering the passing of contemporaries scarcely cheered Tom, who endured a chill caught in France while dining 'in a very cold house with some Carmelite monks' after being received into the Académie Septentrionale.[73] Having approved proofs of the forthcoming published version, he was taking *The Elder Statesman*'s relative failure with good grace. Still, concerned for his emphysema and morale, Valerie had arranged they holiday in the Bahamas early in 1959, escaping the worst of London's winter.

By early March, she was reporting from Nassau that Tom was as brown as a 'handsome Indian'.[74] They returned to London late that month. While it was good to see *The Elder Statesman* published in April, their pleasure was compromised by continuing anxieties about Geoffrey Faber's health. Having suffered a stroke the previous autumn, he was largely confined to his Minsted home. The Eliots mourned Collin Brooks, the mutual friend responsible for bringing them together, and whose 'loveableness' (Tom used that word again) they had enjoyed.[75] Not long after Tom spoke at Brooks's memorial service on 1 May, the *Paris Review* published a long interview which Donald Hall had recorded with him in New York when the Eliots were returning from Nassau. Not having met him for two years, Hall was struck to see Tom looking 'debonair, sophisticated, lean, and handsome, with a fine tan'. Throughout the revealing, far-ranging interview, Tom, whom Hall had caught at his most alertly relaxed, 'threw his head back to laugh a hearty, vigorous laugh'. As soon as Valerie entered the room, Hall noticed his interviewee becoming 'more animated'. Afterwards, the couple sat holding hands. Hall recalled that 'A close friend' of the Eliots later told him about Tom 'at a dinner party eating his soup left-handed, with some difficulty, because he was seated on his wife's left, and his right hand was engaged with her left hand under the table'.[76]

When Hall asked if Tom had plans for new poems, he answered, 'No, I haven't any plans for anything at the moment', except 'a little prose writing of a critical sort'.[77] As public man, elder statesman, and critical voice, he remained in demand. In May he headed north with Valerie to speak at the opening of Sheffield University's new library: 'A library can never be new', he contended, somewhat oracularly.[78] An onlooker was struck by Tom's kindly and meticulous concern for the taxi driver who transported the Eliots back to Leeds: Tom helped ensure that the driver 'got a meal' and had somewhere to relax.[79] Also in May, the poet accepted the Dante Gold Medal at the Italian Embassy in London – a signal honour, requiring further public speaking. More than ever, people around him (including Valerie) hung on his words, wanting them preserved for publication. Though he was not slow to champion causes close to his heart (the disappearance of the London Library would be a 'disaster'), some of his eloquence remained sotto voce, as when in July 1959 he requested a 'compassionate grant' for his impoverished German translator, Nora Wydenbruck, 'a highly deserving and courageous woman' who was dying of cancer but still translating Hofmannsthal's *Arabella*, working very slowly on 'an old typewriter which I gave her some years ago'.[80]

That summer saw the start of a 'sort of reconciliation' with Richard Aldington, who wrote to Tom in July, at around the same time as a penitent message came from Pound in Rapallo, who was depressed. 'What on earth is the failure you are talking about, and I don't like the insinuation that I have an unforgiving nature. Please reply quickly', wrote Tom to his difficult old friend.[81] Though wary of Pound's reference to 'myself and Semites', when 'Ez' continued to sound despairing, Tom followed up with a long telegram. Pound was someone 'TO WHOM ALL LIVING POETS ARE INDEBTED' and whose 'ACHIEVEMENT' was 'EPOCH MAKING'. Just in case Pound misunderstood the sentiments, Tom signed off, 'LOVE POSSUM'.[82] By autumn 1959 there were rumours that *The Waste Land* manuscripts were about to resurface. Though they did not, Tom hoped they might, if only to show his 'debt to Ezra'.[83]

When Stravinsky visited that autumn, having called on the Eliots at their flat the previous year, there was a clear rapport between poet and composer. No modern composer had mattered more to the poet of *The Waste Land*; in Tom, Stravinsky recognised a great artistic peer. Robert Craft, Stravinsky's biographer, was struck by how readily Tom explained the meaning of an ancient Greek term, even before consulting his well-worn Greek dictionary for confirmation. His tenacious alertness impressed everyone, and his capacity for travel seemed undiminished. Winter 1959 saw the Eliots in America again. At Brookline, Massachusetts, on 21 October Tom received the Emerson-Thoreau Medal. He spoke about the influence of landscape on poets, and not least on one 'small boy who was a devoted birdwatcher' but who, because his childhood was divided between St Louis and Massachusetts, 'never saw' in New England 'his birds of the season when they were making their nests'.[84] From Brookline he and Valerie travelled to Chicago, where Tom, confessing 'I have never "taught poetry"', lectured 'On Teaching the Appreciation of Poetry' and stated he did not believe 'the work of living poets should be taught formally'.[85] Then from Chicago they headed to St Louis. On this 'very happy' but 'very tiring' visit, Tom showed Valerie the Mississippi and sites connected with his youth. On 11 November he spoke at the Mary Institute's centennial celebration, reminiscing about childhood and remarking, before reading 'The Dry Salvages', 'I don't think I've ever read in St Louis.'[86] Valerie loved being taken to places familiar from his conversation and writings: whether the house at Gloucester on Cape Ann, which for decades he had not been able to bring himself to revisit, or St Louis' Eads Bridge. When they stopped off briefly in New York before sailing to England, Tom smoked an after-dinner cigar: 'A self-indulgence which I only allow myself on special occasions.'[87]

Not long after their return that December, he was writing again to Pound, trying to reassure him his work was not worthless, and telling him that Valerie 'gives me the first happiness I have ever known'.[88] Though he dipped into poetry and theology, he maintained he read little fiction now, 'except perhaps a little Simenon'.[89] Following their American peregrinations, Valerie encouraged him to relax, and, after several weeks at the inclement English seaside, they went to Morocco for warmth. There, however, they were unlucky: the Agadir earthquake of 29 February 1960 killed thousands of Moroccans and visitors. Relieved to get back to England, both Eliots felt in need of recovery, but by late April Tom was recounting to his old Lloyds Bank friend Aylward a story about sitting beside Churchill at that year's Royal Academy Dinner. Churchill, Tom wrote, 'asked me what my age was and then informed me that he was 87 – adding, I think, a year more to his age than he is officially given. He went on to say that until he was 80 he felt as able as ever but that since reaching the age of 80 he had felt a decline set in.'[90] Tom, a stripling of seventy-one, had given a toast at this event famous for its 'spirituous vapour and cigar smoke', and found Churchill's anecdote heartening.[91] But from now on he could never be certain of his own health.

Nevertheless, he continued with many habitual activities, albeit more sparingly. As a publisher he had halved his salary, sacrificing £500 per annum, which let Fabers appoint Charles Monteith, who had 'taken over' much of Tom's work, to their board.[92] Though formally Sir Geoffrey remained a director, he was no longer chairman. Tom helped ensure the company was purposefully restructured. Announcing in the *Harvard Class of 1910 Fiftieth Annual Report* that nowadays 'I appear at my office only on three days of the week, and I write very few blurbs', nonetheless he maintained his interest in younger poets.[93] On 4 May 1960 he and Valerie invited the Spenders to dinner at their flat along with the new Faber poet Ted Hughes (whom Tom had just refereed for a Guggenheim award) and his American wife, Sylvia Plath. Very much a junior partner in a conversation focused on Bloomsbury literati, Hughes was impressed to notice Tom's unexpectedly 'huge thick hands'. 'Eliot', Hughes reported to his sister, is whimsical & pleasant – at the same time very remote. He talks staring at the floor between his feet – when he's sitting – & looks up only to smile at his wife. His smile is like that of a person recovering from some serious operation.[94]

Plath sent her mother a differently nuanced description next day:

The Eliots live in a surprisingly drab brick building on the first floor. A comfortable, lavish apartment. His Yorkshire wife, Valerie, is handsome, blond & rosy. He was marvelous. Put us immediately at ease. We exchanged American travel experiences. Had sherry by the coal fire. I felt to be sitting next to a descended god: he has such a nimbus of greatness about him. His wife showed me his baby & little-boy pictures in their bedroom. He was handsome from the start. Wonderfully wry & humorous.[95]

The presence of Spender, by now an old friend, helped the evening go well, though Spender noticed that when conversation flagged Valerie 'gave her husband an encouraging look across the table which positively radiated help'.[96] If, as ever, Tom could be shy with people he did not know well, he was much less so among familiar cronies. 'I now prefer claret to burgundy', he mentioned as an aside to old Harvard classmates, informing them, as he did everyone, that 'the greatest, most complete and abiding satisfactions are those which spring from my marriage'.[97] Standing beside Hughes in the stairwell of 24 Russell Square at a party for Auden on 23 June, and flanked by MacNeice, Auden, and Spender, Tom, glass in hand, looked animated, dapper, and elderly, with his customary pale handkerchief in his dark suit's breast pocket. Plath – Mrs Hughes – was beckoned into the hall by Monteith, to see her husband photographed 'among the great' men.[98]

Tom had been a great man for so long, that gravitas could seem his constituent element. His leather card-holder was stuffed with membership cards for London clubs. Now in his third year on the Archbishop of Canterbury's Commission for the Revision of the Psalter, at the Athenaeum he regaled All Souls Club colleagues on 1 June 1960 with a thoughtful disquisition on 'Religion in America', indicating he was alarmed by a 'lack of God-centredness' and had been attentive to the statistical minutiae of sociologist Will Herberg who 'writes, certainly, as a practising Jew, but with no bias in his examination of the present state of Judaism and the Christian "denominations"'.[99] Yet to several observers who knew him well, marriage had moved him into a new, narrower orbit. Benignly, he offered to read and discuss any verse plays Hughes worked on, but he reacted with sharp annoyance to claims by a 'so-called "close friend"' that '"He never sees any of us now and we have completely lost touch with him. It is a great pity."'[100]

Valerie was anxious to protect him from over-exertion, but they continued to host trusted friends. Dining with them in their flat during autumn 1960, Tomlin noted a 'little ceremony' which, Tom's sister-in-law had earlier informed him, 'preceded every meal'. Valerie stood up, and Tomlin followed suit. Then, 'placing his hand on her shoulder', Tom recited a traditional grace – 'Bless this food to our use, and us to Thy service.' After that, Tom kissed Valerie 'on the cheek with studied precision'. To Tomlin,

> all through the evening the signs of mutual affection were so obvious as, paradoxically, not to intrude, still less to embarrass. He needed her presence. When she occasionally absented herself, in connection with serving the meal, she stroked his hand several times in succession, in order, so to speak, to build up a credit of reassurance on which he could draw until her [re]turn.[101]

Something exercising him at this time was that Penguin Books had decided to publish the unexpurgated *Lady Chatterley's Lover*, opening themselves to prosecution under the 1959 Obscene Publications Act. At Penguin's request, Tom had supplied a statement indicating he did not think Lawrence's novel 'obscene'. Soon, he was providing a formal legal deposition. The lawyer cast this document, Tom felt, 'in his idiom rather than mine'; it contends that the book's merit 'outweighs by far any desire to protect from shock or dismay readers for whom sex has long been a subject which arouses guilty feelings'. As a result, 'good should come' from its publication.[102] Such a stance was at odds with Tom's criticism of Lawrence in *After Strange Gods*, but he felt it his 'duty to go into the witness box', if called.[103] Weeks passed. Tom and Valerie spent much of August in Yorkshire, then returned to London for September; the trial was scheduled for the following month. Tom appeared at the Old Bailey on 28 October, but 'felt rather let down' when, like thirty-five other witnesses, he was not called to testify.[104] Mary Hutchinson's son, Jeremy, a solicitor tasked with finding defence witnesses, recalled Tom 'was *determined*' to 'put the record straight'; but Hutchinson, having reflected on Tom's earlier 'hostile' comments on Lawrence, decided it 'would have been a disaster' to call him, because the prosecution could have asked the jury to accept his earlier, rather than his current, views.[105] Soon, once the book had been judged not obscene and Penguin was selling it energetically, Tom felt 'glad not to have been called'. He found it odd that 'the Crown chose Lawrence's book for prosecution', instead of, for instance, *Lolita* – a work he thought 'really evil'.[106]

Concerned about his possible Old Bailey testimony and other commitments, Valerie had been keeping a protective eye on him. Kensington Court Gardens was, he told Eleanor, 'the first "home" I have ever had, since I was a boy in my father's house'.[107] There, ensconced in his seat to the right of the hearth, surrounded by treasured possessions – an Edward Lear watercolour, his library, family photographs – he relished solving crosswords, or playing Scrabble with Valerie. He would leave her messages on their magnetic Scrabble board, and they saved their scores. They drank Drambuie. They laughed together. She came to realise, as she put it later, that there was 'a little boy in him that had never been released'.[108] Often he told her stories of his American youth: how his earliest 'few little verses', written around the age of nine, were 'about the sadness of having to start school again every Monday morning'; how in boyhood he read through 'the works of Poe, in his dentist's waiting room'; he recalled accompanying his brother as a young man to see 'his first Broadway musical, *The Merry Widow*'.[109] He detailed frankly the hurt of his earlier relationships. 'He said', Valerie recalled many years later, 'he could imagine the husband Vivien should have married and he could have imagined the right husband for Emily. But neither was him.'[110] Given his earlier life's painful complexity, some anecdotes mixed humour with ironic poignancy. He

> loved to recount how late one evening he stopped a taxi. As he got in, the driver said: 'You're T. S. Eliot.' When asked how he knew, he replied: 'Ah, I've got an eye for a celebrity. Only the other evening I picked up Bertrand Russell, and I said to him: "Well, Lord Russell, what's it all about", and, do you know, he couldn't tell me.[111]

Valerie collected such fragments, just as she made sure they kept a hoard of annotated theatre programmes, invitations, finished and unfinished crosswords, and menus on which they had scribbled details of what they ate. She knew, as she put it later, 'there was a human love he needed to complete his life, someone who loved him for himself. I felt he'd gone through a great spiritual crisis and had been purged of human love to do the work he did, and finally he was to have it.'[112] But she was also gathering a shared treasury that might outlast them. This collection would include his letters to her: 'he always wrote to me once a week, although when he went to the Brompton Hospital it became difficult. But he managed by writing on lavatory paper, and I'd smuggle in a bottle of whisky for him.'[113] Yet she valued, too, sight of his letters to other people, and, deliberately (because he knew she wanted his letters preserved for publication) she 'used to read to him every evening and I inserted into the reading a lot of poets' letters and so on. Finally, one evening he burst out laughing and said: "All right, you win!" '[114] In December 1960 he signed a legal memorandum for his executors, permitting posthumous publication of his letters, provided 'the selection is made by my wife' to whom he assigned 'sole control' over his correspondence, including the right to destroy incoming or outgoing letters. She determined to collect and preserve it all, but was aware on one point he remained adamant: 'I do not wish my Executors to facilitate or countenance the writing of any biography of me.'[115]

He had been troubled to hear that Emily had been adding 'some sort of commentary of her own' to his letters at Princeton. With Valerie's agreement, he had drafted on 25 November 1960 a narrative to counter Emily's. Not to be opened until the Princeton letters were released, Tom's 'painful' account emerged from intense self-scrutiny. Expressing his suspicion of autobiography, he stated, 'In my experience, there is much for which one cannot find words even in the confessional; much which springs from weakness, irresolution and timidity, from petty self-centredness rather than from inclination towards evil or cruelty, from error rather than ill-nature.' Explaining that throughout much of their correspondence he had hoped their letters might be preserved and made public fifty years after their deaths, but that Emily's interest in the letters now appeared like Henry James's story of archival obsession '*The Aspern Papers* in reverse', Tom recounted briefly how he had fallen in love with Emily in 1912, but that when he had declared his love in 1914 she had not appeared to return his feelings. He had come to believe in 1916, one year into his marriage, that he was still in love with her, though this 'may have been merely my reaction against my misery with Vivienne and desire to revert to an earlier situation'. Meeting Pound in 1914 had been life-changing, convincing him to stay in England and commit to poetry. His marriage had been part of that.

I think that all I wanted of Vivienne was a flirtation or a mild affair: I was too shy and unpractised to achieve either with anybody. I believe that I came to persuade myself that I was in love with her simply because I wanted to burn my boats and commit myself to staying in England. And she persuaded herself (also under the influence of Pound) that she would save the poet by keeping him in England. To her the marriage brought no happiness: the last seven years of her life were spent in a mental home. To me, it brought the state of mind out of which came *The Waste Land*. And it saved me from marrying Emily Hale.

Emily Hale would have killed the poet in me; Vivienne nearly was the death of *me*, but she kept the poet alive. In retrospect, the nightmare agony of my seventeen years with Vivienne seems to me preferable to the dull misery of the mediocre teacher of philosophy which would have been the alternative.

For years I was a divided man (just as, in a different way, I had been a divided man in the years 1911–1915). In 1932 I was appointed Charles Eliot Norton Professor of Poetry at Harvard for one year; and even Vivienne's mother agreed that it was out of the question for Vivienne to go to America with me. I saw Emily Hale in California (where she was teaching in a girls' college) early in 1933, and I saw her from time to time every summer, I think from 1934 on, as she always joined her aunt and uncle who took a house every summer at Chipping Campden.

Tom's account then passes over the period 1933–46, but explains that on Vivien's death he realised 'suddenly' that he was not in love with Emily, and that 'gradually' he realised instead he had been in love with his memory of how he had felt towards her when young. He suggests he fell in love with no other woman while he was with his wife, and that after Vivien's death he came to realise increasingly 'how little Emily Hale and I had in common'. He had come to perceive she 'was not a lover of poetry' and not very interested 'in *my* poetry'. He had been unsettled by elements of her 'insensitiveness and bad taste'. If he thought it 'too harsh' to think she had cared more about his reputation than his writing, nonetheless, he thought her uncle's views mattered more to her than his. Tom thought perhaps she did love him 'according to her capacity for love', but he indicated clear annoyance at her failure to comprehend how 'shocked' he was at her taking Anglican communion while remaining a Unitarian, and at her relaxed attitude towards 'the Christian and Catholic view of divorce'. He contended that 'if she had truly loved me she would have respected my feelings if not my theology', and went on to express his wholehearted love for Valerie.[116] Reproachful as well as self-reproachful and self-exculpating, this document appears written with Valerie, not just Emily, in mind. Not made public until 2020 when the Hale letters were unsealed, it sought to right perceived wrongs, and to control the historical narrative through having the last word, but it could not wholly do so. It has about it the sting of hurt. Uneasily, Tom would return to it before his death.

Though writing this document involved emotional turmoil, visitors perceived none of it. On Christmas Day 1960 the Eliots invited David Jones to lunch, along with Valerie's mother, visiting from Leeds. Jones, who lived alone and was poorly, appreciated this kindness and left with a sense of Tom as 'a really great man & a good one' to whom he felt 'deeply attached'.[117] Not long afterwards, anxious again about emphysema, Valerie travelled with him to the Caribbean. Before sailing for the Jamaica Inn, Ocho Rios, Jamaica, he wrote a tribute to Bruce Richmond, former 'great editor' of the *Times Literary Supplement*, whose ninetieth birthday fell in January; at *The Times*'s request he updated his obituary for Geoffrey Faber, whose health had worsened. When the Eliots returned from Jamaica via New York in March, Faber was dying. Tom's 'Sir Geoffrey Faber: A Poet among Publishers' appeared in the 1 April *Times*.[118] Speaking at Faber's memorial service on 10 May at the church of St Giles-in-the-Fields, Holborn, with Enid Faber, Tom's Faber godsons, and Valerie among the large congregation, he recalled his friend and colleague of thirty-five years, saluting Faber's trust, geniality, courage, and 'the poet in him'. He concluded, 'I loved the man, and part of my own life is in the grave with him. May he rest in peace.'[119]

Though conscious of his own mortality, Tom remained engaged with life around him. After prefacing Jones's *In Parenthesis* ('a work of genius'), he commissioned Jones to design a bookplate featuring an elephant's head ('the family crest'), the words 'THE CERTAINTY OF LOVE UNCHANGING' (spoken by Monica to the man she will marry, at the end of *The Elder Statesman*), and the full names of Tom and Valerie.[120] As one of the judges, he was active in choosing poets to benefit from the recently instituted Gregory awards for British writers under thirty; in summer 1961 these awards went to two very different poets: Geoffrey Hill and Adrian Mitchell. He embarked, too, on a relentless series of *Times* letters about linguistic 'debasement' in the recently published *New English Bible*, but spared time, also, to write a quatrain to adorn a lawnmower presented to Faber's long-serving sales director, W. J. Crawley, at Crawley's retirement dinner on 1 June. Devoting additional time (as often) to answer a child's inquiry about his cat poems, Tom explained he had 'had a Jellicle Cat which ran away' during a thunderstorm: 'His name was Jellylorum.'[121]

A larger-scale project was the survey of his own criticism which he proposed to offer on 1 July as a Convocation Lecture at Leeds University, while he and Valerie were in Yorkshire. His 'unedifying' criticism had fared badly in a recent *Times Literary Supplement* overview (written anonymously by John Gross) which regarded *The Elder Statesman* as 'glib' and rebuked Tom as 'not a systematic thinker'.[122] At Leeds, mixing wry humour and hauteur, he claimed, 'there is no other critic, living or dead, about whose work I am so well informed as I am about my own'. Often upbraiding his younger displays as the 'braggadocio of the mild-mannered man safely entrenched behind his typewriter', he spoke as a 'critic who is also a poet'. Dividing his criticism into three period-based groupings – in essence, early, middle, and late – he dispensed revised versions of earlier pronouncements: 'I am strongly in favour of the maintenance of the monarchy in all countries which have a monarchy; as for Classicism and Romanticism, I find that the terms have no longer the importance to me that they once had.'[123] Yet to some 1960s students in his audience 'this spidery well clothed person' with a 'pernickety appearance' whose voice was just on 'the healthy side of croaky or hoarse' and who 'spoke very slowly' with a 'dry delivery' seemed 'sleep-inducing', his lecture 'dull as ditch water'.[124] In the era of Elvis Presley, Petula Clark, and Shirley Bassey, Tom, with his 'Retrospective View of My Own Literary Criticism', sounded like a figure from another age.[125]

Yet he could sense, and respond to, some emerging energies. When he and Valerie attended 1961's controversial revue *Beyond the Fringe* (which made famous the young Alan Bennett, Peter Cook, Dudley Moore, and Jonathan Miller), Tom scribbled on the programme, 'An amazingly vigorous quartet of young men: their show well produced and fast moving, a mixture of brilliance, juvenility and bad taste.'[126] Shaped by vaudeville, he preferred more old-fashioned humour. 1961 saw him writing in jokey verse 'as your biggest fan' to Groucho Marx, requesting 'a signed picture'. Groucho, two years younger than Tom, obliged, and, on receiving Tom's photograph in return, told him he had no idea the poet was so handsome. Why had no casting director offered him a leading role 'in some sexy movies'? Tom asked for a further picture of Groucho in character. As promised, he had it framed for his Fabers office, for display there 'snuggled up to Yeats'.[127]

As he had for decades, he veered between comic turns and po-faced solemnity. He greatly enjoyed having acquired, through marriage, a four-year-old nephew, Graham Fletcher. Graham thought Uncle Tom's voice singing 'Happy Birthday' sounded like 'the bleat of a sheep'. He sang 'a little more slowly than everybody else' because 'he respected every word'. The boy liked singing hymns to his uncle, relished presents including Edward Lear's collected poems, and was impressed when Tom chanted ' "The Owl and the Pussycat" with great enthusiasm'. Graham also remembered how, later, Uncle Tom 'surprised me by knowing all the words of "Hitler Had Only Got One Ball" and singing it along with me when we were supposed to be being serious in his study'. Sometimes Tom took his nephew by 'cab down Southampton Row, near Bedford Square, to Alan Alan's Magic Spot where we'd buy jokes and tricks to tease the rest of the family'. This side of Tom (the aspect that had gleefully set off fireworks in Faber's boardroom) was the little boy that Valerie, too, detected in him and loved; though perhaps not in quite the same way as Graham:

Clutching our purchases from Alan Alan's, including such useful items as fake plaster dog poo, metal plates and a chinagraph pencil for simulating broken glass, and perhaps the hardy perennial 'jumping cut finger', we'd cross the road to the foyer of the Bedford Hotel, where (with the wisdom of not reserving them to annoy Valerie) we'd crush the glass ampoules of the stink bombs we'd just bought, and then run away. He had a good turn of speed for a septuagenarian with emphysema and a fit of hysterical giggles, flourishing his stick in the manner of Charlie Chaplin.[128]

This Chaplinesque flourish can be seen in the cine footage Valerie took of Tom outdoors in the earlier years of their marriage, but was counterbalanced by the imposing solemnity with which in late August 1961 he testified to a committee investigating BBC sound broadcasting. Richard Hoggart recalled Tom uttering 'a sentence so finely phrased that you could easily identify the semi-colon before the final assertion: "Those who claim to give the public what the public want – (*pause*) – begin by underestimating public taste; they end by *debauching* it.'[129] Seldom challenged to his face, 'Great Tom' – as journalist T. S. Matthews styled him – liked to be commandingly forthright: a commentator's speculations about Tom's dominant mother were 'utter nonsense'; poetry could be a form of 'defecation'.[130] Spending part of November and December 1961 in the States, the Eliots saw family and friends again. Though he read in New York and the Boston area, and lectured at Yale, Tom had accepted fewer public engagements.

When he read at Boston College on 4 December, pronouncing 'Little Gidding' as 'my best', he impressed a *Harvard Crimson* reviewer as 'a mellow, gracefully old and sceptical man, who was perfectly relaxed', even if 'he stoops a little, like an old professor'. Better disposed than some of the Leeds students, this listener was not uncritical: 'his voice rather gets on your nerves'; 'some of the poems were nearly impossible to follow in a reading'.[131] Where once young intellectuals had lionised Tom, now, in the era of the Beat Poets, sceptical notes increased. He was annoyed, during his Massachusetts stay, when he perused the typescript of Herbert Howarth's *Notes on Some Figures behind T. S. Eliot*. On 26 December he informed Howarth the book seemed unpublishable: 'you have set out to demonstrate a thesis: which is that my poetry can be accounted for largely in terms of my devotion to, and of my reaction against, my family'.[132] The monograph must be reconstructed. Over subsequent months, a tussle ensued. Howarth, needing Tom's permission to quote material, substantially backed down.

'Bent over and walking very slowly with the aid of a cane', Tom was 'exhausted' when he and Valerie reached New York. They stayed at the

River Club, inviting the Reverend Levy to lunch in early January 1962. When the elevator doors opened, Levy was 'shocked': Tom's 'physiognomy was altered; not only was he an ashen color, but the very features themselves seemed soft and flabby'.[133] Yet as conversation developed, Tom signalled his tenacity, revealing he had completed a short study of George Herbert due later that year in the British Council's 'Writers and their Work' series, and that Faber & Faber planned to publish his Harvard doctoral thesis on F. H. Bradley's philosophy. Some English friends thought his memory was clouding, but he remained resilient, however tired. Conversation turned to 'Little Gidding'; soon it would be twenty years since publication of his last major poem. Prompted by Levy, Tom, who hoped to see the American priest for longer on his next trip, spoke thoughtfully and with characteristic precision: 'We cannot fully understand a person, grasp the totality of his being, until he is dead.'[134] He left, leaning on Valerie's arm.

For their fifth wedding anniversary they sailed to St James, Barbados. Valerie encouraged him to swim with her daily. Sea, sun, and uninterrupted relaxation helped revive him. He slept late, ate well, and again proudly developed a tan. On an idyllic beach at the exclusive Sandy Lane resort, he caught up with correspondence, assisted by Valerie. He wrote affectionately to Tomlin, who had given him a Peter Sellers record – *The Best of Sellers* – which both Eliots enjoyed. Yet at Sandy Lane they had a sense of being in an artificial world, surrounded by American holidaymakers. Tom complained later that the hotel manager had wanted to exploit their presence by arranging a huge party to present them to all the guests, and would not accept that the Eliots, though content to visit the manager and his wife in private, just wanted peace and quiet. This put Tom off Barbados, though the vacation helped his emphysema.

Return to London in March brought the pleasures and penalties of work. *Old Possum's Book of Practical Cats* was published in paperback for the first time in April; that same month Tom protested astonishment that anyone should regard his using the surname 'Rabinovitch' in 'Sweeney among the Nightingales' as 'evidence of anti-Semitic bias'.[135] Soon afterwards, he was happy for William Kolodney to print his 1953 letter on 'anti-Semitic movements'.[136] In June he did his best to exculpate Pound too, though not everyone would be convinced: 'I think that Ezra's mind was living in an imaginary past in which all Jews were bankers and usurers. And I gather that he has more recently spoken to the effect that if he had been aware of the Nazi persecution in Germany he would have spoken very differently at the time.'[137] Where he could, he sought to smooth over old wounds; in June, signing himself 'Affectionately, Tom', he promised to send Hayward further Eliotica for his book collection.[138] That summer the Eliots returned again to Yorkshire, and Tom continued generously saluting contemporaries who had died, including 'brave, generous and very lovable' Sylvia Beach, and, 'after a long illness', Violet Schiff.[139] Inevitably, illness, death, and posterity's verdicts occupied his mind. Despite his annoyance at Howarth's contentions, the first sentence of Tom's forthcoming study of George Herbert asserted that 'The family background of a man of genius is always of interest', and his account of the 'somewhat haughty' seventeenth-century poet who learned to become a 'proud and humble man' (and who had enjoyed, not many years before his death, 'a happy marriage') followed the customary 'Writers and their Work' format in providing a full biographical account.[140] It was a life story which some readers might relate to aspects of Tom's own. Still, intrusions on authors' dignity should be limited. That autumn he wrote to *The Times*, joining protests against 'the opening of Shakespeare's grave'.[141]

As always, and with patient encouragement to anyone who took a careful, sensitive interest, he replied to requests for information about his poems' background, recalling encounters with earlier texts that had shaped his work, and sometimes countering interpretations which seemed forced. Nevertheless, there were bounds to how much he wished to reveal. He was delighted to see his *Collected Plays* published that August, but grew impatient with what he called that November (in a letter about Howarth's researches) source-hunting 'Xanadu stuff'.[142] Searching through his Russell Square office, on 10 September he had come across a copy of his 1944 lecture *What is a Classic?* and now inscribed it for Valerie; but he was also aware of documents he wanted destroyed before his death.

Not long after writing that his 'personal bias' favoured 'Britain's entering into the Common Market', and a few weeks after *George Herbert* was published on 26 November, in the exceptionally bitter winter of December 1962 successive days of smog took their toll.[143] Even indoors, 'bowed', Tom now walked with difficulty. Visiting Kensington Court Gardens, Tomlin noticed how he hated to be separated from Valerie. 'On his own he walked with difficulty, holding on with each hand to the high beading, which by happy chance ran at a convenient height along the corridors of the flat.'[144] Its windows were kept shut tight that December, but smog seeped in. One night, Valerie helped Tom into bed. He seemed confused and struggled to breathe. For hours she had to hold him up; with no one else present, she could not reach the phone. She tried to kick it off the mantelpiece, to call for help, but failed. Not daring to release her hold on her gasping husband, she struggled to support his considerable weight. She thought he would die. Eventually, she managed to summon an ambulance.

Tom was hospitalised in London's Brompton Hospital – which special-ised in lung problems – for five weeks. 'Very ill indeed', he was given continuous oxygen.[145] He lapsed into a coma. Valerie was constantly at his bedside. 'He has not been very ill, but the smog upset him. He will be com-ing out soon', his protective Faber secretary told the press in mid-January, but he remained at risk, and late that month Valerie confessed to his old Harvard friend Leon Little that he had been 'critically ill'.[146] At one point he talked wildly all day, uttering nonsense that 'rhymed'.[147] Yet he rallied. When she brought him home, Valerie saw him 'excited as a schoolboy', but had to nurse him completely: 'I wash and shave him and see that he swal-lows 26 pills a day.'[148] He liked being shaved by her, though 'sometimes', she recalled, 'it was hazardous because he sang music hall ditties and would not stay still.'[149]

He was determined to live. By 23 February 1963 he was writing a resounding reference for his old friend Dobrée ('far and away the best authority on Kipling').[150] By March, sharing his determination, Valerie had flown with him to Bermuda where, as before, Caribbean sea, sun, and clear air helped restore him. Sadly, while in Bermuda, he heard his sister Marion was dying in Massachusetts. On medical grounds he was forbidden to travel there, but, at Valerie's suggestion, his cousin Martha came to Ber-muda overnight and, to their mutual comfort, passed messages between Tom and Marion. Eventually, Marion died in a Watertown nursing home on 28 April. The Eliots were back in London by then. Though still frail, Tom attended to accumulated correspondence. Annoyingly, mistakes had been made in the publishing of his Harvard thesis, so that in May almost the entire print run of *Knowledge and Experience in the Philosophy of F. H. Bradley* had to be destroyed. Much more confidentially, some weeks earlier, Tom had asked Peter du Sautoy, his younger directorial colleague, to de-stroy a box at Russell Square filled with letters. Du Sautoy set them alight.

In June, solemnly mentioning 'forces of Antichrist' when he wrote to thank New York's Catholic Book Club for its Campion Award, Tom indi-cated he was 'still only convalescent from a long and severe illness of last winter'.[151] Though his memory sometimes failed, he found himself think-ing that summer with vivid recall of people he had not seen for many decades, including Karl Culpin, 'My closest friend at Merton' College, Oxford. With his 'bad eyesight', Culpin had died in May 1917, 'killed, I think, on his first day in the trenches'.[152] Next day, not for the first time, Tom's nephew cheered him up. Tom sent the boy a letter explaining that, though he had not written further cat poems, he had 'a few creatures' left; 'one I like is called *Marching Song of the Pollicle Dogs*'.[153] Dutifully and stringently, he made notes on Northrop Frye's book about himself: 'I joined the Church of England in 1927, but only became interested in Anglo-Catholic practices and opinions later. One does not *join* an Anglo-Catholic wing!'[154] He relinquished neither desire for exactitude nor tetchiness. When Donald Hall visited him at Russell Square on 28 August, a 'fragile' and 'affectionate' Tom seemed 'frail, sickly, and happy'; Tom looked forward to meeting Groucho Marx. Yet, after remarking resignedly that Pound's judgements about people were 'extremely poor', he then 'rambled on' about an American academic whom he feared was trying to snaffle manuscripts from a poet's widow. Hall, who realised Tom must be thinking about Valerie's future, heard 'his voice tense with anger' verging on 'panic'.[155]

Louis MacNeice, who had struggled with alcohol, and was almost twenty years Tom's junior, died on 3 September. Tom felt 'grief and shock'.[156] Two weeks later, with 'nothing left but feelings of friendliness and regard', he sent off a tribute to his former friend, and one-time enemy, Aldington, who had died the previous year. Meanwhile, after several years of silence, a letter arrived from Emily, hoping that rather than having their correspondence sequestered for fifty years after their deaths, it might be made available sooner. If he still had her letters, might Tom deposit them at Princeton, rather than (as he had once considered) at the Bodleian Library? Emily felt slighted, and feared that very little of herself had found its way into Tom's poetry. By this stage, she had already given away a good number of the books and typescripts he had given her. Signalling her awareness of his meticulousness regarding intellectual property, she attempted to sound objective. In an awkward letter perhaps guided by the Princeton professor Thorp and his eager librarian colleagues, she pleaded with Tom, signing off, 'In thought of past friendship'.[157] He did not reply. She was correct in what she feared might have happened: almost all her letters to him had been burned by Peter du Sautoy.

To other contemporaries, including Conrad Aiken, and younger friends like Allen Tate, Tom was more benign, but they perceived his frailty. Dining with the Eliots and Tates at the flat on 4 September 1963, Tomlin was struck by how 'bitterly' Tom spoke of the Profumo scandal, and about critic Kenneth Tynan, but there were also 'touches of the old dry wit'. After dinner, Tomlin noticed in 'the matrimonial bedroom' a 'large oxygen cylinder' stood 'beside the bed on the left'.[158] Tom's existence grew increasingly precarious. Yet 25 September brought his *Collected Poems 1909–62*, a landmark volume published in London by Fabers the day before the poet's seventy-fifth birthday. There was a celebratory birthday dinner at

London's Ivy Restaurant with Valerie, Enid Faber, du Sautoy and about a dozen others – Faber colleagues and their wives. In New York the American edition of the *Collected Poems* appeared from Harcourt, Brace on the birthday itself.

If these were causes for celebration, there was also concern at the approach of winter. He turned again to thinking about Emily and his letters to her. On 30 September he altered slightly the final page of his short account of their relationship, which makes clear that 'I never at any time had and [*sic*] sexual relations with Emily Hale.' The awkward typing of 'and' instead of 'any' suggests Tom retyped this page himself. It explains how, after Vivien's death, 'I came to see that my love for Emily was the love of a ghost for a ghost, and that the letters I had been writing to her were the letters of an hallucinated man, a man vainly trying to pretend to himself that he was the same man that he had been in 1914.' His emending of this document shows not just determination to narrate the story of his feelings for Emily, and to elucidate why marrying her would have been a 'mistake'; it also indicates his wish to record his commitment to Valerie: 'It is only within the last few years that I have known what it was tolove [*sic*] a woman who truly, selflessly and whole-heartedly loves me.' In his typing or retyping of these words there is an evident struggle to articulate how much Valerie matters to him, and to renounce Emily.

> The world with my beloved wife Valerie has been a good world such as I have never known before. At the age of 68 the world was transformed for me, and I was transformed by Valerie.
> May we all rest in peace.[159]

Against the odds, and thanks to Valerie's determined attentiveness, he was able to travel with her to America in December 1963. They stayed again at New York's River Club on East 52nd Street, and enjoyed dining with Stravinsky. He remembered Tom bent low over his dinner plate, not eating, and reminiscing about Missouri. Eventually, with an effort, the poet drew himself upright, proposing a toast, wishing he and the composer might live for a further decade. But Tom was worried. Giroux recalled him confiding, 'I'm so concerned about my young wife's future. I don't have a great estate to leave her.'[160] In Manhattan the Eliots ventured out little. A few invited guests, including Donald Gallup, came individually to meet them. Watching him enter the River Club's cocktail lounge, Levy was struck by the 'great effort' with which Tom walked, and by his 'great shortness of breath'. He looked 'bone tired'. Over dinner, reminiscing about his St Louis childhood but also chatting in a kindly, engaged manner, he ate strikingly little. Levy was pleased, though, to see how 'immensely amused' he was by a story about a young man with his girlfriend who were picnicking together in idyllic surroundings when suddenly the young man frowned, cursing, 'Damn it, I forgot the cigarettes!'[161]

From New York Valerie took him to Nassau for a substantial stay in the Bahamas, where he managed to swim in the hotel pool. In London his Bradley thesis, with 'important corrections' and additional material supplied by Professor Anne C. Bolgan, was published in January. A New York edition appeared the following month. Both were dedicated 'To my wife who urged me to publish this essay', but Valerie now focused her energies on helping Tom make the most of their Caribbean stay.[162] He felt well enough to send greetings to his niece, Theodora, on 16 March. Then, returning to England for spring, he garnered his energies. On 3 April he asked for revisions to mentions of influences on him 'at Harvard' in a blurb accompanying a new American edition of his plays, and he asserted that the unpublished early poems in his lost *March Hare* notebook, even if rediscovered, 'were not worth publishing'.[163] Verbal nuances and the future of his work: these things continued to matter, and the alertness of his listening remained disconcertingly acute. 'I remember his pointing out to me once that the metre of Tennyson's *Catullus* was identical with that of Edward Lear's *Yonghy-Bonghy-Bo*', he wrote that spring, putting on paper recollections of the late Aldous Huxley that stretched back almost half a century.[164] At the end of May he joined in a long-running *Daily Telegraph* correspondence about the 'split infinitive', which provided an excuse to correct publicly a fault attributed to an old mentor whom he had known even longer, Vivien's former lover Bertrand Russell.[165]

In June Groucho Marx and his third wife, actress Eden Hartford (four years younger than Valerie), came to dinner at the flat. It was a strain. The two men had corresponded intermittently for several years, and at least one modern commentator has detected hints of 'simmering resentment' as well as wit in the letters. Groucho had sent best wishes to Tom's 'lovely wife, whoever she may be', and Tom, conscious of Groucho's Jewishness, stated 'great admiration' for Israel.[166] According to Groucho's later account, in anxious preparation before meeting the Nobel Prize-winning poet, he had been reading and rereading *The Waste Land*, *Murder in the Cathedral*, and, for good measure, *King Lear*. Tom 'smiled faintly'.[167] Eager to discuss classic Marx Brothers films – *Animal Crackers*, *A Night at the Opera* – and the rapid-fire exchanges of the courtroom scene in *Duck Soup*, Tom began quoting a hilarious line, but Groucho had forgotten how it went. Valerie, unlikely to have been pleased by the 'whoever she may be' comment, remembered Groucho 'kept saying things like "As I was saying to Jack."' Tom, who was carving the meat, 'hissed' to Valerie, 'Who's Jack?' and Valerie hissed back 'Kennedy'. 'Eventually, Tom just sat back looking bored.' The two elderly men realised it was best to share other mutual enthusiasms: cats, puns, and – Groucho's trademark – memorable cigars. Valerie thought Groucho simply 'dull'.[168]

As was now their custom, the Eliots spent part of the summer in Yorkshire, but the journey was difficult. Alan Bennett, passing through Leeds Central Station, noticed Valerie's mother walking among 'a flotilla of porters', followed by 'her daughter Valerie pushing a wheelchair with, under a pile of rugs', Tom.[169] He was failing; but not ready to quit. He still sent Faber internal memos to Charles Monteith; attending its AGM on 21 July, he championed the London Library; and, despite his not infrequent remissness about errors that crept into reprints of his poems, he was still minutely recalibrating them. Concerned about the phrase 'moment after death' in 'To the Indians who Died in Africa', he resolved in June that future editions should read, 'judgment after death'.[170] Writing tributes to the late Edwin Muir (whose 'complete *integrity*' he saluted) and to the long-dead 'faithful secretary Irene Fassett' (for a planned complete reprint of the *Criterion*), Tom reflected on qualities of faith and good living as he prepared to face his own 'judgment after death'.[171] Valerie, treasuring all the many letters he continued to write her, particularly valued 'a wonderful letter in which he said we would be together always, together when one was living and the other dead, and that he would be waiting for me'.[172] Throughout her life, she would show this letter to trusted confidants, including Tomlin and, much later, Christopher Ricks. It maintained that if he died they would meet again in an afterlife and that if they were not going to be able to meet again then he did not want there to be an afterlife. Tomlin was particularly struck by Tom's declaration that if Valerie would not be with him he would prefer 'extinction'.[173]

Tom was too infirm to travel to Washington as one of the thirty people on whom Lyndon B. Johnson in 1964 bestowed the Presidential Medal of Freedom. Instead, he received it from the American ambassador in London in September. Bruce Richmond died on 1 October, on the same day as Richard Cobden-Sanderson, the *Criterion*'s first publisher. Tom sent in an autobiographical note for the *Harvard College Class of 1910* volume, telling classmates his 'emphysema' made the 'English winter increasingly hard to endure. But my wife takes the most wonderful care of me and I enjoy being at home as much as possible.'[174] He had already confessed to Leon Little (who had delighted the Eliots by sharing with them an old logbook chronicling Tom's youthful sailing exploits) that, though he still kept in touch with several Harvard contemporaries, 'nowadays, it may be a bad sign, but names even of old friends frequently escape me' and he was losing track of which classmates were still alive. With difficulty, he visited 'the office two afternoons a week'.[175] His Faber secretary brought mail to the flat.

Then, in October, he collapsed. Paralysed down his left side, he lapsed into a coma and was rushed to hospital. Physicians who examined him thought he would not survive overnight. Valerie knew his mettle, though, and stayed with him for thirteen hours, listening as he struggled to breathe.

> I sat beside him while he fought the crisis. In the morning, barely conscious, he turned over in the bed, placed his face on his cupped left hand and looked at me as if to say: 'I've done it.'[176]

He regained sufficient strength for the doctors to allow her to have him taken home. When he saw the elephant door-knocker on their flat's front door and was carried inside, he exclaimed 'Hurrah, hurrah, hurrah.'[177] But he needed constant access to an oxygen cylinder.

By 11 November, as winter set in, he was corresponding on Faber & Faber notepaper with Pound, whom privately he described in his distinctive accent as a 'silly ahss'.[178] 'Old Ez' must not succumb to the 'temptation' to 'let things go and think one has nothing more to say and that there's nobody wants to hear it if one did. I know all that, and Valerie has had to work hard at times to snap me out of it'. Signing himself 'Yours with love T. Possum', and assuring Pound, 'Damn it, you're still the biggest man in the poetry world', Tom confessed, 'There are still things that I want to do, myself.' Valerie and he aimed to go again to New York and Boston, then on to Barbados in the new year, despite Tom's annoyance at the Barbadian hotel manager in 1963. 'Some day,' he told Pound, 'I want to meet you in Italy. Valerie would love to meet you and I should like you to meet her.'[179]

Though he lacked energy to revise the work, encouraged by her, he had asked Valerie to prepare for publication a new book of his essays. *To Criticize the Critic* would feature his Chicago lectures on 'The Aims of Education', though not the 'review of his sociological writings' he had hoped to produce to accompany the title essay. 'In response to many requests', too, he had 'promised' the book would include early uncollected pieces, including 'Ezra Pound: His Metric and Poetry'.[180] In late November Valerie wrote to Conrad Aiken, acknowledging the gift of his recent *A Seizure of Limericks*, and letting Aiken know 'we laugh over them together'.[181] More solemnly, Tom composed a telegram dated 25 November. Requested by Jacqueline Kennedy for reading aloud at the opening of the Kennedy Center for the Performing Arts, it paid tribute to JFK, two years after his assassination, as 'a great and gifted man'.[182]

Graham Fletcher usually received books as presents from the Eliots – Edward Lear, Rudyard Kipling, or *Old Possum's Book of Practical Cats*. But the nephew knew his old uncle was also 'a fan of Dame Ngaio Marsh's Roderick Alleyn detective novels, and of James Bond, both as written by Ian Fleming and as played in the cinema by Sean Connery'. *Goldfinger*, the first movie in which Connery drove an Aston Martin DB5, had been released in Britain in September, and in December the boy's gift came as a surprise. Visiting the Eliots' flat, Graham was struck by how Uncle Tom 'played with the remote-control James Bond Aston Martin he'd already bought for my Christmas present, before patiently allowing me to have a go, and answering some of my more foolish enquiries into his opinions'.[183] More traditionally, Tom and Valerie sent friends their customary Christmas cards featuring high-quality reproductions of classic religious paintings. It was Valerie who inscribed 'To John' on their 1964 card featuring Hans Memling's serene *Madonna and Child and Angels*, then signed her name first on the card for Hayward; but the words 'and Tom' added by her husband have a confident flourish beneath them.[184]

In late December, however, he became seriously ill again. Valerie wrote to Giroux during the Christmas holidays: London bad weather had set back Tom's health. Her mother was with them, providing help and consolation. On New Year's day when Giroux phoned to wish Tom and Valerie a happy New Year, he was told, to his 'delight, that Tom was in his chair beside the fireplace'. In the background, Giroux recalled, 'I could hear his cheerful tones of greeting.'[185] Soon, though, Tom was bedridden. Valerie tried to stay by his side all the time. 'He bore his sufferings', she wrote that year, 'with great patience and sweetness. Even when he became so weak that I had to lift him in my arms and feed him like a child he was prepared to endure anything rather than we should be parted.'[186] Yet sometimes she had to leave him. His doctor called on the morning of Monday 4 January 1965, giving her a prescription which she took to the nearest chemist, just across the road in Thackeray Street. Tom did not notice her go, and her mother stayed with him, 'gently stroking his head'.[187] After about four minutes, Valerie returned, and, hoping he was asleep, entered as quietly as she could. Even her mother did not hear her coming back. But just then, as Valerie recounted to Eleanor Hinkley not long afterwards, 'he came out of his final coma suddenly, like a diver breaking the surface, spoke my name, then relapsed, never to speak again'.[188]

Next morning in London *The Times* published the obituary of 'The Most Influential English Poet of his Time'. Across the Atlantic, in the *New York Times*, Robert Lowell, calling him 'a dear personal friend', stated, 'Our American literature has had no greater poet or critic.'[189] Obituaries and tributes appeared around the world. His words were quoted, savoured, argued over, and recognised as unique: a reaction which continues to this day, and which has led to his poetry – whether in the original or in its many translations – having become a detectable presence in literatures as different as Gaelic, Greek, and Chinese. Very soon after his death, Tom's body was taken for cremation at London's Golders Green Crematorium; a small, 'private' funeral service was held at St Stephen's Church on 7 January, and a 'Requiem Mass' arranged there for 17 February.[190] At that Mass Canon Demant quoted from a letter in which Father Frank Lucas Hillier, who had been Tom's confessor in his later years, wrote that the poet had possessed 'along with that full grown stature of mind, a truly child-like heart', adding that 'To his refinedness of character is due the fact that like his poetry he himself was not easily understood – but unbelievers always recognized his faith.'[191] The Requiem Mass at St Stephen's had been preceded by a much larger-scale Westminster Abbey memorial service on 4 February. Later, with his young widow's permission, there would be a 'Homage to T. S. Eliot' at London's Globe Theatre on 13 June: Auden was lined up to select Eliot poems for reading; there was to be music by Stravinsky and John Dankworth, with artwork by Henry Moore and Bridget Riley. On the night, though, the standout performer was seventy-four-year-old Groucho Marx. The audience loved his vaudeville gags and his reading of 'Gus: The Theatre Cat' who 'was, in his youth, quite the smartest of Cats'.[192]

On Good Friday, 16 April 1965, Valerie took Tom's ashes to be laid to rest, as he had wished, in the north-west corner of the parish church at East Coker. She tried to ensure everything was done in accord with his wishes; and, as far as possible, she went on doing so for the rest of her life. She would edit for publication the manuscripts of *The Waste Land* when it was realised they were in New York Public Library; she would gather his voluminous letters for editing and begin their long-delayed publication. She would tell and retell anecdotes. Tom 'obviously needed to have a happy marriage', she explained to a 1972 interviewer, 'He couldn't die until he had had that.'[193] Though increasingly wary of people seeking to exploit or distort her husband's life and work (she detested the play *Tom and Viv*), eventually she allowed his poems to be used in Andrew Lloyd Webber's 1980 musical *Cats*. Its global success made her rich and let her help preserve the independence of Faber & Faber. She set up a trust, and established the T. S. Eliot Prize for poetry, personally signing the winners' cheques. Living on in the Kensington Court Gardens flat, she always felt Tom's presence, and stayed true to her 1972 remark, 'I still feel married and that I'll never marry again.'[194] When she died in 2012, a neighbour who had lived for two decades in the same mansion block wrote to *The Times*, 'she always kept a very low profile, but the porter told me that every Monday a florist's van would draw up and a large and expensive bouquet of flowers would be delivered to her from her husband Tom, dead since 1965, by posthumous instruction to his solicitor'.[195]

For the Westminster Abbey memorial service on 4 February 1965 there was, appropriately, secretarial assistance provided from 24 Russell Square. There Tom's small office with its striking array of pictures, and with papers in wire trays still awaiting attention, was photographed prior to being cleared. Though invitations were issued, people wishing to attend the Abbey service were also invited to apply in writing to Faber & Faber 'so that appropriate seating arrangements' could be made.[196] There were notable absences. Hayward, who would die later that year at the age of sixty, did not attend. Nor did seventy-three-year-old Emily Hale, though her reaction to Tom's death is evident in her 11 January 1965 letter to Margaret Thorp: 'Poor Man. The family report that Valerie has been *very* remarkable in her nursing as well as other wifely duties —: her life has indeed been devoted to his wants — perhaps I could not have fulfilled the requirement as she has done — perhaps — only perhaps — the decision to marry her was the right one.'[197] Still spirited, Emily would continue to act onstage, and three years later she played her last part: in the Concord Players' production of *My Fair Lady* she was 'Mrs Higgins', one of the 'supporting roles'.[198] Valerie would meet her — once — in the States before Emily 'died in the Colonial Inn in Concord' on 12 October 1969.[199] Her Unitarian funeral, held under the auspices of First Parish Church in Concord, would be very different from Tom's splendid Westminster Abbey commemoration. Emily's mourners were informed that 'In lieu of flowers contributions in her memory' might 'be made to McLean Hospital, Belmont', the asylum to which, more than half a century earlier, her troubled mother had been confined.[200]

At Tom's Westminster Abbey memorial service in February 1965 there were surprising arrivals from abroad. Accompanied at the event by the brother of his mistress, Olga Rudge, Ezra Pound had flown from Venice. The Abbey service included glorious music: pieces by Bach and, as Tom had wished, the Allegretto from Beethoven's Seventh Symphony, an old favourite. The congregation heard, too, Stravinsky's setting of part four of 'Little Gidding' — 'The Dove Descending Breaks the Air' — and Alec Guinness reading from *Ash-Wednesday* as well as from *Four Quartets*. Peter du Sautoy read from St Paul's second epistle to the Corinthians:

We are confident, I say, and willing rather to be absent from the body, and to be present with the Lord.

Wherefore we labour, that, whether present or absent, we may be accepted of him.

For we must all appear before the judgment seat of Christ; that every one may receive the things done in his body, according to that he hath done, whether it be good or bad.[201]

After the service, Pound, who had telephoned Valerie from Venice to make sure she would receive him, called at Kensington Court Gardens. 'He was very loving', Valerie wrote to Eleanor Hinkley, 'and we hugged each other. Sitting in Tom's chair he absorbed everything intently while I was made aware of his deep distress.'[202] He spoke little, but later wrote an eloquent tribute to his old friend, having detected 'on his own hearth, a flame tended, a presence felt'. Nearly eighty, Pound reflected, 'Who is there now for me to share a joke with?' Valerie reprinted Pound's tribute as a prefatory note to her facsimile edition of *The Waste Land* manuscripts. It urges, 'Read him', and praises Tom's 'true Dantescan voice'.[203]

There would be so many memorial readings, after-echoes, legacies, and lingerings that they could fill another book. The sheer immensity of this poet's achievement was marked again on 4 January 1967. On that Wednesday, two years to the day after her husband's death, his young widow returned to Westminster Abbey. After the opening part of a televised ceremony during which the chaplain read a passage from Ecclesiastes beginning 'Let us now praise famous men', Valerie crouched down in Poets' Corner to lay a bouquet of roses on the new memorial tablet beside that of Tennyson.

THOMAS
STEARNS
ELIOT
O.M.
BORN 26 SEPTEMBER 1888
DIED 4 JANUARY 1965
*'the communication
of the dead is tongued with fire beyond
the language of the living'*

Not many onlookers could remember Tom as a younger man, but among those were 'Hopie' and her sister Margot, the now elderly daughters of Mappie Mirrlees, his wartime hostess at Shamley Wood. To passers-by, viewing this new Abbey memorial, they were simply two old ladies. Yet to one another they had remained since childhood, with slyly conspiratorial glee, 'the Hideous Sisters Mirrlees', and they treasured their special memories of the great, chain-smoking poet who had styled himself to their mother 'the puir daft makar'. Relieved the 'beautiful and moving service' was over, they went, as Valerie's guests, for sherry under the recently restored painted ceiling of Westminster Abbey's elaborate, fourteenth-century Jerusalem Chamber where Tom had given a poetry reading just over six years before. There Margot, taking pleasure in an action with which the poet had been only too familiar, lit up an acrid cigarette.[204]

Acknowledgements

TELLING the eventful story of T. S. Eliot's life from the first British publication of *The Waste Land* in book form by Leonard and Virginia Woolf at their Hogarth Press until Eliot's death over four decades later, this book completes my two-volume biography of the writer considered by many as the twentieth-century's greatest poet. All the people acknowledged in *Young Eliot: From St Louis to 'The Waste Land'* (2015) contributed also to the making of this book, and, though I will not repeat each of their names here, my debts to them are lifelong.

First and foremost in *Eliot After 'The Waste Land'* I would like to thank my wife, Alice Crawford, and our children for sustaining me in so many ways through a project made difficult not just by the complexity of the materials involved, but also in its latter stages by the demands of moving house and the restrictions of the global Covid 19 pandemic. The staunch support of my insightful agent, David Godwin, and my shrewd, trusting editors at Cape, Robin Robertson and Bea Hemming, along with my wise and sympathetic editor at Farrar, Straus & Giroux, Jonathan Galassi, helped ensure that this book stayed on track. I would like to thank Frances Dickey of the University of Missouri for extraordinarily generous advice, and Jim McCue for being an exceptional source of guidance at a crucial stage. During two periods of the work, when I was unable to visit libraries in America, I am grateful to my former student SaraGrace Stefan for research assistance at Bryn Mawr.

For over thirty years at the University of St Andrews I taught an undergraduate course on T. S. Eliot, and I have benefitted from contact with generations of committed students, some of whom, including Suzannah V. Evans and Iman Javadi, have gone on to work on Eliot in various ways. Thanks to each and every one of my undergraduate students, and to my postgraduate students. Will Gray, Sarah Jarvis, Iman Javadi, Joshua Richards, and David-Antoine Williams in particular helped me maintain my direction. All my academic and administrative colleagues in the School of English at the University of St Andrews helped nourish this project, and I valued their collegial friendship. Invitations from Yale University and from the Houghton Library at Harvard to give lectures in 2012 and in 2015 helped make research trips possible, as did the generous support of the British Academy, David Godwin Associates, the Leverhulme Trust, and, throughout, the University of St Andrews.

All who work on T. S. Eliot are indebted to his indefatigable and astute editors. Their names form a roll call at the beginning of the notes to this book, but they should be named here too in a blazon: Christopher Ricks and Jim McCue for their annotated text of *The Poems of T. S. Eliot* (Faber & Faber 2015); John Haffenden (general editor), Valerie Eliot, and Hugh Haughton for their ongoing edition of Eliot's *Letters*, which reached volume 9 in 2021 and is published in print by Faber & Faber, with further materials on the website tseliot.com; Ronald Schuchard (general editor) and his team of co-editors – Jewel Spears Brooker, David E. Chinitz, Anthony Cuda, Frances Dickey, Jennifer Formichelli, Jason Harding, Iman Javadi, Jayme Stayer – for their eight-volume edition of Eliot's *Complete Prose* (2014–19) published online as part of Project Muse by Johns Hopkins University Press and Faber & Faber. Among Eliot-related works, special mention should be made of Ann Pasternak Slater's *The Fall of a Sparrow: Vivien Eliot's Life and Writings* (Faber & Faber, 2020), which makes available texts of Vivien Eliot's previously unpublished writings and collects her published work. Though the present book was written before the publication of John Haffenden's edition of Eliot's letters to Emily Hale on tseliot.com, the website conceived by the T. S. Eliot Estate in partnership with Faber & Faber, I have found other materials on that website a valuable resource, and have gained, too, from consulting the websites of the T. S. Eliot Society (UK) and the International T. S. Eliot Society (based in the USA). When I began to write Eliot's biography, none of these resources existed; now all are invaluable.

For time, friendship, hospitality, guidance, practical help, and encouragement, I would like to thank the following individuals: Sarah Baxter; Christopher Bittenbender; Dorran Boyle; Marina Branscombe; Jewel Spears Brooker; Colin Burrow; Laura Cameron-Mackintosh; James Capobianco; Tony Cuda; Frances Dickey; Valerie Eliot; Aisha Farr; Lisa Rosenberg Foley; Crestina Forcina; Nancy Fulford; Andrea Givan; David Godwin; Heather Godwin; Jane Gordon; Lyndall Gordon; Mary Haegert; John Haffenden; Marianne Hansen; Will Harris; Bob Hessian; Lucy

Hughes; Jeremy Hutchinson; Vania Jurkiewicz; Carey Karmel; Neil Kenny; David Kinloch; Joan Langhorne; Angela Leighton; Sara Lodge; Norman McBeath; Jim McCue; Gail McDonald; Hilda McNae; Patricia McGuire; Elizabeth Micakovic; Peter Monteith; Leslie A. Morris; Andrew Murphy; Kylie Murray; Carol Nickson; Graham Pearson; Clare Reihill; Amandine Riche; Adam Roberts; Paige Roberts; Nick Roe; Amy Sansom; Keith and Ronald Schuchard; Max Scott; Susan Sellers; Maia Sheridan; Philippa Sitters; Sophie Smithson; Susanna and John Smithson; Jane Stabler; Dale Stinchcombe; Jeremy Thurlow; Schölin Tipping; Sandra Wallace; Karen Watson; George Abbott White; Margaret Wilson. Over several years, the colleagues, friends, lecturers and students at the T. S. Eliot International Summer School in London were sources of advice and inspiration.

For permission to quote from the published and unpublished work of T. S. Eliot I extend thanks to the Estate of T. S. Eliot, Set Copyrights Ltd and Faber & Faber Ltd; and for permission to quote from published and unpublished works by Vivien Eliot and Valerie Eliot I extend thanks to the Estate of Valerie Eliot and Faber & Faber Ltd; particularly I acknowledge their permission to quote poetry from *The Poems of T. S. Eliot*, edited by Christopher Ricks and Jim McCue; from the volumes of Eliot's *Letters* edited by Valerie Eliot, Hugh Haughton and John Haffenden under the general editorship of John Haffenden; and from the eight-volume online edition of Eliot's *Complete Prose* published as part of Project Muse by Johns Hopkins University Press and Faber & Faber Ltd, under the general editorship of Ronald Schuchard. Full details of all these books are given in the Abbreviations section at the beginning of the present volume's endnotes, which should be regarded as a continuation of these Acknowledgements. In addition, I am grateful for permission to quote excerpts from the volumes of Eliot's *Letters* which are published in the United States by Yale University Press. I owe a continuing debt of gratitude to Clare Reihill of the T. S. Eliot Foundation and Set Copyrights Ltd for permission to quote from uncollected prose, property of the Estate of T. S. Eliot, and from unpublished letters the contents of which are also property of the Estate of T. S. Eliot. Thanks are due too, to Emma Cheshire and Hattie Cooke of Faber & Faber for processing and advising on permissions requests. Quotations from the previously unpublished notebooks of Aurelia Bolliger Hodgson appear with the kind permission of Bryn Mawr College, which holds copyright in Aurelia Hodgson's work. Other quotations from published works in *Eliot After 'The Waste Land'* are used under the terms of fair use, and sources are cited in detail in the endnotes to this book.

Gratitude is due, too, to the many scholars, collections and libraries mentioned in the endnotes to this book. I would like to extend special thanks to the staff of the following libraries which hold Eliot and Eliot-related collections in paper and/or digital form: Balliol College Library and Archive Centre; the Beinecke Library, Yale University; the Bodleian Library, University of Oxford; the British Library; the Brotherton Library, University of Leeds; Bryn Mawr College Library; Chipping Campden History Society; Cornell University Library; Corpus Christi College Library, Cambridge; Edinburgh University Library; the Ella Strong Denison Library, Scripps College; the Estate of T. S. Eliot, the T. S. Eliot Archive and tseliot.com; Faber & Faber archives; Glasgow University Library; the Harry Ransom Center, University of Texas, Austin; Harvard University Archives and the Houghton Library, Harvard University; the Irving Penn Foundation; the King's College Archive Centre, University of Cambridge; the Lilly Library, Indiana University, Bloomington; the London Library; McKeldin Library, University of Maryland; Magdalene College Library, University of Cambridge; Milton Academy Archives, Massachusetts; the Morgan Library and Museum, New York; Morris Library, Southern Illinois University; the National Library of Scotland; the National Portrait Gallery, London; New York Public Library; Northwestern University Library; Orradre Library, Santa Clara University; Phillips Academy, Andover; Princeton University Library; the Rosenbach, Philadelphia; the Royal Borough of Kensington and Chelsea Archives; the Royal Horticultural Society; Smith College Archives; University College London Library; the University of St Andrews Library; University of Sussex Library; the University of Victoria Libraries, British Columbia; University of Wisconsin-Milwaukee Libraries; Washington State University Department of Manuscripts, Archives, and Special Collections; Washington University Library, St Louis. Thank you also to the several private collectors who shared material with me, and who wish to remain anonymous.

Though any mistakes in the text are my responsibility, I would like to thank my assiduous and good-humoured copy-editor David Milner, proofreader Fiona Brown, and indexer Vicki Robinson, for their patient, meticulous work.

R.C., 2021

Abbreviations

Beinecke The Beinecke Rare Book and Manuscript Library, Yale University

Berg The Henry W. and Albert A. Berg Collection of English and American Literature, New York Public Library

Bodleian The Bodleian Library, University of Oxford

CP1 *The Complete Prose of T. S. Eliot: Volume 1: Apprentice Years, 1905–1918*, ed. Jewel Spears Brooker and Ronald Schuchard (published online as part of Project Muse by Johns Hopkins University Press and Faber & Faber Ltd, 2014)

CP2 *The Complete Prose of T. S. Eliot: Volume 2: The Perfect Critic, 1919–1926*, ed. Anthony Cuda and Ronald Schuchard (published online as part of Project Muse by Johns Hopkins University Press and Faber & Faber Ltd, 2014)

CP3 *The Complete Prose of T. S. Eliot: Volume 3: Literature, Politics, Belief, 1927–1929*, ed. Frances Dickey, Jennifer Formichelli, and Ronald Schuchard (published online as part of Project Muse by Johns Hopkins University Press and Faber & Faber Ltd, 2015)

CP4 *The Complete Prose of T. S. Eliot: Volume 4: English Lion, 1930–1933*, ed. Jason Harding and Ronald Schuchard (published online as part of Project Muse by Johns Hopkins University Press and Faber & Faber Ltd, 2015)

CP5 *The Complete Prose of T. S. Eliot: Volume 5: Tradition and Orthodoxy, 1934–1939*, ed. Iman Javadi, Ronald Schuchard, and Jayme Stayer (published online as part of Project Muse by Johns Hopkins University Press and Faber & Faber Ltd, 2017)

CP6 *The Complete Prose of T. S. Eliot: Volume 6: The War Years, 1940–1946*, ed. David E. Chinitz and Ronald Schuchard (published online as part of Project Muse by Johns Hopkins University Press and Faber & Faber Ltd, 2017)

CP7 *The Complete Prose of T. S. Eliot: Volume 7: A European Society, 1947–1953*, ed. Iman Javadi and Ronald Schuchard (published online as part of Project Muse by Johns Hopkins University Press and Faber & Faber Ltd, 2018)

CP8 *The Complete Prose of T. S. Eliot: Volume 8: Still and Still Moving, 1954–1965*, ed. Jewel Spears Brooker and Ronald Schuchard (published online as part of Project Muse by Johns Hopkins University Press and Faber & Faber Ltd, 2019)

CPP *The Complete Poems and Plays of T. S. Eliot* (London: Faber & Faber, 1969; reprinted 1973)

EH T. S. Eliot's letters to Emily Hale and other materials in the Emily Hale Archive, Princeton University Library (scheduled for online publication on tseliot.com in 2022)

Facsimile T. S. Eliot, *The Waste Land: A Facsimile and Transcript of the Original Drafts including the Annotations of Ezra Pound*, edited by Valerie Eliot (London: Faber & Faber, 1971)

Gallup Donald Gallup, *T. S. Eliot: A Bibliography* (London: Faber & Faber, 1969)

Houghton Houghton Library, Harvard University

KCA King's College Archive Centre, King's College, Cambridge

L1 *The Letters of T. S. Eliot, Volume 1: 1898–1922, Revised Edition*, ed. Valerie Eliot and Hugh Haughton; general editor John Haffenden (London: Faber & Faber, 2009; this volume is published in the United States by Yale University Press)

L2 *The Letters of T. S. Eliot, Volume 2: 1923–1925*, ed. Valerie Eliot and Hugh Haughton; general editor John Haffenden (London: Faber & Faber, 2009; this volume is published in the United States by Yale University Press)

L3 *The Letters of T. S. Eliot, Volume 3: 1926–1927*, ed. Valerie Eliot and John Haffenden (London: Faber & Faber, 2012; this volume is published in the United States by Yale University Press)

L4 *The Letters of T. S. Eliot, Volume 4: 1928–1929*, ed. Valerie Eliot and John Haffenden (London: Faber & Faber, 2013; this volume is published in the United States by Yale University Press)

L5 *The Letters of T. S. Eliot, Volume 5: 1930–1931*, ed. Valerie Eliot and John Haffenden (London: Faber & Faber, 2014; this volume is published in the United States by Yale University Press)

L6 *The Letters of T. S. Eliot, Volume 6: 1932–1933*, ed. Valerie Eliot and John Haffenden (London: Faber & Faber, 2016; this volume is published in the United States by Yale University Press)

L7 *The Letters of T. S. Eliot, Volume 7: 1934–1935*, ed. Valerie Eliot and John Haffenden (London: Faber & Faber, 2017)

L8 *The Letters of T. S. Eliot, Volume 8: 1936–1938*, ed. Valerie Eliot and John Haffenden (London: Faber & Faber, 2019)

L9 *The Letters of T. S. Eliot, Volume 9: 1939–1941*, ed. Valerie Eliot and John Haffenden (London: Faber & Faber, 2021)

NYPL New York Public Library

P1 *The Poems of T. S. Eliot, Volume I, Collected and Uncollected Poems*, ed. Christopher Ricks and Jim McCue (London: Faber & Faber, 2015; this volume is published in the United States by Johns Hopkins University Press)

P2 *The Poems of T. S. Eliot, Volume II, Practical Cats and Further Verses*, ed. Christopher Ricks and Jim McCue (London: Faber & Faber, 2015; this volume is published in the United States by Johns Hopkins University Press)

Ransom Harry Ransom Center, University of Texas, Austin

VMP T. S. Eliot, *The Varieties of Metaphysical Poetry*, ed. and introduced by Ronald Schuchard (London: Faber & Faber, 1993; this volume is published in the United States by Harcourt, Brace, 1994)

Notes

Introduction

1   *P1*, 775.

2   *The Diary of Virginia Woolf, Volume 2, 1920–24*, ed. Anne Olivier Bell and Andrew McNeillie (Harmondsworth: Penguin, 1981), 91.

3   Marian Eliot, quoted in Frederick Tomlin, *T. S. Eliot, A Friendship* (London: Routledge, 1988), 220.

4   Siegfried Sassoon, *Diaries 1920–1922*, ed. Rupert Hart-Davis (London: Faber & Faber, 1981), 132, 133.

5   William Wordsworth, *The Prelude* (1805 text), XII, 208.

1. 'I Cannot Go On'

1   John Peale Bishop, letter to Edmund Wilson [*c.*10 November 1922], quoted in Lawrence Rainey, *Revisiting 'The Waste Land'* (New Haven: Yale University Press, 2005), 104; the original letter is in the Edmund Wilson Papers at the Beinecke Library, Yale.

2   Ibid., 105.

3   John Peale Bishop and Edmund Wilson Jr., *The Undertaker's Garland* (New York: Knopf, 1922), 13, 15, 16, 18.

4   *L2*, 75.

5   *L2*, 124; *The Diary of Virginia Woolf, Volume 2, 1920–24*, ed. Anne Olivier Bell and Andrew McNeillie (Harmondsworth: Penguin, 1981), 178; Conrad Aiken (1923) in Jewel Spears Brooker, ed., *T. S. Eliot: The Contemporary Reviews* (Cambridge: Cambridge University Press, 2004), 99.

6   *CP2*, 106; *L5*, 288.

7   *L1*, 804.

8   *L1*, 803; *L2*, 74, 75.

9   *L2*, 44.

10   *EH*, 3 November 1930.

11   *EH*, 19 March 1933.

12   Daphne Fielding, *Those Remarkable Cunards, Emerald and Nancy* (New York: Atheneum, 1968), 43.

13   'Lady Cunard', *Times*, 17 July 1948, 7.

14   *EH*, 14 July 1932.

15   *EH*, 23 February 1931.

16   *L1*, 365, 280.

17   *P1*, 332, 333, 334, 644.

18 Aldington, quoted in Lois Gordon, *Nancy Cunard* (New York: Columbia University Press, 2007), 29; Leonard Woolf, 'Nancy Cunard', in Hugh Ford, ed., *Nancy Cunard* (Philadelphia: Chilton Book Co., 1968), 58.

19 Nancy Cunard, *Outlaws* (London: Elkin Matthews, 1921), 54, 57.

20 *P1*, 333.

21 Nancy Cunard, 1919 diary, quoted in Anne Chisholm, *Nancy Cunard* (London: Sidgwick & Jackson, 1979), 48; *P2*, 339; *P1*, 33.

22 Mary Hutchinson, 'Nancy: An Impression', in Ford, ed., *Nancy Cunard*, 97.

23 Chisholm, *Nancy Cunard*, 73, 50, 73, 86.

24 Nancy Cunard, letter and enclosure to John Hayward, 1965, quoted in Gordon, *Nancy Cunard*, 36.

25 *L1*, 680.

26 Cunard and Hayward, quoted in Gordon, *Nancy Cunard*, 36, 37.

27 *L3*, 712; *EH*, 3 November 1930 and 7 April 1936.

28 *EH*, 3 November 1930; Chisholm, *Nancy Cunard*, 88.

29 Peter Ackroyd, *T. S. Eliot* (London: Hamish Hamilton, 1984), 85; *EH*, 7 March 1933.

30 *L3*, 3.

31 *EH*, 2 March 1931.

32 'Dramatic Club Officers', *The Microcosm: The Simmons College Annual*, Vol. 10 (Boston: Simmons College, 1919), 154.

33 'Dramatics', *The Microcosm: The Simmons College Annual*, Vol. 9 (Boston: Simmons College, 1918), 146; the performances were favourably reviewed in the *Boston Globe*, 13 May 1917, 63.

34 *P1*, 57; *L9*, 550.

35 *EH*, 3 November 1930.

36 *EH*, 2 March 1931.

37 John Quinn to TSE, 4 December 1922, Quinn papers, Letterbook 26, New York Public Library.

38 A. E. Housman, *A Shropshire Lad* (1896; repr. London: Grant Richards, 1922), 57.

39 Charlotte Eliot's inscribed copy of *A Shropshire Lad* was advertised for sale in Blackwell's Rare Books *Modernisms* catalogue (Oxford), Spring 2018, 24–5.

40 *CP2*, 428. Sydney Schiff published under the pseudonym Stephen Hudson.

41 *CP2*, 418, 433.

42 *CP2*, 420.

43 *P1*, 57, 73.

44 'Eliot, Thomas Stearns', staff card dated 31.3.20, Lloyds Bank Archives, London.

45 *L2*, 56.

46 *L2*, 2.

47 [T. S. Eliot], 'Foreign Exchanges', *Lloyds Bank Monthly*, August 1923, 48–9; *L2*, 68.

48 London Metropolitan Archives, Holborn St Giles and St George, Register of Birth for 1879; *1881 England Census*, Class: *RG11*; Piece: 89; Page: 27; GSU roll: 1341020 (National Archives, Kew); *1901 England Census*, Class: *RG13*; Piece: 30; Folio: 99; Page 6 (National Archives, Kew); London Metropolitan Archives, Saint Clement, Notting Hill, Register of Marriages, P84/CLE, Item 019; Certified copy of the marriage certificate of William Fisher Sollory and Ellen Kellond, 3 April 1926, at the Register Office, Paddington; all the preceding documents are available on the ancestry.com online database, Provo, Utah, USA; the date of George Kellond's death is recorded in the UK Government Records Office Register of Deaths for Kensington, March 1915, available in digital summary on the FreeBMD website.

49 *Facsimile*, 127.

50 Ellen Kellond (1878–1930) was born Ellen Barton, married George Kellond in 1912, then later, on her remarriage in 1926, became Ellen Sollory; information about her is drawn from the FreeBMD website; *Facsimile*, 127.

51   *L2*, 58, 390.
52   *L2*, 389.
53   *L2*, 59.
54   *L2*, 60.
55   *CP2*, 419.
56   *CP2*, 419.
57   'Death of Marie Lloyd', *Times*, 9 October 1922, 14.
58   *CP2*, 418.
59   *CP2*, 419, 420.
60   Harry Bedford and Terry Sullivan, *It's a Bit of a Ruin that Cromwell Knocked About a Bit* (London: B. Feldman & Co., n.d.), unnumbered page.
61   *P1*, 71.
62   *P1*, 77.
63   *P1*, 77.
64   *L2*, 76.
65   *L2*, 124.
66   *CP2*, 479, 476, 478.
67   *Diary of Virginia Woolf, Vol. 2*, 236.
68   *L2*, 3.
69   *L2*, 3.
70   *L2*, 55, 56.
71   *L2*, 7.
72   *L2*, 7; [T. S. Eliot], 'Foreign Exchanges', *Lloyds Bank Monthly*, August 1923, 49.
73   *L2*, 244.
74   *L2*, 7, 3.
75   *L2*, 2, 3.
76   *L2*, 35.
77   *L2*, 8, 9.
78   *L2*, 8, 9.
79   *L2*, 167.
80   *L2*, 17.
81   *L2*, 9.
82   *L2*, 60.
83   *L2*, xx.
84   *L2*, 43.
85   *L2*, 205, 206.
86   *L2*, 220; *EH*, 9 February 1932.
87   Julien Benda, 'A Preface', *Criterion*, I (January 1923), 238.
88   *L2*, 236; Aurelia Bolliger, Notebooks concerning T. S. Eliot, Box 25, item 6 [unnumbered pages], Ralph Hodgson and Aurelia Bolliger Hodgson Papers, Special Collections Department, Bryn Mawr College Library.
89   Aurelia Bolliger, Notebooks concerning T. S. Eliot, Box 25, item 6.
90   *L2*, 207.
91   *L2*, 72.
92   *L2*, 32.
93   *L1*, 630.
94   *L2*, 39, 11.
95   Alfred Kreymborg, *Troubadour* (1925; repr. New York: Sagamore Press, 1957), 316, 317.
96   *CP2*, 434, 435.
97   *EH*, 19 February 1932.
98   *L2*, 72, 71.
99   *The Diary of Virginia Woolf, Volume 3, 1925–1930*, ed. Anne Olivier Bell and Andrew McNeillie (Harmondsworth: Penguin, 1982), 20.

100   *Diary of Virginia Woolf, Vol. 2*, 239.

101   *Diary of Virginia Woolf, Vol. 2*, 236.

102   L2, 83, 105.

103   L2, 86, 84.

104   *Bosham Parish Church Visitors' Book 1915*, entry for 14 July 1919 (Bosham Parish Church). I am grateful to Joan Langhorne for this information.

105   L2, 66.

106   L2, 64.

107   James C. Whorton, *Inner Hygiene* (Oxford: Oxford University Press, 2000), 121.

108   L2, 66.

109   L2, 103.

110   L2, 79.

111   L2, 80.

112   L2, 87, 89.

113   L2, 90.

114   L2, 90.

115   L2, 93.

116   L2, 95.

117   L2, 98.

118   L2, 98.

119   L2, 98.

120   Hubert Higgins, 'The Results of Re-mineralisation in Conditions of Faulty Metabolism, such as Neurasthenia, etc.', *Lancet*, 19 February 1910, 482–91; on Higgins and Fletcher, see James C. Whorton, ' "Physiologic Optimism": Horace Fletcher and Hygienic Ideology in Progressive America', *Bulletin of the History of Medicine*, Vol. 55 (1981), 72.

121   Hubert Higgins, *Humaniculture* (New York: Frederick A. Stokes, [1906]), 185.

122   Hubert Higgins, 'To the Editor', *Times*, 25 April 1922, 13.

123   L2, 104, 103.

124   L2, 108, 109.

125   L2, 115, 116.

126   L2, 116, 117, 118.

127   L2, 114.

128   L2, 114.

129   L2, 138.

130   French text from Paul Auster, ed., *The Random House Book of Twentieth-Century French Poetry* (New York: Vintage, 1984), 94; English version by Robert Crawford.

131   L2, 285.

132   *A Change of Perspective: The Letters of Virginia Woolf, Volume 3, 1923–1928*, ed. Nigel Nicolson and Joanne Trautmann (London: Hogarth Press, 1977), 38.

133   L2, 140.

134   L2, 143.

135   L2, 146.

136   CP2, 442.

137   CP2, 446.

138   L2, 170.

139   L2, 171.

140   Advertisement for Sanatorium Hoven, *Der Tag*, 20 September 1914, Entertainment Supplement, 4.

141   L2, 184, 175.

142   L2, 177.

143   L2, 200.

144   L2, 199, 177.

145   *L2*, 199.

146   *L2*, 185.

147   Alfred Kreymborg, *Puppet Plays* (New York: Harcourt, Brace, 1923), 49.

148   *L2*, 192.

149   *L2*, 209.

150   *EH*, 3 November 1930, 7 April 1936; see also Phil Hanrahan, 'T. S. Eliot's Secret Love', *Milwaukee* (November 1989), 81–5.

151   *EH*, 13 July 1942, 21–24 July 1931.

152   *EH*, 2 April 1935.

153   Edward Hale, 'In Weariness', *Harvard Advocate*, Vol. XXV, no. 9 (7 June 1878), 97.

154   Elmer Osgood Cappers, *History of the First Church in Chestnut Hill* (Newton, Mass.: First Church in Chestnut Hill, 1986), 21, 18, 19.

155   *EH*, 12 April 1943 and 28 November 1944. It seems likely that the painting described is the unattributed 'presentation portrait' reproduced as the first plate in Lyndall Gordon, *Eliot's New Life* (Oxford: Oxford University Press, 1988), opp. p. 20; its present whereabouts are unknown.

156   Cappers, *History of the First Church*, 13.

157   Susan Stewart and Joshua Kotin, 'A Conversation with Sally Foss about Emily Hale', *Time Present: The Newsletter of the International T. S. Eliot Society*, No. 100, Spring 2020, 18, 22.

158   Sixteenth Census of the United States: 1940, Population Schedule for Middlesex County, Massachusetts (Belmont County, S. D. No. 5, E. D. No. 9–53), available online.

159   'Officers of Administration', *Microcosm*, Vol. 10, 13.

160   'The Dramatic Club', *Microcosm*, Vol. 10, 157.

161   'Dramatic Club', *Microcosm*, Vol. 12, 161.

162   Grace Norton Kieckhefer, *The History of Milwaukee-Downer College, 1851–1951*, *Milwaukee-Downer College Bulletin*, Series 3, No. 7 (1951), 101.

163   Course titles and students' recollections cited in Phil Hanrahan, 'T. S. Eliot's Secret Love', *Milwaukee*, November 1989, 83, 84.

164   *EH*, 3(?) October 1930 and 3 November 1930.

165   *P1*, 1149, 268; 'Dramatic Club', *Microcosm*, Vol. 11, 164.

166   *EH*, 3 November 1930.

167   Emily Hale, statement dated '4/19/65' accompanying her letters from Eliot (Princeton University Library); in this document the elderly Hale dates her visit to 'the summer of 1922', but other misdating in the document combined with Eliot's letters to her of 7 April 1936 (indicating his adultery was 'fourteen years ago') with 3 November 1930 (placing his adultery 'a year before I saw you first') indicate that their first meeting in England was in 1923.

168   Robert Bridges, ed., *The Chiswell Book of English Poetry compiled and edited for the use of schools* (London: Longmans, Green & Company, 1924), vii. Emily Hale's copy bears a Christmas 1925 inscription from her Uncle John and was later presented by her to the young Robert D. Richardson; it is now in a private collection.

169   Inscription from Sotheby's catalogue, *The Library of an English Bibliophile, Part II* (New York: Sotheby's, 20 October 2011), entry 47.

170   *L2*, 212.

171   *L2*, 212.

172   *L2*, 203.

173   Brooker, ed., *T. S. Eliot: The Contemporary Reviews*, 111, 113, 115, 116, 117, 118, 119; *L2*, 232.

174   *L2*, 387.

175   *L2*, 242.

176   *CP2*, 460, 461.

177   Richard Aldington, *Life for Life's Sake* (London: Cassell, 1968), 220–1.
178   *L1*, 592, 593.
179   *CP2*, 463; *L2*, 237, 238.
180   *L2*, 356; *CP2*, 461.
181   *CP2*, 462.
182   *L2*, 215, 400.
183   *CP2*, 463.
184   *CP2*, 469.
185   *L2*, 230.
186   *L2*, 302, 301.
187   *CP2*, 471, 473, 474.
188   *CP2*, 498.
189   *CP2*, 583, 582.
190   *L2*, 223, 243, 245.
191   *L2*, 251, 245.

2. Hell-Broth

1   *L2*, 257.
2   *L2*, 256, 271.
3   *L2*, 260.
4   *L2*, 261.
5   *L2*, 284.
6   Gilbert Seldes, 'Toujours Jazz', repr. in *The Seven Lively Arts* (New York: Harper, 1924), 83, 88, 99, 106, 107.
7   *L2*, 268.
8   *L2*, 287.
9   Alison Flood, 'Copy of T. S. Eliot's *The Waste Land* inscribed to his therapist goes on sale', *Guardian*, 5 February 2016, accessed online.
10   *The Diary of Virginia Woolf, Volume 2, 1920–24*, ed. Anne Olivier Bell and Andrew McNeillie (Harmondsworth: Penguin, 1981), 278.
11   *L2*, 311.
12   *L2*, 311, 312.
13   *P1*, 53.
14   Feiron Morris, 'Thé Dansant', *Criterion*, III.9 (October 1924), 76.
15   *Facsimile*, 10–11.
16   Vivien Eliot notebook, Bodleian Library, MS. Eng. misc. c.624, folios 3–4; an edited version of this passage is published in Ann Pasternak Slater, *The Fall of a Sparrow: Vivien Eliot's Life and Writings* (London: Faber & Faber, 2020), 598 and 716.
17   *P1*, 59
18   Vivien Eliot notebook, Bodleian Library, MS. Eng. misc. c.624, folio 136; edited version published in Pasternak Slater, *Fall*, 601.
19   Osbert Sitwell, unpublished memoir (Harry Ransom Center, Texas), quoted in *L2*, 318.
20   *L2*, 317, 318.
21   *Diary of Virginia Woolf, Vol. 2*, 302; *Leave the Letters Till We're Dead: The Letters of Virginia Woolf, Volume 6, 1936–1941*, ed. Nigel Nicolson and Joanne Trautmann (London: Hogarth Press, 1980), 505.
22   *L2*, 320.
23   *L2*, 321, 408.
24   *L2*, 320; Anon., 'Annjuta Kellgren-Cyriax', *British Medical Journal*, I, 5435 (6 March 1965), 664.
25   *L2*, 320–1.

26   *L2*, 321.

27   *L2*, 343.

28   *L4*, 105; on the Culpin family see https://www.flickr.com/photos/sherbornes
      choolarchives/9362337109.

29   Vivien Eliot notebook, Bodleian Library, MS. Eng. misc. c.624, folio 11.

30   Herbert Read, 'T.S.E. – A Memoir', in Allen Tate, ed., *T. S. Eliot: The Man and his
      Work* (London: Chatto & Windus, 1967), 24; *L2*, 409.

31   *L2*, 331.

32   *L2*, 350.

33   *L8*, 221.

34   F. M., 'Letters of the Moment, I', *Criterion*, II (February 1924), 220.

35   *Diary of Virginia Woolf, Vol. 2*, 302; *CP2*, 503, 525; *L2*, 350.

36   *L2*, 342, 412.

37   *L2*, 413.

38   *L2*, 438.

39   *L2*, 463.

40   *EH*, 1 October 1937.

41   See Heiko Weigmann, 'Das ehemalige Sanatorium Hoven', *Herdermer Bürgerbrief*,
      October 2015, 19–23 (quotation comes from p. 23).

42   *P1*, 711, 81, 82.

43   *L2*, 703.

44   Pasternak Slater, *Fall*, 213, argues that the 'story' is 'fantastical'.

45   *L2*, 478.

46   *L2*, 468.

47   *L2*, 412; 'Eastbourne Crime', *Times*, 5 May 1924, 11; 'Bungalow Crime', *Times*, 8 May
      1924, 11; and 9 May 1924, 11; *L2*, 483.

48   *CP1*, 526, 527.

49   *L2*, 771; 'Colonel W. G. Johns', *Times*, 22 March 1941, 7.

50   *L2*, 771.

51   *L2*, 469.

52   *L2*, 468.

53   *L2*, 487.

54   *L2*, 480, 468.

55   *L2*, 467; 473; 470.

56   Aurelia Bolliger, Notebooks concerning T. S. Eliot, Box 25, item 6, [unnumbered
      pages], Ralph Hodgson and Aurelia Bolliger Hodgson Papers, Special Collections
      Department, Bryn Mawr College Library.

57   *L2*, 478.

58   *L2*, 479.

59   *L2*, 493.

60   *CP2*, 540.

61   Vivien Eliot notebook, Bodleian Library, MS. Eng. misc. c.624, folio 13.

62   *L2*, 496; *P1*, 126.

63   *L2*, 504.

64   *P1*, 139, 140, 82.

65   *EH*, 20 March 1933.

66   *P1*, 81.

67   *The Journals of Arnold Bennett, 1921–1928*, ed. Newman Flower (London: Cassell, 1933),
      52.

68   *L2*, 505.

69   *P1*, 793, 791.

70   *P1*, 788.

71   F. M. Cornford, *The Origin of Attic Comedy* (London: Arnold, 1914), 215, 212.

72   *P1*, 797.
73   *L2*, 520; *P1*, 121, 124, 122.
74   *P1*, 124.
75   *P1*, 124.
76   *L2*, 264.
77   *L2*, 627.
78   *L2*, 514, 515, 516.
79   *L2*, 412.
80   *CP2*, 489.
81   *L2*, 189, 190.
82   *L2*, 616.
83   *L2*, 597.
84   *L2*, 611.
85   See Albert Thibaudet, 'L'Esthétique des trois traditions', *La Nouvelle Revue française*, 51
       (March 1913), 355–93; useful is Vesna Rodic, 'Lyricism, Aesthetic Tradition, and the
       Debates on Nationalism in *La Nouvelle Revue française*, 1909–1914', *Modern Language
       Notes*, 77 (September 2012), 806–25.
86   *L2*, 520.
87   *L2*, 536.
88   *L2*, 537.
89   *CP2*, 546; *L2*, 506.
90   *L2*, 538, 521.
91   *L2*, 545.
92   *CP2*, 549, 552, 553, 554, 555.
93   *L2*, 546.
94   *P1*, 81, 84.
95   *P1*, 83.
96   *P1*, 721.
97   *CP2*, 556, 554.
98   *CP2*, 561–2.
99   *L2*, 593.
100   *L2*, 543.
101   *L2*, 543.
102   *L2*, 547.
103   *L2*, 549.
104   *L2*, 551.
105   *L2*, 553.
106   Vivien Eliot notebook, Bodleian Library, MS. Eng. misc. c.624, folio 14; edited ver-
       sion published in Pasternak Slater, *Fall*, 636–7.
107   *L2*, 577.
108   *L2*, 583.
109   *L2*, 585, 589, 591.
110   *L2*, 592.
111   Memo from Lloyds Bank colleagues, 30 April 1925 (Eliot archive at tseliot.com).
112   Vivien Eliot notebook, Bodleian Library MS. Eng. Misc. c. 936/2, folios 1, 7, 12;
       edited version published in Pasternak Slater, *Fall*, 618, 620–21, 622, 730.
113   *L2*, 598.
114   *L2*, 683.
115   Pasternak Slater, *Fall*, 207.
116   *L2*, 684.
117   *L2*, 683.
118   Pasternak Slater, *Fall*, 117, 115.
119   Pasternak Slater, *Fall*, 11, 117.

120   *L2*, 599.
121   *L2*, 600.
122   *L2*, 621.
123   *L2*, 600.
124   *L2*, 601.
125   *L2*, 615.
126   *L2*, 616.
127   *L2*, 606, 611.
128   *L2*, 611.
129   *L2*, 624, 640.
130   *Diary of Virginia Woolf, Vol. 3*, 27.
131   *L2*, 627.
132   *L2*, 627–8.
133   *L2*, 631, 636.
134   *L2*, 645, 652.
135   Vivien Eliot notebook, Bodleian Library MS. Eng. Misc. c. 936/3, folio 20; edited text published in Pasternak Slater, *Fall*, 624–5.
136   *L2*, 639.
137   *L2*, 648.
138   *L2*, 635, 648.
139   *L2*, 704.
140   *L2*, 629, 628.
141   *P1*, 81.
142   *L2*, 633, 703.
143   Vivien Eliot notebook, Bodleian Library, MS. Eng. misc. c.624, folios 71– 79; edited text published in Pasternak Slater, *Fall*, 579–88.
144   *L2*, 632.
145   *L2*, 648.
146   *L2*, 651.
147   *L2*, 703.
148   *L2*, 646.
149   *L2*, 645, 652.
150   Vivien Eliot notebook, Bodleian Library, MS. Eng. misc. c.624, folio 46.
151   *L2*, 652.
152   *L2*, 648.
153   F. M., 'Necesse est Perstare?', *Criterion*, III.11 (April 1925) , 364.
154   Vivien Eliot notebook, Bodleian Library, MS. Eng. misc. c.624, folios 42–3; edited text published in Pasternak Slater, *Fall*, 607.
155   *P1*, 125.
156   *L2*, 665.
157   *L2*, 660.
158   *L2*, 683.
159   *L2*, 686.
160   *L2*, 686.
161   *L2*, 689, 707.
162   *L2*, 704, 705.
163   *L2*, 799.
164   *L2*, 716.
165   *L2*, 722, 723.
166   *L2*, 714.
167   *L2*, 730.
168   *L2*, 759.
169   *L2*, 742, 739.

170   *L2*, 740.
171   *L9*, 534.
172   *L2*, 741.
173   *L2*, 743.
174   *Leave the Letters Till We're Dead: The Letters of Virginia Woolf, Volume 6, 1936–1941*, ed. Nigel Nicolson and Joanne Trautmann (London: Hogarth Press, 1980), 508.
175   *L2*, 764, 798, 797.
176   *L2*, 754.
177   *L2*, 757.
178   *L2*, 769.
179   *L2*, 772.
180   *L2*, 788, 784, 790.
181   *L2*, 773.
182   T. A. Hawkesworth, 'Some Common Emotional States', *Canadian Journal of Medicine and Surgery*, Vols. 73–4 (1933), 55.
183   *L2*, advertisement reproduced as plate 13.
184   *L2*, 783, 784.
185   *L2*, 807–8.
186   *L2*, 772, 773.
187   *L2*, 799, 800.
188   *L2*, 807.
189   *L2*, 803.
190   TSE's caption on photographic enclosure, *EH*, 22 December 1931.
191   *L2*, 799.
192   *L2*, 804.
193   *L2*, 804.
194   *L2*, 806.
195   *L2*, 807, 806.
196   *L2*, 802.
197   *P1*, 84.

3. Crisis

1   *L3*, 33; *L2*, 789.
2   *VMP*, 75 n.30.
3   *VMP*, 41, 175.
4   *VMP*, 58, 59.
5   *VMP*, 51.
6   *P1*, 56.
7   *L2*, 683.
8   *VMP*, 80.
9   *VMP*, 80.
10   *VMP*, 86.
11   *L2*, 680.
12   *VMP*, 92.
13   *VMP*, 115.
14   *L2*, 798.
15   *VMP*, 145.
16   *VMP*, 155, 212.
17   *L3*, 19.
18   *L2*, 796, 797.
19   *L2*, 798.
20   *L2*, 811.

21   Quoted in B. C. Southam, *A Student's Guide to the Selected Poems of T. S. Eliot* (London: Faber & Faber, 1990), 28.

22   *L2*, 790.

23   *L2*, 811.

24   *L2*, 812.

25   *L2*, 813.

26   *L3*, 1.

27   *L3*, 3.

28   *L3*, 8, 31.

29   *L3*, 20.

30   *L3*, 45.

31   *L3*, 43.

32   Ann Pasternak Slater, *The Fall of a Sparrow: Vivien Eliot's Life and Writings* (London: Faber & Faber, 2020), 242.

33   Maurice Haigh-Wood, interview with Michael Hastings, 4 March 1980, quoted in Carole Seymour-Jones, *Painted Shadow: The Life of Vivienne Eliot* (London: Constable & Robinson, 2001), 116.

34   *L3*, 19.

35   *L3*, 18, 19.

36   *CP2*, 773–4.

37   *L3*, 419.

38   *VMP*, 44.

39   *VMP*, 16.

40   Henn and Bennett quoted in George Watson, 'The Cambridge Lectures of T. S. Eliot', *Sewanee Review*, 99.4 (Fall 1991), 577, 578.

41   *L9*, 60.

42   *VMP*, 12.

43   *VMP*, frontispiece and 221.

44   *L3*, 93.

45   *L3*, 90.

46   *L3*, 79, 78.

47   Anon., 'R. H. Miller, M.D., F.R.C.P.', *British Medical Journal*, 8 January 1949, 76.

48   *L3*, 78, 79.

49   *L3*, 90.

50   *L3*, 93.

51   *L3*, 111.

52   Miranda Seymour, *Ottoline Morrell* (London: Hodder & Stoughton, 1992), 348.

53   *L3*, 111, 110.

54   *L3*, 120.

55   *L3*, 114.

56   *L3*, 111.

57   *L3*, 118.

58   *L3*, 121, 120.

59   Certified copy of an Entry of Marriage pursuant to the Marriage Act 1949 for the marriage of William Fisher Sollory and Ellen Kellond (3 April 1926).

60   *L3*, 126.

61   *L3*, 129.

62   *L3*, 129; *VMP*, 75 n.29; *L3*, 131.

63   *L3*, 137.

64   *CP2*, 764–5.

65   *L3*, 138.

66   *L3*, 139.

67   *L3*, 156n.

68 *L3*, 144.
69 *L3*, 145.
70 Aurelia Bolliger, Notebook concerning T. S. Eliot, Box 25, item 6 [unnumbered pages], Ralph Hodgson and Aurelia Bolliger Hodgson Papers, Special Collections Department, Bryn Mawr College Library.
71 *L3*, 145.
72 *L3*, 146.
73 *L3*, 146 n.2; Karl Baedeker, *Central Italy and Rome* (Leipzig: Baedeker, 1909), 150.
74 *L3*, 146.
75 *L3*, 147.
76 *CP2*, 796.
77 *L3*, 148.
78 *EH*, 20 February 1935.
79 *EH*, 18 August 1932.
80 *L3*, 152.
81 *L3*, 151.
82 *L3*, 153, 154.
83 *VMP*, 40.
84 Berton Bradley, *Things as they Are, Ballads* (New York: George H. Doran Co., 1916), 102.
85 *VMP*, 40.
86 *L3*, 154.
87 *L6*, 201.
88 *L3*, 159.
89 *L3*, 160.
90 *L3*, 184–5.
91 *EH*, 19 February 1932.
92 'Parliament', *Times*, 16 July 1926, 8; *P1*, 64, 75.
93 George Every, recollection cited in Barry Spurr, *'Anglo-Catholic in Religion': T. S. Eliot and Christianity* (Cambridge: Lutterworth Press, 2010), 19.
94 'A Threatened City Church', *Times*, 27 August 1926, 13.
95 *CP2*, 831, 832.
96 *L3*, 185, 200.
97 *L3*, 185.
98 *L3*, 197.
99 *L3*, 187.
100 *L3*, 200.
101 *L3*, 208.
102 *L3*, 221, 222.
103 *L3*, 223–4.
104 *L3*, 224.

4. Birth or Death?

1 *P1*, 122.
2 *L3*, 228.
3 *L3*, 229, 228.
4 *L3*, 229.
5 *L3*, 238.
6 *L3*, 229.
7 *L3*, 229.
8 *L3*, 215 n4.
9 *Facsimile*, 12, 13, 126.

Notes to pages 87–92

|---|---|
10	*L3*, 223, 224.
11	*L2*, 628.
12	*L2*, 652; *L3*, 223–4.
13	*L2*, 800, 802.
14	*L3*, 208.
15	*L3*, 250.
16	*L3*, 224.
17	*CP2*, 769.
18	*L3*, 243.
19	*L3*, 260.
20	*VMP*, 40.
21	*P1*, 89, 90; see also *P2*, 727.
22	*EH*, 3 October 1930.
23	*Criterion*, IV.4 (October 1926), 713; *P1*, [113].
24	*L3*, 255, 254, 287.
25	Robert Sencourt, *T. S. Eliot: A Memoir* (London: Garnstone Press, 1971), 105.
26	*L3*, 255.
27	Sencourt, *T. S. Eliot*, 105.
28	*L3*, 281.
29	*L3*, 259 n.2.
30	*L3*, 274.
31	*L3*, 277, 279.
32	*L3*, 279.
33	*L3*, 279.
34	*L3*, 287.
35	*L3*, 287.
36	*CP2*, 820.
37	*L3*, 736.
38	Sencourt, *T. S. Eliot*, 107.
39	*Prayers for the Week from the Private Devotions of Lancelot Andrewes* (Edinburgh: Oliphant, Anderson & Ferrier, 1897), 18–19.
40	*The Preces Privatae of Lancelot Andrewes*, ed. F. E. Brightman (London: Methuen, 1903), xxxviii; *CP2*, 821.
41	*L5*, 726.
42	*L3*, 344, 317.
43	*L3*, 329.
44	*L3*, 333, 334.
45	*L3*, 343.
46	*L3*, 348.
47	*L2*, 660; *L3,* 350.
48	'Mrs Cobden-Sanderson', *Times*, 4 November 1926, 8; *L3*, 306.
49	William Force Stead, *The Shadow of Mount Carmel: A Pilgrimage* (London: Cobden-Sanderson, 1926), jacket.
50	*L3*, 360; Richard J. Finneran et al., ed., *Letters to W. B. Yeats* (London: Macmillan, 1977), 455; Sencourt, *T. S. Eliot*, 105.
51	On Stead, see David Bradshaw, '"Oxford Poets": Yeats, T. S. Eliot and William Force Stead', *Yeats's Mask – Yeats Annual No. 19*; on Morrell and the mystics, see Stead's manuscript recollections of her (Beinecke).
52	*L3*, 306.
53	*L3*, 913.
54	*L3*, 360, 359.
55	*Monthly Weather Report of the Meteorological Office,* 43.12, December 1926.
56	*CP2*, 824.

507

57   *L3*, 360.
58   *L3*, 404.
59   'Mr Stead Presents An Old Friend', *Alumnal Journal of Trinity College* [Washington], XXXVIII.2, Winter 1965, 64.
60   Stead, 'Lady Ottoline Morrell' (Beinecke).
61   *L3*, 392.
62   *L3*, 387.
63   *CP2*, 877.
64   *CP3*, 72, 76, 74.
65   *CP3*, 66.
66   *EH*, 31 May 1932.
67   *CP3*, 141.
68   *L3*, 422.
69   *L3*, 416.
70   *CP3*, 20, 19.
71   *CP3*, 156; *CP2*, 819.
72   Elizabeth Joan Micaković, 'T. S. Eliot's Voice: A Cultural History', University of Exeter PhD thesis, 2015 (available online), 92–3; *L3*, 810.
73   *CP3*, 137, 156.
74   *L3*, 453, 454.
75   *CP3*, 20.
76   *CP2*, 846; Stéphane Mallarmé, *Collected Poems*, trans. Henry Weinfield (Berkeley: University of California Press, 1996), 71 (I have modified Weinfield's translation).
77   *CP3*, 48.
78   *CP3*, 31.
79   *CP3*, 44.
80   *L3*, 425.
81   *CP3*, 68.
82   *L3*, 447.
83   *L3*, 483.
84   *L3*, 448.
85   Charles Haigh-Wood's death certificate, Bodleian Library MS. Eng. Misc.c.624, folio 151; *L3*, 458.
86   *L3*, 483.
87   *L3*, 506.
88   *L3*, 483.
89   *L3*, 485.
90   *CP3*, 38.
91   *L3*, 487.
92   *L3*, 641.
93   *L3*, 487; *CP3*, 136.
94   *L3*, 487.
95   *CP3*, 64.
96   *CP3*, 112, 129.
97   *L3*, 498n.
98   *L3*, 509.
99   *CP3*, 162; *L3*, 518.
100   *L3*, 568.
101   *L3*, 519n.
102   *L3*, 524.
103   *CP3*, 91.
104   *L3*, 543.
105   Phil Hanrahan, 'T. S. Eliot's Secret Love', *Milwaukee*, November 1989, 83.

106　Emily Hale, travel piece from 'a Downer College literary magazine', quoted in Phil Hanrahan, 'T. S. Eliot's Secret Love', *Lawrence Today* [alumni magazine of Lawrence University], 70.3 (Summer 1990), 10. This piece is a later, different version of the article with the same title cited in the previous note.

107　Stead, manuscript recollections, 'T. S. Eliot', April 29, 30, 1940 (Beinecke).

108　*EH*, 15 January 1932.

109　*L3*, 508.

110　'Mr Stead Presents An Old Friend', 65.

111　This was pointed out by T. S. Matthews (whose father was a dean of the Episcopalian Church) in his *Great Tom: Notes Towards the Definition of T. S. Eliot* (London: Weidenfeld & Nicolson, 1974), 99.

112　'Mr Stead Presents An Old Friend', 65.

113　*L3*, 700.

114　*P1*, 126, 102.

115　*P1*, 102.

116　*L3*, 647.

117　*L3*, 573.

118　*L3*, 595–6.

119　*L3*, 599.

120　*L3*, 624.

121　*L3*, 647.

122　*L3*, 647, 648.

123　*L3*, 647, 648.

124　*L3*, 649.

125　*L3*, 659–60, 667.

126　*CP3*, 246, 253; book inscriptions are quoted in William Baker, 'T. S. Eliot and Emily Hale: Some Fresh Evidence', *English Studies*, 66.5 (1985), 433.

127　*P1*, 727.

128　'Salutation', *Criterion*, VII.1 (January 1928), 32; *CP3*, 241.

129　*P1*, 90.

130　*L3*, 682–3.

131　*P1*, 732, 733.

132　*P1*, 87; *L3*, 703; Ezra Pound, trans. and intro., *The Sonnets and Ballate of Guido Cavalcanti* (Boston: Small, Maynard & Co., 1912), xix.

133　Pound, *Cavalcanti*, 11; *P1*, 89.

134　*L3*, 619.

135　*L3*, 669.

136　*L3*, 641, 631.

137　*L3*, 674.

138　*L3*, 674.

139　*L3*, 682.

140　Faber & Gwyer advertisement, *Times Literary Supplement*, 7 January 1926, 5.

141　H. L. Mencken, 'The Library', *American Mercury*, April 1926, 507.

142　Geoffrey Faber, *A Publisher Speaks* (London: Faber & Faber, 1934), 21.

143　Faber & Gwyer advertisement, *Times Literary Supplement*, 17 March 1927, 190.

144　'Five Modern Poets', *Times Literary Supplement*, 21 February 1927, 113; Faber & Gwyer advertisement for poetry books, *TLS*, 11 November 1926, 794; *L3*, 768.

145　*L3*, 709, 710, 707, 708.

146　*L3*, 711 and 713.

147　*P1*, 89; *P2*, 423.

148　*L3*, 712.

149　*L3*, 793.

150　Matthew 5:27.

151	*L3*, 712.
152	*L3*, 718, 719.
153	*L3*, 739.
154	*L3*, 739.
155	*L3*, 762.
156	*L3*, 756.
157	*L4*, 169.
158	*L3*, 863.
159	'Arrangements for To-day', *Times*, 2 July 1926, 17.
160	*L3*, 773.
161	*L3*, 749, 772.
162	*L3*, 780, 836.
163	*L3*, 780.
164	*L3*, 829n.
165	*L3*, 780.
166	*L3*, 786.
167	*L3*, 801.
168	*L3*, 776, 810.
169	*L3*, 810.
170	*L3*, 819, 836.
171	*L3*, 822n.
172	*L3*, 836.
173	*L3*, 851.
174	*CP3*, 316.
175	*L3*, 854.
176	*L3*, 855.
177	*L3*, 863, 864.
178	*L3*, 872.
179	*CP3*, 307, 308.
180	*CP3*, 310.
181	*L3*, 868.
182	*L3*, 692.

5. Churchman

1	*L3*, 872.
2	*L4*, 18.
3	'Marriages', *Times*, 25 January 1928, 17; unknown photographer, The Wedding of Julian Morrell and Victor Goodman, National Portrait Gallery (London), NPG Ax142917.
4	*L6*, 171.
5	*L4*, 18.
6	*A Change of Perspective: The Letters of Virginia Woolf, Volume 3, 1923–1928*, ed. Nigel Nicolson and Joanne Trautmann (London: Hogarth Press, 1977), 457–8.
7	*Leave the Letters Till We're Dead: The Letters of Virginia Woolf, Volume 6, 1936–1941*, ed. Nigel Nicolson and Joanne Trautmann (London: Hogarth Press, 1980), 519.
8	*L4*, 96.
9	Francis Underhill, *The Life of Prayer in the World* (London: A. R. Mowbray, 1925), 2, 3, 4, 7.
10	*CP3*, 446.
11	Underhill, *The Life of Prayer in the World*, 11, 20, 21, 31, 38, 41, 61, 42, 55, 56, 57, 58.
12	Michael Yelton, *Outposts of the Faith* (Norwich: Canterbury Press, 2009), 90–91.
13	*L4*, 432.

14   *L5*, 438.
15   'Obituary', *The Radleian*, No. 611, March 1949, 25; 'Prayer and Contemplation' by the Abbot of Pershore, *Graham Street Quarterly*, July 1926, 115, 117.
16   *L4*, 96.
17   *L4*, 92, 152; *CP3*, 419. 'Sidesmen', *Graham Street Quarterly*, July 1926, [96].
18   *The Book of Common Prayer . . . The Book of 1662 with Additions & Deviations approved in 1927* (London: Oxford University Press, Cambridge University Press, and Eyre & Spottiswoode, 1927), 188.
19   *The Book of Common Prayer*, 431.
20   *P1*, 103; *P2*, 434.
21   *L4*, 45.
22   *The Book of Common Prayer*, 132.
23   *P1*, 87, 733.
24   *P1*, 741; *CP*, 382.
25   *L7*, 618.
26   *L4*, 21.
27   *L4*, 12.
28   *L4*, 37.
29   *L4*, 28 and 29.
30   *L4*, 30.
31   *L4*, 31.
32   *L4*, 51.
33   Francis Underhill, *Prayer in Modern Life* (London: Mowbray, 1929), 35, 34.
34   *L4*, 44.
35   *L4*, 96.
36   Lyndall Gordon, *Eliot's New Life* (Oxford: Oxford University Press, 1988), 15, 66.
37   *L3*, 711.
38   *P1*, 87–8.
39   *P1*, 88.
40   *P1*, 91.
41   Underhill, *The Life of Prayer*, 13.
42   *P1*, 739.
43   *P1*, 89; Dante, *The Vita Nuova and Canzoniere* (London: Dent, 1911), 6.
44   *L5*, 171.
45   *P1*, 92.
46   *P1*, 97, 96.
47   *L4*, 38.
48   *L4*, 55.
49   *CP3*, 330.
50   *CP3*, 386.
51   *L4*, 87.
52   A. D. Moody, *Tracing T. S. Eliot's Spirit* (Cambridge: Cambridge University Press, 1996), 135–43.
53   *L3*, 681.
54   *L4*, 8.
55   *CP3*, 349, 356.
56   *L4*, 86.
57   *L4*, 71.
58   *CP3*, 367.
59   *L4*, 71.
60   *L4*, 10.
61   *L4*, 10.
62   *L4*, 36, 27.

63   *CP3*, 343.

64   *L4*, 73.

65   *L4*, 95.

66   *L4*, 127, 128.

67   *EH*, 3 November 1930.

68   *L6*, 563.

69   William Baker, 'T. S. Eliot and Emily Hale: Some Fresh Evidence', *English Studies*, 66.5 (1985), 433.

70   *CP3*, 399, 400, 402.

71   *CP3*, 400; 'Preface', *The English Holy-Week Book* (London: The Society of SS. Peter and Paul, 1924), iv.

72   'Preface', *The English Holy-Week Book*, v; Underhill, *Prayer in Modern Life*, 198, 51, 57, 56, 57, 55.

73   *CP3*, 414.

74   Underhill, *Prayer in Modern Life*, 32, 88, 72.

75   Underhill, *Prayer in Modern Life*, 93.

76   Underhill, *Prayer in Modern Life*, 139.

77   *L4*, 131.

78   *L4, 183*.

79   *L4*, 137, 138; *P1*, 96.

80   *L4*, 150.

81   *L4*, 160.

82   *L4*, 157.

83   *L4*, 172.

84   *L4*, 178, 184, 207.

85   *Letters of Virginia Woolf, Vol. 3*, 508.

86   *L4*, 165.

87   *L4*, 170, 617.

88   Underhill, *Prayer in Modern Life*, 38–9; *L4*, 203.

89   *CP3*, 447.

90   *L4*, 269.

91   *L4*, 224.

92   *L4*, 269, 258.

93   *L4*, 339.

94   *L4*, 325.

95   *CP3*, 546.

96   *CP3*, 589; *L4*, 245.

97   *CP3*, 614.

98   *CP3*, 514.

99   *CP3*, 487.

100   *CP3*, 502.

101   *CP3*, 489, 535, 536.

102   *CP3*, 513.

103   *L4*, 258.

104   *L4*, 265.

105   *L4*, 265, 266.

106   Eliot household accounts, September 1928, Bodleian Library MS. Eng. Lett. c.384.

107   *L4*, 270, 278.

108   *Letters of Virginia Woolf, Vol. 6*, 523.

109   *L4*, 331.

110   *L4*, 286.

111   *L4*, 698, 405.

112   Leonard Woolf in George Spater and Ian Parsons, *A Marriage of True Minds: An Intimate Portrait of Leonard and Virginia Woolf* (London: Jonathan Cape and The Hogarth Press, 1977), 156.

113   Victoria Glendinning, *Leonard Woolf, A Life* (London: Simon & Schuster, 2006), 261.

114   Stephen Spender, *World within World* (London: Hamish Hamilton and the Book Society, 1951), 145–6.

115   *CP3*, 565.

116   Charles A. Claye, *The Merry Masque of Our Lady in London Town* (London: SSPP, 1928), 5, 23, 44; *CP3*, 564.

117   *P1*, 96, 94, 89.

118   *L4*, 351.

119   *CP3*, 563, 564.

120   *L4*, 311.

121   *L4*, 323, 324.

122   *L4*, 312.

123   *L4*, 463.

124   *L4*, 326.

125   *L4*, 330.

126   *L4*, 361.

127   *L4*, 388.

128   *L4*, 454.

129   *L4*, 373.

130   *L4*, 460; *CP3*, 596.

131   *CP3*, 625; *L4*, 399.

132   Toby Faber, *Faber & Faber: The Untold Story* (London: Faber & Faber, 2019), 66–7.

133   *L4*, 435.

134   *L4*, 652.

135   *L4*, 412.

136   *L4*, 413.

137   *L4*, 414.

138   *L4*, 428.

139   Ottoline Morrell may have suggested this to Vivien. See *L4*, 453.

140   *L4*, 431.

141   *L4*, 432–3.

142   *L4*, 437.

143   *L4*, 519.

144   *L4*, 479.

145   *CP3*, 654, 655.

146   *CP3*, 658.

147   *CP3*, 662.

148   Spender, *World within World*, 147.

149   *L4*, 490.

150   Eliot household accounts, Sept. 1928, Bodleian Library MS. Eng. Lett.c.384; *L4*, 490, 489.

151   *L4*, 497.

152   *L4*, 505.

153   *L4*, 505.

154   *CP3*, 695.

155   *CP3*, 697, 696; *P1*, 53.

156   *L4*, 261.

157   *CP3*, 711, 695, 697–9.

158   *CP3*, 742.

159   *CP3*, 701.

160   *CP3*, 702.
161   *CP3*, 702.
162   *CP3*, 704.
163   *L4*, 506.
164   *CP3*, 722, 723.
165   *CP3*, 732, 733.
166   *CP3*, 711.
167   *P1*, 91, 96, 97; *CP3*, 724.
168   *L4*, 699; *CP3*, 716.
169   *L4*, 433, 128.
170   *L4*, 520, 534.
171   *L4*, 524.
172   *L4*, 547.
173   *L4*, 548.
174   *L4*, 545, 548, 547.
175   *L4*, 555.
176   *L4*, 554.
177   *L4*, 576.
178   *L4*, 583, 584.
179   *CP4*, 37, 39, 38.
180   *P1*, 97.
181   *L6*, 448.
182   *L4*, 586.
183   *L4*, 602, 601.
184   *L4*, 614, 615.
185   *L4*, 615; Aurelia Bolliger, Notebooks concerning T. S. Eliot, Box 25, item 7, [unnumbered pages], Ralph Hodgson and Aurelia Bolliger Hodgson Papers, Special Collections Department, Bryn Mawr College Library.
186   'Rehearsals for "The Goose Hangs High" Under Way', *Simmons News*, 7 November 1929, 3.
187   *EH*, 20 August 1934.
188   *L4*, 616.
189   *L9*, 165.
190   *L4*, 618.
191   *L4*, 600; John Haffenden thinks the number '400' 'presumably' refers to short stories in the Five Reviews competition, but it matches exactly the print-run of the limited edition of 'Animula' – see Gallup A14b.
192   *L4*, 736; *P1*, 768, 105–6.
193   Baker, 'T. S. Eliot and Emily Hale: Some Fresh Evidence', 433.
194   *L4*, 626.
195   *L4*, 643.
196   *L4*, 623.
197   *L4*, 640.
198   *L4*, 650, 651, 652–3.
199   *L4*, 654; Aurelia Bolliger, Notebooks concerning T. S. Eliot, Box 25, item 7.
200   *L4*, 655, 656.
201   *L4*, 685.
202   *L4*, 691.
203   *CP4*, 157, 161, 158, 163.
204   *CP4*, 162, 163.
205   *L4*, 730.
206   *L4*, 730.
207   *L4*, 732.

208	*L4*, 740, 741.
209	*L4*, 744.
210	*L4*, 742.

6. Love and Separation

1	*L5*, 4.
2	*CP4*, 29, 40.
3	*CP4*, 9.
4	*L5*, 93.
5	*L5*, 20.
6	*CP4*, 13.
7	*L5*, 55.
8	*L5*, 38.
9	*L5*, 69.
10	*L6*, 416.
11	*L5*, 76.
12	*CP4*, 50.
13	*L5*, 79, 117.
14	*EH*, 3 November 1930.
15	*L5*, 85.
16	*L5*, 123.
17	*L5*, 83.
18	*L5*, 100.
19	*L5*, 127.
20	*L5*, 126.
21	*L5*, 127.
22	VHE, Lists of 'Furniture to go to 43 Chester Terrace' and to go to storage, 31 March 1930, Bodleian Library MS. Eng. Lett.c.384.
23	*L5*, 127.
24	*L5*, 137.
25	'Miss Emily Hale Talks on American Theater', *Simmons News*, 13 March 1930, 1.
26	*L5*, 162.
27	*L5*, 96.
28	*L5*, 163.
29	*L5*, 166.
30	*P1*, 774.
31	*L5*, 270.
32	*L9*, 348.
33	*P1*, 774; G. Wilson Knight, 'My romantic tendencies', *Studies in Romanticism*, 21 (1982), 556–7.
34	*L5*, 368.
35	*P1*, 107.
36	*P1*, 107.
37	*P1*, 108.
38	*L5*, 166, 167.
39	*P2*, 438.
40	*P2*, 134, 139.
41	*L5*, 271.
42	*L5*, 282.
43	*L5*, 175, 174.
44	*L5*, 175.
45	Richard Aldington, *Death of a Hero* (1929; rpt. London: Penguin, 2013), 94.

46   *L5*, 246.
47   *L5*, 190.
48   *L5*, 202, 203.
49   *L5*, 203.
50   *L5*, 309.
51   *L5*, 217.
52   *L5*, 229.
53   *L5*, 257.
54   *L5*, 210, 292, 293.
55   *L5*, 220.
56   *L5*, 258.
57   *L7*, 643.
58   *L5*, 206.
59   *L5*, 207.
60   *L5*, 271, 290.
61   *L5*, 345; *EH*, 3 October 1930.
62   *L5*, 345; *EH*, 3 October 1930.
63   Paul Keegan, 'Emily of Fire & Violence', *London Review of Books*, 42.20 (22 October 2020), 9.
64   *EH*, 3 October 1930.
65   [Emily Hale], *Mary Lee Ware* (n.p., [1937]), unnumbered pages; Emily Hale's authorship is confirmed on the copy of this pamphlet in the Harvard Botany Libraries.
66   *EH*, 20 January 1931.
67   Lecture notes, Emily Hale Papers, Smith College, cited in Lyndall Gordon, *The Imperfect Life of T. S. Eliot* (London: Virago, 2012), 230.
68   *L6*, 779, 780.
69   *L6*, 780, 781.
70   *EH*, 3[?] October 1930 (the word which looks like 'unsullying' is hard to read).
71   William Baker, 'T. S. Eliot and Emily Hale: Some Fresh Evidence', *English Studies*, 66.5 (1985), 433.
72   *EH*, 3 November 1930.
73   *EH*, 3 November 1930.
74   *EH*, 3 November 1930.
75   *EH*, 31 March 1931.
76   *EH*, 8 December 1930.
77   *EH*, 3 November 1930.
78   *L5*, 337.
79   *L6*, 629.
80   Aurelia Bolliger, Notebook concerning T. S. Eliot, Box 25, item 6 [unnumbered pages], Ralph Hodgson and Aurelia Bolliger Hodgson Papers, Special Collections Department, Bryn Mawr College Library.
81   *L5*, 311.
82   Aurelia Bolliger, Notebook concerning T. S. Eliot, Box 25, item 7 [unnumbered pages].
83   *L5*, 338.
84   *L5*, 363.
85   *L5*, 371.
86   *L5*, 371.
87   *L5*, 353, 354.
88   *EH*, 1 December 1930.
89   *EH*, 1 December 1930.
90   *EH*, 29 December 1930.
91   Francis Underhill, 'Divorce', *Spectator*, 6 December 1930, 9.

92   *EH*, 2 December 1930.

93   *L5*, 379.

94   *L5*, 380.

95   *CP4*, 164.

96   *CP4*, 172.

97   *CP4*, 173.

98   *L5*, 375, 376.

99   *L5*, 451.

100   *L5*, 368.

101   *L5*, 353.

102   *L5*, 362.

103   *L5*, 372.

104   *L5*, 410.

105   *L5*, 391; *CP4*, 372.

106   *L6*, 231.

107   Eliot household accounts in Bodleian Library MS. Eng. misc.c.621; see also MS. Eng. Misc.c.623.

108   *L5*, 397.

109   *EH*, 19 March 1931.

110   *L5*, 402.

111   *L5*, 437.

112   *L5*, 418.

113   *L5*, 413–4.

114   *EH*, 7 January and 4 February 1931.

115   *L5*, 450.

116   *L5*, 434, 435.

117   *L5*, 444, 440.

118   *EH*, 29 December 1930.

119   *L7*, 739; *L5*, 762, 457.

120   *CP4*, 297.

121   *CP4*, 223, 240–41.

122   *L5*, 460, 583.

123   *L5*, 462.

124   *EH*, 20 January 1931; *L5*, 464, 534.

125   *L5*, 534.

126   *L5*, 468.

127   *L5*, 478.

128   *CP4*, 313, 314, 316, 317, 230, 218.

129   *EH*, 4 February 1931.

130   *L5*, 472.

131   *L5*, 480.

132   *EH*, 14 June 1932.

133   *EH*, 27 January and 3 February 1931.

134   *L5*, 485.

135   *L5*, 484, 485, 491.

136   *CP4*, 390.

137   *L5*, 495.

138   *CP4*, 335.

139   *L5*, 484.

140   *EH*, 24 March 1931.

141   *EH*, 24 March 1931.

142   *EH*, 24 March 1931.

143   *L5*, 526, 539.

144   *P1*, 825; Erich Ludendorff, *The Coming War*, trans. Christopher Turner (London: Faber & Faber, 1931), dust jacket and 175.
145   *L5*, 529.
146   *L5*, 507.
147   'National Government', *Times*, 3 March 1931, 13.
148   *CP4*, 254.
149   Donald Davidson et al., *I'll Take My Stand: The South and the Agrarian Tradition* (New York: Harper, 1930), 'Introduction'; *CP4*, 255, 256.
150   *CP4*, 325, 256.
151   *L5*, 638.
152   *L6*, 231.
153   *EH*, 31 March 1931.
154   *L5*, 578.
155   *L5*, 529.
156   *EH*, 2 April 1931.
157   *CP4*, 265–6, 276, 281.
158   *CP4*, 290.
159   *CP4*, 298.
160   *CP4*, 340, 353.
161   *CP4*, 340, 342.
162   *CP4*, 342.
163   *CP4*, 344, 345, 349.
164   *CP4*, 347.
165   *EH*, 14 and 20 April 1931.
166   *CP4*, 345.
167   *L5*, 568.
168   *CP4*, 368.
169   *L5*, 575.
170   *P1*, 820.
171   *P1*, 818.
172   *P1*, 824, 825.
173   *P1*, 131.
174   *CP4*, 309.
175   *P1*, 817.
176   *CP4*, 313.
177   *P1*, 133, 132, 134, 135.
178   *P1*, 818.
179   *EH*, 4 March 1931.
180   *EH*, 14 April 1931.
181   *EH*, 19 March 1931.
182   *EH*, 1 May 1931.
183   *EH*, 19 July 1932.
184   *L5*, 581.
185   *L5*, 608.
186   *L5*, 597.
187   *L5*, 591.
188   *L5*, 594; *EH*, 1 June 1931.
189   *L5*, 618.
190   *EH*, 9 June 1931.
191   *EH*, 18 August and 5 June 1931.
192   *L5*, 606.
193   *EH*, 16 July 1931.
194   *L5*, 707.

195   *L5*, 691.
196   *L5*, 639, 635.
197   *L5*, 635.
198   *L5*, 691.
199   *EH*, 21 and 25 August 1931.
200   *EH*, 25 August 1931.
201   *EH*, 25 August 1931.
202   *EH*, 11 August 1931.
203   *EH*, 31 August 1931.
204   *EH*, 31 August and 4 September 1931.
205   *L5*, 654, 658; *EH*, 27 October 1931.
206   *EH*, 8 December 1931.
207   Aurelia Bolliger, Notebooks concerning T. S. Eliot, Box 25, item 7 (Bryn Mawr archives)
208   *EH*, 23 February 1932; Bolliger, Notebooks, Box 25, items 6 and 7.
209   G. Orioli advertisement, *Times Literary Supplement*, 30 July 1931, 589.
210   Chatto & Windus advertisement, *Times Literary Supplement*, 26 November 1931, 937; Richard Aldington, *Stepping Heavenward: A Record* (London: Chatto & Windus, 1931), 1, 2, 8, 33.
211   Aldington, *Stepping Heavenward*, 33.
212   Aldington, *Stepping Heavenward*, 41, 47.
213   Aldington, *Stepping Heavenward*, 53, 56, 57.
214   Aldington, *Stepping Heavenward*, 60, 62.
215   'New Books and Reprints', *Times Literary Supplement*, 26 November 1931, 961; *L5*, 733, 735.
216   *L5*, 735.
217   *EH*, 20 November 1931.
218   *L6*, 17.
219   *L5*, 765, 766.
220   *L5*, 768.
221   *L5*, 769.
222   *L5*, 770.
223   *L5*, 787, 777.
224   *L5*, 780, 781.
225   *L5*, 784; *L6*, 11.
226   *L5*, 785.
227   *L5*, 785.
228   *EH*, 31 December 1931.
229   *L6*, 13.
230   *EH*, 15 January 1932.
231   *EH*, 12 January 1932.
232   *EH*, 2 February 1932.
233   *EH*, Pound letter of 18 December 1931.
234   *L6*, 62.
235   *L6*, 65.
236   *L6*, 23.
237   *L6*, 58.
238   Bolliger, Notebook, Box 25, item 6.
239   Bolliger, Notebook, Box 25, item 7.
240   Bolliger, Notebook, Box 25, item 7.
241   Bolliger, Notebook, Box 25, item 7.
242   Bolliger, Notebook, Box 25, item 7.
243   Bolliger, Notebook, Box 25, item 7.

244 Bolliger, Notebook, Box 25, item 7.
245 Bolliger, Notebook, Box 25, item 6.
246 Bolliger, Notebook, Box 25, items 6 and 7; Peter F. Anson, *The Quest of Solitude* (London: Dent, 1932), 261.
247 Bolliger, Notebook, Box 25, item 7.
248 *L6*, 70.
249 *L6*, 102.
250 *L6*, 81.
251 *L6*, 87.
252 Bolliger, Notebook, Box 25, item 7.
253 *EH*, 11 August 1932.
254 *EH*, 11 August 1932.
255 *L6*, 153.
256 *L5*, 704.
257 *L6*, 90.
258 *L6*, 91, 92.
259 *EH*, 9 February 1932.
260 *EH*, 9 February 1932; *L6*, 92.
261 *L6*, 136, 137.
262 *L6*, 215.
263 *EH*, 19 February 1932.
264 *EH*, 15 March 1932.
265 *L6*, 229.
266 VHE to Philip Morrell, 27 April 1932 (private collection; text from Paul Rassam, *Late 19th and 20th Century Literature 31* [dealer's catalogue] (Charlbury, Oxon., [2019]), 15 (lot 45).
267 TSE to Philip Morrell, 28 April 1938 (private collection; text from Rassam catalogue as detailed above).
268 *L6*, 153.
269 *L6*, 156.
270 *L6*, 186.
271 *CP4*, 415, 413.
272 *CP4*, 419.
273 *CP4*, 423.
274 *L6*, 183.
275 *CP4*, 427–8.
276 *L5*, 763.
277 *L6*, 154.
278 *L6*, 155.
279 *L6*, 168.
280 *CP4*, 464.
281 *L6*, 168, 169.
282 *CP*, 439.
283 Bolliger, Notebook, Box 25, item 6.
284 *EH*, 3 May 1932.
285 *CP4*, 471.
286 Bolliger, Notebook, Box 25, item 7.
287 Bolliger, Notebook, Box 25, item 7.
288 *L6*, 185.
289 *L6*, 259.
290 *L6*, 193.
291 *L6*, 189.
292 *L6*, 216.

293   *L6*, 205.
294   *CP4*, 433.
295   *L6*, 225.
296   *L6*, 212, 144.
297   *L6*, 230.
298   *L6*, 230–1.
299   *L6*, 231, 232, 233.
300   *L6*, 242.
301   *L6*, 243.
302   *L6*, 269.
303   *EH*, 13 May 1932.
304   *CP4*, 478.
305   *L6*, 259.
306   Bolliger, Notebook, Box 25, item 6.
307   T. S. Eliot, pocket diary entry for 21 July 1932, reproduced at http://tseliot.com/foundation/a-first-look-at-eliots-pocket-diaries/(accessed 14 January 2019).
308   *CP4*, 489, 490.
309   *L6*, 291.
310   Bolliger, Notebook, Box 25, item 6.
311   *L6*, 273.
312   *L6*, 299; Robert Sencourt, *T. S. Eliot: A Memoir*, ed. Donald Adamson (London: Garnstone Press, 1971), 120.
313   Sencourt, *T. S. Eliot*, 120, 121, 122.
314   Bolliger, Notebook, Box 25, item 6.
315   Interview with Hope Mirrlees in BBC documentary, *The Mysterious Mr Eliot*, 1 January 1971.
316   *L6*, 275.
317   Victoria Glendinning, *Elizabeth Bowen* (1977; repr. Harmondsworth: Penguin, 1985), 80.
318   *L6*, 339.
319   *L6*, 320.
320   *L6*, 354, 339.
321   *EH*, 14 June 1932.
322   *EH*, 26 July 1932.
323   *EH*, 18 August 1932.
324   *L6*, 277, 300, 367, 277.
325   *L6*, 317, 376.
326   Bolliger, Notebook, Box 25, item 7.
327   *L6*, 378.
328   *L6*, 386.
329   *L6*, 387.
330   *L6*, 406.
331   *L6*, 407.
332   Bolliger, Notebook, Box 25, item 6.
333   Interview with Jeremy Hutchinson, 3 December 2013; *L6*, 395.
334   *The Diary of Virginia Woolf, Volume 4, 1931–35*, ed. Anne Olivier Bell and Andrew McNeillie (Harmondsworth: Penguin, 1982), 123.
335   *The Sickle Side of the Moon: The Letters of Virginia Woolf, Volume 5, 1932–1935*, ed. Nigel Nicolson and Joanne Trautmann (London: Hogarth Press, 1979), 100.
336   *Letters of Virginia Woolf, Vol. 5*, 107.
337   *L6*, 398.
338   *L6*, 412.
339   *L6*, 416.

340	*Diary of Virginia Woolf, Vol. 4*, 123.
341	*L6*, 441, 439.
342	*L6*, 464.
343	*L6*, 439.

7. America

1	*L6*, 489.
2	*EH*, 18 August 1932.
3	*L6*, 458, 459, 488.
4	*L6*, 459.
5	*EH*, Michaelmas [29 September] 1932.
6	*L6*, 457.
7	*L6*, 628; 'Eliot House', *Harvard Crimson*, 8 March 1933.
8	*L6*, 459.
9	*EH*, 9 September 1932.
10	*EH*, 2 November and 6 October 1932.
11	*EH*, 10 October 1932.
12	'No Real Distinction Between Poetry of England and America, T. S. Eliot Believes – Good Poets Fairly Well Distributed', *Harvard Crimson*, 5 October 1932.
13	*L6*, 459.
14	*L6*, 496.
15	*L6*, 475.
16	*L6*, 462.
17	Sencourt, quoted in *L6*, 463; *L6*, 506.
18	Woolf, quoted in *L6*, 463.
19	*L6*, 506.
20	*L6*, 467; 'Eliot House', *Harvard Crimson*.
21	'Eliot House', *Harvard Crimson*.
22	*L6*, 471, 473.
23	More, quoted in *L6*, 480.
24	*L6*, 475.
25	*L6*, 500.
26	*L6*, 485, 495, 498.
27	*L6*, 507; 'Eliot to give Series of Norton Lectures', *Harvard Crimson*, 28 October 1932; Wallace Fowlie, *Journal of Rehearsals: A Memoir* (Durham, NC: Duke University Press, 1977), 135.
28	*EH*, 18 and 14 November 1932.
29	*EH*, 9 November 1932.
30	'Eliot to Give Series of Norton Lectures', *Harvard Crimson*.
31	*CP4*, 607.
32	*CP4*, 701.
33	*L8*, 803.
34	*P1*, 72, 606, 89.
35	*CP4*, 625–6, 637.
36	*CP4*, 692.
37	*EH*, 3 December 1932.
38	See Eldridge Pendleton, 'T. S. Eliot, Cambridge, and the Society of St John the Evangelist', *Cowley*, Vol. 33, No. 2, 15–17, quoting accounts by Wallace Fowlie; *L6*, 571; I am grateful to Father Geoffrey Tristram, SSJE, who showed me around the monastery and explained to me the nature of the SSJE spiritual direction Eliot would have received.
39	*EH*, 18 November 1932.

40 *L6*, 562; *CP4*, 815.

41 *CP4*, 813.

42 F. P. Harton, *The Elements of the Spiritual Life: A Study in Ascetical Theology* (London: Society for Promoting Christian Knowledge, 1932), 38, 177, 316. Eliot's copy is in Magdalene College Library, Cambridge.

43 Spence Burton, *The Atonement* (Milwaukee: Morehouse Publishing Co., 1931), 49.

44 Fowlie, *Journal*, 138.

45 'Eliot, in Second Norton Lecture, Discusses Elizabethan Poetry and Criticism', *Harvard Crimson*, 26 November 1932.

46 *L6*, 514.

47 *EH*, 9 December 1932.

48 Wallace Fowlie, *Dante Today: A Personal Essay* (Asheville, NC: French Broad Press, 1994), 11.

49 *L6*, 529.

50 *EH*, 20 December 1932.

51 *L6*, 546.

52 See Edward Huntsman-Trout Architectural Landscape Drawings Collection, Ella Strong Denison Library, Scripps College, Box 1, Folder 23; Claremont College website.

53 *EH*, 29 and 13 January 1933.

54 *EH*, 13 February 1933.

55 *EH*, 13 February 1933.

56 *EH*, 14 February 1933.

57 *L6*, 535, 536.

58 *L6*, 539, 543, 545.

59 *L6*, 546.

60 Aldous Huxley, *On the Margin* (London: Chatto & Windus, 1923), 267, 168.

61 *CP4*, 828–33; Edward Lear, *The Complete Nonsense and Other Verse*, ed. Vivien Noakes (London: Penguin, 2002), 325, 238.

62 Marie McSpadden, quoted in Kay Koeninger, 'Search for Eliot's Claremont Connection', *Los Angeles Times*, 18 November 1982, V, 34

63 *EH*, 13 January 1933; McSpadden, quoted in Koeninger, 'Search', V, 34.

64 *L6*, 536.

65 *CP4*, 847.

66 *EH*, 26 February 1933.

67 *EH*, 17 January 1933.

68 *EH*, 14 February 1933; 23 January 1934.

69 Faith McAlister in 1983, quoted in Lyndall Gordon, *The Imperfect Life of T. S. Eliot* (revised edn; London: Virago, 2012), 245.

70 *EH*, 23 January 1934.

71 *EH*, 14 February 1933.

72 Francis Underhill, *The Life of Prayer in the World* (London: Mowbray, 1925), 2, 3.

73 *L6*, 546.

74 *L6*, 546.

75 *EH*, 17 January 1933.

76 McSpadden, quoted in Gordon, *The Imperfect Life*, 244.

77 *EH*, 7 February 1933.

78 *L6*, 686, 687.

79 *CP4*, 731.

80 *CP4*, 748–9.

81 'T. S. Eliot to Lecture on Shelley and Keats', *Harvard Crimson*, 17 February 1933.

82 *CP4*, 656, 664.

83 *CP4*, 668, 673, 685, 686.

84   *CP4*, 688, 687.
85   *CP4*, 690, 691.
86   *L6*, 562.
87   *CP4*, 663–4.
88   *P2*, 287.
89   *The Diary of H. L. Mencken*, ed. Charles A. Fechter (New York: Knopf, 1989), 55.
90   'Eliot House Play', *Harvard Crimson*, 1 March 1933.
91   *L6*, 524–5
92   Fowlie, *Dante Today*, 11.
93   *EH*, 18 November 1932.
94   *CP4*, 792.
95   *CP4*, 758.
96   *CP4*, 768.
97   *CP4*, 773; 'T. S. Eliot Optimistic about Future of English Language', *Harvard Crimson*, 3 March 1933.
98   *CP4*, 788.
99   *CP4*, 773.
100   *L6*, 551, 564.
101   *L6*, 543.
102   *L6*, 570.
103   *L6*, 552, 553.
104   *L6*, 563.
105   *EH*, 7 February 1933; *CP4*, 812, 810, 816, 814.
106   *EH*, 26 and 27 February 1933.
107   *EH*, 27 February 1933.
108   *EH*, 5 March 1933.
109   *EH*, 14 March 1933.
110   *L6*, 592.
111   *EH*, 7 March 1933.
112   *L6*, 569.
113   *L6*, 569–70.
114   *L6*, 571.
115   *EH*, Holy Saturday 1933.
116   *EH*, 26 and 19 April 1933.
117   *EH*, 30 April 1933.
118   Pound, quoted in Harry Levin, 'Old Possum at Possum House', *Southern Review*, Vol. 21, No. 4 (October 1985), 1008.
119   *L6*, 590; *EH*, 16 May 1933.
120   *EH*, 16 May 1933.
121   *CP5*, 17, 18; *I'll Take My Stand: The South and the Agrarian Tradition* by Twelve Southerners (New York: Harper, 1930), Introduction.
122   *CP5*, 19, 20.
123   *CP5*, 14.
124   *L6*, 594.
125   'Anti-Hitler Meeting to be Held by Liberal Club', *Harvard Crimson*, 14 April 1933.
126   *L6*, 593.
127   *CP5*, 16.
128   *CP5*, 50.
129   *L6*, 286.
130   *CP5*, 34, 41, 44, 43.
131   *EH*, 6 March 1933.
132   *CP5*, 15, 16.
133   *EH*, 30 April and 1 March 1933.

134	*EH*, 12 March 1933.
135	*L6*, 584.
136	*EH*, 30 April 1933.
137	*L6*, 587.
138	*EH*, 25 May 1933.
139	*L6*, 594.
140	*EH*, 24 June and 13 July 1933.
141	*EH*, 21 May 1933.
142	*EH*, 1 June 1933.
143	[English poets as letter writers], MS and TS notes, Houghton Library, Harvard, bMSAm1691(134); *A Little Love, A Little Kiss*, English words by Adrian Ross (London: Chappell & Co., 1912), 5–6.
144	*CP4*, 818.
145	Bob Cohen, 'T. S. Eliot Fondly Remembered in Milton', *Patriot Ledger* (Quincy), 24 November 1983, 48.
146	*CP4*, 821, 822, 823.

8. Irrevocable

1	*L6*, 599.
2	Enid Faber, '10 November 1950 Recollections of Vivienne Eliot', in Ann Pasternak Slater, *The Fall of a Sparrow: Vivien Eliot's Life and Writings* (London: Faber & Faber, 2020), 495; *L6*, 593.
3	Enid Faber, 'Recollections', 496.
4	*L6*, 603.
5	*L6*, 578.
6	*L6*, 600.
7	*L6*, 598.
8	*L6*, 601.
9	*L6*, 600.
10	*L6*, 601.
11	*L6*, 601.
12	*L6*, 603.
13	*L6*, 603.
14	*EH*, 28 July 1933.
15	*L6*, 603.
16	*L6*, 603.
17	*L6*, 603.
18	*L6*, 603, 604.
19	*L6*, 618.
20	*L6*, 593.
21	*L6*, 608, 607.
22	*L6*, 607.
23	*P2*, 18.
24	*EH*, 16 and 22 July 1933.
25	*EH*, 9 August 1933.
26	*L6*, 741.
27	*CP4*, 683.
28	*L6*, 614, 671.
29	*EH*, 20 September 1933.
30	*L6*, 577.
31	*L7*, 223.
32	*EH*, 26 September 1933.

33   *L6*, 622, 705.

34   *L6*, 771.

35   Ezra Pound, 'Mr Eliot's Mare's Nest', *New English Weekly*, 8 March 1934, 500.

36   *L6*, 706.

37   *P1*, 144.

38   Carl Sandburg, 'Bringers', *Poetry*, April 1917, 11.

39   *CP4*, 632.

40   *P1*, 145.

41   *EH*, 17 August 1933.

42   *EH*, 2 September 1933.

43   *L6* 631.

44   *L6*, 632.

45   *L6*, 652.

46   *L6*, 637.

47   *The Diary of Virginia Woolf, Volume 4, 1931–1935*, ed. Anne Olivier Bell and Andrew McNeillie (Harmondsworth: Penguin, 1982), 178–9.

48   *L6*, 664, 665.

49   *L6*, 741.

50   *L6*, 641.

51   *L6*, 768.

52   Frank Morley, 'A Few Recollections of Eliot', in Allen Tate, ed., *T. S. Eliot: The Man and his Work* (London: Chatto & Windus, 1967), 107.

53   *EH*, 26 November 1933.

54   *L6*, 711.

55   Neil M. Gunn, *Selected Letters*, ed. J. B. Pick (Edinburgh: Polygon, 1987), 35.

56   *EH*, 2 November 1933.

57   *L6*, 412.

58   Ronald C. D. Jasper, *George Bell* (London: Oxford University Press, 1967), 41.

59   'The Acts of St Richard', *Times*, 19 June 1933, 8.

60   Jasper, *George Bell*, 124.

61   *L6*, 634, 712.

62   *EH*, 11 August 1933.

63   *EH*, 7 October 1933.

64   *P2*, 469; *L6*, 690.

65   *EH*, 7 October 1933.

66   T. S. Eliot, *The Rock: A Pageant Play* (London: Faber & Faber, 1934), Prefatory Note.

67   *P1*, 165.

68   This advertisement ran, for instance, on some early twentieth-century London buses; *Rock*, 44.

69   *CP5*, 91; *L6*, 725.

70   *P1*, 860, 867.

71   *EH*, 14 October 1933.

72   *EH*, 14 and 28 October 1933.

73   *EH*, 19 November 1933.

74   T. S. Matthews, *Great Tom: Notes Towards the Definition of T. S. Eliot* (London: Weidenfeld & Nicolson, 1974), 148.

75   *L6*, 740.

76   *L6*, 691.

77   John Smart, *Tarantula's Web: John Hayward, T. S. Eliot and their Circle* (Norwich: Michael Russell, 2013), 85.

78   *L6*, 740, 741.

79   *L6*, 770.

80   *L6*, 693.

81   *L6*, 704.
82   *L7*, 3, 30.
83   *L6*, 693.
84   *L7*, 3.
85   *CP5*, 4; *L7*, 14.
86   *EH*, 26 January 1934; *P1*, 205.
87   *EH*, 26 January 1934.
88   *EH*, 20 February 1934.
89   *EH*, 16 February 1934.
90   *L7*, 685.
91   *L7*, 28.
92   *L7*, 37.
93   Eric Cheetham, *Odd Moments* (The Vestry, St Stephen's Church, n.d.), [4]; *L7*, 35.
94   *L7*, 35, 38.
95   *L7*, 47.
96   *L7*, 125; *CP5*, 62.
97   *L7*, 569.
98   *L7*, 131, 132.
99   *CP5*, 65.
100   *CP5*, 81, 82; *L7*, 428.
101   *L7*, 57.
102   *L7*, 42.
103   *L7*, 56.
104   *L7*, 80.
105   *L7*, 81.
106   *L7*, 118, 83.
107   *L7*, 37, 86.
108   *L7*, 174.
109   *L7*, 100.
110   *EH*, 16 February and 27 April 1934.
111   *EH*, 16 February 1934; *L7*, 37.
112   *L7*, 196, 137, 138.
113   *L7*, 179, 181.
114   *P2*, 165.
115   'Church Pageant at Sadler's Wells', *Times*, 29 May 1934, 12.
116   Faber & Faber advertisement, *Times Literary Supplement*, 21 June 1934, 440.
117   'Church Pageant', 12.
118   *CP5*, 93.
119   *L7*, 116.
120   L. A. G. Strong, 'Church Building', *Observer*, 22 July 1934, 8; [G.H.P. Buchanan], 'Mr Eliot's Passion Play', *Times Literary Supplement*, 7 June 1934, 404.
121   [A. Clutton-Brock], 'After Strange Gods', *TLS*, 19 April 1934, 278; [G.H.P. Buchanan], 'New Poetic Drama', *TLS*, 24 January 1935, 37.
122   *L6*, 637.
123   *L7*, xxx–xxxi.
124   *L7*, 194.
125   *L7*, 343.
126   *CP4*, 522, 692.
127   *L7*, 228.
128   *L7*, 238.
129   *EH*, 7 April 1934.
130   *L7*, 243.
131   *L7*, 243, 244.

132   *L7*, 252.

133   *L7*, 263.

134   *L7*, 238.

135   'By Burford Spire', *Times*, 6 June 1933, 13.

136   Emily Hale, 'Extract from "They Flash Upon the Inward Eye"', *Campden & District Historical and Archaeological Society Notes Queries*, Spring 2007, 47.

137   *L7*, 791.

138   *CP7*, 104.

139   *L7*, 238.

140   Mrs John Carroll Perkins, 'Beauty in Gardens', *The Town Crier* (Seattle), 16 December 1922, 23.

141   *CP5*, 118; Graham Pearson, 'Mrs Edith Carroll Perkins and Chipping Campden Gardens', *Signpost: The Journal of Chipping Campden History Society*, Issue 8, Spring 2018, 13.

142   *L7*, 779.

143   *P1*, 903.

144   *EH*, 30 July 1934.

145   *EH*, 2 August 1934.

146   *EH*, 6 August 1934.

147   *EH*, 30 July and 6 August 1934.

148   *EH*, 17 and 20 August 1934.

149   *EH*, 19 October 1934.

150   *EH*, 29 August 1934.

151   *L7*, 338; *EH*, 20 August and 19 September 1934.

152   *L7*, 338.

153   *L7*, 453, 461.

154   *L7*, 327.

155   *EH*, 22 October 1934.

156   *EH*, October 1934.

157   *L7*, 332.

158   *L7*, 333.

159   *L7*, 340.

160   *EH*, 29 November 1934.

161   *L7*, 357.

162   *EH*, 29 November 1934.

163   *EH*, 13 December 1934.

164   *L7*, 356, 358; *EH*, 28 December 1934; *L7*, 356.

165   *EH*, 9 December 1934.

166   *L7*, 416.

167   *EH*, 7 December 1934.

168   *EH*, 7 December 1934.

169   *CP5*, 138.

170   *L7*, 436, 371, 676.

171   *L7*, 298.

172   *CP5*, 120.

173   *L7*, 403.

174   *L7*, 411.

175   *L7*, 459; *CP5*, 170.

176   *EH*, 14 December 1934.

177   *L7*, 445.

178   *CP5*, 139; E. Martin Browne, *The Making of T. S. Eliot's Plays* (Cambridge: Cambridge University Press, 1969), 36.

179   Browne, *Making*, 55.

180   *L7*, 449.

181   Browne, *Making*, 39.
182   *L7*, 465.
183   *CP5*, 154.
184   *CP5*, 154.
185   *L7*, 708.
186   *L7*, 35, 36.
187   'Mothers' Union Pageant', *Times*, 4 July 1936, 16; *The Mother's Union Pageant of 1936* (London: Mothers' Union, 1936); *L7*, 550.
188   *L7*, 309, xxiii.
189   'Ecclesiastical News', *Times*, 4 February 1935, 17; see also John Haydn Tyers, 'Borrowed Silence: A History of the Practice of Retreat in the Church of England', University of Liverpool PhD thesis, 2012; *L7*, 500.
190   *L8*, 184.
191   *CP5*, 166.
192   Andrew Chandler, *George Bell, Bishop of Chichester* (Grand Rapids: William B. Eerdmans, 2016), 34, 47, 53, 54.
193   Spender to Eliot, 10 March 1932, quoted in John Sutherland, *Stephen Spender: The Authorized Biography* (London: Viking, 2004), 136; see also 161.
194   'A Schismatic Church in Germany', *Times*, 22 October 1934, 15.
195   *CP5*, 185.
196   J. H. Oldham, *Church, Community and State: A World Issue* (London: Student Christian Movement Press, 1935), 20.
197   Keith Clements, *Faith on the Frontier: A Life of J. H. Oldham* (Edinburgh: T&T Clark, 1999), 302; *L7*, 665.
198   *L7*, 665.
199   *L7*, 489.
200   *EH*, 30 January 1935.
201   *L7*, 499.
202   *L7*, 502; *CP5*, 258.
203   *CP5*, 201–2.
204   *EH*, 30 January 1935.
205   *CP5*, 198, 199.
206   Draft (now in Houghton) quoted in Browne, *Making*, 41.
207   *L7*, 508, 509; Browne, *Making*, 42.
208   *L7*, 523.
209   *L7*, 516.
210   *L7*, 800, 580.
211   *L7*, 799.
212   *EH*, 12 February 1935
213   *EH*, 2 April 1935.
214   *L7*, 515, 516; *CP5*, 205.
215   *L7*, 568.
216   *L7*, 541
217   *L7*, 544.
218   *L7*, 619.
219   *L7*, 562.
220   *L7*, 566.
221   *L7*, 570.
222   *L7*, 544.
223   Geoffrey Faber, *A Publisher Speaks* (London: Faber & Faber, 1934), 133–4.
224   *L7*, 579.
225   Helen Gardner, *The Composition of Four Quartets* (London: Faber & Faber, 1978), 39.
226   *P1*, 904.

227   *P1*, 909.
228   *L7*, 627.
229   *EH*, Ascension Day 1935; *L7*, 637.
230   *CPP*, 240.
231   *EH*, Trinity Sunday 1935.
232   *L8*, 31.
233   Browne, *Making*, 42.
234   *CPP*, 269.
235   *York Plays*, ed. Lucy Toulmain Smith (Oxford: Clarendon Press, 1885), 351.
236   *CPP*, 278.
237   *EH*, Trinity Sunday and 13 June 1935.
238   *CPP*, 261; *CP5*, 154; *L7*, 498.
239   *L7*, 589.
240   Gordon Daviot [i.e., Elizabeth Mackintosh], *Richard of Bordeaux* (London: Victor Gollancz, 1935), 20, 21.
241   'Murder in the Cathedral', *Times*, 17 June 1935, 10.
242   Samuel Jeake, Jr., 'London Letter', *New Yorker*, 3 July 1935, cited in Browne, *Making*, 63, 64.
243   'Broadcasting', *Times*, 9 December 1935, 7; 'Drama in the Air', *Times*, 1 August 1936, 10; *L7*, 718.
244   'The Theatres', *Times*, 10 February 1936, 10.
245   'Concerts &c.', *Times*, 23 December 1936, 8.
246   *CP5*, 260.
247   *L7*, 700.
248   *P1*, 290, 1193.
249   *L7*, 600.
250   *P1*, 1194, 180, 290.
251   Frank Morley, *Literary Britain* (London: Hutchinson, 1980), 463.
252   *L7*, 657.
253   Morley, *Literary Britain*, 463; *P1*, 147.
254   *P1*, 147; *CPP*, 265.
255   *P1*, 147.
256   *EH*, 27, 1 and 11 August 1935.
257   *L7*, 726.
258   *EH*, 10 September 1935.
259   *EH*, 23 August 1935.
260   *EH*, 27 August 1935.
261   *EH*, 10 September 1935.
262   *L7*, 648.
263   *L7*, 656.
264   *L7*, 781.
265   *L7*, 778, 779, 780.
266   *P1*, 903
267   *P1*, 903.
268   *EH*, 30 September and 3 October 1935.
269   *EH*, 3 October 1935.
270   *EH*, 30 October 1935.
271   *EH*, 22 November 1935.
272   *EH*, 16 January 1936.
273   *EH*, 11 December 1935.
274   *EH*, 11 December 1935.
275   D. H. Lawrence, *The Prussian Officer and Other Stories* (1914; rpt. Harmondsworth: Penguin, 1978), 151; *CP5*, 30.

276   *CP4*, 784.
277   *L7*, 414, 415.876.
278   *L7*, 415.
279   *L7*, 876.
280   *L7*, 647.
281   *L7*, 656, 657.
282   *L7*, 362; J. M. Barrie, *The Plays*, ed. A. E. Wilson (London: Hodder & Stoughton, 1942), 1040.
283   *P1*, 179.
284   These lines of Shelley's 'Music, when soft voices die' are quoted in 'Swinburne', *CP2*, 182; see also Robert Crawford, *Young Eliot* (London: Jonathan Cape, 2015), 72–3 and 347.
285   *P1*, 180.
286   *P1*, 56; Shree Purohit Swami and W. B. Yeats, tr., *The Ten Principal Upanishads* (London: Faber & Faber, 1934), 106, 129; see Eliot's '[Notes on Eastern Philosophy]', Houghton MS Am 1691.14(12).
287   *L7*, 749.
288   *P1*, 149.
289   *L7*, 629; *P1*, 183.
290   *CP5*, 361.
291   *P1*, 182, 184.
292   *EH*, 12 December 1935.
293   *P1*, 184.
294   *L7*, 700; *P2*, 490.
295   Enid Faber, 'Recollections', 497.
296   *L7*, 841.
297   *L7*, 841.
298   *L7*, 854.
299   *L7*, 827; *The Sickle Side of the Moon: The Letters of Virginia Woolf, Volume 5, 1932–1935*, ed. Nigel Nicolson and Joanne Trautmann (London: Hogarth Press, 1979), 451.
300   Emily Hale to Ruth George, 6 December 1935 (Denison Library, Scripps College, Claremont).
301   *EH*, 30 September 1935.
302   *EH*, 14 October 1935.
303   *EH*, 22 November 1935.
304   *EH*, 11 December 1935.
305   *EH*, 31 December 1935.
306   *EH*, 12 December 1935.
307   *EH*, 16 December 1935.
308   *EH*, 12 December 1935.
309   *EH*, 13 December 1935.

9. Pursued

1   Frank Morley, 'A Few Recollections of Eliot', in Allen Tate, ed., *T. S. Eliot: The Man and his Work* (London: Chatto & Windus, 1967), 110.
2   *EH*, 10 January 1936.
3   *EH*, 2 January 1936.
4   *EH*, 6 January 1936.
5   *EH*, 14 January and 21 February 1936.
6   *EH*, 21 February 1936.
7   *EH*, 3 March 1936.
8   *EH*, 10 January 1936.

9   *L8*, 4, 40.
10   *EH*, 13 January 1936.
11   *EH*, 13 January 1936.
12   Frances Dickey, 'May the Record Speak: The Correspondence of T. S. Eliot and Emily Hale', *Twentieth-Century Literature*, 66.4 (December 2020), 449.
13   *EH*, 16 January 1936.
14   Anne Ridler, *Working for T. S. Eliot* (London: Enitharmon Press, 2000), 6.
15   *L8*, 8.
16   Ridler, *Working*, 10.
17   *L8*, 170.
18   *L8*, 60.
19   *L8*, 175.
20   *EH*, 10 January 1936; *L8*, 193.
21   *L8*, 103.
22   *L8*, 151.
23   *L8*, 140.
24   *L8*, 38.
25   *CP5*, 290, 286.
26   *L8*, xxi.
27   *L8*, 73.
28   *L8*, 61.
29   Ridler, *Working*, 8, 9.
30   *L8*, 39.
31   *L8*, 54; *CP5*, 294.
32   *L8*, 25.
33   *L8*, 286.
34   *L8*, 137; *P1*, 191, 94.
35   *CP5*, 325, 326, 330, 327, 330.
36   *L8*, 10.
37   *L8*, 11, 7.
38   *L8*, 11, 13.
39   *P2*, 24, 69; *L8*, 17.
40   *L8*, 16.
41   *L8*, 79, 63.
42   *L8*, 65, 66.
43   *L8*, 78, 81.
44   *L8*, 82.
45   *CPP*, 290.
46   *L8*, 98.
47   *L8*, 112.
48   *L8*, 153.
49   *L8*, 112.
50   *EH*, 5 March 1936.
51   Samuel Atkins Eliot, ed., *Heralds of a Liberal Faith, IV: The Pilots* (Boston: Beacon Press, 1952), 255.
52   *EH*, 19 March 1936.
53   *EH*, 24 March 1936.
54   *P1*, 728.
55   *P1*, 113.
56   *L8*, 168, 169.
57   *L8*, 201.
58   *EH*, 11 May 1936.
59   *L8*, 181.

60   *L8*, 185.
61   *L8*, 201.
62   *L8*, 208, 209.
63   Ridler, *Working*, 9, 10.
64   *L8*, 220.
65   *L8*, 99.
66   *L8*, 211.
67   J. H. Shorthouse, *John Inglesant*, 2 vols. (London: Macmillan, 1881), I, 84, 86, 87.
68   T. O. Beachcroft, 'Nicholas Ferrar and George Herbert', *Criterion*, XII.46 (October 1932), 26, 25.
69   *L8*, 273; *EH*, 26 May 1936.
70   *EH*, 26 May 1936.
71   *L8*, 133.
72   *L8*, 133, 134.
73   *P1*, 303, 1207.
74   *L7*, 243.
75   Walter Graeme Eliot, *A Sketch of the Eliot Family* (New York: Livingston Middleditch, 1897), 5, 11, 12.
76   *L8*, 241.
77   G. W. Wade and J. H. Wade, *Somerset*, Eighth Edition (London: Methuen, 1929), 287, 288.
78   *P1*, 185.
79   *L6*, 239; see also TSE, letter to H. S. Häussermann (May 1940), quoted in Helen Gardner, *The Composition of 'Four Quartets'* (London: Faber & Faber, 1978), 43.
80   'The Fairest Villages in England', *Times*, 22 October 1934, 11; Wade and Wade, *Somerset*, 104; *L8*, 241, 239.
81   *P1*, 185.
82   *L8*, 239.
83   *EH*, 18 June 1936.
84   Plaque, St Michael's Church; see also 'The Dampier Memorial at East Coker', *Western Gazette*, 22 May 1908, 5.
85   *P1*, 191, 188.
86   Plaque, St Michael's Church.
87   *L8*, 239.
88   *EH*, 18 June 1936.
89   *L8*, 241; *L9*, 492.
90   *P1*, 188.
91   *L9*, 488.
92   *P1*, 186.
93   *L8*, 260.
94   *P1*, 186, 192.
95   *EH*, 12 June 1936.
96   *L8*, 230.
97   *L8*, 246.
98   *L8*, 255, 256.
99   *EH*, 20 July 1936; *L8*, 298.
100   *L8*, 305.
101   *L2*, 628.
102   *L8*, 802, 846, 847.
103   *L8*, 155, 311; Leon Gordon, *White Cargo* (Boston: Four Seasons, 1925).
104   *EH*, 30 July 1936.
105   *L8*, 316.
106   *L8*, 312.

107   *L8*, 335; *EH*, 24 July 1936.
108   *L8*, 360.
109   *L8*, 360.
110   *EH*, 17 October 1936.
111   *L8*, 346.
112   *L8*, 346.
113   *L8*, 851.
114   TSE to Henry Eliot, [8 September 1936], at tseliot.com
115   *EH*, 30 September 1936.
116   *L8*, 381.
117   *L8*, 446, 442, 445.
118   *L8*, 446.
119   *L8*, 360.
120   *CPP*, 340.
121   TSE, letter to John Cournos, 30 September 1926, at tseliot.com
122   *L8*, 609.
123   *CP5*, 453; *L8*, 347.
124   *L8*, 507.
125   *L8*, 502.
126   *L8*, 469.
127   *L8*, 577.
128   *L8*, 534, 536.
129   *L8*, 563.
130   [Emily Hale], *Mary Lee Ware* (n.p., [1937]), unnumbered pages.
131   *EH*, 17 October 1936.
132   *EH*, 25 November 1936.
133   *EH*, 12 February 1937.
134   *EH*, 16 December 1936.
135   *CP5*, 407.
136   *CP5*, 431, 460.
137   *L8*, 370.
138   *L8*, 362.
139   Charles Williams, *Descent into Hell* (1937; rpt. Grand Rapids: Eerdmans, 1973), 19, 96, 211.
140   Draft of *The Family Reunion*, quoted in E. Martin Browne, *The Making of T. S. Eliot's Plays* (Cambridge: Cambridge University Press, 1969), 129.
141   *L8*, 519, 518.
142   *EH*, 5 December 1936.
143   *EH*, 15 January 1937.
144   *EH*, 23 March 1937; *L8*, 783.
145   *CP5*, 511, 512.
146   *L8*, 571; *P1*, 187.
147   *L8*, 521–2.
148   *CP5*, 480.
149   Robert Sencourt, *T. S. Eliot, A Memoir*, ed. Donald Adamson (London: Garnstone Press, 1971), 133.
150   *L8*, 566.
151   *L8*, 555.
152   *L8*, 562, 565.
153   *EH*, 7 April 1937; *L8*, 579.
154   *L8*, 567.
155   *EH*, 31 March 1937.
156   *L8*, 595.

157   Houghton Library *Family Reunion* scenario, quoted in Browne, *Making*, 92–3.
158   *L8*, 567.
159   'Greek Play at Bradfield', *Times*, 21 June 1937, 12; *L8*, 578.
160   *CP5*, 522.
161   *L8*, 578.
162   *EH*, 25 May 1937.
163   *L8*, 621.
164   *CP5*, 528.
165   *L8*, 631; *EH*, 26 July 1937.
166   *L8*, 644.
167   *L8*, 644; Matthew Nathan, *The Annals of West Coker* (Cambridge: Cambridge University Press, 1957), 163.
168   *P1*, 185.
169   *L8*, 649.
170   Nathan's 1937 diary, Bodleian Library.
171   David Foot, 'When Dad Had T. S. Eliot Caught Behind the Font', *Guardian*, 22 July 2008.
172   *L8*, 810.
173   *L8*, 654.
174   *L8*, 658; *P2*, 211.
175   *L8*, 662.
176   *EH*, 24 September 1937.
177   *L8*, 861, 675, 674.
178   *L8*, 704, 699, 701.
179   Browne, *Making*, 117.
180   *L8*, 818.
181   *L8*, 801.
182   *L8*, 782.
183   *L8*, 723.
184   *L8*, 736.
185   *L8*, 747, 733; TSE's inscription on Woolf's copy of *Men, Women and Things: Memories of the Duke of Portland,* Washington State University Libraries Department of Manuscripts, Archives, and Special Collections.
186   *L8*, 737.
187   *L8*, 737.
188   *L8*, 741.
189   *EH*, 7 December 1937.
190   *L8*, 797, 755.
191   *L8*, 825 (the words are Ronald Duncan's).
192   *EH*, 19 October 1937; Mulk Raj Anand, *Conversations in Bloomsbury* (London: Wildwood House, 1981), 24.
193   *CP5*, 594, 590, 591.
194   [Charles Smyth], review of *English Constitutional Affairs in the Fifteenth Century*, *Criterion*, XVI, No. LXV (July 1937), 685; Frank McEachran, 'A Pattern for Reality', *Criterion*, XVII, No. LXVII (January 1938), 218–32.
195   *L8*, 857, 849.
196   *L8*, 777.
197   *L8*, 757.
198   *CPP*, 315, 316.
199   *L8*, 757.
200   *L8*, 816.
201   *EH*, 14 January 1938.
202   *L8*, 777.

203   *L8*, 770; *EH*, 29 March 1938.

204   *L8*, 770.

205   John Middleton Murry, *Heaven – and Earth* (London: Jonathan Cape, 1938), 31; Murry, *The Price of Leadership* (London: Student Christian Movement Press, 1939), 84, 76.

206   *L8*, 793.

207   *L8*, 795.

208   *L8*, 790, 196.

209   *L8*, 778.

210   *L8*, 799.

211   *L8*, 799.

212   *L8*, 800.

213   *EH*, 15 February 1938.

214   *P2*, 208, 233, 237, 207.

215   *P2*, 205, 208.

216   *L8*, 837, 800, 809.

217   *L8*, 802, 803.

218   *L8*, 833; *P2*, 29.

219   *L8*, 809.

220   *L8*, 882.

221   *L8*, 873.

222   *L8*, 822, 821.

223   *L8*, 822.

224   *L8*, 845–6.

225   *L8*, 846, 847.

226   *EH*, 29 March 1938.

227   *L8*, 845; *CPP*, 291, 286.

228   *L8*, 874.

229   *L8*, 893.

230   *L8*, 844.

231   *L8*, 877.

232   *CP6*, 109.

233   *L8*, 844.

234   'Kensington ARP Test', *Times*, 7 May 1938, 14; 'Bombing Display at Kensington', *Times*, 27 May 1938, 9.

235   *EH*, 29 March 1938.

236   *L8*, 885.

237   *L8*, 905.

238   *L8*, 742.

239   *L8*, 902.

240   *L8*, 909, 910.

241   *L8*, 911.

242   *L8*, 929, 927.

243   *L8*, 926, 928.

244   *L8*, 928.

245   *L8*, 931.

246   Bernard Hart, *The Psychology of Insanity* (Cambridge: Cambridge University Press, 1912), vii.

247   Mapother, quoted in Aubrey Lewis, 'Edward Mapother and the Making of the Maudsley Hospital', *British Journal of Psychiatry*, Vol. 115, No. 529 (1969), 1364.

248   *L8*, 931.

249   Frederick Dillon, 'A Practical Note on Suicide', *British Medical Journal*, II, 3858 (15 December 1934), 1099.

250   Frederick Dillon, 'Mental Factors in Medicine' [letter], *British Medical Journal*, II, 4050 (20 August 1938), 425.
251   *L8*, 932.
252   *L8*, 931.
253   *L8*, 932.
254   *EH*, 1 August 1938.
255   *L8*, 930.
256   *L8*, 930.
257   *L8*, 933.
258   *L8*, 948.
259   *EH*, 23 August 1938.
260   *L8*, 945.
261   *L8*, 945.
262   *L8*, 946; I am grateful to Professor Olav Gjelsvik (personal communication) for the etymological information.
263   Virginia Woolf, *Orlando: A Biography* (1928; repr. London: Grafton Books, 1977), 60.
264   *EH*, 18 September 1938.
265   *EH*, 27 September 1938.
266   *L8*, 959.
267   *EH*, 27 September 1938.
268   *L8*, 951.
269   *L8*, 987.
270   *L8*, 972.
271   *L8*, 973.

10. War

1   *L8*, 959.
2   *L8*, 960.
3   Keith Clements, ed., *The Moot Papers: Faith, Freedom and Society 1938–1947* (London: T&T Clark, 2010), 28, 39, 54, 55.
4   *CP5*, 649.
5   Clements, ed., *Moot*, 79, 82.
6   *L8*, 1026.
7   Clements, ed., *Moot*, 91, 121, 122.
8   *CP5*, 737; *L8*, 906.
9   *L8*, 961.
10   *CP5*, 717, 730.
11   'Ovation in London', *Times*, 1 October 1938, 12; 'House of Commons', *Times*, 4 October 1938, 8.
12   *L8*, 966.
13   *EH*, 4 October 1938.
14   *L8*, 991.
15   *L8*, 976, 977.
16   *CP5*, 655.
17   *L8*, 976, 978.
18   *L8*, 1011.
19   T. S. Matthews, *Great Tom: Notes Towards the Definition of T. S. Eliot* (London: Weidenfeld & Nicolson, 1974), 148.
20   *EH*, 18 November 1938.
21   *L8*, 989–90.
22   *L8*, 999.
23   *L8*, 1000, 996.

24 'The German Camps', *Times*, 24 January 1935, 13; 'Nazi Treatment of Viennese Jews: "Special Train" to Dachau', *Times*, 3 June 1938, 13; 'Threats to Vienna Jews: "Dachau, or Worse"', *Times*, 7 October 1938, 13; 'German Jews Rounded Up', *Times*, 12 November 1938, 12; '600 Jewish Children Leave Vienna', *Times*, 6 December 1938, 13.

25 *L8*, 1000.

26 *EH*, 27 January 1939.

27 *EH*, 16 December 1938.

28 *L8*, 1011.

29 *L8*, 1018.

30 *Criterion*, XVIII, No. LXXI (January 1939), 367.

31 *EH*, 13 January 1939.

32 *CP5*, 659.

33 *L9*, 25; *Leave the Letters Till We're Dead: The Letters of Virginia Woolf, Volume 6, 1936–1941*, ed. Nigel Nicolson and Joanne Trautmann (London: Hogarth Press, 1980), 313.

34 *The Diary of Virginia Woolf, Volume 5, 1936–1941*, ed. Anne Olivier Bell and Andrew McNeillie (London: Hogarth Press, 1984), 203, 202.

35 *CP5*, 660, 661, 662, 663.

36 Clements, ed., *Moot*, 127, 172, 164, 161; Jacques Maritain, *True Humanism*, tr. M. R. Adamson (London: Bles, 1938), 205, 121.

37 Clements, ed., *Moot*, 167.

38 *CP5*, 672.

39 *CP5*, 770, 769.

40 *L8*, 470.

41 *CP5*, 683.

42 *EH*, 10 February 1939.

43 J. H. Oldham, 'Lessons of the Crisis' [letter], *Times*, 5 October 1938, 15.

44 Clements, ed., *Moot*, 142; *CP5*, 683.

45 *CP5*, 668.

46 [J. Middleton Murry], 'Towards a Christian Society', *Times Literary Supplement*, 28 January 1939, 54.

47 *L9*, 84.

48 *CP5*, 695, 696, 697.

49 *CP5*, 698, 707, 708.

50 *CP5*, 710, 711, 712, 715.

51 *CP5*, 716.

52 K. E. Barlow, *The Discipline of Peace* (London: Faber & Faber, 1942), 102.

53 *L9*, 27.

54 *CP5*, 717.

55 *CP5*, 669.

56 *EH*, 10 February 1939.

57 *EH*, 10 March 1939.

58 *CPP*, 343, 309.

59 *L9*, 84.

60 'Poet's Play', *Picture Post*, 8 April 1939, 34.

61 *L9*, 96.

62 'Westminster Theatre', *Times*, 22 March 1939, 12.

63 'A Miscellany', *Times*, 1 January 1940, 22.

64 Jewel Spears Brooker, ed., *T. S. Eliot: The Contemporary Reviews* (Cambridge: Cambridge University Press, 2004), 379.

65 Brooker, ed., *T. S. Eliot: The Contemporary Reviews*, 389.

66 Brooker, ed., *T. S. Eliot: The Contemporary Reviews*, 401.

67 *Diary of Virginia Woolf, Vol. 5*, 210.

68   *EH*, 14 April 1939.
69   *L9*, 122.
70   *Letters of Louis MacNeice*, ed. Jonathan Allison (London: Faber & Faber, 2010), 327, 346.
71   'Nazi Camp', *Sydney Morning Herald*, 18 September 1933, 9.
72   'The Literary Society', *Felstedian*, June 1939, 56, 57.
73   *L9*, 155.
74   Clements, ed., *Moot*, 218, 219.
75   *L9*, 172, 171.
76   *L9*, 170.
77   *EH*, 12 May 1939.
78   *CP5*, 48.
79   Helena M. Tomko, 'Word Creatures: Theodor Haecker and Walter Benjamin between *Geschwätz* and Pure Language in the Late Weimar Republic', *New German Critique*, 45.1 (February 2018), 23.
80   [TSE], front jacket blurb to Bernard Walke, *Plays from St Hilary* (London: Faber & Faber, 1939).
81   *L9*, 165.
82   *EH*, 26 May 1939.
83   *EH*, 24 July 1939.
84   *EH*, 6 July 1939.
85   *L9*, 221.
86   *L9*, 202.
87   *L9*, 204.
88   *L9*, 249.
89   'In Defence of the Jews', *Times Literary Supplement*, 25 March 1939, 170.
90   *L9*, 206.
91   *EH*, 1 September 1939.
92   'Cabinet Reply to Last German Note', *Times*, 31 August 1939, 8.
93   *EH*, 'Thursday 6:15 p. m.' [31 August 1939].
94   'ARP Controllers Assume Duty', *Times*, 1 September 1939, 7.
95   http://news.bbc.co.uk/onthisday/hi/dates/stories/september/3/newsid_3493000/3493279.stm
96   *EH*, 4 September 1939.
97   *L9*, 234.
98   *EH*, 8 September 1939.
99   *EH*, 4 September 1939.
100   *EH*, 15 September 1939.
101   *EH*, 26 September 1936.
102   *L9*, 241.
103   *L9*, 244.
104   *L9*, 244–5.
105   *L9*, 245.
106   *L9*, 247.
107   *L9*, 247.
108   *L9*, 249.
109   *EH*, 26 September 1939.
110   *CP5*, 677.
111   Clements, ed., *Moot*, 225, 227, 233, 229.
112   V. A. Demant, *The Religious Prospect* (London: Frederick Muller, 1939), 221.
113   Clements, ed., *Moot*, 231.
114   *L9*, 264; *CP5*, 679, 680.

115   Clements, ed., *Moot*, 235.
116   Lord Hambleden, 'The Church in War-Time' [letter], *Times*, 7 December 1939, 6.
117   Alec Vidler, *Scenes from a Clerical Life* (London: Collins, 1977), 120; *Christian News-Letter, Supplement No. 6* (6 December 1939), [1]; Clements, ed., *Moot*, 238, 235.
118   Vidler, *Scenes*, 120.
119   Keith Clements, *Faith on the Frontier: A Life of J. H. Oldham* (Edinburgh: T&T Clark, 1999), 390.
120   *Christian News-Letter*, No. 0 (18 October 1939), [2], [3]; *Christian News-Letter, Supplement* No. 0 (18 October 1939), [2], [3].
121   *EH*, 19 October 1939.
122   *L9*, 267.
123   John Smart, *Tarantula's Web: John Hayward, T. S. Eliot and their Circle* (Norwich: Michael Russell, 2013), 143.
124   *L9*, 307.
125   *EH*, 7 October 1939.
126   *L9*, 268, 269.
127   *L9*, 280, 277.
128   *L9*, 278.
129   *L9*, 281.
130   *L9*, 284; *P1*, 191.
131   *L9*, 289, 284.
132   'Going on to the End', *Times*, 2 October 1939, 10.
133   *L9*, 286, 285.
134   'France Will Fight On', *Times*, 11 October 1939, 8.
135   Charles Williams, *The Descent of the Dove* (London: The Religious Book Club, 1939), 233.
136   *L9*, 294, 295.
137   *L9*, 304; *EH,* 26 October 1939.
138   *L9*, 313.
139   Stephen Spender, 'Cats and Dogs', *Listener*, 26 October 1939, Early Autumn Book Supplement, viii; [Anon.], 'The Listener's Book Chronicle', 30 November 1939, 1086.
140   Victoria Glendinning, *Leonard Woolf* (London: Simon & Schuster, 2006), 334.
141   *CP5*, 718.
142   *L9*, 339.
143   *EH*, 24 November 1939.
144   *L9*, 314.
145   *L9*, 326.
146   *L9*, 323, 322, 318.
147   *L9*, 318; *Diary of Virginia Woolf, Vol. 5*, 245.
148   *L9*, 338.
149   *EH*, 28 December 1939.
150   *L9*, 349.
151   *CP5,* 750; Williams, *Descent of the Dove*, 173.
152   *Diary of Virginia Woolf, Vol. 5*, 268.
153   *P1*, 189.
154   *EH*, 28 December 1939.
155   Mary Trevelyan, *From the Ends of the Earth* (London: Faber & Faber, 1942), 138 and plate opp. 112.
156   *L9*, 322.
157   *L9*, 355; J. H. Oldham, 'Prayer in Time of War', *Christian News-Letter*, No. 7, 13 December 1939, [3].
158   *L9*, 355.
159   *L9*, 359.

160   *L9*, 371, 370.

161   TSE to Mappie Mirrlees, 19 December 1939 (McKeldin Library, University of Maryland).

162   *L9*, 372.

163   *L9*, 384.

164   *L9*, 397.

165   'The Queen's Visit to Seamen', *Times*, 1 February 1940, 5.

166   *EH*, 11 January 1940.

167   *EH*, 15 January 1940.

168   *L9*, 390.

169   *L9*, 392.

170   *P1*, 190.

171   *L9*, 420.

172   *L9*, 421–2.

173   *EH*, Shrove Tuesday 1940.

174   *L9*, 374.

175   *L9*, 382, 380.

176   *P1*, 188, 189.

177   *P1*, 191, 192.

178   *CP6*, 10; *L9*, 429.

179   *Diary of Virginia Woolf, Vol. 5*, 268.

180   TSE to Herbert Read, 9 February 1940 (University of Victoria, British Columbia); J. H. Oldham, 'A Declaration by American Christians', *Christian News-Letter*, No. 15, 7 February 1940, [1]; *CP6*, 4, 3.

181   *EH*, 9 February 1940.

182   *L9*, 411. In fact, Hitler was born in April (see L9, 411, note 1).

183   *Diary of Virginia Woolf, Vol. 5*, 268.

184   *P1*, 189.

11. Puir Daft Makar

1   *EH*, 22 February 1940; *L9*, 566.

2   *EH*, 9 March 1940.

3   T. S. Matthews, *Great Tom: Notes Towards the Definition of T. S. Eliot* (London: Weidenfeld & Nicolson, 1974), 144.

4   *EH*, 1 March 1940.

5   *EH*, 9 March 1940.

6   *EH*, 16 March 1940.

7   *EH*, 31 March (incorrectly dated 31 April) 1940.

8   *CP6*, 15, 16.

9   *L9*, 439.

10   *L9*, 435, 437.

11   *L9*, 692, 695.

12   *L9*, 751.

13   *L9*, 786.

14   Margaret Behrens, *Miss Mackay* (London: Herbert Jenkins, 1932), 206, 223.

15   TSE to Frank Morley, Whit Monday 1944 (*P2*, 173); *L9*, 171.

16   *L9*, 651.

17   Typed Faber & Faber gummed label inside Mappie Mirrlees's copy of *For Lancelot Andrewes* (Private Collection); though this item is undated, it may be significant that TSE mentions 'gumming labels' in February 1941, the day before sending Hayward verses in Scots (*L9*, 747, 749).

18   J. H. Oldham, 'A Letter from Germany', *Christian News-Letter*, 6 March 1940, [2], [3].

19   *L9*, 443.
20   *L9*, 452.
21   *EH*, 31 March 1940.
22   *EH*, 6 April and 24 January 1940.
23   *EH*, 6 April 1940.
24   *L9*, 445.
25   *EH*, 12 April 1940.
26   *EH*, 12 April 1940.
27   *L9*, 451.
28   *L9*, 468, 469.
29   *P1*, 200.
30   *EH*, 12 April 1940.
31   J. H. Oldham, 'Non-Aryans in Germany', *Christian News-Letter*, 1 May 1940, [1].
32   *L9*, 453.
33   *L9*, 502–3.
34   *L9*, 528.
35   Adolf Löwe, 'Social Transformation and the War', *Christian News-Letter*, Supplement 29, 15 May 1940, [1], [2], [3].
36   Keith Clements, ed., *The Moot Papers: Faith, Freedom and Society 1938–1947* (London: T&T Clark, 2010), 308.
37   J. H. Oldham, 'American Christians and the War', *Christian News-Letter*, 29 May 1940, [3].
38   *L9*, 518.
39   See Anthony Julius, *T. S. Eliot, Anti-Semitism, and Literary Form* (new edn; London: Thames & Hudson, 2003), 204–5; *L9*, 561.
40   *EH*, 10 May 1940.
41   *EH*, 17 May 1940.
42   TSE to Mappie Mirrlees, 16 May 1940 (McKeldin Library, University of Maryland).
43   *L9*, 529.
44   *L9*, 530.
45   *The Diary of Virginia Woolf, Volume 5, 1936–1941*, ed. Anne Olivier Bell and Andrew McNeillie (London: Hogarth Press, 1984), 287.
46   *Diary of Virginia Woolf, Vol. 5*, 288.
47   *L9*, 530.
48   'The Challenge', *Times*, 25 May 1940, 7.
49   ' "Old and True" – CCXIV', *Times*, 3 June 1940, 9.
50   *CP6*, 130.
51   'Dunkirk', *New York Times*, 1 June 1940, quoted in Nicholas John Cull, *Selling War: The British Propaganda Campaign Against American 'Neutrality' in World War II* (Cambridge: Cambridge University Press, 1995), 71.
52   'Triumph of an Army', *Times*, 3 June 1940, 3.
53   'Mr Churchill Surveys the War', *Times*, 5 June 1940, 6.
54   *P1*, 1046.
55   *P1*, 213, 214.
56   *L9*, 559.
57   J. F. Hendry, 'London Before Invasion, 1940', in M. J. Tambimuttu, ed., *Poetry in War Time* (London: Faber & Faber, 1942), 79.
58   *L9*, 548–9.
59   *L9*, 554, 555.
60   TSE to McKnight Kauffer, 5 June 1940 (Pierpont Morgan Library).
61   *L9*, 563.
62   'Parliament', *Times*, 19 June 1940, 2.
63   *L9*, 564.

64   *P1*, 187, 188, 191; Marina Mackay, *Modernism and World War II* (Cambridge: Cambridge University Press, 2007), 74.
65   James Stourton, *Kenneth Clark: Life, Art and Civilisation* (New York: Knopf, 2016), 185, 186.
66   *L9*, 505.
67   Kenneth Clark, 'The Artist in Wartime', *Listener*, 26 October 1939, 810.
68   *L9*, 568.
69   *L9*, 569.
70   *EH*, 24 June 1940.
71   *L9*, 569.
72   *L9*, 575.
73   *CP6*, 64.
74   *CP6*, 88, 79, 82, 87.
75   *CP6*, 92.
76   *CP6*, 81.
77   *L9*, 574, 575.
78   *L9*, 602.
79   *L9*, 581.
80   'The Token of Freedom', *Times*, 22 August 1940, 2; *L9*, 587.
81   *EH*, 6 July 1940.
82   *P1*, 1046.
83   *L9*, 581.
84   *L9*, 582.
85   Clements, ed., *Moot*, 318, 320, 324.
86   *CP6*, 98.
87   *CP6*, 103, 101.
88   *EH*, 26 July 1940.
89   'Prime Minister's Call to the Nation', *Times*, 15 July 1940, 5.
90   'US and Battle for Britain', *Times*, 14 August 1940, 3.
91   Freda Utley, *The Dream We Lost* (New York: John Day, 1940), 359.
92   *L9*, 604.
93   *L9*, 590.
94   *CP6*, 137.
95   *L9*, 604.
96   *CP6*, 105, 108, 109, 114.
97   *L9*, 606.
98   *L9*, 613.
99   *L9*, 573.
100   *L9*, 618, 619; Royal Borough of Kensington and Chelsea archives, LHvf 940.549.
101   TSE to Enid Faber, 20 August 1940, quoted in *Presentation Copies and Letters from T. S. Eliot to the Faber family,* auction sale catalogue, 20 September 2005 (London: Bonhams, 2005), 6.
102   *P1*, 194, 196.
103   *CP6*, 122, 125.
104   *EH*, 3 September 1940.
105   'House of Commons', 21 August 1940, 2.
106   'Parliament', *Times,* 6 September 1940, 2.
107   'American Destroyers for Britain', *Times*, 4 September 1940, 4.
108   'Mr Churchill's Words of Cheer', *Times*, 12 September 1940, 4.
109   Geoffrey Faber, 'Britain's Ambassadors', *Times Literary Supplement*, 7 September 1940, 441.
110   Cull, *Selling War*, 72–3, 77.
111   Henry Ware Eliot to TSE, 14 November 1940 (Houghton).

112   Henry Ware Eliot to TSE, 22 January 1941 (Houghton).

113   'Mr T. S. Eliot's Confession', *Times Literary Supplement*, 14 September 1940, 472; Desmond Hawkins, 'Mr Eliot's New Poem', *Listener*, 17 October 1940, 567; [Hugh l'Anson Fausset], 'Poets of the Year', *Times Literary Supplement*, 7 December 1940, 624.

114   *EH*, 20 September 1940.

115   *L9*, 627, 628.

116   *EH*, 28 September 1940.

117   *EH*, 28 September 1940.

118   *L9*, 632, 633.

119   *L9*, 687.

120   Helen Gardner, *The Composition of Four Quartets* (London: Faber & Faber, 1978), 118.

121   *P1*, 193, 194, 195.

122   *P1*, 196.

123   *P1*, 198, 199, 200.

124   *EH*, 10 October 1940.

125   1 Corinthians 11 : 28–9 (Authorised Version). I am grateful to Jewel Spears Brooker for calling my attention to this passage.

126   *EH*, 22 October 1940.

127   *EH*, 30 October 1940.

128   *L9, 698*.

129   Eric Cheetham, *Odd Moments* (London: The Vestry, St Stephen's Church, n.d.), 6.

130   'Perilous Living', *Times Literary Supplement*, 3 May 1941, 213.

131   *P1*, 195, 194.

132   *EH*, 10 December 1940.

133   *EH*, 17 December 1940.

134   *EH*, 3 December 1940.

135   Cull, *Selling War*, 163.

136   *EH*, 17 December 1940.

137   *L9*, 679; Henry James, *Selected Stories*, ed. Gerard Hopkins (London: Oxford University Press, 1967), 255.

138   *P1*, 193.

139   *L9*, 646.

140   *L9*, 636.

141   *P1*, 200.

142   Henry Ware Eliot to TSE, 22 January 1941 (Houghton); *L9*, 760; John Paull, 'Lord Northbourne, the Man who Invented Organic Farming, a Biography', *Journal of Organic Systems*, 9.1 (2014), 31.

143   *Leave the Letters Till We're Dead: The Letters of Virginia Woolf, Volume 6, 1936–1941*, ed. Nigel Nicolson and Joanne Trautmann (London: Hogarth Press, 1980), 441.

144   *L9*, 636.

145   *L9*, 639.

146   *L9*, 646, 640, 641.

147   *L9*, 645, 646.

148   *L9*, 647.

149   Geoffrey Faber, diary entry, 30 March 1940, in Toby Faber, *Faber & Faber: The Untold Story* (London: Faber & Faber, 2019), 156–7.

150   *L9*, 640.

151   *L9*, 649–50.

152   *L9*, 658.

153   *CP6*, 135; *L9*, 659.

154   *L9*, 698.

12. Little Gidding

1   *L9*, 705.
2   *L9*, 704; 'Pater Noster', Supplement, *Christian News-Letter*, No. 62, 1 January 1941, [4]; *Christian News-Letter*, 8 January 1941, [2].
3   *EH*, 5 January 1941.
4   *The Life of the Church and the Order of Society* (London: Longmans, Green, 1941), 7.
5   'A New Order after the War', *Times*, 8 January 1941, 2.
6   Ian Jones, 'Faith in the Public Square in 1941 and 1991: Two Malvern Conferences Reviewed', *Journal of Beliefs and Values*, 37.3 (2016), 252.
7   *CP6*, 248, 246, 250, 253, 254.
8   Jones, 'Faith in the Public Square', 251.
9   *CP6*, 795.
10   Keith Clements, ed., *The Moot Papers: Faith, Freedom and Society 1938–1947* (London: T&T Clark, 2010), 348, 350, 352, 354, 343; *P1*, 188.
11   *P1*, 204.
12   *CP6*, 158; 'Mr James Joyce', *Times*, 14 January 1941, 7.
13   *CP6*, 159, 158, 160.
14   *L9*, 961.
15   *L9*, 714, 729.
16   *EH*, 9 February 1941.
17   *Leave the Letters Till We're Dead: The Letters of Virginia Woolf, Volume 6, 1936–1941*, ed. Nigel Nicolson and Joanne Trautmann (London: Hogarth Press, 1980), 472.
18   *CP6*, 162, 164, 167.
19   Edward Mendelson, *Later Auden* (London: Faber & Faber, 1999), 124.
20   *L9*, 802.
21   *P1*, 204, 207.
22   *L9*, 740.
23   *L9*, 757.
24   *EH*, 9 February 1941.
25   *EH*, 9 February 1941.
26   *L9*, 736.
27   *L9*, 756.
28   *L9*, 761.
29   *L9*, 765, 766.
30   *L9*, 809.
31   *EH*, 17 February 1941.
32   *EH*, 2 March 1941.
33   *L9*, 779.
34   *EH*, 1 and 7 April 1941.
35   *EH*, 22 April 1941.
36   *Letters of Virginia Woolf, Vol. 6*, 477; *L9*, 775, 776.
37   *L9*, 786, 787.
38   'Eclipse of the Highbrow', *Times*, 25 March 1941, 5; Geoffrey Faber, 'Eclipse of the Highbrow' [letter], *Times*, 28 March 1941, 5.
39   Mervyn Peake, 'London, 1941', in M. J. Tambimuttu, ed., *Poetry in War Time* (London: Faber & Faber, 1942), 117.
40   *L9*, 793.
41   TSE to Bonamy Dobrée, 29 March [1941] (Brotherton Library, University of Leeds).
42   *Letters of Virginia Woolf, Vol. 6*, 479.
43   *L9*, 786.
44   'Obituary, Mrs Virginia Woolf', *Times*, 3 May 1941, 7.
45   *L9*, 794.

46   *Letters of Virginia Woolf, Vol. 6*, 487.

47   *Letters of Virginia Woolf, Vol. 6*, 487.

48   George Cicestr. [i.e., Bell], 'The Pope's Appeal' [letter], *Times*, 17 April 1941, 5; *L9*, 803; *EH*, 20 May 1941.

49   *Letters of Virginia Woolf, Vol. 6*, 59.

50   *L9*, 803, 804, 805.

51   *L9*, 819–20.

52   *L9*, 814.

53   See A. David Moody, *Ezra Pound: Poet, A Portrait of the Man and his Work, Volume III: The Tragic Years 1939–1972* (Oxford: Oxford University Press, 2015), 27.

54   *CP6*, 150.

55   *CP6*, 172.

56   *CP6*, 169, 170, 171, 170.

57   *L9*, 839.

58   George Barker, 'To T. S. Eliot', in Tambimuttu, ed., *Poetry in War Time*, 23.

59   Geoffrey Faber to Frank Morley, 13 January 1941, in Toby Faber, *Faber & Faber, The Untold Story* (London: Faber & Faber, 2019), 158.

60   *EH*, 28 and 22 April 1941.

61   Faber to Morley, 15 May 1941, in Faber, *Faber & Faber*, 159–60.

62   *EH*, 20 May 1941.

63   *EH*, 20 May 1941.

64   Hayward to Frank Morley, June 1941, quoted in Helen Gardner, *The Composition of Four Quartets* (London: Faber & Faber, 1978), 21.

65   *EH*, 29 June 1941.

66   E. Martin Browne, *The Making of T. S. Eliot's Plays* (Cambridge: Cambridge University Press, 1969), 157.

67   *L9*, 858; *EH*, 7 July 1941.

68   Quoted in Gardner, *Composition*, 157; see also *P2*, 512.

69   *L9*, 858.

70   *L9*, 858.

71   *EH*, 14 July 1941.

72   *L9*, 864.

73   *L9*, 870.

74   *EH*, 28 July 1941.

75   Clements, ed., *Moot*, 420, 436, 428, 434, 436, 437.

76   *L9*, 877.

77   *L9*, 888.

78   *CP6*, 223, 227, 226, 230, 232.

79   *CP6*, 403.

80   *CP6*, 183, 180, 185, 180.

81   'France', *Christian News-Letter*, 12 March 1941, [1].

82   'Anti-Jewish Feeling', *Christian News-Letter*, 30 July 1941, [1].

83   *L9*, 912.

84   '10,000 Jews Arrested in Paris', *Times*, 22 August 1941, 3; '"Communists" in Paris', *Times*, 11 September 1941, 3.

85   *L9*, 914.

86   James Parkes, 'The Jewish Question To-Day', *Christian News-Letter Supplement*, 10 October 1941, [4].

87   Louis MacNeice, 'Bar-room Matins', in Tambimuttu, ed., *Poetry in War Time*, 100.

88   *L9*, 914, 915.

89   *L9*, 925, 949.

90   *EH*, 13 October 1941.

91   *CP6*, 208; *L9*, 946.

92   *L9*, 958.
93   *EH*, 3 November 1941.
94   *L9*, 960.
95   *CP6*, 196, 197, 198.
96   *CP6*, 202.
97   *CP6*, 242.
98   *EH*, 8 December 1941.
99   *L9*, 996.
100   *L9*, 999.
101   *L9*, 997.
102   *L9*, 534, 824.
103   *EH*, 15 December 1941.
104   *EH*, 8 December 1941.
105   T. S. Matthews, *Great Tom: Notes Towards the Definition of T. S. Eliot* (London: Weidenfeld & Nicolson, 1974), 146.
106   *CP6*, 800.
107   TSE to Hayward, Candlemas [2 February] 1942 (KCA).
108   *P1*, 1054, 1055.
109   *P1*, 216.
110   TSE to Hayward, [1 March 1942] (KCA).
111   *CP6*, 324, 310, 315, 321, 311, 322.
112   TSE to Hayward, [1 March 1942] (KCA).
113   TSE to Hayward, 17 August 1942 (KCA).
114   Sally Blake's anecdote is recounted in the Bonhams London auction catalogue, *Fine Books, Manuscripts, Atlases and Historical Photographs*, 15 March 2015, lot 135.
115   Adam Roberts, personal communication.
116   Susanna Smithson, interview with Robert Crawford, 29 August 2015.
117   TSE to Hayward, 21 December 1942 (KCA).
118   *EH*, 16 March 1942.
119   *CP6*, 295.
120   TSE to Hayward, 14 June 1942 (KCA).
121   TSE to Herbert Read, 30 May 1942 (University of Victoria); *CP6*, 285, 283.
122   TSE to Henry Eliot, 1 June 1942 (Houghton).
123   TSE to Hayward, 14 June 1942 (KCA); *CP6*, 287.
124   Mary Trevelyan, *From the Ends of the Earth* (London: Faber & Faber, 1942), 72.
125   TSE to Mary Trevelyan, 21 February 1942 (Houghton).
126   TSE to Mary Trevelyan, 16 March 1942 (Houghton).
127   TSE to Mary Trevelyan, [29 June] 1942 (Houghton).
128   *P1*, 215.
129   TSE to Hayward, 26 July 1942 (KCA); TSE to Christina Morley, 27 July 1942 (Berg Collection).
130   TSE to John Hayward, 27 November 1942 (KCA).
131   TSE to Mary Trevelyan, 16 November 1942 (Houghton).
132   *EH*, Easter Monday 1942.
133   TSE to Mary Trevelyan, [7 September 1942] (Houghton).
134   *EH*, 1 June 1942.
135   *CP6*, 811; Gardner, *Composition*, 24; *P1*, 215.
136   TSE to Hayward, 17 and 27 August 1942 (KCA).
137   *P1*, 209.
138   *P1*, 1031–3.
139   *EH*, 4 August 1942.
140   TSE to Hayward, 13 September 1942 (KCA).
141   *P1*, 202, 204, 1010.

142 Kathleen Raine, 'London Revisited', in Tambimuttu, ed., *Poetry in War Time*, 120 (Read's poem begins on this same page).

143 *P1*, 203, 204, 205.

144 *P1*, 205, 207.

145 *P1*, 208, 209.

13. Deaths

1 *CP6*, 326.

2 *P1*, 208.

3 William Shakespeare, *Richard II*, II.i, 40, 50; Rupert Brooke, *The Complete Poems* (London: Sidgwick & Jackson, 1942), 150.

4 *EH*, 18 August 1942.

5 *CP6*, 326.

6 Jewel Spears Brooker, ed., *T. S. Eliot: The Contemporary Reviews* (Cambridge: Cambridge University Press, 2004), 459.

7 Brooker, ed., *Eliot: The Contemporary Reviews*, 467.

8 Mary Lee Settle, 'How Pleasant to Meet Mr. Eliot', *New York Times*, 16 December 1984.

9 TSE to Helen Gardner, 2 December 1942 (Bodleian).

10 *P1*, 209.

11 *EH*, 13 July 1942.

12 *P1*, 780.

13 *EH*, 27 August 1942.

14 *EH*, 13 October and 27 August 1942.

15 *EH*, 13 October 1942.

16 *EH*, 13 October 1942.

17 *L7*, 414.

18 *EH*, 20 October 1942.

19 *EH*, 30 November 1942.

20 *EH*, early January 1943.

21 TSE to Polly Tandy, 25 October 1942 (British Library); TSE to Hayward, 16 October 1942 (KCA).

22 TSE to Polly Tandy, 25 October 1942 (British Library).

23 TSE to Djuna Barnes, 20 October 1942 (McKeldin Library, University of Maryland).

24 *EH*, 21 December 1942.

25 TSE to Robert Waller, 21 September 1942 (British Library).

26 TSE to Hayward, 21 December 1942 (KCA).

27 TSE to Polly Tandy, 25 October 1942 (British Library).

28 TSE to Hayward, 8 November 1942 (KCA).

29 *EH*, 10 January 1943.

30 *EH*, 7 December and 30 November 1942.

31 *CP6*, 337–8, 339, 340.

32 *CP6*, 346, 347, 349, 353.

33 Ada Eliot Sheffield, quoted in Ian Shaw, ' "Let Us Go Then, You and I" – Journeying with Ada Eliot Sheffield', *Qualitative Social Work*, 18 (1), 2019, 131.

34 Alfred D. Sheffield and Ada Eliot Sheffield, *The Mind of a 'Member'* (New York: Exposition Press, 1951), vii, 162–202, 179.

35 *CP6*, 358, 360.

36 TSE to Hayward, 20 February 1943 (KCA).

37 Ada Eliot Sheffield, quoted in Shaw, ' "Let Us Go Then" ', 135, 118, 131.

38 *EH*, 19 February 1943.

39   *EH*, 9 March 1943.

40   *CP6*, 448.

41   Lumir Soukup and Catriona Soukup, 'Edwin and Willa Muir: A Memoir' (National Library of Scotland), 74.

42   'The Queen and Princesses at Reading of Poetry', *Times*, 15 April 1943, 7.

43   *EH*, Easter Monday [postmarked 21 April] 1943.

44   Marcus Eliason, 'Sharp Words over Publication of Private Royal Chitchat', Associated Press, 12 July 1990; Eliason's report of the story places it at Windsor Castle, and has the Queen Mother recalling *The Waste Land* as 'The Desert', but it seems more likely that the incident recalled was the Aeolian Hall reading.

45   *CP6*, 809.

46   Philip Mairet, 'Memories of T.S.E.', in Neville Braybrooke, ed., *T. S. Eliot: A Symposium for his Seventieth Birthday* (London: Rupert Hart-Davis, 1958), 41.

47   TSE to Hayward, 29 May 1943 (KCA).

48   Keith Clements, ed., *The Moot Papers: Faith, Freedom and Society 1938–1947* (London: T&T Clark, 2010), 601.

49   *CP6*, 448.

50   *CP6*, 406.

51   *CP6*, 474, 414.

52   *CP6*, 434.

53   *CP6*, 442, 436.

54   *CP6*, 458, 463; TSE to Hayward, 2 November 1943 (KCA).

55   *EH*, 16 October 1943.

56   *CP6*, 487; TSE to Hayward, 15 December 1943 (KCA).

57   *EH*, 14 November 1943.

58   Julian P. Boyd to Emily Hale, 7 July 1942, quoted in Don Skemer, 'Sealed Treasure: T. S. Eliot Letters to Emily Hale', blog on Princeton University Library RBSC Manuscripts Division News page, 16 May 2017.

59   Frederick Tomlin, *T. S. Eliot, A Friendship* (London: Routledge, 1988), 218.

60   *EH*, 14 June 1943.

61   *EH*, 16 October 1943.

62   TSE to Hayward, 3 March 1944 (KCA).

63   TSE to Hayward, 26 February and 3 March 1944 (KCA).

64   *EH*, 30 August 1943.

65   *EH*, 20 March 1944.

66   TSE to Hayward, 3 March 1944 (KCA).

67   *EH*, 28 February 1944.

68   TSE to I. A. Richards, 20 February 1944 (Magdalene College, Cambridge).

69   *CP6*, 490, 497.

70   TSE to Mary Trevelyan, 27 February 1944 (Houghton).

71   *EH*, 4 March 1944.

72   *EH*, 4 March 1944.

73   TSE to Hayward, 14 April 1944 (KCA).

74   TSE to Hayward, 14 April 1944 (KCA).

75   *CP6*, 499.

76   TSE to Djuna Barnes, Whit Monday 1944 (McKeldin Library, University of Maryland).

77   TSE to Mary Trevelyan, Whit Monday 1944 (Houghton); TSE to Frank Morley, Whit Monday 1944 (Berg).

78   TSE to Morley, Whit Monday 1944 (Berg).

79   A. David Moody, *Ezra Pound: Poet, A Portrait of the Man and his Work, Volume III: The Tragic Years 1939–1972* (Oxford: Oxford University Press, 2015), 129.

80   *EH*, 5 June 1944.

81   *CP6*, 508.
82   TSE to Margot Coker, 6 June 1944 (Bodleian).
83   *CP6*, 514, 513, 515.
84   *EH*, 26 June 1944.
85   *EH*, 19 June 1944.
86   TSE to Hayward, 19 June 1944 (KCA); TSE to Mary Trevelyan, 19 June 1944 (Houghton).
87   TSE to Herbert Read, 24 June 1944 (University of Victoria).
88   TSE to Hayward, 3 July 1944 (KCA).
89   TSE to Hayward, 31 July 1944 (KCA).
90   TSE to George Orwell, 13 July 1944 (University College London Library).
91   *EH*, 17 July 1944.
92   *EH*, 31 July 1944.
93   TSE to Hayward, 21 August 1944 (KCA).
94   TSE to Hayward, 7 September 1944 (KCA).
95   TSE to Hayward, 24 September 1944 (KCA).
96   *EH*, 31 July 1944.
97   TSE to Hayward, 12 November 1944 (KCA); *CP6*, 543.
98   *EH*, cable of 27 October 1944.
99   Mary Trevelyan, *I'll Walk Beside You, Letters from Belgium: September 1944–May 1945* (London: Longmans, Green, 1946), 40, 54.
100   TSE to Mary Trevelyan, 19 December 1944 (Houghton).
101   TSE to Hayward, 21 December 1944 (KCA).
102   *EH*, 31 October 1944.
103   Trevelyan, *I'll Walk*, 64.
104   TSE to Bill Castle, 21 December 1944 (Houghton).
105   *L9*, 826; *CP6*, 581, 582.
106   'German Atrocities in Poland', *Times*, 20 May 1941, 4; 'Tortured Poles', *Times*, 11 June 1941, 3.
107   'Poles' Martyrdom', *Times*, 6 March 1943, 3.
108   'Nazi Brutality to Jews', *Times*, 1 June 1943, 4; on Koestler's piece, see Will Loxley, *Writing in the Dark: Bloomsbury, the Blitz and Horizon Magazine* (London: Weidenfeld & Nicolson, 2021), 286–8.
109   'Poland's Martyrdom', *Times*, 1 September 1943, 5.
110   'Hungarian Jews' Fate', *Times*, 8 July 1944, 3.
111   *CP6*, 584.
112   *CP6*, 582, 584; Joanna Rzepa, 'The "demonic forces" at Auschwitz: T. S. Eliot reads Jerzy Andrzejewski's *Roll Call*', *Modernism/Modernity*, 26.2 (April 2019), 349, n75.
113   '4,000,000 Deaths at Oswiecim Camp', *Times*, 8 May 1945, 5.
114   *EH*, 29 April 1945.
115   *CP6*, 593.
116   TSE to Henzie Browne, 12 January 1945 (Houghton).
117   TSE to Hayward, 12 January 1945 (KCA).
118   *CP6*, 586.
119   TSE to Mary Trevelyan, 21 January 1945 (Houghton).
120   TSE to Mary Trevelyan, 29 January 1945 (Houghton).
121   TSE to Hayward, 12 February 1945 (KCA).
122   TSE to Theodore Spencer, 19 February 1945 (Harvard University Archives).
123   *CP6*, 601.
124   *CP6*, 610, 619, 606.
125   TSE to Allen Tate, 13 March 1945 (Princeton) and 26 March 1945 (Orradre Library, Santa Clara University).
126   TSE to Hayward, 16 April 1945 (KCA).

127   *EH*, EH to TSE, 26 April 1945.
128   *EH*, 28 May 1945.
129   *EH*, EH to TSE, 26 April 1945.
130   *EH*, 3 April 1945.
131   TSE to Edmund Wilson, 14 April 1945 (Beinecke).
132   TSE to Hayward, 4 May 1945 (KCA); *EH*, 29 April 1945.
133   TSE to Polly Tandy, 22 May 1945 (British Library); TSE to Hayward, 22 May 1945 (KCA).
134   *CP6*, 639, 651.
135   *CP6*, 624.
136   'Ezra Pound Captured', *Times*, 7 May 1945, 3.
137   Moody, *Ezra Pound: Poet, Vol. III*, 115.
138   TSE to Djuna Barnes, 23 July 1945 (McKeldin Library, University of Maryland); TSE to Frank Morley, 21 July 1945 (Berg Collection).
139   *EH*, 22 May 1945.
140   TSE to Morley, 21 July 1945 (Berg).
141   *EH*, 15 July 1945.
142   *CP6*, 653.
143   *EH*, 15 July 1945.
144   TSE to Philip Mairet, 24 August 1945 (Harry Ransom Center, Texas).
145   *EH*, 30 July 1945.
146   TSE to Robert Waller, 1 September 1945 (British Library).
147   *EH*, 26 August 1945.
148   *EH*, 9 September 1945.
149   TSE to Hayward, 2 September 1945 (KCA).
150   TSE to Mappie Mirrlees, 10 September 1945 (McKeldin Library).
151   TSE to Czesław Miłosz, 5 October 1945 (Beinecke).
152   TSE to Ezra Pound, 19 October 1945 (Lilly Library, Indiana University).
153   *CP6*, 696.
154   Peter D. McDonald, *Artefacts of Writing: Ideas of the State and Communities of Letters from Matthew Arnold to Xu Bing* (Oxford: Oxford University Press, 2017), 93.
155   *CP6*, 680.
156   *CP6*, 699.
157   TSE to Hayward, 8 December 1945 and 10 November 1945 (KCA).
158   TSE to E. E. Cummings, 10 December 1945 (Houghton).
159   *EH*, 17 December 1945.
160   TSE to Hayward, 29 December 1945 (KCA).
161   *EH*, 12 January 1946 [misdated 1945].
162   TSE to Hayward, 8 January 1946 (KCA).
163   James Laughlin to TSE, 13 February 1946, cited in Moody, *Ezra Pound: Poet, Vol. III*, 218.
164   TSE to C M Grieve, 4 February 1946 (Edinburgh University Library).
165   TSE to Allen Tate, 27 February 1946 (Princeton University Library).
166   TSE to Hayward, 3 March 1946 (KCA).
167   *CP6*, 767.
168   TSE to I. A. and Dorothea Richards, 9 March 1946 (Magdalene College, Cambridge); *CP6*, 825.
169   *CP6*, 736, 738, 712, 718.
170   TSE to Mary Trevelyan, 28 March 1946 (Houghton).
171   *CP6*, 751, 748.
172   TSE to Mappie Mirrlees, [early June 1946] (McKeldin Library, University of Maryland).
173   Moody, *Ezra Pound: Poet, Vol. III*, 241.

174   John Carroll Perkins to Meg Nason, 14 June 1946 (Private Collection).

175   TSE to Mappie Mirrlees, 3 July 1946 (McKeldin Library).

176   Susan Stewart and Joshua Kotin, 'A Conversation with Sally Foss about Emily Hale', *Time Present: The Newsletter of the International T. S. Eliot Society*, 100 (Spring 2020), 18, 20.

177   TSE to Allen Tate, 10 July and 7 August 1946 (Princeton University Library).

178   TSE to Christina Morley, 5 September 1946 (Berg).

179   TSE to Ronald Bottrall, 20 August 1946 (Harry Ransom Center, University of Texas).

180   TSE to Browne, 27 August 1946 (Houghton).

181   TSE to Polly Tandy, 9 September 1946 (British Library).

182   TSE to Henry Treece, 16 September 1946 (Harry Ransom Center).

183   Settle, 'How Pleasant'.

184   John Smart, *Tarantula's Web: John Hayward, T. S. Eliot and their Circle* (Norwich: Michael Russell, 2013), 263.

185   *L5*, xix.

186   *L5*, xix.

187   *ODNB*, Valerie Eliot.

188   Valerie Eliot to Eleanor Hinkley, 26 October 1957 (Houghton).

189   TSE to Frank Morley, 5 October 1946 (Berg).

190   TSE to Morley, 10 November 1946 (Berg).

191   TSE to Christina Morley, 8 December 1946 (Berg).

192   *CP6*, 777.

193   *CP7*, 5.

194   TSE to Christina Morley, 24 January 1947 (Berg); *L9*, 99.

195   Robert Sencourt, *T. S. Eliot: A Memoir* (London: Garnstone Press, 1971), 154.

196   *EH*, 22 January 1947.

197   TSE to Christina Morley, 24 January 1947 (Berg).

198   *CP7*, xii.

199   TSE to Mappie Mirrlees, 28 January 1947 (McKeldin Library, University of Maryland).

200   Enid Faber, '10 November 1950 Recollections of Vivienne Eliot', in Ann Pasternak Slater, *The Fall of a Sparrow: Vivien Eliot's Life and Writings* (London: Faber & Faber, 2020), 498.

201   TSE to Frank and Christina Morley, 3 February 1947 (Berg).

202   *CPP*, 350.

203   *EH*, 3 February 1947.

204   *CP3*, 722, 723.

205   *EH*, 14 February 1947.

206   *EH*, 1 March 1947.

207   TSE to Frank Morley, 13 February 1947 (Berg).

208   TSE to Frank Morley, 13 February 1947 (Berg).

209   TSE to Stephen Spender, 15 February 1947 (Northwestern University).

210   TSE to Dorothy Pound, 26 February 1947 (Lilly Library).

211   *EH*, 10 March 1947.

212   TSE to I. A. Richards, 7 March 1947 (Magdalene College, Cambridge).

213   TSE to Edward Field, 17 March 1947 (Harry Ransom Center).

214   TSE to Edward Field, 17 March 1947 (Harry Ransom Center).

215   *EH*, 20 March 1947.

216   *EH*, Easter 1947.

217   TSE to Douglas Young, 10 April 1947 (National Library of Scotland).

218   *CP7*, 30.

219   TSE to Mappie Mirrlees, 14 May 1947 (McKeldin Library).

220   TSE to Mappie Mirrlees, 14 May 1947 (McKeldin Library).

221 Frederick Tomlin, *T. S. Eliot, A Friendship* (London: Routledge, 1988), 219.
222 Tomlin, *T. S. Eliot*, 219.
223 Emily Hale to Lorraine Havens, 7 August 1947, quoted in *CP7*, xv.
224 *EH*, 25 June 1947.
225 'T. S. Eliot Reads Poetry, Describes His Next Project', *Harvard Crimson*, 14 May 1947.
226 *CP7*, 11, 14, 12, 13, 17–18.
227 'Degrees to Bradley, Marshall, Oppenheimer', *Harvard Crimson*, 5 June 1947.
228 TSE to Frank Morley, 5 July 1947 (Berg).
229 *EH*, 25 June 1947.

14. Honours

1   *EH*, 25 June 1947.
2   TSE to Frank Morley, 5 July 1947 (Berg).
3   TSE to Hayward, 'Thursday' [July 1947], (KCA).
4   TSE to George Platt Lynes, September 1947, quoted on National Portrait Gallery (London) website.
5   *CP7*, 9; TSE to E H W Meyerstein, 11 October 1947 (KCA).
6   *CP7*, 46.
7   TSE to Djuna Barnes, 1 November 1947 (McKeldin Library).
8   *CP7*, 47.
9   TSE to Sir Allan Lascelles, 26 November 1947 (KCA).
10 *Pound/Lewis: The Letters of Ezra Pound and Wyndham Lewis*, ed. Timothy Materer (London: Faber & Faber, 1985), 239.
11 TSE to Leonard Woolf, 9 January 1948 (University of Sussex Library).
12 TSE to John Middleton Murry, 14 January 1948 (Northwestern University Library).
13 Martin Browne to TSE, 19 January 1948 and TSE to Browne, 25 January 1945, quoted in E. Martin Browne, *The Making of T. S. Eliot's Plays* (Cambridge: Cambridge University Press, 1969), 170.
14 'Classified Advertisements', *Scotsman*, 27 August 1947, 1.
15 TSE to Browne, 25 January 1945, quoted in Browne, *Making*, 170.
16 TSE to Mary Trevelyan, Septuagesima [26 January] 1948 (Houghton).
17 Mary Trevelyan, *I'll Walk Beside You* (London: Longmans, Green, 1946), 54, 43.
18 'Court Circular', *Times*, 13 February 1948, 7.
19 TSE to I. A. Richards, 22 February 1948 (Magdalene College, Cambridge).
20 *CP7*, 118.
21 *CP7*, 112, 114.
22 A. David Moody, *Ezra Pound: Poet, A Portrait of the Man and his Work, Volume III: The Tragic Years 1939–1972* (Oxford: Oxford University Press, 2015), 271.
23 TSE to Olga Rudge, 12 June 1948 and 11 April 1948 (Beinecke).
24 *CP7*, 169.
25 TSE to Hope Mirrlees, 5 April 1948 (McKeldin Library).
26 TSE to Murry, 11 April 1948 (Northwestern University Library).
27 TSE to Theodora Eliot Smith, 2 May 1948 (Houghton).
28 *CP7*, 122; TSE to Pound, 2 May 1948 (Lilly Library).
29 TSE to Dorothy Pound, 2 May 1948 (Lilly Library).
30 TSE to Richards, 10 May 1948 (Magdalene).
31 TSE to Theodora Eliot Smith, 5 June 1948 (Houghton).
32 Emily Lina Mirrlees and Margaret Lina Mirrlees, *Wishful Cooking* (London: Faber & Faber, 1949), 83, 57, 122, front jacket flap.
33 TSE to Philip Mairet, 22 May 1948 (Harry Ransom Center).
34 *CP7*, 176.
35 Browne, *Making*, 172.

36 'T. S. Eliot Reads Poetry', *Harvard Crimson*, 14 May 1947.
37 Browne, *Making*, 173.
38 Browne, *Making*, 174.
39 Browne, *Making*, 176.
40 TSE to Lawrence Durrell, 11 July 1948 (Morris Library, Southern Illinois University).
41 TSE to Mary Trevelyan, 2 July 1948 (Houghton).
42 *CP7*, 222, 199.
43 *CP7*, 224.
44 *CP7*, 232, 247.
45 TSE to Mary Trevelyan [15 September 1948] (Houghton).
46 TSE to Polly Tandy, 20 September 1948 (British Library).
47 TSE to Hayward, 27 September 1948 (KCA).
48 TSE to Mary Trevelyan, 15 October 1948 (Houghton).
49 TSE to Mary Hutchinson, 10 October 1948 (Harry Ransom Center).
50 TSE to Mary Trevelyan, 15 October 1948 (Houghton).
51 TSE to Mary Trevelyan, 15 October 1948 (Houghton).
52 *CP7*, 329, 331.
53 TSE to Marianne Moore, 7 November 1948 (The Rosenbach, Philadelphia).
54 Quoted in Peter Ackroyd, *T. S. Eliot* (London: Hamish Hamilton, 1984), 290.
55 TSE to Hayward, 14 November 1948 (KCA).
56 Anders Osterling, 'Presentation Speech' for T. S. Eliot, 1948, Nobel Prize website (NobelPrize.org. Nobel Media AB 2019).
57 *CP7*, 466, 467.
58 TSE to Marion Eliot, 18 December 1948 (Houghton).
59 TSE to Hope Mirrlees, 18 December 1948 (McKeldin Library).
60 TSE to Violet Schiff, 14 January 1949 (British Library).
61 *CP7*, 315.
62 *CP7*, 453.
63 TSE to Mary Hutchinson, [14 February] 1949 (Harry Ransom Center).
64 Browne, *Making*, 180.
65 Henry Sherek, *Not in Front of the Children* (London: Heinemann, 1959), 139, 140, 141.
66 Browne, *Making*, 181.
67 Browne, *Making*, 184.
68 Browne, *Making*, 184.
69 TSE to Mary Trevelyan, 13 March 1949 (Houghton).
70 TSE to Mary Trevelyan, and her diary entry for 24 November 1949, quoted in Humphrey Carpenter, 'Poor Tom: Mary Trevelyan's View of T. S. Eliot', *English*, 38 (issue 160), 1 March 1989, 48.
71 TSE to Browne, 15 March 1949 (Houghton).
72 *L9*, 384.
73 TSE to Allen Tate, 19 April 1949 (Princeton).
74 Draft of *The Cocktail Party*, quoted in Browne, *Making*, 192.
75 Mary Trevelyan, 'The Pope of Russell Square', II, quoted in Carpenter, 'Poor Tom', 45.
76 TSE to Mary Trevelyan, 27 April 1949 (Houghton).
77 TSE to Mary Trevelyan, 27 April 1949 (Houghton).
78 TSE quoted in National Portrait Gallery (London) news release, 'Patrick Heron's unseen sketches of T. S. Eliot go on display at National Portrait Gallery for the first time', 31 January 2013 (NPG website).
79 TSE to Allen Tate, 20 May 1949 (Princeton).
80 TSE to Mary Trevelyan, 20 May 1949 (Houghton).
81 *CP7*, 357, 358.

82   *CP7*, 363.
83   TSE to Browne, 2 July 1949 (Houghton).
84   *CP8*, 428.
85   TSE to Wyndham Lewis, 13 July 1949 (Cornell University Library).
86   TSE to Polly Tandy, 21 July 1949 (British Library).
87   *CP7*, 361.
88   'Festival Notes', *Scotsman*, 22 August 1949, 6.
89   Browne, *Making*, 233.
90   *CPP*, 353.
91   Browne, *Making*, 238.
92   Browne, *Making*, 238.
93   *CPP*, 379.
94   *CPP*, 407.
95   *CPP*, 402, 381.
96   *CPP*, 380.
97   Lyndall Gordon, *The Imperfect Life of T. S. Eliot*, revised edn (London: Virago, 2012), 407–8; *CPP*, 441.
98   *CPP*, 420.
99   *CPP*, 419.
100   'Festival Notes', *Scotsman*, 26 August 1949, 4; 'The Festival: Glyndebourne Opera', *Scotsman*, 23 August 1949, 6; 'Scots View on Life: Mr Ivor Brown at Edinburgh', *Scotsman*, 29 August 1949, 3.
101   'The Edinburgh Festival', *Times*, 24 August 1949, 8.
102   TSE to Alan Pryce Jones, 12 September 1949 (Beinecke); Craig Raine, 'Eliot, Valerie', *ODNB*.
103   'T. S. Eliot and I' (Valerie Eliot interview with Timothy Wilson), *Observer*, 20 February 1972, 21.
104   'A poet's life and letters' (interview with Valerie Eliot by Bryan Appleyard), *Times*, 17 September 1988, Review section, 35.
105   Alzina Stone Dale, *T. S. Eliot, The Philosopher Poet* (Wheaton, Illinois: Harold Shaw Publishers, 1988), 179.
106   TSE to Mary Hutchinson, 'Sunday' [*c*.September 1949] (Harry Ransom Center).
107   *CP7*, 374, 406.
108   *CP7*, 383.
109   *CP7*, 446.

15. Alone

1   'Social News', *Times*, 6 January 1950, 7.
2   *CP7*, 481.
3   TSE to Hayward, 7 January 1950 (KCA).
4   TSE to Hayward, [?24] January 1950 (KCA).
5   [TSE] to Geoffrey Faber, 28 February 1950, quoted in Toby Faber, *Faber & Faber: The Untold Story* (London: Faber & Faber, 2019), 195–6.
6   *L6*, 628.
7   *CP7*, 469.
8   TSE to Mary Trevelyan, 15 March 1950 (Houghton).
9   TSE to Mary Trevelyan, 2 June 1950 (Houghton).
10   TSE to Mary Trevelyan, 2 June 1950 (Houghton).
11   TSE to Mary Trevelyan, 2 June 1950 (Houghton).
12   *L8*, 1044.
13   *CP7*, 487, 502, 503.
14   John Malcolm Brinnin, *Sextet* (London: André Deutsch, 1982), 253.

15   Mary Hutchinson, 'T. S. Eliot', manuscript photocopy supplied by Jeremy Hutchinson.

16   Stephen Spender, *Eliot* (Glasgow: Fontana/Collins, 1975), 240.

17   *CP7*, 521.

18   *CP7*, 528, 536.

19   Stanley Rosen, 'Kojève's Paris: A Memoir', in Florence de Lussy, ed., *Hommage à Alexandre Kojève* (Paris: Editions de la Bibliothèque nationale de France, 2007), 80.

20   *CP7*, 558.

21   TSE to Hayward, 28 October 1950 (KCA).

22   *CP7*, 606, 601.

23   *L2*, 593.

24   TSE to Mary Trevelyan, 28 October 1950 (Houghton).

25   Hayward to TSE, 26 November 1950 (KCA).

26   Donald Hall, *Remembering Poets* (New York: Harper Colophon, 1979), 86.

27   William Turner Levy and Victor Scherle, *Affectionately, T. S. Eliot* (London: Dent, 1968), 18.

28   *L8*, 54.

29   'Poet attacks – and in walks T. S. Eliot', *Daily Mail*, 16 February 1951, 3.

30   'Poet attacks', 3.

31   *L6*, 286.

32   *CP7*, 664, 669, 662.

33   Emily Hale, 'All the World's a Stage', *Abbot Academy Bulletin*, May 1951, 3.

34   T. S. Matthews, *Great Tom: Notes Towards the Definition of T. S. Eliot* (London: Weidenfeld & Nicolson, 1974), 147.

35   'T. S. Eliot and I' (Valerie Eliot interviewed by Timothy Wilson), *Observer*, 20 February 1972, 21.

36   Valerie Fletcher to Violet Schiff, 22 March 1951 (British Library).

37   *CP7*, 630, 634.

38   *CP7*, 618, 647.

39   *CP7*, 647, 648.

40   Hall, *Remembering*, 88.

41   *P2*, 35.

42   E. Martin Browne, *The Making of T. S. Eliot's Plays* (Cambridge: Cambridge University Press, 1969), 249.

43   Frederick Tomlin, *T. S. Eliot, A Friendship* (London: Routledge, 1988), 159, 160; *CP7*, 641.

44   'William Foyle Poetry Prize Award', *Times*, 18 January 1952, 7.

45   *CP7*, 700, 671.

46   *CP7*, 717; 'Queen Mary to See Eliot Film', *Daily Mail*, 29 January 1952, 3.

47   *CP7*, 743.

48   *CP7*, 752, 757.

49   John Peter, 'A New Interpretation of *The Waste Land*', *Essays in Criticism*, July 1952, 245.

50   *P1*, 579.

51   Tomlin, *T. S. Eliot*, 184.

52   TSE to Charles Maurras, 24 August 1952 (University of St Andrews Library).

53   TSE to Geoffrey Faber, 18 October 1952, quoted in Faber, *Faber & Faber*, 209.

54   TSE to Geoffrey Faber, 26 October 1952, quoted in Faber, *Faber & Faber*, 212.

55   *CP7*, 766.

56   TSE to Alice Quinn, in Stephen Spender, ed., *Hockney's Alphabet* (New York: Random House, 1992), n.p.

57   Browne, *Making*, 249, 250, 253; annotated typescripts of *The Confidential Clerk* (KCA).

58   Browne, *Making*, 260.
59   *P2*, 441.
60   *P1*, 780.
61   Browne, *Making*, 285.
62   Browne, *Making*, 286.
63   *CP7*, 775.
64   Mary Trevelyan, 'The Pope of Russell Square', quoted in Lyndall Gordon, *The Imperfect Life of T. S. Eliot* (revised edn; London: Virago, 2012), 462.
65   TSE to Violet Schiff, 11 January 1953 (British Library).
66   *CP8*, 550.
67   Tomlin, *T. S. Eliot*, 164.
68   Schölin Tipping, letter to the author, 2 July 2014.
69   George D. Stoddard, 'Introduction of Mr T. S. Eliot', 4 June 1953 (Houghton).
70   'Portraits in Bronze', *Times*, 12 June 1953, 2.
71   *CP7*, 792.
72   Levy, *Affectionately*, 37.
73   TSE to Barbara (Welch) Sturtevant, 27 July 1953 (Houghton).
74   Trevelyan, 'The Pope of Russell Square', quoted in Gordon, *The Imperfect Life*, 415.
75   Henry Sherek, *Not in Front of the Children* (London: Heinemann, 1959), 186; *CPP*, 506.
76   'Mr Eliot's Play in London', *Times*, 14 September 1953, 11.
77   Sherek, *Not in Front*, 187.
78   Jewel Spears Brooker, ed., *T. S. Eliot: The Contemporary Reviews* (Cambridge: Cambridge University Press, 2004), 550.
79   Sherek, *Not in Front*, 188.
80   'The Queen sits in the dress circle', *Daily Mail*, 11 November 1953, 1.
81   TSE letter to Enid Faber, quoted in *Presentation Copies and Letters from T. S. Eliot to the Faber Family, 20 September 2005 auction catalogue* (London: Bonhams, 2005), 10.
82   *CP7*, 879.
83   *CP7*, 818, 825.
84   'The Confidential Clerk', *Boston Globe*, 19 November 1953, 4.
85   Tomlin, *T. S. Eliot*, 170, 172, 173, 174; *CP8*, 3.
86   *CP8*, 14.
87   John Hayward to Helen Gardner, 17 April 1954 (KCA).
88   'T. S. Eliot told to rest', *Daily Mail*, 21 April 1954, 1.
89   John Hayward, *Tarantula's Web* (Norwich: Michael Russell, 2013), 257.
90   Levy, *Affectionately*, 48.
91   *P2*, 440.
92   *CP8*, 22.
93   *L6*, 287.
94   *P1*, 977.
95   Levy, *Affectionately*, 51.
96   *P1*, 780.
97   Levy, *Affectionately*, 53.
98   *CP8*, 44, 45.
99   TSE to Rupert Doone, 16 November 1954 (New York Public Library).
100   Faber, *Faber & Faber*, 222.
101   Levy, *Affectionately*, 53, 54.
102   TSE to Mary Trevelyan, 26 February 1955 (Houghton).
103   TSE to Allen Tate, 21 February 1955 (Princeton).
104   *CP8*, 99.
105   Mary Trevelyan to John Hayward, 21 April [1955] (KCA).
106   Smart, *Tarantula's Web*, 259.

107   *CP8*, 57, 60.

108   *CP8*, 86, 90.

109   *P1*, 944.

110   TSE to Ezra Pound, 12 October 1956 (Beinecke).

111   Levy, *Affectionately*, 91.

112   Tomlin, *T. S. Eliot*, 180.

113   *CP8*, 62, 63, 75, 76.

114   J[ames] C[ampbell], 'N.B., High Heels', *Times Literary Supplement*, 16 November 2012, 38.

115   TSE to Hayward, 30 May 1955 (KCA).

116   Walter Jackson Bate, personal communication, August 1983.

117   Tomlin, *T. S. Eliot*, 178.

118   *CP8*, 99, 100.

119   *CP8*, 109.

120   Faber, *Faber & Faber*, 237.

121   TSE to Mary Trevelyan, 18 January 1956 (Houghton).

122   *CP8*, 114.

123   Quoted in Valerie Eliot, 'What Keats drank' [letter], *Times*, 21 February 1977, 11; *The Poems of John Keats*, ed. Miriam Allott (London: Longman, 1970), 529.

124   TSE to Mary Trevelyan, 13 April 1956 (Houghton).

125   *CP8*, 128, 134.

126   TSE to Hayward, [25 April 1956] (KCA).

127   Hayward to TSE, 12 May 1956 (KCA).

128   'T. S. Eliot's Sister Dies in Cambridge', *Boston Globe*, 19 June 1956 (cutting in Houghton).

129   TSE to Mary Trevelyan, 17 May [1956] (Houghton).

130   TSE, 'Instructions to be carried out at the time of my death', 29 June 1956 (KCA).

131   Mary Trevelyan, quoted in Humphrey Carpenter, 'Poor Tom: Mary Trevelyan's View of T. S. Eliot', *English*, 38, issue 160, 1 March 1989, 49.

132   Tomlin, *T. S. Eliot*, 188.

133   Levy, *Affectionately*, 90, 92.

134   TSE to Winthrop Sprague Brooks, 18 July 1956 (Houghton).

135   Tomlin, *T. S. Eliot*, 191, 190.

136   Tomlin, *T. S. Eliot*, 190.

137   Rosemary Goad, quoted in Damian Whitworth, 'A tale of men, Martinis and manuscripts', *Times*, Saturday supplement, 16 May 2009, [1].

138   Inscribed copy of *American Literature and the American Language* (St Louis: Washington University, 1953) (Magdalene College, Cambridge).

139   Rosemary Goad, quoted in Robert McCrum, 'Revealed: The Remarkable Story of T. S. Eliot's Late Love Affair', *Observer*, 24 May 2009; Tomlin, *T. S. Eliot*, 191.

140   Goad, quoted in McCrum, 'Revealed'.

141   Brinnin, *Sextet*, 274.

142   *EH*, 6 October 1956.

143   *EH*, 14 October 1956.

144   *EH*, 27 October 1956.

145   TSE to Helen Gardner, 29 October 1956 (Bodleian).

146   *L5*, xix.

147   'T. S. Eliot and I', 21.

148   'T. S. Eliot and I', 21.

149   Goad, quoted in McCrum, 'Revealed'.

150   Smart, *Tarantula's Web*, 263.

151   TSE to Dwight Macdonald, 29 December 1956 (Beinecke).

152   Valerie Eliot to Eleanor Hinkley, 11 May 1965 (Houghton).

153 Tomlin, *T. S. Eliot*, 195.
154 *EH*, 24 December 1956.
155 *EH*, 10 February 1957.
156 *EH*, 10 February 1957.
157 TSE to Hayward, 7 January 1957 (KCA).
158 Hayward to Anne Ridler, 3 February 1957 (British Library).
159 Smart, *Tarantula's Web*, 269.

16. Together

1 *P1*, 1220.
2 *CP8*, 422.
3 'T. S. Eliot and I' (Valerie Eliot interviewed by Timothy Wilson), *Observer*, 20 February 1972, 21.
4 'Marriage', *Times*, 11 January 1957, 10.
5 'T. S. Eliot weds his secretary', *Daily Mail*, 11 January 1957, 1.
6 TSE to Hayward, [January] 1957 (KCA).
7 'The Confidential Bride', *Daily Express* cutting from January 1957 in Margaret Rosalys Coker, 'Celebration Book', Vol. 22 (1957–9), entry for 28 July 1957 (Bodleian Library).
8 TSE, with attached cutting, to Winthrop Sprague Brooks, 21 February 1957 (Houghton).
9 TSE to Hayward, [January] 1957 (KCA).
10 'The Confidential Bride'.
11 *CP8*, 488; Valerie Eliot to Faber & Faber secretaries, January 1957, quoted in Robert McCrum, 'Revealed: The Remarkable Tale of T. S. Eliot's Late Love Affair', *Observer*, 24 May 2009.
12 TSE to Violet Schiff [?February 1957] (British Library).
13 'Emeralds and diamonds for a confidential wife' (Tanfield's Diary), *Daily Mail*, 1 February 1957.
14 'Emeralds and diamonds'.
15 TSE to Eleanor Hinkley, 10 February 1957 (Houghton).
16 Inscribed copy of *American Literature and the American Language* (St Louis: Washington University, 1953) (Magdalene College, Cambridge).
17 'Dinners', *Times*, 12 February 1957, 10.
18 *L8*, 153.
19 William Turner Levy and Victor Scherle, *Affectionately, T. S. Eliot* (London: J. M. Dent, 1968), 98–9.
20 *L8*, 289.
21 *CP8*, 169.
22 *CP8*, 174.
23 Toby Faber, *Faber & Faber, The Untold Story* (London: Faber & Faber, 2019), 245–6.
24 TSE to Eleanor Hinkley, 12 April 1957 (Houghton).
25 Inscribed copies of *Dante* and *Sweeney Agonistes* in the Valerie Eliot Bequest (Magdalene College, Cambridge).
26 Inscribed copies of *The Idea of a Christian Society*, *Selected Prose* and *Homage to John Dryden* in Valerie Eliot Bequest (Magdalene College, Cambridge).
27 *P1*, 316.
28 *P1*, 317.
29 *P1*, 319.
30 *P1*, 319.
31 Rosemary Goad, quoted in McCrum, 'Revealed'.
32 *P1*, 1102.

33   'Mr Robert Frost in Discursive Mood', *Times*, 22 May 1957, 12.

34   Frederick Tomlin, *T. S. Eliot, A Friendship* (London: Routledge, 1988), 202.

35   *CP8*, 172.

36   *CP8*, 178; TSE to Eleanor Hinkley, 27 May 1957 (Houghton).

37   'Mr T. S. Eliot's Foie-Gras Sandwich', *Times*, 16 September 1957, 13.

38   'Debut', *Evening Standard*, 29 May 1957.

39   Alan Bennett, *Writing Home* (revised edn; London: Faber & Faber, 1994), x; 'T. S. Eliot and I', 21.

40   *CP8*, 240, 236.

41   Mary Trevelyan, 'The Pope of Russell Square', quoted in Humphrey Carpenter, 'Poor Tom: Mary Trevelyan's View of T. S. Eliot', *English*, 38, issue 160, 1 March 1989, 51.

42   Carpenter, 'Poor Tom', 51.

43   TSE to Eleanor Hinkley, 26 October 1957 (Houghton).

44   TSE to Eleanor Hinkley, 12 December 1957 (Houghton).

45   TSE to Eleanor Hinkley, 12 December 1957 (Houghton).

46   Valerie Eliot to Lillian Brooks, 'Friday' [n.d.], (Manuscripts and Special Collections, Washington University, St Louis).

47   Henry Sherek, *Not in Front of the Children* (London: Heinemann, 1959), 221.

48   'The Art of Poetry I: T. S. Eliot' (interview with Donald Hall), *Paris Review*, 21 (Spring/Summer 1959), 61.

49   *CP8*, 245.

50   A. David Moody, *Ezra Pound: Poet, A Portrait of the Man and his Work, Volume III: The Tragic Years 1939–1972* (Oxford: Oxford University Press, 2015), 447.

51   Inscribed copy of *Prufrock and Other Observations* in Valerie Eliot Bequest (Magdalene, Cambridge).

52   McCrum, 'Revealed'.

53   Levy and Scherle, *Affectionately*, 107.

54   Levy and Scherle, *Affectionately*, 109, 110.

55   'Robert Giroux, The Art of Publishing No. 3' (interview by George Plimpton), *Paris Review* website.

56   William J. Lewis, 'Introducing Valerie to US', *Boston Globe*, May 1958, press cutting (Houghton).

57   Valerie Eliot photographs of 1958 visit to Boston and Cambridge (Houghton).

58   I. A. Richards, Notes for lecture on TSE delivered at Eliot House, 12 May 1958, 19 (Houghton).

59   John Finley, personal communication, September 1983.

60   'Eliot Gives Poetry Commentary', *Harvard Crimson*, 15 May 1958.

61   Sherek, *Not in Front*, 223; Jewel Spears Brooker, ed., *T. S. Eliot: The Contemporary Reviews* (Cambridge: Cambridge University Press, 2004), 567.

62   Edinburgh text of *The Elder Statesman* (later revised), quoted in E. Martin Browne, *The Making of T. S. Eliot's Plays* (Cambridge: Cambridge University Press, 1969), 331.

63   Sherek, *Not in Front*, 224, 225.

64   Brooker, ed., *T. S. Eliot: The Contemporary Reviews*, 569.

65   *P1*, 219, 1061; *P2*, 558.

66   TSE to Robert Lowell, 22 October 1958 (Houghton).

67   TSE to Eleanor Hinkley, 25 October 1958 (Houghton).

68   Brooker, ed., *T. S. Eliot: The Contemporary Reviews*, 567.

69   'The Eliot play is coming off after 11 weeks', *Daily Mail*, 28 November 1958, 3.

70   Valerie Eliot, personal communication, 1993.

71   *CP8*, 315, 332.

72   *CP8*, 344.

73   *CP8*, 309.

74   Valerie Eliot, postcard to Barbara Sturtevant, 1 March 1959 (Houghton).

75   *CP8*, 337.

76   Donald Hall, *Remembering Poets* (New York: Harper Colophon, 1979), 98, 99.

77   'The Art of Poetry I: T. S. Eliot', 57.

78   *CP8*, 339.

79   Ian Hainsworth, personal communication, 2015.

80   *CP8*, 370, 365.

81   *CP8*, 556; *P1*, 582.

82   TSE to Pound, 3 September 1959 (Beinecke); *P1*, 582.

83   *P1*, 585.

84   *CP8*, 389.

85   *CP8*, 405, 412.

86   *CP8*, 376, 375.

87   Levy and Scherle, *Affectionately*, 117.

88   *P1*, 1061.

89   *L5*, 751.

90   *CP8*, 391.

91   *CP8*, 392.

92   Faber, *Faber & Faber*, 257.

93   *CP8*, 421.

94   *Letters of Ted Hughes*, ed. Christopher Reid (New York: Farrar, Straus & Giroux, 2007), 159–60.

95   *The Letters of Sylvia Plath, Volume 2, 1956–1963*, ed. Peter K. Steinberg and Karen V. Kukil (London: Faber & Faber, 2018), 469.

96   Stephen Spender, *New Selected Journals*, ed. Lara Feigel and John Sutherland (London: Faber & Faber, 2012), 285.

97   *CP8*, 420, 422.

98   Faber, *Faber & Faber*, 256.

99   *CP8*, 402, 399.

100   *CP8*, 425.

101   Tomlin, *T. S. Eliot*, 225.

102   *CP8*, 474; TSE to Helen Gardner, 8 December 1960 (Bodleian).

103   *CP8*, 474.

104   TSE to Helen Gardner, 8 December 1960 (Bodleian).

105   Jeremy Hutchinson, interview with the author, 3 December 2013.

106   TSE to Helen Gardner, 8 December 1960 (Bodleian).

107   TSE to Eleanor Hinkley, 24 October 1960 (Houghton).

108   Valerie Eliot in BBC TV's *Arena: T. S. Eliot*, broadcast on 6 June 2009 (this remark was first made in a 1971 interview for the BBC documentary *The Mysterious Mr Eliot*).

109   *P1*, 1067, 1186, 1102.

110   'A poet's wife and letters' (interview with Valerie Eliot by Bryan Appleyard), *Times*, 17 September 1988, Review section, 35.

111   Valerie Eliot, 'Bertrand Russell' [letter], *Times*, 10 February 1970, 11.

112   'T. S. Eliot and I', 21.

113   'T. S. Eliot and I', 21.

114   'A poet's wife and letters', 35.

115   *L5*, xx.

116   TSE, 'Directions to my Executors' and untitled statement, 25 November 1960 (Houghton).

117   Thomas Dilworth, *David Jones* (London: Jonathan Cape, 2017), 313.

118   *CP8*, 432.

119   *CP8*, 454, 455.

120   *CP8*, 479, 481; Dilworth, *David Jones*, 313.

121   *CP8*, 447; *L5*, 534.

122   [John Gross], 'An Individual Talent', *Times Literary Supplement*, 10 March 1961, 152.

123   *CP8*, 456, 458, 459–60.

124   I am grateful to Marina Branscombe for gathering comments in 2013 from Susan Katemann, Jane Brown, and Alison Wright; they all attended the Leeds lecture.

125   *CP8*, 469.

126   *P1*, 785.

127   See *The Groucho Letters: Letters from and to Groucho Marx* (London: Michael Joseph, 1967), 154–62; *P2*, 202, 203.

128   Graham Fletcher, 'The Silly Songs of T. Stearns Eliot – a Private Memoir Made Public', *Exchanges: The T. S. Eliot Society (UK) Quarterly*, 6.1 (Summer 2013), 6, 7.

129   *CP8*, 593–4.

130   T. S. Matthews, *Great Tom: Notes Towards the Definition of T. S. Eliot* (London: Weidenfeld & Nicolson, 1974); *P1*, 766, 1089.

131   Joseph L. Featherstone, 'T. S. Eliot', *Harvard Crimson*, 6 December 1961.

132   TSE to Herbert Howarth, 26 December 1961, quoted in Timothy Materer, 'T. S. Eliot and his Biographical Critics', *Essays in Criticism*, 62.1 (2012), 47.

133   Levy and Scherle, *Affectionately*, 126.

134   Levy and Scherle, *Affectionately*, 128–9.

135   *P1*, 51; *L6*, 287.

136   *CP8*, 550.

137   *L6*, 287.

138   TSE to Hayward, 7 June 1962 (KCA).

139   *CP8*, 494, 487.

140   *CP8*, 498, 504, 523, 509.

141   *CP8*, 490.

142   TSE to Ian Parsons, 9 November 1962, quoted in Materer, 'T. S. Eliot and his Biographical Critics', 53.

143   *CP8*, 529.

144   Tomlin, *T. S. Eliot*, 234.

145   TSE to Eleanor Hinkley, 25 August 1963 (Houghton).

146   'Mr T. S. Eliot to Leave Hospital Soon', *Times*, 16 January 1963, 8; Valerie Eliot to Leon Little, 25 January 1963 (Houghton).

147   Valerie Eliot to Eleanor Hinkley, 10 March 1963 (Houghton).

148   Valerie Eliot to W. T. Levy, 11 February 1963, in Levy and Scherle, *Affectionately*, 131.

149   'T. S. Eliot and I', 21.

150   *L4*, 754.

151   *CP8*, 540.

152   *L1*, 199.

153   *L8*, 133.

154   *L3*, 573.

155   Hall, *Remembering Poets*, 109, 106, 107.

156   *CP8*, 548.

157   Emily Hale to TSE, 12 September 1963, in Lyndall Gordon, *The Imperfect Life of T. S. Eliot* (London: Virago, 2012), 420.

158   Tomlin, *T. S. Eliot*, 236.

159   TSE, untitled statement, revised 30 September 1963 (Houghton).

160   'Robert Giroux, The Art of Publishing No. 3' (interview by George Plimpton), *Paris Review* website.

161   Levy and Scherle, *Affectionately*, 134, 136, 141.

162   T. S. Eliot, *Knowledge and Experience in the Philosophy of F. H. Bradley* (London: Faber & Faber, 1964), 10, [7].

163   *L3*, 866; *P1*, 581.

164   *CP8*, 559–60.

165   *CP8*, 563.

166   Lee Siegel, 'The Fraught Friendship of T. S. Eliot and Groucho Marx', *New Yorker*, 25 June 2014, *New Yorker* website.

167   *The Groucho Letters*, 162.

168   'A poet's wife and letters', 35.

169   Alan Bennett, *Keeping On Keeping On* (London: Faber & Faber and Profile Books, 2016), 296.

170   *P1*, 1057.

171   *CP8*, 564, 570.

172   Valerie Eliot to Eleanor Hinkley, 11 May 1965 (Houghton).

173   Tomlin, *T. S. Eliot*, 225.

174   *CP8*, 573.

175   TSE to Leon M. Little, 7 August 1964 (Houghton).

176   'T. S. Eliot and I', 21.

177   McCrum, 'Revealed'.

178   Tomlin, *T. S. Eliot*, 237.

179   TSE to Ezra Pound, 11 November 1964 (Beinecke).

180   Valerie Eliot, 'Note', in T. S. Eliot, *To Criticize the Critic and Other Writings* (London: Faber & Faber, 1965), [7].

181   *P2*, 249.

182   *CP8*, 572.

183   Fletcher, 'The Silly Songs', 7.

184   TSE and Valerie Eliot, 1964 Christmas card to John Hayward (KCA).

185   Robert Giroux, 'A Personal Memoir', in Allen Tate, ed., *T. S. Eliot: The Man and his Work* (London: Chatto & Windus, 1967), 344.

186   Valerie Eliot to Eleanor Hinkley, 11 May 1965 (Houghton).

187   Tomlin, *T. S. Eliot*, 240.

188   Valerie Eliot to Eleanor Hinkley, 11 May 1965 (Houghton).

189   'Mr T. S. Eliot, OM', *Times*, 5 January 1965, 12; 'T. S. Eliot, American-Born Poet, Dies in London', *New York Times*, 5 January 1965.

190   'Private service for Mr T. S. Eliot', *Guardian*, 8 January 1965; 'Today's Arrangements', *Times*, 17 February 1965, 13.

191   *L6*, 53.

192   'Artists to Pay Homage to Eliot', *Times*, 21 April 1965, 13; *P1*, 783; *P2*, 25.

193   'T. S. Eliot and I', 21.

194   'T. S. Eliot and I', 21.

195   Roger J. Morgan, 'Valerie Eliot' [letter], *Times*, 22 November 2012, 61.

196   'Mr T. S. Eliot', 11 January 1965, 10.

197   Emily Hale to Margaret Thorp, 11 January 1965 (Princeton University Library), quoted in Gordon, *The Imperfect Life*, 519.

198   Priscilla A. Korell, 'My Fair Lady: A Review', *Concord Journal*, 3 May 1968.

199   Susan Stewart and Joshua Kotin, 'A Conversation with Sally Foss about Emily Hale', *Time Present: The Newsletter of the International T. S. Eliot Society*, 100, Spring 2020, 23.

200   Deaths notices, *Boston Globe*, 15 October 1969, 52.

201   2 Corinthians 5: 8–10 (Authorised Version).

202   Valerie Eliot to Eleanor Hinkley, 11 May 1965 (Houghton).

203   Ezra Pound, 'For T.S.E.', *Sewanee Review*, 74.1 (1966), 109.

204   'Celebration Book of Margaret Rosalys Coker', Vol. 30, MCMLXVI–MCMLXVII, 138, 406, 170 (Bodleian).

Index

T. S. Eliot is referred to as TSE throughout.

Bertrand Russell 37; plans to leave
bank 37; ill 38; drinking 38;
encourages Vivien's writing 38, 40;
and *Criterion* 41, 49–50, 51; in fancy
dress 41; and *King Lear* 42; annoys
V. Woolf 42; helped financially by
brother 42; psychoanalysed 43; has
surgery on hand 43, 44; and mother's
visit 44–6; and Eastbourne murder
44–5; debates leaving bank 46; and
F. H. Bradley's death 47; situation
with Vivien worsens 47; poetry
bursts from him 47–8; writes drama
in two nights 48–9; influenced by
Maurras 50–51; in Paris 51;
overworks 51; paper to Cam Literary
Society 51–2, 57; meets Faber 52–4;
'breakdown' 54–5; Murry proposes
for Clark Lectures (*see* Lectures,
below) 55; continues at bank 55; and
Lucy Thayer's sexual advance on
Vivien 55–6, 61; discusses new
quarterly with Faber 56–7; in agonies
over Vivien 58; seeks Russell's advice
58–9; guilt about Vivien 60, 61; seeks
British nationality 62, 76, 88; agrees
to edit *New Criterion* for Faber 62; on
Vivien's symptoms 62; and medical
costs 62–3; further help from brother
63; visits Fabers in Wales 63;
reconciles with Aldington 64; takes
on too much 64–5; publishes Pound
65; resigns from bank 65; apart from
Vivien 65, 68; in France 65, 66, 68, 69,
70; sees Pound at Rapallo 66, 68;
displeased with *Poems* 67; gives first
Clark Lecture 70; reads *The Great
Gatsby* 71; back with Vivien 71; and
article on 'Vaginal Discharges' 72;
prepares *Savonarola* 72, 73; lectures at
Cambridge 73; tensions with Vivien
74; at Ottoline Morrell's 74; moves to
Chester Terrace 74, 75; learns to drive
76; witnesses Ellen Kellond's
marriage 76; dines with *New Criterion*

contributors 76; fails in application to
All Souls 76–7; quarrels with Vivien
77; in Paris and Rome 77–8; prays in
St Peter's 77–8; and Vivien's suicide
attempt 79–80; resigns from Phoenix
Society 80; opposes 'Disposal of
Churches' bill 80–81; in Paris 81;
translates Perse's *Anabase* 81–2; and
Vivien's stay at Malmaison 80, 81, 82,
85, 86, 88; consults L. Woolf, Murry,
Russell 83, 87; 'rest cure' at
Malmaison 85–6; drinking 86;
religious commitment deepens 88;
with Vivien at Divonne-les-Bains
88–9, 92; and sister's death 89–90, 91;
and Lancelot Andrewes 90–91, 92,
126; returns to London 91; mollifies
Lady Rothermere 91; and Stead 92,
93
1927–30 anthropological interests 93;
on Baudelaire 93; conversion 93–4,
95, 96, 102; becomes British subject
93, 94–5, 108, 109, 119; in St Leonard's
with Vivien 96; as father-in-law's
executor 96, 98, 143; begs mother to
destroy letters 97; friendship with
Faber 97, 98; at boxing match 98; and
young poets 98; at *Criterion* dinners
98; sends Dobrée ridiculous letters
98, 102, 105; returns Russell's money
98; flirts with V. Woolf 99; and
unexpected letter from Emily Hale
99–100; with Vivien in Eastbourne
100, 101; baptism and confirmation
98, 100, 101; godfather to Faber's son
101, 102; relationship with mother
102–3, 127, 132; cannot leave Vivien
and go to USA 103; gifts to Emily
103; denounced by Roth 104; calms
Graves 104; annoyed by Lady
Rothermere 104; enjoys *Criterion*
dinners 104–5; poetry list
unspectacular 106; drinks heavily 107,
122; returns Vivien to Malmaison
107, 108, 109; and Clive Bell 107; at

Index

Index

Eliot, Valerie (née Fletcher) (cont.)
478, 479; and Groucho Marx 479–80;
pushes TSE in a wheelchair 480; sees
him through another illness 481;
prepares his essays for publication
481; and his death 482; takes his ashes
to East Coker 483; does everything in
accord with his wishes for the rest of
her life 483; receives flowers from
TSE every week 484; hugs Pound
485; lays roses on TSE's tablet in
Poets' corner 485; meets Emily Hale
484; death 483

Eliot, Vivien(ne) (née Haigh-Wood): affair
with Bertrand Russell 6, 7, 19, 91, 98;
and *The Waste Land* 6; lives in the
countryside 7, 9; and TSE's affair
with Nancy Cunard 10; and medical
bills 12, 23, 62–3, 81; her daily
routine 13; friendship with Ellen
Kellond 13; her politics 17, 34;
detests Whibley 17, 52; in Eastbourne
17; on the *Criterion* 18–19; and search
for country cottage 21, 22;
depression 22; and TSE's mother 22,
37, 44; with Dr Higgins 22; very ill
at Fishbourne 23; literary styles she
likes 24; in the country with mother
24; contemplates suicide 24; returns
to London 25; in 'real despair' 25;
too ill to see people 25; with further
physicians 25, 37, 40–41, 43; at
Fishbourne again 25, 37; and Mary
Hutchinson 25–6, 183; paints
furniture 26; takes up writing 26,
38–40, 54, 55, 58, 59–61, 72–3; assists
TSE with *Criterion* 40, 51; effect of
her illnesses on TSE 40; finds
weekends a strain 41; at *King Lear* 42;
does not share TSE's religious
commitment 42; traumatised by
psychoanalysis 43–4; TSE stays with
44; in Paris with him 51; back in
Eastbourne 54; and TSE's quarrel
with Jack Culpin 54; and Lucy

Thayer's sexual advances 55–6, 61;
TSE's guilt towards 58; fearful when
he leaves home 58; under different
physicians 62; complains TSE's busy
life saps her energy 63; in 'nursing
home' 65–6; at The Stanboroughs
66–7, 70; fears and distrusts doctor
70, 71; back in London 71–2; and
menstruation 72; in Cambridge
73–4; and Henry and Theresa Eliot
74; consults Dr Reginald Miller 74;
threatens to sue TSE for putting her
in a mental home 74; and move to
Chester Terrace 74; and arrival of
her parents 74–5; and loss of Ellen
Kellond 75; immerses herself in law
75; retreats to Clarence Gate Gardens
75–6; at Ellen's wedding 76; quarrels
with TSE 77; in Paris and Rome
with him 77–8; encourages him to
dominate her 78, 79; attempts suicide
in Paris 79–80, 83; is committed to
the Malmaison 80, 81, 82; writes to
Murry about TSE 82–3, 84, 86, 87;
with TSE in Paris and Divonne-les-
Bains 85–6, 87, 88–9; 'utter isolation'
with him 86–7; communicates
regularly with TSE 87; her female
confidantes 87; sojourns in Cannes
before returning to Chester Terrace
91; visits father 96; too ill to go to his
funeral 96; in Eastbourne 100; tours
Sussex with TSE 101; reconciled
with Lucy Thayer 101, 105; prevents
TSE from going to USA 103, 105;
with him at Malmaison 107; her
letters censored by TSE 108; shows
'some improvement' 108, 109; and
TSE's visits 109, 110, 111; returns
with him to London 115–16; and
Ottoline Morrell 119, 122, 127, 148,
165–6, 168, 176, 183; terrified of
having children 120; and TSE's
conversion 120; nervous at meeting
people 121–2; and Pearl Fassett's

584